PLACE-NAMES OF NORTH

Volume Seven

COUNTY ANTRI

BALLYCASTLE AND NORTH-EAST ANTRIM

Published 1997
The Institute of Irish Studies
The Queen's University of Belfast
Belfast

Research and Publication funded by the
Central Community Relations Unit

ISBN 0 85389 664 X (hb)

ISBN 0 85389 665 8 (pb)

Printed by W. & G. Baird Ltd, Antrim.

Place-Names of Northern Ireland

VOLUME SEVEN

County Antrim II
Ballycastle and North-East Antrim

Fiachra Mac Gabhann

The Northern Ireland Place-Name Project
Department of Celtic
The Queen's University of Belfast

General Editor: Nollaig Ó Muraíle

RESEARCH GROUP

Dr Nollaig Ó Muraíle

Fiachra Mac Gabhann MA
Dr Patrick McKay
Dr Kay Muhr
Mícheál B. Ó Mainnín MA
Dr Gregory Toner

LIST OF ILLUSTRATIONS

Cover: A section of John Speed's map entitled *Antrym and Downe* (AD 1610).

The cover logo is the pattern on one face of a standing stone found at Derrykeighan, Co. Antrim. The art style is a local variant of the widespread "Celtic Art" of the European Iron Age and dates to about the 1st century AD. The opposite side of the stone is similarly decorated. (Drawing by Deirdre Crone, copyright Ulster Museum).

The townland maps have been prepared from OSNI digitalized data, with the permission of the Director, Ordnance Survey of Northern Ireland.

ACKNOWLEDGEMENTS

Gabhaim buíochas speisialta le mo chomhghleacaithe sa Tionscadal Logainmneacha, agus le Nollaig Ó Muraíle, Gearóid Stockman agus Rhian Andrews. Tá mé go mór faoi chomaoin fosta ag na daoine seo a leanas: Art Ó Maolfabhail, Dónall Mac Giolla Easpaig, Pádraig Ó Cearbhaill, Pádraig Ó Dálaigh agus Seán Ó Cearnaigh i mBrainse Logainmneacha na Suirbhéireachta Ordanáis, Ciarán Ó Duibhín, John Curran agus Tony Sheehan in Ollscoil na Banríona, Antaine Ó Donnaile agus Annraoi Ó Préith a léigh luathdhréachtaí agus Fionntán Mac Giolla Chiaráin a rinne moltaí éagsúla.

Profound thanks are due to all those who assisted with the fieldwork and who happily shared their knowledge of the locality, and to those who answered inquiries pertaining to the study. In particular I would like to thank Cahal Dallat, Paddy and Séamus McBride, Gerard and Mary Burns, Angela Laverty, Maurice and Marie McHenry, Francis McHenry, Peggy McLyster, Sammy Wilkinson, Tony and Kathleen Martin, Matt Scally, Séamas Mac Giolla Chiaráin, Billy Boylan, Rachel and Brendan Jennings, Peter Montgomery, Maria Paterson, Mícheál Ó Breisleáin, Nevin Taggart, Simon Taylor, Ian Frazer, Rosemary Power and Geraldine Tallon.

The Place-Names Project has recieved the assistance of many individuals too numerous to mention here, but special thanks are due to the staff of the Special Collections Library at Queen's, to Margaret McNulty of I.I.S., and to the members of the Steering Committee: Michael Brand, Professor Ronnie Buchanan, Dr Maurna Crozier, Dr Alan Gailey, Dr Ann Hamlin, Dr Maurice Hayes, Tony McCusker, Dr Brian Walker.

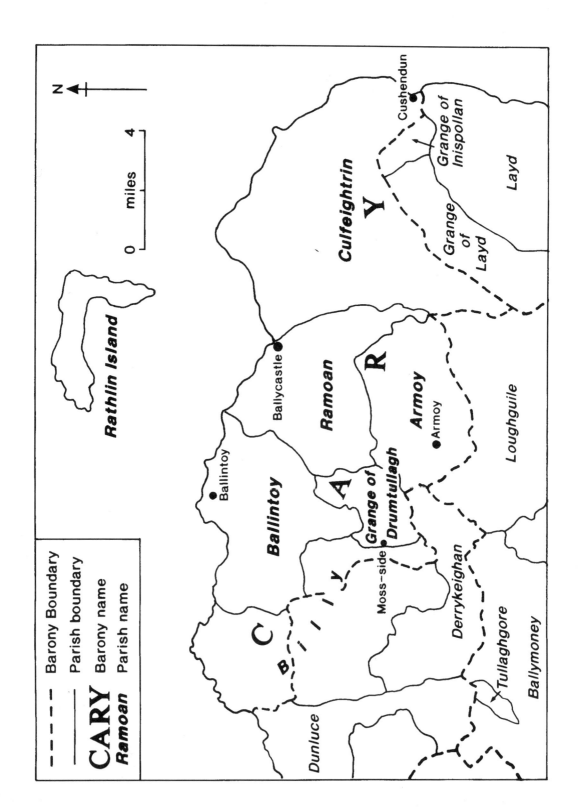

N

0 miles 4

CARY Barony name
Ramoan Parish name

--- Barony Boundary
—— Parish boundary

Rathlin Island

Cushendun

Grange of Inispollan

Layd

Grange of Layd

Culfeightrin

Y

Ballycastle

Ramoan

R

Armoy

Armoy

Loughguile

Ballintoy

Ballintoy

Grange of Drumtullagh

A

Moss-side

Derrykeighan

C

B

Y

Dunluce

Tullaghgore

Ballymoney

CONTENTS

GENERAL INTRODUCTION

BRIEF HISTORY OF PLACE-NAME STUDY IN IRELAND

Place-name lore or *dindsenchas* was a valued type of knowledge in early Ireland, to be learnt by students of secular learning in their eighth year of study. Stories about the origin of place-names appear regularly in early Irish literature. At the end of the epic "Cattle Raid of Cooley" the triumphal charge of the Brown Bull of Cooley around Ireland is said to have given rise to names such as Athlone (Irish *Áth Luain*), so called from the loin *(luan)* of the White-horned Bull slain by the Brown Bull. In the 10th, 11th and 12th centuries legends about the naming of famous places were gathered together into a number of great collections. Frequently, different explanations of the same name are offered in these legends, usually with no preference being expressed. In an entry on the naming of *Cleitech*, the palace on the Boyne of the early king *Muirchertach mac Erca,* five separate explanations of the name are offered, none of which can be correct in modern scholarly terms. Place-name study was cultivated as a branch of literature.

Knowledge of Irish place-names was of practical importance during the English conquest and exploration of Ireland in the 16th century. Recurring elements in the place-names were noted by surveyors, and a table giving a few English equivalents appears on some maps of this period. There was concern that Irish names were "uncouth and unintelligible". William Petty, the great 17th-century surveyor and map-maker, commented that "it would not be amiss if the significant part of the Irish names were interpreted, where they are not nor cannot be abolished" (Petty 1672, 72–3). However, although the English-speaking settlers created many new names, they did not usually change the names of the lands they were granted, and the names of land units remained as they were, albeit in an anglicized form.

Interest in the meaning of Irish place-names developed further towards the end of the 18th century. The contributors to William Shaw Mason's *Parochial Survey of Ireland* often included a table explaining their local townland names, and this aspect was retained in the Statistical Reports compiled by the officers of the Royal Engineers on the parishes they surveyed for the first six-inch survey of Ireland in the late 1820s and early 1830s. Information on the spelling of place-names for the maps was collected in "name-books", and the Ordnance Survey was concerned to find that a variety of anglicized spellings was in use for many Irish place-names. The assistant director, Thomas Larcom, decided that the maps should use the anglicized spellings that most accurately represented the original Irish (Andrews 1975, 122) and he employed an Irish scholar, John O'Donovan, to comment on the name-books and recommend standard forms of names. O'Donovan was sent to the areas being surveyed to talk to local inhabitants, where possible Irish speakers, to find out the Irish forms. These were entered in the name-books, but were not intended for publication.

In 1855, a reader of *Ulster Journal of Archaeology* calling himself "De Campo" asked "that a list of all the townlands should be given in their Irish and English nomenclature, with an explanation of their Irish names" (*UJA* ser. 1, vol. iii, 25 1b). Meanwhile William Reeves, the Church of Ireland Bishop of Connor, had decided to compile a "monster Index" of all Irish townlands, which would eventually include the etymology of the names, "where attainable" (Reeves 1861, 486) . Reeves' project was cited favourably by William Donnelly, the Registrar General, in his introduction to the first Topographical Index to the Census of Ireland: "It would greatly increase the value of a publication of this nature if it were accompanied by a glossary or explanation of the names, and an account of their origin" *(Census 1851* 1, 11–12).

However, it was left to another scholar, P. W. Joyce, to publish the first major work dealing exclusively with the interpretation of Irish place-names, and in his first chapter he acknowledges his debt to both O'Donovan and Reeves (*Joyce* i 7–8, 10). At this period the progress made by Irish place-name scholarship was envied in England (Taylor 1896, 205). The high standard of Joyce's work has made him an authority to the present day, but it is regrettable that most popular books published since on Irish place-names have drawn almost entirely on the selection and arrangement of names discussed by Joyce, ignoring the advances in place-name scholarship over the last hundred years (Flanagan D. 1979(f); 1981–2(b)).

Seosamh Laoide's *Post-Sheanchas*, published in 1905, provided an Irish-language form for modern post towns, districts and counties, and research on place-names found in early Irish texts resulted in Edmund Hogan's *Onomasticon Goedelicum* (1910). Local studies have been published by Alfred Moore Munn (Co. Derry, 1925), and P. McAleer (*Townland Names of County Tyrone*, 1936). The idea of a comprehensive official survey was taken up again by Risteard Ó Foghludha in the introduction to his *Log-ainmneacha* (1935). A Place-Names Commission was founded in Dublin in 1946 to advise on the correct forms of Irish place-names for official use and this was followed by the Place-Names Branch of the Ordnance Survey. They have published the Irish names for postal towns (*AGBP* 1969), a gazetteer covering many of the more important names in Ireland (*GÉ* 1989), a townland survey for Co. Limerick (1990), and most recently bilingual lists of the place-names of a number of individual Irish counties.

John O'Donovan became the first professor of Celtic in Queen's University, Belfast, and in the 20th century members of the Celtic Department continued research on the place-names of the North of Ireland. The Ulster Place-Name Society was founded by the then head of department, Seán Mac Airt, in 1952 (Arthurs 1955–6, 80–82). Its primary aims were, (a) to undertake a survey of Ulster place-names; and (b) to issue periodically to members a bulletin devoted to aspects of place-name study, and ultimately to publish a series of volumes embodying the results of the survey. Several members undertook to do research on particular areas, much of which remains unpublished (Deirdre Flanagan on Lecale, and Dean Bernard Mooney on the names of the Diocese of Dromore).

The primary objective of the Ulster Place-Name Society was partly realized in 1987, when the Department of Celtic was commissioned by the Department of the Environment for Northern Ireland to do research into, "the origin of all names of settlements and physical features appearing on the 1:50,000 scale map; to indicate their meaning and to note any historical or other relevant information". In 1990, under the Central Community Relations Unit, the brief of the scheme was extended: to include work on all townlands in Northern Ireland, and to bring the work to publication. Although individual articles have already been published by various scholars, the *Place-Names of Northern Ireland* series is the first attempt in the North at a complete survey based on original research into the historical sources.

METHOD OF PLACE-NAME RESEARCH

The method employed by the Project has been to gather early spellings of each name from a variety of historical records written mainly in Irish, Latin and English, and arrange them in chronological order. These, then, with due weight being given to those which are demonstrably the oldest and most accurate, provide the evidence necessary for deducing the etymology. The same name may be applied to different places, sometimes only a few miles apart, and all forms are checked to ensure that they are entered under the correct modern name. For example, there are a number of references to a place called *Crosgare* in 17th-century sources, none of which refer to the well-known town of Crossgar in Co. Down, but to a townland also called Crossgar a few miles away near Dromara. Identification of forms is most readily facilitated by those sources which list adjoining lands together or give the name

of the landholder. Indeed, one of the greatest difficulties in using Irish sources and some
early Latin or English documents is the lack of context which would enable firm location of
the place-names which occur in them.

Fieldwork is an essential complement of research on earlier written sources and maps.
Sometimes unrecorded features in local topography or land use are well-known to local
inhabitants. More frequently the pronunciation represented by the early written forms is
obscure, and, especially in areas where there has been little movement of people, the traditional local pronunciation provides valuable evidence. The members of the research team
visited their respective areas of study, to interview and tape-record informants recom-
mended by local historical societies etc., but many others met in the course of fieldwork
kindly offered their assistance and we record here our gratitude. The local pronunciations
have been transcribed in phonetic script and these are given at the end of each list of historical forms. The tapes themselves will become archive material for the future. The transcription used is based on the principles of the International Phonetic Alphabet, modified in
accordance with the general practice in descriptions of Irish and Scottish Gaelic dialects.
The following diagram illustrates the relative position of each of the vowels used:

Front	Central	Back	
i		ʌ u	High
ï			
e		o	High-mid
	ə		
ɛ		ɔ	Low-mid
	a	ɑ	Low

Although this research was originally based on the names appearing on the 1:50,000 scale
map, it soon became clear that many townland names, important in the past and still known
to people today, were not given on the published version. Townlands form the smallest unit
in the historical territorial administrative system of provinces, counties, baronies, parishes,
and townlands. This system, which is that followed by the first Ordnance Survey of Ireland
in its name-books, has been used in the organization of the books in this series. The names
of all the relevant units are explained in Appendix B. Maps of the relevant barony and parish
divisions within the county are supplied for the area covered in each book, to complement
the published 1:50,000 series, and to make the historical context more accessible.

In the process of collecting and interpreting early forms for the *Place-Names of Northern
Ireland* each researcher normally works on a group of parishes. Some books will, therefore,
have joint authorship, and there may be differences of style and emphasis in the discussions
within and between books. It seemed better to retain individuality rather than edit every-
thing into committee prose. The suggested original Irish forms of the place-names were
decided after group discussion with the general editor. In cases of joint authorship the members of the group responsible for the text of each book will be distinguished by name on the
contents page.

All the information in this book is also preserved in a computer database in Queen's
University Belfast. It is hoped that this database will eventually become a permanent
resource for scholars searching for examples of a particular type of name or name element.
Modern map information, lists of the townlands making up historical parishes and baronies,
historical sources and modern Irish forms are all available on separate files which can be
searched and interrelated. The database was designed by Eilís McDaniel, and the Project
gratefully acknowledges her continuing interest.

LANGUAGE

Since Ulster was almost wholly Irish-speaking until the 17th century, most names of town-lands are of Irish-language origin. Some early names were also given Latin equivalents for use in ecclesiastical and secular documents but few probably ever gained wide currency. Norse influence on northern place-names is surprisingly slight and is largely confined to coastal features such as **Strangford Lough** and **Carlingford Lough.** The arrival of the Anglo-Normans in the 12th century brought with it a new phase of naming and its influence is particularly strong in east Ulster, most notably in the Barony of Ards. Here, the names of many of their settlements were formed from a compound of the owner's name plus the English word *tūn* "settlement" which gives us Modern English "town". Names such as **Hogstown** and **Audleystown** have retained their original form, but a considerable number, such as **Ballyphilip** and **Ballyrolly,** derive from forms that were later gaelicized.

By the time of the Plantation of Ulster in the 17th century the system of townland units and their names already existed and this was adopted more or less wholesale by the English and Scots-speaking settlers. These settlers have, nevertheless, left their mark on a sizeable body of names, particularly those of market towns, country houses, villages and farms which did not exist before the 17th century. What made the 17th-century Plantation different from the earlier ones was its extent and intensity, and it was the first time that the Irish language itself, rather than the Irish aristocracy, came under threat. The change from Irish to English speaking was a gradual one, and Irish survived into the 20th century in parts of Antrim and Tyrone. However, the language shift, assisted by an official policy that discriminated against Irish, eventually led to the anglicization of all names to the exclusion of Irish versions.

SPELLING AND PRONUNCIATION

Most of the historical sources used in this series were originally handwritten and this inevitably led to a considerable number of errors, both by contemporary copyists and by modern editors. Many of the documents, particularly grants, were copied time and again, while other sources sometimes only survive in late copies or published calendars. Mistakes could occur in any transcription but were particularly likely when the language or names being copied were unfamiliar. There is a long history of confusion in the Roman alphabet between letters of the type *i, u, n, m, w*. U and *n* are frequently confused, as are *m* and *w*. Where two or more of these letters occur together, the minims (vertical strokes) may be read in different combinations: the simple pair *ui* may be read as *iu, ni, in, m,* or *w*. Another common error is the confusion of long *s* (∫) and *f*. The name **Ballyhaft** (par. Newtownards, Dn) is frequently spelt in 17th-century sources with *s* instead of *f* and the modern form of the name may result from confusion of the written forms. In early sources, horizontal strokes (suspension strokes) could be written over a vowel as shorthand for a following *n* or *m*, but they were easily overlooked by scribes or editors. Spellings such as *Ballemulle* for **Ballymullan** (par. Bangor, Dn) may be explained in this way.

As well as taking account of spelling mistakes, there is sometimes difficulty in interpret-ing just what the spellings were intended to represent. For example, *gh*, which is usually silent in modern English dialects (e.g. night, fought) often retained its original value in the 17th century and was pronounced like the *ch* in Scots *loch* and *nicht*. Thus, *gh* was the obvious way to represent the Irish sound in words like *mullach* "summit", although both the English and Irish sounds were being weakened to [h] in certain positions at the time.

In Irish the spelling *th* was originally pronounced as in modern English *thick*, but in the 13th century it came to be pronounced [h]. The original Irish sound was anglicized as *th* or as *gh* at different periods, but where the older form of the spelling has survived the sound *th* has often been restored by English speakers. In names such as **Rathmullen** and **Rathfriland,** where the initial element represents *ráth* "a ringfort", the *th* has almost invariably been re-established.

It is clear that some spellings used in place-names no longer signify what they did when first anglicized. The *-y* in the common elements "bally-" and "derry-" was selected to represent the final vowel in the corresponding Irish words *baile* and *doire* (the same sound as the *a* in "above") but this vowel is now usually pronounced as a short *ee* as in English words such as *happy, sorry.* In modern Ulster English, the vowel in words ending in *-ane*, such as *mane, crane*, is a diphthong, but in the 17th century it was pronounced as a long *a.* Thus, Irish *bán* "white" was usually represented in anglicized forms of names as *bane* as, for example, in the names **Kinbane** (Ant.) and **Carnbane** (Arm.) and this is frequently how the names are still pronounced locally.

SOURCES

The earliest representations of Irish place-names are found in a broad range of native material, written mostly in Irish although occasionally in Latin, beginning in the 7th or 8th centuries. The Irish annals, probably begun about 550 AD (Byrne 1973, 2) but preserved in manuscripts of much later date, contain a large number of place-names, particularly those of tribes, settlements, and topographical features. Tribal names and those of the areas they inhabited frequently appear among genealogical material, a substantial proportion of which is preserved in a 12th-century manuscript, Rawlinson B 502, but is probably much older. Ecclesiastical records include martyrologies or calendars giving saints' names, often with the names and locations of their churches. The Latin and Irish accounts of the life of St Patrick, which depict him travelling around Ireland founding a series of churches, contain the first lists of place-names which refer to places owned by a particular institution. Later Irish saints' lives also may list lands dedicated to the founder of a church. Medieval Irish narrative shows a great interest in places, often giving, for example, long lists of place-names passed through on journeys. Although many of these sources may date back to the 7th or 8th centuries, the copies we have often survive only in manuscripts of the 12th century and later, in which the spelling may have been modernized or later forms of names substituted.

The administrative records of the reformed Church of the 12th century are among the first to provide detailed grants of land. There are also records from the international Church, such as the papal taxation of 1302–06 (*Eccles. Tax.*). These records are more productive for place-name study, since the names are usually of the same type (either parishes or other land units owned by the church) and are usually geographically related, making them easier to identify with their modern counterparts. However, the place-names in these documents are not usually spelled as they would be in Irish.

Paradoxically, perhaps, the 17th-century Plantation provides a massive amount of evidence for the place-names of Ulster. Grants to and holdings by individuals were written down by government officials in fiants, patents and inquisitions (in the latter case, the lands held by an individual at death). A series of detailed surveys, such as the *Escheated Counties* maps of 1609, the *Civil Survey* of 1654–6, and Sir William Petty's Down Survey (*DS (Par. Maps)*, *Hib. Del.* and *Hib. Reg.*), together with the records of the confiscation and redistribution of land found in the *Books of Survey and Distribution* (*BSD*) and the *Act of Settlement* (*ASE*), meant that, for the first time, almost all the names of smaller land units such as townlands were recorded. Unfortunately the richness of these resources has been depleted by two serious fires among the Irish public records, one in 1711 and the other in the Four Courts in Dublin in 1922. As a result, some of the original maps, and the Civil Survey covering the north-eastern counties, are lost, and the fiants, patents, inquisitions and Act of Settlement now only exist in abridged form in calendars made by the Irish Record Commission in the early 19th century. These calendars were criticized even at the time of publication for their degree of précis and for inaccurate transcription of names.

After the 17th century, little surveying of an official nature was carried out in Ireland, despite the clearance of woods and bogs and reclamation of waste land. The best sources for the 18th century, therefore, are family papers, leases, wills and sometimes estate maps, most of which remain unpublished. It became clear in the early 19th century that much of the taxation system was based on records that were out of date. The Ordnance Survey came to Ireland in 1824 and began in 1825 to do the first large-scale (six inches to the mile) survey of the country. Most of the variant spellings which they collected in their name-books were of the 18th or early 19th centuries, though in some cases local landowners or churchmen allowed access to earlier records, and these again provide a convenient and invaluable source of place-names. Minor names were also recorded in the descriptive remarks of the namebooks, in the fuller treatment of local names (water features, ancient monuments, church sites and other landmarks) in the associated Ordnance Survey Memoirs (*OSM*) and in the Ordnance Survey Revision Name-Books (OSRNB), dating from the second half of the 19th century.

Early maps are an extremely valuable source, since they show the geographical relationship between names that is often crucial for identification purposes, and in many cases they are precise enough to locate lost townlands or to identify the older name of a townland. In parts of Ulster, maps by 16th-century surveyors may antedate texts recording place-names, thus providing the earliest attestation of the names in those areas.

However, maps have their own problems. Like other written texts they often copy from each other, borrowing names or outline or both. Inaccuracies are frequent, especially in the plotting of inland water features, whether due to seasonal flooding, or the lack of a vantage point for viewing the course of a river. Frequently the surveyor of the ground was not the person who drew or published the surviving map. The great continental and English map and atlas publishers, such as Ortelius, Mercator and Speed, all drew on earlier maps, and this custom undoubtedly led to the initiation and prolongation of errors of form and orthography. Sixteenth-century maps of Lough Neagh, for example, regularly show rivers entering the lake on the south between the Blackwater and the Bann where there are known to be none (Andrews 1978, plate 22). Unsurveyed territory was not always drawn to scale. Modern Co. Donegal, for example, is usually drawn too large on 16th-century maps, while Co. Derry is frequently shown too small. The *Escheated County* maps appear to have been partly drawn from verbal information and, in the map for the barony of Armagh, the draughtsman has produced a mirror image reversing east and west (Andrews 1974, 152).

William Petty's Down Survey provided the standard map of Ireland for the 17th century. In the 18th and early 19th centuries various individuals produced local county maps: Roque (1760) Co. Armagh; Lendrick (1780) Co. Antrim; Sampson (1814) Co. Derry; Sloane, Harris, Kennedy and Williamson (1739–1810) Co. Down; Knox and McCrea (1813) Co. Tyrone. These were consulted for the place-names on their own maps by the Ordnance Survey in the 1830s. Apart from published maps, a number of manuscript maps, some anonymous, others the original work of the 16th-century surveyors Lythe and Jobson, still exist. Richard Bartlett and Thomas Raven left important manuscript maps of Ulster from the early 17th century.

HOW TO USE THIS SERIES

Throughout the series, the editors have tried to adhere to the traditional territorial and administrative divisions used in Ireland, but this has not always proved possible. The convenient unit on which to base both research and publication has been the civil parish and all townland names and minor names are discussed under the relevant parish, regardless of whether they are in the same barony or county. Each book normally deals with the parishes in one or more barony, but where the barony is too large they are split into different books, some of which may contain material from geographically adjacent baronies. Every effort has been made to accommodate the historical system in a series of volumes of regular size. Each parish, barony and county is prefaced by an introduction which sets forth its location and history, and discusses some of the sources from which the older spellings of names have been extracted.

Within each parish, townland and other names are arranged in alphabetical order in separate sections following a discussion of the parish name. The first section deals with townland names. The second section deals with names of towns, villages, hills and water features which appear on the OS 1:50,000 map, but which are not classified as townlands. This section may also include a few names of historical importance which do not appear on the map but which may be of interest to the reader. Lesser names on the 1:50,000 are only treated if relevant material has been forthcoming. An index of all the names discussed in each book is given at the back of the relevant volume.

Each name to be discussed is given in bold print on the left-hand side of the page. Bold print is also used elsewhere in the text to cross-refer the reader to another name discussed in the series. The four-figure grid-reference given under each place-name should enable it to be located on modern Ordnance Survey maps.

Beneath the map name[1] and its grid reference, all the pre-1700 spellings that have been found are listed, together with their source and date, followed by a selection of post-1700 forms. Early Irish-language forms are placed above anglicized or latinized spellings because of their importance in establishing the origin of the name. Irish forms suggested by 19th- and 20th-century scholars are listed below the historical spellings. Irish-language forms collected by O'Donovan in the last century, when Irish was still spoken in many parts of the North, require careful assessment. Some may be traditional, but there are many cases where the suggestion made by the local informant is contradicted by the earlier spellings, and it is clear that sometimes informants merely analysed the current form of the name. The current local pronunciation as collected by the editors appears below these Irish forms in phonetic script.

Spellings of names are cited exactly as they occur in the sources. Manuscript contractions have been expanded within square brackets, e.g. [ar]. Square brackets are also used to indicate other editorial readings: [...] indicates three letters in the name which could not be read, while a question mark in front of one or more letters enclosed in square brackets, e.g. [?agh], denotes obscure letters. A question mark in round brackets before a spelling indicates a form which cannot be safely identified as the name under discussion.

The dates of all historical spellings collected are given in the right-hand column, followed, where necessary, by c when the date is approximate. Here, we have departed from the normal practice, employed elsewhere in the books, because the database would otherwise have been unable to sort these dates in numeric order. In Latin and English sources a *circa* date usually indicates an uncertainty of a year or two. Irish language sources, however, rarely have exact dates and *circa* here represents a much longer time-span, perhaps of one or two centuries where the dating is based purely on the language of a text. Where no date has been established for a text, forms from that text are given the date of the earliest MS in which they appear. Following normal practice, dates in the Irish annals are given as in the source, although this may give certain spellings an appearance of antiquity which they do not deserve. The Annals of the Four Masters, for example, were compiled in the early 17th century using earlier material, and many of the names in the text were modernized by the compilers. Moreover, annals were written later for dates before the mid-6th-century, and the names, let alone the spellings, may not be that old. Another difficulty with dates concerns English administrative sources. The civil year in England and Ireland began on March 25th (Lady Day) until the year 1752, when the calendar was brought into line with changes made in the rest of Europe in 1582. Thus, the date of any document written between 1st of January and 24th of March inclusive has had to be adjusted to reconcile it with the current system by adding a year.

The original or most likely original Irish form of a name, where one is known to have existed, is given in italics on the top line to the right of the current spelling, with an English translation below. This includes Norse, Anglo-Norman and English names for which a Gaelic form once existed, as well as those of purely Irish origin. *Loch Cairlinn,* for example, was used by Irish-speakers for *Carlingford Lough* and this, rather than the original Norse, is printed on the top line. Although the name may have originally been coined at an early period of the language, standard modern Irish orthography is employed throughout, except in rare cases where this may obscure the meaning or origin of the name. The rules of modern Irish grammar are usually followed when not contradicted by the historical evidence. Where some doubt concerning the origin or form of a name may exist, or where alternatives may seem equally likely, plausible suggestions made by previous authorities, particularly the *OSNB* informants, are given preference and are printed at the top of the relevant entry. Nevertheless, where there is firm evidence of an origin other than that proposed by earlier scholars, the form suggested by our own research is given prominence.

Names for which no Irish original is proposed are described according to their appearance, that is, English, Scots etc. The form and meaning is usually obvious, and there is no evidence that they replace or translate an original Irish name. Names which are composed of two elements, one originally Irish and the other English or Scots, are described as hybrid forms. An important exception to this rule is names of townlands which are compounded from a name derived from Irish and an English word such as "upper", "east" etc. In these cases, the original Irish elements are given on the right-hand side but the later English appendage is not translated.

In the discussion of each name, difficulties have not been ignored but the basic consideration has been to give a clear and readable explanation of the probable origin of the name, and its relationship to the place. Other relevant information, on the language of the name, on other similar names, on historical events, on past owners or inhabitants, on physical changes or local place-name legends, may also be included, to set the name more fully in context.

The townland maps which appear at the beginning of each parish show the layout of all the townlands in that parish. They are based on printouts from the Ordnance Survey's digitized version of the 1:50,000 map.

The rules of Irish grammar as they relate to place-names are discussed in Appendix A, and the historical system of land divisions in Ulster is described in Appendix B. The bibliography separates primary sources and secondary works (the latter being referred to by author and date of publication). This is followed by a glossary of technical terms used in this series. The place-name index, as well as providing page references, gives the 1:50,000 sheet numbers for all names on the published map, and sheet numbers for the 1:10,000 series and the earlier 6-inch county series for townland names. The index of Irish forms gives a semi-phonetic pronunciation for all names for which an Irish form has been postulated.

SUGGESTIONS FOR FURTHER INVESTIGATION

A work like this on individual names cannot give a clear picture of any area at a particular time in the past. Any source in the bibliography could be used, in conjunction with town-land or other maps, to plot the references to a particular locality at that date, or to lands with a particular owner. Also the Public Record Office of Northern Ireland holds a considerable amount of unpublished material from the eighteenth century and later, which awaits inves-tigation for information on place-names arising at that period.

Although fieldwork forms an integral part of place-name research, it is difficult for a library researcher to acquire the familiarity with an area that the local inhabitants have. Local people can walk the bounds of their townlands, or compare boundary features with those of the early 6-inch maps. Written or tape-recorded collections of local names (especially those of smaller features such as fields, rocks, streams, houses, bridges, etc.), where exactly they are to be found, how written and pronounced, and any stories about them or the people who lived there, would be a valuable resource for the future. The Place-Name Project will be happy to talk to anyone engaged on a venture of this kind.

Footnote

(1) On the OS maps apostrophes are sometimes omitted, e.g. Mahulas Well, Deers Meadow. In this series they have been inserted when there is evidence to indicate whether the possessive is singular or plural, e.g. Mahula's Well, Deers' Meadow.

Kay Muhr
Senior Research Fellow

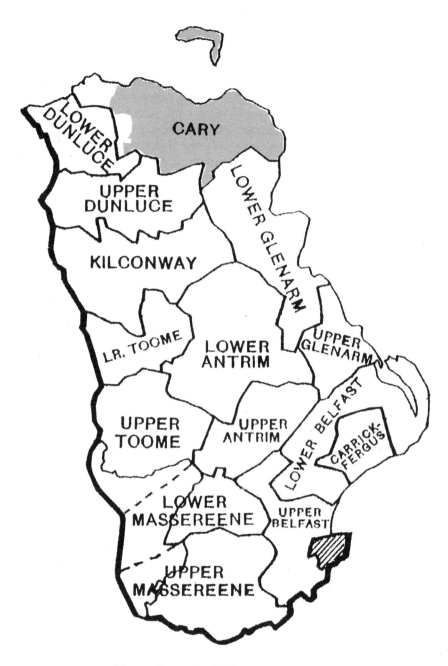

Maps of baronies in Co. Antrim

Antrim Lower
Antrim Upper
Belfast Lower
Belfast Upper
Cary
Carrickfergus
Dunluce Lower
Dunluce Upper

Glenarm Lower
Glenarm Upper
Kilconway
Massereene Lower
Massereene Upper
Toome Lower
Toome Upper

The area described in this volume lies within the barony of Cary and has been shaded to indicate its position.

xviii

INTRODUCTION TO COUNTY ANTRIM

The counties of Ulster as they now stand were established under English rule in the early 17th century. They were built up out of pre-existing smaller districts, some of which were preserved as baronies within the county. County Antrim is bounded by the sea to the north and east and on the south-west by Lough Neagh. On the west the boundary follows the course of the Upper Bann from Toomebridge northwards, but a short distance south of Coleraine it runs eastwards from the Bann to the sea, leaving a small district to the east of the river (i.e. the barony of North-East Liberties of Coleraine) in Co. Derry. On the south it is bounded by the Lagan canal and the river Lagan to the sea.

The county town is named from an early monastery which in Old Irish was known as *Oentreb* "single dwelling". The site is marked by a round tower which stands a little to the north of the centre of the modern town of Antrim. At a later stage, the name *Aontreibh* (<O. Ir. *Oentreb*) was reinterpreted as *Aontroim* "single ridge" which is the accepted modern form of the name.

There are nine barony names, including Carrickfergus, which was formerly known as "the county of the town of Carrickfergus" (*O'Laverty* iii 44). The baronies of Antrim, Belfast, Dunluce, Glenarm, Massereene and Toome are each divided into upper (southern) and lower (northern) halves, while Carrickfergus, Cary and Kilconway are undivided. The native administrative unit of the *tuath* or tribal kingdom (anglicized "tuogh") was well preserved in Antrim and most of the baronies are made up of an amalgamation of these native divisions. For example, the barony of Toome Lower represents a combination of the tuoghs of *Muntercallie* and *Clanagherty* (EA 344–5) while Dunluce Upper is coterminous with the tuoghs of Ballymoney and Loughguile.

The *Ulaid* were once the most powerful tribal group in the north of Ireland and it is from them that the province of Ulster derives its name (Flanagan 1978(d)). However, in the 4th and 5th centuries they were driven eastwards into the modern counties of Antrim and Down under pressure from the *Uí Néill* (who originated in Connaught) and the related *Airgialla*. *Dál Fiatach*, the "true Ulaid", settled in mid-Down, in Lecale and in the vicinity of Strangford Lough. Among the other groups which made up the wider federation of the Ulaid or Ulstermen were several whose ethnic origin was *Cruthin*, a name closely related to *Briton*. The main Cruthin tribe, *Dál nAraide*, was situated east of Lough Neagh and the Lower Bann. Their chief seat appears to have been at *Ráith Mór Maige Line* "Rathmore of Moylinny". Both Rathmore and Moylinny are now mere townlands lying to the east of the town of Antrim, but Moylinny was formerly a tuogh (coextensive with the barony of Antrim Upper) (*EA* 345) and also a medieval deanery (*ibid.* 62). Lying to the north west of this, along the Lower Bann to the sea, was the subkingdom of *Eilne*.

South of Lough Neagh, along the Upper Bann, was a tribe related to *Dál nAraide*, i.e. *Uí Echach Coba* (Iveagh barony in Co. Down). Other more northern kingdoms within the reduced Ulster included *Lathairne* and *Semne* around Larne and Island Magee, *Dál mBuain* and *Uí Earca Céin* near Lough Neagh and the Lagan (all Cruthin) and in the Glens of Antrim the unrelated tribe of *Dál Riata*. Their boundary with *Dál nAraide* was the rivers *Fregabhail* (Glenravel Water) (*AFM* i 32–3) and *Buas* (Bush) (*Céitinn* i 164–6).

From the 6th to 10th centuries the kingship of the Ulaid was shared by Dál Fiatach, Dál nAraide and Uí Echach Coba, but in the 8th century Dál Fiatach extended their influence northward over the area east of Lough Neagh. Benmadigan (*Beann Mhadagáin* "*Madagán's* cliff", now Cave Hill at Belfast), Glengormley (*Clann Ghormlaithe* "descendants of *Gormlaith*") and Clandermot (*Clann Diarmada* "descendants of Dermot"), a now-obsolete district name west of Belfast, are named from chieftains of Dál Fiatach (*Descendants Ir* 82, 85).

The 8th and 9th centuries saw a great advance southwards and eastwards on the part of the *Cenél nEógain*, a branch of the Uí Néill who originated in the Donegal peninsula of Inishowen (Byrne 1973, 114). This had the effect of forcing some of the Airgialla tribes eastwards, further weakening Dál nAraide. One of the most powerful of these tribes was the *Uí Thuirtre* who began to move east across the north shore of Lough Neagh. In the 10th century they took over Eilne, since their lands in Tyrone and Derry had come under the lordship of Cenél nEógain whose dynastic centre was now at *Tulach Óc* (**Tullyhogue**) near Dungannon (*ibid.* 125). Another tribe, the *Fir Lí*, moved east of the Bann into Eilne when their lands in Derry were taken over by the Cenél nEógain sub-king Ó Catháin (O'Kane) of *Ciannachta Glinne Geimin* (Dungiven). By the 12th century we find Uí Thuirtre calling themselves kings of Dál nAraide (*ibid* 126) and their name had come to be applied to a district coterminous with the baronies of Toome Upper and Lower (*EA* 294).

After the Anglo-Norman invasion the whole area east of the Upper and Lower Bann became the feudal Earldom of Ulster, and English shire government was established in the territory of the Ulaid. It was divided into various native and other areas: the "bailiwicks of Antrim, Carrickfergus, Art, Blathewyc, Ladcathel" in 1226, the "counties of Cragfergus, Antrim, Blathewyc, Dun and Coulrath" in 1333 (*Inq. Earldom Ulster* i 31; ii 136, 141; iii 60,63; iv 127). Uí Thuirtre survived as a largely independent Irish district within the Norman Earldom and it gave name to the medieval rural deanery of *Turtrye* which, as well as the baronies of Toome Upper and Lower, also comprised the baronies of Antrim Lower, Glenarm Lower and part of Kilconway (*EA* 83).

In 1549 we find a reference to "the county of Ulster, that is to say the baronies of Grenecastle, Dondalk, Lacayll, Arde, Differens, Gallagh, Bentry, Kroghfergous, Maulyn, Twscard and Glyns" (*Cal. Carew MSS* 1515–74, 223–4). The Antrim districts represented here are *Kroghfergous* (Carrickfergus), *Maulyn*, *Twscard* and *Glyns* (the Glens). The name *Maulyn* has been met with above in the form Moylinny and in this case it refers to the valley of the Six-Mile Water, while *Twscard* is derived from Irish *Tuaisceart* "north" and, as its name suggests, lay to the north and had its capital at Coleraine (*Coulrath* in the aforementioned inquisition of 1333). In 1571 a commission was set up "to survey the countries of Lecale, the Duffrens, M'Carton's country, Slaight M'Oneiles country, Kilvarlyn, Evaghe, M'Ghenes's country, Morne, the lands of the Nury, and O'Handlone's country, and to form them into one county, or to join them to any neighbouring counties or baronies" (*Fiants Eliz.* §1736). This led to the separation from Antrim of the modern county of Down.

A description of Ulster written in 1586 informs us that Antrim "stretching from the haven of Knockfergus to the going out of the Bann" contained the "countreis" of "*North Clandeboy, Iland Magye* (Island Magee), *Brian Caraghe's countrey, Glynnes* (the Glens) and the *Rowte* (the Route)" (*Bagenal's Desc. Ulst.* 154). The name Clandeboy is derived from Irish *Clann Aodha Buí* (earlier *Clann Aodha Buidhe*) "family of *Aodh Buí* or yellow-haired Hugh" and refers to a branch of the O'Neills of Tyrone who after the decline of the Anglo-Norman Earldom of Ulster from the mid-14th century onwards gained control of the area to the north and east of Lough Neagh. In 1584, the territory was divided into Upper and Lower (i.e. North) Clandeboy, the former being represented by the modern baronies of Castlereagh Upper and Lower in Co. Down and the latter by the baronies of Toome, Antrim, Belfast, Massereene Lower and Carrickfergus in Co. Antrim. An alternative name for Clandeboy from Irish literature was *Trian Conghail* "*Conghal's* third or portion". It was named from *Conghal Cláiringhneach* who is said to have ruled Ireland shortly before the coming of Christ and is the central character in the early Modern Irish tale *Caithréim Conghail Cláiringhnigh* "the martial career of *Conghal Cláiringhneach*" (*C. Conghail Cláir.*). *Brian Caraghe's countrey* was named from Brian O'Neill, a member of the Clandeboy O'Neills, who died in 1586 and was grandson of *Domhnall Donn* O'Neill, the founder of a sept named *Clann Domhnaill Doinn na Banna* "the Clann of Donnell Donn, of the Bann" who were located west of the Bann, to the north of Maghera (*GUH* 32). However, *Brian Caraghe's countrey* also comprised territory on the Antrim side of the Bann and, according to Reeves (*EA* 388), it included the parish of Ahoghill in Co. Antrim and the barony of Loughinsholin in Co. Derry. The *Rowte* (Route) refers to the area between the Glens of Antrim and the river Bann, extending as far south as the Glenravel Water to the north of Ballymena. According to MacNeill (1932, 27) its name is derived from Norman French *route* "road" and was originally applied to the northern section of the *Slige Midluachra*, an ancient roadway which ran from Tara to Dunseverick on the north Antrim coast.

The county boundaries were not settled all at once. Jobson's set of Ulster maps (c. 1590) and Norden's map of Ireland (1610) show the names and bounds of the three counties of Antrim, Down and Armagh. According to Jobson, Down included Killultagh on the east bank of Lough Neagh (later the barony of Massereene Upper in Co. Antrim). A document in the state papers of 1603 gives *Kilulto* as a separate "country" (*Cal. Carew MSS* 1601–3, 451). In 1605 Killultagh was annexed to Co. Antrim (*CSP Ire.* 1603–6, 321). In the same year an inquisition on Clandeboy states that the most noted boundary between the parts of it called Killultagh and Upper Clandeboy (later Castlereagh) was the river Lagan (*Inq. Ult.* §2 Jac. I), and the Lagan remains the boundary between Cos Antrim and Down to this day.

INTRODUCTION TO THE BARONY OF CARY

The barony of Cary is the most north-easterly in Ireland. It is bounded on the west by the barony of Dunluce Lower, on the south by the barony of Dunluce Upper, and on the south-east by the barony of Glenarm Lower. It contains six civil parishes, viz. Armoy, Ballintoy, Culfeightrin, Grange of Drumtullagh, Ramoan and Rathlin Island, as well as part of the parish of Billy. The greater part of Billy lies in the barony of Dunluce Lower; therefore that part of it in Cary is not covered by this book.

The earliest reference to Cary is found in a list of churches founded by St Patrick (form 1 below), in a text (c. 700 AD) from the Book of Armagh. The church in this instance was called *Domnuch Cainri*; its precise location remains unknown (see however **Cross** townland in Culfeightrin and **Killaleenan** and **Drumnakill Point** in Other Names, Culfeightrin). In the list it is preceded by the church of Ramoan and followed by the church of Drumeeny (a townland in Ramoan). It appears that at this time Cary referred to the territory lying east of Ramoan, that is, approximately, the area covered today by the parish of Culfeightrin. Cary was understood to refer to such a territory in English documents until the early 17th century (see below), and until the present day in local tradition (see discussion of Culfeightrin). A list of churches from c. 900 (*Trip Life (Stokes)* 162) similar to that alluded to above includes the church of Culfeightrin, entered next to *Domnuch Camri* (*sic*). As the original church in Culfeightrin was in the west of the parish (see **Churchfield** townland), this reference suggests either that Culfeightrin was a territory within Cary or that it was recognised as being distinct from it. In any event, Culfeightrin and Cary later appeared to represent names for the same territory. As Cary lay within the territory of *Dál Riada* (O.Ir. *Dál Riata*), it is open to interpretation whether it was a constituent tribe (and hence a tribal territory) of that kingdom, or whether the name was applied to a population group prior to the foundation of Dál Riada.

Regarding the origin, extent and history of Dál Riada, see, for example, *Céitinn* ii 270, *O'Flaherty's Ogygia* 322–3, *Ogygia Vindicated* 162–9, *Trias Thaum.* 377 n.3, *AFM* i 106–7 n.w, *Leabhar na g-Ceart (JOD)* 161–2 n.a. *EA* 318–34 *et passim, Onom. Goed.* 335, *O'Laverty* 1–12, *MacDonnells Antrim* 2–12, Mac Néill 1933, 10, Mahr 1938, 329 *et passim*, O'Rahilly 1946, 81 *et passim*, Byrne 1973 *passim* and Bannerman 1974, 1–8 *et passim*. It must suffice here to quote MacNeill:

> The kingdom of Dál Riata [in Ireland] in the seventh century should thus have extended no farther than from the Giant's Causeway to Glenarm Bay . . . [although] at a [later time it] gained territory southward along the coast (Mac Néill 1932, 28).

Dál has been translated "a part share; a division, a sept, tribe; the land inhabited by a tribe" (*DIL* sv.). O'Rahilly postulates that *Riada* (often interpreted as meaning "long-armed") derives from the mythical ancestor of the population group (O'Rahilly 1946, 6), and interprets it as meaning:

> 'travelling (on horseback, or in a chariot)', Celt. *Rédodios, I.E. root *reidh-*. So the cognate Gaulish tribal name Rédones (preserved in the placename Rennes), meaning 'riders on horseback, travellers in chariots', probably implies the existence of a sing. *Rédú as a name for the otherworld deity . . . (*ibid.* 295).

We can thus explain Dál Riada as "the territory of the (descendants of the) ancestor *Riada*".

References to Dál Riada, including references to events which occurred within the territory of the modern barony of Cary, abound in the annals. The last mention is in 1247 in a reference to Armoy *(AFM* iii 322; *AU* ii 308). Cary, however, receives no mention in the annals. References occur in medieval sources to a tribe (and/or territory) called *Crotraidhe/ Crotraighe.* This name is tentatively equated with Cary by O'Donovan *(Leabhar na g-Ceart (JOD)* 171–2 n.r; *AFM* ii 1064–5 n.h; cf. also map at rear of *Lebor na Cert).* Dobbs however is probably correct to locate them to the south of Larne, as in a genealogical list of c. 1200 they are treated as a sub-sept of *Uí Dhearca (Descendants Ir* 103 n.9; see also *ibid.* 105 §19–20, and 105 n.6). The latter tribe was apparently located "in the north of the county of Down, or on the confines of Down and Antrim" *(EA* 339 n.a; see also *PNI* vi 229).

The dearth of references to Cary, due to the use of Dál Riada in the sources, continues even after the demise of the latter kingdom in the late 12th and early 13th centuries with the establishment of the Anglo-Norman earldom of Ulster. At this time, the name *An Tuaisceart* "the north" appears in Anglo-Norman literature (cf. *Cul-in-thueskert* in *de Courcy Charters* 6 (1180c AD); *Gweskard* in *Rot. Litt. Pat.* 98a (1213 AD); *Twescart* in *CDI* §565 (1215 AD)). References to such a region appear in the annals prior to this (e. g. *AFM saa.* 907, 1171). There is some doubt about the exact origin of this designation, although it may have referred to that part of *Dál nArai* (O. Ir. *Dál nAraide)* which extended along the Lower Bann to the sea (see county introduction). (Confusingly, the term was also generally employed "in the Irish annals to denote the country of the northern Uí-Neill" *(AFM* i 344 n.k)). It was apparently borrowed by "English settlers to denote the area around Coleraine" *(EA* 71 n.a), and in a document dating to 1213 it is separate from Dál Riada *(Rot. Litt. Pat.* 98a). By c. 1306, the deanery of *Twescard* had been established (see *Inq. Earl. Ulster* 123), covering "the modern baronies of Cary, Dunluce, N.E. Liberties of Coleraine, and most of Kilconway" *(EA* 71 n.a), while Dál Riada now ceases to appear in non-Irish sources (other than native literature translated into English). This ecclesiastical unit of Twescard continued to be used until at least c. 1615 when a further garbled form appears *(Decantus de Inscarde* in *Terrier (Reeves)* 67; in *EA* 71 n.a this form is spelt *Tuscardie).*

Two other regional names were employed to denote local territory in both native and nonnative literature. They account somewhat for the absence of parish names and of the barony name, especially from English sources, until the late 16th century. The first of these regional names, *The Route,* is possibly used for the first time in the sources in an obscure reference to *Ruta Midal* in 1210 *(CDI* §406); the next English reference appears to be in 1543 ("Rory McCuyllen, chief of his nation and captain of Route"; *Cal. Carew MSS* 202). The earliest reference in the annals to The Route appears to be in 1357: "*i rúta meic uidhilin*" *(AFM* iii 612; cf. also *AU* ii 504, *A. Conn.* 316 §10 and *ALC* ii 16). As in the case of Dál Riada, it is not possible to list the historical citations here; what concerns us is that, although it is predominantly portrayed as having lain west of the Bush River (cf. *Ulster Map [1570c]* and subsequent maps), in some cases the Route was used to refer to parts of Cary. Bonamargy townland in Culfeightrin was referred to as *Bunanmargaidh in Patria Ruta* in 1617, for example *(Donatus Moneyus* 103 §5). In 1838, it was recorded locally that "this part of the country is locally called the Root from Bannside to Cushendall . . . The people are called the Root people" *(OSM* xvi 103). Regarding the origin of the term, which for centuries was considered to be derived from Dál Riada, we may note the following:

> I take this name to have been introduced by the feudal colonists and to represent the French *route* applied to the most northern section of the ancient main road, Slige Midluachra, which ended at Dún Sobairche, Dunseverick. Neither etymologically nor topographically is there any identity between Dal Riata and Ruta . . . (MacNeill 1932, 27).

2

Regarding this ancient road-way, see Lawlor 1938 and Hamilton 1913.

The second regional term alluded to above is *The Glens/Glynns*. The earliest form of this name comes from a Scottish document dated to c. 1400 in which John MacDonnell, who acquired much of north Antrim by marriage in 1399 (see below) is described as "*Dominus de Dunwage et de Glynns*" (*ALI* 293). *Dunwage* is identified as Dunivaig in south-east Islay (*ibid.* xxii). The earliest attested Irish references to The Glens occur in 1419 ("*is na glindibh*"; *AFM* iv 838) and 1422 (*na glinne*; *AFM* iv 854). The popular current form, *Na Glinntí*, is not widely attested, although it has been used in some cases in the Irish literature of the past 150 years (cf. *Mac Bionaid* 218 §3; there are frequent examples in *An Claidheamh Soluis*). The form in late local Irish may have been *Na Gleanna* ([nə gl'anə]; *Irish of the Glens* 116). The earliest English forms may be in a document dated to c. 1481 from "John De Islis (McDonnell), Lord of the Glens" (*Cal. Carew MSS* v 428). The next English references date to 1549 ("Besetes of the Glyns . . .; baronies of . . . Twscard, and Glyns"; *Cal. Carew MSS* 223–4). References to both The Glens and The Route become very common in the later half of the 16th century and are equally prolific throughout the 17th century. Regarding the extent of The Glens, see the discussion of English sources below.

Irish references to Cary in the 17th century occur in works by Colgan based on earlier biographies of St Patrick (forms 4–7), and in *SMMD II* (form 3). The latter is an Early Mod. Ir. redaction of an earlier story which was apparently altered to reflect local encounters between Shane O'Neill and the MacDonnells in 1565–7, and which provides us with a small handful of Irish forms for local place-names (*SMMD II* 48–56).

As stated, Cary appears anonymously as part of other territories in the earliest Anglo-Norman sources. Dál Riada was but one of many territories mentioned in a grant from King John of England to one Alan de Galweia (Galloway in Scotland) in 1213: ".s. *tota Dalreth cu Insuł de Rathliñ . . . tota tra de Gweskarð . . .*" (*Rot. Litt. Pat.* 98a §6; see also *EA* 323–4). It appears again in affirmations of this grant in 1215 (*Dalred*; *CDI* §564) and in 1220 (*Dalrede*; *CD* §942). An account dating from 1226–7 relating to the Anglo-Norman earldom of Ulster, "did not include Coleraine and Twescard, or the northern part of the present county of Antrim", indicating that "the district appears to have been held directly of the crown" at this time (*Inq. Earl. Ulster* 31). Alan of Galloway died in 1234, and also around this time, Patrick, Earl of Athol in Scotland and son of Alan's brother, Thomas of Galloway, was murdered. Members of the Biset family were accused, and they consequently fled from Scotland and took refuge in The Glens (*EA* 325), where they obtained a settlement under the Earl of Ulster, Richard de Burgo (*MacDonnells Antrim* 22). Regarding the Bisets (variant spellings of this name include *Myssett*), see *MacDonnells Antrim* 21 and *EA* 325 n.o.

Cary is first mentioned in English sources in the year 1272 (forms 8–9), when on the 27th of December an inquisition taken at "Finale burn in Twiscard, by Sir W(illiam) FitzWarin, seneschal of the land of the Lord Edward in Ulster" found that "the Irish of Turtria burnt the land of Ocaynymery and Cachery and killed 22 English . . ." and that "Sir Walter de Burgh, late Earl of Ulster, was seized at his death as custodee of Mamym' and Cachery . . ." (*CDI* §929; regarding the *Uí Thuirtre*, see the county introduction). In 1278, on the 27th of October, at an inquisition "before Nicholas Bishop of Down" and several named jurors, in the *village of Oul*, the rents of several territories were fixed, including that of Cary at 20 marks (*ibid.* §1500; form 13). It is likely that at this time the territory of Cary still represented only the area approximately covered by the modern parish of Culfeightrin. It is uncertain whether the reference from c. 1280 to the *vill of Catheran* (form 10) refers to Cary. It was located thus by Sweetman and Handcock (*CDI* index sv.), but none of the places or surnames associated with this reference can be conclusively ascribed to north-east Antrim.

In 1279 it was found by inquisition that one Joh'es Biset held extensive tracts of land in north and east Antrim, including *Catherich, [and] Racry* (*Cal. Inq. Post Mortem I* 63b; cf. also *EA* 325). From this Joh'es or John Biset was derived the local patronymic *Mac Eoin* (*ibid.*). The last reference in medieval times to Cary occurs in 1333, when one William de Welles was tenant of the Earl of Ulster in *Manybery and Cary* (that is, in Ramoan/Grange of Drumtullagh and Culfeightrin; *EA* 332) although it appears that by the end of the century the Bisets again held this land (*MacDonnells Antrim* 22). In 1399 all the lands held by the Bisets passed into the hands of the MacDonnells of the Western Isles of Scotland via the marriage of Margery Byset in this year to John Mór (*ibid.*).

Cary appears to be absent from English sources from 1333 until around 1567 (appearing anonymously as a constituent element of An Tuaisceart, The Route, or The Glens) when Somhairle Buí MacDonnell requested "that he might have quiet and immediate possession of the Glynnes, by grant from the crown, which were his family possessions, and also the lands of Monery and Cary" (*MacDonnells Antrim* 147; unfortunately, Hill does not source these forms). We have a more definite reference dated to the 4th of May, 1570, when "William Piers, esq. seneschal of Clannyboy, sir Brian McPhelim, knt., the mayor of Carrickfergus for the time being, captain Thomas Cheston, gent., Robert Munckeman, provost marshal, and Thomas Stephenson, burgess" were obliged to:

> survey and make enquiry in the countries and territories . . . that are not shire ground, or are doubtful to what shire they belong; to limit and nominate them a shire or county; to divide them into counties, baronies, or hundreds, or to join them to any existing shire or barony; and to certify their proceedings to the lord deputy with all convenient speed, (the following lands): the countries or territories of Arde, as well this side Blackstafe as the other side, Copelande islands, the Dufferin, Clandeboy, Kilultoghe, the Glynes with the Raughlines, Momerie, and Carie, the Rowte McWilliam (McQuillan), and all lands between lough Coine and lough Eaghe, and the water of Strangforde and the Banne. To certify their proceedings before the 1st August (*Fiants Eliz.* §§1486, 1530).

Again, *Carie* here only denoted that part of the modern barony covered by Culfeightrin parish (*EA* 332; regarding *Momerie* see the introduction to Ramoan parish). We can assume the *Rowte McWilliam* lay to the west of Ramoan, while *the Glynes* may have been regarded as lying to the immediate south of Ramoan and Culfeightrin (regarding the surname *Mac Uidhilín*, later anglicized as MacQuillan, see *MacQuillan of the Route, EA* 72 n.a, *O'Laverty* iv 11, *MacDonnells Antrim* 123 *et passim*, and MacLysaght 1985, 251). In 1586, Bagenal described the territory of *the Glynnes*, "so called because it is full of rockie and woodie dales", as follows:

> it stetchethe in length 24 miles (on the one side being backed with a very steepe and bogie mounteyne and on th'other parte with the sea) on which side there are many small creekes betweene rockes and thickets, where the Scottische gallies do commonlie land . . . The Glynnes conteyne 7 Baronyes, where the Ile of raghlins is counted half a Barony, the names of the Baronies are these: Larne, Park, Glenarme, Redbaye, Lade, Cary, Mawbray . . . The force of this countrey is uncertaine, for that they are supplied as nede requireth from Scotland, with what numbers they list to call, by makings of fiers upon certain steepe rockes hanginge over the sea . . . The auncient followers of this countrey are these – the Myssetts some few remayninge, but in poor estate, the McKayes, the Omulrenies, the Mac y Gillies, the MacAwnleys, the MacCarnocks, and the Clanalsters . . . (*Bagenal's Descr. Ulst.* 155; cf. also: "the seven baronies in the Glynns be granted to angus McDonnell" in *CSP* 69 §62, dated May, 1586)).

4

The division of The Glens into seven territories was followed 13 years later in John Dymmok's *Treatice of Ireland*: "the ile of glimes [*sic*] contayneth seavon Baronyes of which the Raughlines being six miles, is counted half a barony, the rest are Larnparke, glanan, Redbay, Layde, Carye and Mowbray" (*Treatice of Ire. (Butler)* 23), and again in 1618 (see "The seven troohes or cantreds of the Glens" in *Cal. Carew MSS* 374). The use of a seven-fold divison of The Glens wanes in the sources after c. 1610 (see below). The idea of there being seven territories in The Glens was also used in Irish sources: "*secht dtuatha na nGlinneadh darab ainm Dál Riada*" (*LCA Buidhe* 52 §10; 1618 AD). Similar descriptions of the divisions of The Route, which in the late 1500s was probably considered as including the modern civil parishes of Ballintoy and Billy, do not appear until 1603 (see below).

In a "Grant from the king to sir Randal McDonnel of Dunluce, knt." dated 28th of May, 1603, of "the estate of the Rowte and the Glynnes", Randal, the first Earl of Antrim, received the following denominations:

> the 9 tuoghes in the Rowte, viz. that between the Bande and the Bois, Dunsevericke and Ballenatoy, Ballelagh, Loughgill or Loghill, Ballamoney and Dromart, Killeoconway, Killioquin, Killiomorrie, and Maghareunagh ... the Glynns, containing seven tuoghes, viz. Munerie, the cynomond of Armoy and Raghlines, Carey, Glinmiconogh, the Largie, the Parke, – and the 4 towns, villages or hamlets, called the Creggs, being parcel of the Rowte ... (*CPR* Jas. I 58a; for further information on the Route and its divisions, see *EA* 325–332, and the parish introduction to Ballintoy).

This grant was confirmed on the 6th of July, 1603 (*ibid.*) and again in 1610 (*LP 8 Jas I (PRONI)*). O'Rahilly (1932, 163) estimated that MacDonnell was granted about two-thirds of Co. Antrim. The use of the word *tough/tuogh* in English sources, where it had the approximate meaning "barony", began now to wane. (It represents *tuath* "people, tribe, nation; country, territory, petty kingdom" (*DIL* sv. *túath*)). Forms 39 and 45 below, which contain the word *tuogh*, date to the mid-17th century, but come from sources which contain forms which in some cases appear antiquated if not otherwise obsolete: they have been copied from older documentation.

In 1611, in a grant of lands constituting "the Ballycastle estate" to one Hugh MacNeill, "constable and gentleman" of Dunineny Castle (see Other Names, Ramoan), an administrative unit called the *Barony of Dunluce and Carie* was used (form 28; see also O'Laverty iv 415). The first reference to the barony of Cary as used administratively today may be in 1625 (form 30), when the *territory or precinct of Ardmoy* is ascribed to *the barony of Carie (MacDonnells Antrim* 411 n.24).

Some scattered references to townlands prior to the mid-1600s are found in the *Inquisitions of Ulster (Inq. Ult.*), but the earliest references to townland names in the barony are normally found in the mid-17th-century English-language sources (*Hib. Reg., DS (Par. Map), Census, BSD, HMR, Hib. Del. Antrim*). The mid-17th-century sources invariably exhibit bad spelling and repetition of scribal errors. An *Act of Settlement* which dates from 1668 (*ASE* 116a §19), and which shows "Sir Martin Noell, knt. [and] Geo. Blake, and John Robinson, of London [to be] trustees for ye barony of Cary, ye lordship of Ballycastle, and ye island of Rathcline (to ye uses in a clause in ye act of explanation)", lists many townland names whose spellings appear to be based on the *Down Survey (Hib. Reg.), Census* or *Book of Survey and Distribution (BSD)*. More independent sources from this period include records of a court case in c. 1662 (*Court of Claims*) which contain forms of place-names copied from earlier documents, and the "Decree of Innocence in favour of the Marquis of Antrim" (*Decree of Innocence; MacDonnells Antrim* 430–44) which is dated to 1663, but which contains a copy of Randal MacDonnell's will (d. 1636) and other documents written earlier in the century. The *Lapsed Money Book,* dated by Hill to 1663, appears to be practically identical to the *Antrim Forfeitures (Ant. Forfeit.;* kept in PRONI D2977/5/1/3/19/1), which was dated to c. 1700 by PRONI and which thus may constitute a copy (if not the original). The *Lapsed Money Book* contains a list of townland names in the baronies of Dunluce Lower and Cary, their acreage, and sums levied per townland for the payment of a debt to Martin Noell, a "London scrivener, who had accommodated Lord Antrim with the loan of money to a large extent" *(Hill's Stewarts* 151). The forms of the names appear to be based on other documents compiled in the years immediately prior to 1663, especially the *Book of Survey and Distribution (BSD)* of 1661. Hill *(MacDonnells Antrim, Hill's Stewarts)* seems to have had access to many documents of worth to this study, but often failed to source his information. PRONI keeps a broad selection of land indentures relating to the Antrim estate of the MacDonnells *(PRONI D2977/3A/2).* The earliest of these dates to 1611 although the vast majority postdate c. 1675. Maps and surveys of the Antrim estate were also useful (including *Stewart's Survey* of 1734, *Sur. A.E.* of 1782 and *Culfeightrin Map [1789]/[1812]).* Other local sources include the *Religious Survey* of 1734 which gives a religious break-down of the barony population, townland by townland. The place-name variants in this survey and in the similar *Religious Census* of Ballintoy (1766) appear to be reasonably independent.

Notwithstanding the influence of Scottish Gaelic on the local Irish dialect (see for example O'Rahilly 1932, 161–166 and Ó Baoill 1978), only a tiny minority of townland and sub-townland names (mainly on Rathlin Island) contain what one might consider to be specific features of Scottish Gaelic. The *Ordnance Survey Memoirs (OSM),* compiled in the 1830s, refer to the local Irish-speaking "old natives", and their historical and place-name lore is noted on several occasions. Adams's study of Irish speakers in Ulster based on census returns in 1891 reveals:

> Irish speakers in north east Antrim were concentrated in the eastern half of the barony of Cary and the northern half of the barony of Lower Glenarm, the other halves of these baronies being almost entirely English speaking (Adams 1974, 65).

While between 10% and 30% of people in the 30–90 age group were monoglot or bilingual Irish speakers, less than 10% in the 1–30 age group were monoglot or bilingual in this area at this time *(ibid.).* By 1937, when the linguistic scholar Nils Holmer visited the area, only "three or four people could be found who might be called 'native speakers' of the Antrim dialect, and even these were by no means fluent speakers of Irish" *(Irish of the Glens* 5). He noted, however, the Irish of several people who learned the language in classes given by a local teacher and was satisfied it was of a genuinely local character. Most of these came from the parishes of Culfeightrin and Ramoan *(ibid.* 9–10). Irish forms of some local place-names appeared in publications earlier this century (notably *An Claidheamh Soluis* and *An tUltach);* it is difficult to ascertain how accurately these reflect late local Irish. Preference is given to forms in Holmer's works *(Irish of the Glens, Irish of Rathlin).*

BARONY NAME

Cary   *Cothraí*
                                       A tribal name

1. iCothrugu, .ii. Cheinn[fhin]dán in
   Domnuch Cainri   Tírechán 349   700c

6

2. hiCothrugu, daChenn[fh]indán in Domnuch Camri	Trip. Life (Stokes) 162	900c
3. gCathraoi, i	SMMD II, 42–3	1638c
4. in regione Dalreidiae Cathrugia dicta, & in Deconatu de Tuascheart	Acta SS Colgan 455b	1645
5. Cathrigiae, in regione etiam	Trias Thaum. 146b	1647
6. Cat-rige est regio Dal-riediae quae Reuta vocatur	Trias Thaum. 182b	1647
7. Cathrige, in regione	Trias Thaum. 182b	1647
8. Cachery, the land of Ocaynymery and	CDI §929	1272
9. Cachery, Mamym' and	CDI §929	1272
10. Catherick, Rent of	CDI §1500	1278
11. Catherich	Cal. Inq. Post Mortem i 63b l.28	1279
12. (?)Catheran, the vill of	CDI §1782	1280c
13. Cary, Manyberv and	EA 332	1333
14. (?)Monery and Carey	MacDonnells Antrim 147	1567c
15. the Glynes with the Raughlines, Momerie and Carie, the Rowte McWilliam (McQuillan)	Fiants Eliz. §1530	1570
16. Cary	Ulster Map [1570c]	1570
17. Cary	North Ulster Coast Map	1570c
18. Mowbray and Cary, the countries of	MacDonnells Antrim 417	1575c
19. Cary	Bagenal's Descr. Ulst. 155	1586
20. Cary	Mercator's Ire.	1595
21. Carey	Boazio's Map (BM)	1599
22. Carye	Treatice of Ire. (Butler) 23	1599c
23. Cary	Treatise on Ire. (NLI) 110	1599c
24. Carey (tough of)	CPR Jas. 1 58a	1603
25. Carry, the tough of	LP 8 Jas. I (PRONI)	1610
26. Carie, the Barony of Dunluce and	PRONI D2977/3A/2/1/2	1611
27. Carie, barony of	MacDonnells Antrim 441	1625
28. Cary, barony of	Inq. Ult. (Antrim) §23 Car. I	1633
29. Carey, barony of	MacDonnells Antrim 150	1637
30. Cary, barrony of	MacDonnells Antrim 437	1637
31. Carie	Civ. Surv. x §60	1655
32. Cary, Bar: of	MacDonnells Antrim 283–4	1655c
33. Carie, barony of	Hib. Reg. Cary	1657c
34. Cary, The Barony of	DS (Par. Map) 58	1657c
35. Baronyes of Dunluce Carry and Kilconrie	Census 10	1659
36. Carey	Census 19	1659
37. Cary, the island of Racklyn and the barony of	CSP Ire. 70	1660
38. Carie	BSD 165	1661
39. Carie	Court of Claims §923	1661
40. Cary, the Tough of	Court of Claims §923	1661

41. Carey	MacDonnells Antrim 147	1662
42. Cary, the Island of Rackins and the barony of	CSP Ire. 697	1662c
43. Carre Barro.	Lapsed Money Book 155	1663
44. Carie, the Tough of	Decree of Innocence 437	1663
45. Cary, Barrony of	Decree of Innocence 437	1663
46. Cary, barony of	CSP Ire. 338, 340	1663
47. Cary	CSP Ire. 686	1665
48. Cary Barony	HMR (1666) 111	1666
49. Cary, barony of	CSP Ire. 59, 67	1666
50. Cary	ASE 143b §30	1667
51. Cary, ye barony of	ASE 116a §19	1668
52. Carey,	HMR Ant. 1	1669
53. Cary	Hib. Del. Antrim	1672c
54. Carey	PRONI D2977/3A/2/10/1	1678
55. Cary	PRONI D2977/3A/2/11/1	1681
56. Cary	PRONI D2977/3a/2/1/5A	1682
57. Cary	MacDonnells Antrim 386	1683
58. Cary	Dan. Force 147	1690
59. Cary, Carie	PRONI D2977/3A/2/24/1	1692
60. Carie	PRONI D2977/3A/2/28/1	1696
61. Cary	PRONI D2977/3A/2/1/13, 15	1696
62. Carrie	PRONI D2977/3A/2/1/16	1696
63. Carie	PRONI D2977/3A/2/3/2A	1696
64. Carie	PRONI D2977/3A/2/9/1	1696
65. Carie	PRONI D2977/3A/2/14/1	1696
66. Cary, Carie	PRONI D2977/3A/2/24/1	1696
67. Carie	Ire. Map	1711
68. Carey, Cary	Reg. Deeds abstracts i §265	1722
69. Cary	Religious Survey	1734
70. Cary	Stewart's Survey	1734
71. Carey	MacDonnells Antrim 117	1738
72. Kerry, Carey	MacDonnells Antrim 220	1740c
73. Carye i.e. Cathrugia	Mon. Hib. 11	1779
74. Carey	Lendrick Map	1780
75. Carey	Sur. A.E.	1782
76. Cary, The Barony Lordship or Manor of Ballycastle otherwise	PRONI D2977/3A/2/1/40	1812
77. Carey	Report on the A.E	1812
78. Carey	Dubourdieu Map	1812
79. Carey	Grants on the A.E.	1814
80. Cathraighe, the name of an ancient tribe seated in this barony	J O'D (OSNR) B 24 B 37	1831
81. Caithrighe, the barony of	O'Donovan (DPJ) 321	1833
82. Cathraidhe	Leabhar na g-Ceart (JOD) 171–2 n.r	1847
83. Carraigh "The rocky (place)"	Ó Dubhthaigh 134	1905

84. Cathair ríogh "the seat of the King",
    or Cathraighe "the battling sept"   Rev. Magill 11   1923

85. 'kari   Local pronunciation   1993

Old Irish tribal names which have survived as place-names take a variety of forms (Mac Néill 1907, 43; MacNeill 1911: see also Appendix B, Tribal and Family Names). Some consist of the ancestor's name, or some other element, followed by a (normally collective) suffix. *Cothraí* (earlier *Cothraighe*), anglicized Cary, belongs to this type. MacNeill (1911, 67) correlates the suffix *righe/raighe* with the (O.Ir.) neuter noun *ríge* "kingship": "Hence it would appear that (tribes of this name type) originally formed petty states each under its king". MacNeill (*ibid.* 81) also notes that names of this type often bear the name of an animal for the eponym, while others appear to be based on the occupations of the people. The exact origin of the first element of *Cothraí* remains unclear, however. That it is derived from *coth* "food, sustenance" (*DIL*), which gave rise to the verb *cothad* "act of supporting, maintaining, preserving; act of sustaining, feeding" (*ibid.*) might be considered. The tribal name *Cothraí* recurs elsewhere in Ireland in the obsolete place-names latinized as *Petra(m) Coithrigi* in counties Tipperary and Westmeath, and the tribe called *Catrige* (recté *Cotrige*) in Co. Carlow (Harvey 1985, 7–8). In late local tradition, Cary was interpreted as deriving from *Cathaoir Rí* "king's chair" or *Cath na Rí* "battle of the kings" (*OSM* xxiv 36).

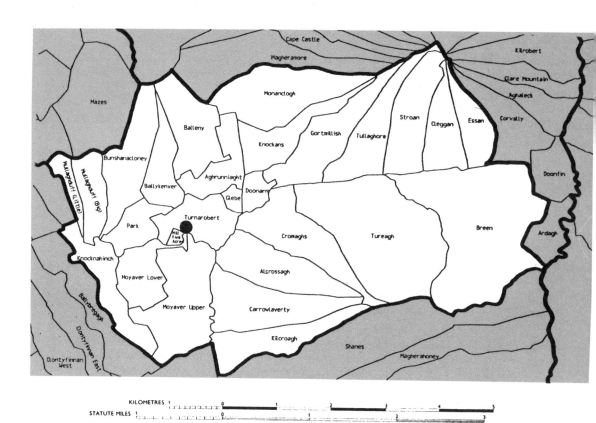

KILOMETRES 1 ⊢⊣⊢⊣⊢⊣ 0   1   2   3   4   5

STATUTE MILES 1 ⊢⊣⊢⊣ 0   1   2   3

Parish of Armoy

Townlands

Aghrunniaght	Knocknahinch
Alcrossagh	Milll Five Acres
Balleny	Monanclogh
Ballykenver	Moyaver Lower
Breen	Moyaver Upper
Bunshanacloney	Mullaghduff Big
Carrowlaverty	Mullaghduff Little
Cleggan	Park
Cromaghs	Stroan
Doonans	Tullaghore
Essan	Tureagh
Glebe	Turnarobert
Gortmillish	
Kilcroagh	*Town*
Knockans	Armoy

PARISH OF ARMOY

The civil parish of Armoy contains 27 townlands and c. 9349 acres (*OSM* xxiv 1). It is bounded to the north and east by the parish of Ramoan, to the north-west by the parish of Grange of Drumtullagh, to the south by the parish of Loughguile in the barony of Dunluce Upper, and to the west by the parish of Derrykeighan in the barony of Dunluce Lower. The Armoy townlands of Moyaver Lower, Moyaver Upper and Knocknahinch are considered to be in the barony of Dunluce Upper; they lie south of the Bush River which forms part of Armoy's southern boundary. The Bush River was formerly a boundary (*Céitinn* i 164) separating Dál Riada from Dál nAraí (see the county and barony introductions regarding these territories).

The earliest reference to Armoy occurs in the context of St Patrick's visit to Dál Riada:

> He heard the crying of the infant out of the earth. The cairn is broken up, the grave opened. A smell of wine comes around them out of the grave. They see the live son with the dead mother, a woman who had died of ague. She was taken by them oversea to Ireland, and after her death brought forth the infant, who lived, they say, seven days in the cairn. "*Olc* ('bad') is that" saith the king. "Let Olcán be his name", saith the druid. Patrick baptized him. He is bishop Olcán of Patrick's household in Airthir Maige, a noble city of Dál Riatai (*Trip. Life (Stokes)* 161–3; see also *O'Laverty* iv 445–6).

The description of Armoy as a "noble city" is derived from form 1 below. *Cathair*, however, might be better translated as "a stone enclosure, fortress, castle; dwelling; monastic settlement, enclosure; monastery; episcopal chair, see, diocese" (*DIL* sv. *cathair*). In 1639, Ussher ventured that the church of Armoy was founded in the year 474 (*Brit. Eccles. Antiq.* 1117). He also stated that St Patrick, having baptized *Olcán* "on the subsequent evidence of his great advance in piety and learning", placed him as bishop over the church of Armoy, "the chief town of *Dál Riada*" (as translated by Reeves in *EA* 80; see also "*Vita S. Olcani Seu Bolcani*" in *Acta SS Colgan* 375–7).

Olcán's feast day is the 20th of February (cf. *Mart. Tal.* 18, and *Mart. Gorm.* 40–1, where he is called "*Bolcán ógnar, idan*", "Bolcán, virgin-bashful, pure"). This male personal name has been recently translated as "a wolf" (Ó Corráin & Maguire 1981, 149). O'Laverty describes Olcán as the only "bishop" of the "see of Armoy" (note that the ecclesiastical territory implied in form 1 seems to be not of Armoy, but of Dál Riada). He continues: "It seems to have been at a very early date absorbed into the see of Connor, perhaps owing to the weakness of the Irish Dal-riadan kingdom", and suggests that this event is the subject of the legend (*Trip. Life (Stokes)* 166) in which St Patrick prophesies to Olcán that the establishment at Armoy "should be thrice destroyed, as was afterwards fulfilled . . ." (*O'Laverty* iv 447–8; regarding the three destructions of Armoy, by three chieftains of Dál nAraí, see *ibid.* and *Trip. Life (Stokes)* loc. cit.; cf. also *Acta SS Colgan* 377–8 and *Mon. Hib.* 23–4). Thus "the church of Armoy sunk into the position of a parochial church of which the bishop was rector, and its property merged into the see lands of Connor" (*O'Laverty* iv 448). The church lands in this parish were sometimes referred to in recent centuries as "the sixteen townlands of Balleeny" and consisted of the townlands of Aghrunniaght, Alcrossagh, Balleny, Breen, Carrowlaverty, Cleggan, Cronaghs, Doonans, Essan, Gortmillish, Kilcroagh, Knockans, Monanclogh, Stroan, Tullaghore and Turnarobert (*ibid.* 448–9). The Glebe, containing the church (now Church of Ireland; see below) and round tower, was apparently formerly part of Doonans (*EA* 260). In 1615, however, these lands were called "the Temporalities of 4

11

Towns" (*ibid.* 259), while O'Laverty says they were called "the four townlands of Armoy, in the territory of the Route" in a parliamentary return of 1833 (*O'Laverty* iv 449).

Armoy appears first in the annals in association with John de Courcy's attack on east Ulster in 1177 (forms 5–7). It is possible that at this time Armoy was considered part of the territory of the *Uí Thuirtre* or *Fir Lí* (see county introduction), as it is with these tribes that it was mentioned in this instance. It seems that one *Cúmidhe ua flainn* burned Armoy before it could be taken by de Courcy; the latter went on to burn Coleraine "and many other churches on this incursion" (*AFM* iii 32–3). However, it is specifically located in Dál Riada by the annals 70 years later (form 8). There is some doubt regarding the two references (3–4) in the 11th-century *Lebor na Cert* to a *rí an Oirthir* ("king of *An tOirthear*"). Dillon (see map at rear of *ibid.*) placed this territory in that part of *Oirghialla* (angl. Oriel) where the baronies of Orior in Co. Armagh are today; O'Donovan believed that these references did not refer to this south Ulster territory (possibly as Orior usually appears in Irish sources in a plural form; see *Onom. Goed.* 26 sv. *airthir*) but was uncertain as to the exact location of this place (*Leabhar na gCeart (JOD)* 161 n.x). These forms occur in the text between references to the kings of Dál Riada and *Uí Dhearca Chéin* (apparently located around the Down/Antrim border; see barony introduction), and it might be considered that they refer to Armoy. The implication would then be that at some time prior to the 11th century the territory of Armoy was being considered as separate from Dál Riada.

Earliest references to Armoy in non-Irish sources relate to Armoy's position in the Anglo-Norman earldom of Ulster. In an account of Henry de Mandeville, "custos of Twescard" (see barony introduction), dated to 1262, Armoy was valued at £20 (*Inq. Earl. Ulster* i 38). In c. 1306 however it was valued at £4 11s. 4d. (*Eccles. Tax (CDI)* 209). Armoy is mentioned again in the *Inquisition Post Mortem* of William de Burgo in 1333 (forms 32–3). In 1586 several people mainly from the Ballymoney area received pardons from the English crown, but the list also includes the "dean (deacañs) of Armoye" (35), suggesting that the territory was for a time recognised as a deanery. In the administration of the Church of Ireland, the rectory of Armoy, consisting of most of the parish less a few townlands and part of the village, was appropriate to the archdeaconry of the see of Connor from 1609 (see *Jas 1 to Connor Cath (EA)* 262) until 1831. During this time the living was a vicarage, and only became a rectory in this latter year (*Lewis' Top. Dict.* 73). The present Church of Ireland parish church, built in 1820 (*EA* 80) or 1829 (*O'Laverty* iv 449), stands upon the foundations of the ancient Patrician one, except at the east end "where it is 23.5 feet shorter . . . At the distance of 28 feet from the N.W. angle are the remains of a Round Tower, 35 feet high, and 47.5 feet in circumference . . ." (*EA* 80).

In 1603, Armoy was amalgamated with Rathlin Island to form a cinament (see form 36), forming one of *the seven tuoghs of the Glynnes* (see barony introduction), and leased to Randal MacDonnell (*CPR Jas I* 58a), who was made the first Earl of Antrim in 1620 (Frey 1953, 93). His grant was confirmed in 1610 (form 38). Rathlin Island, along with other modern Catholic parishes, also appears to have come under the administration of the Catholic parish of Armoy "from the period of the Reformation until 1782" (JDCHS (anon.) 1930, 53): Ramoan or Ballycastle parish was separated from Armoy in 1825, while Ballintoy was separated from it around 1872 (*ibid.*; see also the introductions to the named parishes).

PARISH NAME

Armoy
D 0733

Oirthear Maí
"(the) east of the plain"

12

1. inAirtiur [Maigi] soirchaithir Dáil Riatai	Trip. Life (Stokes) 162	900c
2. Airther Maigi	Trip. Life (Stokes) 162	900c
3. (?)Airrthir, ríg an	Lebor na Cert 84 l.1244	1050c
4. (?)Airthir, ríg an	Lebor na Cert 88 l.2912	1050c
5. airthear mhaighe	AFM iii 32	1177
6. Airthear-Maighi	AU ii 188	1177
7. Airrther Maighe	ALC i 157	1177
8. hairthear mhaighe in ndáilriada, go	AFM iii 322	1247
9. co hAirther-muighi i n-Dail-riatai	AU ii 308	1247
10. Airther Maigi Coba	Trip. Life (Stokes) lix	1400c
11. Airther Maigi Cobhai i nDáil Araidhi	Book of Lismore (Hogan) fo. 5a	1400c
12. Arthir-mughiae seu vt alij Rath-mughia, oppido Dalredinorum	Acta SS Colgan 375a	1645
13. (?)Dercanensi in Dalrieda, Ecclesia	Acta SS Colgan 375b	1645
14. (?)Derkane[n]sis Ecclesiae	Acta SS Colgan 375b	1645
15. Airther Mugia, oppidum de	Acta SS Colgan 375b	1645
16. (?)[Ecclesia] Derekon	Acta SS Colgan 376a	1645
17. Airthermuge, ab	Acta SS Colgan 377a	1645
18. (?)Kill-Easpuic-Bolcain	Acta SS Colgan 377a	1645
19. Airthermugia	Acta SS Colgan 377b	1645
20. (?)[Ecclesia] Derekan	Acta SS Colgan 377b	1645
21. (?)[Ecclesia] Derkan	Acta SS Colgan 377b	1645
22. Airthermuighe, ab	Acta SS Colgan 377b	1645
23. Arthermugensis	Acta SS Colgan 377b	1645
24. Ecclesiae Rath-mugiae seu ut alii Arthir-mugia oppido Dalredinorum	Trias Thaum. 146b	1647
25. Airther Mugiae, oppidum de	Trias Thaum. 147b	1647
26. Airthermugiam seu Rathmugiam cum territorio Derchon in Dalriedia	L. Gen. DF 418	1650
27. Rathmuighe	Mon. Hib. 23	1786
28. Rathmuighe-haonaigh/Arthur-muighe/ Arther-muighe-haonaigh	Mon. Hib. 23 n.c	1786
29. (?)Dercan	EA 80	1182c
30. Erthermoy	Inq. Earl. Ulster 38	1262
31. Ethirmoy	Eccles. Tax. (CDI) 209	1306c
32. Athermoy, the water-mill of	Eccles. Tax. 80 n.t	1333
33. Erthermoy, lands of	Eccles. Tax. 80 n.t	1333
34. (?)Condon or Canton of Armoy	CSP Ire. 90	1576
35. Cone McCoine dean (deacoñs) of Ardmoye	Fiants Eliz. §4897	1586
36. Armoy and Raghlines, the Cynamond of	CPR Jas I 58a	1603
37. Armoye	Jas I to Connor Cath. (EA) 263	1609
38. Armoy and Raghlynns, the tough called the Cinemond of	LP 8 Jas I (PRONI)	1610

39. Armoy, Ecclesia de	Terrier (Reeves) 259	1615
40. Armoy, Ecclia de	Ulster Visit. (Reeves) 63	1622
41. Ardmoy, the territory or precinct of	MacDonnells Antrim 441	1625
42. Armoy	Regal Visit. (Reeves) 121	1633
43. (?)Derkelan, in loco qui dicitur	Brit. Eccles. Ant. 610	1639
44. (?)Derkanensis, Ecclesiæ	Brit. Eccles. Ant. 951, 1117	1639
45. (?)territorio Clonderkan	Brit. Eccles. Ant. 951	1639
46. Armoy, parish of	Hill's Stewarts 86	1643
47. Parish of Admoy	Hib. Reg. Cary	1657c
48. Ardmoy, Parish of	DS (Par. Map) 62	1657c
49. Ardmoy	BSD 177	1659
50. Armoy	Census 19	1659
51. Armoy	Trien. Visit. (Bramhall) 3	1661
52. Armoy	Court of Claims §923	1662c
53. the Finamont of Armoy and the Raghlins	Court of Claims §923	1662c
54. the sinamount of Armoy and the Raghlins	Decree of Innocence 431	1663
55. Armoy	Trien. Visit. (Margetson) 28	1664
56. Armoy, Parish of	HMR (1666) 96	1666
57. Ardmoy	ASE 117a §19	1668
58. Armoy	Shaw Mason's Par. Sur. 517	1668
59. Armoy, parish of	HMR Ant. 11	1669
60. Ardmoy	Hib. Del. Antrim	1672c
61. Armoy	Trien. Visit. (Boyle) 34	1679
62. Armory, a well called	Dobbs' Desc. Antrim 384	1683
63. Armoy	Danish Force 147	1690
64. Ardmoy	Lamb Maps	1690c
65. Armoy	Lhuyd's Tour 222	1699
66. Ardmoy	Ire. Map	1711
67. Armoy	Religious Survey	1734
68. Ardmy, parish of	Hill's Stewarts 220	1740c
69. Armoy	Hill's Stewarts 16	1750
70. Ardmoy	Merchant's Book 41	1752
71. Armoy	Lendrick Map	1780
72. Armoy vi	Dubourdieu Map	1812
73. Armoy	Bnd. Sur. (OSNB) B 21	1830
74. Ardmoy	OSNB B 21	1832
75. Ard-moy, i.e. "yellow hill"	Hamilton's Letters 244	1822
76. Ard-Magh "high plain"	OSM xxiv 1	1832
77. Airthear Maighe "East of the plain"	J O'D (OSNB) B 21	1832
78. Airther-muighe "the eastern plain"	Mon. Hib. 14 n.35	1873
79. Oirthear Muighe	Post-Sheanchas 22	1905
80. Airtear-Mag "The Eastern plain"	Ó Dubhthaigh 131	1905
81. Airthear-Maighe "eastern plain"	Joyce iii 49	1913

82. Airthear Muighe "East part of the plain"	Rev. Magill 5	1923
83. Airthear Maighe	Dallat's Armoy 53	1987
84. Oirthear Maí	Éire Thuaidh	1988
85. Oirthear Maí	GÉ 144	1989
86. ˌarəˈmɔi	Local pronunciation	1995

Joyce notes:

> When we find the term for one of the cardinal points forming part of a local name, we may infer that the object or place was so called on account of its direction, either from the people who gave it its name, or from some other place or object or territory lying near it (*Joyce* ii 447).

O'Laverty suggests that *oirthear* "east, eastern part" was used in this name as the territory lay on the eastern side of the Bush, which is thought to have been a boundary between Dál Riada and the Dál nAraí (*O'Laverty* iv 450; see also the parish introduction above). *Oirthear* has also been used with the meaning "front part" (*DIL* sv. *airther*). The genitive form of the second element *maigh* "plain" (*maighe*) has been shortened to *maí* (forms 84–5) following the conventions of the modern language.

Reeves notes that Armoy should not be confused "with *Rath Maighe hAonaigh* or Rathenaich, in Tirenna, a district of Donegal . . . nor with *Airther Maighe* of *Tuaith Ratha* or Toora, one of the three territories which constituted the barony of Magheraboy in Fermanagh" (*EA* 80 n.t). This is what Colgan appears to have done in forms 12 and 24. Hogan (*Onom. Goed.* 349) further correlates a *Domnach Airthir Maige* (*Trip. Life (Stokes)* 174) with this Armoy, but Mac Neill (1932, 30) points out that this was more probably in central Tyrone. Early association of this Tyrone *domnach-* name to Armoy may have prompted further confusion with the place-name *Domhnach Mór Maí Cobha* (**Donaghmore** in Co. Down; see *PNI* i 85–8 and *ibid.* vi 5, *EA* 111 n.m, *Onom. Goed.* 352), leading to the addition of *Cobha* (cf. *EA* 349) in forms 10 and 11.

Reeves quotes the medieval English historian Jocelyn as having called the church at Armoy *Dercan* (form 29). From Colgan's biography of Olcán (cf. forms 13–23), it appears that he built a church dedicated to one *Derkan* in the district allotted to him (presumably Armoy). Derkan here would represent a diminutive form of one of the personal names *Dearc* (O. Ir. *Dercc*; *CGH* §121 b 15) or *Dearg* (O. Ir. *Derg*; see *CGH* 585 sv. *Derg*). Ussher also mentioned this church (forms 43–5), and called the territory around it *Clonderkan* (translated in *Mon. Hib.* 15 n.35 as "the plain of Derkin"), and Olcán "*ecclesiae Derkanensis episcopus*", or "bishop of the church of Derkan" (see *EA* 80 n.t and *Mon. Hib. loc. cit.*; see also *EA* 345). Colgan was unsure as to the exact location of this church of *Dearcán/Deargán*, and pondered whether it was in fact the name of the original church of Armoy, or arose from a confusion with the south Antrim tribe and territorial name *Uí Dhearca Chéin* (*Acta SS Colgan* 375b, 377b n.8; see also barony introduction and *Trip. Life (Stokes)* 164) and so referred to a church founded by Olcán in that district, or represented a garbled form of Connor, the diocesan name. The latter two explanations seem particularly unlikely. Also unlikely is that the name represents a diminutive of *derc* "cavity, hollow or cave" (*DIL* sv. *derc*) and that it arose from the legend surrounding the birth of Olcán referred to in the parish introduction; neither does it seem very possible that it represents a corrupted form of the name of the neighbouring parish, Derrykeighan. Colgan further noted that there was a church somewhere in Dál Riada or The Route (he confused these two territories; see barony introduction) known locally by the name *Cill Easpaig Bolcán* "church of Bishop Olcán", but was unsure whether this represented another name for the church of Dearcán/Deargán (*Acta SS Colgan* 377b n.8; see also *Mon. Hib.* 14).

TOWNLAND NAMES

Aghrunniaght
D 075335

Achadh Cruithneachta
"field of (the) wheat"

1.	Accrunogh	Hib. Reg. Cary	1657c
2.	Accrunagh	DS (Par. Map) 61	1657c
3.	Attrunaugh	DS (Par. Map) 62	1657c
4.	Accrunagh	BSD 177	1661
5.	Acernahg	Lapsed Money Book 157	1663
6.	Attrunagh	ASE 117a §19	1668
7.	Accrunogh	Hib. Del. Antrim	1672c
8.	Aghnenogh	Religious Survey	1734
9.	Aghrunniaght	Lendrick Map	1780
10.	Aucronaught	Bnd. Sur. (OSNB) B 21	1830
11.	Altcrinaght	Tithe App. Book 1	1833
12.	Achadh cruithneachta "field of the wheat"	J O'D (OSNB) B 21	1832
13.	Achadh cruithneacht "The wheat field" or "field of the picts"	Dallat's Armoy 53	1987
14.	ˌaxˈrọnjəxt	Local pronunciation	1995

As in the townland names of Aughnaholle and Aughnasillagh in Culfeightrin parish, the unstressed second syllable of the first element *achadh* "field" was elided at an early stage. The second element is the gen. form of *cruithneacht* "wheat". The loss of the final syllable of this gen. form can again be ascribed to its unstressed position. The final *t* is absent from all the earliest forms (1–8). Joyce has noted other townland names containing this element, including Tullanacrunat near Castleblayney, and **Tullycreenaght** near Antrim (*Joyce* ii 320). The central *-tt-* in forms 3 and 6 indicates scribal error.

Alcrossagh
D 0932

Ail Chrosach
"transverse stone(?)"

1.	Altrassagh	Hib. Reg. Cary	1657c
2.	Alcrosagh	Census 19	1659
3.	Altrassagh	BSD 177	1661
4.	Altrassagh 1 Qur.	Lapsed Money Book 158	1663
5.	Altrassagh	ASE 117a §19	1668
6.	Altirashagh	HMR Ant. 12	1669
7.	Altvassa	Hib. Del. Ant.	1672c
8.	Altirossogh	Religious Survey	1734
9.	Alcrossagh	Lendrick Map	1780

16

10. Allcrossagh	Bnd. Sur. (OSNB) B 21	1830
11. Altcrossagh	Tithe App. Book 3	1833
12. Aill Crosach "crossed cliff" or "intersected declevity"	J O'D (OSNB) B 21	1832
13. "the Cross valley"	OSRNB sh.13, 1	1855c
14. Ail crosach "the streaked cliff"	Ó Dubhthaigh 131	1905
15. Aill crosach "streaked cliff"	Rev. Magill 5	1923
16. Alt croise achaidh "The height of the field of the cross"	Dallat's Armoy 53	1987
17. ˌalˈcrɔsə	Local pronunciation	1995

There are a number of possibilities regarding the first element. It might be argued, for example, that the final *t* of *allt* "steep glen, cliff, stream" was lost due to coalescence with the *c* of the following element. But as we have no historical forms featuring -*tc*-, it seems that the appearance of the *t* in early forms (1, 3–8) is due to scribal error: *t* is often mistaken for *c* in 17th- and 18th-century sources (cf. early forms of **Aghrunniaght**). The first element is therefore more likely to have been either *aill* "cliff, precipice" (*Ó Dónaill*) or *ail* "stone, rock". The eastern end of this townland is mountainous ground, lying on the western slopes of Croaghan mountain. Topographically then, *aill* may seem suitable, but examples of *aill* in the townland names of east Ulster seem to be quite rare, while the use of *allt* seems to have been much more widespread. This suggests that *ail* was the first element in Alcrossagh. A standing stone in this townland was thus described in 1835: "It is 4 feet by 1 and a quarter feet by a quarter of a foot. It is on what was once a small fort but is now much torn away. The remainder is an irregular circle 40 feet in diameter, of earth. It is called Alcrossagh Fort" (*OSM* xxiv 8). The stone itself was called *Clough Berragh* (*ibid.*), perhaps from *Cloch Bhéarra* "stone of the *Cailleach Bhéarra*" (*O'Laverty* iv 451n), or from *Cloch Bhiorach* "pointed stone". The *Cailleach Bhéarra* is "a mythical old woman in Irish literature and folklore, associated with the Beare peninsula in west Cork . . . undoubtedly a goddess in origin . . . Standing stones are often said to have been people and animals transformed by her" (Ó hÓgáin 1990, 67–8). It is uncertain, however, whether this was the *ail* referred to in the townland name.

The adjective *crosach* (suggested in forms 12, 14–5) has several meanings, including "crosswise; scarred, pock-marked; dirty-faced, grimy" (*Ó Dónaill*). Cross River in the Mournes has the Irish form *Crosabhainn* which has been translated "tranverse river" (*PNI* iii 179). It seems unlikely that *Ail Chrosach* could have referred to a cross which formerly stood in this townland alongside "an ancient and disused graveyard", a "holy well", and the remains of what was possibly an old church (see O'Laverty iv 451). Little else is known about the ecclesiastical history of this site, although the well alluded to above appears to have been that referred to by an English writer in 1683: "There is a well called Armory [i.e. Armoy] well, not far from the highway that leads from Clogh to Bally Castle, much frequented by Scotch and Irish on Midsummer eve. The water flows out in such abundance that till you come to the well, you would take it for an ordinary river" (*Dobbs' Desc. Antrim* 384. This tradition was still current in the 1850s; see *OSRNB* sh.13, 1; see also **Well Water**, Other Names).

One final possibility we might also consider is *Ail Chrosachaidh* "stone of the cross-field", in which the final element is the gen. of *achadh* "field" prefixed by *cros* "cross-, slant-, trans-" (*Dinneen*). We could account for the loss of the final syllable as being due to its unstressed position (cf. **Ardaghmore or Glentop** townland in Culfeightrin, and **Cooraghy Bay** in Other Names, Rathlin).

Balleny	*Baile Uí Éinigh (?)*	
D 0634	"Heaney's townland"	

1. Ballany	Hib. Reg. Cary	1657c
2. Ballyany	Census 19	1659
3. Ballony	BSD 177	1661
4. Balleny	Court of Claims §923	1662c
5. Bellany, the qtr. of	Decree of Innocence 431	1663
6. Ballany 1 Qur.	Lapsed Money Book 158	1663
7. Bellany	ASE 117a §19	1668
8. Ballyny	HMR Ant. 13	1669
9. Ballany	Hib. Del. Antrim	1672c
10. Balleney	Religious Survey	1734
11. Balleny	Stewart's Survey 17	1734
12. Ballenys	Lendrick Map	1780
13. Baleny	Bnd. Sur. (OSNB) B 21	1830
14. Baleny	OSM xxiv 1	1832
15. Baile Eithne "Eithne's town"	J O'D (OSNB) B 21	1832
16. Baile léana "Townland of the meadow"	Dallat's Armoy 53	1987
17. ˌbalˈini	Local pronunciation	1995

Baile is first found in place-names in the 12th century when it denoted "a piece of land held by a family group". The later meaning "the land and holding of an individual" probably did not come into use until after the Anglo-Norman invasion. The further meaning "farmstead" developed from "the spread among the English settlers of the word 'town' from the 13th century onwards", while *baile* also had the sense "town" from the beginning of the 14th century or earlier (Price 1967, 495–6). "Townland" (used in *PNI* i–vi) is the meaning adopted here. The medial vowel in this element in modern local pronunciation is lower than that ([ɔ]) recorded by Holmer (note, for example, the nearby place-name of **Ballycastle**, pronounced [bɔlə xɪsˈlʲən]; *Irish of the Glens* 100). In late local Irish, *ai* was pronounced [ɔ] after a labial consonant (*ibid.* 75).

Form 15 seems an unlikely origin insofar as *baile* followed by a female personal name is a very rare place-name type. **Balleny** in Co. Down may be analogous here. It derives from *Baile Uí Éinigh* "Heaney's townland" (*PNI* vi 110–1). This surname (earlier *Ó hÉighnigh*), of which Hegney is a variant, was "important and wisespread in Oriel, formerly stretching its influence into Fermanagh . . . another family of the name in Ulster were erenaghs of Banagher in Co. Derry" (MacLysaght 1985, 151). It is not associated specifically with north Antrim, but surnames most commonly qualify *baile* names in northern counties, and other surnames which are otherwise unattested locally appear in some local place-names (cf. **Drumaridly** in Culfeightrin, **Turrybrennan** in Other Names, Culfeightrin and **Bellennan** in Other Names, Ramoan). The male personal names *Éineach* (O. Ir. *Éicnech*; see *CGH* 610), on which the surname is based, and *Éinne* (cf. **Killeany**, Other Names, Rathlin) remain possibilities. We might have expected more *-ea-/-ay-* spellings to reflect the [eː] in

18

these names. The initial vowel of the final element is not long in modern pronunciation, but this could be construed as a late development in English; however, the shortening of long accented vowels can also occur in Irish (see Stockman 1986). The first [i] in modern pronunciation could indicate the following tendency in late local Irish: "Before the so-called 'palatal' consonants . . . an *i* is always apt to develop. Usually it is a mere glide . . . but not seldom a full vowel is developed" (*Irish of the Glens* 30 §32). The form *Baile Eanaigh* "townland of the marsh" accords well with those historical forms in *-any*, but there is uncertainty regarding the reliablity of early spellings; form 5 was probably copied from form 4 but contains *a* for *e*, for example. The second element in this form is the gen. sing. of *eanach* "marsh, swamp, fen; passage through swamp; narrow path, pass" (*Ó Dónaill*). *Ei* sometimes became [i] in certain positions in the late local dialect, such as after a nasal consonant (*Irish of the Glens* 29 §29), but the pronunciation of the penultimate vowel, Irish *ea*, as [i] (form 17), would have to be regarded as a late development in English. In 1832 it was recorded that the "principal bog [in this parish] is a large flow situated in the north of the townlands of Baleny [*sic*], Ballykenver and Bunchanacloney. It is called Baleny flow" (*OSM* xxiv 1). Dallat's form (16) may also be considered although even earliest variants do not indicate a central [ə].

Form 12 suggests that some internal division of this territory gave rise to the addition to the name of the English plural suffix.

Ballykenver
D 0633

Of uncertain origin

1. (?)Ballykenbuite	PRONI D2977/3A/2/1/2	1611
2. Ballykinvar	Inq. Ult. (Antrim) §64 Car.I	1635
3. Tulloughpatricke	DS (Par. Map) 62	1657c
4. Ballycaver	Census 19	1659
5. Tulloghpatrick, Bunshanclony &	BSD 178	1661
6. Ballykenvir	Court of Claims §923	1662c
7. Tulloughpatrick, Bunshamlong and	Lapsed Money Book 158	1663
8. Tulloghpatricke	ASE 117a §19	1668
9. Tullaghpatrick	Hib. Del. Antrim	1672c
10. (?)Ballyclanirey	Religious Survey	1734
11. B:chanaver	Lendrick Map	1780
12. Ballykenver	Bnd. Sur. (OSNB) B 21	1830
13. Baile Cinn Bhior "Town of the head of the stream"	J O'D (OSNB) B 21	1832
14. Baile cianmhar "sad or sorrowful townland"	Dallat's Armoy 53	1987
15. ˌbɑliˈkɛnvɪr	Local pronunciation	1995
16. ˌtɒ̈ləxˈpatrək	Local pronunciation	1995

The stress in the form *Baile Cinn Bhiorra* "townland of the end of the marshy place" does not reflect that in modern pronunciation, but we could consider that it has been recently altered in English (compare **Bunshanacloney**). The use of the adjective *biorra* "watery, marshy, abounding in streams" (*Dinneen*) as a substantive noun in place-names has been suggested by Joyce who took Ballinvir in Co. Tipperary to derive from *Baile an Bhiorra* "town of the *biorra* or watery place" (*Joyce* iii 66). *Biorra* is also the Irish form of Birr in Co. Offaly

19

(*GÉ* 36). *Ceann* (gen. sing. *cinn*) "head, front or highest part of anything" (see *Joyce* i 522) is also well attested in the sense "end, extremity" (*Ó Dónaill* sv.; see also Ó Maolfabhail 1987, 76–8). In the last century, the northern part of this townland was comprised of bog (cf. **Balleny**).

Biorra derives from *bior* (gen. *beara*) "water" which Ó Dónaill suggests is now restricted to literary use, but which Mac Giolla Easpaig (1986, 70) has noted in the Donegal place-names *Loch Beara* (previously called *Bior*), *Gaoth Beara* and *Abhainn Bheara*; the Co. Louth river now called the Blackstaff used also to be known as *Bior* (*ibid.*). *Baile Cinn Bheara* "townland of the head of the stream" (cf. form 13) is an unlikely original form for this name insofar as no streams rise in or near this townland. *Bior*, which can also mean "pointed rod or shaft; spit, spike; point" (*Ó Dónaill* sv.) is attested in the names of two headlands on the Ards coast in Co. Down (cf. **Ringburr** and **Burr Point** in *PNI* ii 38, 111), and in some mountain names including Birreencarragh and Birreen Hill in Co. Mayo (*Joyce* ii 18–9), but such meanings here are unlikely.

Dallat's form, *Baile Cianmhar* "sorrowful townland" reflects modern stress but represents an unusual etymology. Holmer recorded examples of velar *mh* pronounced as [v] in the late local dialect (*Irish of the Glens* 115 sv. *gamhain* and *ibid.* 125 sv. *reamhar*; see also **Kinramer Lower** in Rathlin). Joyce suggests that the townland name **Ballysugagh** in south-east Co. Down derives from *Baile Súgach* "merry townland" which might be analogous here.

Form 1 is taken from a grant of lands which seem to lie primarily around Ballycastle; it may refer to an obsolete land division in Ramoan. Forms 3, 5 and 7–9 derive from *Tulach Pádraig* "hillock of (St) Patrick". This name may have referred originally to some internal division of this townland. It is still known today (form 16). No tradition connecting the saint to the townland appears to have been recorded, although he was of course associated with the founding of the parish church of Armoy (see introduction to the parish).

Breen *Bruíon*
D 1134 "fairy dwelling"

1. Braun als Breene	Hib. Reg. Cary	1657c
2. Brum	Census 19	1659
3. Brume als Breene	BSD 178	1661
4. Brine	Court of Claims §923	1662c
5. Bruine, the 20 acres [of]	Court of Claims §923	1662c
6. Bruyne, the twenty acres of	Decree of Innocence 431	1663
7. Braum als Breeme	Lapsed Money Book 158	1663
8. Breen	Hib. Del. Antrim	1672c
9. Breen	PRONI D2977/3A/2/19/1	1709
10. Bruian	Stewart's Survey 3	1734
11. Breen	Lendrick Map	1780
12. Breen	Bnd. Sur. (OSNB) B 21	1830
13. Bruighin "a fairy fort"	J O'D (OSNB) B 21	1832
14. Bruighean "the fairy palace"	Ó Dubhthaigh 133	1905
15. Bruighean "Fairy Mansion"	Rev. Magill 8	1923
16. Bruighean "Fairy mansion"	Dallat's Armoy 53	1987
17. 'brin	Local pronunciation	1995

The fem. noun *bruíon* (earlier *bruidhean*) "fairy dwelling" (*Ó Dónaill*) appears to be the origin of this place-name. In the earlier language, *bruíon* was used to denote a "hostel; large banqueting hall; house, mansion" (*DIL* sv. *bruiden*). In literature, a *bruíon* was often associated with the otherworld (see Ó hÓgáin 1987, 221–2) and "in Modern Irish *bruidhean* has come to be applied to a residence of the 'fairies' within a hill or in an old fort" (O'Rahilly 1946, 121 n.3). *Dinneen* translates it as follows: "a hostel, a caravanserai; a castle, a royal residence, a fairy palace; . . . a dwelling, a mansion (common in placenames)". Unfortunately, no tradition regarding this name appears to have been recorded. Other townlands of this name recur in counties Donegal and Tyrone (*Census 1851*), while Joyce suggests that the south Antrim townland of **Bryantang** also contains this word (*Joyce* ii 427).

Bunshanacloney	*Bun Seanchluana*	
D 0634	"bottom of the old meadow"	

1.	Bunshaclony	Hib. Reg. Cary	1657c
2.	Bunshunclony	DS (Par. Map) 62	1657c
3.	Bunshenclony	Census 19	1659
4.	Bunshanclony & Tulloghpatrick	BSD 178	1661
5.	Bunshamlong and Tulloughpatrick	Lapsed Money Book 158	1663
6.	Buchamlonge	ASE 117a §19	1668
7.	Bonshinclony	HMR Ant. 13	1669
8.	Bushancloy	Hib. Del. Antrim	1672c
9.	Bonehanaghty	Religious Survey	1734
10.	Bunchanchlon	Stewart's Survey 35	1734
11.	Bunchanaclony	Lendrick Map	1780
12.	Bunchanacloney	Bnd. Sur. (OSNB) B 21	1830
13.	Bunchanacloney	OSM ix 1	1832
14.	Bunsanacloney	Tithe Applot. 13	1833

15.	Bun Sean Cluana "bottom of the old lawn or meadow"	J O'D (OSNB) B 21	1832
16.	Bun-Sean Chluana "the foot of the old meadow"	Antrim Place Names 84	1913
17.	Bun an sean cluaine "Foot of the old meadow"	Dallat's Armoy 53	1987

18.	ˌbɒnʃɛnəˈcloːni	Local pronunciation	1995

Form 15 makes the obvious suggestion that the original form was *Bun Seanchluana* "bottom of the old meadow", but this does not take account of vowel stress and the introduction of an epenthetic vowel (note forms 11-14). The element *bun* "base, bottom" occurs elsewhere locally in **Bonamargy** and in early forms of **Cushendun** (in Culfeightrin). Joyce describes it as follows: "*Bun*, an end, the end or foot of anything, such as a hill, the land, a stream (source or mouth), &c., often also applied to bottom land, i.e. at the lower end of the farm, or at the bottom of a hill" (*Joyce* iii 152). *Cluain* "meadow; after-grass" (*Ó Dónaill*), prefixed here by *sean* "old", is described by Joyce as meaning " . . . a fertile piece of land, or a green arable spot, surrounded or nearly surrounded by bog or marsh on one side, and water on the other" (*Joyce* i 233). This seems over-specific although in this instance, much of the north of the townland is dominated by the *Balleny Flow*, the largest bog in the parish

(*OSM* xxiv 1). Mac Giolla Easpaig (1981, 156) has noted that *cluain* (gen. sing. *cluana*) is one of the most common elements in Irish place-names "although it appears to have become obsolete as a productive element at an early period", and suggests the original meaning of the word was "hip, thigh": "*cluain* is therefore yet another example of the use of words referring to parts of the human body as placename elements". The -*(e)y* endings in historical variants possibly indicate the use of a variant gen. form such as *cluanadh* or *cluanaidh*.

A shift backward in stress to the final element in a compound word is uncommon although not unknown. MacKay has noted such a change in the south-west Co. Antrim townland names of *Ardchluain* (anglicized **Artlone**) and *Breacghort* (**Brecart**; *PNI* iv 86, 95).

We may also consider that there has been no shift of stress in the name, and that the central element was *seang*, perhaps "slender land division/ridge" or "narrow place". This is rare in place-names, although we may note a possible fem. variant in the townland name of *An tSeanga Mheáin* (anglicized Tangaveane) in central Co. Donegal (O'Kane 1970, 109; this form could represent a late reinterpretation of *teanga* "tongue", however), and the subtownland name *The Shang* in Gortconny in Ramoan (*Pers. comm.* 27.10.95). We would not expect the *ng* to have been vocalized in late local Irish (cf. **Tenaghs** in Culfeightrin), due to its unstressed position; it could alternatively have been assimilated to the *n* of a following fem. definite article. The absence of a vowel between the second *n* and the *c* in early forms could be explained as due to the article's unstressed position, or as indicating its late introduction. Thus *Bun Seaing Chluana* and *Bun Sheang na Cluana* may be possible origins; both might be translated "bottom of the slender land division of the meadow". However, the lack of attested place-names containing this central element raises considerable doubt over these forms and it is best to accept O'Donovan's suggested form (15).

| **Carrowlaverty** | *Ceathrú Uí Laifeartaigh* | |
| D 0831 | "O'Laverty's quarterland" | |

1. Torilverty	Census 19	1659
2. Kellylawerty	HMR Ant. 12	1669
3. Knyleferty	Religious Survey	1734
4. Carolevertys	Lendrick Map	1780
5. Carolaverty	Bnd. Sur. (OSNB) B 21	1830
6. Carralaverty	Tithe Applot. 13	1833
7. Ceathramh Uí Laithbheartaigh		
"O'Laverty's quarter"	J O'D (OSNB) B 21	1832
8. Ceathramha Ui Labhartaigh		
"O'Laverty's corner"	Antrim Place Names 84	1913
9. Ceathramha Ua Fhlaithbheartaigh		
"O'Lavertys' quarterland"	Dallat's Armoy 53	1987
10. ˌkɛrəˈlavərti	Local pronunciation	1995

The surname *Ó Laifeartaigh* (earlier *Ó Laithbheartaigh*), anglicized as O'Laverty, is that of an Ulster sept associated especially with Tyrone and Donegal (MacLysaght 1985, 190). It is etymologically the same as the Connaught and Munster surnames O'Flaherty and O'Flaverty, and means "descendant of the bright ruler" (*ibid.*, 110). There does not appear to be any other evidence associating this name with the parish. O'Laverty noted "from the return of the Protestant and Papist inhabitants of Armoy, made in 1766 to the House of

Lords by the Vicar, it appears that there was not then in the parish any family of that name, but in the adjoining parishes there were 19 families in Loughguile, 3 in Ballintoy, 2 in Ramoan, and 2 in Culfeightrin" (*O'Laverty* iv 448–9).

Forms 4–6 probably represent *Ceathrú Uí Laifeartaigh* as suggested in form 7. *Ceathrú* (earlier *ceathramha*) "quarterland" is a common element in local townland names. It has been anglicized into several forms, including *carrow*, which begins the names of more than 700 townlands throughout Ireland (*Joyce* i 244).

Earlier forms (1–3) of this name might be construed as containing different first elements, such as *tor* "rocky height" (form 1; cf. **East Torr** in Culfeightrin). However, it is probably better to consider these variant forms as scribal errors.

Cleggan	*An Cloigeann*	
D 1134	"the round hill(?)"	
1. Cleggin	Hib. Reg. Cary	1657c
2. Cleggine	DS (Par. Map) 61	1657c
3. Cleggin	BSD 178	1661
4. Cleggine	ASE 117a §19	1668
5. Clegan	HMR Ant. 12	1669
6. Cleggin	Hib. Del. Antrim	1672c
7. Cleggan	Lendrick Map	1780
8. Clegan	Bnd. Sur. (OSNB) B 21	1830
9. Claigeann "a round hill"	J O'D (OSNB) B 21	1832
10. Cloigean "Skull-shaped hillock"	Dallat's Armoy 53	1987
11. 'klɛgən	Local pronunciation	1995

Cloigeann has been translated "the skull, the head; a headland; land lying on the borders of a swamp" by *Dinneen*. Ó Maolfabhail suggests that this word comes originally from a compound of *cloch* "stone" plus *ceann* "head", and that in place-names it most often denotes something like "high place of bare rocks" (Ó Maolfabhail 1987, 80). *DIL* (sv. *cloicenn*) derives *cloigeann* from *clog* "bell" plus *ceann* "head". The apparent recurrence of *clog* followed by collective suffixes in townland names like **Clagernagh** (Co. Tyrone), Claggarnagh East (Co. Mayo), and Cloggarnagh (Co. Roscommon; *Census 1851*; see also **Clegnagh** in Ballintoy) may support the *DIL* derivation. Joyce suggests that *clog* in place-names of this type denotes "a round bell-like or skull-like hill" (*Joyce* ii 17; note also O'Donovan's translation in form 9). Topographically, this townland is situated on the southern face of Knocklayd mountain and would otherwise accord well with Ó Maolfabhail's derivation. It is worth noting that MacKillop has noted the place-name *Cnoc nan Claigeann* "the knoll of the skulls" on the island of Berneray off western Scotland. It seems possible that some instances of Cleggan and Clegnagh may have simply denoted "place of skulls".

DIL (*ibid.*) indicates that *cloigeann* was originally of neuter gender but had a later fem. variant. Ó Dónaill and Dinneen list it as a masc. noun although both give a fem. variant. Cleggan in Co. Galway has the standard Irish form *An Cloigeann* (*GÉ* 65). There is a townland called **Cleggan** in Rathlin; in this latter case, *cloigeann* was feminine.

Cromaghs	*Cromóg*	
D 0832	"sloping land(?)"	
1. Cromoge	Hib. Reg. Cary	1657c
2. Crumage	Census 19	1659

3. Crummoge	BSD 177	1661
4. Crumogt 1 Qur.	Lapsed Money Book 158	1663
5. Crumoge	ASE 117a §19	1668
6. Crumagh	HMR Ant. 12	1669
7. Crumog	Hib. Dcl. Antrim	1672c
8. Crumoges	Religious Survey	1734
9. Crommaghs	Lendrick Map	1780
10. Cromaghs	Bnd. Sur. (OSNB) B 21	1830
11. Cromachs	Tithe Applot. 21	1833
12. Crom Achadh "sloping or inclining field"	J O'D (OSNB) B 21	1832
13. Crom achaidh "Humpy fields"	Dallat's Armoy 53	1987
14. 'krɒməxs	Local pronunciation	1995

Although some forms (6, 9–11) reflect the origin postulated in form 12, the earliest forms suggest a different etymology. *Cromóg* corresponds to these earlier variants most closely. The recent change from [əgs] to [əxs] is reflected elsewhere in modern pronunciation of the Culfeightrin townland name **Coolnagoppoge**. The English plural suffix, probably denoting some internal division of this territory, appears as early as 1734 (form 8).

Cromóg, anglicized Cromoge, appears to be the name of three further townlands in Cork, Laois and Wexford (*Census 1851*). It is also the origin of the Belfast street name, Cromac Street. In the latter instance it may have referred to a bend in the Lagan River, or may have been a local name for the river itself (Uí Fhlannagáin 1982, 55).

Cromóg is derived from the adj. *crom* "bent, inclined, stooped, or crooked" (*Joyce* ii 422) plus the substantive (more usually diminutive) suffix *-óg*, and may "signify anything sloping or bending including glens, hills, fields and streams" (*ibid.*). This is a hilly townland which is bounded to the north and west by the Well Water, and it is difficult to ascertain the original meaning of the place-name.

Doonans   *Dúnáin*
D 0833   "little forts"

1. Dunane	DS (Par. Map) 61	1657c
2. Duenane	DS (Par. Map) 62	1657c
3. Dunnane	BSD 177	1661
4. Dimane	Lapsed Money Book 158	1663
5. Dunane	ASE 117a §19	1668
6. Downayeglid	HMR Ant. 13	1669
7. Duenan	Hib. Del. Antrim	1672c
8. Doonans	Lendrick Map	1780
9. (?)Dunaine	PRONI D2977/£A/2/1/40	1812
10. Doonans	Bnd. Sur. (OSNB) B 21	1830
11. Dúnain "small forts"	J O'D (OSNB) B 21	1832
12. Dúnan "a little fort"	Rev. Magill 13	1923
13. Dúnáin "Little forts"	Dallat's Armoy 53	1987
14. 'dunənz	Local pronunciation	1995

Dúnán (form 12) is usually interpreted as deriving from *dún* "fort" plus the diminutive suffix *-án*, and thus as denoting "little fort". The *-án* suffix can also have a collective meaning, which seems unlikely here, but its further use as a locative suffix might be considered (cf. **Carnanmore** in Other Names, Culfeightrin). It is uncertain whether the place-name took a nom. sing. or nom. pl. form (*Dúnáin*). The English suffix, which dates to at least 1780 (form 8), is found in several other local townland names including **Cromaghs** and **Knockans** in this parish, and could indicate that the name was originally in a plural form, although it could also indicate some internal division of the townland at this time.

There is no apparent recorded documentary or field evidence extant indicating the presence of any forts in this townland. We might consider, however, that the territory once extended beyond its present boundaries and encompassed two forts, recorded by the Ordnance Survey, now in Knockans to the immediate north of here (*OSM* xxiv 8).

Essan	*An tEasán*	
D 1235	"the small stream(?)"	
1. Nesson	Hib. Reg. Cary	1657c
2. Nesson	BSD 177	1661
3. Nessane	Court of Claims §923	1662c
4. Nessane, the twenty acres of	Decree of Innocence 431	1663
5. Messon	Lapsed Money Book 158	1663
6. Nesson or Nelson	ASE 117a §19	1668
7. Besin	HMR Ant. 12	1669
8. Nesson	Hib. Del. Antrim	1672c
9. esen	Religious Survey	1734
10. Essan	Stewart's Survey 3	1734
11. Essan	Lendrick Map	1780
12. Essan	Bnd. Sur. (OSNB) B 21	1830
13. Easan "a small cataract"	J O'D (OSNB) B 21	1832
14. Easán "Little waterfall"	Rev. Magill 15	1923
15. Easan	Dallat's Armoy 53	1987
16. 'ɛsən	Local pronunciation	1995

Except for forms 5, 6(b) and 7, which contain scribal errors, the historical variants indicate that *An tEasán*, from a diminutive of *eas*, formed the original name. *Eas* is defined by *Dinneen* as "a waterfall, a cascade, a stream, a spring, a rapid"; a development of any of the latter three meanings seems possible here. Two small tributaries of the Inver Burn rise in this townland. Mac Giolla Easpaig translated the Rathlin place-name *Easán* as "the place of the waterfalls or streams", that is, as consisting of *eas* plus the collective suffix *-án*, but noted that the diminutive form *easán* from *eas* plus the diminutive suffix *-án* was used for "a (mountain) stream" in east Donegal (*Place-Names of Rathlin* 41). In Scottish Gaelic, *easan* can denote "a small waterfall or cascade" (*Dwelly*).

The initial *n* in early forms may have resulted from the use of the place-name in the dative case (cf. **Novilly** in Ramoan). There is another townland called Essan in Termonamongan parish in Co. Tyrone.

Glebe   An English form
D 0833

1. (?)Bishops Land	DS (Par. Map) 62	1657c
2. Gleab land of Ardmoy	BSD 178	1661
3. Gleab	Religious Survey	1734
4. Glebe	Bnd. Sur. (OSNB) B 21	1830
5. 'glib	Local pronunciation	1995

This glebe, which consists of over 37 acres, was apparently formerly part of Doonans (*EA* 260). It is the site of the round tower (see *PSAMNI 15*) and ancient church of Armoy (on which the modern Church of Ireland church has been built; *OSM* xxiv 6–7). "An attempt was made to pull the whole [round tower] down and use the stone for building the Glebe House. This happened about the year 1805 but it was resisted by the parishioners and the monument subsequently preserved" (*ibid.* 6).

The place-name form *Glebe* is normally gaelicized as *An Ghléib* (see Ó Maolfabhail 1990, 190–1; see also **Gortmillish** and *Dinneen* sv. *forba* and *tearmann*).

Gortmillish   *An Gort Milis*
D 0934   "the sweet field"

1. Gortmillish	Hib. Reg. Cary	1657c
2. Gortmilles	Census 19	1659
3. Gortmillish	BSD 177	1661
4. Knockangartmillis	Court of Claims §923	1662c
5. Gortnulis, the quarter of	Court of Claims §923	1662c
6. (?)Cormilis, the quarter of	Decree of Innocence 431	1663
7. Gortanillagh	Lapsed Money Book 158	1663
8. Gortmillish	ASE 117a §19	1668
9. Gortmillis	HMR Ant. 12	1669
10. Gortmillish	Hib. Del. Antrim	1672c
11. Gortmillish, Gortmore	Religious Survey	1734
12. Gortmillish	Lendrick Map	1780
13. Gortmillish	Bnd. Sur. (OSNB) B 21	1830
14. Parkmore, or Gortmillish	O'Laverty iv 443	1887
15. Gort milis "sweet field"	J O'D (OSNB) B 21	1832
16. Gort milis "The sweet tilled field"	Ó Dubhthaigh 181	1905
17. Gort-milis "the Sweet field"	Antrim Place Names 84	1913
18. Gort milis "sweet field"	Rev. Magill 17	1923
19. Gort milis "Sweet tilled field"	Dallat's Armoy 53	1987
20. ˌgɔrtˈmïləʃ	Local pronunciation	1995

The element *gort* "field" occurs elsewhere locally in the townland names of **Gortamaddy** and **Gortconny** in Ramoan. Here it is qualified by *milis* "sweet", which may occur in the Belfast place-name **Stranmillis**, possibly derived from *An Sruthán Milis* (Uí Fhlannagáin

1982, 58). *Gort* has been rendered more specifically elsewhere as an "enclosed field" (*Joyce iii* 370) and "a field or plantation, a corn-field and *esp.* a field of oats" (*Dinneen*). Originally, this word probably "signified any type of enclosure" (Mac Giolla Easpaig 1981, 156). It forms the first element of over 1130 townland names (*Census 1851*). Reeves noted that sometimes *gort* "is used to describe 'old glebe'" (*Ulster Visit. (Reeves)* 95). Gortmillish townland was one of sixteen townlands in the parish held by the diocese of Connor (see parish introduction).

Form 7 can be accounted for as resulting from scribal errors. Mistranscription of *g* for a tall *s* occurs elsewhere in this source. It is not certain whether form 11(b) refers to some former internal division of this townland, or to a separate territory. It is derived from *An Gort Mór* "the big field". Note also form 14(a), derived from *An Pháirc Mhór* "the big field". Gortmillish may have been formerly amalgamated with **Knockans**, but form 4 may be the result of an editorial error..

Kilcroagh	*Cill Chruaiche*	
D 0830	"burial-ground of the (mountain) stack"	
1. Kilcroe	Hib. Reg. Cary	1657c
2. Killcroce	Census 19	1659
3. Killcroe	BSD 177	1661
4. Killeroe ½ Town Land	Lapsed Money Book 158	1663
5. Killcroe	ASE 117a §19	1668
6. Kilcrogh	HMR Ant. 12	1669
7. Kilcroe	Hib. Del. Antrim	1672c
8. Killkragh	Religious Survey	1734
9. Kilcroe	Lendrick Map	1780
10. Killcroagh	Bnd. Sur. (OSNB) B 21	1830
11. Kilcroagh	Tithe Applot. 30	1833
12. Coill Cruaiche "wood of the round hill"	J O'D (OSNB) B 21	1832
13. Coill cruaiche "wood of the stacklike hill"	Dallat's Armoy 54	1987
14. kïl'kroəx	Local pronunciation	1995

An early Ordnance Survey map marked a site in this townland *Ancient Burying Ground* (*EA* 287), and the *Statistical Account* of 1832 records it was one of two "old burying grounds [in the parish], of which only [Kilcroagh] is now used and for children soley" (*OSM* xxiv 2). The *Ordnance Survey Memoirs* also record that:

> The burying ground at Kilcrogh is known by the name of Kilcroagh Fort or the 'hard burying ground'. At the time the Danes were in that part of the country, a battle is said to have been fought near it and the slain deposited in the graveyard (*ibid.*).

Later they noted that "there is a tradition that there was once a church at it" (*ibid.* 7). O'Donovan was probably unaware of this tradition as he preferred to explain the first element as *coill* "wood" (form 12) rather than *cill* "a church, a graveyard, a burial place" (*Dinneen*).

Notwithstanding that many forms suggest the gen. pl. form of *cruach* (*cruach*), the structure of the place-name favours the gen. sing. (*cruaiche*). We may account for the loss of the final syllable as due to its unstressed position. *Cruach* may variously mean "a heap, a stack, rick, a clamp (of turf); a rampart; a symmetrically shaped mountain" (*Dinneen*), or "(mountain) stack" (*Ó Dónaill*). The townland is situated on the western slopes of Croaghan mountain.

Knockans
D 1351

Na Cnocáin
"the hillocks"

1. Knockans	Hib. Reg. Cary	1657c
2. Knockanes	Census 19	1659
3. Knockans	BSD 178	1661
4. Knockangartmillis	Court of Claims §923	1662c
5. Knockane, the quarter of	Court of Claims §923	1662c
6. Knockans	Lapsed Money Book 158	1663
7. Knockane	ASE 117a §19	1668
8. Knouckneston	HMR Ant. 12	1669
9. Knockans	Hib. Del. Antrim	1672c
10. Knockans	Religious Survey	1734
11. Nockans	Lendrick Map	1780
12. Knockans	Bnd. Sur. (OSNB) B 21	1830
13. Cnocáin "hillocks"	J O'D (OSNB) B 21	1832
14. Cnocáin "Hillocks"	Dallat's Armoy 54	1987
15. ˈnɔkənz	Local pronunciation	1995

It is uncertain which of *cnocán* "hillock, a height; a heap" or its nom. pl. *cnocáin* formed the original place-name. The *-ane* ending in forms 2 and 5 do not necessarily favour the latter. The English plural suffix has been used at least since c. 1657 (form 1). It may have been used in the knowledge that the place-name was in a plural form, although it could also have resulted from some division of the territory.

Form 4 suggests a temporary amalgamation of the territories of Gortmillish and Knockans. Form 8 may contain scribal errors and been intended as something like *Knockanestown* (cf. **Park**). Regarding the pronunciation of *knock-*, see **Knockbrack** in Culfeightrin.

Knocknahinch
D 0531

Cnoc na hInse
"hill of the holm"

1. Crocknahinch	Lendrick Map	1780
2. Knocknahinch	Bnd. Sur. (OSNB) B 21	1830
3. Cnoc na hinnse "hill of the island"	J O'D (OSNB) B 21	1832
4. Cnoc na h-inse "Hill of the island"	Rev. Magill 19	1904

28

5. Cnoc na hinse "The hill of the island"	Ó Dubhthaigh 183	1905
6. ˌnɔknəˈhïntʃ	Local pronunciation	1995

The surveys of the mid-1600s considered this townland as part of Ballybregagh, a townland in the neighbouring parish of Loughguile in the barony of Dunluce Upper (Carleton 1991, 57–8), which accounts in part for its late appearance in the sources. Knocknahinch is still considered to be in that barony (*Census 1851*).

The *cnoc* "hill, height, mountain" (*Dinneen*) of the place-name may be a small hill of just over 100 metres in the centre of the townland, being the only noticeable undulation in the territory. The final element *inse* has been translated "inch, holm, water-meadow" (*Ó Dónaill* sv. *inse*). A tributary stream of the Bush River runs through this townland past the aforementioned hill, while the latter river also forms the northern boundaries of this territory.

Mill Five Acres　　　　　　　An English form
D 0733

1. Mill Five Acres	Bnd. Sur. (OSNB) B 21	1832
2. mïl faiv 'ekər	Local pronunciation	1995

In c. 1832, the townland was described as follows: "Good soil and very productive; the principal part of Armoy village is in it, and composes [*sic*] the gardens belonging to the village; there is also a flax mill in it" (*OSNB* B 21). The townland contains 11 acres, 3 roods and 28 perches (*Census 1851*). Curiously, the *Religious Survey* of 1734 and the *Tithe Applotment Book* (*Tithe Applot.* 12) of 1832 list two apparently contiguous land divisions near Ballycastle (perhaps in **Drumawillin**) called *Tuckmill* and *Five Acres*.

Monanclogh　　　　　　　*Móin na Cloiche(?)*
D 0835　　　　　　　　　　　"bogland of the stone"

1. Munaghcloye	Hib. Reg. Cary	1657c
2. Munaghiloy	DS (Par. Map) 61	1657c
3. Munaghcloy	DS (Par. Map) 61	1657c
4. Moninalegh	Census 19	1659
5. Munnaghcloy	BSD 178	1661
6. Monenaclogh, the qtr. of land of	Decree of Innocence 431	1663
7. Munagh-Cloy	ASE 117a §19	1668
8. Moninagloy	HMR Ant. 11	1669
9. Munenacloy	Religious Survey	1734
10. Muninacloych	Religious Survey	1734
11. Monynecloegh	Stewart's Survey 17	1734
12. Munnanacloicks	Lendrick Map	1780
13. Monanclough	Bnd. Sur. (OSNB) B 21	1830
14. Moonenacloigh	Tithe Applot. 35	1833
15. Monancleugh	OSM xxiv 8	1838
16. Móin na gcloch "bog of the stones"	J O'D (OSNB) B 21	1832

29

17. Móin na gclocha "Peat bog of the stones"	Dallat's Armoy 54	1987
18. ˌmɒnəˈклɔіx	Local pronunciation	1995

As the first element of this name is in an unstressed position, it is very difficult to discern which of several elements including *móin* "bogland, moor", *muine* "thicket, brushwood, scrub", *móinín* "grassy patch (in bog)" (*Ó Dónaill*) or "a little bog, moor, fen, or marsh; a place for burned tillage; a place for hurling or dancing" (*Dinneen*), or perhaps (the less common) *muin* "neck, hill" (Price 1983, 503) formed the initial word. We could also consider *mong* "a thick growth of grass, underwood, trees; fen, morass or swamp". Forms 1–3 and 5–7 further suggest *muineach* "scrubland, scrub" or the presence of a central element such as *achadh* "field" as possibilities. These forms come from related sources and may reflect the copying of scribal errors, but they may alternatively reflect the *-aidh* in the dative form of *móin* (*mónaidh*; see **Ballycleagh** and **Tornaroan** in Culfeightrin regarding this feature). The *Ordnance Survey Memoirs* record that there was a "large turf bog" in this townland (*OSM* xxiv 1), and later describe it as follows:

> The patches of the bog in Monanclogh and Cromaghs townland are very deep, particularly in the centre where they reach a depth of 14 feet. They seem to have been formerly lakes or lodgements of water which have since been drained or blocked . . . (*ibid.* 3).

The final element is most likely to be the gen. sing. of *cloch* "stone; (stone) castle" (*cloiche*; see also **Ballycleagh** in Culfeightrin and **Cloghanmurry** in Ramoan). Form 8 probably contains a scribal error of *g* for *gh*, rather than indicating a variant form where *cloch* was in the genitive plural. In 1838, it was recorded: "In the townland of Monancleugh [*sic*] there is another standing stone. It is 4 feet 7 inches by 1 foot 4 inches by 3 feet 10 inches" (*OSM* xxiv 8) and it may well have been to this stone that the place-name originally referred (see also *O'Laverty* iv 443–4).

Moyaver Lower, Moyaver Upper
D 0632, 0732

Of uncertain origin

1. Moyawer	Inq. Ult. (Antrim) §144 Car. I	1641
2. Moyover	Hib. Reg. Cary	1657c
3. Mogaver	Census 19	1659
4. Moyavirr	Court of Claims §923	1662c
5. Moyover	Lapsed Money Book 152	1663
6. Moganer, 4 Qrs of Ballybregack &	HMR Ant. 67	1669
7. Mayevers	Lendrick Map	1780
8. Moyaver Upper, Moyaver Lower	Bnd. Sur. (OSNB) B 21	1830
9. Moyaver	OSNB B 21	1832
10. Magh Éibhir "Ever's plain"	J O'D (OSNB) B 21	1832
11. Magh amhair "plain of music"	Rev. Magill 21	1923
12. ˌmɔiˈɑvər	Local pronunciation	1995

In the *Hearth Money Rolls* of 1669, the territory of Moyaver was included with the townlands of Loughguile parish (form 3). The townlands of Moyaver Lower and Upper lie on the south side of the Bush River, and are still considered to be in the barony of Dunluce Upper (*Census 1851*).

The first element in this name was probably *maigh*, a variant form of *magh* "a plain, campus or field, a level district; a battle-field" (*Dinneen*). Form 10 suggests that it was qualified by the male personal name *Éibhear* (earlier *Éber*), but the lowering of an initial [eː] to [a(ː)]/[ɑ(ː)] is unlikely. The personal name *Abor* occurs once in the prehistoric genealogy of the *Laigin* (*CGH* 115b 52) but there does not appear to be any record of its use in the historical period. Some references in medieval literature suggest that the place-name *Mag Adhair* or *Mag Agar* (in Co. Clare) contains the male personal name *Adhar/Aghar* (*Onom. Goed.* 511 sv.; see also *ibid.* 12 svv. *adhair mic umhoir* and *adar*). We could argue that the central gutteral fricative developed to [v] in Moyaver (cf. **Drumavoley** and **Ballydurnian** in Ramoan), but these personal names seem to be otherwise unattested, and the medieval references could represent fanciful etymology. Form 11 reflects the historical forms, but *amhar* (gen. sing. *amhair*) "singing; wailing, moaning" (*DIL*) or "music, speech, singing, chanting" (*Dinneen*) would represent a very unusual element.

Another possible original form is *Maigh Fhobhair*, in which the second element is the gen. sing. of *fobhar* "well" (*DIL* sv. *fofor*), "spring" (*Ó Dónaill*) or "subterranean river passage" (*Dinneen*). The first syllable of the final element in this form would then have suffered a drop from [o]/[ɔ] to [ɑ], a relatively common feature (cf. **Ballycarry** in Rathlin). Intervocalic velar -*bh*- was not vocalized in some circumstances in the late local dialect (cf. *Irish of the Glens* 125 sv. *sábhailte, sabhall*). There are small streams in Moyaver Upper and Lower which run into the Bush River. *Fobhar* was anglicized as Fore in the Co. Westmeath place-name (standard modern form *Baile Fhobhair* (*GÉ* 18)), but Watson (1926, 504) notes a diminutive anglicized as Foveran in the Aberdeenshire place-name. *DIL* also lists *fodair*, a word of uncertain form and meaning, although possibly denoting "neighbouring", which might also be considered as a possible second element, referring to the plain's position south of the Bush River.

The division of Moyaver into two townlands first becomes apparent in the sources in 1780 (form 7). Ballybregagh (form 6(b)) is a townland in the neighbouring parish of Loughguile.

Mullaghduff Big,	*An Mullach Dubh*	
Mullaghduff Little	"the black summit"	
D 0533, 0434		

1. Mullaghduff	Hib. Reg. Cary	1657c
2. Mallughduffe	DS (Par. Map) 61	1657c
3. Mulloughduffe	DS (Par. Map) 62	1657c
4. Mullaghdou, Mullaghdow-Gorther	Census 19	1659
5. Mullaghduffe, ½ qtr	BSD 177	1661
6. Mullaghduffe	Lapsed Money Book 157	1663
7. Mullaghduffe	ASE 117a §19	1668
8. Mullaghdomore, Mullaghdobeg	HMR Ant. 12–3	1669
9. Mulladuff, Mulladuf	Hib. Del. Antrim	1672c
10. Mullaghduffe, the half quarterland of	PRONI D2977/3A/2/1/14	1696
11. Mulloghduff	Religious Survey	1734
12. Mullaghdoe	Lendrick Map	1780

13. Little Mullaghduff, Big Mullaghduff	Bnd. Sur. (OSNB) B 21	1830
14. Mulloghduff (Little), Mulloghduff	Tithe App. Book 46–7	1833
15. Mullach Dubh "black summit"	J O'D (OSNB) B 21	1832
16. Mullach dubh "Black summit"	Dallat's Armoy 54	1987
17. ˌmọləx'dọf	Local pronunciation	1995
18. ˌmọləx'duː	Local pronunciation	1995

There is a third townland of the name Mullaghduff to the immediate west of Mullaghduff Little, in Loughguile parish. The division of Mullaghduff is at least as old as 1659 (forms 4(a)–(b)).

Mullach "summit; elevated ground, height, eminence" is qualified here by *dubh* "black". As in **Carnduff** townland in Ramoan, the adjective may describe an outcrop of basaltic rock. *Dubh* was pronounced [dʌ] in late local Irish (*Irish of the Glens* 111) although the older pronunciation has been retained somewhat in the Armoy and Ramoan townland names. Evidence of a change in pronunciation is shown in forms 4, 8, 12 and 18.

Mullaghduff Little is denoted by a separate epithet in form 4(b). It is not certain what the original form was in this case.

Park
D 0633

An Pháirc
"the field"

1. Parke	Census 19	1659
2. Parketowne	HMR Ant. 13	1669
3. (?)Park	Reg. Deeds Abstracts i §265	1722
4. Park	Religious Survey	1734
5. Parks	Lendrick Map	1780
6. Park	Bnd. Sur. (OSNB) B 21	1830
7. Páirc "The pasture field"	Ó Dubhthaigh 184	1905
8. Páirc "a grazing field"	Rev. Magill 22	1923
9. Pairc "Pasture field"	Dallat's Armoy 54	1987
10. ðə 'park	Local pronunciation	1995

Páirc "a field, esp. a pasture-field, a pasture" (*Dinneen*) recurs in the form *Park* in townland names throughout Ireland (cf. also **White Park** in Ballintoy). The epithet *towne* in form 2 probably denotes a whimsical English addition. It was also added to forms of Broomore in Ramoan, East Torr in Culfeightrin, and possibly Knockans in this parish, and features also in early forms of Ballycastle (Other Names, Ramoan) and Ballycastle Bay (Other Names, Culfeightrin).

Stroan
D 1035

An Sruthán
"the stream"

1. Stravangalmore	Hib. Reg. Cary	1657c
2. Struangallmore	DS (Par. Map) 61	1657c

3. Struangellmore	DS (Par. Map) 62	1657c
4. Shruangalmor	Census 19	1659
5. Stranangallmore	BSD 178	1661
6. Sruanagallmore	Court of Claims §923	1662c
7. Sruanagalmore, the 20 acres of	Court of Claims §923	1662c
8. Srunagalmore, twenty acres of	Decree of Innocence 431	1663
9. Strnangallmore	Lapsed Money Book 158	1663
10. Struangallmore	ASE 117a §19	1668
11. Strandgallmore	HMR Ant. 12	1669
12. Struangellmore	Hib. Del. Antrim	1672c
13. Struangilmore	Lendrick Map	1780
14. Stroan	Bnd. Sur. (OSNB) B 21	1830
15. Strowan	Tithe Applot. 49	1833
16. Srothan "a streamlet"	J O'D (OSNB) B 21	1832
17. Sruthan "The stream"	Dallat's Armoy 54	1987
18. 'stroən	Local pronunciation	1995

Many place-names beginning with *sr* suffer the intrusion of a *t* in the process of anglicization. The common place-name *An Sráidbhaile* "the village" is usually anglicized *Stradbally*, for example (see *GÉ* 160; Ó Maolfabhail 1990, 249), while the same phenomenon has affected the Ballintoy townland name of **Ballynastraid** and subtownland names of **Straid** and **Straidkillen**, and the Rathlin subtownland name of **Stroanlea**.

The standard English form of the name, from *sruthán* "(small) stream; rivulet, brook" (Ó *Dónaill*) is a truncated form of the variants recorded prior to the 19th century (1–13). These latter forms may have been based on something like *Sruthán Gall Mór* "stream of the big foreigners/standing stones", or indicate that two separate land divisions, one called *An Sruthán* and the other called *(An) Gall Mór* "(the) big standing-stone" were amalgamated.

A tributary stream of Inver Burn (see Other Names) runs through the townland. Holmer recorded locally that as with *sliabh* (dat. *tsliabh*), the dat. sing. form (*tsruthán*; [trʌən]) was generally used for the nom. in late local Irish (*Irish of the Glens* §55, 41).

Tullaghore
D 1034

Tulaigh Chorra(?)
"Corr's hill"

1. Tullaghore	Hib. Reg. Cary	1657c
2. Tulicor	Census 19	1659
3. Tullaghore	BSD 177	1661
4. Tullaghroara	Court of Claims §923	1662c
5. (?)Tallaghmarry	Court of Claims §923	1662c
6. Tulloyhore	Lapsed Money Book 158	1663
7. Tulloghroe	ASE 117a §19	1668
8. Tullycogher	HMR Ant. 12	1669
9. Tullaghore	Hib. Del. Antrim	1672c
10. Tolocher	Religious Survey	1734
11. Tulloghore	Lendrick Map	1780
12. Tulahorra	Bnd. Sur. (OSNB) B 21	1830
13. Tullycorogh	Tithe Applot. 52	1833

14. (locally called) Tullaghora or Tullaghoragh	PSAMNI 15	1940
15. Tulaigh odhra "pale or greyish hill"	J O'D (OSNB) B 21	1832
16. Tulach odhar "pale or dunn height"	Rev. Magill 25	1923
17. Tulach odhar "Pale or brown hill"	Dallat's Armoy 54	1987
18. ˌtʊləˈhɔːrə	Local pronuncaition	1995

The first element is almost certainly *tulach* "low hill; hillock, mound" (*Ó Dónaill*), also translated as "a hill or mound, an assembly-hill, 'arena'" (*Dinneen*), or its dative form *tulaigh*. Forms 2, 8 and 13 appear to reflect the latter (regarding this element see also **Grange of Drumtullagh**). These forms also suggest that the final element began with *c*, and so we could interpret the central *-gh-* in many English forms as indicating the lenition of the first consonant of the final element. The *Ordnance Survey Memoirs* recorded that "on the top of a high commanding hill" in the south of this townland there were 2 stone crosses "of a rude description and standing about 3 and a half feet out of the ground" which stood about ten yards apart (*OSM* xxiv 7). Perhaps this is the *tulach* of the place-name.

The second element may be the early male personal name *Corr* (gen. *Chorra*), attested in early east Ulster genealogies (see *Descendants Ir* 100, 354). The Ulster surname *Ó Corra* (anglicized forms include O'Corry, Corr, and Corra) may be derived from this personal name (see *PNI* vi 36–7). Woulfe (1923, 448, 452, 481) believed this surname to be a variant of *Ó Carra/Cairre* (from *carr* "spear"; anglicized forms include Carr and Kerr), and as O'Carr is attested locally (cf. **Magheranahar** in Ballintoy), we could also consider *Tulaigh Uí Chorra* "O'Corr's hillock" as a possible original form. Further possible final elements include *cora* "weir; rocky crossing-place in river" (*Ó Dónaill*); the Well Water forms the southern boundary of the townland.

Tureagh
D 1032

Tuar Riabhach
"streaked cattle-field"

1. Tinereagh als Tonaghreagh	Hib. Reg. Cary	1657c
2. Torreagh	Census 19	1659
3. Tinereagh als Towaghreagh	BSD 177	1661
4. Tuarriagh	Court of Claims §923	1662c
5. Tarreagh, the quarter of	Decree of Innocence 431	1663
6. Finercagh als Towaghreagh	Lapsed Money Book 158	1663
7. Tinereagh alias Toppaghveagh	ASE 117a §19	1668
8. Torreagh	HMR Ant. 12	1669
9. Tinereagh	Hib. Del. Antrim	1672c
10. Tureagh	Religious Survey	1734
11. Toureaghs	Lendrick Map	1780
12. Tureagh	Bnd. Sur. (OSNB) B 21	1830
13. Turreagh	Tithe Applot. 35	1833
14. Tor Riach "grey tower or round hill"	J O'D (OSNB) B 21	1832

34

15. Tor riabhach "Grey height"	Rev. Magill 25	1923
16. An Torr Riabhach	AGMB 100	1969
17. Tor riabhach "Grey round hill"	Dallat's Armoy 54	1987
18. tur'iə	Local pronunciation	1995

Forms 1, 3, 5–7 and 9 come from related sources. Some (1(b), 3(b), 6(b) and 7(b)) contain a central -gh- and suggest a first element such as torach "place of tors; high rocky place", from tor "steep rocky height" (cf. **East Torr** in Culfeightrin) plus the collective suffix ach. It could be argued that this central syllable was later lost by haplology. However, these forms exhibit copying of scribal errors, such as n for r, and perhaps -ine- for -ure-, and are entirely unreliable.

The u in forms 4, 10–3 and modern pronunciation suggests tuar "manured land; cattle-field; sheep-run; pasture, lea; bleaching green" formed the first element. Topographically, the greater part of the townland lies on the rocky upper slopes of Croaghan, but there is also a more low-lying undulating tract in the north of the territory.

The adjective riabhach is translated "streaked, striped; brindled; (speckled) grey; dun, drab" by Ó Dónaill (see also **Ballyreagh** in Culfeightrin).

Turnarobert	*Tuar na Roibeard*
D 0732	"cattle-field of the people called *Roibeard*"

1. Twornyrobbert	Inq. Ult. (Antrim) §38 Car. I	1635
2. Tinenerobert	Hib. Reg. Cary	1657c
3. Tianenevebatt	DS (Par. Map) 62	1657c
4. Tornirobert	Census 19	1659
5. Tinenerobert	BSD 177	1661
6. Tynene Robart	Lapsed Money Book 157	1663
7. Tworin Robert, the mill of	Decree of Innocence 440	1663
8. Fernrobert	ASE 117a §19	1668
9. Tornerobert	HMR Ant. 13	1669
10. Tennerobert	Hib. Del. Antrim	1672c
11. Tournerabert	Lendrick Map	1780
12. Turnarobert	Bnd. Sur. (OSNB) B 21	1830
13. Tournarobert	Tithe App. Book 51	1833
14. Tor na Roibeárd "tower of the Roberts"	J O'D (OSNB) B 21	1832
15. Tor na robaire "The round hill of the robber"	Dallat's Armoy 54	1987
16. 'turnə'rɔbərt	Local pronunciation	1995

The first element in forms 2–5, 8 and 10 of this name reflects to a large extent that in the early forms of the previous townland name. There thus appears to have been a large degree of copying of spellings. The -ine- in forms 2 and 5 could represent a misspelling of -ure-. Tuar "manured land; cattle-field; sheep-run; pasture, lea; bleaching green" (Ó Dónaill sv.) seems most likely to have formed the first element. Túr "tower" (note form 14) is rare in place-names, and *tor* was used locally to denote "a tall rock" (see also **Tornabodagh** in Culfeightrin). In any event, *tuar* seems more likely here considering the topography.

The final element in the name appears to be the gen. pl. form of the male personal name *Roibeard*. Woulfe (1923, 50) lists several other variants of this name including *Riobárd* and *Riobart*. Personal names in the gen. pl. form in place-names are uncommon although not unknown. Note, for example, the Co. Mayo parish name of *Cill na nGarbhán* (anglicized Kilgarvan) "the church of the people named *Garbhán*" and the Co. Tipperary place-name *Doire na bhFlann* (Derrynaflan) "(oak-)wood of the people called *Flann*" (Ó Muraíle 1985, 57). Murphy (*Murphy's Rathlin* 164) noted the name *Tober-na-Brendan*, perhaps from *Tobar na mBreandán* "well of the people called Brendan" in Rathlin (possibly in Ballygill Middle townland). Ó Catháin recorded some subtownland examples including *Sídheán na Micks* "The fairy mound of the Micks" and *Garraí na Réamoinn* "The garden of the Réamoinn" in north-west Co. Mayo (Ó Catháin & O'Flanagan 1975, 42, 55). It might also be considered, however, that *Tuairín Roibeaird* "Roibeard's grassy plot/patch of lea" (see Ó Dónaill sv. *tuairín*; *tuairín* is a diminutive of *tuar*) formed the original name and that the -*ín* was latter affected by metathesis (compare **Portnathalin** in Other Names, Culfeightrin).

OTHER NAMES

Altmore Burn   A hybrid form
D 1134

1. Altmore Burn	OSRNB sh.13, 1	1855c
2. ˌaltˈmor ˈbọrn	Local pronunciation	1995

The *Ordnance Survey Revision Name Books*, which were compiled in c. 1855, recorded that: "This stream has its source in the mountain part of Breen. It flows north westwards in a serpentine course through a deep glen . . . and unites with one of the head streams of the Well Water" (*OSRNB* sh.13, 1).

Allt has several meanings, including "a ravine, a gully; a deep precipitous narrow glen; a height or cliff". Ó Baoill notes that this word usually means "stream" or "burn" in Scotland, "and where it occurs in Ireland it generally retains an older meaning, 'wooded valley' or 'deep glen': this is the meaning in Rathlin" (Ó Baoill 1978, 74–5). Ó Baoill also notes, however, that Holmer recorded *allt* from informants in Murlough Bay and Glenarriff as meaning specifically "stream, brook" (*ibid*; *Irish of the Glens* 99: *allt* "deep valley with stream"). *Alt* "hillock" (*Ó Dónaill*) appears to be inappropriate in the interpretation of *alt*-names locally. Regarding these elements, see also **Altagore** in Culfeightrin.

One may thus postulate the original form for this name *An tAllt Mór* "the big stream/steep glen". The suffix *burn*, literally "a small stream" (*Longman Dict.*), is a word of Scottish origin which is commonly used in local names for streams.

Altnamuck Burn   A hybrid form
D 0932

1. Altnamuck	OSRNB sh.13, 1	1855c
2. Alt na muc "the pig's valley"	J O'D (OSRNB) sh.13, 1	1855c

3. ˌaltnəˌmǫk 'bǫrn   Local pronunciation   1995

"This stream has its rise in the mountain part of Tureagh townland. It flows north westward and unites with the Well Water" (*OSRNB* sh.13, 1).

Allt na Muc "stream/steep glen of the pigs" is the likely original form of the Irish elements.

Bohilbreaga   *An Buachaill Bréagach*
D 1134   "the false boy"

1. Breen Hill   OSRNB sh.14   1855c
2. Bohilbreaga   OSRNB sh.14   1855c

3. Buachaill bréige "pseudo boy"   J O'D (OSRNB) sh.14   1855c
4. "The false boy"   OSRNB sh.14   1855c

5. ˌbɔhïl'bregə   Local pronunciation   1995

"A large heathy hill . . . It signifies 'The false boy' from a standing stone which formerly
stood where the trigonometrical station has been erected" (*OSRNB* sh.14).

The term *buachaill bréige/bréagach* "false boy" is one of several metaphoric terms used
elsewhere in Ireland to denote a standing stone (*Joyce* ii 435; see also Ó Maolfabhail 1990,
76 sv. *Buachaill Bó*). *Bréagach* is perhaps preferable to *bréige* in this case as we might have
expected the latter to yield an anglicized form in *-breagy* (cf. early forms of **Lisnabrague** in
PNI vi 43–4). Bohilbreaga is now also the name of a mountain, 330 metres high, in Breen;
the name is not widely known.

Carneagh   *Carn Eachach*(?)
D 0733   "*Eochu's* cairn"

1. Carneagh   OSRNB sh.13, 1   1855c

2. carn eich "hill of the horse"   OSRNB sh.13, 1   1855c
3. "the Ravens Carn"   OSRNB sh.13, 1   1855c

4. kɑr'neː   Local pronunciation   1995

"A low cultivated hill . . . The name signifies the Ravens Carn but it is not understood
that there existed an ancient carn here at any time. The word carn in this part of the country is often applied to isolated hills" (*OSRNB* sh.13, 1).

This height of 131 metres lies to the immediate north-east of Armoy village, in the townland of Glebe. *Eachach* is the gen. form of the male personal name *Eochu* (compare *Loch
nEachach*/**Lough Neagh**). Modern pronunciation (the name is only vaguely known locally)
might otherwise favour *Carn Fhéich* "cairn of the raven" (the lenition of the *f* could be
ascribed to the use of the place-name in the dative case) to *Carn Eich* "cairn of the horse",
but the final vowel may have been recently lengthened in English. The absence of a central
definite article might also point to the latter form as *féich* appears to be a relatively late genitive form (*DIL* sv. *fiach*). The rare gen. form *féidh* "of the deer" (nom. *fia*) seems unlikely.
See also the somewhat similar subtownland name of **Carnaneigh** in Culfeightrin.

Castlebane	*An Caistéal Bán*	
D 0632	"the white castle"	

1. (?)Castlebawn	OSM ix 2	1832
2. (?)Castlebane	OSM ix 8	1838
3. Castle Bane	OSRNB sh.13, 1	1855c
4. ˌkasəlˈbaːn	Local pronunciation	1995

It was recorded in 1832 that: "There is the site of an old castle, called Castlebawn, in Park townland. Of this, the site alone appears and that very imperfectly" (*OSM* xxiv 2; see also *ibid.* 8). The Ordnance Survey later noted two sites, both called *Castle Bane*, but located them both in the townland of Moyaver Lower (*OSRNB* sh.13, 1). This Castlebane is a small hamlet in Moyaver Lower and appears to be that described as "a few farm houses situate in the vicinity of where a castle formerly stood" in the *OSRNB* (*ibid.*). See also **Cashel** in Other Names, Culfeightrin, and **Ballycastle** in Other Names, Ramoan.

Clinery Burn	A hybrid form	
D 1231		

1. Clynary	Civ. Surv. x §60	1655c
2. ˈklïnəri	Local pronunciation	1995

The first element of this name is possibly the adjectival prefix *claon-* "crooked, sloping, inclined" (*Ó Dónaill*) or "bent/diverted" (Ó Maolfabhail 1990, 110, sv. *An Chlaonghlais Thuaidh*). *Claondoire* "sloping oakwood", with the loss of the *d* next to the *n*, is a possible origin. We may also consider that the place-name was formed by the adj. *claon* plus the substantive suffix *aire* (*Joyce* ii 11–2); *claonaire* could be translated as "sloping place" (see also **Flughery Burn** in Other Names, Culfeightrin). For further possible final elements, see **Araboy** in Ballintoy.

Crockachara	*Cnoc an Chártha(?)*	
D 1033	"hill of the (standing-)stone"	

1. (?)Crockahanagh	Tithe Applot. 19	1833
2. Cruckahara	OSRNB sh.13, 1	1855c
3. Crockachard	O'Laverty iv 443	1887
4. cnoc a chartha "hill of the standing stone"	OSRNB sh.13, 1	1855c
5. ˌkrukəˈhara	Local pronunciation	1995

"A small village of farmhouses near the base of [Croaghan] mountain. It also includes (i.e. denotes) a subdivision of the townland of Tureagh extending westwards from the boundary of Crockatinny to the boundary of Breen" (*OSRNB* sh.13, 1).

The first element of this name was *cnoc* "hill". Holmer recorded this word, which he spelt *cruc*, as [krʌk] (*Irish of the Glens* 106; see also **Crockateemore** in Other Names, Culfeightrin).

Form 1 may contain a scribal error or refer to a different (and since lost) place-name. Form 3 on the other hand seems to contain the scribal error of a final *d* for *a*. *Cártha*, used in the suggested form (note form 4), is a variant form of *coirthe* "(standing-)stone" (*Ó Dónaill*). *Carra* is a variant masc. gen. form of *carr* "rocky patch" (cf. **Maghernahar** in Ballintoy), and so *Cnoc an Charra* "hill of the rocky patch" may also be considered.

Crockatinny	*Cnoc an tSionnaigh*	
D 1033	"hill of the fox"	
1. Crokentiney	Religious Survey	1734
2. Crockathinagh	Tithe Applot. 19	1833
3. Crockatinny	OSRNB sh.13, 1	1855c
4. cnoc a tsionnaigh "hill of the ox"	OSRNB sh.13, 1	1855c
5. Creag an teine "rock of the fire"	Rev. Magill (JDCHS) iii 79	1934
6. ˌkrukəˈtʃïni	Local pronunciation	1995

"A subdivision comprising about one-third of the townland of Turreagh, it is bounded on the east and west by two small streams and on the north by the 'Well Water'" (*OSRNB* sh.13, 1).

Cnocán Tine "hillock of the fire" seems a less likely possible origin.

Doughery Bridge	A hybrid form	
D 0434		
1. Doughery Bridge	OSRNB sh.13, 1	1855c
2. ˈduxəri ˈbrïdʒ	Local pronunciation	1995

"An old stone bridge of 1 arch with parapets about 68 feet long and spans the Doughery Water (connecting the townlands of Mazes and Mullaghduff Big)" (*OSRNB* sh. 13, 1).

The Doughery Water, after joining other streams and undergoing several changes of name, eventually empties into the Bush River. The Irish element appears to derive from *Dúchoraidh* "black weir or crossing place". *Coraidh* was originally a dative form of *cora* but was used here for the nominative. *An Dúchoraidh* anglicized Doochary, and of similar etymology, is in Donegal (*GÉ 96*). A grant dated the 3rd of July, 1620, from "the first earl of Antrim to Alexander Magee of Ballygicon" shows that Ballyukin (see Other Names, Culfeightrin) contained a division called *Dowcorry*, which may have been of similar origin (*MacDonnells Antrim* 117).

Drumnagardeen	*Droim na gCuirdín(?)*	
D 1133	"ridge of the wild carrots"	
1. Drumnagardin	Court of Claims §923	1662c
2. Drumnagorten	Religious Survey	1734
3. Drimnagordon	Lendrick Map	1780

4. Drumnagardeen	OSRNB sh.13, 1	1855c
5. Druim an ghairdín "back of the garden"	OSRNB sh.13, 1	1855c
6. "the Garden Hill" or "Back Garden"	OSRNB sh.13, 1	1855c
7. ˌdrǫməˈgardən	Local pronuncaition	1995

"A subdivision of Breen townland comprising the holdings occupied by Anthony and Patrick McClaine. The Altmore Burn traces the boundary of this division on the west side and the Inver Burn on the north" (*OSRNB* sh. 13,1).

Cuirdín "wild carrot" (*Ó Dónaill*; standard Mod. Ir. gen. pl. *cuirdíní*) appears in a variant form in the Co. Donegal name *Cúil na gCuirridín* (Killygordon; *GÉ* 85).

The first element may have been a derivative of *droim* "ridge" such as *dromainn* "ridge, mound". Metathesis of a central article following *droim* is also a possibility. It is possible that a central [t] in the last element could have become voiced in English variants. This could be explained as occurring amoung English speakers by analogy with *garden*. Thus gen. forms of *goirtín* "small field; a small field of corn" (*Dinneen*) or its variant *goirteán* "small field" (see *Irish of Rathlin* 202 sv. *goirtean*) may be considered. (Power has translated *goirtín* as "little garden" (1952, 130 sv. Gorteen)). *Dinneen* translates *gairdín* (forms 4–5) as "a garden; (also) a haggard, a yard" but its use here is doubtful. Holmer recorded an adoption of Scottish Gaelic *gàirdean* "arm; hand; part of a spinning wheel" (*Dwelly*) locally as [gɑːrdə] "wrist or arm" (*Irish of the Glens* 115), but the occurrence of this element in local place-names is also doubtful.

High Town
D 0831

An English form

1. High Town	OSRNB sh.13, 1	1855c
2. the High Town	OSRNB sh.13, 1	1855c
3. ˈhai təun	Local pronunciation	1995

"A few farm houses. This being the uppermost village in the townland [Carrowlaverty] it is called the High Town" (*OSRNB* sh.13, 1).

Inver Burn
D 1134

A hybrid form

1. (?)abhann an yInnbhir	Antrim Notebooks i 107	1925c
2. Inver Burn	OSRNB sh.13, 1	1855c
3. ˌinəvïr ˈbǫrn	Local pronunciation	1995

"A small stream having its source in a bog north of Breen House . . . it flows westward through a flat valley and forms one of the head streams of the 'Well Water'" (*OSRNB* sh.13, 1).

There is another Inver Burn in the parish, while there is also another Inver Burn which lies along the boundary of the parishes of Ballintoy and Billy. Form 1 suggests the original form was *Abhainn an Inbhir* "river of the *inbhear*". The exact meaning of the last element (nom. sing. *inbhear*) here is not certain. *Ó Dónaill* translates it as "river-mouth, estuary" but the streams of this name locally are but tributaries ultimately feeding the Bush River (Holmer recorded *inbhear* on Rathlin as [inˈəvər] meaning "port; inlet" (*Irish of Rathlin* 205)). *Inbhear* is also an earlier form of *iníor* "(act of) grazing; pasturage" (*Ó Dónaill*); it does not appear to have been used in late Ulster Irish (see for example, *LASID* i 16), and although a place-name might maintain an older form, it still seems doubtful that this was the final element in question. *Dwelly* (sv. *ionbhar* recté *inbhir*) lists other meanings for this word however, including "confluence of waters; angular piece of ground at the confluence of two waters", which can be considered in this case.

Inver Burn D 0735	A hybrid form	
1. (?)abhann an yInnbhir	Antrim Notebooks i 107	1925c
2. Inver Burn	OSRNB sh.8, 3	1855c
3. ˌinəvïr ˈbọrn	Local pronunciation	1995

This stream lies along the north-western boundary of the parish and eventually forms the Doughery Water (see Doughery Bridge above). See above regarding the Irish element.

Killen Vale House D 0735	A hybrid form	
1. Killinvale	OSM xxiv 4	1832
2. ˌkïlənˈveːl	Local pronunciation	1995

This house is in Monanclogh. It has been recorded locally that it took its name from a Fr. Killen who used to live here (Ní Choragáin 1994, 40).

Knocklayd D 1136	*Cnoc Leithid* "mountain of breadth(?)"	
1. (?)Síth Leithet Lachtmaige	LL 1120 l.32917	1100c
2. (?)Lethead, Dun mBaedan a	Descendants Ir 322 l.4	1200c
3. cnoc lea, go	AFM v 1470	1542
4. Cnoc Leaaid	A. Conn. 722 §8	1542
5. Chnuic lán-álainn Leathaid, i mbun abhann	SMMD II, 43	1638c
6. Cnoc Leithid, as cúl	Irish of Rathlin 183	1942
7. Chroc Léithid, as Chúl	Iarsmaí ó Reachrainn 250	1948
8. Knock Glaide	Jobson's Ulster (TCD)	1590c
9. Knock Glade	Dartmouth Map 25	1590c

10. Knock Glad	Bartlett Maps (Esch. Co. Maps) 1	1603
11. Knock Glad	Speed's Ulster	1610
12. Knocklayde	Ulst. Roll Gaol Deliv. 265	1613
13. Knocklayd	BSD 170	1661
14. Knocklayde, Part of	BSD 178	1661
15. Knocklead	Court of Claims §923	1662c
16. Knockleay, the hill of	Court of Claims §923	1662c
17. Knockleg, the Hill of	Decree of Innocence 431	1663
18. Knocklayde (part)	ASE 117a §19	1668
19. Knocklaid	Hib. Del. Antrim	1672c
20. Knocklead	Lendrick Map	1780
21. Knock Lead Mt.	Dubourdieu Map	1812
22. Knocklaid	Bnd. Sur. (OSNB) B 17	1830
23. Knockleade or Knocklaid "the Broad Mountain"	Rev. Connolly 500	1812
24. Knocklead "the broad mountain"	Hamilton's Letters 243	1822
25. Knoc-lade "The broad mountain"	McSkimin (DPJ) 321	1833
26. Cnoc leithid "hill of the breadth"	J O'D (OSNB) B 17	1831
27. Cnoc Leithid	Rev. Magill 19	1904
28. Cnoc leithid "The broad hill"	Ó Dubhthaigh 182	1905
29. Cnoc Leithid	Éire Thuaidh	1988
30. Cnoc Leithid	GÉ 70	1989
31. ɑs kʌːl (kʌːŋ) krɔk lˈɛˈidʒ	Irish of Rathlin 183	1942
32. nɔkˈleːd	Local pronunciation	1993

The boundaries of four Armoy townlands and six Ramoan townlands radiate from the summit of this 514 metre mountain. *Cnoc Leithid* is the likely original form. *Cnoc* "a hill, a height, a mountain" (*Dinneen*) is qualified here by the gen. of *leathad/leithead* "breadth, width, area, space, expanse" (*Dinneen*; *DIL* sv. *leithet*). Ó Mainnín has noticed that in Scottish Gaelic the latter word can be applied to a "declivity, side of a hill, (broad) slope, etc." (*Dwelly*) and claims that "this is clearly true of Ireland also" (*PNI* iii 92; *Leithidean Ard* "high slopes" was noted by Mac Giolla Easpaig in Rathlin (*Place-names of Rathlin* 37)). It seems that form 3 contains a scribal error; this form relates to an attack by O'Donnells and other clans on the MacQuillans.

O'Donovan believed references in the annals c. 622 to a battle between the tribes *Dál bhFiadach* (O.Ir. *Dál Fiatach*) and *Dál nAraí* (O.Ir. *Dál nAraide*) fought at a place called *Lethed Midind i nDruing* to refer to Knocklayd (*AFM* i 246 n.k). The combatants were not associated with this area (see county and barony introductions) and the place-name *Dru(i)ng* remains unidentified. Hogan lists further references to the event and tentatively suggests that this place was in south Co. Down (*Onom. Goed.* 485; see also *AU* i 96 n.1); in any event, north-east Antrim is implausible. The original fort of *Baodán* in or on *Leathad* referred to in form 1 appears in fact to have been at **Leode** in south Co. Down (see *PNI* iii 91–2 and *ibid.* vi 33–5). The scribe seems to have purposefully confused it with Knocklayd so as to extol the extent of the kingdom of the Dál bhFiadach king, *Baodán* (see Byrne 1973, 109). We might also consider that the scribe had the nearby parish of Lade in the barony of Glenarm Lower in mind; Lade is usually called *Leithead Lachtmhaí* in Irish language sources (cf. *Onom. Goed.* 484). The word *sí* (which appears in form 1), usually translated "fairy mound", is also used of mountains and hills considered to be the residences of the fairies (see *Joyce* i 179–188).

Ordnance Survey Memoirs written in 1838 recorded the local tradition that the first element of this name, *cnoc*, was qualified by the name of a "Scottish princess", who, when pregnant, fled from cruel parents only to die at the birth of her two miscarried children at the top of this mountain from starvation (*OSM* xxiv 118). This is the same princess ("Lead or McLade") who supposedly gave her name to Layd parish in the barony of Glenarm Lower (*ibid.*). See also **Carn an Truagh** in Other Names, Ramoan.

Legahapple Bridge	A hybrid form	
D 0631		
1. Lag a chapaill "hollow of the horse"	Rev. Magill 20	1904
2. ˌlɛgəhapəl ˈbrïdʒ	Local pronunciation	1995

Log an Chapaill "hollow of the horse/mare" appears to be the origin of the Irish elements. Holmer recorded *capall* locally as meaning specifically "mare" ([kɑpəl]; *Irish of the Glens* 104).

Limepark	An English form	
D 0631		
1. Lime Park	OSRNB sh.13, 1	1838c
2. Moyaver	OSRNB sh.13, 1	1855c
3. laim ˈpɑrk	Local pronunciation	1995

"A good substantial dwelling house [in Bunshanacloney townland] with a portion of ornamental ground handsomely situated, on the leading road from Ballymena to Ballycastle . . . The present proprietor, B.G. Brooke Esq. requests the name be changed from 'Lime Park' to 'Moyaver'" (*OSRNB* sh.13, 1). There was once a lime quarry in a field called [ˈgoʃək] near here (*Pers. comm.* 07.10.96).

Low Town	An English form	
D 0731		
1. Low Town	OSRNB sh.13, 1	1855c
2. ˈlo təun	Local pronunciation	1995

"A village of houses [in Carrowlaverty townland] partly in ruins . . . so called because it is the lowest village in the townland" (*OSRNB* sh.13, 1). See also **High Town**.

New Bridge	An English form	
D 0632		
1. The New Bridge	OSRNB sh.13, 1	1855c
2. ðə ˌnjəu ˈbrïdʒ	Local pronunciation	1995

"A good modern bridge of 1 arch spanning the Bush River. It was erected about 13 years ago in conjunction with the new line of road from B.Castle to Ballymena. It is called the New Bridge to distinguish it from the Old Bridge over the same river" (*OSRNB* sh.13, 1).

This bridge in Armoy village connects the townlands of Turnarobert and Moyaver Lower.

Peacocks Bridge	An English form	
D 0532		
1. Peacock's Bridge	OSRNB sh.13, 1	1855c
2. ˈpiːkɔks brïdʒ	Local pronunciation	1995

"An old stone bridge of one arch with parapets about 60 feet long. It spans the Bush river ³/₄ mile west of Armoy on a private road leading to Summer Hill. This bridge was built at the private expense of Mr. Peacock about the year 1775" (*OSRNB* sh.13, 1).

MacLysaght (1991, 242) notes that the surname Peacock is of English origin, but it has also been on record in Scotland since the 14th century (Black 1946, 653).

Stick Bridge, The	An English form	
D 0833		
1. The Stick Bridge	OSRNB sh.13, 1	1855c
2. ˈstïk brïdʒ	Local pronunciation	1995

"A stone bridge of one arch with parapets about 33 feet long. Previous to this bridge being erected, it was a temporary bridge constructed of sticks which crossed the river and from which the present one derived the name" (*OSRNB* sh.13, 1).

This bridge spans the Well Water and connects the townlands of Doonans and Cromaghs.

Summer Hill	An English form(?)	
D 0532		
1. Summer Hill	OSRNB sh.13, 1	1855c
2. sọmər ˈhïl	Local pronunciation	1995

"A substantial farmhouse seated on elevated ground [in Park townland] is the residence of Mr. C. Peacock. The land is well cultivated and altogether has a comfortable appearance, with a portion of ornamental ground" (*OSRNB* sh.13, 1).

Some places of this name in Ireland may represent a translation of *Cnoc an tSamhraidh* "hill of the summer" (see *PNI* v 125), while a confusion with *teamhair* (gen. sing. *teamhrach*) "eminence, hill" also seems possible (see *SCtSiadhail* 87n).

Well Water	An English form	
D 1035		
1. Well Water	OSRNB sh.13, 1	1855c
2. ˌðə ˌwɛl ˈwɔtər	Local pronunciation	1995

"A river having its source from Altmore Burn and Inver Burn and empties itself into the Bush river, and takes its name from a Holy Well situated in the townland of Alcrossagh which lies contiguous to this river. This river is called the 'Well Water' from the School House at Breen until it unites with the Bush River" (*OSRNB* sh.13, 1). The well was described as follows: "A Holy Well where Roman Catholics attend on a midsummers eve, for the purpose of performing stations, chiefly for the cure of ulcerated eyes. It is not dedicated to any particular saint and has no distinguishing name" (*ibid.*). See also **Alcrossagh**.

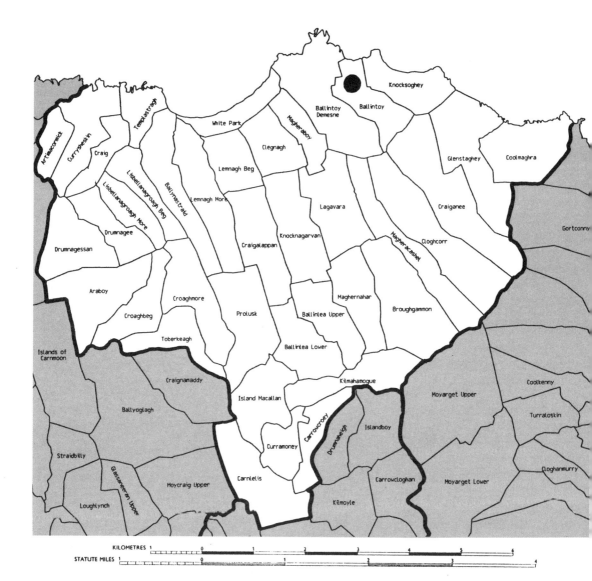

Parust of Ballintoy

Townlands

Araboy
Artimacormick
Ballinlea Lower
Ballinlea Upper
Ballintoy
Ballintoy Demesne
Ballynastraid
Broughgammon
Carnlelis
Carrowcroey
Clegnagh
Cloghcorr
Coolmaghra
Craig

Craigalappan
Craiganee
Croaghbeg
Croaghmore
Curramoney
Currysheskin
Drumnagee
Drumnagessan
Glenstaghey
Island Macallan
Kilmahamogue
Knocknagarvan
Knocksoghey
Lagavara
Lemnagh Beg

Lemnagh More
Lisbellanagroagh Beg
Lisbellangroagh More
Magheraboy
Maghercashel
Maghernahar
Prolusk
Templastragh
Toberkeagh
White Park

Town

Ballintoy

Based upon Ordnance Survey 1:50,000 mapping, with permission of the Director of the Ordnance Survey of Northern Ireland, Crown copyright preserved.

PARISH OF BALLINTOY

The coastal civil parish of Ballintoy contains 39 townlands and c. 12,753 acres (*OSM* xxiv 10). It is bounded on the west and south-west by the parish of Billy, on the south by the parish of Grange of Drumtullagh and to the east by the parish of Ramoan.

The parish makes a belated first appearance in the sources, as the *Tuogh of Dunseverick and Ballentoy*, one of the "nine tuoghs" of The Route, in a grant to Randal MacDonnell (*CPR Jas I* 58a; see also barony introduction). Today, Dunseverick lies to the immediate west of Ballintoy parish in the townland of Feigh alias Dunseverick, in Billy parish. Ballintoy is entirely absent from early Irish and medieval sources. Its structure is of a relatively recent form for a parish name, but it was also formerly annexed to Billy parish, and this accounts for its omission from the *Ecclesiastical Taxation (Eccles. Tax.)* of c. 1306, for example (*EA* 78 n.p). It was still being treated as a constituent part of Billy in mid-17th-century sources (Carleton 1991, 60–1) and the corresponding forms below thus refer to the townland name. Reeves suggests that only in 1745 was the civil parish of Ballintoy separated from Billy (*EA* 285) although Rankin (1984, 41) suggests a date of not later than 1670. In 1814, the Rev. Robert Trail of the Church of Ireland noted: "The Lord Bishop is the patron of this parish, which is a rectory, and not united to any other parish: there is no place of worship in it, except the established church" (*Shaw Mason's Par. Sur.* 159). There is no townland called Glebe in this parish although Rev. Trail wrote: "there was neither glebe nor glebe-house in this parish, until 1788, at which period I obtained a grant of 40 Irish acres for a glebe, on which I built a house with suitable offices" (*ibid.*). The Protestant church alluded to above was built in the townland of Ballintoy Demesne and is described elsewhere as "a neat edifice with a neat spire . . . built on the site of an ancient structure in 1814" (*Lewis' Top. Dict.* 115). In the 1830s it was recorded that this church had been rebuilt in 1813 (*OSM* xxiv 15). Rankin (*ibid.*) claims that this church "occupies the site of an earlier building which stood as a chapel-of-ease to Ballintoy Castle; this church became the parish church of the newly erected parish c.1670" (unfortunately he does not give the source of this information). Modern Catholic churches were erected in Ballinlea in 1816 and in Ballintoy in 1878 (*O'Laverty* iv 347; regarding religious sites used in penal times see *ibid.*) but more ancient ecclesiastical sites are found in Templastragh and possibly also in Kilmahamogue. The Catholic parish was latterly united to that of Armoy until 1872 (JDCHS (anon.) 1930) or 1873 (*O'Laverty* iv 452).

The townlands of Kilmahamogue and Carrowcroey, probably the entire townland of Curramoney, and part of the townland of Islandmacallan were formerly part of the parish of the Grange of Drumtullagh and considered as such at least as late as the mid-17th century (*DS (Par. Map)* 63; Carleton 1991, 69; *O'Laverty* iv 342).

PARISH AND TOWNLAND NAME

Ballintoy
D 045445

Baile an Tuathaigh(?)
"townland of the ruler of the *tuath*"

1. Ballenatoy, Tuogh of Dunseverick and	CPR Jas I 58a	1603
2. Ballentoy, faires and markets of	PRONI D2977/3A/2/4/1	1625
3. Ballintoy	Inq. Ult. (Antrim) §37 Car. I	1635
4. Ballintoy . . . Ballentoy	Inq. Ult. (Antrim) §59 Car. I	1635
5. Ballintoy	Inq. Ult. (Antrim) §102 Car. I	1635

6. Ballentoy	MacDonnells Antrim 437	1637
7. Ballintoy	Hill's Stewarts 84	1642
8. Ballentoy	Hill's Stewarts 86	1643
9. Ballintioy	Hickson's Ire. i 280	1652
10. Ballentoy	Hib. Reg. Cary	1657c
11. Balentoy, The 5 qtrs of	DS (Par. Map) 50	1657c
12. Ballentoy	DS (Par. Map) 51	1657c
13. Ballantoy	Census 13	1659
14. Ballie cu Ballintoy Rectoria	Trien. Visit. (Bramhall) 3	1661
15. Ballintoy	MacDonnells Antrim 312	1663
16. Ballintoy	Decree of Innocence 437	1663
17. Ballentoy, the towne lands of	Decree of Innocence 440	1663
18. Ballyntoy	Lapsed Money Book 157	1663
19. Ballentoy	Trien. Visit. (Margetson) 27	1664
20. Ballyntoy, the Castle of	MacDonnells Antrim 329	1665
21. Ballintoye, Parish of Billey and	HMR (1666) 94	1666
22. Ballintoy	ASE 117a §19	1668
23. Ballyntoy	HMR Ant. 2	1669
24. Ballentoy	Hib. Del. Antrim	1672c
25. Ballentoy	Trien. Visit. (Boyle) 34	1679
26. Ballintoy	Lamb Maps Co. Antrim	1690c
27. Ballintoy	MacDonnells Antrim 386	1683
28. Ballintoy	Ire. Map	1711
29. Balluntoy	PRONI D2977/3A/2/1/25	1714c
30. Ballentoy	PRONI D2977/3A/2/1/28	1720
31. Ballentoy	Religious Survey	1734
32. Ballentoy	Stewart's Survey 25	1734
33. Ballantoy	PRONI D2977/3A/2/1/36A	1738
34. colliery of Ballintoy, the	Hill's Stewarts 16	1749
35. Ballintoy	Reg. Deeds abstracts ii §267	1751
36. Ballantoy	Merchant's Book 19	1752
37. Ballintoy	Reg. Deeds abstracts ii §425	1760
38. Ballentoy, Balentoy	Religious Census	1766
39. Ballantoy	PRONI D2977/3A/2/14/4	1770
40. Ballintoy	Taylor and Skinner 270	1777
41. Ballintoy vi.	Dubourdieu Map	1812
42. Ballintoy . . . from . . . north and town	Shaw Mason's Par. Sur. 150	1814
43. Ballintoy, i.e. "North town"	Hamilton's Letters 247	1822
44. balle, a town, tough, north	OSM xxiv 10	1830
45. Baile an Tuaithe "town' of the tuagh or cinnament"	J O'D (OSNB) B 26	1827
46. Baile an Tuaidhe "town of the north"	EA 285	1847
47. Baile-an-tuaighe "the town of the north"	Joyce ii 20	1873
48. Baile an tuaidh "the town of the north"	O'Laverty iv 335	1887

49. Baile an Tuaidhe	Post-Sheanchas 27	1905
50. Baile 'n Túaith "North Town"	Ó Dubhthaigh 133	1905
51. baile an tuaidh	Onom. Goed. 77	1910
52. Baile an tSaoi	Alasdair Mac Colla vi	1914
53. Baile na Tuaighe	Alasdair Mac Colla vi	1914
54. Baile an Tuaith "Town of the north"	Rev. Magill 8	1923
55. Baile an Tuaighe	GÉ 15	1989
56. ˌbalïntɔi	Local pronunciation	1995

We have noted that the *Tuogh of Dunseverick and Ballentoy* was regarded as one of the "nine tuoghs" in the The Route in the early 17th century. *Tuath* "country, territory" (cf. *DIL* sv. *túath*) has been noted in some place-names (*Joyce* i 124–5; Ó Maolfabhail 1990, 258), but appears to have been universally feminine, and as such is not reflected in the forms (note form 45), with the anomalous exception of form 1. However, *Baile an Tuathaigh* "townland of the ruler of the *tuath*" does concur with the historical variants. The final element in this form is the gen. sing. of *tuathach* "territorial king; lord, chieftain" (*Ó Dónaill*) or "ruler of a tuath" (*Dinneen*). We would not necessarily expect early forms to indicate the presence of the intervocalic -*th*-; compare early 17th-century forms of the south Co. Down townland name *Beitheanach* (anglicized **Benagh**), for example (*PNI* i 10). The development of *ua* to [oː]/[ɔ] was noted in the late local dialect by Holmer (*Irish of the Glens* 32) but this feature is quite old (compare, for example, early forms of **Tornaroan** in Culfeightrin). *Baile* may have other meanings such as "homestead" (see **Balleny** in Armoy). Old settlement sites in the immediate locality include **Dundriff** and **The Castle** in Ballintoy Demesne and **Larry Bane Head** in Knocksoghey (see Other Names).

Previous commentators suggest that the adverb and adj. *thuaidh* "(in the) north" formed the final element in this name. Although it seems unusual that the *t* would remain unlenited in a name of relatively recent construction (post-12th century; cf. **Balleny** in Armoy), we may note that Holmer recorded the word locally as [tʌə] (*Irish of the Glens 132*), and that the *t* remains unlenited in Scotish Gaelic (*Dwelly* sv. *tuath*). Its use as a noun, as suggested in forms 42–44, 46–50 and 54 is somewhat improbable however, and a form such as *Baile Abhann Tuaidh* "townland of the northern river/townland of the river, north" also seems unlikely.

Form 55 suggests an Irish origin which reflects the historical forms but which contains an uncertain second element. *Tua* (earlier *tuagh*, gen. sing. *tuaighe*) has been translated "arch, curve; axe, hatchet" (*DIL* sv. *túag*), but again appears to have been universally feminine, notwithstanding that it also appears in the modern language in the masc. variant form *stua* (*DIL* (sv. *stúag*) has this as a fem. noun). This word is possibly the first element in the Irish name for the mouth of the Bann River, *Tuagh Inbhir* (see *AFM* ii 572 n.m; regarding a medieval etymology which explains *Tuagh* as a female personal name, see *ibid.*; see also *EA* 341 n.g). *Cnoc Tuagh* in Co. Galway (*AFM* v 1274) may contain a gen. pl. form. The townland of Ballytoohey in Co. Roscommon is written *Baile Tuaighe* in an 18th-century local poem, but *Baile Tuaithe* may have been intended (Ó Tuathail 1950, 284). There is a natural arch on the coast of Ballintoy Demesne near to Dundriff.

From Ó Murchadha's (1994–5) discussion of the element *sódh* "weir" in place-names, it appears that the use of this word was confined to a limited area around the Shannon from Lough Derg to Limerick. It derives from *soud* "the act of turning" (*DIL*; see Ó Murchadha 1994–5, 129) which had the later (masc.) gen. sing. form *sóidh* (nom. sing *sódh*). The exact meaning of *Baile an tSóidh* "townland of the turning(?)" would be uncertain, although it might be interpreted as referring to a point on the stream which passes through the modern village and forms the north-eastern boundary of the townland. The use of *sódh* in a place-name would also be somewhat unusual, although we could compare *An tIompú Deiseal* (angl. **Tempo**) "the right-hand turn" in Co. Fermanagh (*GÉ* 119). It seems unlikely that *só* (earlier gen. sing. *sóigh*) "joy, ease, luxury, prosperity" (*Dinneen* sv. *sógh*) would have formed an element in a townland name. *DIL* lists the word *túae* (tentatively ascribed a masculine gender) "rampart, fortification", but it is doubtful whether this word could have given rise to the forms listed above.

TOWNLAND NAMES

Araboy Of uncertain origin
C 9940

1.	Ardins	PRONI D2977/3A/2/1/6	1681
2.	Araboy	C. McG. (OSNB) B 26	1734
3.	Araboy	Stewart's Survey 23	1734
4.	Arboy	Religious Survey	1734
5.	Ardbuy alias Ardins alias Ardboy	PRONI D2977/3A/2/1/33A	1737
6.	Arboy	Religious Census	1766
7.	Arabooey	Lendrick Map	1780
8.	Arabuy	Shaw Mason's Par. Sur. 170	1803
9.	Arbuy	PRONI D2977/3A/2/1/40	1812
10.	Arrabwee	Bnd. Sur. (OSNB) B 26	1827c
11.	Arabuy	Tithe Applot. 1	1833
12.	Arraboy	OSM xxiv 23	1838
13.	Aradh Buidhe "yellow land"	J O'D (OSNB) B 26	1827
14.	ˌarəˈbɔi	Local pronunciation	1995

There are several possible origins of this name. O'Donovan may have had a derivative of the fem. noun *ar* "ploughed land; cultivated land" (cf. *DIL* sv.) in mind in form 13, but while we might compare *dúnadh* derived from *dún* "fort" (see Ó Dónaill svv.), the reflex *aradh* remains unattested. Alternatively he may have had in mind the fem. noun *ára* (dat. sing. *árainn*, gen. sing. *árann*) "kidney, loins", which is used in place-names to denote a "ridge of land" (Ó Máille 1957 *passim*; see also *PNI* ii 172 and *ibid.* vi 337). Thus *Ára Bhuí* "yellow ridge" may be a possible original form. Ó Máille (*loc. cit.*) notes several examples of *ára* in townland names, including **Coolaran** in Co. Fermanagh, Ara in Co. Mayo and Narrabaun North in Co. Kilkenny. The latter name has recently been ascribed the Irish form of *An Fhorrach Bhán Thuaidh* (*L. Log. C. Ch.* 31), however. Local examples of [ɔ] being lowered to [ɑ] have been noted elsewhere (see **Ballycarry** in Rathlin), and so *An Fhorrach Bhuí* "the yellow measure of land/meeting-place" (see *DIL* sv. *forrach*) may be considered here. Another possible first element based on this lowering may be the masc. noun *foradh* "mound; fort, residence, place of meeting" (*ibid.* sv. *forad*).

Other possible original forms include *Oirear Buí* "yellow border region" (see Ó Dónaill sv. *oirear*). *Oirear* has several meanings including "a border, a shore; a borderland; a territory or district" (*Dinneen* sv. *airear, oirear*). Araboy lies on the boundary of the baronies of Cary and Dunluce Lower. Less likely first elements are the nom. pl. of *earr* (*earra*) "end, extremity"

50

(see **Maghernahar**), *aire* "dam, fence (on a stream)" (*DIL, Dinneen* sv.) and *áirí* (earlier *áirghe*) "milking place for cows, byre" (*DIL* sv. *áirge*).

Forms 5(a) and 5(c) suggest that *ard* "height, hillock" (*Ó Dónaill*) formed the first element. This is not supported by forms 2–3, however; the *d* could have been introduced by association with a similar name (see below), or represent a mistranscription of *a* (compare also forms of **Armoy**, and of **Finnard**/*Fionnúir* in *PNI* i 26).

Forms 1 and 5(b) suggest that a separate name, perhaps of a contiguous or internal territory, was formerly current. They may contain the English plural suffix, indicating some internal division, or represent a form such as *Ard Inse* "height of the holm". Sources in the mid-1600s included Araboy under Croaghbeg (Carleton 1991, 59).

Artimacormick	*Ard Tí Mhic Cormaic*	
C 9944	"height of MacCormick's house"	

1. Shanrally	Hib. Reg. Cary	1657c
2. Shavally	DS (Par. Map) 51	1657c
3. Altimacarinick	Census 12	1659
4. (?)Ardomarky, the halfe towne of Kilnoghe and	Decree of Innocence 431	1663
5. Shanvally	Lapsed Money Book 170	1663
6. Shanvally	ASE 117a §19	1668
7. Shanrally	Hib. Del. Antrim	1672c
8. artemacormick	Religious Survey	1734
9. Artimacormick	Stewart's Survey 22	1734
10. Artimacormick	Religious Census	1766
11. Artemacormick	Lendrick Map	1780
12. Artimacormick	Shaw Mason's Par. Sur. 170	1803
13. Artymacormack	Bnd. Sur. (OSNB) B 26	1827c
14. Artimacormick	Tithe Applot. 1	1833
15. Ard Tighe Mic Cormaic "Hill of the House of MacCormick"	J O'D (OSNB) B 26	1827
16. Artimacormick "the height of Mac Cormick's house"	Joyce i 386	1869
17. Ard-Tighe-Mhic-Cormaic "MacCormack's house height"	Antrim Place Names 85	1913
18. ˌɑrtiməˈkɔrmïk	Local pronunciation	1995

It is likely that *ard toighe* (standard Mod. Ir. *ard tí*) "height of the house" indeed formed the first elements in this name (forms 15–7). The *d* must be assumed as having been lost due to amalgamation with the *t* at an early stage, for there is no trace of it in the historical variants. Joyce notes that the *d* "is usually omitted" when these elements come together in placenames, and cites the further example of **Artiferrall** townland in Kilraghts parish, Co. Antrim (*Joyce* i 386). Form 3 might suggest that the first element was based on *allt* (regarding this element see **Altnamuck Burn** in Other Names, Armoy), but this is obviously a scribal error.

The surname *Mac Cormaic* "son of *Cormac*" is usually anglicized MacCormick in Ulster, where the name is often of Scottish origin (MacLysaght 1985, 59). The name is on record elsewhere locally at least as early as 1669 when one Art McCormuck lived in the neighbouring parish of Billy (*HMR Ant.* 2). There were also McCormucks in Culfeightrin, Rathlin and Grange of Drumtullagh at this time (*ibid.* 8–11, 13–4).

Forms 1–2 and 5–7 represent an obsolete name which covered, as well as Artimacormack, the townlands of Carrowreagh, Feigh alias Dunseverick and Carncolp, in the neighbouring parish of Billy (Carleton 1991, 59, 61). It appears to be derived from *Seanbhaile* "old townland". The name *Artimacormick* seems to be falling out of use.

Ballinlea Lower,	*Baile an Leá*
Ballinlea Upper	"townland of the physician"
D 0339, 0340	

1.	(?)Ballenland	PRONI D2977/3A/2/4/1	1625
2.	Ballinlea	Hib. Reg. Cary	1657c
3.	Ballynkea	Census 13	1659
4.	Ballinlea	BSD 173	1661
5.	Ballelea	Court of Claims §923	1662c
6.	Ballinlea 1 Qur.	Lapsed Money Book 157	1663
7.	Ballinlew	ASE 116b §19	1668
8.	Ballyaynels	HMR Ant. 2	1669
9.	Balinlea	Hib. Del. Antrim	1672c
10.	Ballyenlea	PRONI D2977/3A/2/3/1	1696
11.	Ballinlea	PRONI D2977/3A/2/3/2A	1696
12.	Ballyinlea	PRONI D2977/3A/2/3/3, 4	1709
13.	Ballynalea	Hill's Stewarts 11	1720
14.	Ballinlea O'Cahan, Ballinlea-Stewart	Religious Survey	1734
15.	Upper Ballenlea, Lower Ballinlea	Stewart's Survey 19	1734
16.	Bellanlea	Merchant's Book 58	1753
17.	Ballinlea	Religious Census	1766
18.	Ballinlae	Shaw Mason's Par. Sur. 170	1803
19.	(?)Ballynalia	PRONI D2977/3A/2/1/40	1812
20.	Ballinloe	Shaw Mason's Par. Sur. 150	1814
21.	Ballinlea Upper, Ballinlea Lower	Bnd. Sur. (OSNB) B 26	1827c
22.	Ballenlae	OSM xxiv 11	1830
23.	Ballinlea Upper, Ballinlea Lower	Tithe Applot. 1	1833
24.	Baile an Leagha "Town of the physician"	Rev. Magill 7	1923
25.	ˌbalənˈleː	Local pronunciation	1995

With the exception of forms 13 and 19 (which are related and appear to contain scribal errors), the historical variants indicate that the final element was the gen. sing. form of a masc. noun. If we accept the recent lowering of the final vowel from [ʎ]/[iː] to [eː], we could consider *lao* "calf" as a possible final element (see also **Broughanlea** in Culfeightrin).

Dinneen (sv. *liaigh*) gives *leagha*, for which is ascribed the standard Mod. Ir. form *leá*, as a gen. sing. form of *lia* "healer, physician" (*Ó Dónaill* sv. 2 *lia*; *leá* is wrongly listed by *Ó Dónaill* as a variant gen. sing. of *lia* "stone; pillar-stone"). This reflects modern pronunciation most closely. "Each of the great Irish families had attached to it a physician whose office was hereditary, and who usually held a tract of land in return for service" (*Joyce* ii 77). Professions are well represented in Irish place-names (*ibid.* ii 90–121). Other local examples include *Baile na gCeard* (anglicized **Ballynagard**) "townland of the artificers" in Culfeightrin.

There appears to have been some division of Ballinlea as early as 1669 (form 8).

Ballintoy	*Baile an Tuathaigh(?)*
D 0444	"townland of the ruler of the *tuath*"

See under the parish name.

Ballintoy Demesne	A hybrid form
D 4445	

1. (?)the parke of Ballentoy	PRONI D2977/3A/2/1/17	1706
2. (?)Ballentoy Freehold	Stewart's Survey 18	1734
3. (?)Big Park of Ballintoy	Hill's Stewarts 219	1741c
4. (?)Ballentoy park	PRONI D2977/3A/2/1/40	1812
5. Demesne	OSM xxiv 30–1	1838
6. dəm'eːən	Local pronunciation	1995

It is uncertain if forms 1–4 refer in fact to this townland or to a separate (and since obsolete) division. The name *Ballintoy Demesne* only appears at the time of the Ordnance Survey. In earlier sources, this territory was probably included under Ballintoy townland (Carleton 1991, 59). The epithet *demesne* may have been inspired by the remains of a building in the north of this townland, called **The Castle** (see Other Names).

Ballynastraid	*Baile na Sráide*
D 0043	"townland of the village"

1. Ballinstrraid	Hib. Reg. Cary	1657c
2. Ballinstrade	DS (Par. Map) 50	1657c
3. Ballnastrad	Census 13	1659
4. Ballenstraid	BSD 172	1661
5. Ballenstread	ASE 116b §19	1668
6. Ballagnestred	HMR Ant. 3	1669
7. Ballinstrade	Hib. Del. Antrim	1672c
8. Ballynesstrade	PRONI D2977/3A/2/1/5A	1682
9. (?)Ballyneshade and Ballyneshadd	Forfeit. Estates 375b §45	1703
10. Ballaghnastraid	C. McG. (OSNB)	1734
11. Ballynastraidmore	Religious Survey	1734
12. Bellaghnastraidmore	Stewart's Survey 21	1734
13. Ballinastraid	Religious Census	1766
14. Bːnastrade	Lendrick Map	1780
15. Ballnastraid	Shaw Mason's Par. Sur. 170	1803
16. Ballaghnastraidmore	PRONI D2977/3A/2/1/40	1812
17. Ballynastraid	Bnd. Sur (OSNB) B 26	1827c
18. Baile na Sráide "town of the street"	J O'D (OSNB) B 26	1827

19. Baile na sráid "Townland of the village"	Rev. Magill 7	1923
20. ˌbɑlnəˈstraːd	Local pronunciation	1995

The intrusion of a *t* in anglicized forms of *sráid* was noted under **Stroan** in Armoy. This word, in the gen. sing. form, forms the latter element in this name. *Sráid* "street; level (surfaced) ground around a house" is most often translated "village" in townland names. It is not certain to what it originally referred; there are two hamlets in the north of the townland. A complex of the ruins of "2 forts, a battery and some other enclosures" on "an eminence" in this townland was noted and described in the 1830s (*OSM* xxiv 21), and could also have given rise to the place-name.

Forms 11, 12 and 16 probably represent *Baile na Sráide Mór* "townland of the village, big" rather than *Baile na Sráide Móire* "townland of the big village". Indication of an internal division of this townland may also appear in form 9. Perhaps, rather than inventing a new name for the new division, surveyors changed the spelling of the anglicized place-name in some small regard. Forms 6, 10, 12 and 16 suggest that there existed the variant form *Bealach na Sráide* "road of the village".

Broughgammon
D 0540

Bruach gCamán
"bank of the (stream-)bends"

1.	Bruaghmore	Hib. Reg. Cary	1657c
2.	Bruaghmore, Bruaghgammon	DS (Par. Map) 51	1657c
3.	Bruaghmore als Bruaghgammon	DS (Par. Map) 51	1657c
4.	Broughmore, Bruaghgammon	BSD 171	1661
5.	Broughgamon	Lapsed Money Book 157	1663
6.	Broughmore alias Broughgamon	ASE 116b §19	1668
7.	Bruaghmore	Hib. Del. Antrim	1672c
8.	Bruaghgamon	PRONI D2977/3A/2/1/17	1706
9.	Broghgamon	Religious Survey	1734
10.	Broaghgamon	Stewart's Survey 19	1734
11.	Broughgemmon	Hill's Stewarts 22	1741c
12.	Broughgamon	Religious Census	1766
13.	Brughgammon	Lendrick Map	1780
14.	Broughgammon	Shaw Mason's Par. Sur. 170	1803
15.	Broughgammon	Bnd. Sur. (OSNB) B 26	1827c
16.	Bruach Gamáin "Gammon's border or brink"	J O'D (OSNB) B 26	1827
17.	Bruach g-caman "The border of the bends"	Ó Dubhthaigh 133	1905
18.	Bruach gcamán "fort of the camans"	Rev. Magill 9	1923
19.	ˌbrɔxˈgamən	Local pronunciation	1995

Bruach "a brink, edge, a bank (of river), border, boundary; a shore, a coast" (*Dinneen*) is probably the first element in question here. The south-eastern boundary of this townland runs along a tributary stream of Inver Burn, and separates the parishes of Ballintoy and

Ramoan. Holmer recorded *bruach* as meaning "hill, slope or brae" locally, although one suspects that these usages were late developments (*Irish of the Glens* 105; cf. also **Broughanlea** in Culfeightrin).

Form 17 may have been based on the assumption that *bruach* was of neuter gender and hence caused eclipsis in following nouns. Indeed, *DIL* tentatively suggests that *bruach* was originally neuter *(DIL* sv. *bruach)*. As this gender fell out of use around the 10th century (Mac Giolla Easpaig 1984, 59), this would suggest quite an early date for this place-name. Alternatively, this eclipsis could have arisen from the use of the name in the acc. sing. case; such eclipsis fell out of use around the same period. The second element in either case would most likely be the gen. sing. or gen. pl. of *camán*, which appears elsewhere locally in the townland name of **Drumahaman** in Culfeightrin. *Camán* may variously mean "a bend; a stick with a crooked head; a hurley for ball-playing" (*Dinneen*). The first of these meanings, referring to a bend or bends in the boundary stream, may have been that originally intended.

The initial *c* of the second element is unlikely to have undergone an early transformation to *g*, as such change seems to occur to Irish place-names most often in the English language (cf. **Gloonan**, *PNI* iv 181). One might consider however that the second element was originally *Damhán*, a male personal name, or *damhán* "little ox", with lenition of the *d* possibly caused by the use of the place-name in oblique cases, and an early delenition of the central *m* (cf. **Kinramer** in Rathlin). The rare Anglo-Norman surname Gammon is associated with counties Cork and Waterford and is unlikely here (see Woulfe 1923, 290 and MacLysaght 1985, 118).

Another form representing *An Bruach Mór*, perhaps "the large bank" (forms 1, 2(a), 3(a), 4(a), 6(a), 7) is no longer current.

Carnlelis	*Ceathrúin Leithlis(?)*	
D 0237	"quarterland of the half-fort"	

1. Carnelolons	Hib. Reg. Cary	1657c
2. Carnelolous	DS (Par. Map) 63	1657c
3. Kerulelues	Census 11	1659
4. Carnelolus	BSD 179	1661
5. Carelolus	Lapsed Money Book 158	1663
6. Carnelelan, 1 qr.	ASE 117a §19	1668
7. Carneluske	HMR Ant. 14	1669
8. Carnelolons	Hib. Del. Ant.	1672c
9. Carivelelish	C. McG. (OSNB) B 26	1734
10. Carriveleluss	Stewart's Survey 24	1734
11. Carrivelelish	Stewart's Survey 32	1734
12. Carvelealuss	Religious Survey	1734
13. Carnlelish	Religious Census	1766
14. Carroleles	Lendrick Map	1780
15. Cairnlelis	Shaw Mason's Par. Sur. 170	1803
16. Cairnlelis	Bnd. Sur. (OSNB) B 26	1827c
17. Carnlelis	Tithe Applot. 2	1833
18. Carn Lilis "Lelis's carn"	J O'D (OSNB) B 26	1827
19. Carn an léith-lios "The cairn of the half-fort"	Ó Dubhthaigh 135	1905

20. Carn leith leasa "carn of the half fort"	Rev. Magill 9	1923
21. ˌkɑrnˈleliˑs	Local pronunciation	1995

Forms 3, 9–12 and 14 suggest that the first element was originally *ceathrú* "quarterland" (see also the following townland name) and that the anglicized *carn-* variants reflect its dat. sing. form *ceathrúin*. It was recorded in the 1830s however that: "on an eminence in [Carnlelis], and holding of William Hopkin, there stood an ancient cairn of earth and stones. The ruin is now 4 by 3 yards and 4 feet high" (*OSM* xxiv 27), and *carn* "cairn; heap, pile" remains a possible first element. A confusion in English sources of *ceathrúin/carn* (compare **Carrowreagh** in Grange of Drumtullagh), the copying of mistranscriptions (such as *carne-* for *carive-*) in related sources, and a local reinterpretation of the unstressed first element may all be factors here.

Lios has several meanings including "enclosed ground of (ancient) dwelling house; enclosed space, garth; ring-fort; fairy mound" (*Ó Dónaill*). The variant gen. sing. form *lis* appears to be reflected in the forms (cf. *Rinn an Lis*, anglicized **Ringolish**, in *PNI* i 107), prefixed by *leith* "lying, turned, to one side; lopsided, tilted; one-sided, partial; half-, hemi-, semi-; one of two, of a pair" (*Ó Dónaill* sv. *leath-*).

Lillis is a variant of the surname Lawless used in counties Clare and Limerick, and is arguably reflected to some extent in the forms. This surname, which was introduced to Ireland sometime after the Anglo-Norman invasion, and which comes from Old English *laghles* "outlaw" and is gaelicized *Laighléis*, is apparently not associated with Ulster (MacLysaght 1985, 191; Woulfe 1923, 301), and this militates against accepting it here. The Culfeightrin townland name of **Drumaridley** may also contain a locally unattested surname, however.

Carrowcroey
D 0438

An Cheathrú Chrua
"the hard quarterland"

1. Carverog	Religious Survey	1734
2. Carrivecroy, Kittall and	Stewart's Survey 36	1734
3. Carvecroy	Religious Census	1766
4. Carracroey	Lendrick Map	1780
5. Caracroey	Shaw Mason's Par. Sur. 170	1803
6. Carncrooy	PRONI D2977/3A/2/1/40	1812
7. Carrowcroey	Bnd. Sur. (OSNB) B 26	1827c
8. Ceathramh chruadh "hard quarter"	J O'D (OSNB) B 26	1827
9. Ceathramhadh croa "The quarter of the gallows"	Ó Dubhthaigh 135	1905
10. ˌkarəˈkroˑi	Local pronunciation	1995

The older pronunciation of the first element *ceathrú* (earlier *ceathramha*) "quarter (of land)" is reflected in forms 1–3. The internal [v] had been lost by 1780 (form 4), however. Form 6 may contain a scribal error or reflect the dat. form of *ceathrú*, *ceathrúin*; it is unlikely to indicate the presence of a medial definite article. The second element appears to have been the adjective *crua* (historically *cruaidh*) "hard"; Irish *ua* is frequently anglicized [oː] in townland names. Joyce notes that this element is used in place-names to "designate hard surfaced land, a soil difficult to till on account of tough clay, surface rocks", and notes examples including **Cargacroy** in Co. Down and **Mullaghcroy** in Co. Westmeath (*Joyce* ii 477). Mac Giolla Easpaig noted the subtownland example of *Droim Cruaidh* "hard ridge" in Rathlin (*Place-Names of Rathlin* 26).

The townland of Carrowcroey appeared as part of Kittal (see Other Names) in mid-17th-century sources (Carleton 1991, 69).

Clegnagh D 0343	*Cloigneach* "place of round hills"		
1. (?)Cloigneach	Irish of the Glens 106	1940	
2. Cregenagh	Hib. Reg. Cary	1657c	
3. Clegnagh	DS (Par. Map) 50	1657c	
4. Clegenagh	Census 12	1659	
5. Cregenagh & Knocknegarven	BSD 172	1661	
6. Clagne	Court of Claims §923	1662c	
7. Creganagh and Knocknagarvin	Lapsed Money Book 157	1663	
8. Gregenagh, Knocknegarvin and	ASE 116b §19	1668	
9. Cleanugh	HMR Ant. 3	1669	
10. (?)Clegnagh	PRONI D2977/3A/2/1/5A	1682	
11. Clegnagh	PRONI D2977/3A/2/1/15	1696	
12. Clagnagh	C. McG. (OSNB) B 26	1734	
13. Clegneagh	Religious Survey	1734	
14. Clagnagh	Stewart's Survey 20	1734	
15. Clegneagh	Hill's Stewarts 222	1741c	
16. Clegnagh	Religious Census	1766	
17. Clegnagh	Shaw Mason's Par. Sur. 170	1803	
18. Clecnogh	PRONI D2977/3A/2/1/40	1812	
19. Clegnagh	Bnd. Sur. (OSNB) B 26	1827c	
20. Claigeannach "The hillocks like skulls"	Ó Dubhthaigh 134	1905	
21. Claigeanach "skull-like hillocks"	Rev. Magill 11	1923	
22. klEg′n′ax	Irish of the Glens 106	1940	
23. ˌklɛgnəx	Local pronunciation	1995	

Notwithstanding scribal errors, forms 2–8 could be interpreted as *cloigeann* "the skull, the head; a headland; land lying on the borders of a swamp" (*Dinneen*) or "round hill" (see also **Cleggan** in Armoy) followed by the (possibly collective) suffix *-ach*, with eventual shortening by syncope to *cloigneach* (forms 9–19). The meaning "place of round hills" seems most likely. Ó Maolfabhail (1987, 80) suggests that as with the suffixless *cloigeann*, *cloigneach* probably denotes something like "high place of bare rocks" in place-names. In this event we could consider that the place-name could have referred originally to high rocky ground in the south of the townland.

Clegnagh is the name of another townland in Grange of Drumtullagh parish, and it is uncertain to which of these Holmer's informant was referring (forms 1 and 22).

Cloghcorr	*Cloch Chorr*	
D 0541	"odd/pointed stone"	
1. (?)Cloch Corr	Antrim Notebooks i 108	1925c
2. Cloghcor	Inq. Ult. (Antrim) §101 Car. I	1635
3. Cologhcor	Hib. Reg. Cary	1657c
4. Cloghcor	DS (Par. Map) 50	1657c
5. Clocher	Census 13	1659
6. Clogher	BSD 171	1661
7. Cloghcorre 1 Qur	Lapsed Money Book 156	1663
8. Cloghcare	HMR Ant. 4	1669
9. Coolocor	Hib. Del. Antrim	1672c
10. Cloghcorr, one quarter land of	PRONI D2977/3A/2/1/24	1711
11. Cloghcorr	C. McG. (OSNB) B 26	1734
12. Cloghcorr	Stewart's Survey 18	1734
13. Cloghcorr	Religious Survey	1734
14. Cloughcor	Hill's Stewarts 222	1741c
15. Cloghcore	Religious Census	1766
16. Cloghcor	Lendrick Map	1780
17. Cloughcorr	Shaw Mason's Par. Sur. 170	1803
18. Cloughcorr	Bnd. Sur. (OSNB) B 26	1827c
19. Cloghcor	Bnd. Sur. (OSNB) B 26	1827c
20. Cloch corr "odd stone"	J O'D (OSNB) B 26	1827
21. Cloch cor "The round stone"	Ó Dubhthaigh 135	1905
22. Cloch cor "stone of the bends"	Ó Dubhthiagh 135	1905
23. Cloch corra "boundary stone"	Rev. Magill 11	1923
24. klɔxˈkɔːr	Local pronunciation	1995

Cloch may variously denote "stone; rocky shore; rocky island; (stone) castle" (*Ó Dónaill*). This townland is situated inland, and there is no record of a castle of any description within the territory (or indeed, the near vicinity). The adjective *corr* "odd; tapering, pointed" probably formed the second element. Neither the fem. noun *corr* (gen. sing. *coirre*, gen. pl. *corr*), which has several meanings (see **Corrymellagh** and **Torcorr** in Culfeightrin), nor the masc. noun *cor* "bend" (a tributary stream of Inver Burn runs through this townland) seem likely.

Coolmaghra	*Cúil Mhachaire*	
D 0743	"corner of the field(?)"	
1. Culmagher	Religious Survey	1734
2. Coulmaghra	Shaw Mason's Par. Sur. 170	1803
3. Coulmaghra	Bnd. Sur. (OSNB) B 26	1827c

4. Coolmaghry	OSRNB sh.4, 1	1855c
5. Cúl Machaire "back plain"	J O'D (OSNB) B 26	1827
6. cul maghaire "back part of the plain"	OSRNB sh.4, 1	1855c
7. Cúl Machaire "The back of the (plain) field"	Ó Dubhthaigh 135	1905
8. Cúl-machaire "back of the plain or field"	Joyce iii 246	1913
9. ˌkul'maxri	Local pronunciation	1995

Cúl "back", often applied to sides of hills in place-names (*Joyce* i 200), is usually indistinguishable from *cúil* "corner, recess, nook" in anglicized spelling. One or other of these words begins several local names including three townland names in Culfeightrin (also in the form *cool-*), while Culfeightrin itself contains an attested *cúil* as the first element. O'Donovan and Joyce chose *cúl* (forms 5 and 8 respectively). Joyce also assumed similar explanations for the townlands of Coolmaghery and Coolmaghry in Tyrone (*Joyce* iii 246). *Cúil* is more common in townland names, however (cf. **Coolaveely**, Culfeightrin).

The second element *machaire* has several connotations, including "a plain, a flat or low-lying country, a field, a riding or playing-field, a race-course, a battle-field" (*Dinneen*). See also **Magheraboy** regarding this element. Topographically, this townland is generally hilly. The minor place-name **Maghralough** (see Other Names), in the south of this townland, contains the same element and perhaps refers to the same feature.

Craig	*An Chreag*	
D 2028	"the rocky hill"	
1. Ballynoe	Hib. Reg. Cary	1657c
2. Crogballyno	Census 12	1659
3. Ballinoe	BSD 172	1661
4. Ballynoe 1 Qur.	Lapsed Money Book 157	1663
5. Ballynoe	ASE 116a §19	1668
6. Creghballynoe	HMR Ant. 2	1669
7. Cregballynoe	PRONI D2977/3A/2/1/30	1720
8. Craigsballynoe	Stewart's Survey 22	1734
9. Craigballynoe, the quarter land of	PRONI D2977/3A/2/1/37A	1739
10. Craigballyno	Religious Census	1766
11. Craigs	Lendrick Map	1780
12. Craige	Shaw Mason's Par. Sur. 170	1803
13. Craighballynoe	PRONI D2977/3A/2/1/40	1812
14. Craige	Bnd. Sur. (OSNB) B 26	1827c
15. Craig	Bnd. Sur. (OSNB) B 26	1827c
16. Creag "a rock"	J O'D (OSNB) B 26	1827
17. ˌkreːg	Local pronunciation	1995

Creig was originally an acc. or dat. form of *creag*. It is impossible to distinguish between *creag* and *creig* in anglicized form (cf. **Craigban**, Culfeightrin). *Creig* is translated "craig;

rocky eminence, rock; stony, barren, ground; rocky shore" by *Ó Dónaill*. Holmer noted *creig* as the local nominative form and translated it as "rock; cliff, crag" ([kreg']; *Irish of the Glens* 108). It may have referred in this case to a "rocky hill" in this townland, "locally called the Craig hill . . . situated south of and contiguous to the leading road from Bushmills to Ballycastle . . ." (*OSM* xxiv 33).

The form *Craig* appears initially in the sources only in 1780 (form 11). Form 11 also suggests that there may have been some internal division of this territory, but the English plural suffix has since been lost. The form *Creag Bhaile Nua* "(crag) of the new townland" may have formerly been current in Irish (forms 2, 6–10 and 13). It is more likely, however, that these variants are English scribal forms reflecting an amalgamation of two formerly distinct divisions (compare **Brackaghlislea** in *PNI* v 114). Forms 1 and 3–5 are similar to the townland name of **Ballynoe** in Rathlin Island.

Craigalappan
D 0242

Creag na Leapan
"rock of the bed"

1. Cregillapan	Hib. Reg. Cary	1657c
2. Creggillanppan	BSD 172	1661
3. Cregglappan	Lapsed Money Book 157	1663
4. Ams-Cregillappan	ASE 116b §19	1668
5. Creggilapan, 2 quarters of Prolusk and	PRONI D2977/3A/2/1/5A	1682
6. Creggalapan	C. McG. (OSNB) B 26	1734
7. Creggalapan	Stewart's Survey 19	1734
8. Craiglapan	Religious Survey	1734
9. Craigalappan	Religious Census	1766
10. Craigalapan	Lendrick Map	1780
11. Craigalappan	Shaw Mason's Par. Sur. 170	1803
12. Craigalapen	PRONI D2977/3A/2/1/40	1812
13. Craigalappan	Bnd. Sur. (OSNB) B 26	1827c
14. Craigalppin	Tithe App. Book 3	1833
15. Creag na Leapthan "rock of the bed"	J O'D (OSNB) B 26	1827
16. Carraig an leapthain "The rock of the (bed) grave"	Ó Dubhthaigh 135	1905
17. Craig a leapthain "Rock of the bed"	Rev. Magill 12	1923
18. ˌkreːgəˈlapən	Local pronunciation	1995

Forms 15–7 appear to be correct in their interpretation of this place-name. It is unlikely that the first element was in the plural form *creaga* (instances of pl. forms in such a position in place-names are rare). If in the sing., it was possibly in the variant form *creig*. *Creig/creag* has several meanings (cf. **Craig**).

Leapan (earlier *leapthan*) is a variant gen. sing. form of *leapa*, itself a form of *leaba* "a bed, couch, resting-place; a site, position or region" (*Dinneen*). Joyce also notes the meaning "grave" (*Joyce* i 102). It recurs in the nom. form in the south Co. Derry townland name of **Labby** (*PNI* v 26) and as an initial element in about 13 other townlands around the country (*Census 1851*), including the Co. Waterford townland name *Leaba na Cailli*, possibly "the hag's bed" (anglicized Labbanacallee; *L. Log. Ph. Láirge* 36).

Craiganee	*Creag an Fhia*	
D 0642	"rock of the deer"	
1. Creggenee	Hib. Reg. Cary	1657c
2. Cregence	DS (Par. Map) 50	1657c
3. Creggence	DS (Par. Map) 51	1657c
4. Creanivie	Census 13	1659
5. Creggence	BSD 172	1661
6. Crogenie	Lapsed Money Book 157	1663
7. Cregine	ASE 116b §19	1668
8. Creigenen	HMR Ant. 4	1669
9. Cregence	Hib. Del. Antrim	1672c
10. Cregganey	C. McG. (OSNB) B 26	1734
11. Cregganey	Stewart's Survey 18	1734
12. Craiganie	Religious Survey	1734
13. Craiganewey	Hill's Stewarts 222	1741c
14. Craiganie	Religious Census	1766
15. Creganie	Lendrick Map	1780
16. Craiganee	Shaw Mason's Par. Sur. 170	1803
17. Craiganee	Bnd. Sur. (OSNB) B 26	1827c
18. Creagán Aodha "Hugh's rock land"	J O'D (OSNB) B 26	1827
19. ˌkreːgənˈiː	Local pronunciation	1995

Possible etymologies of this place-name include *Creag an Fhia* "rock of the deer" and *Creag an Fhiaigh* "rock of the raven/hunt or chase". Toner regards *fia*, which has been similarly anglicized in a number of place-names throughout Ireland, as most likely in the south Co. Derry name **Drumanee Lower** for which he postulates the Irish form *Droim an Fhia* "ridge of the deer" (*PNI* v 66). Considering forms 4 and 13, we might suggest that the final element derived from one of the fem. nouns *fíobha* "a wood, grove, thicket" (Dinneen sv. *fiod-hbhadh*) and *fíobhach* "a woody district, hence place-names Feevagh, Fivy" (Dinneen sv. *fiod-hbhach*). However, these forms can be accounted for as containing scribal errors, or as indicating that a variant such as *Creag na bhFia* "rock of the deers" was formerly current.

Many of the historical variants arguably reflect the interpretation in form 18, *Creagán Aodha/Aoidh* "Hugh's rocky ground". *Creagán* "rocky eminence; (patch of) stony, barren, ground" (Ó Dónaill), normally anglicized *creggan*, is a common place-name and place-name element. *Dinneen* has translated it as "a little rock; a rocky or stony place; a blank spot in a growing crop". The male personal name *Aodh*, meaning "fire", "was the commonest of all names in use in early Ireland and is now everywhere anglicized Hugh, a name with which it has no connection" (Ó Corráin & Maguire 1981, 13).

Croaghbeg	*An Chruach Bheag*
D 0041	"the heap, little"

See **Croaghmore**.

Croaghmore

D 0040

An Chruach Mhór

"the heap, big"

1. Cruaghbeg, the halfe towneland of	Civ. Surv. x §60	1655
2. Croghmore, Croaghbegg	Hib. Reg. Cary	1657c
3. Croaghbegge	DS (Par. Map) 50	1657c
4. Crnachbeg	Census 13	1659
5. Croghmore, Croghbeg	BSD 171, 173	1661
6. Cruoghmore, Cruoghbegg	Court of Claims §923	1662c
7. Croghmore 1 Qur., Croghbegg 2 Qurs.	Lapsed Money Book 157	1663
8. Croghmore, Croghbegg	ASE 116b §19	1668
9. Croghbeg	HMR Ant. 4	1669
10. Croagh	Hib. Del. Antrim	1672c
11. Croaghmore, the quarter land of	PRONI D2977/3A/2/1/6	1681
12. Creagh-more	C. McG. (OSNB) B 26	1734
13. Croaghmore, Croaghbegg	Stewart's Survey 23	1734
14. Croghmore	Religious Survey	1734
15. the ¼ land of Croaghbegg, Croaghmore	PRONI D2977/3A/2/1/33A	1737
16. Croaghbeg	Religious Census	1766
17. Croaghmore, Croghbeg	Lendrick Map	1780
18. Croagh	Shaw Mason's Par. Sur. 170	1803
19. Croaghmore, Croaghbeg	Bnd. Sur. (OSNB) B 26	1827c
20. Croaghmore "large stack"	Shaw Mason's Par. Sur. 150	1814
21. Croaghmore "large stack"	OSM xxiv 10	1830
22. Cruach "a round hill"	J O'D (OSNB) B 26	1827
23. cruach mor "great stack"	OSRNB sh.3, 4	1855c
24. Crnach mór "The large stack"	Ó Dubhthaigh 135	1905
25. Cruach mór "Big stack-like hill"	Rev. Magill 12	1923
26. krox'moːr	Local pronunciation	1995
27. krox'bɛg	Local pronunciation	1995

Cruach has several meanings including "a heap, a stack, a rick, a clamp (of turf); a rampart; a symmetrically shaped mountain" (*Dinneen*) and "(mountain) stack" (*Ó Dónaill*). It is not certain whether it referred originally to the hill called *Croaghmore* of c. 170 metres in the centre of the townland of the same name, to the cairn complex which lies at its summit, or to one or other of the basalt outcrops of columnar form which are found on this hill (*OSM* xxiv 10). The megalithic complex was described in the 1830s as follows:

On the summit of that lofty hill . . . there stand the ruins of two ancient cairns of stones, one of which stood on the north west side of the hill but now clearly destroyed. It seems to have been circular, 15 yards in diameter. The stones which were of middle size, were cleared away to build fences . . . About 85 yards south east of the latter stood the second of these cairns. It was also of the middle-size stones and approached to circular shape, 20 yards in diameter (*ibid.* 24).

Neither of these cairns lies within Croaghbeg. In c. 1855, it was recorded that Croaghmore was the name of "a hill from which the townland has derived its name. On the face and near the summit is a precipice [beside] tall ranges of basaltic columns" (*OSRNB* sh.3, 4).

It seems more likely that the epithets *beag* "little, small" and *mór* "big, great, large" were used to differentiate the sizes of the territories, rather than qualify a topographical feature in their respective divisions.

Curramoney
D 9538

Cúl re Mónaidh
"(place with its) back to the bog"

1.	Cowllremony, Coulremony	Inq. Ult. (Antrim) §84 Car. I	1635
2.	(?)Cooleremony	Inq. Ult. (Antrim) §101 Car. I	1635
3.	Cooleremony	Inq. Ult. (Antrim) §102 Car. I	1635
4.	Cullramony	Census 12	1659
5.	Curramoney	C. McG. (OSNB)	1734
6.	Cullramony	Stewart's Survey 19	1734
7.	Curramony & Carnanmore	Stewart's Survey 32	1734
8.	Cullymuney	Religious Survey	1734
9.	Coulramoney	Religious Census	1766
10.	Coulramoney	Shaw Mason's Par. Sur. 170	1803
11.	Cullianmoney	PRONI D2977/3A/2/1/40	1812
12.	Culramony	Bnd. Sur. (OSNB) B 26	1827c
13.	Culramony	OSNB B 26	1827
14.	Coulramoney	Tithe Applot. 3	1833
15.	Currach móna "moor of the turf"	J O'D (OSNB) B 26	1827
16.	Carrach móna "The morass of the bog"	Ó Dubhthaigh 135	1905
17.	Cúl re Mónadh	Ó Maolfabhail (T re G) 372	1982
18.	ˌkɔrəˈmoːni	Local pronunciation	1995

The historical forms suggest that this name contained the preposition *re* "in the direction of" or "before, in front of" (*Ó Maolfabhail (T re G)* 371–2), which is followed by the dative case (it was sometimes followed by the accusative, formerly). This word became *le* in the later language. It seems more likely that *cúl* "back" and not *cúil* "recess corner" formed the first element here (see **Coolaveely** in Culfeightrin). The *Ordnance Survey Memoirs* noted two burial grounds in this townland (*OSM* xxiv 27–8), but *ceallrach*, a variant of *cealldrach* "old burial ground; burial place for unbaptized children; dreary old place; ruinous old church or house" (*Ó Dónaill*) is not reflected in historical variants. *Cúl ráth-* "back of the fort" and *cúil ráth-* "recess or corner of the fort" also seem somewhat unlikely.

The long *o* in modern pronunciation suggests that the final element was the dat. sing. (*mónaidh*) of *móin* "turf, peat; bogland, moor" (cf. also **Tornamoney** in Culfeightrin). The Scottish Gaelic noun *monadh* "hilly ground, region" is "not attested in the Irish lexicon and there are no examples of its occurrence as an Irish place-name element in any native source" (Toner 1991–3, 52–3). *Muine* "thicket; brushwood, shrub" (*Ó Dónaill*) would be more likely to have yielded [mɔni].

Form 2 may refer in fact to **Culramoney** townland in Ballymoney parish (barony of Dunluce Upper). Historical forms of this townland are very similar to those in question here (Carleton 1991, 79).

Currysheskin		*Cúl re Seisceann*	
D 9944		"(place with its) back to the sedgy bog"	
1.	Culrasheskin	Hib. Reg. Cary	1657c
2.	Cubrasheskan	Census 12	1659
3.	Cubrasheskin	BSD 172	1661
4.	Curasheskin	Lapsed Money Book 157	1663
5.	Calrasheskin	ASE 116b §19	1668
6.	Carrnisskan	HMR Ant. 2	1669
7.	Coulreshkan	PRONI D2977/3A/2/1/30	1720
8.	Coolrasheskan	Stewart's Survey 22	1734
9.	Coulrashiskan	C. McG. (OSNB)	1734
10.	Coresseskin	Religious Survey	1734
11.	Cullraseskin otherwise		
	Coulreshaskin	PRONI D2977/3A/2/1/37A	1739
12.	Coulrashiskan	Religious Census	1766
13.	Coulrasheskin	Shaw Mason's Par. Sur. 170	1803
14.	Currysheskin	Bnd. Sur. (OSNB) B 26	1827c
15.	Coulrasheskin	Tithe Applot. 3	1833
16.	Coolresheskin	OSRNB sh.3, 2	1855c
17.	Currach Seiscin "moor of the quaw		
	or quagmire"	J O'D (OSNB) B 26	1827
18.	currach seisgin "a marshy sedge"		
	plain	OSRNB sh.3, 2	1855c
19.	Currach seascainn "The quagmire		
	of the marsh"	Ó Dubhthaigh 135	1905
20.	ˌkɔriˈʃeskïn	Local pronunciation	1995

Although the first element in forms 2–3 resembles to some extent *cabrach* "pole structure, hut; copse" (*Ó Dónaill*) or "bad, rough, unprofitable land" (*Joyce* iii 155), these forms come from related sources and probably contain scribal errors, as may form 6. The standardized anglicized form appears to have an antecedent from as early as 1734 (form 10), but *culra*-variants, probably derived from *cúl re* (see **Curramoney**) seem to have survived up to the time of the Ordnance Survey (form 17). This also appears to have been the case with Curramoney (which is several miles away). Perhaps the name was reinterpreted as containing *currach* "wet bog, marsh". The townland of **Currysheskin** in Ballymoney parish appears to have developed in a similar way to the name in question here. This latter name has forms such as *Culreseskin* and *Colreseskan* dating from the mid-1600s (Carleton 1991, 80).

The last element in this name was probably *seisceann* "sedgy bog; marsh, swamp" (*Ó Dónaill* sv. *seascann*).

Drumnagee		*Droim na Gaoithe*	
D 0041		"ridge of the wind"	
1.	Drumnegee	Hib. Reg. Cary	1657c

2. (?)Drumnagree	DS (Par. Map) 57	1657c
3. Drumegee	BSD 174	1661
4. Drumnaghio	Court of Claims §923	1662c
5. Brunegree 1 Qur.	Lapsed Money Book 157	1663
6. Drumnagee	ASE 116b §19	1668
7. Drumnegee	Hib. Del. Antrim	1672c
8. Drumnagee, one quarter land of	PRONI D2977/3A/2/1/20	1709
9. Drumnagee	Hill's Stewarts 11	1720
10. Drimnagee	C. McG. (OSNB) B 26	1734
11. Drimnagee	Stewart's Survey 22	1734
12. Drumnagee	Religious Survey	1734
13. Drimnagee	Religious Census	1766
14. Drimnagree	Lendrick Map	1780
15. Drimnagee	Shaw Mason's Par. Sur. 170	1803
16. Drumnagee	PRONI D2977/3A/2/1/40	1812
17. Drimnagee	Bnd. Sur. (OSNB) B 26	1827c
18. Druim na Gaoithe "ridge of the wind"	J O'D (OSNB) B 26	1827
19. Druim na n-gaoth "Ridge of the winds"	Rev. Magill 14	1923
20. ˌdrọmnəgiː	Local pronunciation	1995

Form 18 represents the most plausible interpretation of this name. *Droim* denotes "hill, ridge" (*Dinneen*) or "hill-ridge" (*Joyce* iii 313) while *gaoth* has been translated "wind, air, blast, a draught of air or wind" (*Dinneen*). The latter element recurs in the subtownland name of *Bearnas na Gaoithe* (anglicized **Barnesnageeha**) "gap of the wind", in the parish of Grange of Layd in Glenarm Lower barony (*OS 1:50,000* D 2233). Joyce has suggested that it recurs in the townland names of Mastergeeha and Mastergeehy in Co. Kerry, **Masteragwee** near Coleraine and **Mostragee** in Derrykeighan parish (barony of Dunluce Lower), three townlands called Balgeeth in Co. Meath, Ballynageeha in Co. Galway, Ballynagee in Co. Wexford and Ballynageehy in Co. Cork, all so called from "the exposed situation of the places" (*Joyce* i 44). Historical forms of Mostragee from the 17th century (Carleton 1991, 88) suggest that this particular name goes back to something like *Más re Gaoth*, perhaps "hill in front of water", however. In any event, it is unlikely that the masc. noun *gaoth* "water" would be used in a construction such as Drumnagee. There is no evidence of the final syllable of the gen. sing. *gaoithe* "of the wind" in the historical forms but this can be explained as resulting from its unstressed position. There is no trace of eclipsis of the *g* which would suggest the gen. pl. form (form 19). Although place-names rarely retain an eclipsed *g* in anglicized forms, the use of the gen. pl. of this element would be unusual in any case.

It is somewhat less likely that the final element in this name is the gen. pl. of *caoth* "bog-hole, swamp-hole; ditch". No tradition regarding the name appears to have been recorded, although there did exist a mearing ditch between this townland and Araboy (*OSM* xxiv 23). Ó Muraíle (*Ó Maolfabhail (T re G)* 378–9) has noted some townland names in Co. Limerick featuring this element, including *Bun Caoith* (anglicized Bunkey) and *Béal an Chaoith* (anglicized Ballykeeffe).

Drumnagessan
D 9841

Droim na gCeasán
"ridge of the baskets(?)"

1. Drumnegesson	Hib. Reg. Cary	1657c
2. Drumnegosson	DS (Par. Map) 51	1657c
3. Drumnagassen	Census 13	1659
4. Drumegossan	BSD 175	1661
5. Drumnagessana	Court of Claims §923	1662c
6. Drumnegessin	ASE 117a §19	1668
7. Drumnegessan	HMR Ant. 5	1669
8. Drumnegesson	Hib. Del. Antrim	1672c
9. Drumnagessan, one quarterland of	PRONI D2977/3A/2/1/20	1709
10. Drimnagissan	C. McG. (OSNB) B 26	1734
11. Drumnagassan	Religious Survey	1734
12. Drimnagessan	Stewart's Survey 22	1734
13. Drimnagesson	Religious Census	1766
14. Drimagessan	Shaw Mason's Par. Sur. 170	1803
15. Druminagisson	PRONI D2977/3A/2/1/40	1812
16. Drimnagessan	Bnd. Sur. (OSNB) B 26	1827c
17. Druim na gCeasán "ridge of the course wool"	J O'D (OSNB) B 26	1827
18. "Ridge of the pathways"	OSRNB sh.3, 4	1855c
19. Druim na gaisan "The ridge of the streams"	Ó Dubhthaigh 138	1905
20. Druim na gcasán "Ridge of the paths"	Rev. Magill 15	1923
21. ˌdrọmnəˈgɛsən	Local pronunciation	1995

The majority of historical forms do not suggest the first vowel of the final element was [a]/[ɔ], so it seems unlikely that this element was the gen. pl. of *casán/cosán* "path; footway, track" (Holmer recorded this word as [kɑsɑn], meaning "footpath"; *Irish of the Glens* 104). Ó Dubhthaigh (form 19) appears to have had a diminutive of *gaise*, a variant of *caise* "a stream, a brook, a current, a flood" in mind (*Dinneen*). Such a diminutive form has not been attested, although we may note that Holmer recorded a word which he spelt *casan/cosan*, and as meaning "waterfall", in Rathlin (*Irish of Rathlin* 172). There is also no evidence of eclipsis of the *g* in historical variants (although anglicized place-names often omit any trace of this feature). O'Donovan probably had a diminutive of *céas* "matted hair, wool" in mind (form 17). *Dinneen* translates *céasán* as "shaggy hair" but notes also the meaning "a lean or narrow rump" in north Donegal. The forms do not suggest that the first vowel in the final element was [eː], however.

Our suggested form above contains a diminutive of *ceas*, a variant form of *cis* "wicker container; basket, crate; plaited or crossed twigs as support for causeway" (*Ó Dónaill* sv.). Irish *ea* was pronounced [ɛ] before *s* locally (cf. **Craigban** in Culfeightrin). A diminutive of *cis*, *ciseán*, is the most common form in the modern language. We might consider that the final element was a simple gen. pl. of *ceas*, *ceasann* (standard Mod. Ir. *ceasanna*; compare *Sloc na Morann* in **Rathlin Sound** in Other Names, Rathlin). This would agree with many of the early historical forms which suggest that the final vowel was [ə] (compare forms of **Doonans** in Armoy and **Glenmakeerin** in Culfeightrin, for example). However, the -*anna* plural suffix is a relatively late one (see McCone *et al* 1994, 451) and is rare in townland names.

Glenstaghy	*Glais tSochaí*	
D 0743	"stream of the host"	

1.	Glastaghy	Hib. Reg. Cary	1657c
2.	Glastaghie	DS (Par. Map) 51	1657c
3.	Glastachie	Census 13	1659
4.	Glastaghie	BSD 171	1661
5.	Clastaoly	Court of Claims §923	1662c
6.	Glassaghie 2 Qur	Lapsed Money Book 157	1663
7.	Glasstaghy	ASE 116b §19	1668
8.	Glastrogy	HMR Ant. 4	1669
9.	Glastaghy	Hib. Del. Antrim	1672c
10.	Glastaachy	PRONI D2977/3A/2/1/7	1681
11.	Glasstaghey	C. McG. (OSNB) B 26	1734
12.	Glesstaghy	Stewart's Survey 18	1734
13.	Glesstaghie	Religious Survey	1734
14.	Glenstaghie	Religious Census	1766
15.	Glenstaghey	Lendrick Map	1780
16.	Glenstaghy	Shaw Mason's Par. Sur. 170	1803
17.	two Glenstaghys otherwise Glasstaghys	PRONI D2977/3A/2/1/40	1812
18.	Glenstaghy	Bnd. Sur. (OSNB) B 26	1827c
19.	Glais Teach Aodha "Stream of Hugh's house"	J O'D (OSNB) B 26	1827
20.	Gleann stabhaighe "The glen of the wide fork"	Ó Dubhthaigh 181	1905
21.	Gleann Sceathaigh "Glen of the thorn shrubbery"	Rev. Magill 16	1923
22.	ˌglenˈstaːxi	Local pronunciation	1995

Forms 1–13 indicate that the first element in this name was not originally *gleann* "a valley, a glen, a hollow" (*Dinneen*). It appears to have been *glais* "stream, streamlet, rivulet, current" (*DIL*); variants of this word include *glas*, but [ʃ] before *t* is often anglicized *s*, while a velarization of Irish *s* prior to a velar *t* could also have occurred. Ó Dónaill also lists *glais* as a variant of *clais*, which has several meanings, including "water channel; gully, ditch; trench, furrow; spawning bed, redd; rut, groove; pit; soft mass". A stream forms part of the eastern boundary of this townland and empties into Port More, and it seems possible that this feature inspired the original name. Later forms suggest that this element was reinterpreted as *gleann* (forms 14–8).

Form 19 could be reconciled to historical forms but does not reflect modern stress. The second element in form 20 is not attested and in any event does not reflect historical forms. Form 21 is based on the premise of a change from *c* to *t* (cf. **Tenaghs** in Culfeightrin) which would thus have occurred very early, but in any event, the suggested element does not reflect historical variants. The last element was probably *sochaí* (earlier *sochaidhe*) "multitude, crowd, host; (in military sense) army, host" (*DIL* sv. *sochaide*). A lowering of Irish *o* to [a] has been noted elsewhere (cf. **Ballycarry** in Rathlin). The name thus reflects **Knocksoghey** which bounds this townland to the west. The central *t* appears to reflect the lenition of *s* following a fem. noun (cf. also **Kentruan** in Other Names, Rathlin).

Indication of a division of this townland is found as early as 1663 (form 6). The names **Glenstaghy Upper** and **Glenstaghy Lower** are locally current (see Other Names).

| **Island Macallan** | *Oileán Mhic Ailín* | |
| D 0238 | "MacAllen's island" | |

1.	Islandavollen	Hib. Reg. Cary	1657c
2.	Islandmc allen	DS (Par. Map) 51	1657c
3.	Island o callen, part of	DS (Par. Map) 57	1657c
4.	IllandMacallen	Census 13	1659
5.	Island McAllen	BSD 173, 179	1661
6.	EllunMcAllin	Court of Claims §923	1662c
7.	Island MacAllen	Lapsed Money Book 157	1663
8.	Island McAllen	ASE 116b §19	1668
9.	Island McCalen	HMR Ant. 4	1669
10.	IslandmacCalline	PRONI D2977/3A/2/23/1	1709
11.	Islanmacalinnon, the quarter land of	PRONI D2977/3A/2/23/1	1709
12.	Island MacAllan	Hill's Stewarts 11	1720
13.	Islandmacallan	C. McG. (OSNB) B 26	1734
14.	Islandmakallan	Stewart's Survey 19	1734
15.	Illan Mckallan	Religious Survey	1734
16.	Islandmacallan	Religious Census	1766
17.	Islandmacalan	Lendrick Map	1780
18.	Islandmacallan	Shaw Mason's Par. Sur. 171	1803
19.	Islandmackallan	PRONI D2977/3A/2/1/40	1812
20.	Islandmacallan	Bnd. Sur. (OSNB) B 26	1827c
21.	Island McAllen	OSRNB sh.8, 1	1855c
22.	Island Macallan	OSRNB sh.8, 1	1855c
23.	Island McCallion	OSRNB sh.8, 1	1855c
24.	Islandmacallan	OSRNB sh.8, 1	1855c
25.	Oileán Mic Ailín "MacAilen's land"	J O'D (OSNB) B 26	1827
26.	ˌailəndməkˈaljən	Local pronunciation	1995

"An interesting feature of the toponymy of Ulster – East Ulster in particular – is the frequent occurrence in the onomastic lexicon of the word 'island' where it does not refer to a piece of land surrounded by water" (Ó Mainnín 1989–90, 200). Ó Mainnín has shown that these "islands" can denote a "hillock surrounded by bog" or may be used to "delimit an area of either low-lying or high ground. As a rule, however, these islands are also bounded by, or occur in, the vicinity of rivers and this usage of the term would seem to correspond with one of the applications of Irish *inis*, 'a river holm or meadow'" (*ibid.*). This townland, which is situated inland, lies between the Moss-side Water and its tributary the Inver Burn; to the centre of the territory is a small hill. As forms 6 and 15 suggest, surveyors substituted *oileán* "island" for an English equivalent, just as *caisleán* "castle" appears to have been changed in

Ballycastle (Other Names, Ramoan). **Islandarragh** and **Islandnanagh** also feature this element (see Other Names).

The surname which formed the second element is most likely to have been *Mac Ailín*, anglicized MacAllen: "(from) *ail*, rock. Primarily the name of a war-like branch of the Scottish Campbells brought to Ulster by the O'Donnells" (MacLysaght 1985, 4). See also **Farranmacallan** in Culfeigtrin.

Kilmahamogue		*Cill Mochomóg*	
D 0439		"*Mochomóg*'s burial-ground"	
1.	Kilmacammagh	Hib. Reg. Cary	1657c
2.	Kilmacammoge	DS (Par. Map) 63	1657c
3.	Kilmacamagh, mossy bog of	DS (Par. Map) 64	1657c
4.	Kilmacamogh, the ¼ of	DS (Par. Map) 64	1657c
5.	Killmacomoge	Census 11	1659
6.	Killmacammoge	BSD 179	1661
7.	Killmacamoge	Court of Claims §923	1662c
8.	Killmcomeoge	Lapsed Money Book 158	1663
9.	Kilmatomack	HMR Ant. 13	1669
10.	Kilmacama	Hib. Del. Antrim	1672c
11.	Killmahamog	PRONI D2977/3A/2/1/24	1711
12.	Killmachamogue	C. McG. (OSNB) B 26	1734
13.	Killmachamagg	Stewart's Survey 16	1734
14.	Killmahomog	Religious Survey	1734
15.	Killmahamog	Hill's Stewarts 222	1741c
16.	Killmahamog	Religious Census	1766
17.	Killmahammogh	Lendrick Map	1780
18.	Kilmahamogue	Shaw Mason's Par. Sur. 171	1803
19.	Kilmahamogue	Bnd. Sur. (OSNB) B 26	1827c
20.	Kilmahamog	Tithe Applot. 5	1833
21.	Kilmahamoge "church of Mochoemog"	EA 286	1847
22.	Cill mo shamóg "Moshoge's church"	OSRNB sh.8, 2	1855c
23.	Kil-mo-Nem-Og "the church of St. Nem"	O'Laverty iv 342	1887
24.	ˌkïlməˈhaməg	Local pronunciation	1995

In 1835 it was recorded:

> In Kilmahamogue, and holding of Charles McCahan, there stood an ancient graveyard which gave name to the townland. It is now destroyed and the site under tillage. In reclaiming it from time to time there were large quantities of human bones lifted, all [of] which have been buried again on the site (*OSM* xxiv 28).

It is reasonable to assume therefore that the first element in the name was *cill* "a church, a churchyard, a burial place; cell, house" (*Dinneen*).

Form 20 suggests that the second element was the male personal name *Mochaomhóg* (earlier *Mo Cháemóc*) which is a pet-form of the names *Caoimhín* and *Caomhán* (Ó Corráin & Maguire 1981, 41, 137). However, if this were so, we would have expected historical variants to reflect a central [v] (cf. **Kinramer** in Rathlin), while we would also have expected the *ao* to have yielded a spelling reflecting [ʌ]. It thus seems likely the that the second element has its origin in a different name. The male personal name *Mochomóg* (earlier *Mochommóc*) reflects the historical variants most exactly. It may be a pet form of one of the male personal names *Comán* (earlier *Commán*; *ibid.*, 56) or *Colmán*.

This townland was formerly considered part of the Grange of Drumtullagh (see parish introduction).

Knocknagarvan
D 0341

Of uncertain origin

1. Knocknegaroeny	Hib. Reg. Cary	1657c
2. Knocknegarvan	DS (Par. Map) 51	1657c
3. Knockgarvens	DS (Par. Map) 51	1657c
4. Knocknegarven & Cregenagh	BSD 172	1661
5. Knocknagarvin, Creganagh and	Lapsed Money Book 157	1663
6. Knocknegarvin and Gregenagh	ASE 116b §19	1668
7. Knocknegarkin	HMR Ant. 3	1669
8. Knegarveny	Hib. Del. Antrim	1672c
9. Knocknegarvony	PRONI D2977/3A/2/1/15	1696
10. Knockanagarvan	PRONI D2977/3A/2/1/28	1720
11. Knocknagarvony	C. McG. (OSNB) B 26	1734
12. Knockanagarvony	Stewart's Survey 19	1734
13. Knockanagarvaine	Religious Survey	1734
14. Knock-na-Garvon	Hill's Stewarts 223	1741c
15. Knockanagarvan	Merchant's Book 5	1751
16. Knocknagarvon	Religious Census	1766
17. Knockanagarvan	Shaw Mason's Par. Sur. 171	1803
18. Knocknagarvan	PRONI D2977/3A/2/1/40	1812
19. Knockanagarvan	Bnd. Sur. (OSNB) B 26	1827c
20. Knocknagarvon	Tithe Applot. 5	1833
21. Cnoc na ngarbhan "hill of the rough persons"	J O'D (OSNB) B 26	1827
22. Cnoc na ngarbhan "The hill of the coarse spots"	Ó Dubhthaigh 182	1905
23. Cnoc na garbhain "Hill of the wild kale"	Rev. Magill 19	1923
24. ˌnɔknəˈɡɑrvən	Local pronunciation	1995

Forms 10, 12–3, 15, 17, and 19 suggest that the first element of this name was originally *cnocán* "a hillock; a height; a heap", and not *cnoc* "a hill, a height, a mountain". The absence of the second syllable of *cnocán* in many of the forms can be explained as being due to its unstressed position. That *cnocán* latterly replaced *cnoc* is also possible.

Eclipsis is often neglected in the anglicization of place-names (cf. **Drumnagee**), and it is on this premise that forms 21–2 depend. However, forms 1, 8–9 and 11–2, which end in -*y*, suggest that a final unstressed vowel has been lost, and so we can dismiss several elements that might otherwise be considered, including *garbhán* "coarse substance; coarse-grained object or person" (*Ó Dónaill*). Form 23 is also grammatically dubious and linguistically unlikely (see *Ó Dónaill* sv. *garbhán*).

Cnocán an Gharbheanaigh "hillock of the rough bog" and *Cnocán na Garbhanaí* "hillock of the rough place" may be considered as possible original forms. The nom. form of the final element in the last case, *garbhanach*, consists of *garbh* "rough" plus the the adjectival suffix *(e)anach* (cf. also **Brackney** in Culfeightrin and **Derganagh** in *PNI* v 218–9). A further possible original form is *Cnocán na Garbheanga* "hillock of the rough track". The intervocalic [ŋ] sound in the gen. (*eanga*) of the fem. noun *eang* "track, trace; strip of land" could easily have become [n] in unstressed position (see Toner 1994–5). *Eang* is rare in place-names but derived forms may have been used locally (see **Agangarive Hill** in Other Names, Culfeightrin, and **Innananooan** in Other Names, Rathlin). *Garbh* "rough; uneven, rugged" (*Ó Dónaill*) is a common prefix in place-names (cf. **Garvalt Burn** in Other Names, Culfeightrin). Perhaps less likely as an original form is *Cnocán an Gharbhánaigh* which contains the gen. sing. of *garbhánach* "a coarse tall person" (*Dinneen*). *Garbhánach* "sea-bream" (cf. the Rathlin subtownland name *Carraig na nGarbhánach* "the rock of the sea-bream" (*Place-Names of Rathlin* 52)) would represent an unusual element in the name of a townland which lies 1.5 miles from the coast.

Knocksoghey	*Cnoc Sochaí*	
D 0645	"hill of the host"	

1. Knocksochie	Census 13	1659
2. Knocksochy	Court of Claims §923	1662c
3. Knocksocke	HMR Ant. 3	1669
4. Knocksoghie	Religious Survey	1734
5. Knoghsoughy	Religious Census	1766
6. Knocksoghey	Lendrick Map	1780
7. Knocksoghy	Hamilton's Letters 8	1784
8. Knocksoghy	Bnd. Sur. (OSNB) B 26	1827c
9. Knocksaughey	OSRNB sh.4, 1	1855c
10. Cnoc Sochaidhe "hill of the multitude"	J O'D (OSNB) B 26	1827
11. Cnoc na soithighe "The hill of the vessel (ship)"	Ó Dubhthaigh 182	1905
12. Cnoc soithighe "Hill view of the ships"	Rev. Magill 19	1923
13. ˌnɔk'sɔhi	Local pronunciation	1995

Of the three interpretations in forms 10–12, form 10 reflects the historical forms most closely. Intervocalic -*th*- has been known to change from [h] to [x] in some instances (see *Irish of the Glens* 24), but such a transformation as early as the mid-1600s is unlikely (forms 11–12). *Sochaí* (earlier *sochaidhe*) "multitude, crowd, host; (in military sense) army, host" (*DIL*) represents an unusual element in a townland name. No tradition regarding the name seems to have been recorded. See also **Glenstaghy**.

Lagavara

D 0442

Lag an Bheara

"hollow of the stream(?)"

1. Legevare	Hib. Reg. Cary	1657c
2. Lagevarie	Census 13	1659
3. Legevare	BSD 171	1661
4. Legeorre 1 Qur.	Lapsed Money Book 157	1663
5. legevare	ASE 116b §19	1668
6. (?)Lagandrey	HMR Ant. 4	1669
7. Legavare	PRONI D2977/3A/2/1/24	1711
8. Laggavara	Stewart's Survey 19	1734
9. Legavar	Religious Survey	1734
10. Lagavar	Hill's Stewarts 222	1741c
11. Legavare	Religious Census	1766
12. Legavarr	Lendrick Map	1780
13. Lagavara	Shaw Mason's Par. Sur. 171	1803
14. Legavare	PRONI D2977/3A/2/1/40	1812
15. Laggavarra	Bnd. Sur. (OSNB) B 26	1827c
16. (?)Lagava	Bnd. Sur. (OSNB) B 26	1827c
17. Legavar	Tithe Applot. 5	1833
18. Lag a' bheara "hollow of the spit"	J O'D (OSNB) B 26	1827
19. Lug an bhathair "The hollow of the road"	Ó Dubhthaigh 183	1905
20. Lagabhair "Hollow of the marsh"	Rev. Magill 19	1923
21. Lag an Bháire	Éire Thuaidh	1988
22. ˌlɛgə'var	Local pronunciation	1995

As forms 18–21 suggest, the first element of this name was almost certainly *log/lag* "a hollow, cavity or sag; a pool in a river, etc.; a place, arena, locus; socket or pit; a tomb; a pool, flash or dyke of water; a part or portion" (*Dinneen* svv. *lag, log*). Regarding this element, see also **Ligadaughtan** in Culfeightrin.

Form 19 does not accurately reflect the succeeding elements in the name. Form 18 suggests the gen. sing. of *bior* (*beara*), which can also denote "a skewer, a lance, a point, a spike" (*Dinneen*) or "pointed rod or shaft" (*Ó Dónaill*), and by extension "headland; mountain peak" (see **Ballykenver** in Armoy). The north-east of this townland lies on Lannimore Hill (207 metres). *Beara* is also the gen. sing of *bior* "water", which Mac Giolla Easpaig (1986, 70) has identified in some place-names (see **Ballykenver**); perhaps it was used here in the sense "stream". A head-water of the Moss-Side Water runs through the west of the townland, and a small tributary of this stream rises in the centre of the territory. Irish *ea* was pronounced [ɛ] before *d, g* and *s* in the late local dialect (*Irish of the Glens* 76), but otherwise Holmer noted it as [a] (*ibid. et passim*), which is reflected in historical forms. (Holmer used [a] to denote IPA [a] and [ɑ] to denote IPA [ɑ]; *ibid.* 14 §5).

Most historical forms do not suggest that the final element ended with *-ire* (as postulated in form 21). Many other forms do not indicate a vowel following the *r*, although the loss of a final vowel in unstressed position is common (cf. **Craigfad** and **Aughnaholle** in Culfeightrin, and **Coolkenny** in Ramoan, for example).

Lemnagh Beg

D 0243

Léim an Eich Bheag
"leap of the horse, little"

1.	Lemenemore, Lemenebeg	Hib. Reg. Cary	1657c
2.	Lameneghmor	Census 12	1659
3.	Lemneghmore, Lemneghbeg	BSD 172	1661
4.	Lemneghmore 1 Qur., Lemneghbegg 1 Qur.	Lapsed Money Book 157	1663
5.	Lemnaghmore, Lemnaghbegg	ASE 116b §19	1668
6.	Lemoneight, Lamonebeg	HMR Ant. 3	1669
7.	Lemenemore, Lemene beg	Hib. Del. Antrim	1672c
8.	Leminegh begg, quarter of	PRONI D2977/3A/2/1/5A	1682
9.	lamenaghbegg	Forfeit. Estates 375b §45	1703
10.	Lemeneghmore	PRONI D2977/3A/2/1/17	1706
11.	Limnaighmore, Limaneigh beg	C. McG. (OSNB) B 26	1734
12.	Lemanaighmore, Lemnaighbegg	Stewart's Survey 20	1734
13.	Lemeaghmore, Lemneaghbeg	Religious Survey	1734
14.	lemaneaghmore, lemaneaghbeg	Religious Census	1766
15.	Limenaghmore, Limenaghbeg	Lendrick Map	1780
16.	Limeneagh	Shaw Mason's Par. Sur. 171	1803
17.	Lemineaghmore, Leamineaghbegg	PRONI D2977/3A/2/1/40	1812
18.	Limeneaghmore, Limeneaghbeg	Bnd. Sur. (OSNB) B 26	1827c
19.	Lemnaghmore, Lemnaghbeg	Bnd. Sur. (OSNB) B 26	1827c
20.	Lemineaghmore, Lemineaghbeg	Tithe Applot. 6	1833
21.	Lemmaneigh Beg	OSRNB sh.4, 1	1855c
22.	Léim an eich "leap of the horse"	J O'D (OSNB) B 26	1827
23.	Leim-an-eich "the leap of the horse"	O'Laverty iv 319	1887
24.	Léimneach beag "the small leaping"	Ó Dubhthaigh 183	1905
25.	Léimneach mór "the great leaping"	Ó Dubhthaigh 183	1905
26.	Léim an éich "Leap of the horse"	Rev. Magill 20	1923
27.	ˌlɛmnjɔxˈbɛg	Local pronunciation	1995
28.	ˌlɛmnɔxˈmoːr	Local pronunciation	1995

Forms 22, 23 and 26 are correct in their interpretation of the origin of this name. It is likely that the qualifiers *beag* "little, small" in this name, and *mór* "big, great, large" in the neighbouring **Lemnagh More**, were used to designate the divisions of the original territory. The division was already recognised by the mid-1600s (form 1). The initial consonants of these qualifiers are lenited under the action of the fem. noun *léim*.

Regarding *léim* "leap, bound", Joyce noted:

[it] is very often used to designate spots where animals were in the habit of passing - a narrow part of a river where they crossed by bounding from one bank to the other, a rent in a line of rocks affording just enough room to pass across a hill ridge leading from one pasture to another, &c. (*Joyce* ii 317).

If this was indeed the original context in which *léim* was employed, there is little doubt that it soon inspired folk etymologies which feature a literal translation of *léim* "leap" (*ibid.*). O'Laverty notes that the original feature which gave rise to the place-name is on the stream which divides the two townlands and suggests it "was named from some ancient legend now forgotten" (*O'Laverty* iv 319–20). This spot is known today as **The Horse Leap** (see Other Names regarding the folk etymology). *Léim* appears as an element in several townland names anglicized as *leam-, lem* or *-leap*, or as a place-name in its own right anglicized *leam* or *leap*. The Co. Clare townlands of Leamaneh North/Leamaneh South and Leamaneigh Beg/Leamaneigh More are probably etymologically similar to those in question here. The townland of **Lemnalary** in Ardclinis parish in Glenarm Lower barony was probably *Léim na Lárach* "leap of the mare" (*Joyce ibid.*).

Lemnagh More	*Léim an Eich Mhór*
D 0243	"leap of the horse, big"

See **Lemnagh Beg**.

Lisbellanagroagh Beg	*Lios Bhaile na gCruach Beag*
C 9942	"fort of the townland of the stacks, little"

1. Lisballinegroe	Hib. Reg. Cary	1657c
2. Lisballengro	DS (Par. Map) 50	1657c
3. Lisballengrough	DS (Par. Map) 51	1657c
4. Lisvallynagroghmor, Lisvallynagroghbeg	Census 12	1659
5. Lisballynagroagh 1 qtr, Lisballynagroagh other qtr	BSD 174	1661
6. Lispatricknagruagh	Court of Claims §923	1662c
7. Lissbrenine Grogh	Lapsed Money Book 157	1663
8. Lisbalienegrough . . . Lisballenegroagh, 1 qr . . . Lisballenegroagh, other qr.	ASE 116b §19	1668
9. Lisbelnegrough	HMR Ant. 1	1669
10. Lisballnagroaghbegg	PRONI D2977/3A/2/1/5A	1682
11. Lisballynagroghmore, the quarterland of	PRONI D2977/3A/2/24/1	1696
12. Ballynegrath alias Ballynegraghbegg	Forfeit. Estates 375b §45	1703
13. Lisballynagroagh-more, Lisballynagroagh-beg	C. McG. (OSNB) B 26	1734
14. Lissballynagroaghmore, Lissballynagroaghbegg	Stewart's Survey 22	1734
15. Liaballynagroaghmore	Religious Survey	1734
16. Lisbelnagroghmore, Lisbelnagroghbeg	Religious Census	1766
17. Lisbellaghnagroaghmore, Lisbellaghnagroaghbeg	Lendrick Map	1780
18. Lisbellanagroagh	Shaw Mason's Par. Sur. 171	1803

19. Lisbelnagroah, Lissbelnagroaghmore	PRONI D2977/3A/2/1/40	1812
20. Lisbellanagroagh-more, Lisbellanagroagh-beg	Bnd. Sur. (OSNB) B 26	1827c
21. Lisbelnagroaghmore, Lisbelnagroaghbeg	Tithe Applot. 6	1833
22. Lios (bhaile) Baile na gCruach "fort of the town of the ricks or round hills"	J O'D (OSNB) 27	1827
23. Lios bealaigh na g-croidh "The fort of the ford-mouth of the stacks (sic)"	Ó Dubhthaigh 183	1905
24. Lios béil átha na gcruach "fort of the mouth of the ford of the stacks"	Ó Dubhthaigh 188	1905
25. Lios-béil-ath-na-gCruach "the fort of the ford of the mouth of the stacks	Antrim Place Names 84	1913
26. Lios béil-atha na gcruach "Fort of the ford mouth of the corn stacks"	Rev. Magill 20	1923
27. ˌlïsbɛlnəˈgroːx	Local pronunciation	1995

In 1835, it was recorded:

> In Lisbellanagroagh, and holding of Daniel McConaghey, stands the ruins of a fort composed of earth and stone but now nearly destroyed. It seems to have stood circular, 30 yards in diameter . . . Leading out from the fort on the south, north and north west sides are ruins of stone causeways (*OSM* xxiv 22).

The memoirs go on to describe the remains of several houses and other enclosures which lay contiguous to the fort. It is likely that this site was the *lios* "enclosed ground of (ancient) dwelling house; enclosed space, garth; ring-fort; fairy mound" (*Ó Dónaill*) in question.

The second element is somewhat uncertain. Modern pronunciation and some historical forms (forms 15–20) reflect [bɛli] which could have conceivably derived from *béal átha* "mouth of the ford" (forms 23–5) or *bealach* "road, track" (form 22). There is a stream a short distance from the aforementioned fort. More likely is that the [ɛ] vowel implied in these forms, which are generally late, indicates a raising of the medial vowel of *baile* following *lios*.

It is unlikely that *cró* (earlier *crodh*, gen. pl. *crodh*; see **Kilcrue Cross**, Other Names, Ramoan parish) was maintained in local speech as something resembling [kroix'], as suggested in form 23. *Cruach*, the likely element in this case, has been translated "a heap, a stack, a rick, a clamp (of turf); a rampart; a symmetrically shaped mountain" (*Dinneen*; gen. pl. *cruach*). Notwithstanding that Lisbellanagroagh Beg contains over 209 acres while Lisbellanagroagh More contains just over 188 acres (*Census 1851*), the elements *mór* and *beag* probably represented epithets indicating the relative size of the divisions of the original territory (cf. **Ballymacaratty More/Beg** in *PNI* i 94).

Form 6, which was copied from older documentation, possibly suggests that there existed two names (and hence territories), *Lios Pádraig* "Patrick's fort" and *Baile na gCruach*, which were later amalgamated. It may have resulted, however, from scribal error.

Lisbellanagroagh More	*Lios Bhaile na gCruach Mór*
D 0043	"fort of the townland of the stacks, big"

See **Lisbellanagroagh Beg**.

Magheraboy	*An Machaire Buí*
D 0343	"the yellow plain"

1. Maghereboy loer, Maghereboy upper	Census 13	1659
2. Mahereboy	Court of Claims §923	1662c
3. Maghrabuy	Shaw Mason's Par. Sur. 171	1663
4. Mareboy	ASE 117a §19	1668
5. Magherboy	HMR Ant. 3	1669
6. Maghreboy	PRONI D2977/3A/2/1/24	1711
7. Macherebuey	C. McG. (OSNB) B 26	1734
8. Macherebuey	Stewart's Survey 18	1734
9. Maghreboy	Religious Survey	1734
10. Magherabuoy	Hill's Stewarts 222	1741c
11. Maghreboy	Religious Census	1766
12. Magherabuy	Lendrick Map	1780
13. Maghrabuy	Bnd. Sur. (OSNB) B 26	1827c
14. Magherabwee	Bnd. Sur. (OSNB) B 26	1827c
15. Magherabuy	Tithe Applot. 7	1833
16. Machaire Buidhe "yellow plain"	J O'D (OSNB) B 26	1827
17. Machaire buidhe "yellow plain"	Rev. Magill 21	1923
18. ˌmaxərəˈbɔi	Local pronunciation	1995

Forms 16 and 17 are broadly correct in assessing the origin of this name. *Machaire* has several meanings however, including "a plain, a flat or low-lying country, a field, a riding or playing-field, a race-course, a battlefield" (*Dinneen*). *Machaire* may also have an ecclesiastical significance in some names (although there is no such tradition apparent in this case), while the meaning "common land" is also a possibility. Price (1983, 448) adopted the meaning "a large area of level or cleared land". *Machaire* may be either feminine or masculine in Mod. Ir. It was found to be feminine in south-west Co. Antrim (*PNI* iv 53), but historical forms of local names containing this element seem to indicate that it was masculine.

Magheracashel	*Machaire Caisil*
D 0541	"plain of the stone fort"

1. Magherecastle	Hib. Reg. Cary	1657c
2. Magherycastle	DS (Par. Map) 57	1657c
3. Maghrichastle	Census 13	1659

4. Magherecastle	BSD 171	1661
5. Maghere Castle	Lapsed Money Book 157	1663
6. Maghere-Castle	ASE 116b §19	1668
7. Maherricashell	HMR Ant. 4	1669
8. Maghere Castl.	Hib. Del. Ant.	1672c
9. Magherecastle, the 1/4 land of	PRONI D2977/3A/2/1/14	1696
10. Magherecastle	PRONI D2977/3A/2/1/17	1706
11. Macherecashell	C. McG. (OSNB) B 26	1734
12. Macherecashell	Stewart's Survey 18	1734
13. Maghre Castle	Religious Survey	1734
14. Maghrecastle	Hill's Stewarts 222	1741c
15. Maghrecastle	Religious Census	1766
16. Maghracastle	Shaw Mason's Par. Sur. 171	1803
17. Magherry Castle Lower, Maghery Castle Upper	PRONI D2977/3A/2/1/40	1812
18. Maghracastle	Bnd. Sur. (OSNB) B 26	1827c
19. Magheracashel	Bnd. Sur. (OSNB) B 26	1827c
20. Machaire Caisil "plain of the stone fort"	J O'D (OSNB) B 26	1827
21. Machaire Caisil	GÉ 131	1989
22. ˌmaxərəˈkaʃəl	Local pronunciation	1995

Machaire in this case may indeed have meant a "plain, or flat country", as suggested in form 20, as the townland is topographically an undulating territory. It lies next to the townland of **Moyarget Upper** in Ramoan. Other meanings of *machaire* are listed under the previous townland. Here it is followed by *caisil*, the gen. sing. of *caiseal* "a bulwark, a wall; a church boundary wall; a stone building; a clamping of sods, etc.; a stone fort" (*Dinneen*). Most often in place-names it seems to denote "stone fort" (cf. also **Cashel** in Other Names, Culfeightrin). In the 1830s it was recorded:

In Magheracashel, and holding of Pat McEnerney, there stood a large fort of earth and stones. The latter was the chief material. It was enclosed by 2 parapets which were also of stones. It was called Cashel and gave name to the townland. Nothing now remains to denote its existence but the site and a quantity of large stones dug out of it, and caves beneath it. The quantity of stones occupied in this fortress was so great that several dwelling and office houses in its neighbourhood have been erected with them. The fort seems to have stood circular, 40 yards in diameter and is locally said to have been the seat of an ancient castle of great size . . . Paved causeways supposed to have accomodated the castle offices are now occasionally discovered beneath the surface in labouring the ground around the site of the fort . . . (*OSM* xxiv 30–1).

Maghernahar
D 0440

Machairín an Choirthe(?)
"little plain of the standing-stone"

1. Maghereher	Census 13	1659
2. Magherenehere	BSD 171	1661

3. Maghernaher	Court of Claims §923	1662c
4. Magherenhere 1 Qur.	Lapsed Money Book 157	1663
5. Magherenohare	ASE 116b §19	1668
6. Mahereihere	HMR Ant. 4	1669
7. Maghrenegher	Hib. Del. Antrim	1672c
8. Magherneherr	PRONI D2977/3A/2/1/24	1711
9. Macherenachare	C. McG. (OSNB) B 26	1734
10. Macherenahare	Stewart's Survey 18	1734
11. Maghrenahor	Religious Survey	1734
12. Maghernagher	Hill's Stewarts 222	1741c
13. Machhernaharr	Merchant's Book 6	1751
14. Maghrenehare	Religious Census	1766
15. Maghrehare	PRONI D2977/3A/2/14/4	1770
16. Maghernaher	Lendrick Map	1780
17. Maharnahar	Shaw Mason's Par. Sur. 171	1803
18. Maghernagher	PRONI D2977/3A/2/1/40	1812
19. Maharnahar	Bnd. Sur. (OSNB) B 26	1827c
20. Maghernahar	Bnd. Sur. (OSNB) B 26	1827c
21. Machaire na hár "plain of the tillage"	J O'D (OSNB) B 26	1827
22. Machaire na h-Ethiar "plain of the air demon"	Rev. Magill 24	1923
23. ˌmaxərnəˈheːr	Local pronunciation	1995

The north-west Co. Down townland name of **Drumnahare** derives from *Dromainn an Choirthe* "ridge of the standing-stone" and may be somewhat analogous here (*PNI* vi 36–7). Local pronunciation of the final syllable of the Down name is [heːr]. *Machairín an Choirthe* could thus be considered as a possible original form. There is no apparent record of a standing-stone in this townland; the nearest at the time of the Ordnance Survey seems to have been in the neighbouring townland of Lagavara (*OSM* xxiv 31). *Machairín* is a diminutive of *machaire* "plain" (see **Magheraboy**) which appears to occur in the Culfeightrin townland name of **Magherindonnell** but which may be otherwise unattested.

A man whose name was written as Oggin O Carr lived here in 1669 (*HMR Ant.* 4). His surname is an anglicized form of *Ó Carra/Cairre*, "a common Ulster surname" (Woulfe 1923, 452, 481; his first name appears to be *Aodhagán*). This might prompt us to suggest *Machairín Uí Chairre* "O'Corr's little plain" as a possible original form, but it seems unlikely that the final element in this name would come to be pronounced [heːr].

The historical forms might be interpreted as indicating that the final element was the the gen. sing. of a fem. noun. *Earr* (gen. sing. *eirre*) "end, extremity" (*Ó Dónaill*) is attested as meaning "pennant, streamer; remote part; point, spike, sharp edge(?)" (*DIL* sv. *err*) and is also a later form of O. Ir. *eirr* "chariot-fighter; champion, warrior" (*ibid.* sv.). **Tullyear** in Co. Down derives from *Tulaigh Eirre* "hillock of the boundary" but is pronounced [ˌtɔliˈir] (*PNI* vi 320). Maghernahar does not lie on the parish boundary.

O'Donovan was obviously unaware of local pronunciation and based his Irish form (21) on forms 19–20 alone. Regarding the final element in his suggested Irish form, see **Araboy**.

Prolusk *Prolaisc*
D 0240 "cave"

1. Prosucke	Hib. Reg. Cary	1657c
2. Proluske	DS (Par. Map) 51	1657c
3. Proluske	DS (Par. Map) 57	1657c
4. Prolusk	BSD 173	1661
5. Proluske	Lapsed Money Book 157	1663
6. Proluske	ASE 116b §19	1668
7. Prosucke	Hib. Del. Antrim	1672c
8. 2 quarters of Prolusk and Creggilapan	PRONI D2977/3A/2/1/5A	1682
9. Prolusk	C. McG. (OSNB) B 26	1734
10. Prolusk	Stewart's Survey 19	1734
11. Prullisk	Religious Survey	1734
12. Prolusk	Lendrick Map	1780
13. Prolusk	Religious Census	1766
14. Prolisk	Shaw Mason's Par. Sur. 171	1803
15. prollusk	PRONI D2977/3A/2/1/40	1812
16. Prolisk	Bnd. Sur. (OSNB) B 26	1827c
17. Prolisk	Tithe Applot. 7	1833
18. Prolusc "a cave"	J O'D (OSNB) B 26	1827
19. Prolusc "a cave"	Joyce iii 533	1913
20. ˈprɔlọsk	Local pronunciation	1995

This name appears to have derived from *Prochlais*, a recurring townland name anglicized as *Procklis*, *Prucklish* and *Prughlish*, which may variously denote "a badger sett; den; cave; hollow" and possibly "patch of stony ground; a heap of stones (Antr.)" (cf. *An Phrochlais* in *PNI* iv 59). The development of the final [k] cannot be explained as metathesis although there may be a parallel in O.Ir. *echlais/echlasc* "shelter for horses" (*DIL*). Irish [ʃ] before [k] is often anglicized as *s* rather than *sh* (cf. for example *PNI* v 50–1). Ploresk, a townland in Co. Kerry, may have a similar origin (*Joyce* iii 533–4).

There is another townland called Prolusk in Clogher parish and barony, Co. Tyrone.

Templastragh *Teampall Lasrach*
D 0043 "*Lasair*'s church"

1. (?)Eccur Sendomnaig (.i. senbríathar). DunSobairgi	Trip. Life. (Stokes) 250	900c
2. Templelasleagh	Hib. Reg. Cary	1657c
3. Templeassereagh	DS (Par. Map) 50	1657c
4. Templasragh	Census 12	1659
5. Templeastragh	BSD 172	1661
6. (?)Templeloghragh	Court of Claims §923	1662c
7. Templelasoragh	Court of Claims §923	1662c
8. Templeastragh	Lapsed Money Book 157	1663

9. Templeastoragh	ASE 116b §19	1668
10. Templasteragh	HMR Ant. 2	1669
11. Templ:astra	Hib. Del. Antrim	1672c
12. Templeasteragh	C. McG. (OSNB) B 26	1734
13. Templeasteragh	Stewart's Survey 21	1734
14. Templasrie	Religious Survey	1734
15. Templeastra	Religious Census	1766
16. Templestra	Lendrick Map	1780
17. Templastragh	Shaw Mason's Par. Sur. 171	1803
18. Templeaztragh	PRONI D2977/3A/2/1/40	1812
19. Templeustragh	Hamilton's Letters 247	1822
20. Templestragh	Bnd. Sur. (OSNB) B 26	1827c
21. Templastra	Tithe Applot. 7	1833
22. Templeastragh	OSRNB sh.3, 2	1855c
23. Templeasteragh	OSRNB sh.3, 2	1855c
24. Teampull Lastrach "St. Lassera's church"	J O'D (OSNB) B 26	1827
25. "the blazing temple or blazing church"	OSM xxiv 18	1838
26. Teampull Lastrach "Church of Lassara"	EA 285	1847
27. Teampull an tsratha "The temple or church of the river holme"	Ó Dubhthaigh 186	1905
28. Teampull lastrach "the flaming church"	Rev. Magill 24	1923
29. Teampul Lasrach "the Church of the flame"	PSAMNI 4	1940
30. ˌtɛmpˈlastər	Local pronunciation	1995

Flanagan (1981–2, 73) notes that *teampall* "church" is:

[of] frequent occurrence both as a townland name and as a parish name. For the most part, it represents a church (frequently a parish church) of the post-Reform period. In post-12th century annalistic records, *teampall* is the term most commonly used of 'church' . . . There are indications that *teampall* may have been in use as a name-element in the pre-Reform period, particularly in the west of Ireland, with reference to small stone-built churches . . .

The church in question here was in the north of the townland. The ruins of the building "with burying ground contiguous" were noted in the 1830s by the Ordnance Survey which also recorded: "it is supposed to have been formerly the church for the parish of Billy and Ballintoy" (*OSM* xxiv 12). Nearer to the shore was found another "ancient graveyard" in which were to be seen "some traces of an ancient building locally said to be the original foundation of Templeastragh ancient church" (*ibid.* 18). The Archaeological Survey of 1940 noted: "The present church ruin is undoubtedly the successor of the original which apparently was N. of it", and that "the masonry of the church so closely resembles in minute detail that of the castle of Dunineny as to suggest that they are contemporary, early 16th century" (*PSAMNI* 4).

An etymological legend concerning the moving of the church site was formerly current and incorporated the second element in the place-name being interpreted as the adj. *lasrach* "flaming, fiery" or *lasrach*, the gen. sing. or gen. pl. of *lasair* "flame, blaze":

> all built here by day was nightly demolished by some invisible agent, in consequence of which obstruction there was a nightly watch left on the building, which watch observed a blazing light each night on the present site of the above old church. This mysterious light, the founder of the church construed to be a miraculous omen, pointing out the proper site for the church to be erected on. They therefore had the building materials removed from the original ground to the present site on which the church stands, and there completed its erection without experiencing the slightest obstruction by day or by night . . . Of the founder . . . there is little local account, but it is said to have been destroyed by Cromwell (*OSM* xxiv 19).

Also nearby "stood an ancient building locally called the Priest's House, also an ancient spring well called the Priest's well. Between the Priest's House and [the] spring stood a paved causeway" (*OSM ibid.*).

Forms 24 and 26 probably had the personal name *Lasair* (an adaptation of the noun *lasair* "flame, blaze") in mind. Ó Corráin and Maguire (1981, 121) describe this "as a relatively common female name in early Ireland". It occurs in the Co. Waterford townland name of *Cill Lasrach* (anglicized Killosseragh; *L. Log. Ph. Láirge* 20). The *Martyrology of Donegal* lists several saints of the name, some of whom are male (*Mart. Don.* 513 sv. *Lassar*; see also Ó Corráin & Maguire 1981, 121 sv. *Laisre*), although Gwynn (1911, 73) claims that only a diminutive form of the name was used for males. The intrusive *t* appears at least as early as 1661 (form 5; note also form 2).

Reeves believed form 1 to refer to this townland name, but it is unclear from the context if this was so. *Seandomhnach* "old church" (form 1) may have been referring to Dunseverick itself, or to some other site. This form occurs in a list of "consecrated residences" (*Trip. Life (Stokes)* 251).

Toberkeagh	*An Tobar Caoch*	
D 0139	"the disused/dry well"	
1. Tobberbigh	Hib. Reg. Cary	1657c
2. Toberkirk	Census 13	1659
3. Tobberbigh	BSD 173	1661
4. Tobberkeigh	Lapsed Money Book 157	1663
5. Tobberbigh	ASE 116b §19	1668
6. Tubberkeagh	HMR Ant. 4	1669
7. Toberkegh	PRONI D2977/3A/2/1/6	1681
8. Toberkigh	C. McG. (OSNB) B 26	1734
9. Toberkeegh	Stewart's Survey 23	1734
10. Toberkeigh	Religious Survey	1734
11. Tobberkeiogh alias Tubberkeigh alias Toberkeigh	PRONI D2977/3A/2/1/33A	1737
12. Toberkeigh	Religious Census	1766
13. Tobarkeagh	Shaw Mason's Par. Sur. 171	1803
14. Tobberkeiegh	PRONI D2977/3A/2/1/40	1812
15. Tobarkeagh	Bnd. Sur. (OSNB) B 26	1827c

16. Tubberkeagh	Bnd. Sur. (OSNB) B 26	1827c
17. Toberkeigh	Tithe Applot. 7	1833
18. Tobar caoch "blind well"	J O'D (OSNB) B 26	1827
19. Tobar caech "The well of the blind"	Ó Dubhthaigh 187	1905
20. ˌtobərˈkiəx	Local pronunciation	1995

In 1887 O'Laverty noted: "The townland of Toberkeagh is so named from a well in the farm of Mr. Forbes" (*O'Laverty* iv 325–6). The *Ordnance Survey Memoirs* mention other wells in Ballintoy parish, but none specifically in this townland.

Tobar "a well, spring" (*Dinneen* sv.) recurs elsewhere locally in the Ramoan townland name of **Toberbilly**. It is probably qualified by the adjective *caoch*, which usually means "blind" in speech, but which may mean "covered up, empty" in cases like this. Price (1983, 454) has translated *caoch* as "hidden" in the Co. Wicklow townland name of *Coill Chaoch* (anglicized as Blindwood) while *Dinneen* (sv. *caoch*) has translated the term *tobar caoch* as "a disused or dry well".

White Park
D 0144

An Pháirc
"the field"

1. Parke	Census 12	1659
2. (?)Park	Reg. Deeds Abstracts i §265	1722
3. Park	Stewart's Survey 20	1734
4. White Park	Religious Census	1766
5. Whitepark	PRONI D2977/3A/2/21/4	1776
6. White Park	Lendrick Map	1780
7. White Park	Shaw Mason's Par. Sur. 171	1803
8. White Park	Bnd. Sur. (OSNB) B 26	1827c
9. White park	Tithe Applot. 7	1833
10. hwəit ˈpark	Local pronunciation	1995

It seems likely that the original place-name here was *An Pháirc* "the field, esp. a pasture-field, a pasture" (*Dinneen*) which at a later stage was prefixed by the English adjective, possibly from **White Park Bay** (possibly *White Bay*, formerly; see Other Names), along which this townland lies (cf. also **Park** in Armoy). This adj. may have been inspired by the extensive beach on the coast of this townland; the townland also abounds in chalk (*OSM* xxiv 10; see also **Black Park** in Other Names).

Among the older meanings listed for the English word *park* are "an enclosed piece of ground stocked with game and held by royal grant; an enclosed area of lawns, woodland, pasture etc attached to a country house and used as a game reserve for recreation" (*Longman Dict.*). It was recorded in 1838 that White Park House in the west of this townland was built by one "late Squire John Stewart . . . above a century ago" (*OSM* xxiv 30), but it seems unlikely that the English word would have given name to the territory as early as 1659 (form 1).

Ballaghcravey	*Bealach na Creamhaí(?)*	
D 0544	"road of the place of garlic"	
1. bɛlənə'kraːvi	Local pronunciation	1995

The official form and modern pronunciation are somewhat contradictory. The form on the *OS 1:10,000* map is *Ballaghacravey* and introduces other possibilities. The name is not widely known and may have been altered by analogy. It is possible, for example, that the central definite article has been recently affected by metathesis. However, the first element of this name seems likely to have been *bealach* "road, track" as the name refers to a path leading up from the shore at Portaneevey; form 1 has thus been affected by elision. The final element may have been the gen. of a substantive fem. or masc. form of the adjective *creamhach* "garlic, garlic-grown" (*Dinneen*) meaning "place of garlic", a variant form of which, *cneamhach*, Joyce believes to be the etymology of the Co. Galway townland name of Knavagh (*Joyce* ii 349). *Cnáimhfhiach* (gen. sing. *cnáimhfhiaigh*, gen. pl. *cnáimhfhiach*) "black kite" (see *Dinneen*, Ó Dónaill sv. *cnáimhfhiach*; *Dwelly* has this word as *cnàimheach* "crow; jackdaw") could also be considered.

Ballintoy Port	A hybrid form	
D 0446		
1. Portcampley	OSRNB sh.4, 1	1855c
2. ˌportˈkɑmplɪ	Local pronunciation	1995

This lies to the north-west of the village, in Ballintoy Demesne (see the discussion of the parish name regarding the Irish elements). The official name does not appear to be used; Portcampley (*OS 1:10,000*) is preferred. *Port Camplaí* "port of the encampment" may have been the original form of the latter name. The second element is the gen. of a syncopated form of *campa* "camp" plus the collective suffix *-lach*. Joyce believed the townland name **Camplagh** in Co. Fermanagh to have a similar origin (*Joyce* ii 61). We might also consider that the second element was a development of the masc. noun *compal* "ring, enclosure; enclosed space" (Ó Dónaill), such as a fem. variant (*compail*, gen. sing. *compaile*). *Port Compaile* would certainly be topographically suitable. That the masc. noun *pléidhe* "the outer net in a trammel" (*Dinneen*) was used here with the adjectival prefix *cam-* "bent" seems unlikely. In c. 1855 the surveyor noted: "I cannot learn whether Campley is a proper name or not" (*OSRNB* sh.4, 1); *Port an Chaimbéalaigh* "Campbell's port" also seems unlikely.

Black Park	An English form	
D 0443		
1. Black Park	OSRNB sh.8, 1	1855c
2. blak ˈpaərk	Local pronunciation	1995

"2 farm houses and out offices in the possession of Mr. Charles Price of Rock Cottage, but at meantime the occupation of John McNichle and Alexd. Ramage. It is said to have been so called from its black aspect when first enclosed" (*OSRNB* sh.8, 2). This is situated in the south of Ballintoy Demesne. It is uncertain whether there originally existed a place-name *An Pháirc* "the field/pasture", prior to the addition of an English prefix, as appears to have been the case with the townland name of **White Park**. The element *dubh* "black" can refer locally to the appearance of basaltic rock (cf. **Carnduff** in Ramoan).

Boheeshane Bay D 0445	A hybrid form	
1. ˌboˈhiʃan	Local pronunciation	1995

Boheeshane refers to a small cove lined with sand and gravel to the west of what is termed *Boheeshane Bay* on the Ordnance Survey map (*OS 1:50,000*), in Ballintoy townland. Local fishermen do not land here but can collect fresh water from a stream which enters the sea at this point (*Pers. comm.* 12.10.96). The English epithet is not used. The masc. noun *bogha* "a sunken sea-rock, a reef" (*Dinneen*) has passed into the local English dialect as [boː]; Holmer recorded it in the Irish of Rathlin as denoting "reef; wave (breaking over a submerged rock)" (*Irish of Rathlin* 165). *Dwelly* has this word as *bodha* "rock over which the waves break; breaker over sunken rocks" (for some examples in place-names in western Scotland see MacKillop 1989, 38–40). The second element is the gen. form of *taosán*. This seems to be the word (a derivative of *taos* "dough, paste" (*Dinneen*)) which appears in the south-west Co. Antrim townland name **Teeshan** and which has been explained as "muddy/clayey place" (*PNI* iv 210). *Bogha Thaosáin* "sea-rock of the muddy place", then, seems to have formed the original name. The lenition of the *t* may have arisen from the use of the name in the dat. case although it may also indicate that there existed the place-name *Taosán* "muddy place" prior to the addition of *bogha*. Note that the townland name also features a medial [ʃ]; McKay suggests the change occurred after the name was adopted into English, although *Dinneen* lists the variant *taois* from which *taoiseán* could have developed.

Lemawilkin (see *OSRNB* sh.4, 1; local pronunciation [ˌlɛməˈvïlkən]) is used instead to denote Boheeshane Bay and the adjacent shore. The form *Limmavoolkin* was recorded in c. 1855 (*OSRNB* sh.4, 1) and suggests that the initial vowel of the final element was Irish *ao* or *u* or possibly *o* (see *Irish of the Glens* 30–1); this in turn suggests several possible original forms, including *Léim an Mhaolchinn* "leap of the bald-headed person/person with cropped hair". Other possible final elements include gen. forms of *bolcán* "cove; strong, stocky person [or] animal" (*Ó Dónaill* sv.; possibly in variant form), and perhaps a variant unattested diminutive of *molt* "wether", *moiltín* ([tʹ] sometimes became [kʹ] in local Irish; see **Tenaghs** in Culfeightrin). See **Lemnagh Beg** regarding *léim*.

Carnanmore D 0338	*An Carnán Mór* "the big cairn"	
1. Carnanmore	OSRNB sh.8, 2	1855c
2. ˌkɑrnənˈmoːr	Local pronunciation	1995

This hill lies in Curramoney. *Carnán*, which has been translated "a heap, a pile, a hillock" (*Dinneen*) and "(small) heap, mound" (*Ó Dónaill*), consists of *carn* "cairn" plus a suffix which might normally be interpreted as representing a diminutive or a collective, although neither sense seems applicable here (see also **Carnanmore** in Other Names, Culfeightrin).

In c. 1855 it was recorded that Carnanmore "is said to have been formerly a large round carn. It was destroyed by continual encroachments. A portion of its site is now traceable at the junction of the fences. Some years ago human bones were discovered by working parties at this place. Since then no further encroachment has been made . . ." (*OSRNB* sh.8, 2).

The minor name anglicized as Cairnan Glas (perhaps from *An Carnán Glas* "the green hillock") was noted by the Ordnance Survey in 1838 in this townland as referring to a "small green hill . . . [which] in consequence of it being considered a gentle and fairy haunt, [would] not be laboured by the farmers" (*OSM* xxiv 28). It is not certain if it represents another name for Carnanmore.

Carrickarade Island	A hybrid form	
D 0645		

1. Carrickarede	Lendrick Map	1780
2. Carrick a Rede	Dubourdieu Map	1812
3. Carrick-a-rede	Hamilton's Letters 247	1822
4. Carrick a rede	Bnd. Sur. (OSNB) B 26	1827c
5. Carrickaraid	OSRNB sh.4, 1	1855c
6. Carrick-a-raide	O'Laverty iv 338	1887
7. Carraic a ramhad "rock of the road"	J O'D (OSNB) B 26	1827
8. "named from an Irish tribe called Dalriada"	OSRNB sh.4, 1	1855c
9. Carrig-Riada	Hill's Stewarts 154 n.1	1900
10. Carraig a' roid "The rock of the road"	Ó Dubhthaigh 134	1905
11. Carraig a róid "Rock of the road"	Rev. Magill 10	1923
12. Carraig an Ráid	Éire Thuaidh	1988
13. ˌkarïkəˈreːd	Local pronunciation	1995
14. ˌkarïkəˈrid	Local pronunciation	1995

Forms 1–4 appear to suggest that the final vowel was originally [i(ː)], but we could postulate that they contain scribal errors. The revised name books of c. 1855 noted that "the last syllable will be better expressed by 'raid' than 'rede'" (*OSRNB* sh.4, 1). The road intended in forms 7, 10 and 11 may be the Ballintoy-Ballycastle route, although it passes several hundred metres south of this famous rock. The gen. form of *ród* "road" is not reflected in the forms unless we accept that it took a variant form locally. A development from Scottish Gaelic *rathad* "road, way, highway; path, track" (*Dwelly*) to *reathad* (gen. sing. *reathaid*) seems possible but while the loss of intervocalic -*th*- occurred in local Irish (see *Irish of the Glens* 24–5) we would probably expect the vowel sound to remain as [a] (cf. **Craigban** in Culfeightrin). O'Donovan's variant (form 7) is not helpful here. Hill noted:

This . . . [has been] absurdly translated the 'Rock-in-the-Road': meaning, as they say, the rock in the road of the salmon when journeying westward to the net at Larrybawn. But the salmon evidently do not regard the rock in the light of an obstruction; for, on the contrary, they delight to linger round it as they pass. Carrig-Riada was the name originally employed to distinguish it as *the* Rock most remarkable in Dalriada; or it may have been at first so named as being in some way associated with the career of Carbery Riada, the founder of the principality (*Hill's Stewarts* 154 n.1).

The Ordnance Survey also recorded locally that: "This island is said to have been named from an Irish tribe called the [Dál Riada]" (*OSRNB* sh.4, 1). *Carraig Dhál Riada* "(the) rock of *Dál Riada*" is not a plausible origin however (regarding Dál Riada, see the barony introduction). *Carraig an Raid* "rock of the throwing or casting" might be considered; *raid* is a gen. sing. of *rad* "act of giving, casting, discharging, throwing, kicking" (*Dinneen*). The origin of the final element in form 12 is obscure; *An Ráid*, a field name recorded in Tory Island in Co. Donegal by Ó hUrmoltaigh (1967, 100), may represent a fem. form of this noun. Again, however, neither *raid* nor *ráid* reflect the [eː] vowel. *Réad* (gen. sing. *réada*) "star", related to Mod. Ir. *réalt* "star" is now confined to literary use (*Ó Dónaill* sv.) but might be considered. It is tempting to suggest forms such as *Carraigeach Dhroichid* "rocky place of the bridge" and *Carraig Dhroichid* "rock of the bridge" (to which was added a central epenthetic vowel), but the etymology remains uncertain.

Carrickarade (the epithet *island* does not appear to be used) was the site of one of 3 salmon fisheries in the parish in 1830 (*OSM* xxiv 12), at which time the rock was thus described:

> Carrickarede [*sic*] is another little island separated from the mainland by a frightful chasm about 60 feet wide . . . The bridge which connects this island with the mainland . . . is about 100 feet long and is made of ropes suspended from either side of the chasm, at an elevation of about 80 feet above the water. Its breadth is about 3 feet . . . this bridge is used by the persons who have the salmon fishery in the island and also by inhabitants for the purpose of going down to the north side of the island to gather seaweed (*ibid.*).

Carricknaford	*Carraig an Phoirt(?)*	
D 0245	"rock of the port"	
1. Carricknafurd	OSRNB sh.4, 1	1855c
2. creag a phuirt "rock of the ports or harbours"	OSRNB sh.4, 1	1855c
3. ˌkarïknəˈfurd	Local pronunciation	1995

"A large insulated rock or rather an island [in Ballintoy Demesne townland]. The south part of it lies to a considerable height above the level of the sea. It signifies the rock of the ports, which appears to have originated from the number of small creeks . . ." (*OSRNB* sh.4, 1). The central article has been changed by metathesis in other subtownland names locally. See for example **Portnathalin** in Other Names, Culfeightrin. *Port* was pronounced [pʎrt] in late local Irish (*Irish of the Glens* 31).

Castle, The	An English form(?)	
D 0344		
1. (?)Caue ca	Norden's Map	1610
2. ðə ˈkasəl	Local pronunciation	1995

Norden's map depicts a castle in this area (form 1), but its name is likely to have been badly affected by mistranscription and its etymology is obscure. In 1835 it was recorded:

> The ruins of a very large castle or rather a bawn still remain about half a mile north west of [Ballintoy] village. It is within memory when they were inhabited . . . They seem to have been of rather modern erection, as the walls are rather slight. It is said the village formerly stood there and that this castle was built by the MacDonnells (*OSM* xxiv 15).

The present name may represent a translation from *caisleán/caistéal*; see, for example, **Ballycastle** in Ramoan and **Cashel** in Other Names, Culfeightrin.

Clare Wood	A hybrid form
D 0741	

This wood straddles several townlands in both Ballintoy and Ramoan. The first element appears to derive from *clár* "flat surface; plain", which is briefly discussed under **Clare** in Ramoan.

Cloghcorr Middle,	Hybrid forms
Cloghcorr Upper	
D 0543, 0542	

These names are derived from the townland name of **Cloghcorr**. They refer to two farm hamlets (*OS 1:10,000*).

Coolnagorr	*Cúl na gCorr*
D 9941	"back of the rounded hills"

1.	cul na g-cor "sequestered nook of the heights"	OSRNB sh.3, 4	1855c
2.	ˌkulnəˈgɔːr	Local pronunciation	1995

"A long irregular range of farmhouses on elevated ground so called from their position on a height, and their situation in what was once a remote backland district" (*OSRNB* sh.3, 4). The first element in this name seems likely to have been *cúl* "back", sometimes applied to the back of a hill (*Joyce* ii 200), rather than *cúil* "corner, nook", which is more prevalent in townland names (cf. **Coolaveely** in Culfeightrin). The final element, the gen. pl. form *corr*, has several meanings (cf. **Cloghcorr**), but "(of the) rounded hills" seems most likely here.

Craignagolman	*Creag na gColmán*
D 0543	"rock of the pigeons"

1.	ˌkreːgnəˈgolman	Local pronunciation	1995

Colmán "a young pigeon or dove" (*Dinneen*) or "(little) dove; pigeon" (*Ó Dónaill*) appears also in the Rathlin subtownland name of *Uamha na gColmán* "the cave of the pigeons" (anglicized **Oweynagolman**; *Place-Names of Rathlin* 66). It might also be considered that the gen. pl. form of the male personal name *Colmán* formed the last element in this name (cf.

Knocknagarvan). See **Craig** townland regarding *creag*. This name refers to a hill 202 metres high.

| **Crockacollier** | *Cnoc an Choiléir(?)* |
| D 0743 | "hill of the quarry" |

| 1. ˌkrɒknəˈkɒljər | Local pronunciation | 1996 |

The first element in this name was probably *cnoc* "hill, mountain" (see also **Crockateemore** in Other Names, Culfeightrin). *Coiléar* (gen. sing. *coiléir*) is a variant of *cairéal* "quarry". The English word *collier* (cf. **Colliery Bay** and **Pans Rock** in Other Names, Culfeightrin, regarding the local coal industry) might also be considered as a possible final element, but the surname Collier (see *PNI* ii 129–30; see also Black 1946, 162), or one of its variants, seems unlikely. The place-name is only vaguely known locally and modern pronunciation may be unreliable. However, it possibly contains a metathesized medial definite article (compare **Portnathalin** in Other Names, Culfeightrin, and **Portandoon** in Other Names, Rathlin). Alternatively, form 1 may indicate that the final element appeared here in a gen. pl. form: *Cnoc na gCoiléar* "hill of the quarries".

| **Cross Bridge** | An English form(?) |
| D 0338 | |

| 1. The Cross Bridge | OSRNB sh.8, 1 | 1855c |

| 2. krɔs ˈbrïdʒ | Local pronunciation | 1995 |

"Bridge of small arches built with stone and lime and parapet walls. It has been so called from its proximity to a cross roads which lie to the west of it" (*OSRNB* sh.8, 1). There does not appear to be any record of a cross standing at this place, which lies in Curramoney townland. The cross-road is c. 150 metres west of this bridge, which spans Inver Burn.

| **Dundriff** | Of uncertain origin |
| D 0344 | |

1. (?)Dundrif	Inq. Earl. Ulster 37	1262
2. (?)Dundresse	Court of Claims §923	1662c
3. Dundriff	OSRNB sh.4, 1	1855c

| 4. dɒnˈdrïf | Local pronunciation | 1995 |

In c. 1855, Dundriff was described as follows:

> a large insulated rock rising abruptly from the sea, and to a considerable height. Its sides are steep. It tapers to a point at the summit and appears at a distance like a pyramid. Along the summit there is some vegetation. The summit is apparently inaccessible (*OSRNB* sh.4, 1).

This would lead us to believe that the *dún* "fort" element was used figuratively of the rock (cf. **Carravindoon**, Rathlin Island). The Archaeological Survey of 1940 noted that

Dundriff was marked on the 1904 Ordnance Survey maps as a headland, not an antiquity. There may have been some confusion with the nearby minor coastal place-name Dunshammer (*OS 1:10,000*). The Archaeological Survey describes Dundriff as follows:

> A conical outcrop of basalt forming a peninsula of which the northern half is washed by the tides. It is some 100 ft. high on the land side; and 129 ft. next the sea. The sides are very steep, and the artificially flattened top is approximately circular, 45 ft. in diameter (*PSAMNI* 4).

Orpen originally believed form 1 to be Dunluce but later equated it with Dundarave, about 1 mile north-east of Bushmills (*Account Tweskard (Curtis)* 16; *Inq. Earldom Ulster* 38). Lawlor (1938, 6) points out however that the geographical order of names in the account of de Mandeville, "custos of Twescard" (see barony introduction), from which this form is taken, suggests that *Dundrif* lay east of Dunseverick. It was valued at £13 6s. 8d. in this account (*Account Tweskard (Curtis)* ibid.). It is impossible to equate the names on the basis of one form, however, and we must also consider that form 1 may contain scribal errors. Form 2 may contain the common scribal error of confusing a tall *s* with *f*.

The origin of the second element is uncertain. *Dún* was formerly of neuter gender (cf. **Broughgammon**), and would have caused the nasalization of the initial consonant of the following noun. Possible final elements, then, include *treibh* (gen. sing. *treibhe*) "house, farm, holding; household, tribe" (*DIL* sv. *treb*).

Fallgarrive

Fallgarrive	*Fál Garbh*	
D 0040	"rough enclosure"	
1. Fillgarive	OSRNB sh.7, 1	1855c
2. Fallgarrive	OSRNB sh.7, 1	1855c
3. Fál garbh "rough enclosure"	J O'D (OSRNB) sh.7, 1	1855c
4. ˌfalˈgarïv	Local pronunciation	1995

"A small farm village situate on the other side of the road that turns north and south through the townland of Croaghbeg . . ." (*OSRNB* sh.7, 1). Ó Dónaill gives several meanings for *fál*, including "hedge, fence; wall, barrier; enclosure, field".

Falltagart

Falltagart	*Fál tSagairt(?)*	
D 0441	"enclosure of the priest"	
1. Falltaggart	OSRNB sh.8, 2	1855c
2. feall a tagairt "residence or habitation of the priest"	OSRNB sh.8, 2	1855c
3. ˌfalˈtagərt	Local pronunciation	1995

"Two dwelling houses in one range and in the occupation of John White and John McCurdy . . . origin [of the name] is unknown in the locality" (*OSRNB* sh.8, 2). A medial definite article (*an*) may have been recently phonetically lost, although the *t* could have prefixed the *s* even in the absence of the article, by analogy. The Scottish surname Taggart (Black 1946, 761) may also be considered as a possible second element.

Giants Cut	*Buille Chú Chulainn*	
D 0744	"*Cú Chulainn*'s blow"	
1. Buillacoocullian	OSM xxiv 34	1838
2. dʒaiənts 'kɒt	Local pronunciation	1995

The following was recorded in 1838:

> The Giant's Cut, situated to the south east of Carrickarede bridge and adjoining the sea-shore in the townland of Glenstahy [*sic*] . . . is a long deep and narrow passage between two headlands . . . It is called in Irish Buillacoocullian. The latter, or Coocullian, was one of the ancient warriors compory with Finnmacuil, and to whose powerful arm and extraordinary-sized sword the old Irish inhabitants in this part of the neighbourhood attributed the above cut. It still gets the aforesaid name amoungst those who speak the Irish language, and the idea [was] said to prevail amoung the old inhabitants for centuries that the cut was made by one stroke of the above warrior's sword (*OSM* xxiv 34).

Regarding *Cú Chulainn*, see for example Ó hÓgáin 1990, 131–9. In 1835 however, it was recorded that "the natives say [that this gorge] was the effect of a cut of Finn McCoul's wonderful sword" (*OSM* xxiv 14). Regarding *Fionn Mac Cumhail*, see **Doonfinn** in Ramoan.

Gid Point	An English form(?)	
D 0044		
1. Gid Point	OSRNB sh.3, 2	1855c
2. gïd 'pɔint	Local pronunciation	1995

Gid is an obsolete form of the English word *guide*; it is also an obsolete "provincial name for the Jack Snipe" (*OED*). It is furthermore an obsolete form of *ged*, a word of Old Norse origin used in the English of Scotland and north England for "the fish Esox lucius; the pike or luce" (*ibid.*). The English word *gid* which denotes "a disease, esp of sheep . . . characterized by a staggering gait" is derived by back-formation from *giddy* which may sometimes mean "whirling rapidly" (*Longman Dict.*). We may also consider that this element represents a colloquial form of the word *good* (see *Scot. Nat. Dict.* sv. *guid*).

Glennamally	*Gleann na mBáillí(?)*	
D 0240	"valley of the bailiffs"	
1. Glenamally	OSRNB sh.8, 1	1855c
2. Glennamally	OSRNB sh.8, 1	1855c
3. "the Glen of the bailiffs"	OSRNB sh.8, 1	1855c
4. ˌglɛnə'maːli	Local pronunciation	1995

"A subdenomination of the townland of Prolusk . . . it is applied to a strip of land through which a road runs north and south . . ." (*OSRNB* sh.8, 1). *Gleann na Mala/Malaí* "valley of the slope(s)" and *Gleann na Mullaí* "valley of the summits" are further possible original forms. The name refers to a valley of one of the head-waters of Inver Burn.

Glenstaghy Lower,   Hybrid forms
Glenstaghy Upper
D 0744, 0644

1. Glenstaghey Upper, Lower	OSRNB sh.4, 1	1855c
2. Glenstaughey Upper, Lower	OSRNB sh.4, 1	1855c

These forms derive from the townland name **Glenstaghy** and in c. 1855 referred to separate farm hamlets (*OSRNB* sh.4, 1).

Gobe Feagh   *Gob Féich*
or Ravens Point   "point of the raven/raven's beak"
D 0744

1. gobˈfeəx	Local pronunciation	1995

Dinneen gives several meanings for *gob,* including "a pointed or beak-like mouth; a land's end or ness; a point of land jutting into the sea". This headland lies in Coolmaghra townland. *Gob Fiach* "point of the ravens" (see *Dinneen* sv. *fiach; fiaigh* is the standard Mod. Ir. gen. sing. (*Ó Dónaill*)) is a further possible original form (see also **Carnaneigh** and **Tornaveagh** in Other Names, Culfeightrin).

High Carn   A hybrid form
D 0142

1. Carn	Religious Survey	1734
2. Carn	OSM xxiv 30	1838
3. hai ˈkɑrn	Local pronunciation	1995

Low Carn lies less than half a mile south of here; both refer to farm hamlets and are in Lemnagh More. The *carn* "cairn; heap, pile" to which the names referred may be long disappeared.

Horse Leap, The   *Léim an Eich*
D 0143   "leap of the horse"

1. Lemnagh or The Horse Lope	OSRNB sh.3, 4	1855c
2. leim an aigh "the horse's leap"	OSRNB sh.3, 4	1855c
3. ðə hɔrs ˈloːp	Local pronunciation	1995

"A narrow ravine over which a smuggler leaped with a horse when hotly pursued by the military. The horse was killed, and the place is since called Leamnagh, or the horse's leap.

The townlands on either side have derived their names from this stream" (*OSRNB* sh.3, 4). Regarding modern pronunciation of the final element, we may quote the *Scottish National Dictionary*: "Sc. forms correspond to Eng. *lope*, which have now displaced *leap*" (*Scot. Nat. Dict.* sv. *lowp*). See **Lemnagh Beg**.

Islandarragh	*Oileán Darach*	
D 0642	"island of the oak(s)"	
1. ˌailəndara	Local pronunciation	1995

This inland place-name is in Craiganee townland. *Darach* is both the gen. sing. and gen. pl. of *dair* "oak". See **Island Macallan** regarding the first element.

Islandlean	*An tOileán Leathan(?)*	
D 0345	"the broad island"	
1. Islandlean	OSRNB sh.4, 1	1855c
2. ailan a leun "island of woe or lamentation"	OSRNB sh.4, 1	1855c
3. ailənd'jeːn	Local pronunciation	1995

"A large insulated rock over which the sea breaks when rough. The tide does not at any time cover it. There is no vegetation on it. It signifies the rock or island of woe, but nothing is locally known of the reason why . . ." (*OSRNB* sh.4, 1). It lies off the coast of Ballintoy Demesne.

The gen. sing. of *léan* "deep affliction; grief, anguish, woe" (*Ó Dónaill*) may have formed the final element (compare *Port an tSonais*, anglicized **Portantonnish**, in Other Names, Rathlin Island), but in the absence of a central definite article, *An tOileán Leathan* "the broad island" seems a more likely origin. It is somewhat less likely that the final element was the gen. sing. form *lín*, from *líon* "flax, linen/fishing net" and that the final vowel has been recently lowered.

Islandnanagh	*Oileán na nEach*	
D 0540	"island of the horses"	
1. Islandnanagh	OSRNB sh.8, 2	1855c
2. ealan-na-neach "Isle of the horses"	OSRNB sh.8, 2	1855c
3. ˌailənd'njax	Local pronunciation	1855c

"A pretty extensive arable tract, once surrounded by bog, but now opened up by a new road which runs by the north side of it and in part reclaimed from the bog. It was used as a grazing place for horses and from this circumstance it has derived its name . . . A portion is situate in each of [Broughgammon and Magheracashel] townlands . . ." (*OSRNB* sh.8, 2). Modern pronunciation shows evidence of haplology.

Islandoo	*An tOileán Dubh*	
D 0345	"the dark island"	

1. Islandoo	OSRNB sh.4, 1	1855c
2. ailan dubh "black island"	OSRNB sh.4, 1	1855c
3. ailən'duː	Local pronunciation	1995

"A large insulated rock so called from its colour being black. It is situated at the mouth of Portcampley. The sea washes over it when it is rough. There is no vegetation on it" (*OSRNB* sh.4, 1). This lies off Ballintoy Demesne. There is an Island Doo off Goodland in Culfeightrin (cf. **Portdoo** in Other Names, Culfeightrin).

Kilmacromey	*Cill Mochroma*	
D 0040	"*Mochroma*'s burial-ground"	

1. Kilmacromey	OSRNB sh.7, 1	1855c
2. "the burying ground of the hill side"	OSRNB sh.7, 1	1855c
3. ˌkïlmə'krǫmi	Local pronunciation	1995

It was recorded in 1838 that:

> In Arraboy [*sic*], and holding of James Rogers, stood an ancient graveyard locally called Killemacromy, but now destroyed and the site under tillage. In reclaiming the ground from time to time there were large quantities of every description of human bones and decayed coffin boards raised, but buried again on the site (*OSM* xxiv 23).

In c. 1855 it was recorded that this name referred to "a small farm village close to Fillgarive [*sic*] and on the north side of it . . . This village is said to be built on the site of an ancient burying ground, no trace of which remains . . ." (*OSRNB* sh.7, 1).

Cill "burial-ground" seems to be qualified here by the male personal (pet) name *Mochroma* (earlier *Mochromma* (*CSH* 56 §361)) which presumably derives from *crom* "crooked, bent".

Kinmeen	*An Cionn Mín*	
D 064426	"the smooth high ground"	

| 1. kïn'miːn | Local pronunciation | 1995 |

For appproximately 1000 years, *ceann/cionn* "head" has been used in place-names to denote high ground above land or sea (Ó Maolfabhail 1987, 76). In the absence of historical forms, of course, the age of this name will remain unknown; it refers to an inland site on the boundary of Craiganee and Glenstaghy. Holmer recorded *cionn* as the nom. form locally (*Irish of the Glens* 105). See also **Kinkeel** in Rathlin Island and **Barmeen** in Culfeightrin.

Kittall
D 0437

Of uncertain origin

1. Kittillatragh	Hib. Reg. Cary	1657c
2. Killitragh, Killillutragh	DS (Par. Map) 63	1657c
3. Killitragh, Kittillutragh	DS (Par. Map) 63	1657c
4. Killultragh, Killitragh	DS (Par. Map) 64	1657c
5. Killitragh, Kiltillictragh	DS (Par. Map) 57	1657c
6. Kittell	Census 11	1659
7. Koitill	Court of Claims §923	1662c
8. Killault	Lapsed Money Book 158	1663
9. Kettleoghtragh, ½ townland of; Kettilutragh	ASE 117a §19	1668
10. Sittell	HMR Ant. 13	1669
11. Killitragh, Kiltullatra	Hib. Del. Antrim	1672c
12. Kittall and Carrivecroy	Stewart's Survey 36	1734
13. Kihell	Religious Census	1766
14. Kittel	Lendrick Map	1780
15. Kittal	Shaw Mason's Par. Sur. 171	1803
16. Kettall	PRONI D2977/3A/2/1/40	1812
17. Kittall	OSRNB sh.8, 2	1855c
18. Ciot-aill "the left hand cliff or steep"	Ó Dubhthaigh 182	1905
19. Ciot-aill "left hand cliff"	Rev. Magill 19	1923
20. 'kïtəl	Local pronunciation	1995

    "A small farm village [in Carrowcroey] close on the east side to the road from Ballintoy to Armoy. Origin of the name is unknown" (*OSRNB* sh.8, 2). The divisional epithets *íochtarach* "lower" and *uachtarach* "upper" do not recur after c. 1672 (form 11). *Ciot*- forms the root of some words implying "lefthandedness; awkwardness", but its use as a prefix here (as suggested in forms 18–9) is much in doubt. *Cat* "cat", prefixing *aill* "cliff, precipice", would also represent an unusual origin. There is a parish called Kettle in Fife in Scotland, which Taylor (1995, 273–5) believes to be of Celtic origin, and for which he notes the possibility that it might contain *cat* used in a totemic sense. The O. Ir. word *cit* "sheep" (*DIL*) seems to be attested only in glossaries (see also *Dwelly* sv. *ceut*) and again would represent an unusual prefix. The surname *Mac Coitil*, anglicized Kettle, derives from a Norse personal name (Anglo-Saxon *Cytel*; Woulfe 1923, 335) which appears in the Co. Limerick townland name *Carraig Chiotal* (*sic*; anglicized Carrickittle; Ó Maolfabhail 1990, 84) and possibly in the Co. Cork townland name of Dunkettle, but personal names and surnames rarely appear as place-names in their own right in Ireland. Examples include *Aird Mhic Giollagáin*, angl. **Magilligan**, in Co. Derry (*IPN* 237). As Kettle was formerly a townland, perhaps we may postulate that there existed the form *Baile Chiotail* "*Ciotal*'s townland" prior to the loss of the first element.

Knockshanny
D 0041

Cnoc Seanaigh(?)
"*Seanach*'s hill"

1. Cnoc sionaidhe "hill of the fox"	OSRNB sh.3, 4	1855c

2. ˌnɔkˈʃani	Local pronunciation	1995

There is some doubt over the second element. It may have been the male personal name *Seanach* (gen. sing. *S(h)eanaigh*), which is "a diminutive from *sen* 'ancient, old'" (Ó Corráin & Maguire 1981, 164). *Seanadh* (gen. *seanaidh*), an otherwise obsolete noun found in place-names and meaning "hillside, slope, sloping ground" (Ó Máille 1953–4, 499) should also be considered. *Seanadh* (gen. sing. *seanaidh*) "a synod, a senate" would represent an unususal second element. Irish *io* was usually pronounced [ɛ] locally (*Irish of the Glens* 28) but a lowering of the first vowel of *sionnach* "fox" (gen. sing. *sionnaigh*) and anglicization as *-shanny* might be considered. It was anglicized differently in **Crockatinny** in Armoy (see Other Names). The surveyor noted in c. 1855 that the hill was "so called from it being the haunt of foxes" (*OSRNB* sh.3, 4), but this could represent a late reinterpretation; the absence of a medial definite article may militate against *sionnach*. This place-name seems to be only vaguely remembered locally.

Lannimore Hill	A hybrid form	
D 0443		

1. ˌlanjəˈmoːr	Local pronunciation	1996
2. ˌlaŋəˈmoːr	Local pronunciation	1996

This eminence straddles the townlands of Ballintoy Demesne, Lagavara and Cloghcorr (*OS 1:10,000*); the epithet *hill* does not appear to be used. *Loingeach Mhór* "big quaking bog/fen" (see Ó Dónaill sv. *loingeach*) may have formed the original name, with a lowering of the initial unstressed vowel to [a]. This word is the origin of the north-west Co. Donegal name *An Luinneach* (see Mac Giolla Easpaig 1986, 19). We would not have expected the vocalization of the [ŋ'] in unstressed position. The [ŋ'] seems to have been depalatalized in form 2. Alternatively, we could consider that a substantive form of the adjective *longach* "(of sod) quaking" (Ó Dónaill) was used (perhaps as a variant of *loingeach*) and attribute an apparent palatalization of the [ŋ] as anomalous (compare **Corrymeela** in Other Names, Culfeightrin). *Léana* "lowlying grassy place, water-meadow; greensward, lawn" (Ó Dónaill) has been noticed by Bradley (1986, 93) as *lanna* "hillside meadowland" in the English of south Armagh (see also *PNI* vi 297), but this element is not supported by modern pronunciations. It seems unlikely that *leamhnaigh* "place of elms" (cf. *PNI* v 101–2 sv. *Leamhnaigh*) would have given rise to the modern form while *lána* "a lane" seems to be rare in place-names.

Larry Bane Bay	*Port na Láithreach Báine*	
D 0545	"port of the white site"	

1. Portnalarabane	Hill's Stewarts 21	1625
2. Larry bane bay	OSRNB sh.4, 1	1855c
3. Larach ban/ba larach bhan "Bay of the white battle field or of the white wall stead"	OSRNB sh.4, 1	1855c
4. ˌlaribaːn ˈbeː	Local pronunciation	1995

The following was recorded of this name in c. 1855:

> a large bay extending from the headland called Doon to Carrickaraid Island . . . Larry is supposed to owe its origin to some combat or battle on the contiguous shore. Some however think that it signifies the bay of the white wallstead [which] is to be seen along it now. The cliffs which it washes and which bound it on [the] south side are white (*OSRNB* sh.4, 1).

Forms 1–2 appear to indicate that the fem. noun *láthair* (gen. sing. *láithreach*) "place, spot; site, location" (*Ó Dónaill*), which is attested as a component element in several place-names (*Joyce* iii 310), formed the first element here. The dative form *láithrigh* seems to have been latterly used in the nominative. Other elements such as *láir* (gen. sing. *lárach*) "mare" (cf. Ó Catháin & O'Flanagan 1975, 43 sv. *Iomaire na Láire Báine*; see also **Lemnagh Beg**), *leathráth* "half-fort" (see **Larry Bane Bay**) and the masc. noun *laithreach* "spot or venue . . . a site, ruins of a building, a battle-field; a sanctuary" (*Dinneen*) might be considered but seem considerably less likely.

Larry Bane Head
D 0545

1. (?)Sheepe Head	Sea Chart [1590c]	1590c
2. Doon, the headland called	OSRNB sh.4, 1	1855c
3. lárthach bán "the fair (white) site position"	Ó Dubhthaigh 183	1905
4. Laithreach bán "white site or ruins"	Rev. Magill 19	1923
5. Leath Rath Ban "Half White Fort"	Childe's Larry Bane 179	1936
6. ˌlaribaːnˈheːd	Local pronunciation	1995

"The neck of the promontory has been cut off by a rampart and fosse about 100ft from its extremity" (*Childe's Larry Bane* 179). The fort is described elsewhere as "a headland fort, defended by a rock-cut ditch and a stone rampart 15ft. thick, which has been considerably damaged by quarrying operations . . . the fort was occupied at some date between 700 and 900 AD" (*PSAMNI* 4). This was the motivation for the explanation in form 5. *An Láithrigh Bhán* "the white site" appears to be the original form of the Irish elements however, while the fort was known as *Dún* "promontory fort" (see *Ó Dónaill* sv.), latterly at least (see **Larry Bane Bay**). Form 1 echoes **Sheep Island** which lies off this headland.

Long Causeway
D 0244

1. ðə laŋ ˈkasi	Local pronunciation	1995

"A long range of rocks running from the low water line into the sea. Their sides are pretty regular and would appear in the distance to resemble an old pier . . . They are bare at low water and covered when the tide is in. Their length, which is about 350 links, and their regularity have given use to the name" (*OSRNB* sh.4, 1). This lies at the eastern end of White Park Bay.

| **Long Gilbert** | An English form(?) | |
| D 0245 | | |

| 1. lɔŋ ˈgïlbïrt | Local pronunciation | 1995 |

"A large rugged insulated rock, the surface of which appears indented with numerous crevices and chasms. The sea washes over some portions of it . . . There is no vegetation on it" (*OSRNB* sh.4, 1). It lies in the north-east of White Park Bay. The Ordnance Survey recorded another Long Gilbert in Ballymagarry in Billy parish. In this latter instance, it referred to "a cove or an indentation of the sea, with steep precipitous sides. It is said to have been called after a man named Gilbert who is traditionally reported to have sprung over it with his charger" (*OSRNB* sh.2, 1; this might suggest an origin in *Léim Ghilbeirt* "Gilbert's leap"). Gilbert is both a surname and a personal name (Black 1946, 298). *Toigh Ghilbeirt* "the house of Gilbert" in Kilpatrick, and *Cloch Ghilbeirt* "the stone of Gilbert" in Cleggan, are subtownland place-names in Rathlin (*Place-Names of Rathlin* 57; see also *PNI* ii 152 sv. **Ballygilbert**), and it might be considered that this name derives from *Long Ghilbeirt* "Gilbert's ship".

| **Lough-a-verrie** | *Loch an Bhioraigh(?)* | |
| D 0439 | "lake of the heifer" | |

1. (?)inis locha burann	AFM v 1486	1544
2. (?)Inis Locha Burrann	A. Conn. 736 §13	1544
3. (?)Lagandrey	HMR Ant. 4	1669
4. Loughavirry	OSRNB sh.8, 2	1855c
5. loch a biorrae "lake of the		
lagoon or of the marshy plain"	OSRNB sh.8, 2	1855c
6. ˌlɔxəˈvɛri	Local pronunciation	1995

Forms 1 and 2 relate to an expedition by Hugh O'Donnell into the Route. In 1847, Reeves equated forms 1–2 with this name (*EA* 286). O'Donovan, writing in 1856, also equated the lake in these forms with Lough-a-verrie and said it had dried up (*AFM* v 1487 n.d). The first two elements in early forms, *inis locha*, could be translated as "island/water-meadow of the lake". It is possible that the final element is a variant form of *boireann* (gen. sing. *boirne*, gen. pl. *boireann*) "a large rock; a stony district; a rocky hill" (*Dinneen*). It is also possible that the element was misspelt by the scribe.

It is difficult to reconcile forms 1–2 with the modern anglicized form, however, and they may in fact refer to some other unidentified place. Alternative origins of Lough-a-verrie may therefore be considered, including *Loch an Bhioraigh* "lake of the heifer" (see *Irish of the Glens* 101, sv. *biorach* "stirk", [bɛrɑx]) and *Loch an Bhiorraigh* "lake of the bulrushes or reeds/marsh or marshy field" (*Dinneen* sv. *biorrach*). *Biorra* "marshy or watery place" (see **Ballykenver** in Armoy) may also be a possible final element. The Ordnance Survey noted in c. 1855 that Lough-a-verrie referred to "an arable tract forming the extreme south point of the townland of Maghernahar. There are two dwellings in it in the occupation of two men named McConaghy. The name is a locality or subdenomination . . . called from a lough which formerly stood there. The lough is long since drained and [the] site cultivated . . ." (*OSRNB* sh.8, 2).

Low Carn D 0241	A hybrid form	
1. Carn	Religious Survey	1734
2. Carn	OSM xxiv 30	1838
3. loː ˈkɑrn	Local pronunciation	1995

See **High Carn**.

Magheralough D 0742	*Machaire an Locha* "field of the lake(?)"	
1. Maghry Lough	OSRNB sh.4, 1	1855c
2. lach maghaire "lough of the plain"	OSRNB sh.4, 1	1855c
3. ˌmaxərəˈlɔːx	Local pronunciation	1995

Machaire has several meanings (cf. **Magheraboy** townland). It refers to an area in the south of **Coolmaghra** (which may thus refer to the same feature). "A small lough was formerly all covered with water but is now a marsh - the water being drawn away by the gradual cutting away of the turf bank which enclosed it" (*OSRNB* sh.4, 1).

Mount Druid D 0344	An English form	
1. məunt ˈdruəd	Local pronunciation	1995

In 1830 this rectory was the residence of one Reverend Mr. Traill: "In the grounds of Mount Druid, Mr Traill's place in the townland of Magherabuy [*sic*], may be seen a druidical cromlech. The covering stone is 6 feet in length and 5 feet broad. It is supported on a number of large rocks" (*OSM* xxiv 12). In 1835, the Ordnance Survey recorded the following: "Mount Druid . . . is the only gentleman's seat in the parish . . . the house is very substantial, roomy and 3–storeys high . . ." (*ibid.* 15). A brief description of the megalithic chamber is given in *PSAMNI* 5.

New Town D 0336	An English form	
1. New Town	OSRNB sh.8, 2	1855c
2. nju ˈtəun	Local pronunciation	1995

"A small farm village [in Carnlelis] so called from its being of more recent erection than another village in [the] same townland called Old Town . . ." (*OSRNB* sh.8, 2).

Newbuildings
D 9943

An English form

1. new Buildings	PRONI D2977/3A/2/1/40	1812
2. Newbuildings	OSRNB sh.3, 2	1855c

"This is the name given to a locality in the town of Currysheskin. It embraces 5 or 6 scattered farmhouses ... It is an old name, i.e. it is not of recent application" (*OSRNB* sh.3, 2). There are townlands of this name in Antrim, Derry and Tyrone. *Newbuildings* appears as a place-name in Derrykeighan parish, barony of Dunluce Lower, in the *Hearth Money Rolls* of 1669 (Carleton 1991, 88), but it is difficult to ascertain its age in this instance.

Old Town,
Oldtown Bridge
D 0337, 0237

English forms

1. Old Town	OSRNB sh.8, 2	1855c
2. old 'tɔun	Local pronunciation	1995

"A small farm village [in Carnlelis] so named from being it is supposed the oldest village in the townland. It is often pronounced auldtun or altun - but this arises from the prevalence of Scotch idioms in the locality" (*OSRNB* sh.8, 2).
"A small bridge with 2 arches and low stone parapet and named from its proximity to a village called Old Town, on the east side of it" (*ibid.*).

Port More
D 0743

An Port Mór
"the big port"

1. port'moːr	Local pronunciation	1995

This lies along the coast of Coolmaghra. See **Portadoon** in Other Names, Culfeightrin, regarding the element *port*.

Portaneevey
D 0644

Port na nUamhadh(?)
"port of the caves"

1. Portaneevey	OSRNB sh.4, 1	1855c
2. ˌportən'iːvi	Local pronunciation	1995

"A small port [in Knocksoghey] where boats land in calm weather" (*OSRNB* sh.4, 1).
We may consider that the final element consists of a variant of *uaimh* "cave"; there are several caves along this part of the coast of Ballintoy (see *OSM* xxiv 14), including two to the immediate west of this port called The Doors (*Pers. comm.* 12.10.96). Holmer recorded several nom. sing. forms of *uaimh* in Rathlin: *uamh, uamha, uamhach, uamhaidh* (*Irish of Rathlin* 246). We could account for the [iː] in modern pronunciation as an anomalous result of the tendency in late local Irish to pronounce *u* as [ʌ] (*Irish of the Glens* 17; *Irish of Rathlin* 28). This word has only been recorded as a fem. noun, however, so we would be forced to suggest that it appeared in this place-name not as a masc. variant, but undeclined (cf.

Sroanderrig in Other Names, Rathlin). Alternatively, we could suggest instead that this element appears in one of the variant gen. pl. forms *uamhadh* (see *DIL* sv. *úam*) or *uamha* (*Dinneen*). Both final *-adh* and *-a* have been anglicized [i] elsewhere.

Fíobhach "a woody district" (*Dinneen* sv. *fiodhbhach*) and *fíobha* "a wood, a grove, a thicket" (*Dinneen* sv. *fiodhbhadh*) are both fem. nouns and are unlikely to have formed the final element. *Fíobhach* (gen. *fíobhaigh*) is also a masc. noun denoting "some kind of corn" (*ibid.*) but is also unlikely. Ó *Dónaill* lists a masc. variant of the generally fem. noun *iomhá(igh)* "image, statue" but this too would represent an unusual place-name element.

Portbraddan	*Port Bradán*	
D 0044	"port of the salmon"	
1. Portbraddan	OSRNB sh.3, 2	1855c
2. Port bradán	OSRNB sh.3, 2	1855c
3. Port-Bradan, or "Salmon Harbour"	Hamilton's Letters 248	1822
4. Port bradáin "port of the salmon"	Rev. Magill 22	1904
5. ˌportˈbradən	Local pronunciation	1995

"A few farmhouses . . . called from the contiguous port, in which a salmon fishery is situated" (*OSRNB* sh.3, 2). Portbraddan was one of three salmon fisheries in this parish in 1830, and was let for 60 guineas a year (*OSM* xxiv 12). It might be considered that *bráidín*, an unattested diminutive of *bráid* "sheltered land breasting a cliff or rock" (*Dinneen* sv. *braghaid*) formed the second element. Morton (1956–7, 41–2) suggests that *brághdán*, an otherwise unattested diminutive of *brágha* "neck, throat, gullet" appears in the Belfast tuogh name **Braden-Island**, and so this element may also be considered.

Rope Bridge	An English form
D 0644	

See **Carrickarade Island**.

Sheep Island	An English form (?)	
D 0445		
1. Eilean nan gCaorach	Irish of Rathlin 171	1942
2. Shipp Iland	Dartmouth Map 5	1590c
3. Ships Iland	Ulster Map	1590c
4. Lams Iland	Jobson's Ulster (TCD)	1590c
5. Sheape I	Hondius Map	1591
6. Sheap	Mercator's Ire.	1595
7. Shepe Iland	Treatise on Ire. (NLI) 11	1599c
8. Ship Isl	Bartlett Maps (Esch. Co. Maps) 1	1603
9. Lambs Iland	Speed's Ulster	1610
10. Lambs Iland	Speed's Antrim & Down	1610
11. Lambes Ile	Speed's Ireland	1610
12. Sheep Island	Civ. Surv. x §60	1655
13. Lambe's Isle	Hib. Del. Antrim	1672c

14. Sheep I.	Lendrick Map	1780
15. Sheepe Isld	Map Antrim	1807
16. Sheep Isle	Dubourdieu Map	1812
17. Sheep Island	Bnd. Sur. (OSNB) B 26	1827c
18. el'ɛn naŋ gEːrax	Irish of Rathlin 171	1942
19. ʃip 'ail(ənd)	Local pronunciation	1995

Ship and Sheep have been confused in several coastal place-names around Ireland (see Hughes 1988 *passim* and Ó Cearbhaill 1991–3 *passim*). The appearance of *lamb* in some forms here may favour the latter word as that originally used. Note also the form in use in Rathlin, which we may standardize as *Oileán na gCaorach* "island of the sheep" (forms 1 and 18). The island was described as follows in the 1830s:

> [it is] a third of a mile from the shore, being due north of the village of Ballintoy. It contains 3 acres 1 rood 24 perches and its extreme [height] above the sea is about 120 feet. It is a bluff, black basaltic rock, coated with light rich soil which produces good pasture for sheep. There are always a few kept on it . . . The tradition is that this island will fatten 10 sheep: 9 will die with fat and 11 will be starved to death on it (*OSM* xxiv 14).

Skehoge	*An Sceitheog*	
D 028372	"the small thorn bush"	
1. Skehoge	OSRNB sh.8, 2	1855c
2. Sceathóg "a hawthorn"	OSRNB sh.8, 2	1855c
3. 'skɛhoːg	Local pronunciation	1995

"A small farm village [in Carnlelis] close to the east bank of a small stream. Where the village now stands, there formerly stood a large hawthorn bush or tree. The tree disappeared or was destroyed by the villagers, but the village still retained the name . . ." (*OSRNB* sh.8, 2). Holmer recorded this word locally, which he spelt as *sciachóg*, as [sk'iag] (*Irish of the Glens* 25), but this name retains a somewhat older pronunciation. There are several variants of this diminutive in Mod. Ir. (see *Dinneen* sv. *sceachóg*; see also *PNI* iv 73 sv. **Skeiganeagh**). *Sceitheog* appears elsewhere in *Sceitheog an Iarla* "the earl's thorn bush", the standard Irish form of **Skegoneill** in Belfast (*GÉ* 155).

Straid	*An tSráid*	
D 0140	"the village"	
1. (?)Sraid	Court of Claims §923	1662c
2. (?)Stade, the quarter of	Decree of Innocence 431	1663
3. Straid	Shaw Mason's Par. Sur. 171	1803
4. Straid	Bnd. Sur. (OSNB) B 26	1827c
5. Straid	OSRNB sh.7, 1	1855c
6. Sráid "a street"	J O'D (OSNB) B 26	1827
7. 'straːd	Local pronunciation	1995

In c. 1855 it was recorded that Straid referred to "a farm village on either side of the main road from Bushmills to Ballycastle . . . The name also applies to a subdivision of the townland of Croaghmore" (*OSRNB* sh.7, 1). It is derived from *sráid*, probably meaning "village"; further meanings of this word include "a passage-way between houses, a farmyard, the space round a house" (*Dinneen*). Regarding the intrusive *t* in the anglicized place-name, see **Stroan** in Armoy.

Straidkillen
D 0139

Sráid Chillín(?)
"village of the small burial-ground"

1. Stradkillire	Hib. Reg. Cary	1657c
2. Straidkillin	DS (Par. Map) 51	1657c
3. Stradkillin	Census 13	1659
4. Stradkillin	BSD 175	1661
5. Sraidkillin	Court of Claims §923	1662c
6. Stradkillin	Lapsed Money Book 157	1663
7. Stradkillin	ASE 117a §19	1668
8. Streadkilling	HMR Ant. 4	1669
9. Stradkillin	Hib. Del. Antrim	1672c
10. Straidkillin, quarter land of	PRONI D2977/3A/2/1/6	1681
11. Straidkillin	Religious Survey	1734
12. Stradkillin, the quarter land of Straidkillen alias	PRONI D2977/3A/2/1/33A	1737
13. Straidkillen	Religious Census	1766
14. Straidkeller	PRONI D2977/3A/2/1/40	1812
15. Straidkeelan	O'Laverty iv 326	1887
16. Sráid cillín "village of the little church"	Rev. Magill 23	1923
16. ˌstraːdˈkilən	Local pronunciation	1995

Coillín "little wood", the male personal names *Cillín*, *Coilín* and *Caolán* (gen. sing. *Chaoláin*), and the female personal name *Caoileann* (gen. sing. *Chaoilinne*; the loss of its final vowel could be ascribed to its unstressed position) are all possible second elements of this place-name, which is in Croaghmore. A further possibility is that this element was *cillín* "a little church; a churchyard set apart for infants" (*Dinneen*) and that it referred to an "ancient graveyard called Killyharnagh, or Killyvig, which is now under tillage" (*O'Laverty* iv 326). Although these latter names noted by O'Laverty appear to contain *coillidh* "wood", *cill* developed to *cillidh* in other local subtownland names in the late dialect (cf. **Killaleenan** in Other Names, Culfeightrin).

See **Straid**, above, regarding the first element in this place-name.

Tornagrow
D 0441

Tuar na gCró(?)
"pasture of the huts"

1. ˌtoːrnəˈgroː	Local pronunciation	1995

This is in Lagavara. *Cró* has several meanings, including "enclosure; fold, pen; (small) outhouse; mean dwelling, hovel; hollow, hole" (*Ó Dónaill* sv.). In place-names it most often denotes "hut, fold, pen for cattle" (*Joyce* ii 225; see also *PNI* v 121 sv. **Drumcrow**). We may also consider that it represented the gen. pl. form of *cnó* "nut". The element *tor* (cf. **East Torr** in Culfeightrin) which appears to denote "steep rocky height" in local names seems topographically unsuitable in this case; the first element thus seems more likely to have been *tuar* "cattle-field; sheep-run; pasture, lea; bleaching green" (*Ó Dónaill* sv.). See also **Tornabodagh** in Culfeightrin.

| **Wallsteads** | An English form |
| D 0342 | |

This is in Craigalappan.

| **White Park Bay** | A hybrid form |
| D 0244 | |

1.	(?)White Bay	Norden's Map	1610
2.	White Park Bay	Lendrick Map	1780
3.	White Park Bay	Hamilton's Letters 8	1784
4.	White Park Bay	Dubourdieu Map	1812
5.	'hwəit park 'beː	Local pronunciation	1995

The place-name *White Head Bay* appears on *Speed's Ulster* map of 1610 (cf. **Kinbane or White Head** in Other Names, Ramoan), and form 1 may in fact be a corrupted form of this. See **White Park** townland.

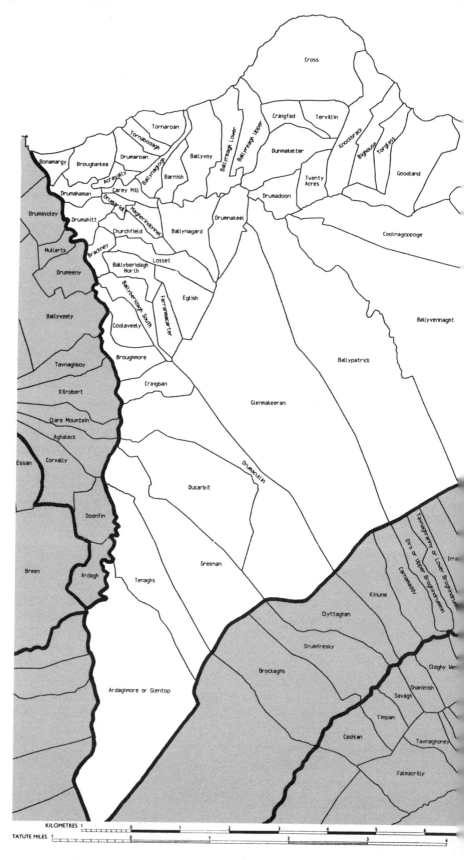

Cross

Tornaroan
Tornabodagh
Craigfad
Tervillin

Bonamargy
Broughanlea
Drumaroan
Ballyvoy
Ballyreagh Lower
Ballyreagh Upper
Dunmakelter
Knockbrack
Bighouse
Torglass

Acravally
Ballynagopp
Barnish
Twenty
Acres
Goodland

Drumahaman
Carey Mill
Drumartin
Magheri-hdonnel
Drumadoon

Drumavoley
Drumahitt
Churchfield
Ballynagard
Drumnakeel

Mullarts
Brackney
Losset
Coolnagoppoge

Drumeeny
Ballyberidagh
North

Ballyveely
Ballyberidagh South
Ferranacarter
Eglish
Ballyvennaght

Tavnaghboy
Coolaveely
Ballypatrick

Kilrobert
Broughmore

Clare Mountain
Craigban
Glenmakeeran

Aghaleck

Essan
Corvally
Drumacullin

Doonfin
Ducarbit

Tavnagrarmy or Lower Broghshane
Dry-a or Upper Broghshane
Irra

Breen
Ardagh
Greenan
Carnasobby

Tenaghs
Kinune

Clyttaghan

Drumfresky
Cloghy Wes

Brockaghs
Shaninish
Savagh

Ardaghmore or Glentop
Timpan
Tavnaghoney

Cashlan

Falmacrilly

Parish of Culfeightrin

Townlands
Acravally
Altagore
Ardaghmore or Glentop
Aughnaholle
Aughnasillagh
Ballindam
Ballinloughan
Ballyberidagh North
Ballyberidagh South
Ballycleagh
Ballynagard
Ballynaglogh
Ballypatrick
Ballyreagh Lower
Ballyreagh Upper
Ballyteerim
Ballyvennaght
Ballyvoy
Barmeen
Barnish
Bighouse
Bonamargy
Brackney
Broughanlea
Broughmore
Carey Mill
Castle Park
Churchfield
Coolaveely
Coolnagoppoge
Coolranny
Corrymellagh
Craigban
Craigfad
Cross
Curragh
Cushendun
Cushleake Mountain
    North

Cushleake Mountain
    Middle
Cushleake Mountain
    South
Drumacullin
Drumadoon
Drumahaman
Drumahitt
Drumaridly
Drumaroan
Drumnakeel
Duncarbit
Dunmakelter
East Torr
Eglish
Farranmacallan
Farranmacarter
Glenmakeeran
Goodland
Greenan
Knockbrack
Knockmacoulusky
Ligadaughtan
Losset
Loughan
Magherindonnell
Tenaghs
Tevillin
Torcorr
Torglass
Tornabodagh
Tornamoney
Tornaroan
Twenty Acres
West Torr
Whitehouse

Town
Cushendun

Based upon Ordnance Survey 1:50,000 mapping, with permission of the Director of the Ordnance Survey of Northern Ireland, Crown copyright preserved.

105

PARISH OF CULFEIGHTRIN

The coastal civil parish of Culfeightrin is the most north-easterly on the mainland. From its south-eastern-most point on the northern banks of the Glendun River in Cushendun, its boundary stretches westwards along a mountainous course marked by the peaks of Crockaneel, Oghtbristacree and Agangarrive Hill, to its most southerly point on the northern slopes of Slieveanorra or Orra More mountain. From here the boundary swings northwards following for the most part the route of the Glenshesk River to its mouth at Ballycastle Bay. The parish is bounded to the south-east by the parish of Layd, to the south by the parishes of Grange of Inispollan and Grange of Layd, all of which are in the barony of Glenarm Lower, to the south-west by the parishes of Loughguile (in the barony of Dunluce Upper) and Armoy, and to the west by the parish of Ramoan. The parish covers over 26,473 acres and contains 72 townlands (*OSM* xxiv 36).

Culfeightrin first appears in the sources in a biography of St. Patrick, which records that he founded a church here and left in charge of it a bishop called *Fiachra* (form 1). The original building apparently stood in the townland now called **Churchfield**. Colgan, who calls the bishop Fiachrius, locates his feast day on the 28th of September on the basis of the martyrologies (*Trias Thaum.* 182b). Note, for example: "*Fiachra, cáid in clerech*" ("Fiachra, chaste was the cleric") in the *Martyrology of Gorman* (*Mart. Gorm.* 186–7; cf. also *Mart. Tal.* 75 and *Mart. Don.* 237). In c. 1306, the parish was valued at £9 4s. 8d. (*Eccles. Tax. (Reeves)* 79), less than the neighbouring (and smaller) parish of Ramoan. This may have been due in part to the extent of moorland in the parish which in 1831 still covered approximately two-thirds of the territory (*OSM* xxiv 40). The following record dates to 1524: "Dominus Bernard O Heyle, cleric of Conor diocese, was presented by George, Abp. of Armagh to the Rectory of the parish church of St. Fechtany of Cowlofeghraine, diocese of Conor, vacant by the promotion of Magonius O Coyne" (*Reg. Cromer* ii §33; see also *EA* 79).

Until the early 1600s, most references to Cary, now the barony name, appear to have implicitly denoted an area roughly coextensive with the modern civil parish of Culfeightrin. They are discussed in the barony introduction. This tradition continues today as the name *Culfeightrin* is not used of the Catholic parish, which is known as ['kari], usually spelt *Carey*. The Catholic parish included the civil parishes of Grange of Inispollan and Grange of Layd until 1848, when these territories, along with parts of East and West Torr and those townlands in Culfeightrin east of Ballyvennaght were amalgamated to form the parish of Cushendun (*O'Laverty* iv 458, 532).

PARISH NAME

Culfeightrin	*Cúil Eachtrann* "corner of the foreigners"	
1. iCuil Ectrann, epscop Fíachrai	Trip. Life (Stokes) 162	900c
2. Cuil-Ectrann, Ecclesiam de	Trias Thaum. 146b	1647
3. Cuil-echtra	Trias Thaum. 182b	1647
4. vulgo Cuil-echtra dicta	Trias Thaum. 182b	1647
5. Kilfeutre	Eccles. Tax. 209	1306c
6. Cowlofeghraine, St. Fechtany of	Reg. Cromer ii §33	1524
7. Cullerton	Dartmouth Map 25	1590c
8. Culfetryn	Jas. I to Connor Cath. (EA) 263	1609

9. Culfetrin	Shaw Mason's Par. Sur. 516	1614
10. Kullfechtrene	Terrier (Reeves) 75	1615
11. Coolfeightron	Regal Visit. (Reeves) 121	1633
12. Culfaghtorin, Parish of	Hill's Stewarts 88	1652
13. C'ulfaghtrim parish	Hill's Stewarts 143	1652
14. Culfeightin R.	Inq. Par. Ant. 4	1657
15. Kilfaghtrim	Hib. Reg.	1657c
16. Culfatrim	DS (Par. Map) 56	1657c
17. Calfachterny	Census 17	1659
18. Kilfaghtrim	BSD 165	1661
19. Culfeightron	Trien. Visit. (Bramhall) 3	1661
20. Culphephtrie	Shaw Mason's Par. Sur. 517	1661
21. Culfieghtrim	Court of Claims §923	1662c
22. Culfreghtrin	Court of Claims §923	1662c
23. Culfortrin, the 20 acres	Court of Claims §923	1662c
24. Coolefeightrim	Ulster Visit. (Reeves) 65	1662
25. Culfeightrin, the twenty acres of	Decree of Innocence 431	1663
26. Culfeightron	Trien. Visit. (Margetson) 28	1664
27. Cullfeightrim	HMR (1666) 97	1666
28. Cullfaten	ASE 116a §19	1668
29. Culfactory	HMR Ant. 8	1669
30. Culfaghtrim	Shaw Mason's Par. Sur. 517	1681
31. Culfeightron	Shaw Mason's Par. Sur. 517	1681
32. Culfaghtrim	Lamb Maps Co. Antrim	1690c
33. (?)Culfeightrim	Religious Survey	1734
34. Culfaughtrin	PRONI D2977/3A/2/13/2	1742
35. Culfeightrin	PRONI D2977/3A/2/21/1	1742
36. Colfeightron	Ulster Visit. (Reeves) 60	1754
37. Collfaughtrean	PRONI D2977/3A/2/6/2	1771
38. Culfayton Ch.	Taylor and Skinner 272	1777
39. Colfeightern	Lendrick Map	1780
40. Culfatrim	PRONI D2977/3A/2/6/3	1792
41. Culfeightrin or Carey P.	Map Antrim	1807
42. Calfieghten	Dubourdieu Map	1812
43. Culfeightrin	Bnd. Sur. (OSNB) B 24 B 37	1830
44. Cuilfeighterin	Bnd. Sur. (OSNB) B 24 B 37	1830
45. Cúil Eachtrann "Corner or angle of the adventurers or foreigners"	J O'D (OSNB) B 24 B 37	1831
46. Cúl fá eachtrann, Cúl eachtrann, "bank or defense of the foreigners"	J O'D (OSNB) B 24 B 37	1831
47. Cúil Feachtrann "The recess of St. Feightrin"	Ó Dubhthaigh 136	1905
48. Cúil f-eachtrann "corner of the stranger"	Rev. Magill 13	1923
49. ˌkɔlˌfitrən	Local pronunciation	1993
50. ˌkɔlˌfitrəm	Local pronunciation	1993

Form 1 indicates that the first element is *cúil* meaning "corner or recess" (*DIL*) or "nook" (*Ó Dónaill*), and not *cúl* "back", often applied to sides of hills in place-names (*Joyce* i 200). O'Donovan's form (45) accurately reflects the earliest historical variant of the name, although forms since c. 1306 (form 5) feature a prosthetic *f* at the beginning of the second element, the gen. pl. *eachtrann* "foreigners, strangers" (see *Dinneen* sv., and *Ó Dónaill* sv. *eachtrannach*). Whether the *f* was included by back formation is uncertain. Examples of a prosthetic *f* prefixing words beginning with a vowel are to be found in all Irish dialects, but examples in place-names are somewhat rare. The Co. Mayo townland name of Cloonfeightrin in Kilturra parish (*Census 1851*) may be analogous here however, while the Co. Mayo parish name Kilfian deriving from *Cill Aodháin* represents a further example (Ó Muraíle 1985, 55–6). Other changes in this parish name include the loss of the medial *ch* sound in *eachtrann* (a feature somewhat typical of East Ulster Irish; see, for example, *Irish of the Glens* 24) and the lowering of the initial vowel sound of *cúil* in unstressed position.

In 1831, it was recorded that the parish was "known here as Carey [*sic*] Parish rather than Culfeightrin, which is unheard of by most lower order inhabitants" (*OSM* xxiv 36; see also *Lewis' Top. Dict.* 427), a phenomenon which which has an old historical basis (see barony introduction and parish introduction above). Carey Mill townland and Carey River (see Other Names) in this parish are also based on what has become the barony name.

TOWNLAND NAMES

Acravally   Of uncertain origin
D 1441

1.	Acruell	Hib. Reg. Cary	1657c
2.	Acrevell, Crosalista	DS (Par. Map) 55	1657c
3.	Crosallister, part of	DS (Par. Map) 56	1657c
4.	Acruell, Crossalister	Lapsed Money Book 155	1663
5.	Acrevell, Cossalister	ASE 116a §19	1668
6.	Acruell	Ant. Forfeit. 91	1700
7.	Achrulla	Religious Survey	1734
8.	Achrevilly	Stewart's Survey 6	1734
9.	Achraveelie	Hills' Stewarts 220	1741c
10.	Acrevally	Lendrick Map (OSNB) B 24 B 37	1780
11.	Ackravally	PRONI D2977/3A/2/1/40	1812
12.	Accrevelly	Bnd. Sur. (OSNB) B 24 B 37	1830
13.	Acrevally	Tithe Applot. 2	1833
14.	Acra bhile "acre of the old tree"	J O'D (OSNB) B 24 B 37	1831
15.	Acra bhile "acre of the old tree"	Rev. Magill 5	1923
16.	Acra bhile "field of the ancient pagan tree"	Dallat's Culfeightrin 34	1981
17.	ˌakra'vɛli	Local pronunciation	1993

Acra "acre" would indeed appear to be the first element in the name of this (31 acre (*Census 1851*)) townland. This element occurs elsewhere locally in a variant form in the subtownland name of *Glaic an (Dá) Acair* "the hollow of the (two) acre(s)" in Ballygill South in Rathlin (*Place-Names of Rathlin* 52). However, we could also consider that it appears here in a calcified plural dative form, *acraibh*.

The second element suggested by forms 14–16 is *bile* "(sacred) tree" (cf. **Toberbilly** in Ramoan). The lenition of the initial consonant of the second element could be ascribed to the regular use of the place-name in oblique cases. The historical variants generally imply a lower vowel than the [ï] associated with modern and historical forms of other local place-names which contain *bile* (such as Toberbilly). The final element in the south-west Co. Antrim townland name of *Éadan an Bhile* (anglicized **Edenvale**), has exhibited some fronting of the central vowel (*PNI* iv 150). In Antrim Irish, [ï] sometimes developed to [i] (see **Drumnakeel**), but in the absence of similar forms, form 9 must be regarded as anomalous. Forms 1–2, and 4–6, which do not feature a vowel following the final *l*, and some of which feature a *u* for a *v*, come from related sources and indicate copies of misspellings. The absence of the final vowel in early forms could also be due to its unstressed position. This would suggest that the final element ended with the central [ə] vowel: Irish *-e* or *-a*. Further possible final elements may include *baile* "townland" (*baile* is rare in final position; see **Drumbally Hill** in *PNI* vi 136; compare also forms of **Aughnasillagh**), *báille* "bailiff", and perhaps the surname *Mailleach*, "a sept of the Scottish clan MacGregor [angl. Mallagh], found in north-east Ulster" (MacLysaght 1985, 206) and *bealach* "road, track". The historical evidence is conflicting, however; there is a possibility that the name was latterly reinterpreted.

On the *Down Survey* parish map (*DS (Par. Map)*), Acravally was divided into *Acrevell* and *Crosalista*. The latter form, which recurs in forms 3, 4(b) and 5(b), may be based on *Cros Alastair* "Alastar's cross(-road?)". *Alastar* is a borrowing of the Greek name Alexander brought into Ireland from Scotland, being popular with Scoto-Irish families including the MacDonnells and MacDowells (Ó Corráin & Maguire 1981, 21–2).

Altagore　　　　　　　　　　　　　*Allt an Ghabhair*
D 2435　　　　　　　　　　　　　　　"steep glen/stream of the goat"

1. Altagoar	C. McG. (OSNB)B 24 B 37	1734
2. Altagoar	Stewart's Survey 11	1734
3. Altagore	Culfeightrin Map [1789] 1	1789
4. Altagore	Culfeightrin Map [1812]	1812
5. Altagore	Bnd. Sur. (OSNB) B 24 B 37	1830
6. Alt a' ghobhair "high cliff or glenside of the goat"	J O'D (OSNB) B 24 B 37	1831
7. Alt gabhair "height of the goat"	Rev. Magill 5	1904
8. Alt an ghabhair "the glenside of the goat"	Ó Dubhthaigh 131	1923
9. Alt gabhair "The height or cliff of the goats"	Dallat's Culfeightrin 34	1981
10. ˌaltəˈɡoːər	Local pronunciation	1993

Alt "a hillock" (*Ó Dónaill*) and *allt* "steep-sided glen; ravine" (*ibid.* sv. *ailt*) both reflect the first element. The topography of this coastal townland, which is located on the stiff eastward falling slopes of Cushleake Mountain South, however, renders the former of these elements unlikely. *Allt* has been adopted as the standardized form of *ailt* in place-names (*PNI* iii 125). *Dinneen* has this word as *ált* "a ravine, a gully; a deep precipitous narrow glen". *Allt* meaning "brook, stream" is common in Scottish Gaelic (Ó Baoill 1978, 74) and this meaning was locally recorded by Holmer (*Irish of the Glens* 99; cf. also **Altmore Burn** in Other Names, Armoy), while we may also note *Dinneen* (sv. *allt*): "cliff, side of glen; brook (chiefly in Scotland); a wooded glen". *Allt* in this instance could refer to a tributary of Tornamoney Burn which has cut a deep and narrow valley through this townland.

The final element is probably the gen. sing. of *gabhar* "goat". Holmer recorded *gabhar* locally as [goər], which reflects the historical forms well (*Irish of the Glens* 115). *Dinneen* lists the further meanings "scad or rock-herring; a horse (early); a bundle; misappropriated goods", but none of these seem likely. *Gabhar* occurs as a place-name element elsewhere in the subtownland name *Carn Gabhair* "(the) goat's cairn" (anglicized **Cairngaver**) in Co. Down (*PNI* ii 237), and the Co. Galway townland name Carrownagower, from *Ceathrú na nGabhar* "quarter-land of the goats" (*Joyce* iii 190; see also Ó Maolfabhail 1990, 226 sv. *Oileán an Ghabhair*). For various reasons, the Anglo-Norman surname Gower (see Spencer 1945, 159) and the English surname Gore (see MacLysaght 1985, 132) are unlikely elements here.

Ardaghmore or Glentop	*Ardach Mór*	
D 1530	"high field, big"	
1. Ardynoy als Ardaghis	DS (Par. Map) 53	1657c
2. Ardimoy	DS (Par. Map) 57	1657c
3. Ardaghmore	Stewart's Survey 4	1734
4. Ardaghmore	Sur. A.E. 80	1782
5. Ardaghmore, the quarterland of	PRONI D2977/3A/2/1/39	1783
6. Ardaghmore or Glentop	Bnd. Sur. (OSNB) B 24 B 37	1830
7. Ardaghmore	Tithe Applot. 1	1833
8. Ardachadh Mór "big highfield"	J O'D (OSNB) B 24 B 37	1831
9. Ard acadh mór "The great high field"	Dallat's Culfeightrin 34	1981
10. ˌardəx'moːr	Local pronunciation	1993

It seems more likely that the adjectival prefix *ard* "high" (*Ó Dónaill* sv.) rather than the noun *ard* "a height, a hill; the top; high ground" (*Dinneen* sv. *árd*; in a noun plus noun compound) formed the first element. Either would be topographically suitable; this territory lies on high mountainous ground in the south of the parish. *Ard* is followed here by *achadh* "field", a common townland-name element. As in other local place-names containing this element, the second and unstressed syllable was elided. The epithet *mór* "large, big" was probably originally used to differentiate it from the smaller townland of **Ardagh**, north-west of here and in Ramoan.

As a place-name form, *ardachadh* has been shortened elsewhere, due to the elision of the final unstressed syllable. The Co. Limerick parish name of Ardagh, although originally *Ardachadh*, latterly became *Ardach* (Ó Maolfabhail 1990, 3). *Ardach* was translated "high field" in this case. Both forms occur in townland names in Co. Louth: *Ardach* has been anglicized Ardagh, while *Ardachadh* has been anglicized Ardaghy (*L. Log. Lú* 27). *Glentop* is a late English appellation for this townland and does not appear to be widely used. It refers to the position of this townland at the top of **Glenshesk** (see Other Names, Ramoan), and was possibly translated from Irish *Barr an Ghleanna* "top of the valley" (see **Ballyberidagh North**).

Aughnaholle
D 2439

Achadh na hOlla
"field of the wool"

1. Aghenholly	Census 17	1659
2. Aughenholl	Culfeightrin Map [1789] 1	1789
3. Aughnaholl	Culfeightrin Map [1812]	1812
4. Aughnaholle	Bnd. Sur. (OSNB) B 24 B 37	1830
5. Aughnaholl	Tithe Applot. 18	1833
6. Achadh na holna "field of the wool"	J O'D (OSNB) B 24 B 37	1831
7. Achadh na holna "The field of the wool"	Ó Dubhthaigh 131	1905
8. Acadh na h-olna "The field of the fleeces"	Dallat's Culfeightrin 34	1981
9. ˌɔxnəˈhɔl	Local pronunciation	1993

The second syllable of the first element *achadh* "field", perhaps discernible in form 1, was elided in later forms. The final element appears indeed to be the fem. gen. sing. of *olann* "wool" (forms 6–8), although *olla* rather than the older variant *olna* is the gen. sing. form suggested by the limited historical variants available. The loss of a final unstressed vowel in local names has been noted elsewhere (cf., for example, **Craigfad**).

Aughnasillagh
D 2537

Achadh na Saileach
"field of the willows"

1. Ardymony, Quarter of Ballytirim called	DS (Par. Map) 55	1657c
2. Ardimony	DS (Par. Map) 56	1657c
3. Achishelag	Census 17	1659
4. Aghensillagh	HMR Ant. 9	1669
5. Aughnasellough	Culfeightrin Map [1789] 1	1789
6. Aughnasillagh	Culfeightrin Map [1812]	1812
7. Aughnasillagh	Bnd. Sur. (OSNB) B 24 B 37	1830
8. Aughnasillagh	Tithe Applot. 17	1833
9. Achadh na saileach "field of the sallows"	J O'D (OSNB) B 24 B 37	1831
10. Achadh na saileach "the field of the sallows"	Ó Dubhthaigh 131	1905
11. Achadh na saileach "field of the sallows"	Rev. Magill 5	1923
12. Achadh na saileach "The field of the willows"	Dallat's Culfeightrin 34	1981
13. ˌɔxnəˈsɛlə	Local pronunciation	1993

The later forms suggest the final element was the gen. sing. or gen. pl. (being identical) of *sail* "willow(-tree), sallow", *saileach*. The gen. pl. form has been adopted in other place-names (cf. *Mullán Saileach* "summit of the willows", angl. **Mullinsallagh**, in *PNI* iv 254). Along with the townlands of Corrymellagh, Knockmacolusky and Ligadaughtan, Aughnasillagh was but a constituent part of a territory called *Ardymony* (form 1; Carleton 1991, 67). Ardymony was itself a quarterland of **Ballyteerim** (*DS (Par. Map)* 55). The modern pronunciation features no semblance of the final *ch* of *saileach*, as one might expect in late East Ulster Irish (see *Irish of the Glens* 24).

Ballindam	*Baile an Daim*	
D 2434	"townland of the dam"	
1. Ballindam	Culfeightrin Map [1812]	1812
2. Ballindam	Bnd. Sur. (OSNB) B 24 B 37	1830
3. Baile an daimh "town of the ox"	J O'D (OSNB) B 24 B 37	1831
4. Baile 'n dáimh "The town of the plague"	Ó Dubhthaigh 131	1905
5. Baile na dtám "town of the plagues"	Rev. Magill 6	1923
6. Baile an dtam "The townland of the plague"	Dallat's Culfeightrin 34	1981
7. ˌbɑlənˈdam	Local pronunciation	1993

The first element, *baile* "townland" appears in 13 townland names in this parish (see also **Balleny**, Armoy).

Forms 3–6 suggest that the modern name features a delenited final *m*. An intervocalic *mh* appears as *m* in anglicized forms of several place-names in northern counties (see **Kinramer North** in Rathlin), but the anglicization of a final palatal *mh* such as in the gen. sing. of *damh* (*daimh*) "ox; stag" (*Ó Dónaill*) seems unlikely. Forms 4–6 are unacceptable for several reasons. The historical variants available do not reflect the gen. sing. (*táimhe*) or the gen. pl. (*támh*) of the fem. noun *támh* "plague, pestilence; swoon, trance, stupor; rest, silence; lethargy, apathy; idleness" (*Ó Dónaill*). The Ordnance Survey, which had access to local Irish speakers, neither recorded any tradition related to such a supposed name, nor suggested such a derivation. In 1905, however, Ó Dubhthaigh claimed that there was "a local tradition of a plague here" (*Ó Dubhthaigh* 131).

It is possible that this element was inspired by the partial damming of the townland's most salient physical feature, Milltown Burn. The *Ordnance Survey Memoirs* recorded the existence of a corn mill, one of three in the parish, at **Milltown** (see Other Names) near the mouth of the river (*OSM* xxiv 45). A small dam or weir to shunt water for the mill could have lent itself to the form *Baile an Daim* "townland of the dam". *Dinneen* also translates *dam* as "a pool". The use of lint-holes and flax-retting dams in the area might also have inspired such a form. We may note in this context "a subdivision of the townland Moss-side" in the parish of Grange of Drumtullagh called **Drumadam**, "said to be so named from a mill-dam at its south end" (*OSRNB* sh.7, 2).

Ballinloughan	*Baile an Locháin*	
D 2439	"townland of the pond"	
1. 2 Loghans	Inq. Ult. (Antrim) §49 Car. I	1635

2. Rumekaddam	Hib. Reg. Cary	1657c
3. Rumckaddum	DS (Par. Map) 55	1657c
4. Ru McAdom	Census 18	1659
5. the two Loghanes	Court of Claims §923	1662c
6. 2 Loghans, the 40 acres of the	Court of Claims §923	1662c
7. two Loghans, the forty acres of the	Decree of Innocence 431	1663
8. two Loghanes, the forty acres of the	Decree of Innocence 440	1663
9. Ramacadine, Ten acres of	Lapsed Money Book 156	1663
10. (?)Ballyloghan	HMR Ant. 9	1669
11. Ballinloughan	C. McG. (OSNB)B 24 B 37	1734
12. Ballyloughan	Stewart's Survey 9	1734
13. Bellenloughan	Stewart's Survey 11	1734
14. Ballyloughan	Culfeightrin Map [1789] 1	1789
15. Ballyloughan	Culfeightrin Map	1812
16. Ballynaloghan	PRONI D2977/3A/2/1/40	1812
17. Ballinloughan	Bnd. Sur. (OSNB) B 24 B 37	1830
18. Baile an locháin "town of the small pool or lough"	J O'D (OSNB) B 24 B 37	1831
19. Baile an lócháin "townland of the chaff"	Dallat's Culfeightrin 34	1981
20. ˌbaliˈlɔːkən	Local pronunciation	1993

There appear to be two valid interpretations of the name of this coastal townland, depending on the final element. The uncertainty is whether the *loughan* element represents *lochán* "small lake or pond" (form 18) or *lóchán* "chaff; light over dried or withered grass, etc; broken seaweed" (*Dinneen*; form 19). *Lóchán* is a rare place-name element but not unknown. It recurs in the townland name of *Droim Lócháin* ("ridge of the chaff"), anglicized Dromlohan, in Co. Limerick (Ó Maolfabhail 1990, 163), and in the variant form *luachán* in the Donegal townland name of *Doire Luacháin*, anglicized Derryloaghan (O'Kane 1970, 79). There does not appear to be any pond in the modern townland, although such a feature may have been long since drained. The form *Baile an Locháin* is a common place-name variously anglicized Ballinloughan, Ballyloughan and Ballyloughaun (*Joyce* i 442). The first vowel in the final element is long (form 20) but it is also long in the local English dialect word *lough* ([lɔːx]). Form 1 seems to refer to the two modern townlands of Ballinloughan and **Loughan** (today .5 km apart), and implies that the relevant elements were interpreted as being identical. Form 10 may in fact be referring to Loughan. The medial [ən] found in the historical forms has recently been lost (form 20).

Ruemacadam (forms 2–4, 9) was denoted as part of Ballinloughan in the *Down Survey* parish map (*DS (Par. Map)*) of c. 1657 (Carleton 1991, 67 n.16). These forms appear to be based on *Rubha Meic Adaim* (standard Mod. Ir. *Rubha Mhic Adaim*) "MacAdam's headland". There are two noteworthy headlands in the townland: **Leckpatrick** and **Crockan Point** (see Other Names), and Ruemacadam may have originally referred to one of these. *Mac Adaim* "'son of Adam', from the unaspirated form of the name" (Black 1946, 449), is probably of Scottish origin in this instance (see MacLysaght 1985, 1 and Woulfe 1923, 304–5). Regarding other meanings of *rubha*, see **Roonivoolin** in Rathlin.

Ballyberidagh North, *Baile Bhairéadach*(?)
Ballyberidagh South "townland of the black guillemots"
D 1439, 1438

1. Bonaghlen	Hib. Reg. Cary	1657c
2. Boneaglen	DS (Par. Map) 55	1657c
3. Bonnaglen	DS (Par. Map) 56	1657c
4. Ballyverie	Census 18	1659
5. (?)Ballerdagh, ye towne of	Decree of Innocence 431	1663
6. Ballyvardy	HMR Ant. 10	1669
7. Ballyveradagh	C. McG. (OSNB)B 24 B 37	1734
8. Ballyvardy	Religious Survey	1734
9. Ballyveredagh	Stewart's Survey 2	1734
10. Ballyveradagh	Stewart's Survey 5	1734
11. Ballyvardogh	Lendrick Map (OSNB) B 24 B 37	1780
12. Ballyveredith	Sur. A.E. 54	1782
13. Ballyveradagh	PRONI D2977/3A/2/6/3	1792
14. Ballyvarady	PRONI D2977/3A/2/1/40	1812
15. Ballyberidagh	Bnd. Sur. (OSNB) B 24 B 37	1830
16. Ballyvardagh, Ballyvardagh North	Tithe Applot. 2, 4	1833
17. Ballyverdough	OSM xxiv 53	1838
18. Ballyverdough Nat. Sch.	OSRNB sh.9, 2	1838
19. Baile 'n bheirtigh "The town of the looms"	Ó Dubhthaigh 133	1905
20. Baile bheartha "town of the shearing (harvest)"	Rev. Magill 5	1923
21. Baile biorraidheach "town land of the osiers or saplings"	Dallat's Culfeightrin 34	1981
22. ˌbɑliˈvɛrdɔx	Local pronunciation	1993

Forms 19–21 are unacceptable in that they cannot be reconciled either to modern pronunciation or to forms gleaned from the sources. The forms appear to indicate that the second element was the gen. pl. of *bairéadach* "black guillemot" (Ballyberidagh North is c. 3 km from the sea), notwithstanding that some seem to suggest a gen. form of *bárdach* "warden". The lenition of the second *b* may be the result of the action of the dative case. Other species of birds are well represented in place-names (cf. *Joyce* ii 296–303) but the use of *bairéadach* with *baile* is somewhat unusual. The townland appears to have been divided only at the time of the Ordnance Survey.

Forms 1–3 probably derive from *Bun an Ghleanna* "end of the valley", referring to **Glenshesk** (see Other Names, Ramoan; see also **Ardaghmore or Glentop**). The *Down Survey* parish map of c. 1657 depicts this territory as comprising North and South Ballyberidagh, Farranmacarter and Brackney (Carleton 1991, 65).

Ballycleagh *Baile Cloicheach*(?)
D 2534 "stony townland"

1. Balleclogh	Inq. Ult. (Antrim) §62 Car. I	1635

2. Balliclogh	Inq. Ult. (Antrim) §119 Car. I	1637
3. Ballicloughagh	DS (Par. Map) 55	1657c
4. Ballicloghagh	DS (Par. Map) 56	1657c
5. Ballelagh	Census 17	1659
6. Ballicloghagh	BSD 166	1661
7. Ballycloghagh	Lapsed Money Book 156	1663
8. Ballycloughach	ASE 116a §19	1668
9. Ballyclogh	HMR Ant. 9	1669
10. Ballyecloghagh	Ant. Forfeit.	1700
11. Sth Ballycleagh, Nth Ballycleagh	Culfeightrin Map [1789] 1	1789
12. Ballycleogh	Culfeightrin Map [1812]	1812
13. Ballycleagh	Bnd. Sur. (OSNB) B 24 B 37	1830
14. Ballycliogh	Tithe Applot. 21	1833
15. Baile cliath "town of the hurdles"	J O'D (OSNB) B 24 B 37	1831
16. Baile Cladhach "Miry town"	Rev. Magill 6	1923
17. Baile claidhe "townland of the mound or rampart"	Dallat's Culfeightrin 34	1981
18. ˌbɑliˈkliː	Local pronunciation	1993

The etymology of this name is complicated somewhat by historical forms offering conflicting evidence. *Baile Cloicheach* "stony townland" is a possible origin, however. *Cloicheach* is an unattested variant of the adj. *clochach* "stony" which would account for the medial -*gh*- in some early forms and later development of the second [i] vowel. We could account for its omission in early forms as indicating haplology. *Baile Cloiche* represents a further possible original form. As forms 3–4, 6–8 and 10 are related, the medial -*gh*- could represent an anomalous spelling (cf. **Tureagh** in Armoy). It should not worry us that there is no evidence of the gen. sing. of *cloch* "stone; rocky shore; (stone) castle" in early forms: compare the townland names **Kilcroagh** in Armoy and **Kilcreg** in Ramoan. The development to [kliː] of the final element is not unlikely; we may note, for example, that Wagner (1959, 188) recorded a dative form of *cloch* (*c(h)loich*) in south Co. Donegal as [xləi]. Ballycleagh is separated from the sea by the tiny and relatively new townland of **Castle Park**; the stone tower-house in this latter townland could be the *cloch* of *Baile Cloiche* (see also **Cloghanmurry** in Ramoan and **Monanclogh** in Armoy).

We might consider that the final element was originally *claidheach*, a variant of *cladhach* "ridged, furrowed" (*Ó Dónaill, Dinneen*; see also O'Kane 1970, 119 and Hughes 1986, 92) and that the medial -*dh*- was still sounded as a guttural fricative in the 17th century and so anglicized as -*gh*-; this sound is reflected in some variants of **Tornaroan** (cf. also *Fiodhóg*/**Feehoge** in *PNI* iv 45–6). However, we would not expect the first vowel in *claidheach* to have been rendered *o* in early forms, even accounting for mistranscriptions of *a*. For similar reasons, *cliathach* "fenced" and *claíocha* "dikes, walls, fences" represent unlikely final elements.

Ballynagard
D 1540

Baile na gCeard
"townland of the artificers"

1. Ballynegard	Hib. Reg. Cary	1657c
2. Ballinegard	DS (Par. Map) 56	1657c

3. Ballynecarde	BSD 165	1661
4. Ballinegard other quarter	BSD 166	1661
5. Ballynagard called Drumnekelly	Lapsed Money Book 155	1663
6. Ballynagare other Qur.	Lapsed Money Book 156	1663
7. Ballynegard	ASE 116a §19	1668
8. Ballynagardy	HMR Ant. 10	1669
9. B:negard	Hib. Del. Antrim	1672c
10. Ballynecarde	Irish Jacobites 56 §38v	1699
11. Ballynegard	Ant. Forfeit.	1700
12. Ballengard, one quarter of	PRONI D2977/3A/2/1/21	1709
13. Ballynagard	C. McG. (OSNB) B 24 B 37	1734
14. Ballygard	Religious Survey	1734
15. Ballynegard	Stewart's Survey 6	1734
16. Ballynagard, the Quarterland of	PRONI D2977/3A/2/6/1	1739
17. Ballynaguard	PRONI D2977/3A/2/21/2,3	1746
18. Ballynaguard	PRONI D2977/3A/2/13/3	1746
19. Ballnagard	Merchant's Book 26	1752
20. Ballynagard	PRONI D2977/3A/2/6/2	1771
21. Ballynagard	Lendrick Map (OSNB) B 24 B 37	1780
22. Ballynagard	Sur. A.E. 60	1782
23. Ballinaguard	PRONI D2977/3A/2/6/3	1792
24. Ballinagard	Bnd. Sur. (OSNB) B 24 B 37	1830
25. Ballynagard	OSNB B 24 B 37	1831
26. Baile na gceard "town of the artificers"	J O'D (OSNB) B 24 B 37	1831
28. Baile na g-ceard "The town of the artificers"	Ó Dubhthaigh 132	1905
27. Baile na gceard "town of the mechanic"	Rev. Magill 6	1923
29. Baile na gceard "Townland of the workmen or masons"	Dallat's Culfeightrin 34	1981
30. ˌbɑlənəˈgjɑrd	Local pronunciation	1993

The forms of this townland name vary very little in the sources, and all point to the interpretations in forms 26–29 as being correct. The word *ceard* has the connotation "tinker" in both Irish (*Dinneen*) and in Scottish Gaelic (*Dieckhoff*, *Dwelly*) and such a meaning was noted by Holmer in Rathlin Island (where it also meant "a garrulous woman"), along with the townland name *Baile na gCeard* (*Irish of Rathlin* 173). *Ceard* appears in other townland names including *Cúl na gCeard* (anglicized **Coolnagard**) "hill back of the artificers" (*Joyce* iii 246) in Co. Tyrone, and *Baile na gCeard* (anglicized Ballynagarde) "the town of the craftsmen" in Co. Limerick (Ó Maolfabhail 1990, 41). Form 8 seems to contain the variant plural form *ceardaithe*, which appears in the Ards townland name *Tulaigh na gCeardaithe*, anglicized **Tullynagardy** (*PNI* ii 236).

Ballynaglogh
D 1540

Baile na gCloch
"townland of the stones"

1. Balleghlogh	Hib. Reg. Cary	1657c

2. Balleghlogh	DS (Par. Map) 50	1657c
3. Ballyneglogh	HMR Ant. 8	1669
4. Ballyeghlogh	Ant. Forfeit.	1700
5. Ballynaglogh	Religious Survey	1734
6. Ballyneglogh	Stewart's Survey 6	1734
7. Ballynaglogh	PRONI D2977/3A/2/28/5	1746
8. Ballynaglogh	Lendrick Map (OSNB) B 24 B 37	1780
9. Ballynaglough	Bnd. Sur. (OSNB) B 24 B 37	1830
10. Baile na gcloch "town of the stones"	J O'D (OSNB) B 24 B 37	1831
11. Baile na gcloch "Townland of the stone"	Dallat's Culfeightrin 34	1981
12. ˌbɑlənə'glɔx	Local pronunciation	1993

The earliest available forms of this name variously retain and omit a medial *n*. Those without it are likely to represent scribal errors or copies of scribal errors.

In 1838, the Ordnance Survey recorded that there were two standing stones in the churchyard of the Church of Ireland parish church in this townland:

> In the church yard also lie several stones of large size, probably left there by nature . . .
> the quantity of standing stones here and in its immediate vicinity at a former period gave
> the townland its present name . . . One of these remarkable columns, which stood con-
> tiguous to those above mentioned, was taken to Ballycastle harbour above 80 years back
> and being of such weight that it took 8 horses to convey it on a slide to the aforesaid har-
> bour (*OSM* xxiv 55).

Ballypatrick
D 1836

Baile Pádraig
"Patrick's townland"

1. Ballypatrick	Hib. Reg. Cary	1657c
2. Magherelogh	Census 18	1659
3. qtr. of Ballypatrick called Dromine, other qtr. called Magheriloghy	BSD 166	1661
4. Ballepatricke	Court of Claims §923	1662c
5. Ballypatrick called Brumeine, 1 Qur.; other Qur. called Maghercloughy	Lapsed Money Book 155	1663
6. part of Ballypatrick called Dromine, other qtr. called Maheriloghy	ASE 116a §19	1668
7. Ballypatricke	HMR Ant. 10	1669
8. Maghernloghy, B.patrick	Hib. Del. Antrim	1672c
9. Ballypatrick	Ant. Forfeit.	1700
10. Ballypatrick	C. McG. (OSNB) B 24 B 37	1734
11. Ballypatrick	Stewart's Survey 7	1734
12. Ballypatrick	PRONI D2977/3A/2/1/33A	1737

13. Ballypatrick, half town of	PRONI D2977/3A/2/1/36A	1738
14. Ballypatrick	PRONI D2977/3A/2/1/33A	1742
15. Ballypatrick	Lendrick Map (OSNB) B 24 B 37	1780
16. Ballypatrick	Sur. A.E. 42	1782
17. Ballypatrick	Report of the A.E.	1812
18. Ballypatrick	Grants on the A.E.	1814
19. Ballypatrick	Bnd. Sur. (OSNB) B 24 B 37	1830
20. Baile Phádraig "Patricks town"	J O'D (OSNB) B 24 B 37	1831
21. Baile Phádraig "St. Patricks townland"	Dallat's Culfeightrin 34	1981
22. ˌbɑliˈpatrək	Local pronunciation	1993

Hill describes Ballypatrick as "an old residence of the McDonnells in the parish of Culfeightrin" (*MacDonnells Antrim* 115). Perhaps it was named after some otherwise unattested family figure. "Patrick came into use among the [Anglo-Norman] colonists in Ireland before it became common among the native Irish" (Ó Corráin & Maguire 1981, 154) and it is possible that *Pádraig* was not widely used as a personal name until the late 1600s (*ibid.*). None of the historical variants exhibit lenition of the *p*, and this grammatical feature will be retained here (as in *Dún Pádraig* (anglicized **Downpatrick**; *GÉ* 100)). Examples of saints' names in a *baile-* structure are very rare (*PNI* iv 10), and no tradition associating the national saint with this townland appears to have been recorded. Other places in the parish have been associated with him however, including perhaps a burial ground for unbaptized infants called *Cillidh Phádraig* in the townland to the immediate north of here (*EA* 283 sv. Killyphadrick; *OSM* xxiv 51; see **Killaleenan** in Other Names regarding this Irish form; see also **Leckpatrick** in Other Names, and **Ballykenver** in Armoy).

Magheralogh (form 2), possibly *Machaire an Locha* "plain of the lake", is revealed to have been a subdivisional quarterland in forms 3 and 4, along with *Dromine*, perhaps *Droimín/Droim Mín* "small/smooth ridge" or *Dromainn* "ridge, mound". Both of these latter names have fallen out of use.

Ballyreagh Lower, Ballyreagh Upper D 1641, 1642

An Baile Riabhach "the dun/grey townland"

1. Ballyreagh	Inq. Ult. (Antrim) §7 Jac. I	1621
2. Ballyreagh	Census 18	1660
3. Ballyreagh	BSD 165	1661
4. Ballereagh	Court of Claims §923	1662c
5. Ballereogh, the town of	Court of Claims §923	1662c
6. Ballyreagh	Lapsed Money Book 155	1663
7. Ballyreagh	ASE 116a §19	1668
8. Ballyreagh	Forfeit. Estates 360b §27	1668
9. Ballyreagh	HMR Ant. 8	1669
10. Ballyrea	Hib. Del. Antrim	1672c
11. Ballreagh	PRONI D2977/3A/2/9/1	1696
12. Ballyreagh	Ant. Forfeit.	1700
13. Ballyreagh	C. McG. (OSNB) B 24 B 37	1734

14. Ballyreaghs	Religious Survey	1734
15. Ballyreagh	Stewart's Survey 7	1734
16. Ballyreagh	Sur. A.E. 42	1782
17. Ballyreagh	PRONI D2977/3A/2/6/3	1792
18. Ballyreagh	Lendrick Map (OSNB)	1780
19. Ballyreagh	Bnd. Sur. (OSNB) B 24 B 37	1830
20. Ballyreags	OSNB B 24 B 37	1831
21. Baile riach "grey town"	J O'D (OSNB) B 24 B 37	1831
22. Baile riabhach "grey townland"	Dallat's Culfeightrin 34	1981
23. ˌbɑliˈriəx	Local pronunciation	1993

In 1831, a local informant stated that *Ballyreags* was the prevalent form used (form 20); the earliest indication of the division between Upper and Lower Ballyreagh appears in 1734 (form 14).

Holmer recorded *riabhach* as [riʌx] (*Irish of the Glens* 125); the medial *bh* had been lost resulting in one syllable. While one might expect some indication of the *bh* in earliest variants, historical forms of the Ards townland name *An Cheathrú Riabhach* (anglicized **Carryreagh**) dating to 1605 do not denote any trace of an internal bilabial fricative (*PNI* ii 189). Variants of the south-east Co. Antrim townland name *An Mhachaire Riabhach* (anglicized **Magherareagh**) suggest that this sound was lost there early in the 17th century (*PNI* iv 54). *Riabhach* may variously denote "streaked, striped; brindled; (speckled) grey; dun, drab" (*Ó Dónaill*) or "fallow, roan, brindled, striped" (*Dinneen*), and its original meaning in place-names is often obscure. *Riabhach* occurs in similar guise in many place-names including the Co. Louth townland name Acarreagh, anglicized from *An tAcra Riabhach* (*L. Log. Lú* 27), and **Carrowreagh** in Grange of Drumtullagh.

Ballyteerim *An Baile Tirim*
D 2545 "the dry townland"

1. B. Tereme	Jobson's Ulster (TCD)	1590c
2. B. Terraine	Dartmouth Map 25	1590c
3. B. Terain	Bartlett Maps (Esch. Co. Maps) 1	1603
4. C. Balltern, Bay Teraine	Speed's Ulster	1610
5. C. Ballitern	Speed's Ireland	1610
6. Balle Terame	Norden's Map	1610
7. Ballytirim	Inq. Ult. (Antrim) §49 Car. I	1635
8. Ballytirrime	Inq. Ult. (Antrim) §133 Car. I	1638
9. Ballytirrime	Inq. Ult. (Antrim) §135 Car. I	1638
10. Ballytermine	Hib. Reg. Cary	1657c
11. quarter of Ballytirim called Ardimony	DS (Par. Map) 55	1657c
12. Costrim	Census 17	1660
13. Ballytermine	BSD 166	1661
14. Balletyrim	Court of Claims §923	1662c
15. Balleterim, the town of	Court of Claims §923	1662c
16. Ballylermine	Lapsed Money Book 156	1663
17. Balleterin, the Towne of	Decree of Innocence 440	1663

18. Ballytren	ASE 116a §19	1668
19. Ballytrym	HMR Ant. 9	1669
20. Ballitermeen, 6 qtrs of	Hib. Del. Antrim	1672c
21. Ballytirrim, the six quarters of land of	PRONI D2977/3A/2/10/1	1678
22. Ballytermine	Ant. Forfeit.	1700
23. Ballyterim, 6 Quarters of land of	PRONI D2977/3A/2/10/2	1761
24. Sth Ballytirim, North Ballytirim	Culfeightrin Map [1789] 1	1789
25. Ballyterim	PRONI D2977/3A/2/1/40	1812
26. Ballyteerim	Culfeightrin Map [1812]	1812
27. Ballyterim	Grants on the A.E.	1814
28. Ballyterim, the six Quarters of land of	PRONI D2977/3A/2/10/3	1820
29. Ballyteerim	Bnd. Sur. (OSNB) B 24 B 37	1830
30. Baile tirim "dry town"	J O'D (OSNB) B 24 B 37	1831
31. Baile tirim "The dry town"	Ó Dubhthaigh 132	1905
32. Baile tirim "dry town"	Rev. Magill 7	1923
33. Baile Tirim "Dry townland"	Dallat's Culfeightrin 35	1981
34. ˌbɑliˈtʃirəm	Local pronunciation	1993

Most of the historical forms underpin O'Donovan's interpretation of this name (form 30). Form 12 appears to represent an obsolete form of the name comprising the elements *cois*, which in this instance might be understood to denote "foot of (the) valley" (cf. also **Cushendun**), and *tirim* "dry". It should also be considered that the surveyor may have substituted the first element in this case by analogy with Cushendun and Cushendall which lie further south along the coast. Presumably the adjective *tirim* referred to a lack of running water. Modern pronunciation of this element reflects somewhat that in the late local dialect. Holmer recorded *tirim* as [kʹirəm]/[tʹʌrəm] (*Irish of the Glens* 131). *Tirim* occurs elsewhere in the Co. Kilkenny townland name *An Tulaigh Thirim*, anglicized Tullaherin (*L. Log. C. Chainnigh* 46). Joyce gives a similar etymology for the townland names of Tullyhirim in counties Monaghan and Armagh (*Joyce* ii 413).

Forms 10, 13, 16, 20 and 22 resemble *Baile Tearmainn* "townland of the church land". There is no record of an ecclesiastical association with this townland, and they can be readily dismissed as scribal errors.

In the late 1500s and early 1600s, Ballytirim referred to a large territory along the the south-east coast of Culfeightrin, and was later regarded as containing "six quarters" (form 20); these quarters are represented by the twenty modern townlands from Farranmacallan to Barmeen inclusive (Carleton 1991, 67 n.14).

Ballyvennght
D 2038

Baile Bheannacht
"townland of the blessings"

1. Ballebennaght	Inq. Ult. (Antrim) §73 Car. I	1635
2. Ballyvannaght	Inq. Ult. (Antrim) §140 Car. I	1640
3. The quarters of Ballyvennaught called Mallendugan, Rodding, Downe		
	DS (Par. Map) 55	1657c

4. Quarter of Ballyveroughy called		
Roddynge	DS (Par. Map) 55	1657c
5. Downe; Mallendugane; Toppland of		
Rodding	DS (Par. Map) 57	1657c
6. Ballibenagh	Court of Claims §923	1662c
7. Ballebonaght	Court of Claims §923	1662c
8. Ballebonaght, the towne of	Decree of Innocence 431	1663
9. Downe; Mullendugane; Part of		
Roddings	Lapsed Money Book 155	1663
10. Redtowne; Ballindeweight;	Downe HMR Ant. 6, 8–9	1669
11. Ballyvenaght; Carivendooen	Stewart's Survey 5	1734
12. B:venaght	Lendrick Map	1780
13. Ballyvennaght	Sur. A.E. 48	1782
14. Ballyvenaght	Bnd. Sur. (OSNB) B 24 B 37	1830
15. Baile bheannacht "town of the		
blessing"	J O'D (OSNB) B 24 B 37	1831
16. Baile bheannachd "town of the		
blessing"	Rev. Magill 7	1923
17. Baile bheannach "town of the		
blessing"	Dallat's Culfeightrin 35	1981
18. ˌbɑliˈvɛnəx	Local pronunciation	1993

The final *t* in this name appears to have been only recently lost. *Baile Bheannacht* "townland of the blessings" is consistent with the historical forms although we may also consider that the final element was in the gen. sing. (*beannachta*), and that the final vowel was lost due to its unstressed position. The consistent lenition of the second element is the result of the use of the name in oblique cases.

There is no current local tradition regarding the name. However, the Ordnance Survey recorded in 1838 that a valley in this townland "was the seat of Roman Catholic worship during the existence of the penal code and also at subsequent periods" (*OSM* xxiv 73; see also *ibid.* 83 and *O'Laverty* iv 496). *Beannacht* is an unusual place-name element although we may note the townland name of *Cúm an Bheannaithe*, (anglicized Coomavanniha and Dughile) south-east of Cahirsiveen in Co. Kerry, translated "the valley of the blessing" (*Joyce* ii 479). *Mallacht* "curse" on other hand is quite common in place-names (*ibid.* ii 479–80); *Dún na Mallacht* "fort of the curses" (angl. **Dun a Mallght**) is the nearest local example (see Other Names, Ramoan).

Two of the three divisions alluded to in early forms of this townland name are still current (cf. **Carrowndoon** and **Mallandeevan** in Other Names). The third (*Rodding*) may have derived from *roideán* "place of reddish mud or bog-mire" (see Ó *Dónaill* sv. *roide*); [rɔdən], apparently denoting "rough track; sheugh; stream" and perhaps from *ródán* "little road", is used in the local English dialect and represents a further possibility. **Coolnagoppoge** may have been a fourth quarter (Carleton 1991, 68 n.32).

Ballyvoy   *Baile Bhuí(?)*
D 1641   "yellow townland"

1. (?)[Slemne] Baile [Á]tha Buidhe	L. Gen. DF 831	1650

2. (?)[A]tha Buidhe, Sleimhne	MacQuillan of the Route 102	1650c
3. (?)Bhaile [Á]tha Buidhe, Sleimhne	MacQuillan of the Route 102	1750c
4. Ballyvoy	Hib. Reg. Cary	1657c
5. Ballyboy	Census 18	1659
6. Ballvoy	BSD 165	1661
7. Ballyvoy	Lapsed Money Book 155	1663
8. Ballyvoy	ASE 116a §19	1668
9. Balli voy	Hib. Del. Antrim	1672c
10. Ballyvoy	Ant. Forfeit.	1700
11. Ballyvoy, 2 quarters of	PRONI D2977/3A/2/1/25	1714c
12. Ballyvoy	PRONI D2977/3A/2/1/26	1714c
13. Ballyvoy	C. McG. (OSNB) B 24 B 37	1734
14. Ballyvoy	Stewart's Survey 7	1734
15. Ballvoy	Lendrick Map (OSNB) B 24 B 37	1780
16. Ballyvoy	PRONI D2977/3A/2/6/3	1782
17. Ballyvoy	Bnd. Sur. (OSNB) B 24 B 37	1830
18. Baile Aodha bhuidhe "Hugh Boy's town"	J O'D (OSNB) B 24 B 37	1831
19. Baile buidhe "The yellow town"	Ó Dubhthaigh 133	1905
20. Baile an Mhuighe	Post-Sheanchas 33	1905
21. Baile bhuidhe "yellow town"	Rev. Magill 8	1923
22. Baile bhuidhe "Yellow townland"	Dallat's Culfeightrin 35	1981
23. Baile Bhóidh	GÉ 16	1989
24. ˌbɑliˈvɔi	Local pronunciation	1993

The Irish forms (1–3) occur in a genealogy of the MacQuillan family, which is associated with north Antrim (see barony introduction). This might lead us to identify *Baile Átha Buí* "townland of the yellow ford" as Ballyvoy, but the lenition (even by analogy) of the second *b* indicated in later English variants seems unlikely to have occured in such an Irish form (see *Joyce* i 356; *Census 1859* sv. Ballyboy). Curtis was unsure of the location of *Baile Átha Buí* and suggested Athboy in Co. Meath (*MacQuillan of the Route* 104–5). *Buí* "yellow" (forms 19, 21–23) is a common place-name element however and could have qualified *baile* in its own right. Joyce believed many townland names of the type *Ballyboy* to be derived from *Baile Buí* "yellow townland" (*Joyce ibid.*), and the lenition in the form *Baile Bhuí* could have resulted from the use of the name in oblique cases (cf. **Ballyvennaght, Ballyberidagh**).

Baile Aoidh Bhuí "yellow (skinned) *Aodh*'s townland" (cf. form 18) is among other possible original forms (*Baile Aodha Bhuí*, of similar meaning and with lenition of the second *b* by analogy might be considered). The male personal name *Aodh*, which denotes "fire", "was the commonest of all names in use in early Ireland and is now everywhere anglicized as Hugh, a name with which it has no connection" (Ó Corráin & Maguire 1981, 13). The further male personal name *Baoth* (gen. sing. *B(h)aoith*), which is possibly found in the south-west Co. Antrim townland name of **Clonboy** (*PNI* iv 36) occurs most frequently in early genealogies and seems less likely to have qualified the relatively recent element *baile* (cf. **Balleny**, Armoy). *Baile Mhaí* "townland of the plain" (note form 20) may also be considered. This form might seem to be at odds with form 5, which suggests that the last element in this place-name began with a *b*, but English *v* was often mistranscribed as *b* in 17th-century sources. *Maigh* "plain" also has other meanings (cf. **Glenmakeerin**). Other possibilities may include *Baile Bhoithe* "townland of the hut" (see *DIL* sv. *both* and *IPN* 32); *Baile Bhoithigh* "townland of the byre" seems unlikely.

The second element in form 23 also seems unlikely: the element *bóidh* would be an unusual element in a *baile-* name. The Scottish Gaelic word *boidh* "neat, tidy, trim" (*Dwelly*) was not noted locally although Holmer recorded *bóidheach* "bonny; pretty", and the subtownland place-name he spelt as *Láthrach Bóidheach* "bonny site", in Rathlin (*Irish of Rathlin* 165, 208).

Barmeen	*An Barr Mín*	
D 2333	"the smooth top"	
1. Barmeen	Culfeightrin Map [1789] 1	1789
2. Barrameen	Culfeightrin Map [1812]	1812
3. Barmeen	Bnd. Sur. (OSNB) B 24 B 37	1830
4. Barrameen	Tithe Applot. 18	1833
5. Barr mín "smooth top"	J O'D (OSNB) B 24 B 37	1831
6. "smooth top"	Joyce i 528	1869
7. Bárr mín "smooth top"	Ó Dubhthaigh 132	1905
8. Barr mín "smooth top"	Rev. Magill 8	1923
9. Barr mín "Smooth top"	Dallat's Culfeightrin 35	1981
10. ˌbɑːrˈmin	Local pronunciation	1993

Joyce notes that *barr* "top; summit; upper part" (*Ó Dónaill* sv.) can have the meaning "high or hilly part [of a townland]" in some northern counties (*Joyce* i 528–9). Topographically, there is no conspicuous summit in this townland, which lies on the southern boundaries of Cushleake Mountain South (a peak and a townland name). We could also consider that the first element was *bearna* "gap", or its variant *bearn* (*Ó Dónaill*). *Bearna* is "usually applied to a gap in a mountain or through high land" (*Joyce* i 433). The Cushendun-Ballycastle road uses a glen in this townland to ascend high ground south of the aforementioned mountain. In the townland name **Barnmeen** in south Co. Down, which derives from *Bearn Mhín* "smooth gap", the medial *n* was not found in several of its historical variants (*PNI* i 119–120) due to coalescence with the delenited *m* (cf. also **Doonmakelter** below). It seems best, however, to explain the second vowel indicated in forms 2 and 4 (which may come from related sources) as either anomalous or epenthetic and accept the etymology suggested by previous authorities (forms 5–9).

The adjective *mín* "smooth, level" (*Ó Dónaill* sv.) probably formed the second element. The noun *mín* "gentle place" (*IPN* 121) or "grassy land on a mountain" (Mac Giolla Easpaig 1984, 54) is rarely used in this position in place-names.

Barnish	*Bearnais*	
D 1541	"gap"	
1. Barnish	Religious Survey	1734
2. Barnish	Bnd. Sur. (OSNB) B 24 B 37	1830
3. Barr-inis "top holm or island"	J O'D (OSNB) B 24 B 37	1831

4. Bearnas "gap"	Ó Dubhthaigh 132	1905
5. Bearnas "a gap"	Antrim Place Names 84	1913
6. beárnas "the gap"	Rev. Magill 8	1923
7. Bearnas "A gap"	Dallat's Culfeightrin 35	1981
8. 'bɑrnəʃ	Local pronunciation	1993

Bearnas "gap, pass" (*Ó Dónaill*) was feminine in some dialects of East Ulster Irish (see *PNI* ii 219 and *PNI* iv 53). It recurs here in the oblique form *bearnais*. Dinneen (sv. *beárna*) lists the forms *béarnais* and *beárnas* as Rathlin Irish variants. Holmer recorded the former of these, which he spelt as *beirneis*, as meaning "bare promontory" ([bɛrn'ɛʃ]/[bʌrn'ɛʃ]; *Irish of Rathlin* 164; see also *Place-Names of Rathlin* 63), but such a form is not reflected in the historical forms here. The use of *barr* as a prefix meaning "top-" as suggested by O'Donovan (form 3) is unlikely.

Big House
D 1942

An English form

1. Big House	Bnd. Sur. (OSNB) B 24 B 37	1830
2. Big House	Tithe Applot. 2	1833
3. 'bɛg haus	Local pronunciation	1993

As the dearth of historical forms suggests, this townland name is relatively new and is one of only seven English townland names in the parish. In 1838 it was recorded: "In Bighouse, on the holding of Michael Scully stand ruins of a once handsome and extensive mansion house erected there some centuries past by Henry Stafford Esquire, related to the Antrim family [MacDonnells]" (*OSM* xxiv 74).

This territory appeared in the earlier sources under the former townland **Ballyukin** (see Other Names). In c. 1855, the Ordnance Survey recorded that Ballyukin was coterminous with the townlands of Big House, Goodland, Torglass and Knockbrack (*OSRNB* sh.9, 1).

Bonamargy
D 1341

Bun na Margaí(?)
"end of the river *Margaigh*"

1. Bunanmargaidh in Patria Ruta	Donatus Moneyus 103 §5	1617c
2. Bun-na-Máirge	Ultach 5:3, 6	1928
3. Bun (na) Margaidh	Irish of the Glens 103	1940
4. mones	Italian Maps 425	1339
5. moneth	Italian Maps 425	1351
6. moneth	Italian Maps 425	1367
7. munax	Italian Maps 425	1373
8. momer	Italian Maps 425	1384
9. monexi	Italian Maps 425	1426
10. moneth	Italian Maps 425	1467
11. moneth	Italian Maps 425	1513
12. momolag	Italian Maps 425	1544
13. the Abbey called the Market town	CSP Ire. 363	1568

14. momo arger	Italian Maps 425	1569
15. Banymargy, the Abbey of	MacDonnells Antrim 167	1584
16. Banymargey	O'Laverty iv 468	1584
17. Bonamergh	Italian Maps 425	1590
18. Mou age	Dartmouth Map 25	1590c
19. Bonamergee	Jobson's Ulster (TCD)	1590c
20. Bonovargo	Jobson's Ulster (BM)	1590c
21. momlus	Italian Maps 425	1593
22. Mo. Bonamarghe	Boazio's Map (BM)	1599
23. Bonamerghey	Treatise on Ire. (NLI) 11	1599c
24. Boneargy	Hill's Bun na Mairge 15	1601
25. Mouarg	Bartlett Maps (Esch. Co. Maps) 1	1603
26. Mouarg	Italian Maps 425	1609
27. Mo. Bonamerghe	Mercator's/Hole's Ire.	1610
28. Banomergh	Norden's Map	1610c
29. Bonamarga	Speed's Antrim & Down	1610
30. Port Britas called Bonavergie	CSP Ire. 58	1615
31. Bunamargy	De Hibernia & Antiq. 183	1654
32. Buiremargy	Hib. Reg. Cary	1657c
33. Bumnargee	DS (Par. Map) 57	1657c
34. Bonemargie	Census 18	1659
35. Bunmargee	BSD 165	1661
36. Bumamargie, the monastery of	Court of Claims §923	1662c
37. Bunamargie	Court of Claims §923	1662c
38. Barnemargie, the townland of	Court of Claims §923	1662c
39. Bunamargie	Decree of Innocence 437	1663
40. Bunargee	Lapsed Money Book 155	1663
41. Bunnumargee	ASE 116a §19	1668
42. Bonnymargy	HMR Ant. 10	1669
43. Bunemargie	Hib. Del. Antrim	1672c
44. Bonamargy	O'Laverty iv 471	1687
45. Bunmargy	Liber Louvan. 184	1687
46. Bunaworgi	Liber Louvan. 191	1690
47. Bunvarge	Liber Louvan. 201	1697
48. Bunavarge	Liber Louvan. 229	1699
49. Bunavargai	Liber Louvan. 244	1700
50. Bunnevargi	Liber Louvan. 281	1702
51. Bunauargi	Liber Louvan. 287	1703
52. Buneuargi	Liber Louvan. 297	1705
53. Bunavargy	Liber Louvan. 304	1706
54. Buneuargis	Liber Louvan. 314	1708
55. Bunevarhy	Liber Louvan. 318	1709
56. Bunevargi	Liber Louvan. 328	1711
57. Buneuargi	Liber Louvan. 336	1714
58. Bunavargy	Liber Louvan. 347	1716
59. Boonowargy	Liber Louvan. 352	1717
60. Bonavirgi	Liber Dublin. 3	1719
61. Bonnevargy	Liber Dublin. 8	1720
62. Bunevargi	Liber Dublin. 13	1724

63. Bunevargii	Liber Dublin. 18	1727
64. Bonavargii	Liber Dublin. 22	1729
65. Bonavargy	Liber Dublin. 27	1733
66. Bunamargy	Stewart's Survey 2	1734
67. Bonavergy	Liber Dublin. 32	1735
68. Bonavergy	Liber Dublin. 42	1738
69. Bonavergi	Liber Dublin. 46	1739
70. Bonnavargy	Liber Dublin. 86	1753
71. Bonnavergy	Liber Dublin. 144	1778
72. Bona Virgi	Liber Dublin. 206	1803
73. Bona Vergi	Liber Dublin. 270	1848
74. Bonavirgi	Liber Dublin. 324	1867
75. Bonavirgensis, Pro conventu Liber	Dublin. 324	1870
76. Bunamargy	C. McG. (OSNB) B 24 B 37	1734
77. Bonymargie	Religious Survey	1734
78. Bunamargy	Sur. A.E.	1734
79. Bonymargy	Taylor and Skinner 272	1777
80. Bonamargy (Bun-na-margy)	Mon. Hib. 4	1786
81. Bonymargy	Lendrick Map (OSNB) B 24 B 37	1780
82. Bonamarga	OSNB B 24 B 37	1809
83. Bonamargie	PRONI D2977/3A/2/1/40	1812
84. Boney Margy	Bnd. Sur. (OSNB) B 24 B 37	1830
85. Bonamargy	OSNB B 24 B 37	1831
86. Bona Marga	McSkimin (DPJ) 321	1833
87. Market Root, the	OSM xvi 103	1838
88. Bun na mairge "mouth of the river margy"	J O'D (OSNB) B 24 B 37	1831
89. Bun na Mairge "the foot of the mouth of the river margy"	O'Donovan (DPJ) 321	1833
90. Bun na Mairge "The foot of R. Mairge"	Ó Dubhthaigh 133	1905
91. Bun na mairge "foot of the river margy"	Rev. Magill 8	1923
92. Bun na mairgeadh "foot of the market"	Dallat's Culfeightrin 35	1981
93. bɔn(ə) mɑrgi	Irish of the Glens 103	1940
94. ˌbɒnə'mɑrgi	Local pronunciation	1993

This townland occupies a coastal stretch of land just east of Ballycastle in Ramoan parish, from which it is separated by the Margy River. In c. 1855, it was recorded that the Margy appellation referred only to that stretch of river extending .75 km inland from the coast to the confluence of the Glenshesk River and the Carey River (*OSRNB* sh.9, 2). The first element *bun* "base, bottom; lower end; extremity" (*Ó Dónaill* sv.) was historically used in variants of Cushendun. Joyce describes it as "an end, the end or foot of anything, such as a hill, the land, a stream (source or mouth), &c., often also applied to bottom land, i.e. at the lower end of a farm, or at the bottom of a hill" (*Joyce* iii 152).

It seems most likely that *margy* reflects a gen. form of the river name. The majority of Irish river names are feminine; many are named from goddesses (especially of fertility; Ó hÓgáin 1991, 243–4; see also O'Rahilly 1933, 217 and *GÉ* 266–7). Previous commentators derive this element from the fem. noun *marg* (gen. *mairge*) "march, boundary" (*Ó Dónaill*): nom. *An Mharg*, dat. *An Mhairg*, gen. *na Mairge* (see forms 88–91). The mountain name *Sliabh Mairge* (anglicized Slievemargie) in Co. Laois (*Onom. Goed.* 610 sv. *Sliab maircce* and 630 sv. *Temair mairci*) may contain the same element. Examples of Scottish place-names containing this element include *Marg an tSruthain* "merkland of the brook" (Watson 1926, 236). However, this would not account for the river being known today as *The Margy River*. Watson (1926, 441) lists several Scottish stream names of the type noun plus the adjectival (originally reductive/gaelicizing) suffix *-aidh* (possibly undeclinable), including four called *Marcaidh* which he translates as "horse-brook", from *marc* "horse" (*DIL*). A development from *marcaidh* to *margaidh* would be unlikely, but *margaidh* "boundary-river" might be considered as an original form of the river name. *Bun na Margaidh* reflects the phonetic form recorded by Holmer (form 93). However, this adjectival *-aidh* suffix is otherwise unattested in stream or river names in Ireland. It is better to assume that the river name took the form *An Mhargaigh* (gen. *na Margai*), an oblique form of *An Mhargach* which itself consists of *marg* plus the collective suffix *-ach*, again denoting "boundary river". Dallat suggests that the *margy* element derives from *margadh* "market", being " . . .an early reference to Ballycastle's fair or market" (Dallat 1981, 35). *Margadh* "market; market-place" (*DIL* sv. *marg(g)ad*) has always been masculine in Irish (*ibid.*, Ó Dónaill, Dinneen) although *Dwelly* notes a fem. form in Scottish Gaelic. It is unlikely that *margadh* would have been used in a townland name in conjunction with *bun* (i.e. in a topographical sense), and that the river is known as *The Margy River* also militates against such an interpretation, notwithstanding that this has clearly been current for some time (note forms 1 and 13).

Several forms (13, 15, 26–7, 36, 75) refer explicitly to the friary (now called Bonamargy Abbey) of the Franciscan Third Order Regular at Bonamargy. The founding of the friary has been variously dated to between c. 1475 and 1509, and variously ascribed to MacQuillans and MacDonnells (see Gwynn and Hadcock 1970, 269; regarding this establishment see also, for example, *Mon. Hib.* 4–5, *Hamilton's Letters* 242, *OSM* xxiv 60–7, *EA* 282, *O'Laverty* iv 468–78, *Hill's Bun na Mairge*, *Biggar's Bun na Mairge*, and *PSAMNI* 10). It is to be noted, however, that the earliest references to a monastery here date to the 14th century (forms 4–8), suggesting that (notwithstanding cartographic errors) there existed a religious institution here, prior to the establishment of a house by the above-mentioned order. Hill has noted that "all writers on Irish monastic affairs are agreed that, in the year 1202, a priory was founded by William de Burgh, to the Honour of God and the Virgin, at some point in this immediate district" (*Hill's Bun ma Mairge* 15), but it remains uncertain whether this priory was at Bonamargy. The ruins of the abbey were apparently formerly on the mouth of the river, but the channel was diverted in 1738 during the construction of Ballycastle harbour (*Mon. Hib.* 4 n.9). The boundary of the Catholic parishes of Carey (see introduction to Culfeightrin) and Ballycastle (also called Ramoan) follow the old channel (*O'Laverty* iv 418).

Brackney	*Breacnaigh*	
D 1439	"speckled place"	
1. Breacnigh [sic]	Ultach 4:2, 3	1929
2. Brackney	PRONI D2977/3A/2/1/16	1696

3.	Brackney	C. McG. (OSNB) B 24 B 37	1734
4.	Brackney	Stewart's Survey 2	1734
5.	Brackney	Lendrick Map (OSNB) B 24 B 37	1790
6.	Brackney	PRONI D2977/3A/2/1/40	1812
7.	Brackney	Bnd. Sur. (OSNB) B 24 B 37	1830
8.	breacnaidh "speckled land"	J O'D (OSNB) B 24 B 37	1831
9.	Breacnach "Speckled place"	Ó Dubhthaigh 133	1905
10.	breacnach "speckled place"	Rev. Magill 8	1923
11.	breacnach "speckled place or place of trout"	Dallat's Culfeightrin 35	1981
12.	ˌbraxni	Local pronunciation	1993

Breacanach "a speckled or spotted place" (anglicized **Brackenagh East**) in Co. Down is analogous with this name (*PNI* iii 30–1). Ó Mainnín notes that the Down name could concievably have resulted from one of three constructions: *breac* "speckled" plus the descriptive/substantive suffix *(e)anach*; *breac* plus the two suffixes *án* (as a substantive) and *ach* (perhaps as a collective); or from *breac* plus *eanach* "marsh". While noting all three forms are almost indistinguishable in Ulster Irish, he considers the first construction as the most likely (*ibid.*). On the other hand, the Co. Kilkenny townland name of Bruckana and the two Co. Offaly townland names Brickanagh and Bracknagh derive from the second of these constructions (*L. Log. C. Chainnigh* 18; *L. Log. Uíbh Fhailí* 11). If we accept Joyce's view that there existed the further distinct collective suffix *-n(e)ach*, we could consider *Breacnach* as a further possible form (*Joyce* ii 6–7).

Both the Down (modern pronunciation ['brakni]; *PNI ibid.*) and Antrim names now consist of only two syllables; this shortening by syncope appears to have occured in Irish here (cf. **Clegnagh** in Ballintoy). Ó Mainnín argues that the modern [ni] endings may reflect the use of the place-names in oblique cases, or may perhaps have resulted from late phonetic development in English (*ibid.*). We may discount the latter possibility in this case. It is difficult to correlate the modern western facing slopes of Brackney with the description "speckled", although of course, it was named to suit a landscape centuries past.

Broughanlea
D 1441

An Bruachán Liath(?)
"the small grey bank"

1.	Brochenlea	Religious Survey	1734
2.	Broughenlea	Stewart's Survey 5	1734
3.	Broughanlea	C. McG. (OSNB) B 24 B 37	1734
4.	Brughanlea	Hill's Stewarts 220	1741c
5.	Brochenlea	Merchant's Book 1	1751
6.	Broughinlea	Lendrick Map (OSNB) B 24 B 37	1780
7.	Broughanlea	Bnd. Sur. (OSNB) B 24 B 37	1830
8.	Broughanlea	OSNB B 24 B 37	1831
9.	Brochenlea	Tithe Applot. 13	1833
10.	Bruaichin liath "little grey border or margin"	J O'D (OSNB) B 24 B 37	1831
11.	Bruachán liath "grey little fort"	Rev. Magill 8	1923

128

12. bruachán liath "little grey place", or bruach an laoigh "the place of the calf"	Dallat's Culfeightrin 35	1981
13. ˌbrɔxən'liː	Local pronunciation	1993

It is uncertain which of *bruach* "bank, brink" (cf. also **Broughmore**) or its diminutive form *bruachán* "(small) bank" (*Ó Dónaill*) or "border; fringe" (*Dinneen*) formed the first element here. The Glenmakeerin River forms the southern boundary of this townland while its northern boundary stretches along the coast. Of several possible original forms, *An Bruachán Liath* "the (small) grey bank" and *Bruach an Lao* "the bank of the calf" are perhaps the most plausible. *Lao* "calf" appears in place-names throughout Ireland (*Joyce* i 470–1; *gamhain* alone was used for "calf" in late local Irish; *Irish of the Glens* 115). *Lao* has also been used in some dialects to refer to a young deer (Hughes 1989, 180). The Ards townland name **Carnalea** appears to have derived from *Carnán Lao* "the small mound of the calf" (*PNI* ii 161). We might also consider that Broughanlea records the Irish name for the Glenmakeerin River. *Lao* "calf" was the original name in Irish for the Lagan River (*ibid.* vi 295–6); Belfast Lough is *Loch Lao* in Irish (*GÉ* 129). *Trá Lí* (angl. Tralee) has been translated "strand of the (river) Lí" (*IPN* 259). The river Lee (Mod. Ir. *An Laoi* (*GÉ* 120)) in Co. Cork contains a calcified dative form of *lua/luae*, probably meaning "water" (cognate with Latin *lavo*), which originally had gen. forms identical to the nom. (O'Rahilly 1933, 215).

Broughmore
D 1537

An Bruach Mór
"the great bank"

1. Bruaghmore	Hib. Reg. Cary	1657c
2. Bruaghmore	BSD 165	1661
3. Creggbane als Bruaghmore	Lapsed Money Book 155	1663
4. Bruagmore	ASE 116a §19	1668
5. Creggbane als Bruagmore	Ant. Forfeit.	1700
6. Broughmore	C. McG. (OSNB) B 24 B 37	1734
7. Broughmore	Stewart's Survey 2	1734
8. Broaghmore	Stewart's Survey 4	1734
9. Broughmore	Lendrick Map (OSNB) B 24 B 37	1780
10. Broughmore	Sur. A.E. 54	1782
11. Broughmore	PRONI D2977/3A/2/1/39	1783
12. Broghmore	PRONI D2977/3A/2/1/40	1812
13. Broughmore	Report of the A.E.	1812
14. Broughmore	Bnd. Sur. (OSNB) B 24 B 37	1830
15. Bruach mór "great brink or margin"	J O'D (OSNB) B 24 B 37	1831
16. Bruach Mór "great fort or boundary"	Rev. Magill 9	1923
17. Bruach mór "great palace"	Dallat's Culfeightrin 35	1981
18. ˌbrɔx'moːr	Local pronunciation	1993

Broughmore has the largest boundary with the Glenshesk River of any townland along its banks, and the townland territory thins considerably inland from the river, suggesting the place-name referred to a parcel of land which stretched for a long distance along the water-course. *Bruach* is translated "a brink, edge, a bank (of river), border, boundary; a shore, a coast" by *Dinneen*.

Holmer recorded the word *bruach* as meaning "hill, slope or brae" in late local Irish ([brʌx]/[bruəx]; *Irish of the Glens* 103). This may represent an adoption of (the derived) Scottish Gaelic *bruthach* "ascent, steep, acclivity, hill-side, brae, precipice" (*Dwelly*). Broughmore is indeed located on a stiff slope, but as the use of *bruthach* locally appears to be a relatively late development, it seems unlikely to have formed the first element here.

| **Carey Mill** | | A hybrid form | |
| D 1440 | | | |

1.	Mill of Carey, the accustomed	PRONI D2977/3A/2/14/2	1709
2.	Mill of Carey, the accustomed	PRONI D2977/3A/2/20/2	1709
3.	Mill of Carey, the accustomed	PRONI D2977/3A/2/1/25	1714c
4.	Carey Mill	C. McG. (OSNB) B 24 B 37	1734
5.	Carry Mill	Stewart's Survey 6	1734
6.	Mill of Cary, the accustomed	PRONI D2977/3A/2/14/3A	1742
7.	Mill of Cary, the accustomed	PRONI D2977/3A/2/28/5	1746
8.	Carey Mill	Lendrick Map (OSNB) B 24 B 37	1780
9.	Carey Mill	Bnd. Sur. (OSNB) B 24 B 37	1830
10.	ˌkariˈmïl	Local pronunciation	1993

The *Ordnance Survey Memoirs*, compiled in the 1830s, recorded that there was still a corn mill here on the Carey River at this time, "propelled by a breast water wheel 12 feet in diameter and 1 foot 4 inches broad" (*OSM* xxiv 45). In the 18th century, the land indentures granting land-holdings on the estate of the MacDonnells sometimes specified that the leasee "shall send all the Corn and Grain which shall be expended on the premises, to be ground at the Accustomed Mill of Cary" (see, for example, *PRONI D2977/3A/2/28/5*).

The element *carey* in the townland name is derived from the (similarly pronounced) name of the barony (see the discussion of the barony name regarding this element). The memoirs note that at this time the parish of Culfeightrin was almost exclusively called *Carey* (see discussion under Culfeightrin).

| **Castle Park** | | Of English origin | |
| D 2533 | | | |

1.	Castle Parke	Ant. Forfeit.	1700
2.	Castle Park	Culfeightrin Map [1812]	1812
3.	Castle Park	Bnd. Sur. (OSNB) B 24 B 37	1830
4.	Castle Park	Tithe Applot. 2	1833
5.	kasəl ˈpɑrk	Local pronunciation	1993

This tiny townland derives its name from the single tower-house found here. The tower itself is called **Castle Carra** (see Other Names) and is the reputed site of Shane O'Neill's death at the hands of Somhairle Buí MacDonnell in 1567 (*PSAMNI* 17). The lateness of the appearance of the name in the sources suggests that this English name, and the townland itself, have been recently forged, being previously considered part of the neighbouring town-lands of Ballycleagh and Ballyteerim (Carleton 1991, 64). A land division in or near Ballycastle was also formerly known as *the Castle Park* (cf. **Town Parks**, Ramoan). See also **Ballycleagh**, and **White Park** in Ballintoy.

Churchfield	*Machaire an Teampaill*	
D 1440	"plain of the church"	
1. Magheritemple	Hib. Reg. Cary	1657c
2. Magheretemple	Census 18	1659
3. Macheretemple	BSD 166	1661
4. Maghera Temple	Lapsed Money Book 156	1663
5. Magherintemple	ASE 116a §19	1668
6. Marghetemple	HMR Ant. 10	1669
7. Magherrtample	Hib. Del. Antrim	1672c
8. Magheretemple, 2 quarters of	PRONI D2977/3A/2/1/16	1696
9. Magheretemple	Ant. Forfeit.	1700
10. Maghretemple	Religious Survey	1734
11. Magherentemple	Stewart's Survey 6	1734
12. Churchfield or Macherientemple	C. McG. (OSNB)B 24 B 37	1734
13. Magherintemple	Hill's Stewarts 220	1741c
14. Churchfield	Lendrick Map (OSNB) B 24 B 37	1780
15. Magherintemple	PRONI D2977/3A/2/1/40	1812
16. Churchfield	Bnd. Sur. (OSNB) B 24 B 37	1830
17. Churchfield	OSNB B 24 B 37	1831
18. Maghera an teampull "The field of the church"	Dallat's Culfeightrin 35	1981
19. ˌmɑhọrən'tɛmpəl	Local pronunciation	1993
20. 'tʃọrtʃfild	Local pronunciation	1993

The Irish form of this name appears to be more popular despite standardization of the translated English form in the 1830s (forms 19, 20).

Machaire has several meanings incuding "a plain, a flat or low-lying country, a field, a rid-ing or playing field, a race-course, a battle-field" (*Dinneen*) although when used in connec-tion with ecclesiastical establishments, it is possible that it denotes "erenagh land". Mac Giolla Easpaig (1986, 82) has noted that in Co. Donegal it often refers to church land, and gives *Machaire an Tearmainn* and *Machaire Chlochair* in *Gaoth Dobhair* as examples. Flanagan (1981–2(c), 73) has noted that *teampall* (from Latin *templum*) "(medieval) church; church-yard" (*Ó Dónaill*) is associated in place-names mainly with churches (frequently parish churches) of the post-Reform period (post-12th century), although "there are indications that *teampall* may have been used as a name-element in the pre-Reform period, particularly in the west of Ireland, with reference to small stone built churches, such as Teampall Mhic Dhuach and Teampall Bhreacáin in the Aran Islands" (*ibid.*). McKay notes that *teampall* can also signify "graveyard of the church" (*PNI* iv 137). There is thus the possibility that the place-name denotes "plain (etc.) of the graveyard" and that the former parish church which stood in this townland was known as *Eaglais* (cf. **Eglish**).

"The church is associated with a 6th century Saint Fiachra, but it is quite uncertain if his church was on this site" (*PSAMNI* 12; see also the introduction to Culfeightrin parish). In 1657, the church was desribed as "ruinous and inconvenient . . . no glebe or incumbent" (*Inq. Par. Ant.* 4). Reeves, writing in 1847, noted that most of the building except for the east gable had "been demolished, but sufficient traces of the foundations remain to show that it was of very large dimensions; the area of the old church and cemetery are now in pasturage" (*EA* 79 n.r). The Ordnance Survey recorded that the original structure measured "100' x 21½' in the clear, with walls 3½' thick" and describes a window in the east gable wall as being in gothic style (*OSM* xxiv 69–70).

There are several townlands of the name Churchfield scattered throughout Ireland (*Census 1851*).

Coolaveely D 1438	*Cúil Uí Bhaothalaigh(?)* "*Ó Baothalaigh*'s corner"		
1. Coolaveely	C. McG. (OSNB) B 24 B 37	1734
2. Cullyvieley	Religious Survey	1734
3. Coolaveely	Stewart's Survey 3	1734
4. Colvilly	Sur. A.E. 54	1782
5. Coollyvealy	Bnd. Sur. (OSNB) B 24 B 37	1830
6. Cultravillon otherwise Ballyvilly	PRONI D2977/3A/2/1/40	1814
7. Cullavilly	Tithe Applot. 2	1833
8. Coolyveally	OSM xxiv 58	1838
9. Cúil a' Mhíle "corner or angle of the soldier"	J O'D (OSNB) B 24 B 37	1831
10. Cúl an bhile "The corner of the tree"	Ó Dubhthaigh 137	1905
11. Cúil an bhile "The corner of the ancient pagan tree"	Dallat's Culfeightrin 35	1981
12. 'kulə'vili	Local pronunciation	1993

It is difficult to discern whether *cúil* meaning "corner, recess, nook" or *cúl* "back" (e.g. of a hill (*Joyce* ii 200)) represents the first element of this place-name. The townland is topographically dominated by the western and northern slopes of a hill in Broughmore. Both words have been anglicized into identical forms elsewhere, and in unstressed position are often pronounced [kọl]. *Cúil* appears to be much more prevalent in townland names, however (*L. Log. C. Chainnigh* 27–28; *L. Log. Luimnigh* 34–5; *GÉ* 84–5 (etc.)).

O'Donovan's explanation of this name (form 9) is a possible origin; we could also consider that the final element took one of the variant gen. forms *mileadh/milidh* (*Dinneen* sv. *míle*). Local military lore, concerning for example Shane O'Neill's campaign in Glenshesk, in which this townland is situated, abounded in the 1830s (see *OSM passim*), but *míle* would represent a somewhat unusual element in a townland name. Forms including *Cúil an Bhile* "corner of the (sacred) tree" (forms 10–11; *bile* is discussed under **Toberbilly** in Ramoan) and perhaps *Cúil an Mhínligh/Mhionlaigh* "corner of the tract of grassland (in mountain)" could also be considered. However, the historical forms closely resemble those of **Ballyveely**, a neighbouring townland in Ramoan, which appears to contain the gen. form of the rare surname *Ó Baothalaigh*. It remains a possibility that Coolaveely has latterly come under the influence of Ballyveely thus masking its etymology.

Coolnagoppoge
D 2040

Cúil na gCopóg
"corner of the docks"

1. Coolenegoppoge	Hib. Reg. Cary	1657c
2. Culnowpog	Census 18	1659
3. Coolenegoppoge	BSD 166	1661
4. Coolenagappage	Lapsed Money Book 155	1663
5. Coolegappoge	ASE 116a §19	1668
6. Cullnagappack	HMR Ant. 8	1669
7. Colnegopoge	Hib. Del. Antrim	1672c
8. Coolenegappage	Ant. Forfeit.	1700
9. Coolenegopog	PRONI D2977/3A/2/13/1	1710
10. Coolnagappage	Hill's Stewarts 11	1720
11. Cullnegapogh	Religious Survey	1734
12. Coolnagopagg	Stewart's Survey 9	1734
13. Coolnagoppag	C. McG. (OSNB) B 24 B 37	1734
14. Coolnegopoge	PRONI D2977/3A/2/12/2	1742
15. Cullnagoppoge	PRONI D2977/3A/2/13/3	1746
16. Coolnagopag	Lendrick Map	1780
17. Culnagapogh	PRONI D2977/3A/2/13/4–6	1781
18. Colenagappog	Sur. A.E. 42	1782
19. Coolnagoppog	Report of the A.E.	1812
20. Culnaboy, Culnagopag	PRONI D2977/3A/2/1/40	1812
21. Coolnagoppog	Grants for the A.E.	1814
22. Coolnagoppag	PRONI D2977/3A/2/13/7–13	1821
23. Coolnagoppag	Bnd. Sur. (OSNB) B 24 B 37	1830
24. Coolnagoppig	Tithe Applot. 6	1833
25. Coolnagoppag	Tithe Applot. 7	1833
26. Cúil na gcopóg "corner or angle of the dock leaves"	J O'D (OSNB) B 24 B 37	1831
27. Cúil na gCopóg "the Docken-nook"	Antrim Place Names 84	1913
28. Cúil na gCopóg "corner-field of the dock-leaves"	Joyce iii 247	1913
29. Cúil na gcopóg "corner of the dockans"	Rev. Magill 12	1923
30. Cúil na gCopóg "The corner of the dockans"	Dallat's Culfeightrin 35	1981
31. ˌkulnəˈgabǫx	Local pronunciation	1993

The historical forms support O'Donovan's interpretation (form 26). *Copóg* may variously mean "large leaf, dock" (*Ó Dónaill*). Holmer recorded the word *copóg* as [kɔpɑg], which he translated "dockans", showing a higher initial vowel than in modern pronunciation (*Irish of the Glens* 107). This final element, which is a very common place-name element throughout Ireland (*Joyce* ii 347), has also suffered further recent degeneration (forms 17, 31). The historical variants do not reflect *ceapóg*, a diminutive of *ceapach* "a plot of land laid out for tillage" (*Joyce* i 228). *Cúil na gCopóg* recurs as a townland name elsewhere in counties Kilkenny (anglicized Coolnambrisklaun or Coolnacoppoge; *L. Log. C. Chainnigh* 28),

Waterford (Coolnagoppoge; *L. Log. P. Láirge* 29), Kerry (Coolnagoppoge; *Joyce* iii 248) and Carlow (Coolnacoppoge; *ibid.* 247).

Coolranny	*Cúil Raithní*	
D 2637	"corner of the bracken"	
1. Coolreeny	Culfeightrin Map [1789] 1	1789
2. Coolranney	Culfeightrin Map [1812]	1812
3. Cullrainey	PRONI D2977/3A/2/1/40	1812
4. Coolranny	Bnd. Sur. (OSNB) B 24 B 37	1830
5. Culranny	Tithe Applot. 16	1833
6. Cuil raithnighe "ferny corner"	J O'D (OSNB) B 24 B 37	1831
7. Cúil Rathaine "the corner of the ferns"	Ó Dubhthaigh 137	1905
8. Cúil raithne "The corner of the ferns"	Dallat's Culfeightrin 35	1981
9. ˌkɔlˈrɑni	Local pronunciation	1993

The word *raithneach* ([rɑnˈɑx]) "bracken" and the field name *Lag Raithnighe* were noted locally by Holmer (*Irish of the Glens* 124). The Co. Limerick townland names Coolrahnee and Coolraine both derive from *Cúil Raithní* "corner of the bracken" (Ó Maolfabhail 1990, 149), as does the Co. Kilkenny townland name of Coolrainey (*L. Log. C. Chainnigh* 28).

Corrymellagh	*Coraidh Mheallach*	
D 2635	"lumpy crossing-place"	
1. Carmillagh	Census 17	1659
2. Corramela	Culfeightrin Map [1789] 1	1789
3. Coramelia	Culfeightrin Map [1812]	1812
4. Corrymellagh	Bnd. Sur. (OSNB) B 24 B 37	1830
5. Coramela	Tithe App. 16	1833
6. Corr meallach "rocky hillocks"	J O'D (OSNB) B 24 B 37	1831
7. Cor na mbealach "round hill of the pass"	Dallat's Culfeightrin 35	1981
8. ˌkɑriˈmiləx	Local pronunciation	1993
9. ˌkɔriˈmɛləx	Local pronunciation	1996

Corr "projection, edge or peak; angle, nook or corner; hut, enclosure or paddock; pit, pool or well; conical or rounded hill" (see *PNI* iii 33) is unlikely to have formed the first element in this name (as suggested in forms 6–7). The last of these meanings, which is the most common in place-names (*PNI* v 45–6), would hardly have been intended here in any case, as this tiny townland generally consists of steeply sloping rocky ground with no distinct summits. The pl. form *corra* resembles the historical forms to some extent but pl. forms of nouns in this position in place-names are very rare. The first element could also be construed as *coire* "corrie, deep mountain hollow; mountain tarn", but there does not appear to be any such feature here. *Coraidh* "weir; rocky crossing place in a river" (see *O Dónaill* sv. *cora*; *coraidh* was originally a dative form) probably reflects the historical forms most accurately. It could have referred to some point on a tributary of Tornamoney Burn which rises in this townland.

The second element appears to have been *meallach* "globular; protuberant; lumpy, knobby" (*Ó Dónaill*). This element also means "beguiling, pleasant, delightful" (*ibid.*); the somewhat similar *álainn* "beautiful, lovely" (*ibid.*) has been noted in place-names (see *Joyce* ii 65). It appears that this place-name has recently been affected by the much more well known **Corrymeela** (see Other Names; note form 8), and that the first vowel of the second element was historically pronounced [a]/[ɛ] (form 9). **Corrymeela** derives in fact from Corrymellagh.

Craigban	*An Chreag Bhán*	
D 1537	"the white rock"	
1. Creigbane	Hib. Reg. Cary	1657c
2. Cregbane	BSD 165	1661
3. Creggbane als Bruaghmore	Lapsed Money Book 155	1663
4. Cragbane	ASE 116a §19	1668
5. Cregban	Hib. Del. Antrim	1672c
6. Creggbane als. Bruagmore	Ant. Forfeit.	1700
7. Cregbane	Stewart's Survey 4	1734
8. Creggbane	C. McG. (OSNB) B 24 B 37	1734
9. Cregbane	Sur. A.E. 54	1782
10. Craigban	PRONI D2977/3A/2/1/39	1783
11. Creigbane	Report of the A.E.	1812
12. Craigbane	PRONI D2977/3A/2/1/40	1812
13. Craigbane	Bnd. Sur. (OSNB) B 24 B 37	1830
14. Creag bán "white rock"	J O'D (OSNB) B 24 B 37	1831
15. Craigban "white rock"	Joyce iii 270	1913
16. Craig bán "white rock"	Rev. Magill 12	1923
17. Craig bán "White rock"	Dallat's Culfeightrin 35	1981
18. kreg'ban	Local pronunciation	1993

Ó Dónaill translates *creig* as "crag; rocky eminence, rock; stony, barren ground; rocky shore". *Creig* is an acc. or dat. form of the fem. noun *creag* (*PNI* iii 132). Holmer recorded *creig* as the local nom. form, and as meaning "rock or cliff" ([kreg']; *Irish of the Glens* 108) but it is still not certain what form was used in the original name of this inland townland, as *ea* was pronounced [ɛ] before *d*, *g* and *s* in late local Irish (*ibid.* 76; this feature probably extended throughout east Ulster; see, for example, *PNI* iii 40). However, *creag* has normally been adopted on these occasions in modern works on place-names. See also **Craig** in Ballintoy regarding this element.

The qualifying element *bán* "white" does not feature a lenited *b*, even in the earliest forms. Adjectives following fem. nouns are often left unlenited in the process of anglicization.

Craigfad	*An Chreag Fhada*	
D 1842	"the long rock"	
1. Creagfadd	C. McG. (OSNB) B 24 B 37	1734

2. Craigfad	Religious Survey	1734
3. Cregfadd	Stewart's Survey 8	1734
4. Cregfadd	PRONI D2977/3A/2/1/34	1737
5. Cregfad	Lendrick Map (OSNB) B 24 B 37	1780
6. Craigfadd	Bnd. Sur. (OSNB) B 24 B 37	1830
7. Craigfadd	OSNB B 24 B 37	1831
8. Creag fada "long rock"	J O'D (OSNB) B 24 B 37	1831
9. Craig fada "The long rock"	Ó Dubhthaigh 136	1905
10. Craigfad "long rock"	Joyce iii 270	1913
11. Craig fada "long rock"	Rev. Magill 12	1923
12. Craig fada "Long rock"	Dallat's Culfeightrin 35	1981
13. kreg'fɑd	Local pronunciation	1993

As in the previous townland name there is no evidence of the lenition of the first letter of the final element of this name under the action of the fem. noun, *creag* "rocky eminence or cliff (etc.)". This final element, *fada* "long", has long since lost its final and unstressed syllable. Notably, Holmer recorded the word *fada* as [fɑd] from two separate local informants (*Irish of the Glens* 112). The final syllable was also absent in early 17th-century forms of the south-west Co. Antrim name *An Choillidh Fhada* (anglicized **Killyfad**; *PNI* iv 49–50). **Ballyfad** in the neighbouring parish of Layd probably contains a similar form of *fada* although in the *Hearth Money Rolls* (*HMR Ant.*) of 1669 it was spelt *Ballyfadye* (Carleton 1991, 113). We may also note a stone circle in Tervillan called **Cloghafadd** (*OSRNB* sh.5). Joyce postulated that the townlands called Drummod in counties Clare and Roscommon were derived from "Druim-fhad, long ridge" (*Joyce* iii 331).

It was recorded in c. 1855 that Craigfad refers to "a long ridge of rock with steep sides, and very narrow at the summit. The direction of the ridge is nearly north and south, and is almost crescent like in shape" (*OSRNB* sh.5).

Cross
D 1843

An Chros
"the cross"

1. Dunard	Hib. Reg. Cary	1657c
2. Dunard	Census 18	1659
3. Dunard	BSD 165	1661
4. Dunard	Court of Claims §923	1662c
5. Dunard, the forty acres of	Decree of Innocence 431	1663
6. Dunards	Lapsed Money Book 155	1663
7. Denard	HMR Ant. 10	1669
8. Dunard	Hib. Del. Antrim	1672c
9. Cross	Irish Jacobites 55 §38	1699
10. Dunards	Ant. Forfeit.	1700
11. Duanard	PRONI D2977/3A/2/18/1	1719
12. Dunard	PRONI D2977/3A/2/1/34	1734
13. Crosse	Religious Survey	1734
14. Doonard	Stewart's Survey 7	1734
15. Dunard, Cross, Coolnalough	Stewart's Survey 8	1734
16. Cross	C. McG. (OSNB) B 24 B 37	1734

17. Dunard Als Drumaduan, the quarterland of	PRONI D2977/3A/2/18/2	1746
18. Dunard	Lendrick Map	1780
19. Cross, Dunard	PRONI D2977/3A/2/1/40	1812
20. Cross	Bnd. Sur. (OSNB) B 24 B 37	1830
21. Cross alias Dunaird	OSNB B 24 B 37	1831
22. Cros "a cross" ; Dún aird "fort of the height"	J O'D (OSNB) B 24 B 37	1831
23. Cros, A market cross	Dallat's Culfeightrin 35	1981
24. 'krɔs	Local pronunciation	1993

The following was recorded in 1838:

> In Cross, and holding of Patrick Jameson, there stood an ancient church and graveyard locally called Kille Owen or 'John's Church', being probably dedicated to him. However, the site of the graveyard is now under tillage and occupied as a kitchen garden, and nothing left to denote its existence at any period, save the ruins of the church or foundation walls which are grown over with soil . . . Here also stood a font stone and a cross, from which the townland derived its name, both now disappear[ed] (*OSM* xxiv 67).

The Archaeological Survey of 1940 (*PSAMNI*) makes no mention of this church, which was about 35 perches west of Lough na Cranagh in an area called Coolanlough (*EA* 283). Reeves described the foundations as being 33' by 16' and noted that unbaptised children had occasionally been interred here (*ibid.*). The following was entered under the name *Capella de Killoan* in *Terrier (Reeves)* 75 (1615 AD): "The chappell of St. James in Mowllocke near the Fair Foreland: it is usurped and concealed by the parson of Kullfechtrene a long time, and tis exempted". Reeves considered this passage to refer to another old church at Drumnakill Point (*EA* 282–3), however, although this latter church appears previously to have been named after a different saint (cf. **Drumnakill Point**, Other Names). Both sites are within 1.5 miles of Murlough Bay. Reeves also noted the further place-name *Killowen* in East Torr, where "adults are still occasionally buried" (*ibid.* 283). *Cill Eoin/Eoghain* "Eoin's/Eoghan's Church" can be postulated as original forms of *Kille Owen*. Holmer recorded the form [k'i'l'ɔn] locally, which he spelt as *Cill Eoin* (*Irish of the Glens* 105).

Price (1945–67, 233, 268) has noted some instances in Co. Wicklow where the element *cross* in townland names appears to denote "church land". The name *Cross* only appears in the sources in 1734. Prior to this an obsolete form, probably *Dún Ard* "high fort", was used. This may have referred to **Doonmore**, a motte and bailey in the west of the townland dating from c. 1180 (*PSAMNI* 8; see Other Names). See also **Lough na Cranagh** in Other Names.

Curragh	*Currach*	
D 2433	"marsh"	
1. Corragh	Hib. Reg. Cary	1657c
2. Corragh	BSD 166	1661
3. Corragh	Lapsed Money Book 156	1663

4. Coragh, Coragh beg	HMR Ant. 9	1669
5. Corragh	Ant. Forfeit.	1700
6. Curragh	C. McG. (OSNB) B 24 B 37	1734
7. Curraghmore, Curraghbage	Religious Survey	1734
8. Curraghs	Stewart's Survey 13	1734
9. McVeas Corragh, Martin's Corragh	Culfeightrin Map [1789] 1	1789
10. Curraghmore, Curraghbegg	PRONI D2977/3A/2/1/40	1812
11. Curragh	Bnd. Sur. (OSNB) B 24 B 37	1830
12. Curragh, Curragh or Brablagh	Tithe Applot. 19	1833
13. Currach "a moor"	J O'D (OSNB) B 24 B 37	1831
14. Currach "a marsh"	Rev. Magill 13	1923
15. Currach "A marsh"	Dallat's Culfeightrin 35	1981
16. ˈkɒrəx	Local pronunciation	1993

This townland lies between the Glendun and Milltown rivers. Its name is probably derived from *currach* "wet bog, marsh" (*Ó Dónaill* sv. *corrach* recté *currach*). Form 8 takes a plural form which probably resulted from the townland being divided. There is evidence of a division of the territory from the late 1660s (form 4). Form 7(a) is derived from *Currach Mór* "marsh, big" i.e. "bigger division of the marsh", while form 7(b) derives from *Currach Beag* "marsh, small". Regarding form 12(b), which refers to the western and most mountainous part of the townland, see **Brablagh** in Other Names.

Cushendun
D 2533

Bun Abhann Doinne
"end of the river *Donn*"

1. Bun-abhann Duine	AFM v 1616	1567
2. mBun Abhonn Duine, i	LCABuidhe 38 §54	1578c
3. Bun 'ann Duinne	Irisleabhar na Gaedhilge 6, 109	1895
4. Bun Abhann Duinne	Irisleabhar na Gaedhilge 6, 109	1895
5. mBun Abhann Duine, i	Claidheamh Soluis 28 Mn.F., 5	1912
6. mBun Abhann Duinne, i	Iris. MN 88	1914
7. mBun Abhann Duinne, i	Antrim Notebooks i 108	1925c
8. Bun an duine	Antrim Notebooks i 91	1926
9. mBun Abhann Duinne, i	DCCU 104	1934
10. Cois-Abhainn-Dúinne	Ultach 12:5, 13	1935
11. Bun Abhann Duinne	Ultach 12:6, 5	1935
12. mBun (mBon) an Duinne, in	Irish of the Glens 103	1940
13. Chois Abhann Duinne, ar	Ultach 30:11, 11	1954
14. Bonondony	Jobson's Ulster (TCD)	1590c
15. Bounondunne	Jobson's Ulster (TCD)	1590c
16. Bundunon	Dartmouth Map 25	1590c
17. Barnadowne	Mercator's Ire.	1595
18. Bunondune	Bartlett Maps (Esch. Co. Maps) 1	1603
19. Bunondune	Norden's Map	1610
20. Bonnodrinny	Speed's Antrim & Down	1610
21. Bonodrumy	Speed's Ireland	1610

22. Bonodrumy	Speed's Ulster	1610
23. C'oshendonn	Hill Stewart's 143	1652
24. Cushandin	Civ. Surv. x §60	1655
25. Cushandin	Hib. Reg. Cary	1657c
26. Coshendune	ASE 116a §19	1668
27. Coshendune alias Gleadun, alias Glendun	ASE 169b §13	1668
28. Coshandun	Dobbs' Desc. Antrim 386	1683
29. Cosh'n Den	Lhuyd's Tour 221	1699
30. CwshinDun	Lhuyd's Tour 222	1699
31. Cashendon R.	Ire. Map	1711
32. Cossendon Bay	Stewart's Survey 13	1734
33. Cushendun	Taylor and Skinner 272	1777
34. Cushendun	Culfeightrin Map [1789] 1	1789
35. Cushendun	Lendrick Map	1780
36. Cushindun	Bnd. Sur. (OSNB) B 24 B 37	1830
37. Cois Abhann Dúine "mouth or foot of the river Dun"	J O'D (OSNB) B 24 B 37	1831
38. Cos abhann duine "The foot of the river Duine"	Ó Dubhthaigh 136	1905
39. Bun Abhann Duine	Post-Sheanchas 57	1905
40. Cois Abhann Duinn "foot of the brown river"	Rev. Magill 13	1923
41. Cois abhainn duinn "The foot of the brown river"	Dallat's Culfeightrin 35	1981
42. Bun Abhann Duinne	GÉ 40	1989
43. ə mɔn ən dʌn'ə	Irish of the Glens 103	1940
44. ˌkoʃən'dɔn	Local pronunciation	1993
45. ˌkoʃən'dïn	Local pronunciation	1993

The element *bun* "foot, bottom, base, end (of a valley, etc.)" (cf. **Bonamargy**) does not recur among English historical forms after 1610, at which time forms appear beginning with *cois*, a locative form of *cos* "leg, foot" meaning "at the foot of; along, beside" (Ó Dónaill sv.). The Co. Limerick barony name *Cois Sléibhe* (anglicized Coshlea) has been translated "(place) beside (the) mountain" by Ó Maolfabhail (1990, 138). Ó Maolfabhail also notes that *cos* may denote a measure of land in some instances in place-names (*ibid.* sv. *An Chois*; see also *Dinneen* sv. *gníomh*). Mac Giolla Easpaig (*Place-Names of Rathlin* 29) has translated the Rathlin subtownland name of *Cois an Locha* as "the side of the lake", while Ó Mainnín has translated the south Co. Down name *Baile Cois Abhann* (which has given rise to the anglicized townland names Ballycoshone Lower and Ballycoshone Upper) as "townland by the river" (*PNI* iii 77). *Cois* may however have been used in the sense "foot or bottom of the valley" in a historical variant of the townland name of **Ballyteerim**, so it is not certain whether the *bon-* and *cush-* variants originally represented two distinct names or indicate the replacement of the first element.

The place-name beginning with *bun* appears in the local Irish song *Aird a' Chumhaing*. Recensions of this song collected locally furnished forms 3–4 and 6–10. This song appears to have been composed in the early 19th century, which suggests that *Bun Abhann Doinne* survived longer than the English variants would otherwise indicate.

The final syllable of the place-name has long been lost in anglicized variants. The river called the Dun or the Glendun River enters the sea in this townland. The river name in this case, *An Donn* "the brown (river)" (nom.; dat. *An Doinn*), seems to be a substantive fem. noun alluding to the colour of the river. *DIL* notes the use of the adj. *donn* to denote "dun, brown, apparently a light brown inclining to yellow or red" and gives some examples of its use to describe water. *An Fhinn* (**Finn River**, mainly in Co. Donegal) from *fionn* "white" and *An Dearg* (as in *Caisleán na Deirge* anglicized **Castlederg** in Co. Tyrone) from *dearg* "red" appear to be somewhat similar river names (*GÉ* 105, 42). Both *Dinneen* and *Dwelly* list *duinne* as the fem. gen. form of *donn* "brown" but *doinne* is the spelling in standard Modern Irish. Forms 1–2 (on which forms 37–9 may be based), which contain only one *n* in the final element, may have omitted a second *n* by the non-transcription of a shortening mark. The medial element, the gen. form of *abhainn* "river", is barely perceptible in anglicized variants due to its unstressed position.

This place-name appears in the *Annals of the Four Masters* (form 1) in connection with the assassination of Shane O'Neill by the MacDonnells (see, for example, *MacDonnells Antrim* 122–46). He was reputedly buried nearby at Cross Skreen (see Other Names). Reeves (*EA* 284) noted in 1847 that there was a small mound in Cushendun which he called *Cruik-na-Dhuine* (perhaps *Cnoc na Doinne*), where "according to local tradition, O Neill and Mac Donnell fought in single combat".

Cushleake Mountain Middle,	*Cois Leice*
Cushleake Mountain North,	"(place) beside the flagstone"
Cushleake Mountain South	
D 2138, 2336, 2236	

1. Cushleack	Lendrick Map	1780
2. Cushleake undivided Mountain	Culfeightrin Map [1789] 1	1789
3. Cushleake Mt.	Bnd. Sur. (OSNB) B 24 B 37	1830
4. Cosleak	Tithe Applot. 16	1833
5. Cois leac "foot of the flagstones"	J O'D (OSNB) B 24 B 37	1831
6. Cos leacaigh "The foot of the hill slopes"; pronounced Cush-leak-ey by the natives	Ó Dubhthaigh 136	1905
7. Cois lice "foot of the flagstones"	Rev. Magill 13	1923
8. Cois leice "The foot of the flagstone"	Dallat's Culfeightrin 35	1981
9. koʃ'liːk	Local pronunciation	1993
10. koʃ'leːk	Local pronunciation	1993

These three mountainous and practically uninhabited townlands appear to have been drawn up by the Boundary Survey of 1830, each surrounding its own eponymous mountain peak. *Cois* "(place) beside" or "at the foot of" is briefly discussed under **Cushendun**.

It seems likely that the second element was the gen. sing. (*leice/lice*) of *leac* "flat stone or rock; flagstone, slab" (*Ó Dónaill*). Holmer noticed that through the narrowing effect of a nasal consonant, *ei* could become [i] locally (*Irish of the Glens* 29). The loss of the final syllable can be explained as being due to its unstressed position. It is tempting to suggest that the most northerly of the three peaks was the original Cushleak, being so called as it is the lower of the two peaks on a ridge where the second and more northerly summit, Carnanmore, has a chambered grave or cairn with a large covering flagstone (*PSAMNI* 3). Toner has suggested that *leac* has probably been used in many place-names in the sense "grave-stone" (*PNI* v 100). Cushleake Mountain Middle and South form a separate ridge south-east of Cushleake Mountain North.

Drumacullin	*Droim an Chuilinn*	
D 1535	"ridge of the holly"	

1. (?)Drumholly	Ant. Forfeit.	1700
2. Drimachullin	Stewart's Survey 4	1734
3. Drumcullen	Sur. A.E. 54	1782
4. Drimacullin	Bnd. Sur. (OSNB) B 24 B 37	1830
5. Drumahoolen	Tithe Applot. 8	1833
6. Druin a chuillin "ridge of the holly"	J O'D (OSNB) B 24 B 37	1831
7. Druim an cuilinn "The hill ridge of the holly tree"	Dallat's Culfeightrin 36	1981
8. ˌdrọmaˈkọljən	Local pronunciation	1993

Droim meaning "a ridge, a hill" is a common element in townland names in this parish. It is often difficult, however, as in the case of this loftily situated and rugged townland, to discern what exactly is the physical eminence in question. The final element seems likely to have been the gen. form (*cuilinn*) of *cuileann* "holly" (forms 6–7). *Coileán* "pup" was pronounced [kʌlʹən] in the late local dialect, thus resembling *cuileann* to some extent (*Irish of the Glens* 109), but we might have expected anglicized variants ending in *-an/-ane* had this formed the final element (cf. **Doonans** in Armoy). The earliest historical form may feature a translation of the final element by the surveyor (this may refer to **Drumavoley** in Ramoan). There is a possibility, albeit unlikely, that the last element of this name was the gen. sing. of the obsolete fem. noun *cuilleann*, a word interpreted by Ó Máille (1960, 64) as meaning "a steep unbroken slope" but which appears in fact to denote something like "place of holly" (see a forthcoming article on this word by G. Toner in *Ainm*, and *PNI* v 92). While most of the forested land in the parish appears to have been cut by the time of the Ordnance Survey in the 1830s, maps of the parish from the late 1500s on (e.g. *Mercator's Ire.*, 1595; *Speed's Ulster*, 1610) continually depict heavy forestation along the Glenshesk valley, in which this townland is situated. It was recorded in the 1830s that the only forested tracts left in the parish were of "hazel, birch and holly brushwood stands in the valley of Glenshesk and on the banks of the Carey river" (*OSM* xxiv 43).

Drumadoon	*Droim an Dúin*	
D 1741	"ridge of the fort"	

1. Drimadune in the barony of Carey	MacDonnells Antrim 117	1620
2. Drimedoone	PRONI D2977/3A/2/18/1	1719
4. Drumadun	Religious Survey	1734

5. Drimadooan	Stewart's Survey 5	1734
6. Drimadoon	C. McG. (OSNB) B 24 B 37	1734
7. Dunard Als Drumaduan, the Quarter land	PRONI D2977/3A/2/18/2	1746
8. Drumadowne	Taylor and Skinner 272	1777
9. Drimadoon	Lendrick Map (OSNB) B 24 B 37	1780
10. Drimadoan	Sur. A.E. 42	1782
11. Drimdoan	Sur. A.E. 66	1782
12. Drimadoon	Bnd. Sur. (OSNB) B 24 B 37	1830
13. Druim an dúin "the ridge of the fort"	J O'D (OSNB) B 24 B 37	1831
14. Druim an dúin "The ridge of the fort"	Ó Dubhthaigh 137	1905
15. Druim an dúin "The hill ridge of the fort"	Dallat's Culfeightrin 36	1981
16. ˈdrɔmədun	Local pronunciation	1993

Dún may be more specifically translated "fort, fortress; (secure) residence, house; promontory fort" (*Ó Dónaill*; regarding this element see also, for example, Flanagan 1980–1(a) and Mac Giolla Easpaig 1981, 162 and 1984, 56). In 1838, the Ordnance Survey recorded that:

> [On the] holding of John McClene, and situated on the summit of a handsome lofty hill there stood a fort which gave the townland its name. It was composed of earth and stones and seemed to have been of circular shape, about 25 yards in diameter and nearly 5–10' high, but nearly half of it has fallen down a great precipice to the south side (*OSM* xxiv 51–2).

In c. 1855 the Ordnance Survey recorded the name of this site as *Doon* and described it as "a small round and apparently natural mound on the summit of a sloping cliff . . . The peasantry venerate it" (*OSRNB* sh.9, 2).

Drumahaman	*Droim an Chamáin*	
D 1340	"ridge of the small river-bend"	
1. Dromcamon	Inq. Ult. (Antrim) §100 Car.I	1635
2. Drumkamon	DS (Par. Map) 56	1657c
3. Drumnacaman	Census 18	1659
4. Drumkannon	BSD 165	1661
5. Drumcomon	Lapsed Money Book 155	1663
6. Drumcannon	ASE 116a §19	1668
7. Drumkamon	HMR Ant. 11	1669
8. Drumcannon	Ant. Forfeit.	1700
9. Drumcammon	PRONI D2977/3A/2/1/27	1720
10. Drimahaman	C. McG. (OSNB) B 24 B 37	1734
11. Drimaman	Religious Survey	1734
12. Drimachaman	Stewart's Survey 2	1734
13. Drumahamon	Lendrick Map	1780

14. Drimacamon	PRONI D2977/3A/2/1/40	1812
15. Drumahaman School	OSRNB sh.9, 2	1829
15. Drimahaman	Bnd. Sur. (OSNB) B 24 B 37	1830
16. Drumacamon	OSNB B 24 B 37	1831
17. Drummahammond School	OSRNB sh.9, 2	1855c
18. Druim a' chamáin "ridge of the wading"	J O'D (OSNB) B 24 B 37	1831
19. Druim a' chamáin "ridge of the camán"	Rev. Magill 14	1923
20. Druim an chamáin "the hillridge of the river bend"	Dallat's Culfeightrin 36	1981
21. ˌdrɔməˈhamən	Local pronunciation	1993

The northern and western boundaries of this townland are formed by the Carey and Glenshesk rivers respectively, towards whose confluence a ridge of land c. 20 metres high notably extends. The final element in the name has been variously interpreted (forms 18–20). Form 20, considering the circuitous routes of both river channels, seems the most likely. The former townland of **Cam** in south-west Co. Antrim derives its name from *cam* "a bend in the river" (*PNI* iv 123). In this instance, the diminutive form *camán* "small bend" appears to have been used. *Cam* can sometimes denote a vessel-shaped hollow in the ground (Ó Máille 1968, 69), however, and a diminutive form, *camán*, might also be considered in this case.

Droim an Chamáin "ridge of the hurley-stick" (form 19), is an attractive interpretation of the name: the ridge in question may have been considered as being in the shape of a *camán*. Notwithstanding this, however, the *Ordnance Survey Memoirs* recorded no contemporary belief that the ridge form inspired this name, or any tradition linking the ridge with the game of hurley. The form suggested by O'Donovan (form 18) may not be directly translated as "ridge of the wading". Perhaps one could infer that a fording point on some bend of one or other of the boundary rivers was what he intended.

Drumahitt	*Droim an Chait*
D 1340	"ridge of the cat"

1. Dromkaite	Inq. Ult. (Antrim) §100 Car. I	1635
2. Drumchett	Hib. Reg. Cary	1657c
3. Drumkett	DS (Par. Map) 55	1657c
4. Drumnakitt	Census 18	1659
5. Drumchett	BSD 165	1661
6. Drumkett	Lapsed Money Book 155	1663
7. Drumchitt	ASE 116a §19	1668
8. Drumkitt	HMR Ant. 11	1669
9. Drumchett	Hib. Del. Antrim	1672c
10. Drumkett	Ant. Forfeit.	1700
11. Drumkitt	PRONI D2977/3A/2/1/27	1720
12. Drimachitt	Stewart's Survey 2	1734
13. Drumachitt	C. McG. (OSNB) B 24 B 37	1734
14. Drumahitt	Bnd. Sur. (OSNB) B 24 B 37	1830

15. Drumahitt	OSNB B 24 B 37	1831
16. Druim a chait "ridge of the cat"	J O'D (OSNB) B 24 B 37	1831
17. Druim-a'-chait "ridge of the cat"; meaning a resort of wild cats	Joyce iii 314	1913
18. Druim a chait "ridge of the cat"	Rev. Magill 14	1923
19. Druim an chait "The hill ridge of the cat"	Dallat's Culfeightrin 36	1981
20. ˌdrɔmaˈhït	Local pronunciation	1993

The following was recorded in 1838:

> [this townland is] said to have been the seat of an ancient parliament locally called The Long Parliament, in consequence, it is said, of [the] long duration of its thirteen month sitting. It was convened here some time about the 6th century by the then monarch of Ireland for various purposes . . .[to which] St. Columcill came over from Scotland . . . [wearing] a cloth or muffle over his eyes . . . of the exact spot on which the assembly sat, there is now little detail to be found, save conjecture, as the grounds have undergone many alterations since the above period . . . (*OSM* xxiv 67).

This event took place in the latter half of the 6th century at *Druim Cett* which has been consistently located in north Co. Derry by commentators since c. 1400 (see *Onom. Goed.* 359–60; *Céitinn* iv 262; *AU* i 66n) on the basis of contextual evidence from Adomnán's biography of St *Colm Cille* (Sharpe 1995, 312). Presumably the similarity in the place-names prompted the local tradition.

The later variants support O'Donovan's etymology (form 16). The apparent absence of the medial article in earlier forms may indicate that the name was originally *Droim C(h)ait* (of similar meaning). Joyce noted that sometimes "in place-names . . . a single animal is put forward to stand for many or all" (*Joyce* iii 11). *Cat* occurs elsewhere in the north Co. Louth townland name of *Corr an Chait*, (anglicized Corrakit; *L. Log. Lú* 12), and in the Rathlin subtownland name of *Rubha an Chait* "the point of the cat", anglicized **Ruecait** (in Ballycarry; Place-Names of Rathlin 64). The subtownland name of *Clochar an Chait* in *Mín an Chuilinn* (Meenachullion) townland in central Co. Donegal is described as "a place frequented by foxes and wild cats" (O'Kane 1970, 96).

Drumaridly
D 1440

Droim an Riodalaigh(?)
"Riddell's ridge"

1. Drumaridly	Bnd. Sur. (OSNB) B 24 B 37	1830
2. Drumaridly	OSNB B 24 B 37	1831
3. Drumariddily	Tithe App. Book 8	1833
4. Druim "ridge"; ridley is a family name	J O'D (OSNB) B 24 B 37	1831
5. Druim an riodaire "the ridge of the rider"	Dallat's Culfeightrin 36	1981
6. ˌdrɔmaˈrïdlı	Local pronunciation	1993

An Anglo-Norman juror called Adam de Ridal was present at an evaluation of lands in the northern areas of the earldom of Ulster, on the 27th of October, 1278 (*CDI* §1500), but this surname is absent from local sources. A gaelicized form of this name, or of Riddell "an English name numerous in Ulster" (MacLysaght 1985, 258; this is presumably a later form of de Ridal. See also Reaney 1958, 294 sv. Ridal and Riddell) in *Droim an Riodalaigh* "de Ridal's/Riddell's ridge", would reflect the few historical forms. The Ards townland name of **Ballyridley** derives from *Baile an Riodalaigh* (*PNI* ii 32–3). *Baile an Ridéalaigh*, a townland in Co. Limerick, was anglicized as Riddlestown (Ó Maolfabhail 1990, 26). Ridley is itself an English locational surname found in Cheshire, Kent, Essex and Northumberland (Barber 1901, 226 and Reaney 1958, 295; it is also listed in *The Surnames of Lancashire* (McKinley 1981, 422)), and although it is also absent from local sources we might consider that a similar gaelicized form of it was used here.

We must take into consideration that the *baile* plus article plus surname structure is quite rare in northern place-names, and that it would be perhaps all the more unusual to find a *droim* plus article plus surname structure. Furthermore, the historical forms are so late that it is a distinct possibility that the name has been latterly reinterpreted, obscuring the correct etymology. Form 5 is based on the assumption that dissimilation of the second *r* to *l* in *ridire/rudaire* "knight" has taken place (and that the vowel between the *d* and *l* has been lost in modern pronunciation). The fem. noun *rideal* "riddle" would represent an unusual element in a townland name. We might consider that the final element consisted of the gen. sing. of one of the nouns *roid* "bog myrtle" (Ó Dónaill) or *roide* "reddish mud, bog-mire; muck, dirt" (*ibid.*) plus the collective suffix -*leach* (see *Joyce* ii 5 sv. *lach*), but such forms are unattested.

Drumaroan	*Droim an Ruáin*	
D 1441	"ridge of the red place"	

1. Drunroan	HMR Ant. 11	1669
2. Drumonan	PRONI D2977/3A/2/1/3	1681
3. Drimroan	Religious Survey	1734
4. Drimaroan	C. McG. (OSNB) B 24 B 37	1734
5. Drimaroan	Lendrick Map (OSNB) B 24 B 37	1780
6. Drimaroan	Bnd. Sur. (OSNB) B 24 B 37	1830
7. Drumaroan	Tithe Applot. 7	1833
8. Druim a' ruadháin "ridge of the reddish surface"	J O'D (OSNB) B 24 B 37	1831
9. Druim a' ruain "ridge of the headland"	Rev. Magill 14	1923
10. Druim an ruadháin "The hill of the moorland"	Dallat's Culfeigthrin 36	1981
11. ˌdrọmaˈroən	Local pronunciation	1993

Regarding further possible interpretations of the final element of this name, see **Drumroan** in Grange of Drumtullagh. Magill seems to have had a variant of *rubha* "headland" in mind in form 9. While this townland has a number of rocky eminences on its coastline that might be construed as headlands, the word he ascribes to the second element (perhaps a diminutive form) is not attested. *Droim an Róin* "ridge of the seal", referring to the shape of the ridge, might be considered, but the *-oa-* in historical forms probably represents a diphthong.

Drumnakeel　　　　　　　　　　*Droim na Cille*
D 1640　　　　　　　　　　　　　　"ridge of the graveyard"

1. (?)Droim na Cille	Irish of the Glens 105	1940
2. Drumnakelly	Hib. Reg. Cary	1657c
3. Drumykilly	DS (Par. Map) 55	1657c
4. Drumnakill	Census 18	1659
5. Drumnekelly	BSD 165	1661
6. Drumnekelly, Ballynagard called	Lapsed Money Book 155	1663
7. Drumnakelly	ASE 116a §19	1668
8. Drumnakill, quart.land of	PRONI D2977/3A/2/20/1	1692
9. Drumnakelly	Ant. Forfeit.	1700
10. Drumnakill	Hill's Stewarts 11	1720
11. Drumkill	Religious Survey	1734
12. Drimnakill	Stewart's Survey 5	1734
13. Drimnakeel	C. McG. (OSNB) B 24 B 37	1734
14. Drumnakeill	PRONI D2977/3A/2/20/3	1738
15. Drimkill	Sur. A.E. 42	1782
16. Drimnakill	Sur. A.E. 60	1782
17. Drumnakill	PRONI D2977/3A//2/6/3	1792
18. Drumnakeel	Lendrick Map (OSNB) B 24 B 37	1780
19. Drumnakeil	PRONI D2977/3A/2/1/40	1812
20. Drumnakell	Grants on the A.E.	1814
21. Drimnakeel	Bnd. Sur. (OSNB) B 24 B 37	1830
22. Droman caol "narrow ridge"	J O'D (OSNB) B 24 B 37	1831
23. Druim na cill "The ridge of the church"	Ó Dubhthaigh 137	1905
24. Druim na cille "ridge of the church"	Rev. Magill 14	1923
25. Druim na cille "The hill ridge of the church"	Dallat's Culfeightrin 36	1981
26. (?)drɔm nə k'il'ə	Irish of the Glens 105	1940
27. ˌdrɔmnaˈkiːl	Local pronunciation	1993

Cill "a church, a churchyard, a burial place" and *coill* "forest" are often indistinguishable from one another in anglicized form. Based on the following, written in 1847, we may suggest that modern pronunciation favours the former: "(Culfeightrin) is remarkable for the number of its small burying grounds. These are called by the people keels, from *cill*, a church, and are principally employed for still born children" (*EA* 282). Reeves noted 14 "keels" in the parish, including one in this townland: "In the townland of Drumnakill [*sic*] is a small place, enclosed in a field where infants have been buried. It is situated in the fork of the Carey and Glenmakeerin rivers" (*ibid.* 283). This site was also noted in 1838: "on the holding of James Kenny, west of and contiguous to the Ballycastle-Cushendun road, are the

146

remains of a local graveyard, locally called kille, from which the [townland] took its name" (*OSM* xxiv 51). This does not reflect O'Donovan's explanation (form 22) which in any event is not supported by the historical forms. The anglicized form *keel* occurs elsewhere in Antrim in 17–19th-century forms for the obsolete townland name of **Churchtown** (originally *Baile na Cille*) in the parish of Cranfield (*PNI* iv 11). The development of [ï] to [i] in some words in Antrim Irish was regarded by Wagner as indicating "a Scottish tendency in pronunciation" (*LASID* iv 284 n.4). Forms 2, 5–7 and 9 which contain *-kelly*, an anglicized form associated more especially with *coill* come from related sources and may exhibit a copied misspelling.

It is not certain whether Holmer's informant (forms 1 and 26) was refering to Drumnakill in Bighouse (see **Drumnakill Point** in Other Names), or to this townland name.

| **Duncarbit** | *Dún Carbaid* | |
| D 1534 | "fort of the chariot(?)" | |

1.	Dún Carbaid, co Dún in Daimh darab comhainm	SMMD II 43	1638c
2.	Duncarbett	Hib. Reg. Cary	1657c
3.	Duncarbitt	Census 18	1659
4.	Duncarbett	BSD 165	1661
5.	Duncarbett	Lapsed Money Book 153	1663
6.	Duncarrbett	ASE 116a §19	1668
7.	Duncarbett	Hib. Del. Antrim	1672c
8.	Duncarbit	Ant. Forfeit.	1700
9.	Duncorbit	Sur. A.E. 80	1782
10.	Duncorbit	Report of the A.E.	1812
11.	Duncorbitt	PRONI D2977/3A/2/1/40	1812
12.	Duncarbit	Bnd. Sur. (OSNB) B 24 B 37	1830
13.	Dún carbaid "fort of the chariot"	J O'D (OSNB) B 24 B 37	1831
14.	Dún carbad "The fort of the coaches"	Ó Dubhthaigh 137	1905
15.	Dún carbaid "fort of the chariot"	Rev. Magill 15	1923
16.	Dún cearbaid "The fort of the chariots"	Dallat's Culfeightrin 36	1981
17.	ˌdọnˈkɑrbət	Local pronunciation	1993

The Ordnance Survey recorded the following in 1838: "On the holding of Archibald McAlister on an eminence east of and contiguous to the River Shesk, there stood a large and well fortified fort which gave its name to the townland . . ." (*OSM* xxiv 68).

The *-bit(t)* endings in historical forms reflect the gen. sing. of *carbad* "jaw; chariot". Joyce wrote of this place-name element: "We may conclude with great probability that at least some of the places whose names contain this word were exercise grounds, where the young warriors and charioteers trained their steeds and practised driving", and noted the place-name Drumcarbit near Malin village in Inishowen (*Joyce* ii 175). *Carbad* is also a variant of *carball* "boulder", and appears as such in Co. Down townland name *An Carbad* (angl. **Corbet**; *PNI* vi 261–2) and the Co. Limerick townland name *Baile an Charbaid Beag*, which might be translated "townland of the boulder, small" (modern anglicized form Corrabul Beg; Ó Maolfabhail 1990, 14). This meaning should also be considered in this case.

The alternative name cited in form 1 (standard Mod. Ir. *Dún an Daimh*) is not reflected in the anglicized variants. It may be translated "fort of the ox/stag".

Dunmakelter   *Dún Mhac Cealtchair(?)*
D 1841   "*Mac Cealtchair*'s fort"

1. Dún Meic Cealtchair	SMMD II 42	1638c
2. Crynagh & Dumakelter	Inq. Ult. (Antrim) §100 Car. I	1635
3. Dunmackelter	Inq. Ult. (Antrim) §100 Car. I	1635
4. Criragh	Hib. Reg. Cary	1657c
5. Crivath	DS (Par. Map) 57	1657c
6. Dunekellber; Crivagh	Census 18	1659
7. Durveceller	Court of Claims §923	1662c
8. Dunacelter	Court of Claims §923	1662c
9. (?)Crisarch	Lapsed Money Book 155	1663
10. Creevagh	HMR Ant. 8	1669
11. Criragh	Hib. Del. Antrim	1672c
12. Crivagh, the quarter land of	PRONI D2977/3A/2/14/1	1696
13. Crevagh	PRONI D2977/3A/2/14/2	1709
14. Creevagh	Hill's Stewarts 11	1720
15. Duniecaltrey	Religious Survey	1734
16. Doonmakalter	Stewart's Survey 8	1734
17. Dunmakalter	C. McG. (OSNB) B 24 B 37	1734
18. Crevagh	PRONI D2977/3A/2/14/3A	1742
19. Doonmakelter otherwise Creevagh, the quarter land of	PRONI D2977/3A/2/14/4	1770
20. Doomakalter	Sur. A.E. 42	1782
21. Doonmakelter	Report for the A.E.	1812
22. Crevagh	PRONI D2977/3A/2/1/40	1812
23. Doonmakalter	Grants of the A.E.	1814
24. Dunmakelter	Bnd. Sur. (OSNB) B 24 B 37	1830
25. Creevagh or Dunnycalter	Tithe Applot. 6	1833
26. Dún Mic Cealtair "fort of the son of Cealtar/Kelter"	J O'D (OSNB) B 24 B 37	1831
27. Dún Uí Chealtair "The fort of Keltair"	Dallat's Culfeightrin 36	1981
28. ˌdɔnaˈkəltïr	Local pronunciation	1993

Forms 2(a), 4–5, 6(b), 9–14, 18, 19(b), 22 and 25(a) indicate an obsolete name for this territory (we may also consider that it referred to an internal or contiguous land division). They appear to be based on *Craobhach* "place of trees/bushy place" (see Ó Dónaill sv. *craobh* and *PNI* vi 31). Carleton (1991, 65) suggested that form 6(a) referred to the contiguous townland of Drumadoon, but it is more likely to contain a scribal error and refer to Dunmakelter.

There is some uncertainty regarding this name. We could interpret the elements following *dún* in three ways: as the patronymic *mac Chealtchair* "son of *Cealtchar*" (gen. *mhac*

Chealtchair; compare *Baile Mhac an Tuaisceartaigh*/**Ballymatoskerty** and *Carn Mic Mhuáin*/**Carmacmoin** *PNI* iv 92, 173); as the otherwise unattested male personal name *Mac Cealtchair* (gen. sing. *Mhac Cealtchair*); or as the otherwise unattested surname *Mac Cealtchair* (gen. sing. *Mhic Cealtchair*). Form 1 points to one of the latter two interpretations (the earlier gen. form of both would have been *Mic Cealtchair*), and as surnames rarely qualify *dún*, we might deem the male personal name most likely. As the grammar in form 1 could have been affected by analogy, however, and referred to some otherwise unknown figure in local tradition, the first interpretation remains a possibility (its earlier gen. form would have been *mic Chealtchair*). The rare personal name *Cealtchar*, used of a "fictional warrior of Ulster" (who appears in the Ulster Cycle) means "mantel" or "concealment", and was a metaphorical term for a spear (Ó hÓgáin 1990, 79). This personal name appears in the obsolete place-name anglicized Rath-Keltair, in or near Downpatrick (Flanagan 1971, 107). As in the Downpatrick place-name, the *ch* following the *t* is seen to have been lost at an early stage. The 17th-century text from in which form 1 appears claims Dunmakelter was named from the *Cealtchar* of the Ulster cycle (*SMMD II* 42), but this may have been to reinforce the story's relocation in north Antrim. The *Ordnance Survey Memoirs* make no reference to the site of a fort in the townland. Reeves noted in 1847 however that near the graveyard alluded to in the discussion of the neighbouring townland of Drumnakeel (see above) "is a conical hill, with some remains of a stone enclosure on the top, called *Dunmakelter*" (*EA* 283).

East Torr,	*Tor*	
West Torr	"tor"	
D 2340, 2141		

1. Torbhuirg, go	Céitinn iii 302	1633c
2. Torbhuirge	MacErlean 7	1646
3. Tor	Irish of Rathlin 243	1942
4. Tor	Nowel's Ire. (1)	1570c
5. Tor	Bartlett Maps (Esch. Co. Maps) 1	1603
6. Tor	Norden's Map	1610
7. Tor	Speed's Antrim & Down	1610
8. Torre	Speed's Ireland	1610
9. Tor	Speed's Ulster	1610
10. the Torr, half a townland in the Route called	CSP Ire. 596	1647
11. Torretwone	Hib. Reg. Cary	1657c
12. Torre	DS (Par. Map) 56	1657c
13. Tor	Census 17	1659
14. Torre	BSD 166	1661
15. Toar	Court of Claims §923	1662c
16. Torre, the ½ town of	Court of Claims §923	1662c
17. Torr, the half towne of	Decree of Innocence 431	1663
18. Torre 2 Qurs.	Lapsed Money Book 154	1663
19. Torre	ASE 116a §19	1668
20. Toretowne	HMR Ant. 9	1669
21. Torre	Hib. Del. Antrim	1672c
22. Torr, the two quarter lands of	PRONI D2977/3A/2/28/1	1696

23. Torre	Ant. Forfeit.	1700
24. that quarterland of Torr sometimes called Iscart	PRONI D2977/3A/2/28/2	1711
25. Cregybryan, Carrivegarave	Stewart's Survey 10	1734
26. Creggbryan	Stewart's Survey 11	1734
27. Torr, the Quarter land of	PRONI D2977/3A/2/1/36A	1738
28. Torr, Quarter land of	PRONI D2977/3A/2/28/3A	1742
29. Torr alias Eskart, the quarter land of	PRONI D2977/3A/2/28/4	1742
30. Torr Als Ischartt, the Quarterland of	PRONI D2977/3A/2/28/5	1746
31. Torr, The Quarter land of	PRONI D2977/3A/2/28/7	1776
32. Tour Point	Lendrick Map	1780
33. The Quarter land of West Torr alias Eskirt	PRONI D2977/3A/2/28/8	1781
34. Cregybryan, Carrivegarive	Sur. A.E. 72	1782
35. Toaar	Culfeightrin Map [1789] 1	1789
36. East Torr or Creigbryan	Report of the A.E.	1812
37. West Torr or Carrivegarrive	Report of the A.E.	1812
38. East Tor, West Torr	Grants on the A.E.	1812
39. Torr otherwise Iskart	PRONI D2977/3A/2/1/40	1812
40. Torr, West	Bnd. Sur. (OSNB) B 24 B 37	1830
41. Torr, East	Bnd. Sur. (OSNB) B 24 B 37	1830
42. Tor "a Tower, tower like hill or rock"	J O'D (OSNB) B 24 B 37	1831
43. Tor Bhuraigh	MacErlean 32	1914
44. Tor "A tower or tall round hill"	Dallat's Culfeightrin 36	1981
45. Torr	Éire Thuaidh	1988
46. 'tɔr	Irish of Rathlin 243	1942
47. 'tɔːr	Local pronunciation	1993

The earliest Irish forms (1, 2) of this name feature a final element which is dropped in even the earliest of the English variants. **Torr Head** (see Other Names) was in one instance called *Torsboro Head* (c. 1580). This element has been interpreted by MacErlean (form 43) as the male personal name found also in *Dún Bharach* (*sic*) or Dunworry Fort on Torr Head (*Irish of the Glens* 101; Holmer describes *Barach* as the "name of a hero of the *Clann Uisnigh*"; this fort name appears as *[i n]Dún Bhorraigh* in *SMMD II* 43). This is unlikely, but the second element in *Torbhuirg* remains unidentified. *Borg* "castle" (see *DIL* sv.) and perhaps even Old Norse *berg* "mountain" might be considered; Irish *buirg* "borough" would be unusual.

Tor variously denoted "a tower, fortified building (latterly *túr*), a flame or blaze, a champion or hero, a bush, or a host or multitude" (*DIL*) in the earlier language. But perhaps most commonly in place-names it has come to mean "tall rock; steep rocky height" (*Ó Dónaill*). The Co. Donegal townland name *An Tor* (anglicized **Tor**) has been translated "rocky height" by Mac Aodha (1989–90, 172). Mac Giolla Easpaig (1986, 86) points out that *tor* is very common in names along the entire northern coast, and that it refers most often to a high projecting rock in the sea. Holmer translated the word as "hill" (*Irish of the Glens* 131), which does not seem to be an entirely accurate interpretation of this word as it appears in local place-names (cf. also **Tornabodagh**). Here, it relates to the rocky, lofty headland of Torr Head.

Forms 25(a), 26, 34(a) and 36 represent a division within Torr, coterminous with East Torr. They may be based on *Creag Bhriain* "Brian's rock". Forms 25(b), 34(b) and 37 represent a distinct name for West Torr, and are probably based on *An Cheathrú Gharbh* "the rough quarterland". These names do not appear to be current, and *Torr* is used indiscriminately of both East and West Torr. Regarding forms 24, 29–30, 33 and 39, see **Escort** in Other Names.

Eglish	*An Eaglais*	
D 1638	"the church"	
1. Eglish	Bnd. Sur. (OSNB) B 24 B 37	1830
2. Eaglais "a church"	J O'D (OSNB) B 24 B 37	1831
3. Eaglais "The church"	Ó Dubhthaigh 138	1905
4. Eaglais "a church"	Antrim Place Names 84	1913
5. Eaglais "the church"	Rev. Magill 15	1923
6. Eaglais "A church"	Dallat's Culfeightrin 36	1981
7. ˈɛglïʃ	Local pronunciation	1993

There appears to be no record of a chuch in this townland. The *Ordnance Survey Memoirs* describe, among other antiquities, a site containing graves and standing stones (*OSM* xxiv 53). O'Laverty suggests that this site proves that a church formerly stood here (*O'Laverty* iv 461). Reeves made no such claim. Perhaps it is more likely that this townland once encompassed a greater area, including **Churchfield** townland (site of the original parish church of Culfeightrin), from which it is separated today by the townland of Losset. *Eaglais* "church" as a place-name element refers to a post-Reform church (post-12th century), and does not appear to have been dialectally different from *teampall* (Flanagan 1981–2(c)), used in the original form of Churchfield. We might also consider that *eaglais* simply denoted "church land" here.

Somewhat less likely possible etymologies include origins in *eachla(i)s*, a variant of *achaill* "view point" (see Ó Máille 1989–90, 127 and 1958, 98), *eachlios* "horse-enclosure" (a pre-Christian place-name structure; Mac Giolla Easpaig (1981, 152)) and *éaglios* "(ancient) burial-ground" (*Ó Dónaill*).

Farranmacallan	*Fearann Mhic Ailín*	
D 2340	"MacAllen's ploughland"	
1. Ferinvecallin	Inq. Ult. (Ant.) §49 Car. I	1635
2. Ferren McKallon	Hib. Reg. Cary	1657c
3. ffarn McMallon	BSD 166	1661
4. Farinvicallin	Court of Claims §923	1662c
5. Farinveckallin, the 20 acres of	Court of Claims §923	1662c
6. arinveckallin, the twenty acres of	Decree of Innocence 431	1663
7. the twenty acres ffarin mcAllin	Decree of Innocence 440	1663
8. Farenmac Mallen	Lapsed Money Book 156	1663
9. Fau McAllen	ASE 116a §19	1668
10. Feronkalwen	HMR Ant. 9	1669
11. Ffaren McMallen	Ant. Forfeit.	1700

12. Faranmakallen	Stewart's Survey 10	1734
13. Ferrenmacollen	Sur. A.E. 72	1782
14. Ferran McCallen	Culfeightrin Map [1789] 1	1789
15. Feranmacollan	Culfeightrin Map [1789] 3	1789
16. ffarmackallan	PRONI D2977/3A/2/1/40	1812
17. Farrinmacallin, Farrinmacallen	Culfeightrin Map [1812]	1812
18. Ferranmacallan	Bnd. Sur. (OSNB) B 24 B 37	1830
19. Ferrinmacallan	OSNB B 24 B 37	1831
20. Fearann Mhic Ailin "Mac Allen's land"	J O'D (OSNB) B 24 B 37	1831
21. Fearann Mhic Calainn "MacCallan's land"	Ó Dubhthaigh 138	1905
22. Fearann Mhic Calainn "McCallon's land"	Rev. Magill 16	1923
23. Fearann Mhic Alainn "McAllan's lands"	Dallat's Culfeightrin 36	1981
24. ˌfɑrənməˈkaljən	Local pronunciation	1993
25. ˌfarməˈkaljən	Local pronunciation	1996

Surname scholars such as Woulfe (1923, 305–6, 325) and MacLysaght (1991, 4, 34) distinguish between the surnames MacAllen, for which they give the Irish form *Mac Ailín*, and MacCallion, for which they give the Irish form *Mac Cailín*. MacLysaght suggests *Mac Ailín* derives from *ail* "stone, rock", and describes it as "the name of a war-like branch of the Scottish Campbells brought to Ulster by the O'Donnells" (MacLysaght 1985, 4); he describes *Mac Cailín* somewhat similarly as "a galloglass family with the O'Donnells (found almost exclusively in Donegal and Derry)" (*ibid.* 34). *Mac Cailín* has also been anglicized MacCallan/MacCallen (Woulfe 1923, 325), although this form of the name is associated especially with Co. Fermanagh (MacLysaght 1985, 34). *Mac Coilín*, a variant of *Mac Cailín*, was "common . . . in Down and Antrim at the end of the 16th century" (*ibid.* 334) but the historical variants militate against such a form here.

Fearann is translated "field, land, farm; ground, country; as land-measure, a ploughland" by *Dinneen*. Forms 3, 8 and 11 appear to indicate misspellings.

Farranmacarter   *Fearann Mhic Artúir*
D 1538   "MacCarter's ploughland"

1. ffarnemcallister	DS (Par. Map) 56	1657
2. ffarn Mc Alistor	BSD 165	1661
3. Ffarne mack allister	Lapsed Money Book 155	1663
4. Farran Mc Alister	ASE 116a §19	1668
5. ffarne mack allister	Ant. Forfeit.	1700
6. Faranmakarter	Stewart's Survey 6	1734
7. Farranmakarter	C. McG. (OSNB) B 24 B 37	1734
8. Ffaronmacartor Mountain	Hill's Stewarts 220	1741c
9. Ferrenmacarter	Bnd. Sur. (OSNB) B 24 B 37	1830
10. Ferrinmarter	OSNB B 24 B 37	1831

11. Fearann Mhic Artuir "Mac Arthur's land"	J O'D (OSNB) B 24 B 37	1831
12. Fearann-Mac Arthur	Antrim Place Names	1913
13. Fearann Mhic Artair "Mc Arthur's lands"	Dallat's Culfeightrin 36	1981
14. ˌfarənmïkjɑrtər	Local pronunciation	1993
15. ˌfarmïkɑrtər	Local pronunciation	1996

MacArthur, from *Mac Artúir*, is "a Scottish name . . . sometimes called MacCarter" (MacLysaght 1985, 8; see also Sellar 1973, 111), while MacAlister, from *Mac Alastair*, is "an Irish-Gaelic family in Scotland, a branch of which returned to Ulster as galloglasses in the 14th century" (MacLysaght 1985, 4). Holmer recorded the former surname in the Rathlin subtownland place-name of *Scairbhigh Dhom'all ic Airteoir* as [(skörvi ɣɔːl) i'kɑrtʃɛr] ("rough stony ground of MacArthur"; *Irish of Rathlin* 229). MacAlister is on record locally from the mid-17th century (*HMR Ant.* 8, 11, 13). *Fearann Mhic Alastair* appears to have been altered to *Fearann Mhic Artúir* in the early 1700s. In Culfeightrin, families of the name MacAllister commonly use the name Arthur for a son (*Pers. comm.* 6.1.93).

Glenmakeerin

D 1736

Gleann Maí Caorthainn
"valley of the field of the rowan"

1. Glenmakerrin	Hib. Reg. Cary	1657c
2. Glenmackerrin	DS (Par. Map) 55	1657c
3. Glenmakin	Census 18	1659
4. Glenmakerin	BSD 165	1661
5. Glanackerine	Lapsed Money Book 155	1663
6. Glenmakerin	ASE 116a §19	1668
7. Glenmakern	HMR Ant. 10	1669
8. Glanackerine	Ant. Forfeit.	1700
9. Glenmakirne, one quarter of	PRONI D2977/3A/2/1/21	1709
10. Glarykiran	Religious Survey	1734
11. Glenmakeerin	Stewart's Survey 5	1734
12. Glenmakeerin	C. McG. (OSNB) B 24 B 37	1734
13. Glenmakerin, Quarterland of	PRONI D2977/3A/2/1/36A	1738
14. Glenackerin, the Quarter land of	PRONI D2977/3A/2/4/1	1742
15. Glenmakeerin, the Quarter land of	PRONI D2977/3A/2/21/2–3	1746
16. Glemakeerin	PRONI D2977/3A/2/21/4	1776
17. Glenmakerin	Lendrick Map	1780
18. Glenmakeeran	Sur. A.E. 54	1782
19. Glenmakeerin	Sur. A.E. 60	1782
20. Glenmakirin	PRONI D2977/3A/2/6/3	1792
21. Glenmakeerin	Report of the A.E.	1812
22. Glenmakerin	PRONI D2977/3A/2/1/40	1812
23. Glenmakeerin	Bnd. Sur. (OSNB) B 24 B 37	1830
24. Gleann Mhic Chiaráin "valley of the son of Kieran"	J O'D (OSNB) B 24 B 37	1831

25. Gleann Mhic Caorthainn "Mackeeran's glen"	Ó Dubhthaigh 180	1905
26. Gleann Maighe Caorthainn "glen of the rowan tree plain"	Rev. Magill 16	1923
27. Gleann na caorthainn "glen of rowan trees or mountain-ash"	Dallat's Culfeightrin 36	1981
28. ˌglɛnməˈkiːrən	Local pronunciation	1993

The *gleann* "valley" referred to in the place-name seems likely to be that occupied by the northward flowing Glenmakeeran River, which runs through the centre of this townland. The patronymic *mac Chiaráin* "son of *Ciarán*" (gen. *mhac Chiaráin*; earlier gen. *mic Chiaráin*) reflects the subsequent elements in historical variants to some degree (note form 24). However, *Ciarán* is somewhat rare in east Ulster genealogies, and we might have expected its gen. *-áin* ending to have yielded *-an/-ane* in some of the historical forms, especially in the 17th century (cf. **Feykeeran Burn** in Other Names, **Carnkirn** in Grange of Drumtullagh, and **Doonans** in Armoy). The latter also applies to the surname *Mac Ciaráin* (anglicized MacKieran), gen. sing. *Mhic Ciaráin* (earlier *Mic Ciaráin*), which is described as "a Donegal name" by MacLysaght (1991, 179).

Form 26 reflects the historical forms well. *Magh* (gen. sing. *maí*, earlier *maighe*) may variously denote "a plain, a campus or field" (*Dinneen*). This element has been somewhat similarly anglicized in the Lough Erne island name **Inishmacsaint** (see *Onom. Goed.* sv. *Inis maige samh*). The gen. sing. (*caorthainn*) rather than the gen. pl. (*caorthann*) form of *caorthann* "rowan or quicken tree or mountain ash" has been adopted elsewhere in the south Co. Derry townland name *Tulaigh Chaorthainn*/**Tullyheran** (*PNI* v 155). Maps from the late 16th and early 17th centuries (such as *Mercator's Ire.*, 1595; *Speed's Ulster*, 1610; etc.) depict this area as being heavily forested. The upper valleys of the Glenmakeerin river and its tributaries are also wooded today; they form the western tracts of the Ballypatrick Forest.

Glentop or Ardaghmore D 1530	A hybrid form(?)

See **Ardaghmore or Glentop**.

Goodland D 2041	An English form

1. Goodalan	Stewart's Survey 9	1734
2. Goodland	Bnd. Sur. (OSNB) B 24 B 37	1830
3. Goodelan	Tithe App. Book 9	1833
4. gọdˈlɑnd	Local pronunciation	1993

Along with the townlands of Bighouse, Knockbrack and Torglass, Goodland formed part of the former townland of **Ballyukin** (see Other Names).

Greenan D 1634	*An Grianán* "the eminent place"	
1. Grianan	Ultach 4:2, 3	1927
2. Greenan	C. McG. (OSNB) B 24 B 37	1734
3. Grianan	Stewart's Survey 4	1734
4. Greenan	Sur. A.E. 80	1782
5. Grainan	PRONI D2977/3A/2/1/39	1783
6. Grenans	PRONI D2977/3A/2/1/40	1812
7. Greenans	Bnd. Sur. (OSNB) B 24 B 37	1830
8. Grianán "sunny land, fort or hill"	J O'D (OSNB) B 24 B 37	1831
9. Gríanan "Palace, or sunny bower"	Ó Dubhthaigh 181	1905
10. Grianán "a sunny bower"	Rev. Magill 17	1923
11. Grianán "A sunny spot"	Dallat's Culfeightrin 36	1981
12. 'griːnənz	Ó Maolfabhail (Grianán) 70	1974
13. 'griːnənz	Local pronunciation	1993

Prior to 1734, Greenan appeared under Duncarbit townland in the sources (Carleton 1991, 67). The English plural suffix in the later forms listed above suggest that there has been some recent division of this territory.

The name derives from *grianán*, a word originally meaning "a sunny chamber, a bower, a soller, an open balcony exposed to the sun; an upper room" (*DIL*). Holmer recorded the place-name *An Grianán Mór* ([ə griənə moːr]), referring to a mountain several miles east of Greenan townland, and tentatively offered the meaning for *grianán* "sun bower, summer dwelling (sunny spot?)" (*Irish of the Glens* 117; see **Greenanmore**, Other Names).

Physically, Greenan townland is a mountainous and northward sloping territory in the shadow of Oghtbristacree mountain (393 metres), which lies on its southern boundary. Toner has argued that the primary meaning of *grianán* in place-names may be "hill, mound". He has noted that the word has been translated "peak of a mountain" by *Dwelly*, and that many places in Ireland which bear this name command a good view of the surrounding district (*PNI* i 29). This is commensurable with this townland and such a meaning was hinted at by O'Donovan in form 8. Ó Maolfabhail suggests that the idea of *grianán* as an upper room or balcony with a view associated with houses of importance led to its initial use as a name for special places in an upland location which people regularly frequented (*Ó Maolfabhail (Grianán)* 68–9). A second and much later series of place-names based on *grianán* seems to mean more specifically "sunny place, a place good for drying (e.g. of turf)" (*ibid.* 69), although it may be impracticable to differentiate between the two place-name strata now because of the paucity of historical forms.

There is another place called *An Grianán* in Ballygill Middle in Rathlin Island (it has been anglicized as **Greenan**; see *Place-Names of Rathlin* 39). It was described as follows in the 1850s: "A small smooth hill rising on a tongue of land that runs into the sea. It forms the crowning point of said tongue or headland. It is supposed to have been so named from its smoothness and sunny aspect. It is well known by the name" (*OSRNB* sh.1, 2), and in 1887 as follows: "the most beautiful of the many beautiful spots on the island, combining the grandest features of ocean, cliff, and cavern scenery" (*O'Laverty* iv 385). Mac Giolla Easpaig translated the name as "the sunny place" (*Place-Names of Rathlin ibid.*). The Co. Limerick townland name of *An Grianán* (anglicized **Greenane**) has been translated "the eminent place" (Ó Maolfabhail 1990, 200).

Knockbrack	*An Cnoc Breac*	
D 1942	"the speckled hill"	
1. Knockbrack	Bnd. Sur. (OSNB) B 24 B 37	1830
2. Cnoc Breac "speckled hill"	J O'D (OSNB) B 24 B 37	1831
3. Cnoc breac "Speckled hill"	Dallat's Culfeightrin 36	1981
4. nɑkˈbrak	Local pronunciation	1993

There are two summits in this townland: one to the south, at 248 metres, being a western extension of Crockanore (see Other Names), and a more northerly hill of c. 200 metres on the north-western boundary with Cross, either of which could have prompted the first element in this name, *cnoc* "a hill, a height, a mountain" (*Dinneen*). Holmer recorded this word in late local Irish as [krʌk] (*Irish of the Glens* 106). The remnants of an older pronunciation are retained in this place-name; the Ordnance Survey (*OSRNB* sh.5) recorded a similar subtownland name in Ballyreagh Lower as *Crookbrack* (it was standardized as **Crockbrack**; *OS 1:10,000*). The second element of the name is *breac* "speckled, spotted" (*Dinneen*). There are some 43 townlands called Knockbrack found throughout Ireland.

Knockmacolusky	*Cnoc Mhic Bhloscaidh*	
D 2635	"MacCloskey's hill"	
1. Knocklesky	Census 17	1659
2. Knokkulliske	HMR Ant. 9	1669
3. Knocknacola	Culfeightrin Map [1789] 1	1789
4. Knocknacoliska	Culfeightrin Map [1812]	1812
5. Knockmacolusky	Bnd. Sur. (OSNB) B 24 B 37	1830
6. Croaghmacolusky	OSNB B 24 B 37	1831
7. Nockmacoliskey	Tithe Applot. 17	1833
8. Knock and Croagh mean hill; "Macolusky's hill"	J O'D (OSNB) B 24 B 37	1831
9. Cnoc na coláisde "The hill of the college or school"	Ó Dubhthaigh 182	1905
10. Cnoc na cúil loiscthe "The hill of the burnt corner"	Dallat's Culfeightrin 36	1981
11. ˌnɔkməkˈɔləski	Local pronunciation	1993

The first element in form 6, which was recorded from local informants, resembles *cruach* "reek or mountain", but this variant does not appear to be current today. The spelling *croagh* may in fact represent the surveyor's reinterpretation of the element based on the local pronunciation of *cnoc* ([krʌk]; *Irish of the Glens* 106). The name refers to an eminence of c. 190 metres dominating the northern end of this small coastal townland on the southern slopes of Carnaneigh (see Other Names).

Form 8 suggests that the first element is qualified by the surname *Mac Bhloscaidh*, angli-cized MacCloskey or MacCluskey, and described as "a branch of the O'Cahans with whom *Bloscaidh* [*sic*] was a favourite forename" (the surname was associated especially with Co. Derry; MacLysaght 1985, 47; see also Bell 1988, 143). The surname is not conspicuous in the sources, although O'Cahans have been associated with the area since at least the late 1600s (see **Kanestown**, Other Names, Ramoan). *Cnoc Bhloscaidh* "*Bloscadh*'s hill" resem-bles earlier historical variants (forms 1–2), but the absence of unstressed syllables in angli-cized forms of place-names is common. Form 1 also resembles *Cnoc Loiscthe* "burnt hill" but such a form could not explain the appearance of the medial *mac* in later forms; forms 9 (which appears to be popular locally and which may be reflected in forms 4–5) and 10 may be similarly dismissed. The vowel between the *k* and *l* in this name may have developed through association with the etymology in form 9.

| **Ligadaughtan** | *Log an Dachtáin* | |
| D 2536 | "hollow of the mud(?)" | |

1. Laghedaghten	Census 17	1659
2. Lagadaghtowne	HMR Ant. 9	1669
3. Lagadarten	C. McG. (OSNB) B 24 B 37	1734
4. Lagadartan	Stewart's Survey 12	1734
5. Ligadaskon	Culfeightrin Map [1789] 1	1789
6. Legadaghton	PRONI D2977/3A/2/1/40	1812
7. Legadaghtin	Culfeightrin Map [1812]	1812
8. Ligadaughtan	Bnd. Sur. (OSNB) B 24 B 37	1830
9. Legadaghton	Tithe Applot. 17	1833
10. Lag a' dartáin "hollow of the herd or drove"	J O'D (OSNB) B 24 B 37	1831
11. lug an tachtain "The hollow of the choking"	Ó Dubhthaigh 183	1905
12. Lag a' dtactáin "hollow of choking"	Rev. Magill 19	1923
13. Lag a dtactán "the hollow of the strangling"	Dallat's Culfeightrin 36	1981
14. ˌlïgəˈdatən	Local pronunciation	1993

Holmer recorded the word *log/lag* "hollow" locally as [lïg] and [lɛg] (*Irish of the Glens* 118). Regarding further possible interpretations of this element, see **Lagavara** in Ballintoy. Joyce has noted that the anglicized forms *log/lag* for the first element of around 100 town-land names, almost all of them in the northern half of the country (*Joyce* i 431).

Dinneen notes that Quiggin recorded *dachtán* "smell (as of food, earth, etc.)" in north-west Co. Donegal earlier this century, but ascribes to it a late usage. Ó Domhnaill (1952, 190) explained the word *dachtán* as meaning *abar* "boggy ground, morass" in roughly the same area. These meanings may be developments of *dachtán* which is otherwise a variant of *dartán* "(little) clod" (*Ó Dónaill*). Although these words seem to be otherwise unattested outside Co. Donegal (*Dinneen* sv. *dachtán*, *dartán*), the gen. sing. of *dachtán*, of uncertain meaning here, is the most likely final element.

Back-formation of *dartán* "calf; herd or drove" (*DIL* sv.) to *dachtán*, which is perhaps what

157

O'Donovan had in mind (form 10), seems unlikely, as the changes in the second element in historical forms seem to reflect natural phonetic development (*ch* prior to a *t* in the late local dialect tended to become [h] (*Irish of the Glens* 24)). Forms 11–13 seem to assume that the initial consonant in the final element has changed from *t* to *d*, which is in itself unlikely, but the unattested *tachtán*, perhaps "strangled object", is not well reflected in the historical forms.

Losset	*Losaid*	
D 1539	"kneading-trough-like land division"	

1. Loslet	Hib. Reg. Cary	1657c
2. Losset	DS (Par. Map) 56	1657c
3. Loskid	Census 18	1659
4. Lossett	BSD 165	1661
5. Lossett	Lapsed Money Book 154	1663
6. Lossett	ASE 116a §19	1668
7. Lossid	HMR Ant. 10	1669
8. Lossett	Hib. Del. Antrim	1672c
9. Losett	PRONI D2977/3A/2/1/16	1696
10. Lossett	Ant. Forfeit.	1700
11. Lossett	C. McG. (OSNB) B 24 B 37	1734
12. Lossett	Stewart's Survey 6	1734
13. losset	PRONI D2977/3A/2/1/40	1812
14. Lossett	Bnd. Sur. (OSNB) B 24 B 37	1830
15. Losad "a kneading trough" (a name applied to good land)	J O'D (OSNB) B 24 B 37	1831
16. Losaid "very fertile land"	Rev. Magill 20	1923
17. 'lɔsət	Local pronunciation	1993

Losaid "a kneading trough" (for making bread; *DIL* sv. *losat*) is used figuratively in place-names to denote a territory which has a resemblence to such a trough, or possibly to land with an attractive appearance, or to fertile soil (*Dinneen*). It may also refer to a "shallow depression" (*Ó Dónaill*). Joyce stated regarding this place-name element that "the allusion seems to be not so much to shape, as to use and production . . . for the word is applied to a well tilled and productive field" (*Joyce* ii 430). The modern townland is indeed of *losaid* form inasmuch as it occupies a long, narrow strip of land either side of a tributary of the Glenshesk river. There are some 12 townlands of this name in the country, including Lossetkillew in Co. Cavan in which it is qualified; all but two are in Ulster (*Census 1851*). The subtownland name *Creag na Loiste* (angl. **Craigalusta**) in Co. Down has been translated "crag/rock of the shallow depression(?)" (*PNI* iii 131).

Loughan	*An Lochán*	
D 2437	"the pond"	

1. 2 Loghans	Inq. Ult. (Antrim) §49 Car. I	1635
2. Loghan	DS (Par. Map) 56	1657c
3. Lochan	Census 17	1659

4. Ballyloughan	Inq. Ult. (Antrim) §3 Car. II	1661
5. Loghan	BSD 166	1661
6. the two Loghanes	Court of Claims §923	1662c
7. 2 Loghans, the 40 acres of the	Court of Claims §923	1662c
8. the two Loghans, the forty acres of	Decree of Innocence 431	1663
9. the two Loghanes, the forty acres of	Decree of Innocence 440	1663
10. Loughan, 1 Qur.	Lapsed Money Book 156	1663
11. Loughan	ASE 116a §19	1668
12. (?)Ballyloghan	HMR Ant. 9	1669
13. Loighan	Ant. Forfeit.	1700
14. Loughan	Stewart's Survey 11	1734
15. Loughan	C. McG. (OSNB) B 24 B 37	1734
16. Loughan	Culfeightrin Map [1789] 1	1789
17. Loughan	Culfeightrin Map [1812]	1812
18. Loughan	Bnd. Sur. (OSNB) B 24 B 37	1830
19. Lochán "a small lough or pool"	J O'D (OSNB) B 24 B 37	1831
20. ˈlɔːxən	Local pronunciation	1993

Form 1, which implies that two territories of similar name existed locally, may refer also to Ballinloughan, c. .5 km to the immediate north of this townland. As with Ballinloughan, there exists today no discernable lake or pool which might have prompted the place-name, as interpreted in form 19, although a *lochán* "a small lake, pool, a shallow rain lake" is necessarily a minor feature. The prefixing of *Bally* to place-names in the *Ulster Inquisitions* (*Inq. Ult.*) is not uncommon (form 4) and although form 12 suggests that the name *Baile Locháin* "townland of the small lake" was formerly current, Carleton (1991, 67) notes that this particular reference is ambiguous and may in fact be referring to **Ballinloughan**.

Magherindonnell
D 1540

Machairín Dónaill(?)
"Dónall's little plain"

1. Magherinedonnell	Court of Claims §923	1662c
2. Magherenindonnell, the 20 acres of	Court of Claims §923	1662c
3. Magheren McDonell, the twenty. acres of	Decree of Innocence 431	1663
4. Magherindonell	PRONI D2977/3A/2/1/26	1714c
5. Macherendoniel	Stewart's Survey 7	1734
6. Macherindonnell	C. McG. (OSNB) B 24 B 37	1734
7. Macherendoniel	Sur. A.E. 60	1782
8. Magrindonnell	PRONI D2977/3A/2/6/3	1792
9. Magherydonnell; Magherindonnell	PRONI D2977/3A/2/1/40	1812
10. Magherindonnel	Bnd. Sur. (OSNB) B 24 B 37	1830
11. Magherendonnell	Tithe Applot. 10	1833
12. Machairín Domhnaill "Donnell's little plain"	J O'D (OSNB) B 24 B 37	1831

13. Machaire Domhnaill "The plain of the McDonnells"	Dallat's Culfeightrin 36	1981
14. ˌmahïrən'dɔnəl	Local pronunciation	1993

Machairín, a diminutive form of *machaire* "a plain, a flat or low lying country" (*Dinneen*) which appears to have formed the first element in this name, may be otherwise unattested (see also **Maghernahar** in Ballintoy). The feature in question is a gently sloping and low-lying territory in Glenshesk. The townland is situated to the immediate north of **Churchfield** which was formerly *Magheretemple* in the sources.

The second element is probably the male personal name *Dónall* (earlier *Domhnall*) in its genitive form; the change from [doːnəl] to [dɔnəl] in anglicized forms mirrors the anglicization of the well known local patronymic, *Mac Dónaill* (MacDonnell).

Machaire an Dónallaigh "plain of MacDonnell" might also be considered as a possible original form. The loss in speech of a short, unstressed final vowel has been attested to elsewhere (see, for example, **Craigfad**). Finally *Machairín Mhic Dhónaill* "MacDonnell's little plain", based on form 3, could also be considered, although the early loss of the *mac* element seems unusual. Perhaps the writer inserted the *Mc* in this form by analogy.

Tenaghs	*Teangach*	
D 1533	"place of tongues of land"	

1. Teaughs	C. McG. (OSNB)	1734
2. Tenagh	Stewart's Survey 4	1734
3. Tenaghs	Sur. A.E. 80	1782
4. Tinagh, the quarter land of	PRONI D2977/3A/2/1/39	1783
5. Tenagh	Report of the A.E.	1812
6. Tenaghs	Bnd. Sur. (OSNB) B 24 B 37	1830
7. Corry Teighs and Ardaghmore	Tithe Applot. 1	1833
8. Taomhach, meaning uncertain	J O'D (OSNB) B 24 B 37	1831
9. Cíoch "a breast"	Dallat's Culfeightrin 36	1981
10. 'tʃiəxs	Local pronunciation	1996
11. 'kiəxs	Local pronunciation	1996

The large disparity between modern pronunciation and that hinted at in the historical variants leads one to suspect that the original form of this name was *teangach* "place of tongues (of land)" or perhaps *teangacha* "tongues (of land)". Such forms could refer to spurs or ridges of land in the west of the townland around which the Glenshesk River winds its course. The vocalization of *ng* is something of a feature of late East Ulster Irish and indeed Holmer recorded *teanga* "tongue" locally as [t's'ʌə] and [t'eə] (*Irish of the Glens* 130; see also *ibid.* 31). *Teanga* "tongue" is found in other Irish place-names including the Co. Westmeath village name *An Teanga* (anglicized Tang; *GÉ* 165), and the Co. Down townland name *Cill Teanga* (anglicized **Kiltonga**) "church of (the) tongue of land" (*PNI* ii 232). Joyce suggests that the townland of **Bryantang** in south Co. Antrim also contains this element (*Joyce* ii 427).

Other possibilities may include the form *An tSeangach*, meaning perhaps "the narrow place" or "the place of thin land divisions/ridges". O'Kane (1970, 109) recorded the town-

land name *An tSeanga Mheáin*, anglicized Tangaveane, in central Co. Donegal (but see also
Bunshanacloney in Armoy).

Sommerfelt (1929, 175) recorded the word *cíoch* "breast" as [t'i:] in late south Armagh
Irish (note form 9). A similar change of [t'] to [k'] in some words in the late local dialect was
not unknown (see *Irish of the Glens* 22). However, there remains some doubt as to how early
such a pronunciation developed, while this etymology also does not account for the medial
-n- in forms 2–6. The pronunciation in form 11 is no longer current but remembered. The
preferred English spelling locally is *Teaughs*. The *s* suffix in most forms suggests that there
has been some internal division of this territory. It seems likely that form 7(a) represents an
obsolete land division; Ardaghmore is a neighbouring townland.

| **Tervillin** | *Tír Mhaoilín(?)* | |
| D 1842 | "*Maoilín*'s land" | |

1. Tervillan	C. McG. (OSNB) B 24 B 37	1734
2. Terullian	Religious Survey	1734
3. Teervillin	Stewart's Survey 8	1734
4. Terveelin	Lendrick Map	1780
5. Treenillan	PRONI D2977/3A/2/1/40	1812
6. Tervillan	Bnd. Sur. (OSNB) B 24 B 37	1830
7. Treemillin	OSNB B 24 B 37	1831
8. Terveelin	OSNB B 24 B 37	1831
9. Turveelin	Tithe App. Book 13	1833
10. Tír Maoilín "Moyleen's district or land"	J O'D (OSNB) B 24 B 37	1831
11. Tír buailean "The place of the little boolies"	Dallat's Culfeightrin 35	1981
12. ˌtÿr'vÿljən	Local pronunciation	1993

The first element of this name appears to have been *tír* "land, region". Dallat has noted
the local pronunciation [tʃÿr'vÿljən] (*Pers. comm.* 06.01.93). The land in question is hilly
ground (c. 220 metres on average) to the north of Crockanore.

There is some doubt regarding the second element. We might consider gen. forms of
muileann "mill", *millín* "small eminence, knoll" and the unattested *bilín* "small tree". The
alteration in historical forms between *-ee-* and *-i-* may suggest that the first vowel in this element was [ʎ] (see also **Ballyveely** in Ramoan), and we might thus consider *maoileann*
"rounded summit, hillock, knoll" (*Ó Dónaill*) in one of the forms *Tír Mhaoilinn/Mhaoileann*
"land of the rounded summit(s)". *Tír Mhaoilín* "land of the hornless cows" (see *Ó Dónaill*
sv. *maoilín*; standard modern gen. pl. *maoilíní*), perhaps with the connotation "place of trans-
humance", is a further possible original form, although unstressed *-in* is rarely anglicized to
-an (forms 1–2, 5–6) elsewhere locally (cf. **Farranmacallan** in Culfeightrin). As *tír* is often
qualified by a personal name however (see *Joyce* ii 381; *L. Log. Mhuineacháin* 50), the suggested form is *Tír Mhaoilín*, which contains the male personal name *Maoilín* (O. Ir. *Muiléne*;
see *CGH* 150 b 3), which occurs in the Co. Meath parish and townland name *Steach Maoilín*
(Stamullen; *GÉ* 162). We might also consider the personal name *Maolán*, but we would then
have to explain the palatalization of the *-l-* in modern pronunciation. The variant of *buaile*
"milking-place in summer pasturage; fold, enclosure; small grazing field; dung-yard" (*Ó*

Dónaill) suggested in form 11 does not appear to be attested, and it is furthermore doubtful whether such a form is reflected in the historical variants.

Torcorr D 2538	*Tor Corr* "odd tor"	
1. Tercor	Census 17	1659
2. (?)Turlagh	HMR Ant. 9	1669
3. Torcorr	Culfeightrin Map [1789] 1	1789
4. Torcorr	Culfeightrin Map [1812]	1812
5. Torcorr	Bnd. Sur. (OSNB) B 24 B 37	1830
6. Tor corr "odd tower", or "tower-like hill of the cranes"	J O'D (OSNB) B 24 B 37	1831
7. Tor cor "The roundhill tower (rock)"	Ó Dubhthaigh 186	1905
8. Tor cor "round hill tower"	Rev. Magill 24	1923
9. Tor corr "The tower-like round hill"	Dallat's Culfeightrin 36	1981
10. tɔrˈkɔr	Local pronunciation	1993

While the place-name element *tor* has various meanings (cf. **East Torr**), "a tall rock; steep rocky height" (*Ó Dónaill*) appears to be the most relevant locally. This is a mountainous townland with a cliff-lined coast, but it is not certain to what feature exactly that *tor* referred. Regarding the translation of *tor* as "hill" in forms 6–9, we may note that Joyce stated that *tur* (*sic*) in place-names could "sometimes (denote) a little round hill, oftener a bush" (*Joyce* iii 595). This could have developed from *tor* "bush" or *tor* "steep rocky height" being associated especially with hills: compare *muine* "brake, thicket" and *doire* "oak grove; wood; thicket", which also came to mean "hill or hillock" in northern counties (see *GUH* 46 n.5 and Mac Giolla Easpaig 1984, 55 and 1986, 85). Watson (1926, 145), possibly following Joyce, translated *tor* in Scottish place-names as "a rounded hill", while Nicolaisen (1969, 12 sv. *torr*) translated it as "hill, mountain of an abrupt or conical form, eminence, mound, tower". Holmer also translated *tor* as "hill" (*Irish of the Glens* 131) but this is somewhat inaccurate in the context of names such as East Torr.

As with the townland name **Cloghcorr** in Armoy, *corr* could conceivably represent one of several words, but in the absence of a medial definite article, the adj. *corr* "odd; uneven, rounded, convex, curved; peaked, projecting; smooth" (*Dinneen*) seems most likely.

Torglass D 1942	*Tor Glas* "grey tor"	
1. Torr Glas	Irish of the Glens 131	1940
2. Torglass	Bnd. Sur. (OSNB) B 24 B 37	1830
3. Torglass	OSNB B 24 B 37	1831
4. Tor glas "green tower, or tower like hill or rock"	J O'D (OSNB) B 24 B 37	1831

5. tɔːr glɑs	Irish of the Glens 131	1940
6. tǫr'glɑs	Local pronunciation	1993

Glas "green" (*Irish of the Glens* 116) may have been used here in its older meaning "grey". *Dinneen* translates *glas* as "green, verdant (as grass); grey (as a horse, cloth, stone, etc.); bluish-grey; silvery, bright, lustrous (of the eye) . . .". This townland was considered part of **Ballyukin** (see Other Names) in the sources until 1830. The first vowel, in unstressed position, has recently been raised (perhaps by analogy with names beginning with *tuar*).

Tornabodagh	*Tuar na mBodach*	
D 1541	"cattle-field of the churls"	
1. Tornabodagh	Bnd. Sur. (OSNB) B 24 B 37	1830
2. Turnabodagg	Tithe App. Book 10	1833
3. Tor na mbodach "tower of the clowns"	J O'D (OSNB) B 24 B 37	1831
4. Tor na bodach "The hill of the clown"	Dallat's Culfeightrin 36	1981
5. ˌturnə'bǫdəx	Local pronunciation	1993

The modern form of this name retains no evidence of eclipsis of the final element but it appears that the gen. pl. form (*bodach*) of *bodach* "lout, churl; codling" (*Dinneen*) was used. Notably, Holmer recorded the word *bodach* ([bɔdɑx]) as meaning "old man" (*Irish of the Glens* 102). The Co. Limerick townland name *Baile na mBodach* (anglicized Ballynamuddagh) has been translated "the town of the low-bred persons" (Ó Maolfabhail 1990, 43). Modern pronunciation suggests that *tuar* "manured land; cattle-field; sheep-run; pasture, lea; bleaching-green" (*Ó Dónaill* sv.) formed the first element. Joyce waywardly claimed that this element "does not occur at all in Ulster counties" (*Joyce* i 236) but note, for example, *Tuar Gabhann* "the cattle-field/pasture of the smith" (anglicized **Terrygowan**) in south-west Co. Antrim (*PNI* iv 68). One would not be suprised at [tuər] developing eventually to [tur]/[tɔr]/[tor] in unstressed position (see also **Turrybrennan** in Other Names).

O'Donovan's translation (form 3) suggests however that *tor* "steep rocky height" (see also **East Torr**) was confused with *túr* "tower" locally. Joyce noted that in many parts of Ireland *tor* "is applied to a tall rock resembling a tower" (*Joyce* iii 399), and *DIL* (sv. *tor*) suggests *tor* has been confused with *tuir* "pillar, column" (*ibid.*) and *túr*. However, in the absence of more definite evidence of an interaction of *tor/túr* to denote the same feature, *tuar* has been adopted here (the varying topographical character of the townland could be invoked to support either *tuar* or *tor/túr*).

This territory appeared under Tornaroan townland in the sources prior to 1830 (Carleton 1991, 64).

Tornamoney	*Tuar na Móna*	
D 2535	"cattle-field of the bogland(?)"	
1. Tornamurie	Census 17	1659
2. Tworenemony	ASE 116a §19	1668
3. Turmone	HMR Ant. 10	1669

4. Touranony	Lamb Maps Co. Antrim	1690c
5. Tornamoney	Culfeightrin Map [1789] 1	1789
6. Tornamoney	Culfeightrin Map [1812]	1812
7. Tornamurey	PRONI D2977/3A/2/1/40	1812
8. Tornamoney	Bnd. Sur. (OSNB) B 24 B 37	1830
9. Turnamoany	Tithe Applot. 16	1833
10. Tor na móna "tower of the bog"	J O'D (OSNB) B 24 B 37	1831
11. Tor na móna "The cliff of the bog"	Ó Dubhthaigh 186	1905
12. Tor na móna "height of the bog"	Rev. Magill 25	1923
13. Tor na mónadh "the hill of the bog"	Dallat's Culfeightrin 36	1981
14. ˌtɔrnəˈmoːnə	Local pronunciation	1996

The standard English form of the name reflects O'Donovan's interpretation (form 10). However, early forms suggest that *tuar* "manured land; cattle-field; sheep-run; pasture, lea; bleaching green" (*Ó Dónaill* sv.) originally formed the first element (regarding forms 10–3 see also **Torcorr** and **Tornabodagh**).

An *-adh* ending, as in the gen. (*mónadh*, later *móna*) of *móin* "turf, peat; bogland, moor" (*Ó Dónaill* sv.) eventually developed to [uː] in most Ulster dialects (see O'Rahilly 1932, 66), but was spelled *-y* in anglicized form in some cases, such as *An Fionnachadh* (anglicized **Finaghy**; *GÉ* 106). Modern local pronunciation does not reflect English *-y* however (form 14). The Scottish Gaelic word *monadh* "hilly ground" does not appear to have been in "either the lexicon or the onomasticon of Ireland" (*PNI* i 105), while the [oː] in modern pronunciation discounts *muine* "thicket; brushwood, scrub" (*Ó Dónaill*) as a possibility.

Tornaroan
D 1542

Tuar na Ruán
"cattle-field of the red patches"

1. Twornarone	MacDonnells Antrim 441	1625
2. Twornarone	Inq. Ult. (Antrim) §61 Car. I	1635
3. (?)Twornaroney	Inq. Ult. (Antrim) §128 Car. I	1638
4. Turnenarone	Hib. Reg. Cary	1657c
5. Towrnaghroaghane	DS (Par. Map) 55	1657c
6. Turenaroughan; Turnaroghan	DS (Par. Map) 56	1657c
7. Twoaroan	Census 18	1659
8. Turnaroaghan	BSD 166	1661
9. Tornooroane	Court of Claims §923	1662c
10. Twornoroane, the fi town of	Court of Claims §923	1662c
11. Turmacroghane	Lapsed Money Book 156	1663
12. the halftowne Towrnarone	Decree of Innocence 440	1663
13. (?)Tinnavaghan, fi town	ASE 116a §19	1668
14. Toronarony	Hib. Del. Antrim	1672c
15. Turmacroghane	Ant. Forfeit.	1700
16. Torarane	Religious Survey	1734
17. Tournaroan	Lendrick Map (OSNB) B 24 B 37	1780
18. Tornaroan	Bnd. Sur. (OSNB) B 24 B 37	1830

19. Turnarooan	Tithe Applot. 11	1833
20. Tor na rón "tower of seals"	J O'D (OSNB) B 24 B 37	1831
21. Tor na run "hill or crest of the secrets"	OSRNB sh.5	1855c
22. Tor na ruadháin "The tor of the moorland"	Dallat's Culfeightrin 36	1981
23. ˌturnəˈrɔn	Local pronunciation	1993

As in the previous name, early variants suggest that the first element was *tuar*, which has several meanings (see also **Tornabodagh**).

Several possibilities exist regarding the interpretation of the second element, including the gen. pl. of *ruán* (earlier *ruadhán*) "plant (that produces red colouring matter)", and the gen. pl. of the male personal name *Rúán* (earlier *Rúadhán*; regarding this latter place-name type, and further possibilities regarding this element, see **Drumroan** in Grange of Drumtullagh). Although the gen. pl. of *rón* is normally *rónta*, the Galway place-name *Cloch na Rón* (Roundstone) contains a variant form (*GÉ* 65), and *Dieckhoff*'s dictionary of Scottish Gaelic lists the gen. pl. *rón*, which would be consistent with O'Donovan's interpretation (form 20). Note also the Rathlin subtownland place-name *Rubha na Rón* "the point of the seals" (*Place-Names of Rathlin* 73). However, the medial -*gh*- in forms 5–6, 8–9 and 11 may reflect the *dh* of *ruadh*- (see **Ballycleagh** regarding this feature), while most forms suggest that the final syllable contained a diphthong. Stressed medial [x] is rarely lost and this -*gh*- is unlikely to represent Irish -*ch*- here.

The integrity of forms 3 and 14, which would suggest the existence of a final syllable which has been lost, is in doubt.

Twenty Acres	*Droim na Meallóg(?)*	
D 1841	"ridge of the small mounds"	
1. Drumnemologe	Hib. Reg. Cary	1657c
2. Drumnemellog	DS (Par. Reg.) 57	1657c
3. 20 Acres	Census 17	1659
4. Drumnemolloge	BSD 165	1661
5. Drumnemelloge	ASE 116a §19	1668
6. Bummemelloge	Lapsed Money Book 155	1663
7. Drumnemolagh	Hib. Del. Antrim	1672c
8. Twenty Acres	Religious Survey	1734
9. Twenty Acres	Stewart's Survey 8	1734
10. Twenty Acres	C. McG. (OSNB) B 24 B 37	1734
11. Twenty Acres	Lendrick Map (OSNB) B 24 B 37	1780
12. Twenty Acres	Sur. A.E. 42	1782
13. Twenty Acres	Bnd. Sur. (OSNB) B 24 B 37	1830
14. ˌdrɔmnə ˈmaləg	Local pronunciation	1993
15. twɛnti ˈeːkərs	Local pronunciation	1993

Although the Irish name for this townland has not appeared in the sources since c. 1672 (form 7), Dallat believes it to be remembered if not still used (*Pers. comm.* 06.1.93) and furnished the pronunciation in form 14. Unfortunately, forms 1–2 and 4–7 are all related and exhibit copying of scribal errors. Possible final elements include gen. pl. forms of *ballóg* "roofless house; ruin" and *meallóg* "small mound or knoll". *Meallóg* is a diminutive of *meall* "knoll"; Flanagan and Flanagan have said the latter is confined to Cork and Kerry in place-names (*IPN* 120; see however *PNI* iv 321). *Bológ* "a yearling bullock, an ox" (*Dinneen*; it has the further meanings "shell; skull, top of the head; heifer" in Scottish Gaelic (*Dwelly* sv. *bollag*)) seems to be a late borrowing from English and so seems less likely, while the first vowel in *mullóg* "small height or mound" would be unlikely to have yielded the [a] in modern pronunciation. This [a] could have arisen from Irish *a, ea* or *o*.

The English name is obviously not based on the forms discussed above. The modern townland covers over 128 acres. There are 6 townlands called Twenty Acres scattered throughout Ireland (*Census 1851*). In c. 1855, the Ordnance Survey also noted a "small farm village" of this name in Carnfeogue townland in nearby Derrykeighan parish (*OSRNB* sh.13, 1).

| **West Torr** | *Tor* |
| D 2141 | "tor" |

See **East Torr**.

| **White House** | *An Toigh Bán* |
| D 2433 | "the white house" |

1. White House	Culfeightrin Map [1789] 1	1789
2. White House	Culfeightrin Map [1812]	1812
3. White House	Bnd. Sur. (OSNB) B 24 B 37	1830
4. Taigh bán "Whitehouse"	Ó Dubhthaigh 187	1905
5. ti'baːn	Local pronunciation	1993
6. 'hwəithaus	Local pronunciation	1993

This land division was formerly a constituent part of **Ballyteerim** and thus it is difficult to trace the now rare Irish form of the name which appears on the *OS 1:50,000* map as *Tyban*, probably from *An Toigh Bán* "the white house". Holmer recorded *toigh* as the local nom. form of *teach* "house" (*Irish of the Glens* 131). A further possibility regarding the first element is *taobh* "side", although this seems less likely: Holmer recorded the non-palatal *bh* sound in this word (in stressed and unstressed position) as [v] ([tʌːv]; *ibid.* 130).

OTHER NAMES

| **Agangarrive Hill** | A hybrid form |
| D 1631 | |

1. Agangarrive Hill	OSRNB sh.14	1855c
2. Eagan garbh "Rough hollow"	Rev. Magill 5	1904
3. Eagan Garbh "Rough bottom"	Ó Dubhthaigh 130	1905
4. ˌagən'garəv	Local pronunciation	1993

"The summit of a mountain range [in Ardaghmore or Glentop] and from its base issues several streams flowing east, west and south and uniting with the Rivers Glenshesk and Glendun. The hill has an altitude of 1,225 feet above sea level" (*OSRNB* sh.14).

Eagán recté *aigeán* (we might expect *eag-* to be anglicized *eg-* locally; cf. **Craigban**) in place-names may be confined to Co. Antrim. Other examples are **Agan Bridge, Aganageeragh** and **Aganlane or Parkmore**. We could consider that it derives from *eag* > *eang* "track, trace; strip of land" (see Ó *Dónaill* sv. and **Innananooan** in Other Names, Rathlin) plus the diminutive suffix *-án*. *Eagán* is translated "bottom, hollow part, pit" by Ó *Dónaill*, which indicates that it represents a development from *aigéan* "ocean". Indeed, *Dwelly* lists Scottish Gaelic *aigeann* as denoting "abyss; deep pool; sea, ocean; bottom of an abyss". From its use in the Antrim names it could be interpreted as denoting something like "path on hilly ground", although we could also consider that the Irish form *Aigeán Garbh* "rough hollow(?)" referred originally to part of a valley of one of the several streams which flow down the slopes of this height. Finally, there may be a parallel here in the development in meaning of *aibhéis* "abyss" (Ó *Dónaill*) to "hill-side; coarse mountain pasture" (see Ó Máille 1981–2, 4–5).

Aganmore	*Aigeán Mór*	
D 1839	"large hollow(?)"	
1. Aganmore	OSRNB sh.9, 1	1855c
2. ˌagənˈmoːr	Local pronunciation	1993

"Two farm houses [in Ballypatrick] with farms attached and in the occupation of James McHenry and James McCollum. The name applies to the houses . . . origin unknown" (*OSRNB* sh.9, 1).

The name may have originally referred to some point in the Carey River valley. See **Agangarrive Hill** above.

Altadreen,	*Allt an Draighin*	
Altadreen Bridge	"steep glen/stream of the blackthorn"	
D 1938		
1. Altadreen, Altadreen bridge	OSRNB sh.9, 1	1855c
2. alt a draoighin "glen of the blackthorn"	OSRNB sh.9, 1	1855c
3. ˌaltəˈdriən	Local pronunciation	1993

"A small glen [in Ballypatrick] bounded on the west side by a steep precipice, on the sides of which thorns and shrubs grow. The glen has been named from these thorns"; "A small stone bridge with stone pararpets . . . It is called from the contiguous glen of the name" (*OSRNB* sh.9, 1).

Allt is a recurring element in local sub-townland names. It has several meanings and variant spellings; it may variously refer to a steep narrow valley, to the valley sides, or to the actual stream contained therein (cf. **Altagore** in this parish, and **Altnamuck** in Other Names, Armoy). *Allt an Draighin* "steep glen/stream of the blackthorn" is the likely original

Irish form; we may note that McKay has translated the south-west Co. Antrim townland name of *Draighean* (anglicized **Dreen**) as "place of blackthorns" (*PNI* iv 200). The masc. noun *dreann* "rough encounter, combat, quarel" (*Ó Dónaill*) seems less likely. Holmer (*Irish of Rathlin* 187) and Mac Giolla Easpaig (*Place-Names of Rathlin* 73) noted the Rathlin subtownland place-name of *Port an Draighin* "port of the blackthorn".

Altahullion Burn	A hybrid form	
D 1430		
1. Altahullin Burn	OSRNB sh.14	1855c
2. Alt a Chuillinn "glen of the holly"	J O'D (OSRNB) sh.14	1855c
3. uilleann "honeysuckle, angle, nook, corner" (or) ullin "a fork, a movement"	OSRNB sh.14	1855c
4. ˌɑltəˈhol̡jən	Local pronunciation	1993

"This stream has its source at the boundary between Beaghs [in the parish of the Grange of Layd] and Ardaghmore or Glentop, and takes a W.N.W. course about ¾ statute mile and falls into the Glenshesk River" (*OSRNB* sh.14).

Allt an Chuilinn "steep glen/stream of the holly" is the probable origin of the Irish elements. See also **Drumacullin**.

Altaneigh Burn	A hybrid form	
D 1439		
1. Altnahigh Burn	OSRNB sh.14	1855c
2. Alɯahieha	OSRNB sh.14	1855c
3. Altnahigh Stream	OSRNB sh.14	1855c
4. Alt an fheich "glen of the raven"	J O'D (OSRNB) sh.14	1855c
5. "The horse's alt or valley"	OSRNB sh.14	1855c
6. ˌɑltəne ˈborn	Local pronunciation	1993

"This stream takes its rise on the west side of 'Agangarrive hill' and flows N. westward about ¾ statute mile and unites with the Glenshesk river" (*OSRNB* sh.14).

Allt na hÁithe "steep glen/stream of the kiln" appears to be the original form of the Irish elements. The standardized spelling may indicate that the name has suffered from metathesis (cf. **Portnathalin**) or mistranscription. See also **Drumnaheigh** in Grange of Drumtullagh.

Altdorragha	*An tAllt Dorcha*	
D 2135	"the dark steep glen"	
1. Altdorragha	OSRNB sh.9, 1	1855c
2. alt dorcha "dark cliff"	J O'D (OSRNB) sh.9, 1	1855c

3. Alt dorcha "dark close ravine"	O Dubhthaigh 131	1905
4. Alt dorcha "Dark height"	Rev. Magill 5	1923
5. ˌaltˈdọrahə	Local pronunciation	1993

"A dark glen with steep sloping sides. In winter, the sun never shines on it, the rays being intercepted by the height of the steeps which surround it. It is so named from its dark aspect. The main road from Ballycastle to Cushendall passes through it" (*OSRNB* sh.9, 1).

This is a north facing and dry glen in the south of Ballyvennaght. The element *dorcha* "dark" occurs elsewhere in the Rathlin subtownland name *An tÍneán Dorcha* "the dark *ineán*" (*Place-Names of Rathlin* 79; see **Inannanooan** in Other Names, Rathlin Island, regarding *ineán recté ingeán*) and in the Co. Limerick townland name *An tOileán Dorcha* "the dark island" (anglicized Dark Island; Ó Maolfabhail 1990, 226).

Altheela Bridge A hybrid form
D 2035

1. Altheela Bridge	OSRNB sh.9, 1	1855c
2. Alt Shíle	J O'D (OSRNB) sh.9, 1	1855c
3. ˌaltəˈhilə	Local pronunciation	1993

"A small stone bridge with stone parapets [in Ballypatrick] . . . It has been so named from the circumstances of a woman called Sheela having missed her way at night being found dead in the glen close to the bridge some time after" (*OSRNB* sh.9, 1).

The medial [ə] in form 3 probably indicates a recently introduced epenthetic vowel. *Allt Shíle* "*Síle*'s steep glen/stream" is the likely original form of the Irish elements. *Síle* is a borrowing of Latin *Caecilia* brought to Ireland by the Anglo-Normans (Ó Corráin & Maguire 1981, 165).

Altiffirnan Glen A hybrid form
D 1536

1. Altiffirnan	OSRNB sh.9, 2	1855c
2. Alt Ifearnain "Iffernan's Glen"	J O'D (OSRNB) sh.9, 2	1855c
3. "Iffernan or Heifernan's Glen"	OSRNB sh.9, 2	1855c
4. ˌaltˈïfərnən	Local pronunciation	1993

"A romantic glen [in Drumacullin] bounded here and there by sloping precipices on either side. A small stream flows westwards through it. Origin of name not locally known. It is supposed that in times of persecution priests were wont to frequent this place and celebrate mass at it, and that the glen has been named from this circumstance. Others suppose it to have been named after a robber and magician called Iffernan (perhaps the same as the proper name now rendered Hefernan) who is said to have frequented this glen." (*OSRNB* sh.9, 2).

Heffernan is essentially a Co. Clare surname (MacLysaght 1985, 153) and seems unlikely to have formed the last element. This element appears instead to have been the male personal name *Ifearnán* (gen. *Ifearnáin*), "a relatively rare early name" (Ó Corráin & Maguire 1981, 116), from which Heffernan derives. We may thus postulate the original form *Allt Ifearnáin* "Ifearnán's steep glen/stream". *Allt (an) Aifrinn* "steep glen/stream of the mass" would not reflect modern stress.

Altinadarragh Burn	A hybrid form	
D 1429		
1. Altinadaragh Burn	OSRNB sh.14	1855c
2. ˌaltnəˈdɑrə	Local pronunciation	1993

"A small stream having its source near the boundary between the townlands of Beaghs [in the parish of Grange of Layd] and Ardaghmore or Glentop. It flows W.N. westward about ½ statute mile and enters the head of the Glenshesk river" (*OSRNB* sh.14).

Local pronunciation does not reflect the medial *i* found in standard spelling; this may have been epenthetic. Modern pronunciation points to *Allt na Darach* "steep glen/stream of the oak(s)" as being the original name.

Altmore Bridge,	Hybrid forms	
Altmore Burn		
D 2339		
1. Altmore Burn	OSRNB sh.10	1855c
2. Altmore Bridge	OSRNB sh.10	1855c
3. Alt mór "great glen"	OSRNB sh.10	1855c
4. Alt mór "Large (ravine)"	Ó Dubhthaigh 131	1905
5. altˈmoːrˈborn	Local pronunciation	1993

The Ordnance Survey noted the following regarding the stream and the bridge in 1855c: "This stream [which forms the boundary between Farranmacallan and Ballinloughan] has its source from the head streams called Altnacartha and Sluggan . . . and enters the sea at Portaleen"; "A small bridge of one arch with parapets 33 feet long . . . [on the boundary of the aforementioned townlands]" (*OSRNB* sh.10).

An tAllt Mór "large steep glen/stream" probably represents the original form of the Irish elements.

Altnacartha Burn	A hybrid form	
D 2238		
1. Altnakartha Burn	OSRNB sh.10	1855c
2. Altnacartha Burn	OSRNB sh.10	1855c
3. Alt na ceartan "glen of the forge"	J O'D (OSRNB) sh.10	1855c
4. ˌaltnəˈkjaːrtə	Local pronunciation	1993

"A small mountain stream [in Cushleake Mountain North] . . . A smith's shop was erected some years ago in this glen but is now defaced" (*OSRNB* sh.10).

Allt na Ceárta "steep glen/stream of the forge" is the likely original form of the Irish elements.

Ballycastle Bay   A hybrid form
D 1342

1.	Market-town Bay	CSP Ire. 375, 377, 378, 381	1568
2.	Market town Bay	CSP Ire. 393	1568
3.	Markettowne baye	North Ulster Coast Map	1570c
4.	Marketon Bay	MacDonnells Antrim 417	1575c
5.	Marketon Bay	MacDonnells Antrim 167	1584
6.	Markenton Bay	Dartmouth Map 5	1590c
7.	Markintton bay	Dartmouth Map 6	1590c
8.	Markenton baye	Dartmouth Map 25	1590c
9.	Marknigton baye	Jobson's Ulster (TCD)	1590c
10.	Marckington baye	Jobson's Ulster (TCD)	1590c.
11.	Marketton bay	Hondius Map	1591
12.	Merkinton Baie	Boazio's Map (BM)	1599
13.	Market towne bay	Treatise on Ire. (NLI) 11	1599c
14.	Markenton baie	Bartlett Maps (Esch. Co. Maps) 1	1603
15.	Markenton baye	Norden's Map	1610
16.	Merkinton bay	Mercator's/Hole's Ire.	1610
17.	Markinton Bay	Speed's Antrim & Down	1610
18.	Markinton Bay	Speed's Ulster	1610
19.	(?)Ballicastlwater	Hib. Del. Antrim	1672c
20.	Ballycastle Bay	Stewart's Survey 2	1734
21.	Ballycastle Bay	Taylor and Skinner 273	1777
22.	B:Castle Bay	Lendrick Map	1780
23.	Ballycastle Bay	Hamilton's Letters 4	1784
24.	Carrick ronan B.	Dubourdieu Map	1812

The earliest variants reflect an appellation for Ballycastle which fell out of use in the early 1600s: this name may have derived from *Margytown* (*Mon. Hib.* 4; the Margy River enters this bay on Ballycastle's eastern boundary; see **Bonamargy**). Form 24 may represent a misrendering of *Carrickmannon Bay* (see Other Names, Ramoan); Carrickmannon lies northwest of Ballycastle Bay, off Kinbane or White Head.

Ballyukin   Of uncertain origin
D 1941

1.	Ballygicon	MacDonnells Antrim 117	1620
2.	Ballegicon	MacDonnells Antrim 441	1625
3.	Ballegicon	Inq. Ult. (Antrim) §61 Car. I	1635
4.	Ballgicon	Inq. Ult. (Antrim) §128 Car. I	1638
5.	Ballicron	Hib. Reg. Cary	1657c
6.	Ballyiocran	DS (Par. Map) 57	1657c
7.	Ballyechin	Census 17	1659

8. Ballyocron	BSD 166	1661
9. Ballegickane	Court of Claims §923	1662c
10. Ballechiron, the 80 acres of	Court of Claims §923	1662c
11. Ballechion, the ffower score acres of	Decree of Innocence 431	1663
12. Ballegigon, eighty acres of country of	Decree of Innocence 440	1663
13. Ballyocran	Lapsed Money Book 156	1663
14. Ballycrou	ASE 116a §19	1668
15. Ballicroa	Hib. Del. Antrim	1672c
16. Balliquan	HMR Ant. 10	1669
17. Ballyocran	Ant. Forfeit.	1700
18. Ballyukan	Religious Survey	1734
19. Ballikuin	Stewart's Survey 10	1734
20. BallyIcon	PRONI D2977/3A/2/18/2	1746
21. B.ukin	Lendrick Map	1780
22. Ballyucan	Sur. A.E. 48	1782
23. Ballyluken	OSM xxiv 52	1838
24. Ballyukin	OSRNB sh.9, 1	1855c
25. Ballyeuchan	MacDonnells Antrim 133	1873
26. Ballyukin "Ukin's town"	J O'D (OSNB) B 24 B 37	1831
27. Baile Feochan "The town of the thistles"	Ó Dubhthaigh 133	1905
28. ˌbɑliˈukən	Local pronunciation	1993

This former townland was coextensive with the modern townlands of Knockbrack, Bighouse, Torglass and Goodland (*OSRNB* sh.9, 1).

The historical forms vary widely and exhibit copying of scribal errors. Note, for example, the recurring *r* in forms 5–6, 8, 10, 13–5 and 17. It is possible that the *g* in early forms should read *gh* and that the final element was the male personal name *Eochagán*, a pet-form of *Eochu* (Ó Corráin & Maguire 1981, 87). *Baile Eochagáin* "*Eochagán*'s townland", then, is a possible original form. *Baile Uí Eochagáin* "O'Houghegan's townland" contains a surname based on this personal name and might also be considered as possible original form. This surname is described by Woulfe (1923, 568) as "an old Ulidian surname . . . now found only in Co. Galway"; there is no other record of it locally. The somewhat similar surname *Mac Eochagáin* has several anglicized forms including Cooken, which may be analogous here (*ibid.* 358). Less likely original forms are *Baile Aodhagáin* "*Aodhagán*'s townland" and *Baile Uí Aodhagáin* "O'Huggain/Hoogan/Heaken's townland" (Woulfe (*ibid.*, 556–7) lists 19 anglicized variants of the surname *Ó hAodhagáin*). Several of the early historical forms might be interpreted as containing a form of *geocán* (gen. sing. *geocáin*, gen. pl. *geocán*) "reed, pipe; drinking straw" (*Ó Dónaill*), a word which also has the variant forms *diúcán* and *deocán* (see *Dinneen* sv.), but which would represent an unusual element in a place-name.

Benmore or Fair Head
D 1844

An Bhinn Mhór
"the big cliff"

1. beinn mhór	Mulcahy's Rathlin 44	1889

2. Cionn Fionn	Irish of the Glens 114	1940
3. Bheinn Mhór, an	Irish of Rathlin 63	1942
4. Fayre forland	Goghe's Map	1567
5. Faire forlande	Nowel's Ire. (1)	1570c
6. The North Forland of Eyerlond	Antrim Coast Sketch	1570c
7. Fairy Foreland, a cape called	Cal. Carew MSS 438	1575
8. faire forland	Dartmouth Map 5	1590c
9. Fayre forelande	Dartmouth Map 6	1590c
10. Faire forland	Dartmouth Map 25	1590c
11. Fayre Forelande	Sea Chart	1590c
12. Fayre Forlande	Ulster Map	1590c
13. The faire forland	Jobson's Ulster (TCD)	1590
14. Faire Forland	Hondius Map	1591
15. Fayre forland	Mercator's Ire.	1595
16. Faire Forlande	Boazio's Map (BM)	1599
17. Fayre forlande	Treatise on Ireland (NLI) 11	1599c
18. Fair foreland	Bartlett Maps (Esch. Co. Maps) 1	1603
19. Faire forelande	Mercator's/Hole's Ire.	1610
20. Fayre forland	Speed's Ireland	1610
21. Fayre Forland Promontory	Speed's Ulster	1610
22. the Fair foreland	Terrier (Reeves) 75	1615
23. Fair Head	Hib. Reg. Cary	1657c
24. Point Ffairehead	DS (Par. Map) 59	1657c
25. Faire head Point	Hib. Del. Antrim	1672c
26. Faire head	Lamb Maps Co. Antrim	1690c
27. Fairehead	Taylor and Skinner 270	1777
28. Fairhead	Hamilton's Letters 8	1784
29. Fair Head	Wright's Diary 31	1806
30. Beeing vore	Mulcahy's Rathlin 44	1889
31. Beann Mór "great ben or peak"	J O'D (OSNB) B 24 B 37	1831
32. Beann Mhór "great peak"	Rev. Magill 8	1923
33. Rubha an Fhir Liaith "the promontory of the grey man"	Dinneen	1927
34. An Bhinn Mhór	GÉ 36	1989
35. k'ɛn fjɛn	Irish of the Glens 114	1940
36. ə ven' voːr	Irish of Rathlin 63	1942
37. bɛn'moːr	Local pronunciation	1993
38. fer 'hɛːd	Local pronunciation	1993

Benmore is not widely used but remembered. It is possible that early English forms were translated from *(An) Cionn Fionn*, literally "(the) fair head(-land)" (see form 2), but the topographical suitability of this designation is in doubt. Early forms of **Kinbane or White Head** were also translated (see Other Names, Ramoan). Regarding the use of *fionn* in place-names, see **Doonfinn** in Ramoan. *Sliabh an Choiligh* and its translated form **Cock Mountain** in Co. Down eventually came to be applied to separate peaks (*PNI* iii 131; compare also *Dubhais* and **Black Mountain** outside Belfast). In this case, however, were we to accept an Irish origin for Fair Head, we might suggest that *An Bhinn Mhór* referred to some other part of the headland; it seems less likely to have been confined to Rathlin (see forms 1, 3). The name given to this headland by Dinneen (form 33) reflects another place-name on the east side of the promontory: **Grey Man's Path**.

It was previously believed that the cape called *Rhobogdiou akrou* by the Greek geographer Ptolemy (*Geographia* II.2.2) represented Benmore or Fair Head (e.g. Orpen 1894, 115). Ptolemy's *Geographia* was compiled shortly before 150 AD but the earliest extant copy dates only to c. 1200 AD and has been extensively altered by scribal errors (Mac an Bhaird 1991–3, 1). Mac an Bhaird (*ibid.*, 3–4) has recently postulated that Ptolemy's tribal name of *Robogdioi* (*Geographia ibid.*), from which the cape name is derived, would have originally been written *Soborgioi*, and thus represented not Dál Riada as tentatively suggested by O'Rahilly (1946, 6–7), but the tribe after which Dunseverick is named (proto-Irish *⋆DŪNON SOBORGION* "the fort of the Soborgii" (Mac an Bhaird *ibid.*, 3); Mod. Ir. *Dún Sobhairce* (*GÉ* 100)). Mac an Bhaird (*ibid.*, 2) identifies the cape name as Benbane Head (*An Bhinn Bhán* (*GÉ* 35)), which lies west of Dunseverick.

Benvan	*An Bhinn Bhán*	
D 2042	"the white cliff"	
1. Binvane	OSRNB sh.5	1855c
2. bin ban "white peak"	OSRNB sh.5	1855c
3. bɛn'van	Local pronunciation	1993

This is on the steep northern slopes of Greenanmore mountain in Goodland. It gave name to a small village (*OSRNB* sh.5). *Binn* was originally the dat. form of *beann*, but standardized forms used by *GÉ* (see **Benmore or Fair Head** above) suggest that it was used in the nom. case in local place-names. Holmer did not record the word on the Antrim mainland, but noted the form *beinn* ([beːnʹ]/[bɛːn]) "rock, cliff" in Rathlin (*Irish of Rathlin* 164).

Brablagh	*Brablach*	
D 2434	"stony land"	
1. Brablagh	OSRNB sh.15	1855c
2. "The refuse or waste part of anything"	OSRNB sh.15	1855c
3. Brabarlach "The rubbish land"	Ó Dubhthaigh 133	1905
4. 'brablə	Local pronunciation	1993

"A name given to a few houses which lie in the centre of Cushendun townland, in consequence of the land in which they are situated being of a bad quality" (*OSRNB* sh.15).

Brablach probably formed the original place-name. It means "rubble; poor, stony land" (*Ó Dónaill*). The form postulated by Ó Dubhthaigh (form 1) does not appear to be attested.

Bushburn Bridge   A Scots/English form
D 2047

1. Bushburn br.	OSRNB sh.9, 1	1855c
2. boʃˈbọrn	Local pronunciation	1993

"A small stone bridge [in Ballyvennaght] with one arch, and stone parapets, and on the road from Ballycastle to Cushendall. It is named from the stream or burn which it spans" (*OSRNB* sh.9, 1). The Ordnance Survey also recorded in c. 1855 that the stream was named from "a large round tree bush which stood on its north bank a short distance west of its junction with Carey River. The bush was cut down some years ago" (*ibid.*).

Carey River   A hybrid form
D 1839, 1640

1. Cary Water	Hib. Reg. Cary	1657c
2. Carie flu.	Hib. Del. Antrim	1672c
3. Cary R	Ire. Map	1711
4. Cary R.	Taylor and Skinner 273	1777
5. Cary River	Lendrick Map	1780
6. ðə kari ˈrïvər	Local pronunciation	1993

It is not certain whether the first element was used in an Irish name for this water course. *Carey* recurs elsewhere in place-names in this parish and is identical in origin to the barony name, which is similarly pronounced but spelt *Cary*. See the barony introduction and introduction to this parish.

Cargismore   *An Carraigeas Mór*
D 2341   "the large rock"

1. Tor Ile	Boazio's Map (BM)	1599
2. Ille torre	Treatise on Ire. (NLI) 11	1599c
3. Tor Ile	Bartlett Maps (Esch. Co. Maps) 1	1603
4. Tor Ile	Mercator's/Hole's Ire.	1610
5. Tor Iland	Speed's Antrim & Down	1610
6. Tor Ile	Speed's Ireland	1610
7. Tor Iland	Speed's Ulster	1610
8. Torill	Norden's Map	1610c
9. Tor Isle	Hib. Del. Antrim	1672c
10. Cargismore	OSRNB sh.10	1855c
11. ˌkargəsˈmɔːr	Local pronunciation	1993

"A large rock visible at high water and without any vegetation. It is connected with the mainland of Torr Head by a narrow ledge of rock at low water" (*OSRNB* sh.10).

The original form of this name may be *Carraig an Smúir* "rock of the ash, dust, rust, soot or grime" (see Ó *Dónaill* sv. *smúr*). However, some place-names feature an *-(e)as* suffix on the noun (cf. **Barnish**) and the forms *corgus* and *cargas-*, both from *carraig* plus *-eas*, have been noted by Ó Máille (1989–90, 128). This rock was known to foreign cartographers in the late 16th and early 17th centuries as *Torr Island/Isle* (forms 1–9; see **Torr Head**).

Carnaneigh	*Carn an Fhéich(?)*	
D 2537	"cairn of the raven"	
1. Carnaneigh	OSRNB sh.10	1855c
2. Carn an fheich "the raven's carn"	OSRNB sh.10	1855c
3. "the crow's carn"	OSRNB sh.10	1855c
4. Carn an fheigh "The cairn of the deer"	Ó Dubhthaigh 134	1905
5. ˌkarnənˈeː	Local pronunciation	1993

"A hill top [in Aughnasillagh] having an altitude of 880 feet above sea level; is one of the principal heights along the coastline between Torr Head and Cushendun . . . so called from a natural rocky mound on its summit and being the resort of the carrion crow" (*OSRNB* sh.10).

Carn "cairn; heap, pile" is perhaps more likely first element than the diminutive *carnán* "(small) heap, mound" (*Ó Dónaill* sv.). See also **Carnduff** in Ramoan and **Carneagh** in Other Names, Armoy.

While *Ó Dónaill* gives *fiaigh* as the gen. sing. of *fiach* "raven", *Dinneen* lists the further gen. sing. form *féich*, suggested by forms 2–4. This gen. form of *fiach* is possibly unattested prior to the advent of Modern Irish (see *DIL* sv.). The rare form *féidh* which *Dinneen* gives as a gen. sing. of *fia* "deer" seems unlikely, and the forms *Carn an Fhiaigh/Fhia* "carn of the hunt/deer" also seem unlikely as *ia* was seldom pronounced as anything resembling [e(ː)] in the late local dialect (see *Irish of the Glens* 32).

We might also consider *Carn an Eich* "cairn of the horse/steed" as a possible original form of the name. *Ei* was normally [e] locally (although in some cases it was raised to [i] after nasal consonants (*Irish of the Glens* 28–9)). Final [x] was often replaced by [h] (*ibid.* 24). The lengthening of the final vowel (form 5) would have to be explained as a recent development in English (compare form 3 of **Portdoo**). See also **Carneighaneigh**.

Carnanmore	*An Carnán Mór*	
D 2239	"the big cairn"	
1. an Carn Mór	Irish of the Glens 104	1940
2. (?)Carnanmore	PRONI D2977/3A/2/1/40	1812
3. Carnleagh	OSNB B 24 B 37	1831
4. Carnan more	OSRNB sh.10	1855c
5. Carnanmore	OSRNB sh.10	1855c
6. Carn liath "grey carn or heap"	J O'D (OSNB) B 24 B 37	1831
7. Carnán mór "The great cairn"	Ó Dubhthaigh 133	1905
8. əŋ karnə moːr	Irish of the Glens 104	1940
9. ˌkarnəˈmoːr	Local pronunciation	1993

"A high mountain [in East Torr] and on its summit is an ancient carn, the base of which measures 50 feet in diameter and about 8 feet at top. In the west side is a cave or entrance 5.5 feet high, 3 feet broad and 8 feet long and covered over by flagstones 4 feet long, 2.5 to 3 feet broad and 6 to 9 inches thick; near the base of this carn are two other flag stones lying prostrate and of similar dimensions with the former. The mound is composed of loose stones covered over with grass" (*OSRNB* sh.10). The cairn of the chambered grave atop this mountain was given the dimensions 25 yards in diameter and 15' high in 1940 (*PSAMNI* 3; regarding this cairn, see also *O'Laverty* iv 523).

Carnán "(small) heap, mound", from *carn* "cairn" plus the diminutive suffix -*án*, would seem unlikely to have been qualified here by the adj. *mór* "big, great". *Carnán* may also mean "hillock" but this particular feature is one of the highest points in the parish (379 metres). The -*án* suffix may indicate the collective meaning "place of cairns" but that *carnán* was adopted as *carn* seems most likely (see also **Carnanmore** in Other Names, Ballintoy, and **Carnmoon** in Ramoan; see also *PNI* v 107). Holmer recorded *carnán* in place-names in Rathlin and translated it as "cairn" (*Irish of Rathlin* 171). The second *n* has been recently assimilated to the *m* of *mór*.

Regarding the alternative name recorded by the Ordnance Survey (form 3), the following was noted in c. 1855: "There is no such name in the country known as Carnlea. The correct and popular name is Carnan more i.e. the Big Carn . . . There is a particular spot near the base of Carnanmore called Carleague which was originally supplied by the Trig. and converted into Carnlea as inserted on the original plan" (*OSRNB* sh.10).

Carneighaneigh	*Carnach Chinn Eich(?)*	
D 1837	"place of cairns of the head of the horse"	
1. Carneighaneigh	OSNB B 24 B 37	1831
2. Carneihaneigh	OSM xxiv 41	1835
3. Carnicaneigh	OSM xxiv 83	1839
4. Carneighaneigh	OSRNB sh.9, 1	1855c
5. Carnacaneogh	OSCNB sh.9	1855c
6. Carnach an eich "hill of the horse"	J O'D (OSNB) B 24 B 37	1831
7. "a giant's cairn"	OSM xxiv 83	1839
8. Carn chinn eich "carn of the horse's head"	J O'D (OSRNB) sh.9, 1	1855c
9. ˌkɑrnehən'eː	Local pronunciation	1993

"A high mountain [in Ballypatrick] with smooth surface, on the summit of which stands an ancient carn from which the mountain has been named . . ." (*OSRNB* sh.9, 1).

Carnach "place of cairns" appears to have formed the first element in this name. The cairn at the summit of this 313 metre height has been noted elsewhere (see *PSAMNI* 13 and *O'Laverty* iv 494), while Evans (1945, 21) has described a site on its southern slopes, marked *Chambered Grave* on the *OS 1:50,000* map, as "the ruins of a great stone monument . . . once surrounded by a circle of small standing stones". McKay has suggested that *carnach* can also represent "place of rocks" in place-names (*PNI* iv 67).

Other place-names of the type *Carnach Chinn Eich* include the subtownland name of *Lios Cinn Eich* (anglicized **Lisconaye**) in Co. Antrim (*PNI* iv 71), the Co. Offaly townland name *Achadh Cinn Chon* (Aghancon; *L. Log. Uíbh Fhailí* 4) and *Ceann Eich* (Kinneigh), a parish name in Co. Cork (*Onom. Goed.* 203). We might also consider *Carnach an Eich* "place of cairns of the horse" as a possible original form. The final vowel in modern pronunciation also suggests *fhéich* "(of the) raven", which on the basis of precedent might seem more likely to appear in the structure *Carnach an Fhéich* than in *Carnach Chinn Fhéich*. We might not expect the late gen. form *féich* to be used with *carnach*, however. See also **Carnaneigh**.

Carrick More	*An Charraig Mhór*	
D 1643	"the big rock"	
1. Carraig mór "Great rock"	Rev. Magill 11	1923
2. ˌkarəxˈmɔːr	Local pronunciation	1993

This lies off the coast of Ballyreagh Upper.

Carrowndoon	*Ceathrú an Dúin*	
D 1840	"quarterland of the fort"	
1. Downe	Hib. Reg. Cary	1657c
2. Down	Census 18	1659
3. Downe	HMR Ant. 6	1669
4. Carriveindan	Religious Survey	1734
5. Carrivendooen	Stewart's Survey 5	1734
6. Carrivendooan	Stewart's Survey 9	1734
7. Doon alias Dune	PRONI D2977/3A/2/1/34	1737
8. Carvinduan	OSRNB sh.9, 1	1790
9. Carriffendoon	Tithe Applot. 12	1833
10. Carrivendoon	Tithe Applot. 22	1833
11. Carrowadoon	OSRNB sh.9, 1	1855c
12. Carrowndoon	OSRNB sh.9, 1	1855c
13. Carvadoon	OSRNB sh.9, 1	1855c
14. "the quarter of the doon"	OSRNB sh.9, 1	1855c
15. ˌkarəvənˈdun	Local pronunciation	1993

This place-name represents a subdivision in the north-west of Ballyvennaght which has been recognised since at least the mid-1600s (forms 1–3; Carleton 1991, 65). The remains of a fort called *Doon* in the west of this subdivision which apparently gave rise to the name was thus described in c. 1855: "A small smooth eminence of natural formation. The sides slope rather abruptly. It is flat on [the] summit. Around the verge of the summit is the remains of some stone structure in the shape of a dry uncemented stone wall – a small portion of the foundation of the said wall only remains" (*OSRNB* sh.9, 1).

Modern pronunciation maintains the medial [v] from *ceathrú* (earlier *ceathramha*) "quarterland", although it is absent from the standard anglicized spelling.

| **Cashel** | *Caiseal* | |
| D 2535 | "stone fort" | |

| 1. Caisil "Round stone fort" | Rev. Magill 11 | 1904 |
| 2. ðə'kɑsəl | Local pronunciation | 1993 |

This name refers to a site in Altagore where a roughly circular wall, 6' to 10' in height and 10' thick, encloses an area about 50' in diameter (*PSAMNI* 16). *Caiseal* has various meanings, including "(ancient) stone fort; unmortared stone wall; (of church, cemetery) boundary wall" (*Ó Dónaill*). The former of these meanings is most applicable in this case. It appears that the place-name has become recently replaced by the English word *castle* (form 2). Both words derive from the same Latin root: *castellum* (*IPN* 39; *Ox. Eng. Dict.*).

| **Castle Carra** | *An Caisleán Carrach* | |
| D 2534 | "the rocky castle" | |

1. Castle Carie	Hib. Del. Antrim	1672c
2. (?)C. Carie	Lamb Maps Co. Antrim	1690c
3. Kerragh Cas.	Hamilton's Letters 1	1788c
4. Cary Castle	OSRNB sh.15	1855c
5. Cashlan Carragh or Castle Carra	OSRNB sh.15	1855c
6. Caislean Carrach "rugged castle"	J O'D (OSNB) B 24 B 37	1831
7. Cashlan Carragh "the rough or rugged castle"	OSRNB sh.15	1855c
8. Caisleán cairthe "The Castle of the pillar stones"	Ó Dubhthaigh 134	1905
9. "kasəl'kara	Local pronunciation	1993

"Cashlan Carragh or Castle Carra is the local name amoung the peasantry. It does not derive from the Barony of Cary . . . [The name refers to] the ruins of an old castle seated on a rock. It measures 18 feet long by 9 feet broad in the interior" (*OSRNB* sh.15). The ruins of this castle are also described in the Archaeological Survey of 1940 (*PSAMNI* 17), which notes that local tradition believed this to be the site of Shane O'Neill's death at the hands of Somhairle Buí MacDonnell in 1567.

It might be considered that the [i] sound in forms 1–2 and 4 resulted from the gen. form of the unattested noun *carrach* "rocky ground" (cf. **Ballycarry** in Rathlin Island), or that the second element was reinterpreted as the barony name. Form 5(a), which is perhaps the most reliable form to hand, suggests that the second element was the adjective *carrach* "rocky; rock-incrusted". Ó Laoide confused Irish forms of Castle Cary in Inishowen in Co. Donegal with this name (*SCtSiadhail* 105).

| **Colliery Bay** | An English form |
| D 1542 | |

The mining of coal in this parish for use in the local production of salt has been attested elsewhere (note Carleton 1991, 67). Two pits were still being worked in the 1830s (*OSM* xxiv 38–9 and 46). It is surely this industry which inspired this place-name. See also **Pans-Rock**.

Coolanlough	*Cúl an Locha(?)*	
D 1842	"back of the lake"	
1. Coolnalough	Stewart's Survey 8	1734
2. Coolanlough	OSRNB sh.5	1855c
3. ˌkulən'laːx	Local pronunciation	1993
4. ˌkuli'lɔːx	Local pronunciation	1993

"A small village of farm houses so called from its being situated at what is locally considered to be the back of the Lough, that is of Lough na Cranagh. The village is situate a short distance to the S.E. of said lough" (*OSRNB* sh.5).

Cúl an Locha "back of the lake" is the origin suggested by the *OSRNB*; *Cúil an Locha* "corner of the lake" remains a possibilty, however (cf. **Culfeightrin** and **Coolaveely**). *Loch* may formerly have been feminine locally (form 1). Regarding the "little rundale village" of the same name, see Evans (1945, 32).

Corratavey Bridge	A hybrid form	
D 2036		
1. Coratvey Bridge	OSRNB sh.9, 1	1855c
2. Cor a tsamha "the hill or angle		
of the sorrel"	OSRNB sh.9, 1	1855c
3. ˌkarə'tavi	Local pronunciation	1993

"A small stone bridge [in Ballypatrick] with one arch and stone parapets on the main road from Ballycastle to Cushendall. It is named from the burn which it spans [Coratavey Burn]" (*OSRNB* sh.9, 1).

Corr an tSamhaidh "rounded hill of the sorrel" and *Corr an tSamhaí* "rounded hill of the easygoing or sleepy, lazy person" would both reflect modern pronunciation. *Samhadh* "sorrel" is more common in place-names, however. It recurs elsewhere, for example, in the south Co. Derry subtownland name of *Sruthán Léana an tSamhaidh* "the stream of the sorrel meadow" (**Sruhanleinantawey**; see *PNI* v 56). *Corr* has several other meanings (cf. **Corrymellagh**). As a similarly named stream flows by here, it could be that the first element was *cor* "bend", while *cora* "weir; rocky crossing-place in river" should also be considered.

Corrymeela	A transferred form	
D 1441		
1. Corrymeela "hill of sweetness"	Dallat's Culfeightrin 35	1981
2. ˌkɔri'milə	Local pronunciation	1993
3. ˌkɔri'miljə	Local pronunciation	1996

This name was used in a poem by Moira O'Neill (see O'Neill 1906, 4–6) and adopted in the 1930s for this residence which is now in the hands of the Corrymeela Community (*Pers. comm.* 6.12.95). It seems likely that O'Neill derived the name from **Corrymellagh** townland in the south-east of the parish.

Coskemnacally
D 1433

Coiscéim na Cailli
"foot-step of the hag"

1. Cuskimnacallie	OSRNB sh.14	1855c
2. coisceim na caillighe "step of the hag"	OSRNB sh.14	1855c
3. ˌkɔskəmnaˈkali	Local pronunciation	1993

"A remarkable passage through a steep rock and on each side of the 'Glenshesk River' [connecting the townlands of Ardaghmore or Glentop and Ardagh]. Here tradition asserts that an old woman of pretended witchcraft in early ages was hunted for her life and in her flight stepped over this rock and having made her way as far as the hill called 'Oghtbristacree' there breathed her last from which circumstance the hill is said to have derived the name" (*OSRNB* sh.14).

Coiscéim na Cailli "foot-step of the hag" appears to be the original form of the name. *Coiscéim* in place-names can be applied to "a narrow road or pass" (*Joyce* ii 386; see also *PNI* vi 29 sv. **Caskum**). Regarding the final element see also **Port Calliagh** in Other Names, Ramoan.

Crockanaskista Burn
D 1430

A hybrid form

1. Knockinaisky Stream	OSRNB sh.14	1855c
2. Crockanaskista Burn	OSRNB sh.14	1855c
3. Cnocan na scíste "hillock of the rest"	J O'D (OSRNB) sh.14	1855c
4. ˌkrɔkənəˈskistə	Local pronunciation	1993

"A small stream having its source near the mutual boundary between the townlands of Beaghs [in the parish of the Grange of Layd] and Ardaghmore or Glentop, and flows W.N. west about ½ of a statute mile and falls into the Glenshesk River" (*OSRNB* sh.14).

Cnocán na Scíste "height of the rest" appears to be the origin of the Irish elements in this name. *Cnocán* may also mean "hillock; heap" (*Dinneen*); Holmer recorded *scíste* as "pause, rest, relaxation" ([skʹiisʹtʹ] (*sic*) ; *Irish of the Glens* 126).

Crockaneel
D 1934

Cnoc an Aoil
"mountain of the limestone"

1. Crockaneel	OSRNB sh.14	1855c
2. Glenmakeerin Top	OSRNB sh.14	1855c
3. Cnoc an Aoil "hill of the lime"	J O'D (OSRNB) sh.14	1855c
4. "Lime Hill"	OSRNB sh.14	1855c
5. Croc an aoil "Hill of lime"	Rev. Magill 12	1923
6. ˌkrɔkənˈiːl	Local pronunciation	1993

"A mountain top [on the southern boundary of Glenmakeerin] having an altitude of 1,321 feet above the level of the sea at low water. It is the principal watershed of a large tract of mountain east of Knocklayd. Several small streams have their source from the east side of Crockaneel and unite with 'Glendun River'" (*OSRNB* sh. 14).

While there are several possibilities, *Cnoc an Aoil* "mountain of the limestone" is the likely origin of the name.

Crockanore	*Cnoc an Óir(?)*	
D 1941	"mountain of the gold"	
1. Crockanoir	OSRNB sh.9, 1	1855c
2. Cnoc an Óir "hill of the gold"	J O'D (OSRNB) sh.9, 1	1855c
3. Croc an Óir "The hill of the gold"	Ó Dubhthaigh 136	1905
4. Cruachán odhar "Pale little stack (or hill)"	Rev. Magill 12	1923
5. ˌkrɔkən'oːr	Local pronunciation	1993

"A small round hill with smooth surface and fine pasture . . . It signifies the hill of gold but nothing is locally known of its origin" (*OSRNB* sh.9, 1). It stands at 255 metres, in the centre of Goodland.

Cnoc an Óir "mountain of the gold" is but one possible original form. *Cnocán* "hillock" and *odhar* "dun, . . .pale, wan, brown [etc]" (*Dinneen*) are among further possible elements (see also **Crockateemore**).

Crockan Point	A hybrid form	
D 2439		
1. Crockan Point	OSRNB sh.10	1855c
2. Cnocán "a hillock"	J O'D (OSRNB) sh.10	1855c
3. 'kruxən	Local pronunciation	1993

"A point or headland at the northern extremity of Loughan Bay [in Aughnaholle], having an altitude of about 100 feet above sea level" (*OSRNB* sh.10).

Cnocán meaning "a hillock, a height" (*Dinneen*) may be the Irish element in this place-name. Holmer recorded the word *cnoc*, which he spelt as *cnuc*, as [krʌk] (*Irish of the Glens* 106). Modern pronunciation suggests that *cruachán* "little hill or mound" (*Dinneen*) is another possibility, although the medial [x] appears to have been a recent development (cf. **Coolnagoppoge**).

Crockateemore	*Cnoc an Tí Mhóir*	
D 1542	"hill of the big house"	
1. Croagh a teighmore	OSNB B 24 B 37	1831
2. Krock-a-thievoir	OSM xxiv 71	1838

3. Crockateemore	OSRNB sh.5	1855c
4. Croagh-ateighmore	OSRNB sh.5	1855c
5. Crockateighmore	OSRNB sh.5	1855c
6. Cruach a tighe mor "round hill of the big house"	J O'D (OSNB) B 24 B 37	1831
7. "big house hill"	OSM xxiv 71	1838
8. Cnoc a tsighe mhoir "The hill of the great or potent fairy"	OSRNB sh.5	1855c
9. Cnoc a tighe mhor "hill of the great house"	OSRNB sh.5	1855c
10. Knockanteemore – "the Hill of the great House"	O'Laverty iv 484	1887
11. ˌkrọkəti'moːr	Local pronunciation	1993

It is possible that *Cruach an Tí Mhóir* "(mountain) stack/symmetrically shaped mountain of the big house" formed the original place-name, and that the pronunciation of the first element has changed under the influence of the standardized spelling or through association with other local place-names containing *cnoc* "a hill, a mountain, a height" (*Dinneen*). It seems more probable, however, that the surveyors who wrote forms 1 and 4 were unaccustomed with the local pronunciation of *cnoc* ([krʌk]; *Irish of the Glens* 106), and so interpreted it as *cruach*. *Cnoc an tSí Mhóir* "hill of the big fairy mound" could also be considered as an origin; *sí* can also denote "fairy" (form 8). This was not how the name was understood by locals in the 1850s, however (*OSRNB* sh.5).

"The hill [in Ballyvoy townland] is said to be called from a large house that once stood at its north face and [was used] as a colliery office" (*OSRNB* sh.5). The site which gave rise to the name was described in 1838 as "an ancient enclosure . . . approaching to circular shape, 16 yards in diameter and enclosed by a row of large stones sunk in the ground . . ." (*OSM* xxiv 71; see also *O'Laverty* iv 484–5). O'Boyle noted a similar subtownland name, which he spelt *Croc an toighe mhóir*, in Craigmacagan in Rathlin (*O'Boyle* 48). Mac Giolla Easpaig recorded the further Rathlin subtownland name of *Glaic an Toighe Mhóir* "hollow of the big house" as [glak ˈən̩ˌtEi'moːr] (in Kinramer South). This pronunciation may indicate the decline of the gen. case or alternatively reflect the treatment of *teach/toigh* as a u-stem masc. noun (compare the Co. Monaghan townland name *Corr an Tí Móir*/Corrateemore (*L. Log. Mhuineacháin* 16)).

Cross Skreen
D 2534

Cros Scríne
"cross of the shrine"

1. (?)Skrine	Court of Claims §923	1662c
2. (?)the 5 acres of Skrine	Court of Claims §923	1662c
3. (?)Skrine, the five acres of	Decree of Innocence 431	1663
4. Crosscrene	EA 283	1847
5. Cross Skreen Burial Ground	OSRNB sh.15	1855c
6. "The Shrine Cross"	OSRNB sh.15	1855c

7. "the faded cross"	OSRNB sh.15	1855c
8. krɔs'skrin	Local pronunciation	1993
9. kɔs'krin	Local pronunciation	1996

In 1847, Reeves (*EA* 283) described this place, which is in Ballyteerim, as "the hill over Cushendun Bay". He noted that it was used as a graveyard, probably for the interment of still-born children. He further noted: "There are some rude remains of a fort here, and the faint traces of a building, measuring 35' by 22'" (*ibid.*). In c. 1855, the Ordnance Survey recorded that this place was:

> a small enclosure resembling a Danish fort. In the west side of it is a flagstone placed firmly in the ground and lying in a horizontal position. It is 4 feet long by 3 feet broad and 4 inches thick; in the middle of this flagstone is a cup like depression 10 inches by 12. This contains water, and many persons have resort to it in order to remove warts by washing with the water contained in the stone; the enclosure is used as a burial ground for unbaptized children (*OSRNB* sh.15).

Bigger (1908, 98) noted that:

> [At Cross Skreen] the mangled body [of Shane O'Neill] was buried after the murder. It is an old site, much older than the time of Sean; it is prehistoric. There is a central fort . . . whose circuit was built with large boulders, now earth covered and grass grown . . . A square sandstone slab from Carrig-Uisneach has been built into the east face of the carn, with the simple name in Gaelic, Séan O'Neill [*sic*], and the date 1567. This is surmounted by the lambh dearg [*sic*] and a little Celtic ornament. (See also **Pans Rock**).

Cros Scríne "cross of the shrine" is the probable original Irish form of the name. There does not appear to be any record of an ecclesiastical cross at this site (although note the explanations given in forms 6–7). It seems unlikely that this element could have referred to a crossroads (a further meaning of *cros*), however. *Scrín* is not a common element in place-names: "the probability is that some, if not all of them, refer to pre-Reform (12th century) sites, distinguished by their possession of a venerated shrine" (Flanagan 1981–2, 72–3). This may not be true of all subtownland names containing this element, however. Holmer recorded an example in the Rathlin name *Fearann na Scríne* (*Irish of Rathlin* 194), to which forms 1–3 may in fact refer. A reference in *AFM* i 396 (790 AD) to the destruction of *scrine* "shrines" on *Reachrainde* may not necessarily be linked to the modern name. The age of this name remains uncertain.

Cushendun Bay A hybrid form
D 2533

1. Cashendon B.	Ire. Map	1711
2. Cossendon Bay	Stewart's Survey 13	1734
3. Cushendun Bay	Lendrick Map	1780

See **Cushendun** townland.

Doey Plantation   A hybrid form
D 1940

1. Dubhaigh, ionns an	Irish of the Glens 111	1940
2. 'əns ən dʌˈi	Irish of the Glens 111	1940
3. dui	Local pronunciation	1993

This is a small wooded area in the south of Knockbrack.

Holmer's forms suggest that the original name was *An Dubhaigh* "the black/dark place". *Dubhaigh* is an oblique form of the fem. noun *dubhach*; *dubhach* here may represent a substantive form of the adjective *dubhach* "black, dark" (*Ó Dónaill*). We might also consider *An Dumhaigh* "the sandy ground" (*Ó Dónaill* sv. *dumhach*; see also *PNI* ii 116) as a possible original form, however.

Doon   *Dún*
D 1743   "fort"

1. Doon	OSRNB sh.5	1855c
2. dun	Local pronunciation	1993

"A small farm village of 3 dwellings occupied by three brothers named Butler. The village has been named from its proximity to an ancient object . . . which lies east of it" (*OSRNB* sh.5).

Dún has been variously translated "a fort, fortress, castle, fortified mansion" (*Dinneen*) and "(secure) residence; promontory fort, bluff" (*Ó Dónaill*). The "ancient object" is **Doonmore Fort**.

Doonmore   *Dún Mór*
D 2536   "large fort"

1. Doonmore	OSRNB sh.10	1855c
2. Dunmore "big fortified hill"	OSRNB sh.10	1855c
3. dunˈmoːr	Local pronunciation	1993

"A small hill or isolated mound forming a natural fortification. It has a steep ascent on every side, a flat surface on top, and when viewed from the north side presents all the appearance of a large fort" (*OSRNB* sh.10). This is in Ligadaughtan. See also **Portadoon**.

Doonmore Fort   A hybrid form
D 1743

1. Doonmore	OSRNB sh.5	1855c
2. duːnˈmoːr	Local pronunciation	1993

Dún Mór "large fort" is the original form of this place-name, which is in Cross. It probably refers to the site of a motte and bailey dating to c. 1180 (*PSAMNI* 8); objects of pre-
Norman age have also been found on this site (Childe 1938, 128). The English suffix in the
standard form of the place-name does not appear to be used.

Drumnakill Point	A hybrid form	
D 2043		
1. (?)Druim na Cille	Irish of the Glens 105	1940
2. Mount of Droimnakill	Wright's Diary 31	1806
3. Drumnakill	OSNB B 24 B 37	1834
4. Drumnakill Point	OSRNB sh.5	1855c
5. Druim na coille "ridge of the wood"	J O'D (OSNB) B 24 B 37	1831
6. ˌdrǫmnə'kiːl	Local pronunciation	1993

The Irish elements in this place-name refer to nearby Drumnakill, originally *Droim na
Cille* "ridge of the church", a "promontory which extends considerably into the sea", and on
which stand the remains of an "ancient church and graveyard . . . anciently called
Killemoiloge . . . At the West of the Church, the remains of St. Moiloge or Malock are supposed to be found" (*OSM* xxiv 57; recorded in 1838). The original form of the saint's name
is uncertain, although we may consider *Maolmhaodhóg* and perhaps *Mo Luóg* (see *PNI* iii 60)
and *Mocheallóg*. In c. 1855 it was noted that unbaptized children were interred here (*OSRNB*
sh.5). The Archaeological Survey of 1940 describes the ruins as the remains of a "very small
church, only 33 ft. by 18 ft. outside" (*PSAMNI* 8). It is not clear whether form 1 refers to
this place or to **Drumnakeel** townland. See also **Cross**.
Drumnakill Point is .5 km north of the old church and lies in Big House.

Eglarudda Burn	A hybrid form	
D 1834		
1. Eglarudda Burn	OSRNB sh.14	1855c
2. Eagla roda	J O'D (OSRNB) sh.14	1855c
3. ˌɛglɑ'rǫdə'bǫrn	Local pronunciation	1993

"This stream takes its rise at the border between Glenmakeerin and Kinune [in the parish
of Grange of Layd]. It takes a north west course . . ." (*OSRNB* sh.14), and forms one of the
head streams of the Glenmakeerin River.
The origin of this name is difficult to determine. The east Co. Donegal townland name of
Egglybane may contain the same first element. *Agaill* "eagle's nest" is attested in plural form
in another Co. Donegal townland name *Na hAgallaí* (Ó Domhnaill 1952, 189); a variant
form such as *eagaill/iogaill* might have formed the first element here and been later affected
by metathesis. This stream rises in the loftiest part of the parish. That it derives from *achaill*
"view point" (see Ó Máille 1989–90, 128) might be considered but is unlikely. *Aigeán*

"hollow(?)", possibly a variant of *aigéan* "ocean" has been noted in local place-names including **Agangarrive Hill** above; it may have developed a local connotation such as "mountainside; sheep-path". Other attested Irish variants are *eagán* and *aigéal* while *Dwelly* lists the further variant (from the Scotish Gaelic of the Western Isles) *aigeall* "abyss; deep pool". We might consider that this name features a further variant, *eagal(l)*.

The final element in this place-name may derive from one of the fem. nouns *roide* "red water (from admixture of mud, bog-stuff or mineral), bog-stuff, mire, refuse, any soft plashy refuse" (this has a variant form *roda* of uncertain gender; *Dinneen*) or *roid* (gen. *roide*) "a dye plant; applied to bog-myrtle, *al.* bog-poppy" (*ibid.*). Possible original forms of the place-name could be constructred from these various elements but there remains considerable doubt over both form and meaning.

| **Escort** | *Ioscart* | |
| D 2241 | "bad land" | |

1. Iscart, quarterland of Torr sometimes called	PRONI D2977/3A/2/28/2	1711
2. Eskart, the quarterland of Torr alias	PRONI D2977/3A/2/28/4	1742
3. Ischartt, quarter land of Torr Als	PRONI D2977/3A/2/28/5	1746
4. Eskirt, the Quarterland of West Torr alias	PRONI D2977/3A/2/28/8	1781
5. Iscart	Tithe App. Book 20	1833
6. ˈïskərt	Local pronunciation	1993

This place-name refers now to a small hamlet, found on high ground in the north of West Torr. It was described in 1835 as "a cluster of about 20 cabins of wretched description. It is situated near the signal staff near Torr Head. The inhabitants are of the poorer class" (*OSM* xxiv 45). It may derive from *eiscir* "ridge of high land" (*Joyce* i 402). Although this element seems to be more usually applied to low glacial sandy ridges (see *ibid.* and Ó Dónaill sv.), both *Dinneen* and *Dwelly* have translated it as "ridge of mountains". A further possibility is that the name consists of *easc(a)* "wet, sedgy, bog; depression, hollow" (Ó Dónaill; see also *Joyce* i 447 and *DIL* sv. *esc(a)*) plus the meaningless suffix *-ar* (see Ó Máille 1987). The somewhat similar *eascar* "a cup, goblet" (*DIL* sv. *escar*) may also be a possibility insofar as vessels are sometimes used in place-names to denote topographical depressions (see *PNI* v 55–6). *Dinneen* gives several meanings for *eascar/ioscar* including "a leap, a fall (esp. from a horse); a cascade", and we might consider that this was used here to describe a mountain stream which runs past the hamlet. In all of these forms, however, we would have to explain the final *t* as a later addition.

The most likely origin appears to be from *eascart* "tow; refuse, offscourings" (*DIL* sv. *escart*), a variant form of which appears in the nom. pl. in the Co. Kilkenny townland name of *Ioscarta* (anglicized Uskerty; *L. Log. C. Ch.* 35). It seems to have been employed in place-names in the sense "bad land".

| **Ess Bridge** | A hybrid form | |
| D 1840 | | |

1. The Ess Bridge	OSRNB sh.9, 2	1855c

2. eas "a waterfall"	J O'D (OSRNB) sh.9, 2	1855c
3. ɛsˈbrïdʒ	Local pronunciation	1993

"A small stone bridge with one arch on the road from Ballycastle to Cushendun – the road is raised on either side of the bridge, and close to it on the south side is a waterfall – from this waterfall the bridge has derived its name" (*OSRNB* sh.9, 2). It lies on the boundary of the townlands of Drumadoon and Coolnagoppoge.

Eas may variously mean "a waterfall, cascade, a stream, a rapid" (*Dinneen*). See also **Essan** in Armoy.

Fair Head
D 1844

An English form

See **Benmore**.

Fall Point
D 1943

An English form

1. The fall Point	OSRNB sh.5	1855c

"A headland sloping to the waters edge and the surface of which is strewn with huge massive rocks. It is situate at the N. base of a towering cliff of great height [south east of Benmore or Fair Head], and some 15 years ago a large breach fell from the cliff and covered all into the sea with rocks and other debris. From this circumstance the place is called 'The Fall Point'" (*OSRNB* sh.5). It seems unlikely that the former element in this name derived from Irish *fál* "a hedge, a dead hedge; a protection; top wall or fence; a pailing, a wall" (*Dinneen*).

Feykeeran Burn
D 1734

A hybrid form

1. Feykeeran Burn	OSRNB sh.14	1855c
2. Faithce caorthainn "green of the rowan trees"	J O'D (OSRNB) sh.14	1855c
3. "The rushy Moor"	OSRNB sh.14	1855c
4. ˌfeːkirənˈbọrn	Local pronunciation	1993

"A small stream which rises in the S. west side of Drumacullin townland. It flows in a northward course about ¾ mile and forms one of the head streams of 'Owen Cam'" (*OSRNB* sh.14).

Féith "a fountain or stream, a swamp" (*Dinneen*) appears to be the first element, and *Féith Chaorthainn* "stream of the rowan" may have constituted the original name. The gen. pl. form of *caorthann* (*caorthann*) "the rowan or quicken tree, mountain ash" (*Dinneen*) and the male personal name *Ciarán* (Mod. Ir. gen. *Chiaráin*) seem somewhat less likely final elements (cf. **Glenmakeerin**). *Feá* "beech" and *caorán* "moor" could be considered however (see *PNI* v 33 sv. **Moykeeran**).

188

Flughery Burn, Hybrid forms
Flughery Bridge
D 2039

1. Flughery	OSRNB sh.9, 2	1855c
2. Flughery Bridge	OSRNB sh.9, 2	1855c
3. Flughery Burn	OSRNB sh.9, 2	1855c
4. fliuchaire "wet land"	J O'D (OSRNB) sh.9, 2	1855c
5. Fliuchre "wet spots"	Rev. Magill 16	1923
6. 'fluxəri	Local pronunciation	1993

Flughery was described in c. 1855 as "a mountain farm with one farm house and in the occupation of Daniel McCormick. It is supposed to have been named from the moisture of the soil" (*OSRNB* sh.9, 2). The bridge and stream were described as follows: "A small bridge with one arch on a mountain road that leads N.W. and S.E. through the townland of Ballyvennaght. It is built on a small burn of the same name . . . the burn is named from a tract [of land] on the N.E. side of it"; "A small stream flowing for the greater part through a moorland district and supposed to have been so named from the moisture of the soil along its course. It flows in a westerly direction and unites with Carey River" (*ibid.*).

There are several possibilities regarding the original form, but one of the more likely is *Fliuchdhoire* "wet oak-wood". The somewhat similar form *An Fhliuchmhuine* "the wet thicket" is the name of three townlands in Co. Kilkenny (Lughinny, Loffanny x2; *L. Log. C. Chainnigh* 31). We could also consider that the original name was formed by *fliuch* plus the meaningless suffix *-ar* plus the collective/substantive suffix *-ach*, with the meaning "wet place": *fliucharach* could later have become *fliucharaigh* through use in oblique cases. McKay has recorded a form based on *fliuchaigh* used as an alternative name for the south-west Co. Antrim subtownland name of **Farranflough**; *fliuchaigh* is an oblique form of *fliuchach* "wet place" (*PNI* iv 71). O'Boyle noted the name *Fleughans* (perhaps from *Fliuchá(i)n*) in Carravindoon in Rathlin, which he understood to mean "wet, marshy place" (*O'Boyle* 46).

Garvalt Burn A hybrid form
D 1432

1. Garvalt Burn	OSRNB sh.14	1855c
2. garbh-alt "rough glen"	OSRNB sh.14	1855c
3. "the coarse valley or glen"	OSRNB sh.14	1855c
4. 'gɑrvalt	Local pronunciation	1993

"This stream takes its rise in the townlands of Tenaghs and Ardaghmore from two small head streams and flows N. westward through a small glen about 1½ statute miles and unites with the Glenshesk River" (*OSRNB* sh.14).

An Garbhallt "the rough steep glen/stream" is the likely original form of the Irish elements.

Glenmakeerin River	A hybrid form	
D 1637, 1640		
1. Glemmakeerin River	OSRNB sh.9, 2	1855c

"A small mountain river flowing north and N.W. through the townlands of Glenmakeerin, Drumnakeel and Ballynagard and uniting with the Carey River at the north side of the [latter] townland" (*OSRNB* sh.9, 2). See also **Glenmakeerin** and **Broughanlea** townlands.

Greenanmore	*An Grianán Mór*	
D 2141	"the eminent place, big"	
1. An Grianán Mór	Irish of the Glens 117	1940
2. Granamore	OSNB B 24 B 37	1831
3. Greenanmore	OSRNB sh.9, 1	1855c
4. Greenan More Hill	OSCNB sh.9	1855c
5. greanan mór "great gravelly hill"	J O'D (OSNB) B 24 B 37	1831
6. Grianan mór "great sunny hill"	J O'D (OSRNB) sh.9, 1	1855c
7. Gríanan mór "The large palace, or sun bower"	Ó Dubhthaigh 181	1905
8. ə griənɑn moːr	Irish of the Glens 117	1940
9. 'griːnənz	Ó Maolfabhail (Grianán) 71	1974
10. ˌgriənə'moːr	Local pronunciation	1993
11. ˌgrɛn'mɔːr	Local pronunciation	1993

In c. 1855, Greenanmore was described as "a green hill with very fine pasture and indented with small nooks. Its surface is very smooth except in some spots where limestone rocks appear through it. It commands an extensive view of the country around, and is supposed to take its name from its sunny aspect" (*OSRNB* sh.9, 1). It stands at 282 metres in West Torr.

Forms 2 and 11 seem to indicate phonetic degeneration rather than suggest that *An Greanach Mór* "the large gravelly place" formed the original name. O'Donovan appears to have had a collective form of *grean* "gravel, grit; coarse sand" in mind in form 5 (cf. *An Greanach* "the gravelly place" anglicized **Granagh**, a townland in east Co. Down, in *PNI* ii 48). The pronunciation in form 9 reflects that of the townland name of **Greenan**, which lies on the opposite (west) side of the parish. In this case however, it was not prompted by a territorial division. There exists another peak, probably that to the immediate south-east of Greenanmore, called *Wee Greenan* (*Pers. comm.* 07.10.96), probably from (*An*) *Grianán Beag* "(the) eminent place, small".

Greenan Water	A hybrid form	
D 1534		
1. Greenan Water	OSRNB sh.14	1855c
2. 'grinən 'ri̇vər	Local pronunciation	1993

"This stream takes its rise in the mountain part of Greenan Townland . . . and flows N. westward about 1½ miles [before joining with] Owen Cam" (*OSRNB* sh.14).

Green Hill
An English form(?)
D 2439

1. Green Hill	OSRNB sh.10	1855c
2. 'grin hïl	Local pronunciation	1993

"The summit of a high hill bordering the sea coast [and on the boundary of Ballinloughan and Aughnaholle townlands]. It has an altitude above sea level of 715 feet. The coast road leading from Cushendall to Ballycastle passes over this hill at an altitude of 650 feet above sea level" (*OSRNB* sh.10).

Although no Irish antecedent to this place-name has been recorded, place-names of this type in Ireland may be pseudo-translations of Irish forms. The Co. Limerick townland name of Greenhills was formerly *Cnoc na Buaile Glaise* "the hill of the green booley" (Ó Maolfabhail 1990, 130). Ó Maolfabhail (*Ó Maolfabhail (Grianán)* 67) has noted that *Greenhills* in Irish place-names may often have originally denoted "hillocks of sand". *Grian* is a variant of *grean* "gravel, grit; coarse sand" but may also denote "(of sea, lake, river) bottom; earth, ground, land" (*Ó Dónaill* sv.).

Grey Man's Path
Casán an Fhir Léith
D 1843
"path of the grey man"

1. Fhirleith or Grey Man's Path	OSM xxiv 81	1835
2. Grayman's Path	Wright's Diary 31	1806
3. ðə 'greː mɑnz 'paθ	Local pronunciation	1993

Dallat has noted the pronunciation [ˌkɑsənfar'liː] locally (*Pers. comm.* 06.01.93). Form 1, which seems to be a truncated locally recorded Irish form, may indicate an origin in *Casán an Fhir Léith* "path of the grey man" although it might also be considered that the last elements of this name were in the gen. pl. case. The translated English form of the name predominates now. A grey man is also referred to in an Irish form of **Benmore or Fair Head** (form 33).

The Ordnance Survey recorded that the name derived from "some aged and grey haired recluses who in ancient times resided in some of the large caves along the base of the rocky eminence [Benmore or Fair Head] and whose only descent to their subterraneous mansion was by this dangerous path" (*OSM* xxiv 81). O'Laverty later wrote that the name was "said to have been so named from some holy man who came here each day from some of the neighbouring churches to pass his time in prayer and meditation . . ." (*O'Laverty* iv 486). The townland name of **Fallinerlea** in Layd parish has been interpreted as *Fál an Fhir Léith* "Greyman's hedge" by Magill (*Rev. Magill* 15; regarding similar elements in other local place-names, see also *Place-Names of Rathlin* 12).

Gribbin
Grabán
D 1642
"rocky ground"

Grabán "patch of rough, rocky ground" (*Ó Dónaill*) appears to be the origin of this coastal place-name which may be obsolete. It is in Ballyreagh Lower.

Killaleenan	*Cill an Líonáin*	
D 1742	"church of the ravine"	
1. Killylyenan	EA 283	1847
2. Killaleenan	OSRNB sh.5	1885c
3. Cill na leanan "burial place of the favourites or lovers"	OSRNB sh.5	1885c
4. Coill na líonan "the wood of the creeks"	Ó Dubhthaigh 182	1905
5. Coill a líonan "Wood of the tidal stream"	Rev. Magill 18	1923
6. ˌkïˈlinən	Local pronunciation	1993

Reeves recorded in 1847 that "S. W. of [Killowen] in a part locally called Cruachan Carrach, is a little glen through which flows a stream, where are the remains of this rudely built chapel, measuring 16.5' by 9.25'" (*EA* 284). This chapel would thus have stood very near to the church of Killowen, discussed under **Cross**. In c. 1855 it was recorded that this name referred to a "a small and nearly circular burial ground situate in a valley and close to the south bank of a small stream which flows west through said valley . . . It is said to have been an ancient place of interment but there is nothing but vague conjecture to support such a claim. It is now used only for the interment of unbaptized children" (*OSRNB* sh.5).

Cill an Líonáin "church/burial-ground of the ravine" accords reasonably with standard anglicized spelling: the modern variant could have suffered from syncope or haplology, or represent the form *Cill Líonáin* (with the same meaning). The nom. *cill* seems to have developed to *cillidh* in some cases in the late local dialect, and this may be reflected in form 1. Something similar occurred in Omeath where the forms *Cillidh Chaoil* and *Cille Chaol* were recorded earlier this century (they refer to *Cill Chaoil*, anglicized **Kilkeel**, in Co. Down; see *PNI* iii 13; cf. also form 1 of **Kilpatrick** in Rathlin). We may also consider that the final element was the somewhat rare male personal name *Liadhnán* (meaning originally perhaps "grey lad"; Ó Corráin & Maguire 1981, 122). Form 3 does not reflect the few historical forms available.

Killuca Burn,	Hybrid forms	
Killuca Bridge		
D 1535, 1485		
1. Killyluke	EA 283	1847
2. Killuca	OSRNB sh.9, 2	1855c
3. Killuca Burn	OSRNB sh.9, 2	1855c
4. Killuca Bridge	OSRNB sh.9, 2	1855c
5. ˌkïlˈuka	Local pronunciation	1993

Reeves describes Killuca, which lies in the townland of Duncarbit, as a "small disused cemetery" (*EA* 284). In c. 1855 it was described as "a rugged uncultivated spot situate in a meadow. It is said to have been formerly a burial place – none have of late been buried in it save unbaptized children. The peasantry venerate it" (*OSRNB* sh.9, 2). The first element thus appears to have been *cill* "church, burial-ground", rather than *coill/coillidh* "wood" (cf. also **Killaleenan**).

The etymology of this name is uncertain, but we should consider that *cill* was qualified by a gaelicized form of the male personal name Luke. A form appears in the Monaghan townland of *Tír Liúc* (Dunnaluck; *L. Log. Mhuineacháin* 50), and Woulfe (1923, 49) lists the further variants *Lúcás* and *Labhcás*. Although it is unattested, this place-name may indicate that there existed the variant form *Liúca*: *Cill Liúca* "Luke's burial-ground". There is also a surname Luke ("rarer and of later introduction than Lucas (itself on record since the 1400s) ... It has sometimes been used as a synonym of the Scottish MacLucas" (MacLysaght 1985, 200)), but surnames in *cill-* names are rare. Further possible final elements include the adj. *slocach* "abounding in pits, hollows or caverns" (*Dinneen*; see also *Irish of the Glens* 128 sv. *slocach*) or "pitted; rutted" (*Ó Dónaill*), *loca* "pen, fold" (*ibid.*) or its variant *loc* (gen. sing. *loic/loca*; *Dinneen*). Irish *o* when pronounced [ǫ] sometimes developed to [ʌ] in the late local dialect, although Holmer did not record any examples which would be particularly analogous here (*Irish of the Glens* 30–1). The unattested adj. *sliúcach* "slanted" may also be a possibility; note also *liuca* "a small half-grown fish of any species" (*Dinneen*).

The stream and the bridge were described in c. 1855 as follows: "A small stream having its source in the south east part of Duncarbit townland . . . It is named from an old graveyard – or what is supposed to be one – close by which it flows"; "A small stone bridge with one arch spanning Killuca Burn and on the old road from Ballycastle to Greenan . . ." (*OSRNB* sh.9, 2).

Lack-na-traw	*Leac na Trá*	
D 1944	"flag-stone of the beach"	
1. Lacknatraw	OSRNB sh.5	1855c
2. Lacknatra	OSRNB sh.5	1855c
3. "flag of the strand"	OSRNB sh.5	1855c
4. ˌlaknəˈtra	Local pronunciation	1993

This is "a low rocky headland running into the sea, and situate at the north base of the towering cliffs of Fair Head. The ground from the base of the sea is strewn with huge rocks. At the low water [-mark] are some rocks upon which some marine plants grow – these are called Lacknatraw or the flag of the strand by the country people . . . who collect dillisk" (*OSRNB* sh.5).

Leckpatrick	*Leac Pádraig*	
D 2440	"St. Patrick's flag-stone"	
1. Leckpatrick	OSRNB sh.10	1855c
2. leic Patraic "Patrick's flagstone"	J O'D (OSRNB) sh.10	1855c
3. ˌlɛkˈpatrək	Local pronunciation	1993

"A point of land sheltering the south side of Portaleen [in Ballinloughan]. Origin unknown" (*OSRNB* sh.10).

St Patrick is reputed to have slept on the stone of this name (*Pers. comm.* 26.2.94) which was adopted for the headland. Nearby is a stone known as *St Columkille's Stone*, "so called in consequence of some impressions on its flat side which in some degree resemble the prints of a hand and foot . . ." (*OSM* xxiv 77). See also **Ballykenver** in Armoy.

Legacapple Burn	A hybrid form	
D 1833		
1. Legacapple Burn	OSRNB sh.14	1855c
2. lag a chapaill "hollow of the		
horse"	OSRNB sh.14	1855c
3. "the Horses Glen"	OSRNB sh.14	1855c
4. ˌlɛgəˈkapəlˈborn	Local pronunciation	1993

"This stream takes its rise . . . at the head of a narrow glen [in Drumacullin]. It flows N. westwards nearly in a direct line until it unites with Feykeeran Burn . . ." (*OSRNB* sh.14).

Log or *lag* has several meanings, including "a hollow, cavity or sag; a pool, in a river, etc" (*Dinneen*; see also **Lagavara** in Ballintoy). *Log an Chapaill* "hollow of the horse/mare", the likely original form of the Irish elements, has since been transferred to the stream. See also **Legahapple Bridge** in Other Names, Armoy.

Lisnacalliagh	*Lios na gCailleach(?)*	
D 1742	"fort of the hags"	
1. Lisnacalliagh	OSRNB sh.5	1855c
2. Lisnakilley	OSRNB sh.5	1855c
3. "fort of the hags"	OSRNB sh.5	1855c
4. ˌlïsnəˈkïli	Local pronunciation	1993

In c. 1855 it was recorded that this place-name, in Ballyreagh Upper, referred to "a small scattered farm village, close to which on the N.W. side stands an old fort. The village was formerly occupied by old women whose sons worked in collieries north of it . . . [giving rise to the name]" (*OSRNB* sh.5).

The discrepancy between form 1 and forms 2 and 4 does not allow us to conclusively decide whether the final element originally represented the gen. sing. or gen. pl. of *cailleach* "old woman, hag; nun". The absence of eclipsis of the *g* could be explained as a typical feature of anglicization. Regarding this element, see also **Port Calliagh** in Other Names, Ramoan. Forms 2 and 4 also reflect gen. forms of *coill* "wood" and *cill* "church; burying ground". Perhaps a confusion of elements gave rise to the etymology noted in the *OSRNB*. *Lios* has several meanings (see **Lismorrity** in Grange of Drumtullagh).

Loughan Bay	A hybrid form	
D 2538		
1. Loughan Bay	OSRNB sh.10	1855c

"A bay or merely a curvation of the sea coast line upon a radius of about 6 furlongs [between Crockan Point and Runabay Head]. It is seldom resorted to by vessels of heavy burden as an anchoring ground in stormy weather, being rather open to the northern gales" (*OSRNB* sh.10). See also **Loughan** townland.

Loughareema (Vanishing Lake)	*Loch an Mhadhma*	
D 2136	"lake of the bursting out(?)"	
1. Lough Avoon	OSM xxiv 42	1835
2. Loughaveema	OSRNB sh.9, 1	1855c
3. Loughaweema	J O'D (OSRNB) sh.9, 1	1855c
4. Loughaveema	PSAMNI 14	1940
5. Loch a mhadhma "lake of the eruption"	J O'D (OSRNB) sh.9, 1	1855c
6. Loch an Rith Amach	Dallat's Glens 71	1989
7. ˌlɑːxəˈrima	Local pronunciation	1993

"A small lough in a mountain district. The main road from Ballycastle to Cushendall passes through it. The lough is full to overflowing in winter, but in summer the water disappears. This appearance and disappearance have given rise to the name it is said. It is situated at the north end of a deep glen called Altdorragha [in Ballypatrick] . . . The local sound of this name cannot be expressed by any combination of English letters. The above [form 2] is the nearest approximation" (*OSRNB* sh.9, 1).

The *r* in the standardized anglicized form seems to be based on a misspelling. It hardly reflects a phonetic development. The "local sound" alluded to above was probably the high back unrounded vowel ([ʌ]) which is also reflected in forms 1–4. We would not be suprised at *-idh* being pronounced [i] (cf. **Ballycleagh**), but [i] and [ʌ] intermixed in certain positions locally, such as after broad consonants (see *Irish of the Glens* 16–7 and 31). *Maidhm* (gen. sing. *maidhme*) "break, burst, eruption; defeat, rout" (*Ó Dónaill*) is normally fem. in the later language although *Ó Dónaill* lists a masc. variant (with gen. sing. *madhma*). *DIL* lists it as neuter and masc. with the meanings "breaking (a battle); defeat, rout, flight; breaking, bursting, giving way (in a physical sense); a breaking forth, bursting out, eruption" (*DIL* sv. *maidm*). It occurs in the Co. Monaghan townland name of *Corr Mhadhma*, anglicized Corvoam (*L. Log. Mhuineacháin* 18). We may note also *tomaidhm* "eruption, outpouring; bursting forth of lake or river" (*DIL*) and consider that *Loch Thomhadhma* "lake of the outpouring(?)" may have constituted the original form.

Lough Bridge	A hybrid form	
D 2136		
1. lɔːxˈbrïdʒ	Local pronunciation	1993

The name refers to the bridge on the main Cushendun-Ballycastle road which spans Loughareema.

Lough Doo	*An Loch Dubh*	
D 1743	"the black lake"	
1. (?)Lough Addy, 4 A. unprof.	ASE 116a §19	1668

2. Loch dubh "Black lough"	Rev. Magill 20	1923
3. lɔːxˈdu	Local pronunciation	1993

This lake is in Cross. See also **Portdoo**.

Lough Fadden
D 1942

Loch Pháidín
"*Páidín*'s lake"

1. Lough called Padyn	DS (Par. Map) 55	1657c
2. Logh Padding	BSD 165	1661
3. Logh Pading, 9 A. unprof.	ASE 116a §19	1668
4. Loch feadáin "lake of the brook or streamlet"	J O'D (OSNB) B 24 B 37	1831
5. ˌlɑxˈfadən	Local pronunciation	1993

Páidín is a form of *Pádraig* (Ó Corráin & Maguire 1981, 152). The pet form *Paidí* was noted locally by Holmer ([padˈi]; *Irish of the Glens* 123). *Loch Feadáin* "lake of the stream" (form 4) would be a reasonable etymology if we assumed the *p* in forms 1–3, which are related, to have resulted from mistranscription. The gen. pl. form *feadán* "(of the) streams" would not correspond to the *-ing* ending (forms 2–3). This is in Knockbrack.

Lough na Cranagh
D 1843

Loch na Crannóige(?)
"lake of the dwelling"

1. Logh Dunard	Dartmouth Map 25	1590c
2. Lo. Dunard	Bartlett Maps (Esch. Co. Maps) 1	1603
3. Lo. Dunnare	Speed's Antrim & Down	1610
4. Lo. Dunnare	Speed's Ulster	1610
5. Logh dunard	BSD 165	1661
6. (?)the Lough of Cary-vizt.	Decree of Innocence 431	1663
7. Lough Dunard 15 A. 1 R. unprof.	ASE 116a §19	1668
8. Lough-na-cressa	OSM xxiv 81	1838
9. Loughnacranagh	OSRNB sh.5	1855c
10. Loch na Cranóige "lake of the wooden house"	J O'D (OSNB) B 24 B 37	1831
11. Lough-na-crannóg	Murphy's Rathlin 165	1953c
12. ˌlɔːxnəˈkranɑx	Local pronunciation	1993

Reeves notes that this lake "covers 24½ acres and derives its name from a small circular island artificially formed in the centre of it" (*EA* 283; see also *PSAMNI* 8). The Ordnance Survey noted that an island in this lake was called *Cranagh* or *Crannoge* locally: "it appears to have been artificially formed. It is faced all round with stone work of the best style masonry. It rises about 4 or 5 feet above the surface of the lake and in shape is like an inverted tub" (*OSRNB* sh. 5). *Loch na Crannóige* "lake of the dwelling" then, is a possible origin. The Ordnance Survey recorded a further instance of this element in the name of a hamlet called **Crannoge** in the Ballintoy townland of Artimacormick (*ibid.* sh.3, 2). We could account for the [ɑx] ending in modern pronunciation by noting a somewhat similar deterioriation in the townland name **Coolnagoppoge**.

The fem. noun *crannach* "trees, grove, wooded place; [of] various objects made of wood; wooden structure; stake-fence" (see *DIL* sv.) is normally ascribed the gen. sing. form *cran-naí*, but we might postulate an alternative form in *Loch na Cranncha* "lake of the wooden structure" (compare *tulach* in *Dinneen* sv.). *Loch na Cránach* "lake of the sow", considering that the island was called *Cranagh* or *Crannoge* locally, seems less likely.

In penal times, the island was resorted to by Catholics as a place of worship until "a boat which was conveying the clergy and the congregation from the mainland was upset with a large number who were on board and consequently perished in the bowels of the lake . . . a cross situated there in the place for religious purposes gave its present name to the lough" (*OSM* xxiv 8; form 8): *Loch na Croise* "lake of the cross". *Loch Dhún Ard/Loch Dúin Aird*, suggested in forms 1–5 and 7, is no longer current (the townland in which this lake is found was once called *Dún Ard*; see **Cross**).

Magheraboy	*An Machaire Buí*	
D 1841	"the yellow plain/field"	
1. Magheraboy	OSRNB sh.9, 1	1855c
2. machaire buidhe "yellow plain"	J O'D (OSRNB) sh.9, 1	1855c
3. ˌmɑxərəˈbɔi	Local pronunciation	1993

"Two farm houses [in Knockbrack] in the occupation of John and Daniel McCormick. The name signifies the yellow plain, and is supposed to have been described from the colour of the soil" (*OSRNB* sh.9, 1).

Machaire has several meanings including "a plain, a flat or low-lying country, a field, a riding or playing field, a race-course, a battlefield" (*Dinneen*). The place-name refers to a gently sloping area on the western side of Crockanore mountain, between this peak and the Carey River. See also **Magheraboy** townland in Grange of Drumtullagh parish.

Mallandeevan	*Mala an Duibhéin(?)*	
D 1839	"hill-slope of the cormorant"	
1. Mallendugane	Hib. Reg. Cary	1657c
2. Mallendugan	DS (Par. Map) 55	1657c
3. Mollindiume	Census 18	1659
4. Mallendugoan	Hib. Del. Antrim	1672c
5. Malnedivan	Reg. Deeds abstracts i §265	1722
6. Mallendeven	Religious Survey	1734
7. Mallindeevan	OSRNB sh.9, 1	1855c
8. Mallindeevan	OSRNB sh.9, 1	1855c
9. Mallanadeevan	OSRNB sh.9, 1	1855c
10. mala na dtaobhan	J O'D (OSRNB) sh.9, 1	1855c
11. "brow of the ricks"	OSRNB sh.9, 1	1855c

12. Mala na doimhne "Hill brow of the deep"	Rev. Magill 21	1923
13. ˌmɑlənəˈdivən	Local pronunciation	1993

"An arable tract comprising 3 or 4 farms and forming a subdenomination of the townland of Ballyvennaght. Formerly and until a recent period, it was covered with wood which supplied the neighbouring farmers with ricks, or teevans, for the roofs of houses, and hence the name . . ." (*OSRNB* sh.9, 1).

The first element in the name could have been one of several words, but *mala* "hill-slope" seems the most likely. The second [ə] in modern pronunciation appears to be a recently introduced epenthetic vowel. If the final element was indeed the gen. pl. of *taobhán* "longitudinal beam (in roof), purlin" (form 10), we must assume that this vowel was hidden in earlier forms due to its unstressed position. Other possibilities regarding the final element in this name include the gen. sing. or gen. pl. of *duibhéan* "cormorant". The first vowel of this element would have been latterly raised to [ʌ] in the late dialect: Holmer recorded the placename [pʌrt ən dʌvən] which he spelt as *Purt an Duibhean* (*Irish of the Glens* 111). The adj. *díomhaoin* "worthless, unoccupied(?)" may also be considered. Note, for example, Tievedeevan townland, from *An Taobh Díomhaoin*, in Co. Donegal (O'Kane 1970, 111). Joyce translates this element in place-name as "idle [i.e. unfarmed]" (*Joyce* i 211).

It is difficult to ascertain to what extent forms 1, 2 and 4 accurately reflect the final element. They come from related documents and may contain scribal errors. An intervocalic *g(h)* appears to have developed to [v] in the Ramoan townland name of **Drumavoley**, but even in this event it remains unclear what the final element could have been. A form of the surname *Ó Dubhagáin*, anglicized Dougan in east Ulster (MacLysaght 1985, 92) might be considered. It is uncertain how long this surname has been found in this part of Ireland (*ibid.*), where it may have been of Scottish origin (regarding which, see Black 1946, 224 and 226).

Mill Town,	English forms	
Milltown Burn		
D 2433, 2434		

1. Milltown	Culfeightrin Map [1789] 1	1789
2. Mill Town	OSRNB sh.15	1855c

"A village of farm houses. It derives its name from a mill being there some time ago. This [village] contains one licenced house"; "This stream takes its rise in the mountain part of Cushleake. It takes a course S. eastward through a narrow defile and crossing the shore road at Milltown it falls into the sea at Rock Port Lodge" (*OSRNB* sh.15). The Ordnance Survey recorded the existence of a corn mill here in the 1830s (*OSM* xxiv 45). See also **Ballindam**.

Murlough Bay	A hybrid form	
D 2042		

1. (?)Cath Murbuilg i nDál Riada (prehist.)	AFM i 10	2859
2. (?)Murbhulg, i	AFM i 322	725
3. (?)Murbulg, im-	A. Tigern. i 235	730

4. (?)Murbuilgg, in	AU i 182	730
5. (?)Murbuilg i nDal Riatai,	Cath LL 20 §630	1100c
6. (?)Murbuilg, Cath	LL 23 §723	1100c
7. (?)mMurbulc, i	LL 57 §1842	1100c
8. (?)mMurbulgi, macne Durthacht a	CGH 284 §158,24	1125c
9. (?)Murbuilg, carraic	CRR 14 §9, 16 §10	1150c
10. (?)na Caenraigi Muirbuilg	Descendants Ir 52	1200c
11. (?)i mmurbulc la dál riatai	Senchus Fer n-Alban 154 §9	1350c
12. (?)i Murbolc	L. Gábala v 170 §487	1350c
13. (?)caenraige muirbuilg	Uí Mhaine (Hogan) 66a	1390c
14. (?)m[uir]bhuilg, cath	BB 11b 14	1390c
15. (?)Murbolg, i	L. Gabála v 166 §483M	1397c
16. (?)Murbholg, i	Geneal. Tracts 195 §189	1400c
17. (?)Murbhuilg, Cath	Céitinn i 178, 180; iii 146	1633c
18. (?)go Torbhuirg is ó Phort Murbhoilg	Céitinn iii 302	1633c
19. (?)Murbhuilg, cath	L. Gen. DF 37	1650
20. (?)Murbholg, i	L. Gen. DF 37, 400	1650
21. (?)Caonraighe Murbuilg	L. Gen. DF 501	1650
22. Mowllacke	Terrier (Reeves) 75	1615
23. murbholg "sea-belly"	Joyce ii 249	1875
24. Murbholg "The sea belly"	Ó Dubhthaigh 184	1905
25. Murlach	GÉ 142	1989
26. 'mɔrlɔx	Local pronunciation	1993

While the standardized anglicized form of this name seems to derive from the form *Murloch*, literally "sea-lake", the original form was *Mu(i)rbholg* (forms 1–21): the modern form probably derives in fact from the action of metathesis. The *o* has been altered to *a* in the standard Mod. Ir. form (25) due to its unstressed position. *DIL* has translated *muirbholg* as "a sea bag; inlet of the sea" (*DIL* sv. *muir*). The English epithet in the name does not appear to be used, and Murlough is used locally also to denote the land adjacent to the bay. In the last century, Murlough was described as a "subdivision of Bighouse [townland]" (*OSM* xxiv 57).

Reeves (*EA* 27 n.c) has noted that the Co. Down parish now called Maghera was previously known as *Rath-murbhuilg* (sic). Part of the latter name is recorded in the townland called **Murlough Upper** in Maghera (*Census 1851*). "*Domonghort raith rogein mac Echdach ó Raith Murbuilcc i nDal Ríada*" (*Mart. Gorm.*, March 24 p.60 (1170c); see also *Mart. Don.*, March 24 p.85 (1630c)) is a confused reference which pertains more correctly in fact to the Co. Down name (*EA* 154) and so was not listed above. Joyce notes that *muirbholg* was generally anglicized *murlough* and locates two further examples of the latter in Co. Donegal (*Joyce* ii 249). Hogan (*Onom. Goed.* 550) also lists two Scottish names containing *muirbholg*.

Form 18 occurs in Céitinn's account of the extent of the diocese of Connor. The extremities of the diocese were used to define the territory and so MacErlean has suggested that *Port Murbhoilg* is unlikely to be Murlough Bay, being so close to *Torbhuirg* (see **East Torr** townland and **Torr Head**, which lies 3 miles to the south east), as it would be contrary to "normal procedure" to have named two places so close together: it probably referred to some coastal site much further west or south (*MacErlean* 26). O'Donovan believed that an early reference to a *[Dun Sobhairce i] Murbholg Dhál Riada* (not listed above) related to the "small bay at Dunseverick", but that Murlough Bay "was also anciently called Murbholg" (see *AFM* i 26–7 n.o; see also *Lebor Gabála* v 68 §431 and 170 §487; see also *Joyce* ii 249). This casts doubt on the identification of most of the forms listed above. The battle referred to in forms 1, 5–6, 17 and 19 seems more likely to have occured at the Dunseverick site.

The location of the tribe mentioned in forms 13 and 22 is much in doubt and again, these may refer to the Co. Down name or indeed, to some other place.

Oghtbristacree
D 1732

Ucht Briste Croí
"mountain breast of the heart-break"

1. Aughtha	OSRNB sh.14	1855c
2. Oghtbristacree	OSRNB sh.14	1855c
3. Greenan Top	OSRNB sh.14	1855c
4. Oghbristacree	OSRNB sh.14	1855c
5. ocht briste croidhe "hill of the heart"	OSRNB sh.14	1855c
6. "The Broken Hearted Bosom"	OSRNB sh.14	1855c
7. ˌo̱xtbrïstə'criː	Local pronunciation	1993

"Oghtbristacree is the popular name amoung the peasantry, and signifies The Broken Hearted Bosom . . . There is a fairy tale tradition respecting the origin of this name which would be ludicrous to insert here" (*OSRNB* sh.14). Regarding this legend, see **Coskemnacally**.

This mountain (393 metres) in Greenan on the southern boundary of Culfeightrin parish has several valleys emanating radially from near the peak, and we could consider that these features prompted the possible original form *Ucht Briste Crí* "fractured mountain breast of the boundary". The etymology suggested by the legend alluded to above is *Ucht Briste Croí* "mountain breast of the heart-break", however, which is reminiscent of the place-name *Bruach an Bhriste Chroidhe* "the slope of the heart-break" in Glebe townland in Rathlin (*Place-Names of Rathlin* 72). The use of *ucht* "chest, breast; bosom" (*Ó Dónaill*) to denote "the front of a hill [or] a projection from its general body" in place-names was noted by Joyce (*Joyce* ii 428; see also *PNI* iii 146–7). Form 1 resembles somewhat *uchtach* "breast of a hill, upward slope, rise" (*Ó Dónaill* sv.), however (cf. the Rathlin place-names *Uchtaigh* and *Ucht* in *Place-Names of Rathlin* 43, 55).

Owencam River
D 1635

A hybrid form

1. ˌðowən'kam	Local pronunciation	1993

The English suffix to this river name does not appear to be used. *An Abhainn Cham* "the twisting river" is the most likely original form.

Pans-rock
D 1442

An English form

1. (?)Salt Panns	HMR Ant. 11	1669
2. (?)Salt pan fields	Tithe Applot. 13	1833
3. Carrig-Uisnech	MacDonnells Antrim 23	1873
4. Carraig Mhic Uisnich "Rock of the sons of Uisnich"	O'Laverty iv 480	1887
5. Carraig Uisnigh "The rock of Uisneach"	Ó Dubhthaigh 134	1905
6. ˌkarəg'oʃnə	Local pronunciation	1993
7. pɑns'rɔːk	Local pronunciation	1993

At the time of the *Down Survey* in the mid-1650s, it was recorded that two salt-pans on Ballyvoy's coast were used for the boiling of salt water with locally mined coal (Carleton 1991, 67 n.7). Form 1 may be referring to the Ballyvoy name (*ibid.* 66 sv. Ballyvoy). In any event, this coastal name in Broughanlea apparently records the existence of further salt-pans in this townland. Form 2 may refer to an obsolete land division adjacent to the shore.

The earliest reference to the local manufacture of salt appears to be in a will of Randal MacDonnell compiled in 1629 (the earliest extant copy dates from 1663), in which he bequeathes " . . . all my saltworkes and coal workes within the tough of Carie" (*MacDonnells Antrim* 437).

The rock is also known by another name derived perhaps from *Carraig Uisnigh* "Uisneach's Rock", after the father of the lover of Deirdre in a pretale of the *Táin* (see, for example, Ó hÓgáin 1991, 155–6). The rock is known locally as the place where Deirdre and the sons of Uisneach landed on their return from Scotland (*Pers. comm.* 02.06.96), which might suggest an original Irish form such as *Carraig Chlann/Mhic Uisnigh* "rock of the children/sons of Uisneach" (cf. form 4). A place-name, spelt *Coill Uisneach* by Séamus Ó Duilearga, was noted from a native speaker in Glenariff in 1920 (*Ultach* 66:10, 10).

Portadoon
D 2241

Port an Dúin
"port of the fort"

1. Portadoon	OSRNB sh.10	1855c
2. port a duin "port of the fort"	J O'D (OSRNB) sh.10	1855c
3. ˌpɔrtə'duːn	Local pronunciation	1993

"A small port or landing place for row boats [in West Torr], and derives its name from a natural mound sloping abruptly towards the sea close to the shore of the south side" (*OSRNB* sh.10).

The Irish word *port* has several meanings other than "landing-place, harbour, port" (Ó Dónaill; see *DIL* sv.). The place-names in this parish containing this element are coastal, and often refer to a small cove at a cliff-side location. *Port* has been translated "bank, brink" in some place-names by Ó Máille (1987, 33). A subtownland place-name in north-west Co.

Mayo, *An Port*, has been translated "the anchorage" by Ó Catháin (Ó Catháin & O'Flanagan 1975, 24). Holmer recorded the word locally as [pʌrt] and translated it as "port, natural inlet" (*Irish of the Glens* 124).

Port an Dúin is the likely original form of this particular place-name, but no record of a fort, other than the place-name, appears to exist. The Ordnance Survey noted several examples of subtownland names in this area where a *dún* element appeared to refer to a rock or to some other natural object (*OSRNB passim*). In many cases these were regarded as the haunts of fairies. See also **Doon Bay** in Other Names in Rathlin Island.

Port-aleen Bay	A hybrid form	
D 2440		
1. Purt an Líon (for Lín)	Irish of the Glens 119	1940
2. Tur baye	Goghe's Map	1567
3. Tor baye	Nowel's Ire. (1)	1570c
4. Torbay	Hondius Map	1591
5. Torboy	Mercator's Ire.	1595
6. Tor bay	Boazio's Map (BM)	1599
7. Torbay	Treatise on Ire. (NLI) 11	1599c
8. Torbaie	Bartlett Maps (Esch. Co. Maps) 1	1603
9. Tor bay	Mercator's/Hole's Ire.	1610
10. Tor baye	Norden's Map	1610c
11. Portaleen Bay	OSRNB sh.10	1838c
12. Portaleen	OSRNB sh.10	1855c
13. port a lín "port of the flax"	OSRNB sh.10	1855c
14. Port an lín "The port of the linen"	Ó Dubhthaigh 185	1905
15. pʌrt ə liən	Irish of the Glens	1940
16. ˌpɔrtə'lin	Local pronunciation	1993

"A small port or landing place for row boats and being free from rocks is easy of access and is frequented by small boats connected with the salmon fishery of this part of the coast . . . Is supposed to have derived its origin from the land adjoining being of a good quality for the production of flax" (*OSRNB* sh.10).

The original form of this name appears to have been *Port an Lín*, which could be variously interpreted "port of the linen/flax" or "port of the (fishing) net". The bay is an inlet on the southern side of Torr Head. The English suffix in this place-name does not appear to be used. The name *Torr Bay* (forms 2–10) appears to have been used only by foreign surveyors.

Portdoo	*An Port Dubh*	
D 1943	"the dark port"	
1. Portdoo	OSRNB sh.5	1855c
2. Port dubh "black port"	OSRNB sh.5	1855c
3. pɔrt'duː	Local pronunciation	1993

"A small port [in Knockbrack] here boats enter to cut and collect sea weeds. The rocks along the bottom of the port are black" (*OSRNB* sh.5).

There is an *Island Doo* off the coast of Goodland (*OS 1:10,000*).

Portmore	*An Port Mór*	
D 2538	"the large port"	
1. Portmore	OSRNB sh.10	1855c
2. port mór "great port"	OSRNB sh.10	1855c
3. pɔrt'moːr	Local pronunciation	1993

"A small port or landing place for row boats [in Torcorr and on Loughan Bay] (*OSRNB* sh.10).

Portnathalin	*Port an tSalainn*	
D 2438	"port of the salt"	
1. Portnathalin	OSRNB sh.10	1855c
2. port a tsálainn "port of the salt"	J O'D (OSRNB) sh.10	1855c
3. ˌpɔrtnə'talən	Local pronunciation	1993

"A small port and landing place for row boats [in Loughan]" (*OSRNB* sh.10).

It seems likely that the name derives from *Port an tSalainn* "port of the salt" and that the medial [nə] has resulted from metathesis. Metathesis may have similarly recently affected the Rathlin subtownland place-name of **Portandoon** (see form 4 of this latter name). Salt was being produced in this parish from at least as early as 1629 (see **Pans-Rock**).

Rock Port	An English form	
D 2533		
1. Rock Port	OSRNB sh.15	1855c

"A small boat port at the entrance of which at low water are several rocks which gives name to this landing place" (*OSRNB* sh.15). This is in Castle Park townland and on Cushendun Bay.

Ruebane Point	A hybrid form	
D 2142		
1. Ruebane Point	OSRNB sh.5	1855c
2. "the point of the foaming ocean current"	OSRNB sh.5	1855c
3. ru'baːn	Local pronunciation	1993

203

"A bold precipitous headland projecting into the sea and overhanging in some parts. The bounds between West Torr and Goodland strikes the sea at it . . . A very rapid (and foaming) current runs past it and it is thought that the name has been suggested by it. The undulations of the current are short and generally crested with foam" (*OSRNB* sh.5).

An Rubha Bán "the white headland" is the likely origin, notwithstanding that *rubha* may also have the meaning "clearing" (*PNI* ii 110). See also **Roonivoolin** in Rathlin.

Runabay Head	A hybrid form		
D 2637			
1. Rinn an buidhe "The yellow point"	Ó Dubhthaigh 185	1905
2. ˌrɔnəˈbeː	Local pronunciation	1993

Rubha na Beithe "headland of the birch tree" seems a more likely origin than *Rubha na Bé* "headland of the woman/wife/fairy". We may also consider that the first element was *rinn* "point of land, cape, promontory" (*Ó Dónaill* sv.) or perhaps even *rann* "divided, partitioned, portion; part, area" (*Ó Dónaill* sv. *roinn*). A form of *bá* "bay" pronounced [beː(i)] was used in Rathlin Irish (see for example **Church Bay** and **Mill Bay** in Other Names, Rathlin Island) but seems unlikely here.

Salmon Port	An English form	
D 2340		
1. Salmon Port	OSRNB sh.15	1855c

"A small cove or fishing port [in Ballyteerim] for salmon. Also a landing place for small boats . . . Here nets are usually set for catching salmon, from which it derives the name" (*OSRNB* sh.15). Compare **Port Bradan** in Other Names, Ballintoy.

Slaght	*An Sleacht*	
D 1535	"the grave"	
1. Slaght	OSRNB sh.14	1855c
2. "slaughter"	OSRNB sh.14	1855c
3. Slaght "the place of slaughter"	Mon. Hib. 4 n.10	1873
4. ˈʃlaxt	Local pronunciation	1993

Joyce notes that *leacht* "grave, grave-mound" was sometimes prefixed by an *s* in northern counties (*Joyce* i 66) and indeed, the two stones standing on this site are said to mark the head and foot of the grave of "Shane Roe or Red John Macdonnel[l]", killed in a battle against the MacQuillans (*OSM* xxiv 78). The name refers both to the "two monumental pillar stones . . . formed of two rude stones set upon their ends about 9 links high" and to "a flat cultivated hill on the west side" (*OSRNB* sh.14). Moran wrongly believed that the word derived from *sleacht/sléacht* "slaughter". O'Laverty recorded the further place-name *Sleacht Bharaigh Mhóir* "great *Barach*'s grave" (*O'Laverty* iv 521) somewhere near Torr Head (see **East Torr** regarding *Barach*). *Sleamhán*, a variant of *leamhán* "elm" found in Ulster Irish (*PNI* iv 126), also features an *l* prefixed by *s*. See also **Sluggan Burn** below.

Slievepin
D 2039

Sliabh Pín(?)
"mountain of the pine"

1.	Slapin	Tithe Applot. 12	1833
2.	Slievepin	OSRNB sh.9, 2	1855c
3.	"the mountain summit"	OSRNB sh.9, 2	1855c
4.	Sliabh Fhionn "Fionn's mountain"	Rev. Magill 23	1923
5.	slïp'ïn	Local pronunciation	1993

"A subdivision of the townland of Ballyvennaght supposed to have been so named from its being the highest part of a moorland district. The name signifies the mountain summit" (*OSRNB* sh.9, 2).

Sliabh Pín "mountain of the pine" may represent the original form of this name. Other possibilities include *Sliabh Pionna* "mountain of the (sheep) pen". *Sliabh* "mountain" can also denote "moor" (*Ó Dónaill*); *Dwelly* noted the meanings "extended heath, alpine plain, moorish ground; extensive tract of dry moorland; mountain grass" in Scottish Gaelic, and these might be considered here. Form 3 suggests the original form was *Sliabh Binne* "mountain of the peak", but the devoicing of *b* to *p* would be unlikely in this instance. Furthermore, there is no peak here. Perhaps we can consider that *slí* "way; road, track" (*Ó Dónaill*) formed the first element and was latterly confused with *sliabh* and standardized in anglicized garb as *slieve*. Holmer noted *sliabh* locally as [sliəv] (*Irish of the Glens* 128).

Sluggan Burn
D 2338

A hybrid form

1.	Sluggan Burn	OSRNB sh.9, 2	1855c
2.	ˌslugən'bọrn	Local pronunciation	1993

"A small mountain stream having its source in the south east side of Cushleake Mtn. North. It passes through a narrow glen north westward. It unites with Altnacartha Burn both forming the head streams of Altmore Burn" (*OSRNB* sh.10).

Slogán "a vortex or quagmire, a throat" (*Dinneen*) may be the Irish word behind this place-name. However, the word *slugan* "gully/hollow", resembling *logán* "little hollow; pit; depression" prefixed by *s* (cf. **Slaght**) was recorded by Holmer ([slʌgən]; *Irish of the Glens* 128), and is another possibility.

Tornamoney Burn,
Tornamoney Bridge,
Tornamoney Point
D 2436, 2536, 2634

Hybrid forms

1.	Tornamoney Burn	OSRNB sh.15	1855c
2.	Tornamoney Bridge	OSRNB sh.15	1855c
3.	Tornamoney Point	OSRNB sh.15	1855c

The following was noted in c. 1855 regarding these three names: "This stream takes its rise chiefly in the mountain part of Cushleake and flows in a south easterly direction through a narrow glen and crossing the coast road from Cushendall to Ballycastle at Tornamoney Bridge it falls into the sea a little N.E. of Salmon Port"; "A small stone bridge, one arch with parapets 37 feet long" [connecting **Tornamoney** and Altagore and spanning Tornamoney Burn]; "The northern point of Cushendun Bay . . . A high bold rocky point of land" (*OSRNB* sh.15).

Tornaveagh	*Tor na bhFiach(?)*	
D 1938	"tor of the ravens"	
1. Tornaveagh	OSRNB sh.9, 1	1855c
2. Tor na bhfiach "raven's rock"	OSRNB sh.9, 1	1855c
3. "The haunt or crest of the deer"	OSRNB sh.9, 1	1855c
4. ˌtɔrnəˈveː	Local pronunciation	1993

"Two farm houses [in Ballypatrick townland] with farms attached and in the occupation of John McHenry and Micheal Butler. The houses are about 13 chains apart, and the name applies to both, and to the space between them . . ." (*OSRNB* sh.9, 1).

It seems likely that *tor* "rocky height or tall rock" rather than *tor* "bush" originally represented the first element (see also **East Torr** townland regarding this element). Given standard spelling, the gen. pl. of *fiach* "raven" would seem more likely than *fia* "deer" (forms 2–3). However, *Tor na bhFéitheacha* "tor of the swampy strips" (see Ó Dónaill sv. *féith* and **Feykeeran** above) may be a possible origin.

Torr	*Tor*
D 2340	"tor"

See **East Torr** townland.

Torr Head	A hybrid form	
D 2340		
1. gob tóir	Mulcahy's Rathlin 44	1889
2. Torsboro hed	Ulster Map	1570c
3. Torr head	Dartmouth Map 6	1590c
4. Kaine Torbaie	Dartmouth Map 25	1590c
5. C. Torbay	Hondius Map	1591
6. Can Torbaie	Bartlett Maps (Esch. Co. Maps) 1	1603
7. Tor he.	Norden's Map	1610
8. Point of Taur	Lendrick's Map	1780
9. Tor Point	Wright's Diary 30	1806
10. Point of Taur	Map Antrim	1807
11. gub tore	Mulcahy's Rathlin 44	1889
12. gob tóir, the beak of the tower[-] like bulwark of rocks	Mulcahy's Rathlin 44	1889

Forms 4 and 6 seem to reflect an Irish form such as *Ceann Toir* "headland of the rocky height", with the English word *bay* added by the cartographer. *Gob Toir*, of similar meaning, was used in Rathlin (forms 1, 11). See **East Torr** townland.

Torteige	*Tor Taidhg*	
D 1739	"*Tadhg*'s tor"	
1. Torteige	OSRNB sh.9, 1	1855c
2. Tor Taidhg "Teige's tower"	J O'D (OSRNB) sh.9, 1	1855c
3. tɔr'te:g	Local pronunciation	1993

"A farm house with out offices [in Ballypatrick townland] in the occupation of Francis McHenry. It stands close to the main road from Ballycastle to Cushendall" (*OSRNB* sh.9, 1).

The name appears to derive from a rocky hill south of the farmhouse (see **East Torr** and **Tornabodagh** regarding *tor*).

Turrybrennan,	*Tuar Uí Bhranáin*	
Turrybrennan Burn	"O'Brennan's cattle-field"	
D 1939		
1. Torryoranan	PRONI D2977/3A/2/1/40	1812
2. Torryvrannen	Tithe App. Book 13	1833
3. Turrybrennan	OSRNB sh.9, 1	1855c
4. Turryvrennan	OSRNB sh.9, 1	1855c
5. Turrybrennan Burn	OSRNB sh.9, 2	1855c
6. Tor uí braonain "O'Brennan's tower or rock"	J O'D (OSRNB) sh.9, 1	1855c
7. ˌtɔri'branən	Local pronunciation	1993
8. ˌtɔri'vranən	Local pronunciation	1993

In c. 1855, Turrybrennan was described as denoting a "small tract comprising a few farms forming a subdivision or subdenomination" (*OSRNB* sh.9, 1) in Ballyvennaght townland. The stream was noted as separating "two subdivisions of Ballyvennaght called Slievepin and Turrybrennan, bounding the later on its north western side" (*ibid.* sh.9, 2).

Woulfe (1923, 440) has noted that the surname *Ó Branáin*, which is "the name of an ecclesiastical family in Ulster, who were erenaghs of the church of Derry and Derryvullan, Co. Fermanagh", has several anglicized forms, including Brennan; the name is based on a diminutive of *bran* "raven". Ó Ceallaigh has described this name as "well known" in the area south of Coleraine in the form Brennan, and has noted its recurrence in place-names there, including **Moneybrannon** (*GUH* 46). Other possible final elements, however, include the gen. sing. of *bronnán* "heap of stones and sand" (*Ó Dónaill*) or perhaps "place of mud" (see *Dinneen* sv. *bronn*). *Tuar* "manured land; cattle-field; sheep-run; pasture, lea; bleaching-green" (see **Tornabodagh**) seems topographically more likely than *tor* "tor; steep rocky height" (see **East Torr**) and is also suggested by forms 3–5.

Tyban
D 2433

An Toigh Bán
"the white house"

See **White House** townland.

Water Top
D 2037

An English form

| 1. Water Top | Tithe App. Book 12 | 1833 |
| 2. Water Top | OSRNB sh.9, 2 | 1855c |

"A mountain district interspersed with some arable patches and forming a subdivision of the townland of Ballyvennaght. It is so named from it being situate near the top or source of the Carey River" (*OSRNB* sh.9, 2).

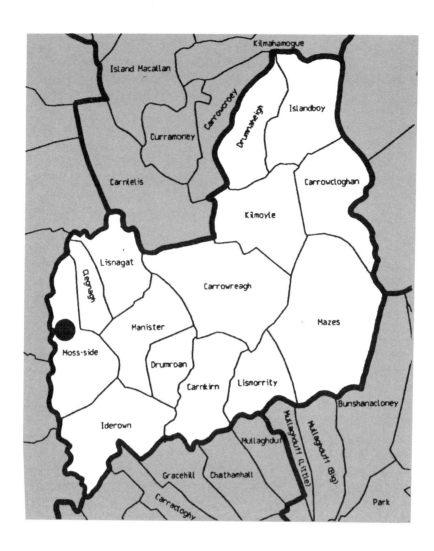

Parish of Grange of Drumtullagh

Townlands Drumroan   Manister
Carnkirn   Iderown   Mazes
Carrowcloghan   Islandboy   Moss-side
Carrowreagh   Kilmoyle
Clegnagh   Lismorrity   *Town*
Drumnaheigh   Lisnagat   Moss-side

Based upon Ordnance Survey 1:50,000 mapping, with permission of the Director of the Ordnance Survey of Northern Ireland, Crown copyright preserved.

PARISH OF GRANGE OF DRUMTULLAGH

This small civil parish contains 14 townlands and comprises c. 3753 acres (*OSM* xxiv 96). It is bounded to the west by the parish of Billy, to the north by the parish of Ballintoy, to the north-east by the parish of Ramoan, to the south-east by the parish of Armoy, and to the south by the parish of Derrykeighan in the barony of Dunluce Lower.

This territory was long considered part of the parish of Derrykeighan, which accounts for the paucity of historical forms below; it was still considered as such in the Church of Ireland in 1832 (*ibid.*): "(the grange) pays tithes with and is generally considered as part of Derrykeighan parish". Lewis suggests that the territory (which is referred to in this source as "the 13 quarters called the Grange of Drumtullagh") was probably "an appendage to a monastery at some remote period" (*Lewis' Top. Dict.* 439). There is a townland called **Manister** in the Grange although there is no other evidence regarding such an institution. In mid-17th-century sources, the townlands of Kilmahamogue and Carrowcroey, as well as part of Islandmacallan and probably the entire townland of Curramoney, which are all now in Ballintoy parish, were considered to be part of the Grange (*DS Par. Map* 53; Carleton 1991, 69; *O'Laverty* iv 342). This was no longer the case by the time of the *Religious Survey* of 1734, however. All of the civil parish of Grange of Drumtullagh lies within the Catholic parish of Ballintoy (*O'Laverty* iv 315).

English sources from medieval times until the 1600s make reference to a territory which apparently covered the modern parishes of Ramoan and Grange of Drumtullagh (*EA* 332). From the late 1500s this territory is referred to as one of the *seven tuoghs of the Glynns* (see barony introduction). The spelling of the name of this "tuogh" varies widely in the sources (*Mamym'*, *Manyberry*, *Mowbray* etc; see forms 8–9, 11–18, 20 and 32 of Ramoan), prohibiting interpretation.

PARISH NAME

Grange of Drumtullagh   A hybrid form

1. (?)Telich Ceniúil Oingosso, epscop Ném i	Tírechán 349	700c
2. (?)Telaig cenéoil Oengusa, epscop Ném hi	Trip. Life (Stokes) 162	900c
3. (?)Tulachensem, cui Nehemium Episcopum praefecit	Acta SS Colgan 455a	1645
4. (?)Fulachensem	Trias Thaum. 146b	1647
5. (?)Tulacensem	Trias Thaum. 182b	1647
6. Part of Derrykighan Parish in Cary Barony,	HMR (1666) 111	1666
7. part of Donnykigan	HMR Ant. 13	1669
8. part of ye parish of Derrykeighan called Drumtullagh	Religious Survey	1734
9. Drumtullagh, Grange of	Lendrick Map	1780
10. Drumtullagh Grange	Bnd. Sur. (OSNB) B 18	1830
11. Crosshan schoolhouse	OSM vxi 102	1838
12. Croshan	EA 251	1847

13. Druim Tulcha "ridge of the hill"	OSM xvi 96	1832
14. Druim Tulcha "ridge of the hill"	J O'D (OSNB) B 18	1832
15. Druim Tulach "The little hill ridge"	Ó Dubhthaigh 138	1905
16. Druim Tulach "Ridge of the hillocks"	Rev. Magill 14	1923
17. ˌdrǫmˈtǫləx	Local pronunciation	1995

Previous commentators have linked the name Drumtullagh with the Patrician church name in forms 1–5 (Reeves in *EA* 251; *O'Laverty* iv 342). The basis for doing so appears to be that the place alluded to in the sources is somewhere in Dál Riada (see *Trip. Life (Stokes)* 162), and that they contain the place-name element *tulach*. The location of the church in these forms remains far from certain, however, although we may note those local place-names which exhibit a distinctively ecclesiastical character: **Kilmoyle**, **Manister** and **Kilmahamogue** (the latter is now in Ballintoy). Very little is known of the bishop *Nem/Ném* associated with forms 1–5. O'Laverty suggests that this is the *Nem* of *Druim Dalláin* who is commemorated in the martyrologies on the 3rd of May (*Mart. Gorm.* 88; *Mart. Don.* 119); the whereabouts of *Druim Dalláin* is also in doubt (*O'Laverty* iv 342). The *Martyrology of Gorman* lists a further bishop *Nem* of *Druim bertach*, possibly Burt in Inishowen, Co. Donegal (*Mart. Gorm.* Feb. 18, p.38 and p.308). *Cineál nAonghusa* "tribe or kindred of *Aonghus*" (forms 1–2) was one of the three original leading tribes of Dál Riada in Scotland, being associated predominantly with Islay (*Senchus Fer n-Alban* 155 §46 and Bannerman 1974, 70). The *Aonghus* of this tribal name is *Aonghus (Mór)*, one of the sons of *Earc* who went to Scotland (*Senchus Fer n-Alban* 154 l.10, 155 l.29, 154 l.1–2; see also *Adomnán's Columba (Anderson)* 36–9). *Earc* died in 474 (*AFM* i 148).

Forms 1–2 contain a dat. form of *telach*, a variant of the fem. noun *tulach* "low hill; hillock, mound" (*Ó Dónaill*). Although forms 8–10 appear to contain the gen. pl. form (or variant gen. sing. form) *tulach*, it is more likely that they contain the variant gen. sing. form *tulcha* and that *Droim Tulcha* "ridge of the mound" was the original form (13–4). The loss of a final unstressed vowel is a common feature of anglicization.

Ó Doibhlin (1971, 3) notes that the incidence of *tulach* in early literature often suggests for it the meaning "a hill of assembly around a ruler or chief". In 1838 it was recorded:

> Drumtullagh Carn is a mere mound situated about 100 perches north of the Crosshan schoolhouse, on the west side of the road leading from Stranocum to Ballintoy, on the farm of William Hopkins. The carn is oval shaped, 29 feet long by 15 feet broad and 4 feet high, of stones and earth. [It] is said to have [been] a standard or citadel of the grange, with the gortin or field attached to the carn and grange, and was given for the support of friars and superannuated clergy who lived amoung the people and were supported by them. The friars could compel the people on every tenth day to drive the cows to the gortin to be milked at the carn, if they could not support them otherwise. This carn is said to have been an altar. The Freemasons used to make this carn a resting place on St John's Day . . . (*OSM* xvi 102).

It is far from certain that this mound inspired the parish name. If this cairn was indeed the site of the original *tulach*, however, the tradition recorded in the *OSM* might indicate something of its former importance.

The use of *grange* here seems to date only to c. 1780 (form 9), and there is no evidence of the use of it in Irish; neither does it appear to be used locally in English. The place-name formation *Grange of . . .* is peculiar to Co. Antrim, there being in all ten parishes and a further three townlands so designated (*PNI* iv 132). In the case of the parish name of Grange of Shilvodan in the south-west of the county, McKay observed that "the element *grange* was appended to the place-name at a fairly late date, possibly with the significance of "small parish" rather than in recognition of its former links with Muckamore Abbey" (*ibid.* 148). In some instances, however, the *grange* element may have an earlier origin. Mullin and Mullan (1966, 56) suggest that as the word "is old French for barn . . . such names mark Anglo-Norman farmsteads".

In 1847, Reeves wrote that the parish was "popularly called *Croshan*" (*EA* 251). In 1887, however, O'Laverty noted that this name referred to "the vicinity of the old church" in **Kilmoyle** (*O'Laverty* iv 344). It may represent a diminutive of *cros* (or of its variant (originally dat.) form *crois*) "(a religious) cross; crossroad".

TOWNLAND NAMES

Carnkirn	*Carn Caorthainn*	
D 0334	"cairn of the rowan"	
1. Carnekynen	Hib. Reg. Cary	1657c
2. Carnkeene	DS (Par. Map) 63	1657c
3. Karnekein als Karnekerrin	DS (Par. Map) 64	1657c
4. Carnkerm	Census 11	1659
5. Carnekeene	BSD 179	1661
6. Carnekeene	Lapsed Money Book 158	1663
7. Carnkeene	ASE 117a §19	1668
8. Carnkean	HMR Ant. 14	1669
9. Carnekeyne	Hib. Del. Antrim	1672c
10. Carnkeeran	Stewart's Survey 33	1734
11. Carnkerin	Religious Survey	1734
12. Carnkirn	Lendrick Map	1780
13. Carnkeirn	Bnd. Sur. (OSNB) B 18	1830
14. Carn Ceirn "Kerrin's carn or heap"	J O'D (OSNB) B 18	1832
15. "the Moss Carn"	OSRNB sh.13, 1	1855c
16. Carn-Caorthinn "the rowan-tree cairn"	O'Laverty iv 346	1887
17. Carn crainn "The carn of the quicken"	Ó Dubhthaigh 135	1905
18. Carn Ciaráin	Duncan 132	1906
19. karn'keərn	Local pronunciation	1995

It was recorded in 1838 that: "There was a carn called the Rowantree Carn in the townland of Carnkirn, on the property of Alexander Stewart Esquire of Gracehill, but not a trace of it remains but is planted with forest trees" (*OSM* xvi 102). This tradition favours O'Laverty's form (16) over Duncan's (18). *Caorthann* "the rowan or quicken tree, mountain ash" (*Dinneen*) is found also in **Glenmakeerin** in Culfeightrin (for which see regarding genitive forms).

Carn- names often feature personal names, and as with Glenmakeerin, the male personal name *Ciarán* (gen. sing. *C(h)iaráin*) may not be decisively dismissed as a possible second elememt. It is relatively rare in east Ulster genealogies however, and more importantly, the variation of *-ee-* with *-e-* in historical forms seems to suggest that the first vowel in this element was [ʌ]. The male personal name *Céirín* (*CSH* 134 §704.157) suggested in form 14 does not reflect the historical forms. A further possible second element may be *caorán* "moor", attested in the Irish of Donegal and Tyrone (see *Dinneen* sv. and Stockman & Wagner 1968, 60; see also **Feykeeran Burn** in Other Names, Culfeightrin), but *-án* would probably have yielded more anglicized *-an* forms, especially in the 17th century (compare **Doonans** in Armoy). Holmer noticed that [ə] between *r* and *n*/*nn* was often suppressed in late local Irish (*Irish of the Glens* 33).

Carrowcloghan   *Ceathrú Chlocháin*
D 0537   "quarterland of the stony ground(?)"

1.	Caretlogh	Hib. Reg. Cary	1657c
2.	Caretlogh als Cernecloghan	DS (Par. Map) 63	1657c
3.	Carneclough, mossy bog of	DS (Par. Map) 64	1657c
4.	Caretlough als Cernecloughan	DS (Par. Map) 64	1657c
5.	Kerucloghan	Census 11	1659
6.	Caretclogh als Carrecloghan	BSD 179	1661
7.	Carkclough als Carnecloughane	Lapsed Money Book 158	1663
8.	Caretclough alias Carecloughane	ASE 117a §19	1668
9.	Caretlogh	Hib. Del. Antrim	1672c
10.	Carrowcloghan, the quarter land of	PRONI D2977/3A/2/11/1	1681
11.	Carrivecloghan	Stewart's Survey 35	1734
12.	Kerrucloghan	Religious Survey	1734
13.	Caracloughan	Bnd. Sur. (OSNB) B 18	1830

14.	Ceathramhadh Chlocháin "quarter of the stony fords"	J O'D (OSNB) B 18	1832

15.	ˌkarvəˈclɔxən	Local pronunciation	1995
16.	ˌgarvəˈclɔxən	Local Pronunciation	1996

The wide range of spelling is found chiefly in related sources. *Ceathrú* "quarter of a *baile fearainn* (i.e. townland)" (*Dinneen*) is probably indeed the first element (see also **Carrowcroey** in Armoy). *Carne-* variants could represent mistranscriptions, but alternatively, they could indicate the dat. form of *ceathrú, ceathrúin.* The second element *clochán* has a variety of meanings including "stepping-stones; stony ground" (*Ó Dónaill*) and "a ruin, remains of an old fort; a heap of stones; a stone circle; a burying ground; village or townland containing the parish church; a causeway; a pavement" (*Dinneen*). It is far from certain what it originally denoted in this case. There is no record of any stone ruins in the townland. Regarding O'Donovan's explanation (form 14), a tributary stream of Inver Burn forms the eastern boundary of this territory. It was formerly believed that an old church stood somewhere in the vicinity of the neighbouring townland of **Kilmoyle** (*OSM* xvi 100) but this hardly proves that the *clochán* referred to some lost ecclesiastical site.

Carrowreagh
D 0336

An Cheathrú Riabhach
"the grey/dun quarterland"

1. Carnereagh	Hib. Reg. Cary	1657c
2. Keruriagh	Census 11	1659
3. Carnereagh	BSD 179	1661
4. Carnereagh	Lapsed Money Book 158	1663
5. Carnereagh, 1 qr.	ASE 117a §19	1668
6. Carrowreagh	HMR Ant. 13	1669
7. Carrive Reagh	Stewart's Survey 33	1734
8. Kerrivereogh	Religious Survey	1734
9. Carroreagh	Lendrick Map	1780
10. Carrevereiogh	PRONI D2977/3A/2/1/40	1812
11. Carryreagh	Bnd. Sur. (OSNB) B 18	1830
12. Ceathramh Riach "grey quarter"	J O'D (OSNB) B 18	1832
13. Ceathramhadh reidh "The mountain-plain quarter"	Ó Dubhthaigh 135	1905
14. Ceathramha-Riabhach "the Grey Quarter"	Antrim Place Names 84	1913
15. karə'riəx	Local pronunciation	1995

Ceathrú "quarter (of land)" appears in several local townland names (see **Carrowcloghan**). The adjective *riabhach* has several meanings, including "brindled, striped, grey, roan, swarthy, grizzled, fallow" (see also **Ballyreagh** in Culfeightrin). One would not expect the noun *ré* "a plain, a level field; . . . more commonly employed in the south of Ireland than elsewhere, and . . . usually applied to a mountain-flat, or a coarse, moory, level piece of land amoung hills" (*Joyce* i 426 sv. *reidh*; see also *Dinneen* sv. *rae* and *réidh*) or the adjective *réidh* "smooth, level, easy to traverse" (*Ó Dónaill*) to have yielded -*gh* endings in late local Irish. *Carne-* variants (forms 1, 3–5) may denote scribal errors, or indicate the dat. of *ceathrú*, *ceathrúin* (there was however a cairn in this townland, used as a source of stones to build a ditch, and variously called *Cairnamena* and *Carnanena* in the *Ordnance Survey Memoirs* (*OSM* xxiv 100, 102)).

Clegnagh
D 0235

Cloigneach
"place of round hills"

1. (?)Cloigneach	Irish of the Glens 106	1940
2. Clymagh	HMR Ant. 14	1669
3. (?)Clegnagh	PRONI D2977/3A/2/1/5A	1682
4. Clagnagh	Stewart's Survey 31	1734
5. Cllegnogh	Religious Survey	1734
6. Clegna	Lendrick Map	1780
7. Clegnagh	Bnd. Sur. (OSNB) B 18	1830
8. Claigneach "abounding in rocky hills"	J O'D (OSNB) B 18	1832

9. Claigeannach "The hillicks like
   skulls"   Ó Dubhthaigh 134   1905

10. (?)klEg′n′ɑx   Irish of the Glens 106   1940
11. ′klɛgnɔx   Local pronunciation   1995

Ó Maolfabhail suggests that the fem. noun *cloigneach* in place-names probably most often denotes something like "high place of bare rocks" (1987, 80) but this would not reflect local topography. There is a small hill in the south of the townland and another to the immediate west just north of Moss-side village. *Cloigneach* is further discussed under the similar Ballintoy townland name of **Clegnagh**.

Drumnaheigh   *Droim na hÁithe*
D 0437   "ridge of the kiln"

1. Drimnahaigh   Stewart's Survey 35   1734
2. Drumnahagh   Religious Survey   1734
3. Drumnahagh   Lendrick Map   1780
4. Drimnaheigh   Bnd. Sur. (OSNB) B 18   1830

5. Druim na faithche "ridge of the
   green"   J O'D (OSNB) B 18   1832

6. ˌdrọmnə′heː   Local pronunciation   1995

As there is no trace of a medial *f* in any of the historical variants, form 5 represents an unlikely origin of the name. More likely is that the final element was formed by the fem. noun *áith* (gen. sing. *áithe*) "a fire or kiln, esp. a corn kiln, a flax kiln, an oast; an eminence" (*Dinneen*). The historical forms indicate that the final *-the* was pronounced something like [x′(ə)], although this syllable has been lost in modern pronunciation (form 6). Such a development in local Irish was not unknown: "strangely enough, x often appears instead of h, in cases where this sound would regularly disappear" (*Irish of the Glens* 24 §19). Holmer recorded *áith* "kiln" as [ɑːix′] locally (*ibid.* 99). The [ɑː] apears to have been raised to [eː] in this instance consequent to 1780 (form 3).

Drumroan   *Droim Rúáin*
D 0334   "ridge of the red place"

1. Drumbruan   Census 11   1659
2. Drumrowan   HMR Ant. 14   1669
3. Drumduan, the quarter of   PRONI D2977/3A/2/1/5A   1682
4. Drimaroan   Stewart's Survey 34   1734
5. Drumroan   Religious Survey   1734
6. Drumroan   Lendrick Map   1780
7. Drimroan   Bnd. Sur. (OSNB) B 18   1830

8. Druim Ruadhain "Ruadhan's or
   Rowan's ridge"   J O'D (OSNB) B 18   1832

9. drọm′roən   Local pronunciation   1995

Several possible origins of this name, depending on the interpretation of the final element, may be considered. The gen. sing. (*ruáin*) or gen. pl. (*ruán*) of *ruán* (earlier *ruadhán*) "a red or reddish-brown person, animal or thing; redness, a red dye, buck-wheat or red-wheat; a fish-line, a moorland" (*Dinneen*) seems most likely. *Ruán* is attested in other place-names, including the Co. Limerick townland name of *Baile an Ruáin* (anglicized Ballinruane) which has been translated "the town of the red place" (Ó Maolfabhail 1990, 48). *Ruán* has elswhere been translated "red patch" (*PNI* iii 150 sv. **The Rowans**). *Ruán* is also a variant of *rabhán* "spasm, fit; thrift (a tufted plant)", but these meanings do not appear to be attested in place-names. Historical forms do not reflect the surname Ó *Ruadhacháin* (anglicized Rohan and Rowan (MacLysaght 1985, 260–1)), while modern pronunciation also militates against the English surname Rowan. The male personal name *Rúan*, which is derived "from *rúad* 'red haired'", may be considered as a possible second element however (Ó Corráin & Maguire 1981, 157 sv. *Rúadhán*; see also O'Rahilly 1946, 294–5 and *Antiquities of Rathlin* 42–3).

The presence of a *b* in form 1, which may have since assimilated to the *m*, increases the number of possible etymologies. We might consider (an unattested) diminutive of *brugh* "a large house; a fort; hillock; district", *brughán*; *bruan* "fragments, crumbs" and *bruán* "after-birth of animal; straggling thing" would represent somewhat unusual place-name elements. It should be remembered however that the source of this form, the *Census*, is notorious for scribal errors. In addition, the *b* in the *mb* complex in English was generally silent by the 17th century (Barbour 1981, 317), and the surveyor may have been following *lamb*, *crumb* (etc.) to anglicize *droim*.

| **Iderown** | *Idir Dhá Abhainn* | |
| D 0234 | "(place) between two rivers" | |

1.	Ederown	Stewart's Survey 31	1734
2.	Ederoan	Lendrick Map	1780
3.	Iderown	Bnd. Sur. (OSNB) B 18	1830
4.	Manisteriderow	OSM xvi 97	1835
5.	Idderoan	Lewis' Top. Dict. 439	1837
6.	Edirowens	OSM xvi 102	1838
7.	Idir Abhainn "between the river", or "central river"	J O'D (OSNB) B 18	1832
8.	idər'oən	Local pronunciation	1995

This townland lies between the Moss-side Water and the Doughery Water which form its southern and western boundaries, and which meet at its southern-most point to form the Black Water. This is broadly the topographical evidence for the interpretations of the place-name in form 7. The preposition *idir* "between", often followed by some reference to rivers, appears in other townland names, including **Ederdaglass or Hollybank** in Co. Fermanagh, Killederowen in Co. Galway, Dromderaown in Co. Cork and Dromdiraowen in Co. Kerry (*Joyce* i 251). The Irish forms of all these examples feature the medial unstressed element *dhá* "two" (*ibid.*), and it also seems to have featured in the Irish form of Iderown. In the north-west Co. Down townland name *Baile idir Dhá Abhainn* "townland between two rivers" (angl. **Ballynadrone**), evidence of *dhá* in historical anglicized forms ceased to be apparent c. 1657 (*PNI* vi 227).

Holmer noted that *eadar* was the late local form of *idir* which seems to have been used here with the sense "(place) between" (*Irish of the Glens* 50). Mac Giolla Easpaig translated the Rathlin subtownland place-name of *Eadar an Dá Staca* as "between the two stacks" (this is in Kebble; *Place-Names of Rathlin* 13). It seems unlikely, given modern stress, that *idir/eadar* was used here as a prefix meaning "mid-" to refer to the Black Water (as suggested in form 7(b)).

The townland of **Manister** lies to the immediate north of Iderown. The reliability of form 4, which suggests that *Mainistir idir Dhá Abhainn* "monastery between two rivers" was formerly current, is difficult to ascertain.

Islandboy
D 0538

An tOileán Buí
"the yellow island"

1. Islandecard	Hib. Reg. Cary	1657c
2. Islandcarde	DS (Par. Map) 63	1657c
3. Islandeard	BSD 179	1661
4. Islande Carde 1 Qur.	Lapsed Money Book 158	1663
5. Islandtickard	Hill's Stewarts 148	1665
6. Island-Card	ASE 117a §19	1668
7. Islandkerd	HMR Ant. 13	1669
8. Islandcard	Hib. Del. Antrim	1672c
9. Ilanticard	PRONI D2977/3A/2/1/5A	1682
10. Ireland Tyecard	Forfeit. Estates 375b §45	1703
11. Islandbay	Stewart's Survey 35	1734
12. Islandnacard	Religious Survey	1734
13. Islandboy	Religious Survey	1734
14. Islandbuy	Lendrick Map	1780
15. Islandbuey	Bnd. Sur. (OSNB) B 18	1830
16. Oileán Buidhe "yellow island"	J O'D (OSNB) B 18	1832
17. ˌailənd'bɔi	Local pronunciation	1995

The first element in this place-name, translated from Irish *oileán* "island" may have represented something like "hillock surrounded by bog" (see also **Island Macallan** in Ballintoy). Modern variants of the name feature the adjective *buí* "yellow" although most earlier forms contain a different ending. As both types appear in the *Religious Survey* of 1734, it is possible that the names represented separate (and perhaps contiguous) territories. The earlier forms may have been based on *Oileán Ceard* "island (etc.) of the artificers", although forms 5, 9 and 10 appear to indicate *Oileán Tí Ceard* "island (etc.) of the house of the artificers" (see **Ballynagard** in Culfeightrin regarding *ceard*).

Kilmoyle
D 0336

An Chill Mhaol
"derelict burial-ground/church"

1. Kilmoole	Hib. Reg. Cary	1657c
2. Killmoole	DS (Par. Map) 63	1657c
3. Killmoyle	Census 11	1659
4. Killmoole	BSD 179	1661

5. Kilmoyle	HMR Ant. 13	1669
6. Killinoole	ASE 117a §19	1668
7. Kilwoole	Hib. Del. Antrim	1672c
8. Killmoyle	Stewart's Survey 32	1734
9. Killmoyle	Religious Survey	1734
10. Killmoyle	Lendrick Map	1780
11. Killmoyle	PRONI D2977/3A/2/1/40	1812
12. Kilmoyle	Bnd. Sur. (OSNB) B 18	1830.
13. Kilmoyle "bare graveyard"	OSM xvi 97	1832
14. Coill maol "bald wood"	J O'D (OSNB) B 18	1832
15. Cill Maol "bald church"	J O'D (OSNB) B 18	1832
16. "The bald or flat church"	OSRNB sh.8, 2	1855c
17. Cill maol "Bare church"	Rev. Magill 18	1923
18. kïl'mɔiəl	Local pronunciation	1995

In 1832 it was recorded that "An old graveyard is the only antiquarian remains to be found [in the parish]. It is situated in the townland of Kilmoyle, on the highest ground in the grange" (*OSM* xvi 98). In 1838, the Ordnance Survey recorded the following:

About 105 feet south of the leading road from Coleraine to Ballycastle in the townland of Killmoyle [*sic*], on the farm of Andrew Maybin, there is an ancient graveyard which is nearly 80 feet in diameter, situated on an eminence without parapet or wall in an open field, and without a gravestone. An old church is said to have stood at the north side of it, but not a trace of it remains to be seen . . . Tradition states that the burial ground at Bonamargy should have stood here, as the consecrated mould which was brought from Rome was deposited here, but from some unknown circumstance it was removed to Bonamargy, whose abbey is also in ruins (*ibid.* 100–1).

In c. 1855 it was further recorded of this place that:

a small uneven spot in the corner of a field is said to have been the site of a church and of an ancient burying ground . . . there is no vestige of the church or its site . . . It is not now used as a burying ground – none but unbaptized children are buried in it (*OSRNB* sh.8, 2).

It appears likely, therefore, that the first element in this place-name was *cill* "a church, a churchyard, a burial place" (*Dinneen*).

The second element seems most likely to have been the adj. *maol*, which has several meanings, including "bare, bald; roofless, dismantled; flattened" (*Dinneen* sv.). The Co. Limerick townland name of *Maoilis* (anglicized Moylish) has been translated as "derelict enclosure" (Ó Maolfabhail 1990, 218). Considering the location of the burial ground, *maoil* (gen. sing. *maoile*) "rounded summit; hillock, knoll; bare, bald, top" could be considered as a further possible second element. There is no trace of the final vowel of the gen. sing. form of this word in the historical variants, although this could have easily resulted from being in an unstressed position (cf. **Kilcroagh** in Armoy).

Lismorrity

D 0434

Lios Muircheartaigh
"Murtagh's fort"

1. Lismarerty	Hib. Reg. Cary	1657c
2. Lismurirty	Census 11	1659
3. Lismalerty	BSD 179	1661
4. Lissmarety	Lapsed Money Book 158	1663
5. Lissmarritie	ASE 117a §19	1668
6. Lismurty	HMR Ant. 14	1669
7. Lismureity	Hill's Stewarts 11	1720
8. Lissmorerty	Stewart's Survey 33	1734
9. Lissmurattie	Religious Survey	1734
10. Lismurrerty	PRONI D2977/3A/2/25/1	1738
11. Lismurerty, one quarter land of	PRONI D2977/3A/2/25/1	1738
12. Lismoratty, Quarter land of	PRONI D2977/3A/2/25/2	1738
13. Lismurrity	Lendrick Map	1780
14. Lissmurratty	PRONI D2977/3A/2/1/40	1812
15. Lismorrity	Bnd. Sur. (OSNB) B 18	1830
16. Lios Muircheartaigh "Murty's fort"	J O'D (OSNB) B 18	1832
17. Lios Muircheartaigh. "Muirceartach's fort"	Ó Dubhthaigh 183	1905
18. Lios Muircheartaigh "Murtagh's fort"	Rev. Magill 20	1923
19. lïs'mɔrəti	Local pronunciation	1995

The *Ordnance Survey Memoirs* record "In the townland of Lismority [*sic*] a common fort was dug away in 1822" (*OSM* xvi 100) and later also note: "There is a fort of earth on the farm of James Quinn, Lismoditty [*sic*], 15 perches west of the road leading from Armoy to Ballintoy, of stones and earth, not remarkable" (*ibid.* 101). Thus the memoirs appear to present two possible locations of the *lios* "a garth, enclosure or court-yard; a small circumvallation or ring-fort; a fairy-fort, rath or liss" (*Dinneen*). *DIL* translates *lios* as "the space about a dwelling house or houses enclosed by a bank or rampart" (*DIL* sv. *les*).

Lios is qualified here by the male personal name *Muircheartach* (gen. *M(h)uircheartaigh*). This name which means "skilled in seacraft, mariner" was "an extremely common name in early and medieval Ireland, and was common to very recent times amoung the Mac Loughlins, O Brollaghans (Bradleys) and other northern families" (Ó Corráin & Maguire 1981, 140). Muircheartach gave rise to the surname *Ó Muircheartaigh* which is generally a Leinster name but which in Ulster "is sometimes Scottish [in origin] and a synonym of Murdoch" (MacLysaght 1985, 231 sv. Murtagh). There is no record of the surname locally.

Lisnagat

D 0236

Lios na gCat
"fort of the cats"

1. Lisnegate	Hib. Reg. Cary	1657c
2. Lisnegat	DS (Par. Map) 57	1657c
3. Lisnegat ¼ of Monester	BSD 179	1661

4. Lisnegett ¼ of Monester	Lapsed Money Book 158	1663
5. (?)Lisnagall	Hill's Stewarts 148	1665
6. Lisnegatt	ASE 117a §19	1668
7. Lisnegate	HMR Ant. 14	1669
8. Lisnegat	Hib. Del. Antrim	1672c
9. Lisnegatt	PRONI D2977/3A/2/1/5A	1682
10. Lissnagatt	Stewart's Survey 33	1734
11. Lisnagatt	Religious Survey	1734
12. Lisnagal	Lendrick Map	1780
13. Lissngratt	PRONI D2977/3A/2/1/40	1812
14. Lisnagat	Bnd. Sur. (OSNB) B 18	1830
15. Lios na gCat "fort of the cats"	J O'D (OSNB) B 18	1832.
16. ˌlïsnə'gɑt	Local pronunciation	1995

Notwithstanding scribal errors, the forms support O'Donovan's interpretation of this name (15). Regarding the first element, see **Lismorrity** above. The *Ordnance Survey Memoirs* make references to objects found in "a fort" in this townland (*OSM* xvi 100, 103), and this may have been the *lios* of the place-name. The element *cat* "cat" appears elsewhere locally in the Culfeightrin townland name of **Drumahitt**. There are three other townlands of the name Lisnagat in the country; one each in counties Armagh, Leitrim and Cork (*Census 1851*).

Manister
D 0235

An Mhainistir
"the monastery"

1. Monester	Hib. Reg. Cary	1657c
2. Monnister ¾ of Novilly	DS (Par. Map) 57	1657c
3. Manister	Census 11	1659
4. Monester	BSD 179	1661
5. Monester	Lapsed Money Book 158	1663
6. Mounester	ASE 117a §19	1668
7. Monster	Hib. Del. Antrim	1672c
8. Monister, the quarter of	PRONI D2977/3A/2/1/5A	1682
9. Monishter	Stewart's Survey 32	1734
10. Mannester	Religious Survey	1734
11. Manister	Lendrick Map	1780
12. Monister	PRONI D2977/3A/2/1/40	1812
13. Manister	Bnd. Sur. (OSNB) B 18	1830
14. Manisteriderow	OSM xvi 97	1835
15. Mainistir "a monastery"	J O'D (OSNB) B 18	1832
16. Manister "a monastery"	Joyce iii 498	1913
17. 'manïstər	Local pronunciation	1995

It was recorded in 1838 that: "There stood, according to tradition, on the farm of John McAlister in the townland of Manister, a monastery, but not a trace of it remains to be seen now. About 70 years ago the last remnant, which was 4 corner stones, was taken away" (*OSM* xvi 103). The tradition reflects the townland name which derives from *mainistir* "monastery, abbey". Flanagan has noted that *mainistir* (from Latin *monasterium*) in place-names, with the one exception of Monasterboice in Co. Louth, is not documented in pre-12th-century sources and so appears to refer to post-Reform monastic houses (Flanagan 1981–2(c), 73). It seems unusual that we have no other documentary evidence regarding such an ecclesiastical institution in this townland; it is tempting to suggest, however, that it was affiliated to the Franciscan friary at **Bonamargy** in Culfeightrin.

Mainistir is usually anglicized *monaster* and occurs in townland names throughout the country, generally as an initial element (*Census 1851*).

Mazes *Na Mása*
D 0535 "the low hills"

1. Masses	Hib. Reg. Cary	1657c
2. Masses, ¼ of Novilly called	DS (Par. Map) 57	1657c
3. Mosses, the Quarter of	DS (Par. Map) 64	1657c
4. Masses	BSD 179	1661
5. Massess 1 Qur	Lapsed Money Book 158	1663
6. Masses	ASE 117a §19	1668
7. Messistowne	HMR Ant. 13	1669
8. Masses	Hib. Del. Antrim	1672c
9. Moasses	PRONI D2977/3A/2/1/6	1681
10. Meazes	Stewart's Survey 35	1734
11. Measis	Religious Survey	1734
12. Measses alias Measis	PRONI D2977/3A/2/1/33A	1737
13. Mazies	Lendrick Map	1780
14. Mosses	PRONI D2977/3A/2/1/40	1812
15. Mazes	Bnd. Sur. (OSNB) B 18	1830
16. Mais "fat hills"	J O'D (OSNB) B 18	1832
17. ˌðə ˈmeːziz	Local pronunciation	1995

The use of *más* "the buttock; hip, thigh, breech" in place-names to denote a hill has been noted by Joyce, who cites for example "Masiness in Donegal; [from] *Más-an-easa*, hill of the cataract" (*Joyce* iii 499). He suggests that *más* is applied specifically to "a long low hill" (*ibid.* i 526–7). The standard nom. pl. form is *mása* (*Ó Dónaill*) although Dinneen also lists the nom. pl. form *máis*. *Mása* is also a variant sing. form (*Dinneen*, Quiggan 1906, 95 §135)). Neither *mása* nor *máis* is likely to have developed an internal [eː] sound in local Irish, and we must presume that this name underwent early degeneration in English due possibly to analogy with the English word *maze* (compare **Cape Castle** in Ramoan). There is a low hill in the north of the territory at Islandreagh and another close by in the neighbouring townland of Carrowreagh. English *s* after a vowel often becomes [z] (compare the Co. Down name **Drumnabreeze** in *PNI* vi 233–5); the spelling in early forms may have been affected by analogy with the English words *mass/moss*. Another Irish word, *meathas*, earlier *methas* "a frontier, march, 'space of unappropriated ground between two territories'" (*DIL*) might also be considered as an origin for this name. Mazes is situated on the border of the parishes of Armoy and Ramoan. However, this word does not appear to be attested in place-names without a qualifying element (*Onom. Goed.* 538 sv. *methus*).

The final syllable seems to indicate an English plural suffix. Such suffixes have been added to other townland names in Cary, and may reflect some internal division of the territory or indicate a knowledge that the original Irish name was a plural form. Modern pronunciation is reminiscent of **Cozies**, a townland in the nearby parish of Billy (17th-century forms of the latter name include *Casey* and *Cossy* (Carleton 1991, 86); an origin in *Na Cuasa* "the hollows" seems possible). The final syllable is unlikely to indicate the meaningless Irish *-as* suffix (Ó Máille 1989–90, 125), while compounds in *más* (plus *ais* "ridge", for example) are unattested (Mac Giolla Easpaig 1981).

Moss-side		*Maigh Saighead(?)*	
D 0135		"plain of (the) arrows"	
1.	(?)Mareside	Inq. Ult. (Antrim) §38 Car. I	1635
2.	Mosside	Hib. Reg. Cary	1657c
3.	Massyde	DS (Par. Map) 57	1657c
4.	Mosside	Census 11	1659
5.	Mosside	BSD 179	1661
6.	(?)Mervide	Decree of Innocence 440	1663
7.	Mossid Towne	HMR Ant. 14	1669
8.	Mossid	Hib. Del. Antrim	1672c
9.	Mosside	Religious Survey	1734
10.	Moss side	Taylor and Skinner 272	1777
11.	Mosside	Lendrick Map	1780
12.	Mosside	Bnd. Sur. (OSNB) B 18	1830
13.	Mosside	OSM xvi 98	1832
14.	Mas Saíde	GÉ 136	1989
15.	mɔs'əid	Local pronunciation	1995

English place-names in Cary which are attested prior to the 18th century are rare but not unknown (see, for example, **Glebe** in Armoy and **Leland** in Other Names, Ramoan). An English origin might appear to be all the more unusual given its inland location, but historical variants of **Taylorstown** in south-west Co. Antrim dating to 1669 have been attested (*PNI* iv 137, 140). Among other meanings, the English word *moss* can denote "*chiefly Scot* a bog, swamp; esp. a peat bog" (*Longman Dict.*) and in this sense could have referred to what was still "a considerable tract of bog in Manisteriderow and the adjoining townlands" in 1832 (*OSM* xvi 97; *Manisteriderow* represents the neighbouring townlands of Manister and Iderown). The substitution of similar sounding English elements for Irish words is well known, however. The element *caisleán* was apparently substituted by *castle* in the name **Ballycastle** as early as 1630, while other examples of substitution of elements in local names can be found in the historical forms of Drumawillin (Ramoan) and Island Macallan (Ballintoy). Modern stress also suggests an Irish origin, although we might also consider that this has been altered by analogy with local Irish names.

We could consider, among other possibilities, that the first element was *meathas* "a frontier, march, 'space of unappropriated ground between two teritories'" (*DIL* sv. *methas*) which is the first element in the Co. Longford place-name *Meathas Troim*, which is anglicized Mostrim but standardized in English as Edgeworthstown (*GÉ* 137). Moss-side lies on the boundary with the parish of Billy, but one suspects that 17th-century pronunciation of this relatively rare element would not have prompted an association with English *moss*. The first element seems most likely to have been *maigh* "plain", which was usually anglicized *moy* locally (*maigh* was originally an oblique form of the nom. *magh*). The second element resembles *saighead* (gen. sing. *saighid*; gen. pl. *saighead*) "arrow". The south-west Co. Antrim townland name of *Cúil Saighead* contains this element (it is anglicized **Coolsythe**; *PNI* iv 39). Joyce suggests that it also occurs in the Co. Roscommon townland name Gortnasythe, and the lake name of Moneenascythe in Co. Tipperary (*Joyce* ii 179).

OTHER NAMES

| **Brevellan Bridge** | A hybrid form | |
| D 0236 | | |

| 1. ˌbrəvˌalən ˈbrïdʒ | Local pronunciation | 1995 |

The bridge spans the Moss-side Water. The townlands of Clegnagh and Lisnagat in this parsish, and Moycraig Hamilton in the parish of Billy, meet at this point. The origin of the name is obscure; there is a possibilty that the name represents a late introduction. Possible original forms, however, include *Bruach/Brágha Mhealláin* "bank/thin neck of land of the small knoll".

| **Calhame Bridge** | A hybrid form | |
| D 0334. | | |

| 1. calˌheːm ˈbrïdʒ | Local pronunciation | 1995 |

The first element in this name derives from the Lowland Scots for "cold home", applied to homesteads in exposed positions (*PNI* iv 257). There is another **Calhame** in Drumnakeel in Culfeightrin (*LGD Map Co. Ant.* 1). The bridge spans the Doughery Water (see Doughery Bridge in Other Names, Armoy), and connects the townlands of Iderown and Gracehill (the latter is in Derrykeighan parish).

| **Castle, The** | An English form(?) | |
| D 0438 | | |

| 1. The Castle | OSRNB sh.8, 2 | 1855c |

| 2. ðə ˈkasəl | Local pronunciation | 1995 |

"Two farm houses with some out offices [in Drumnaheigh] in the occupation of John Taggart and John Wiley. There is a local tradition that these houses were built on the site of an old castle . . . There is at present no vestige of such a structure; none of any of the inhabitants remember to have seen any" (*OSRNB* sh.8, 2). This name may derive from Irish *An Caistéal/Caisleán* "the castle".

| **Crocknahorna** | *Cnoc na hEorna* | |
| D 0436 | "hill of the barley" | |

| 1. Crocknahorna | OSRNB sh.8, 3 | 1855c |

2. "hill of the barley"	OSRNB sh.8, 3	1855c
3. kruknə'hɔːrn	Local pronunciation	1995

"A small farm village [in Carrowreagh] close on the west side to the road from Ballintoy and occupied by families named McLees" (*OSRNB* sh.8, 3).

Dry Arch (Viaduct), The D 0336	An English form	
1. ðə drai 'ɑrtʃ	Local pronunciation	1995

Islandreagh D 0536	*An tOileán Riabhach* "the grey/dun island"	
1. Islandreagh	OSRNB sh.8, 3	1855c
2. ˌailənd'reː	Local pronunciation	1995

"A small arable plot or farm with one dwelling house [in Mazes] in the occupation of Tom Smyth. The farm is surrounded by bog, and was once used [as] a sheepfold. It is supposed to have been named from its isolated position, and from its greyish or swarthy aspect" (*OSRNB* sh.8, 3). See **Island Macallan** in Ballintoy parish regarding the element *island*, and **Carrowreagh** (which borders Mazes) regarding *reagh*.

Knockbane D 0539	*An Cnoc Bán* "the white hill"	
1. nɔk'baːn	Local pronunciation	1995

This is in Islandboy. It refers to a small farm cluster beside a hill c. 110 metres high, in the north of the townland.

Knockmore D 0235	*An Cnoc Mór* "the big hill"	
1. Knockmore	Religious Survey	1734
2. Knockmore	Stewart's Survey 32	1734
3. Knockmore	OSRNB sh.7, 2	1855c
4. Cnoc Mór "great pile"	OSRNB sh.7, 2 (OD)	1855c
5. nɔk'moːr	Local pronunciation	1995

"A farm house and farm in Moss-side townland . . . it is situate on the summit of an elevated ridge and hence the term Knockmore is applied to it" (*OSRNB* sh.7, 2).

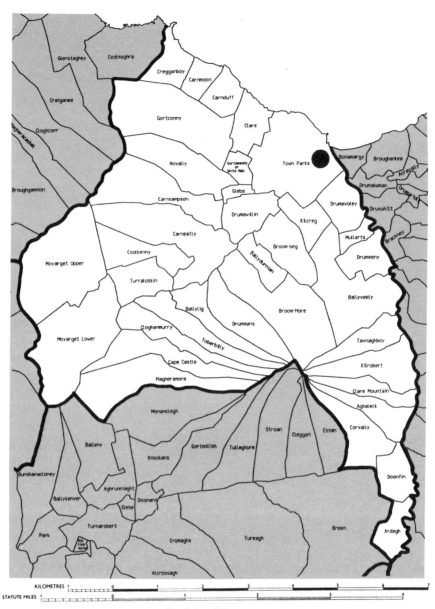

Parish of Ramoan

Townlands
Aghaleck
Ardagh
Ballydurnian
Ballylig
Ballyveely
Broom-beg
Broom-more
Cape Castle
Carnduff
Carneatly
Carnmoon
Carnsampson
Clare

Clare Mountain
Cloghanmurry
Coolkenny
Corvally
Cregganboy
Doonfin
Drumavoley
Drumawillin
Drumeeny
Drummans
Glebe
Gortamaddy or Whitehall
Gortconny
Kilcreg

Kilrobert
Magheramore
Moyarget Lower
Moyarget Upper
Mullarts
Novally
Tavnaghboy
Toberbilly
Townparks
Turraloskin

Town
Ballycastle

PARISH OF RAMOAN

The coastal civil parish of Ramoan lies to the west of the parish of Culfeightrin from which it is separated for the most part by the Glenshesk River. Armoy parish lies to its immediate south, and the parishes of Grange of Drumtullagh and Ballintoy lie on its western boundary. It contains 37 townlands and c. 12,067 acres (*OSM* xxiv 86).

The earliest reference to the parish name occurs in the *Book of Armagh* (form 1), which states that the church of *R[á]th Muadáin* was founded by St Patrick, and that he installed there the presbyter *Erclach* (*Trip. Life (Stokes)* 162–3). Colgan calls the presbyter St. Ereclacius and places his feast day on the 3rd of March, based on the martyrologies (*Acta SS Colgan* 455a; *Mart. Gorm.* 46–7, *Mart. Tal.* 20, *Mart. Don.* 62). Reeves noted in 1847 that the "modern parish church [Church of Ireland] occupies the ancient site" (*EA* 79 n.r; see also *OSM* xxiv 107, *OSRNB* sh.8, 3 and *Hill's Stewarts* 86). It was formerly located in the townland of Drumawillin but now lies within Glebe (*O'Laverty* iv 408).

The parish of Ramoan was evaluated at £10 in the *Ecclesiastical Taxation* of c. 1306, more than the neighbouring, and much larger, parish of Culfeightrin (*Eccles. Tax. (Reeves)* 79). In Church of Ireland administration, "the living was formerly a vicarage united to that of Culfeightrin, the rectories of which, from 1609, were appropriate to the chancellorship of Connor till 1831, when, on the decease of Dr. Trail, the last chancellor, Ramoan became a vicarage . . ." (*Lewis' Top. Dict.* 443; see also see *Jas I to Connor Cath (EA)* 262–3). For a list of some of the resident Church of Ireland clergy in the 17th–18th centuries, see *Shaw Mason's Par. Sur.* 516–7. The Catholic parish is coextensive with the civil parish and is usually called Ballycastle (*Lewis' Top. Dict. ibid.*). Subsequent to the establishment of the Church of Ireland as the religion of the state, the Catholic parish joined with the union of Armoy and Ballintoy, from which it was severed in 1825 (*O'Laverty* iv 436).

PARISH NAME

Ramoan

Ráth Muáin
"*Muán's* fort"

1. iRaith Muadáin, Muadan martrach ocus presbiter Erclach	Tírechán 349	700c
2. Ráith Mudáin	Trip. Life (Stokes) 162	900c
3. Rath-mudhain, Ecclesia de	Acta SS Colgan 455a	1645
4. Rathmudain, regione	Acta SS Colgan 455a	1645
5. *In Rat-mudhain* . . . hodiè vulgo *Rath-moain* corruptè appell[i]tur rectius *Rath-modhain* appellanda	Acta SS Colgan 455b	1645
6. Rath-Mudain	Trias Thaum. 146b	1647
7. Rath-mudain .i. arx Muadain	Trias Thaum. 182b	1647
8. (?)the land of Ocaynymery and Cachery	CDI §929	1272
9. Mamym' and Cachery	CDI §929	1272
10. Rathmohan	Eccles. Tax. 209	1306c
11. Manyberry and Cary	EA 332	1333
12. (?)Monery and Carey	Decree of Innocence 431	1567c
13. Momerie and Carie	Fiants Eliz. §1530	1570

14. Mowbray and Cary, the countries of	MacDonnells Antrim 417	1575c
15. Mowbray	Bagenal's Descr. Ulst. 155	1586
16. Mowbray	Treatice of Ire. (Butler) 23	1599c
17. Moubray	Treatise on Ire. (NLI) 110	1599c
18. Munerie (tough of)	CPR Jas I 58a	1603
19. Ramoan	Jas. I to Connor Cath. (EA) 263	1609
20. Munomer	Ulst. Roll Gaol Deliv. 264	1613
21. Ramoan	Shaw Mason's Par. Sur. 516	1614
22. Rathmoan	Terrier (Reeves) 107	1615
23. Ramoan	Ulster Visit. (Reeves) 65	1622
24. Ramoan	Regal Visit. (Reeves) 121	1633
25. Ramone	Hill's Stewarts 86	1643
26. Ramoane	Hill's Stewarts 89	1652
27. Ramoan R.	Inq. Par. Ant. 2	1657
28. Rathmoane	Hib. Reg. Cary	1657c
29. Rathone	DS (Par. Map) 54	1657c
30. Ramoan	Census 18	1659
31. Rathmoane	BSD 167	1661
32. Ramoan	Trien. Visit. (Bramhall) 3	1661
33. Ramoan	Court of Claims §923	1662c
34. (?)Minmorry	Court of Claims §923	1662c
35. (?)Killmoane	Court of Claims §923	1662c
36. Tough of Minnery	Decree of Innocence 431	1663
37. Ramoan	Trien. Visit. (Margetson) 28	1664
38. Ramone	HMR (1666) 100	1666
39. Ramona	Shaw Mason's Par. Sur. 517	1668
40. Rathmoane	HMR Ant. 5	1669
41. Rathmoane	Hib. Del. Antrim	1672c
42. Romoan	Trien. Visit. (Boyle) 35	1679
43. Ramoan	Shaw Mason's Par. Sur. 517	1681
44. Rath-mount, and móna-bog or marsh	Rev. Connolly 499	1814
45. Ráth Mudháin "Mudhán's fort"	J O'D (OSNB) B 17	1831
46. Rath Mhórain "Moran's fort"	J O'D (OSNB) B 17	1831
47. Rath Maoin "Moan's fort"	J O'D (OSNB) B 17	1831
48. "the fort of Modhan"	Dallat's Ramoan 25	1973
49. ram'oən	Local pronunciation	1993

The noun *ráth* "the circular vallum often palisaded or otherwise strengthened, surrounding ancient Irish residences" (*Dinneen*) may be either feminine or masculine; here it is feminine (forms 1–2). The male personal name *Muán* (earlier *Muadhán*) is derived from (O. Ir.) *muad* "noble, good" (Ó Corráin & Maguire 1981, 139). As early as 1645, Colgan commented that the pronunciation of this name was corrupted (form 5), but the change in the *ua* dipthong he alludes to was widespread in the Irish of east Ulster; see, for example, **Drumroan** in Grange of Drumtullagh. Colgan claimed that *Muán* was the father of *Éanán* who was appointed by St Patrick to the nearby church of **Drumeeny** (*Trias Thaum.* 182b). He obviously based this on references to an *Enan mac Muadan* who is commemorated in the martyrologies on the 25th of March (*Mart. Tal.* p. 27 (830c); *Mart. Gorm.* p.62; *Mart. Don.*

p.86). Form 35, which was probably copied from earlier documents, may indicate the parish church name was *Cill Mhuáin* "Muán's church". See also **Carnmoon**.

The earliest English references refer to a territory which apparently "was about co-extensive with the parish of Ramoan and Grange of Drumtullagh" (*EA* 332; forms 8–9). In 1333, one William de Welles was the tenant of the earl of Ulster in *Manybery and Cary* (*ibid.*). As with Cary, this territory was being called one of the "seven tuoghs" of The Glens by the late 16th century (see barony introduction), but as a denomination it fell into disuse in the early 1600s (forms 34–5 come from copies of earlier documents). The range of spellings of this name prevents meaningful interpretation.

Aghaleck	*Achadh Leice*	
D 1335	"field of the flagstone"	
1. Aghelecke	Inq. Ult. (Antrim) §100 Car. I	1635
2. Acheleke	Hib. Reg. Cary	1657c
3. Atchleake	DS (Par. Map) 53	1657c
4. Acheleake	DS (Par. Map) 54	1657c
5. Agheleck	Census 18	1659
6. Athleake	BSD 168	1661
7. Aghalecke	Court of Claims §923	1662c
8. (?)the town called Aghlouke and Ballytallydor	Court of Claims §923	1662c
9. (?)towne called Aghaleisk and Balletalheor	Decree of Innocence 431	1663
10. Athleake	Lapsed Money Book 156	1663
11. Ackleake	ASE 116a §19	1668
12. Acklack	HMR Ant. 6	1669
13. Achleke	Hib. Del. Antrim	1672c
14. Achenleck	PRONI D2977/3A/2/1/6	1681
15. Athleake	Ant. Forfeit.	1700
16. Aughelack	Stewart's Survey 4	1734
17. Aughaleak	C. McG. (OSNB) B 17	1734
18. Aghelick alias Aghinlesk	PRONI D2977/3A/2/1/33A	1757
19. Agheyleck	Lendrick Map	1780
20. Aghilisk otherwise Aghenlosk	PRONI D2977/3A/2/1/40	1812
21. Aghaleck	Bnd. Sur. (OSNB) B 17	1830
22. Aughalike	Tithe Applot. 1	1833
23. Aghalig, from agh-field, lig-mount	Rev. Connolly 518	1814
24. Ath a' lic "ford of the flag stone"	J O'D (OSNB) B 17	1831
25. Achadh "field of the flagstone"	O'Laverty iv 427	1887
26. Achadh leice "field of the flagstone"	Ó Dubhthaigh 131	1905
27. Achadh lice "field of the flagstone"	Rev. Magill 5	1923
28. "the field of the flagstone"	Dallat's Ramoan 25	1973
29. ˌakə'lɛk	Local pronunciation	1993

Some early forms indicate the tendency to elide the unstressed second syllable of the place-name element *achadh* "field, cultivated field" (*Dinneen*), which has been noted in townland names in Culfeightrin (cf. **Aughnaholle**). Connolly may have had *leaca* "side, slope (of hill)" in mind in form 23. However, although this townland slopes consistently eastwards from the summit of Knocklayd, the historical variants do not reflect the gen. sing. or the gen. pl. (being identical) of this word, *leacan*. This second element is more likely to have been derived from *leac* "a hard surface or layer, a stone, especially a flagstone" (*Dinneen*). The gen. sing. (*leice*) seems more likely than the gen. pl. (*leac*). Forms 14, 18(b) and 20(b) could be interpreted as indicating the presence of a medial definite article. These forms are obviously related and indicate copying of scribal errors, however.

Ardagh	*Ardach*	
D 1333	"high field"	
1. (?)nArdachadh, i	AFM ii 950	1095
2. (?)Arda-achad, Maidm	AU ii 54	1095
3. (?)Ardachad, Maidhm	ALC i 80	1095
4. Ardynoy als Ardaghis	DS (Par. Map) 53	1657c
5. Ardagh	C. McG. (OSNB)	1734
6. Ardagh	Lendrick Map	1780
7. Ardah	Sur. A.E. 80	1782
8. Ardaghy otherwise ardina	PRONI D2977/3A/2/1/40	1812
9. Ardagh	Bnd. Sur. (OSNB) B 17	1830
10. Ardagh "lofty place"	Rev. Connolly 519	1814
11. Ard-achadh "high field"	J O'D (OSNB) B 17	1831
12. Ard achadh "The high field"	Ó Dubhthaigh 132	1905
13. Ard Achadh "High Field"	Antrim Place Names 83	1913
14. Ard Achadh "high field"	Rev. Magill 5	1923
15. "The high field"	Dallat's Ramaon 25	1973
16. 'ardəx	Local pronunciation	1993

This mountainous townland, situated at the south-eastern tip of the parish, is separated from the similarly named **Ardaghmore** (in Culfeightrin) by the Glenshesk River (for a discussion of the elements in Ardagh see the latter townland). O'Donovan believed forms 1–3, which relate to victory in battle of the Dál nAraí over the Ulaidh (see county introduction), to refer to this townland (*AFM* ii 951–1 n.b), but they seem more likely to refer to somewhere in Co. Down.

Ballydurnian	*Baile Uí Dhoirnín*	
D 1139	"O'Durnian's townland"	
1. (?)Ballewirnyne	PRONI D2977/3A/2/1/2	1611
2. (?)Ballyvornyn	Inq. Ult. (Antrim) §64 Car. I	1635
3. Ballydunnie	Religious Survey	1734
4. Ballydurnin	Stewart's Survey 15	1734
5. B:durnian	Lendrick Map	1780

6. Ballydurnian	Bnd. Sur. (OSNB) B 17	1830
7. Ballydurnan	Tithe Applot. 2	1833
8. Ballydurnian "small town", from Bhalla-town, Dhorna-handfull	Rev. Connolly 518	1814
9. Balie Uí Dhuirnín "O'Durneen's or Caffe's town"	J O'D (OSNB) B 24 B 37	1831
10. Baile durnain "The town of the boors or churls"	Ó Dubhthaigh 131	1905
11. "the townland of the boors"	Dallat's Ramoan 25	1973
12. ˌbɑliˈdǫrnjɛn	Local pronunciation	1993

The second element is derived from the Irish surname *Ó Doirnín*, anglicized as Durnan and Durnin; it is associated with "Louth and East Ulster. Ballydurnian is in Co. Antrim but Durnian is the more usual form in West Ulster" (MacLysaght 1985, 94). Regarding the apparent development of a gutteral fricative sound to [v] (forms 1–2), see **Drumavoley**.

Ballylig	*Baile an Loig*	
D 0938	"townland of the hollow"	
1. Baile 'n Lig	Antrim Notebooks i 107	1925c
2. molan Lig, i	Antrim Notebooks i 107	1925c
3. Ballenluge, the quarter land called	PRONI D2977/3A/2/1/2	1611
4. Ballinlugg	Inq. Ult. (Antrim) §64 Car. I	1635
5. Ballilogge	Hib. Reg. Cary	1657c
6. Ballinlugge	DS (Par. Map) 54	1657c
7. Ballylige	Census 19	1659
8. Ballinlugg	BSD 168	1661
9. Balleluig	Decree of Innocence 431	1663
10. Balyynalagge	Lapsed Money Book 156	1663
11. Ballinlugg	ASE 116a §19	1668
12. Ballylig	HMR Ant. 6	1669
13. Ballilug	Hib. Del. Antrim	1672c
14. Ballynlagg	Ant. Forfeit.	1700
15. Ballyluig	Stewart's Survey 15	1734
16. B:lig	Lendrick Map	1780
17. Ballyluig	PRONI D2977/3A/2/1/40	1812
18. Ballylig	Bnd. Sur. (OSNB) B 17	1830
19. Ballylig	Tithe Applot. 1	1833
20. Bally leg "mountain town", from Bhalla-town, leg-mount	Rev. Connolly 518	1814
21. Baile Luig "town of the hollow"	J O'D (OSNB) B 17	1831
22. Baile liag "town of the standing stone"	Rev. Magill 6	1923

231

23. "the townland of the hollow"	Dallat's Ramoan 25	1973
24. ˌbɑliˈlïg	Local pronunciation	1993

Notwithstanding that there is a standing stone in this townland, most forms indicate that the final element of this name is derived from *log/lag* "hollow", and not *lia(g)* "stone". Ballylig House is situated in a dip between two minor summits of approximately 90 metres and 100 metres, to the west of the Tow River, which may have been the inspiration for the name. The rest of the townland is on the lower slopes of Knocklayd. *Log* also has other meaings (see **Lagavara** in Ballintoy).

Ballyveely
D 1338

Baile Uí Bhaothalaigh(?)
"*Ó Baothalaigh*'s townland"

1. (?)Ballyvilly	Inq. Ult. (Antrim) §7 Jac. I	1621
2. Ballybeilly	Inq. Ult. (Antrim) §100 Car. I	1635
3. Ballivelly	Hib. Reg. Cary	1657c
4. Ballyvellie	DS (Par. Map) 53	1657c
5. Ballyvilly	Census 18	1659
6. Ballyvilly	Inq. Ult. (Antrim) §12 Car. II	1661
7. Ballivelly	BSD 168	1661
8. Ballebayly	Court of Claims §923	1662c
9. Ballyvolly	Lapsed Money Book 156	1663
10. Ballyvelly	ASE 116a §19	1668
11. Balliceele	HMR Ant. 6	1669
12. Ballyvelly	Ant. Forfeit.	1700
13. Ballyvelly	PRONI D2977/3A/2/1/27	1720
14. Ballyvely	C. McG. (OSNB) B 17	1734
15. Ballyveelly	Stewart's Survey 2	1734
16. Ballyverleys	Lendrick Map	1780
17. Ballyvilly	Sur. A.E. 54	1782
18. Cultravillon otherwise Ballyvilly	PRONI D2977/3A/2/1/40	1814
19. Ballyveally	Bnd. Sur. (OSNB) B 17	1830
20. Ballyvely	OSNB B 17	1831
21. Ballyveley Nat. Sch.	OSRNB sh.9, 2	1853

22. Ballyvely "Miletown"; Bhalla-town, Millhe-mile	Rev. Connolly 518	1814
23. Balie bhealaigh "town of the road or pass"	J O'D (OSNB) B 17	1831
24. Beal-agh-na-fola "mouth of the bloody ford"	OSM xxiv 79	1838
25. Baile bhile "town of the old tree"	Rev. Magill 7	1923
26. "townland of the blood or slaughter"	Dallat's Ramoan 25	1973

27. ˌbɑliˈvili	Local pronunciation	1993

The variation in the anglicization of the penultimate vowel stongly suggests that it was originally Irish *ao*, a high back unrounded vowel. English *i* (forms 1, 5–6) has been used in other 17th-century forms of place-names for *ao* (cf. *PNI* v 216 sv. **Broagh** and 217–8 sv. **Carricknakielt**). We would not necessarily expect this vowel to yield more *-oy-/-oo-* variants here as these seem to arise more especially when following an unlenited *m* or *b* as a result of a phonetic glide (compare forms of the south-east Co. Down townland name **Lisnamulligan** in *PNI* iii 92; see also **Kilmoyle** in Grange of Drumtullagh). Thus, although Wagner noted the development of [ï] to [i] in some words in Antrim Irish (*LASID* iv 284 n.4; see also **Drumnakeel** in Culfeightrin), we may dimiss such possible final elements as *bile* "(sacred) tree" (compare **Toberbilly**). *Baile Mhaoile* "townland of the rounded summit/hillock" is a possible original form; the lenition of the initial consonant of the final element could be ascribed to the use of the place-name in oblique cases (form 2 suggests that the second element in this name began with *b*, but mistranscription of *v* as *b* in 17th-century English sources is not uncommon). We must take into consideration, however, that *baile*-names are often qualified by personal names and (more commonly in northern counties) surnames. In addition, it is possible that the neighbouring townland of **Coolaveely**, which lies across the Glenshesk River in Culfeightrin parish, contains the same final element. The relatively rare early male personal name *Baothallach* (*CGH* 141 b 34) seems unlikely to have qualified the relatively late place-name element *baile* (see **Balleny** in Armoy). Somewhat more likely is the rare surname *Ó Baothalaigh* (earlier *Ó Baothghalaigh*) which Woulfe (1923, 434) notes is listed as an Ulster surname in a 14th-century text (see *Topog. Poems (JOD)* 16). It appears from this text to be associated with the Inishowen-Derry area. Woulfe (*loc. cit.*) comments on this surname: "I have failed to discover any early angl. forms . . . and am by no means certain that it is still extant". The apparent early loss of the intervocalic *-th-* is not a problem: compare early forms of **Boveagh**, from *Both Bheitheach* "birch hut" in south Co. Derry (*PNI* v 89).

It is difficult to ascertain the importance of form 18(a), as the document from which it is taken is badly affected by scribal errors. It may be a garbled form of Coolaveely.

Broom-beg	*Brú Beag*
D 1139	"fort, little"

See **Broom-more**.

Broom-more	*Brú Mór*
D 1138	"fort, big"

1. Brumemore, the quarter land called the	PRONI D2977/3A/2/1/2	1611
2. Broomore	Inq. Ult. (Antrim) §64 Car. I	1635
3. Broome	Hib. Reg. Cary	1657c
4. Brewrne, the townland of	DS (Par. Map) 53	1657c
5. Brumbeg, Brommore	Census 18	1659
6. Broometowne	BSD 170	1661
7. (?)Birine	Court of Claims §923	1662c
8. Bramine, the ½ town of	Court of Claims §923	1662c
9. Brumine, the half towne of	Decree of Innocence 431	1663
10. Broome Towne	Lapsed Money Book 156	1663
11. Dromine als Broome	ASE 116a §19	1668

12. Drombeg, Broomre	HMR Ant. 7	1669
13. Broombagg	Stewart's Survey 1	1734
14. Broombegg	Stewart's Survey 2	1734
15. Broomore	Stewart's Survey 15	1734
16. Broombeg, Broomore	Lendrick Map (OSNB) B 17	1780
17. Broombeg, Bromore	Bnd. Sur. (OSNB) B 17	1830
18. Brom-Begg, Brom-More	Tithe Applot. 3	1833
19. broombeg "small piece of broom"; from bromh-broom, beg-little	Rev. Connolly 518	1814
20. Brommore "large piece of broom", from bromh-broom, mhor-great	Rev. Connolly 518	1814
21. Brugh mór "great fort"	J O'D (OSNB) B 17	1831
22. Brugh beag "The little mansion"	Ó Dubhthaigh 133	1905
23. Brugh mór "The large mansion"	Ó Dubhthaigh 133	1905
24. Brugh beag "small fort"	Rev. Magill 9	1923
25. Brugh mór "large fort"	Rev. Magill 9	1923
26. broombeg "the small palace"	Dallat's Ramoan 25	1973
27. broomore "the great palace"	Dallat's Ramoan 25	1973
28. brum'bɛg	Local pronunciation	1993
29. bru'moːr	Local pronunciation	1993

The first element of this name was probably *brú* "a large house, a palace, a fort, a fairy mansion, a hillock; a district; a region" (*Dinneen*). It derives from O.Ir. *bruig* for which *DIL* gives several meanings: "land, cultivated land, holding; region, district, border; (farm-) house; abode, hall, mansion". In the case of Broom-beg, the *m* was apparently added by analogy with Broom-more.

The *Ordnance Survey Memoirs* recorded the following in 1838:

> In Broomore, and situated on a lofty eminence in the holding of Charles Boyd, there stands the ruins of a fort that seems circular form (*sic*), 30 yards in diameter at the top. It was composed of earth and stones, and its summit from 10 to 15 feet above the surface of the hill on which it is situate . . . (*OSM* xxiv 116).

> [In Broomore and] situated on a lofty hill in the holding of Robert Clowey, there stands a fort approaching to circular shape and composed chiefly of earth. It is surrounded by a moat averaging 14 feet wide. The fort is 15 yards in diameter on the top and stands from 6 to 10 feet above the bottom of the moate . . . (*ibid.*).

The first element of Broom-more may have referred originally to one of these sites.

In the absence of any field evidence in Broom-beg townland, it seems likely that the epithets *mór* "large, great" and *beag* "small" refer to the relative sizes of the land divisions.

Form 11(a) may refer to the neighbouring townland of **Drummans**, or to some obsolete division, but seems more likely to represent a scribal error.

Cape Castle	*Ceap Caistéil*	
D 0837	"tillage plot of the castle"	
1. Capecastle	Hib. Reg. Cary	1657c

2. Kepcastle	Census 19	1659
3. Capecastle	BSD 170	1661
4. Cape Castle	Lapsed Money Book 156	1663
5. Cape Castle	ASE 116a §19	1668
6. Capcastle	HMR Ant. 7	1669
7. Capcastle	Hib. Del. Antrim	1672c
8. Capcastle	PRONI D2977/3A/2/1/2	1676
9. Cape Castle	Ant. Forfeit.	1700
10. Cape C.	Ire. Map	1711
11. Capcastle	Religious Survey	1734
12. Capcastle	Stewart's Survey 17	1734
13. Capcastle	C. McG. (OSNB) B 17	1734
14. Cape Castle	Lendrick Map	1780
15. Capcastle	PRONI D2977/3A/2/1/40	1812
16. Cape Castle	Bnd. Sur. (OSNB) B 17	1830
17. "Castle of the cape or headland"	J O'D (OSNB) B 17	1831
18. Caislean Cába "Cabe's castle"	Ó Dubhthaigh 134	1905
19. Ceapach Caisleáin "tillage plot of the castle"	Rev. Magill 10	1923
20. "the castle of the tillage plot"	Dallat's Ramoan 25	1973
21. Caisteal an Chába	Éire Thuaidh	1988
22. ˌkepˈkasəl	Local pronunciation	1993

It appears that English surveyors substituted *cape* for Irish *ceap* "a piece of ground, a small cultivated plot" (*Dinneen*). The similar *ceapach* (form 19) is not distinctively reflected in historical forms. There is no record of a castle in this townland, and the name seems to refer instead to the castle in **Cloghanmurry** to the immediate north. It should also be borne in mind that the final element in this name was perhaps originally the gen. sing. (*caisleáin*) of *caisleán* "castle", and that it was replaced with *castle* by English surveyors (see, for example, **Ballycastle** and **Clare** townlands).

Forms 18 and 21 presume that the second element was altered to *cape* and placed before *castle* in anglicized variants. This is difficult to prove however, as the historical forms do not predate c. 1657. Laoide (*SCtSiadhail* 104) noted the name *Caisleán Cába* in a popular traditional song, and believed it to be an Irish form of Cape Castle, and suggested that *Cába* was a late form of *Capa*, one of three fishermen who were believed to have drowned at the mouth of the Bann about the time of the (biblical) deluge (cf. *Céitinn* i 140). It seems most likely, however, that this form refers in fact to some other (unidentified) place (*Duncan* 132).

Carnduff
D 1042

An Carn Dubh
"the black cairn"

1. Carneduffe	Hib. Reg. Cary	1657c
2. Carnduff	Census 18	1659
3. Carneduffe	BSD 170	1661
4. Carneduffe, the halfe towneland of	Decree of Innocence 431	1661
5. Carneduffe	Court of Claims §923	1662c

6. Carneaffe, the ½ townland of	Court of Claims §923	1662c
7. Carnduffe	Lapsed Money Book 156	1663
8. Carndoe	HMR Ant. 7	1669
9. Carneduffe	Hib. Del. Antrim	1672c
10. Carnduffe	Ant. Forfeit.	1700
11. Carnduf, two quarters of	PRONI D2977/3A/2/1/19	1709
12. Carnduffe	Hill's Stewarts 11	1720
13. Carnduff	Religious Survey	1734
14. Carnduff	Stewart's Survey 14	1734
15. Carnduff	C. McG. (OSNB) B 17	1734
16. Carnduff alias Carndoo	PRONI d2977/3A/2/1/34	1737
17. Carnduff	Lendrick Map	1780
18. Carnduff	PRONI D2977/3A/2/1/40	1812
19. Carnduff	Bnd. Sur. (OSNB) B 17	1830
20. Carnduff or Carndoo	OSNB B 17	1831
21. Cairn duff "black hillock"	Rev. Connolly 501	1814
22. Carnduff "dark heap"; carn-heap, dhu-black	Rev. Connolly 518	1814
23. Carn dubh "black carn or heap"	J O'D (OSNB) B 17	1831
24. Carn dubh "the black cairn"	Ó Dubhthaigh 134	1905
25. Carn Dubh "black cairn"	Rev. Magill 9	1923
26. "the black cairn"	Dallat's Ramoan 25	1973
27. kɑrnˈdọf	Local pronunciation	1993
28. kɑrnˈdu	Local pronunciation	1996

Carn "a heap, a cairn, a pile of stones" (*Dinneen*) is qualified here by the adjective *dubh* "black". Holmer recorded the word *dubh* as [dʌ] (*Irish of the Glens* 111), and form 28 of this name, and the Culfeightrin subtownland place-names **Lough Doo** and **Portdoo**, reflect this somewhat.

The existence of a *carn* in the townland has not been recorded, although these features were often removed for building material. Local historian Cahal Dallat has suggested that the name refers to the outcrop of basalt on a summit of 104 metres situated in the west of the townland, which is also the townland's highest point (*Dallat's Ramoan* 25). In c. 1855 this eminence was called Carnduff Hill and descibed as "a small [conical] hill in shape and overgrown with furze . . . The townland has derived its name from this hill" (*OSRNB* sh.4, 1). A natural feature also appears to have inspired the Culfeightrin subtownland name of **Carnaneigh**.

Carneatly	*Carn Tulcha*	
D 1039	"cairn of the mound"	
1. Carnetillagh	Inq. Ult. (Antrim) §42 Car. I	1635
2. Carnetelagh	Inq. Ult. (Antrim) §50 Car. I	1635
3. Carnetullagh	Hib. Reg. Cary	1657c
4. Cornetelagh, a parcell of	DS (Par. Map) 53	1657c
5. Carnetilagh	Census 18	1659
6. Corntullagh	BSD 169	1661

7. Carnetellogh	Court of Claims §923	1662c
8. Cariletellagh	Court of Claims §923	1662c
9. Canetellagh, the towneland of	Decree of Innocence 431	1663
10. Cornetullagh	ASE 116a §19	1668
11. Carnetly	HMR Ant. 8	1669
12. Gortnetulla	Hib. Del. Antrim	1672c
13. Carnetllagh	PRONI D2977/3A/2/1/3	1676
14. Ballycastle and Carnetillagh, Mills of	PRONI D2977/3A/2/1/9A	1693
15. Carnetly	Religious Survey	1734
16. Carnetly	Stewart's Survey 1	1734
17. Carnetley	Stewart's Survey 15	1734
18. Carneatly	C. McG. (OSNB) B 17	1734
19. Carneatly	Lendrick Map	1780
20. Carnately	Bnd. Sur. (OSNB) B 17	1830
21. Carneatly "mount of birds"; from carn-heap, ettalagh-fluttering	Rev. Connolly 518	1814
22. Carn Nataile "Natalai's heap or carn"	J O'D (OSNB) B 17	1831
23. Carn Natluagh, Natluagh being a prince of the Rudrician or Northern Ultonian race	MacDonnell Antrim 403	1873
24. Carn ealta "The cairn of the flocks"	Ó Dubhthaigh 134	1905
25. Carn Natluaigh "Natluach's cairn"	Rev. Magill 9	1923
26. "the cairn of the flocks"	Dallat's Ramoan 25	1973
27. ˌkɑrˈnitlɪ	Local pronunciation	1993
28. ˌkɑrˈnetlɪ	Local pronunciation	1996

Carn Tulcha "cairn of the hillock/mound" is the most plausible origin of this name. The second element is a gen. sing. form of *tulach* "low hill; hillock, mound" (see **Grange of Drumtullagh**); *tulach* is also a gen. sing. and gen. pl. form (see *DIL*, *Ó Dónaill*) but the loss of unstressed final vowels in place-names is common. The rare female personal name *Tai(d)lech* (*CSH* 175 §722.56) might have given a gen. form *Tailche* and could also be considered as a possible final element, although it seems somewhat less likely. The further gen. form *tulaí* of *tulach* may have been adopted towards the end of the 17th century. In any event, at this time the name suffered from metathesis.

The figure to whom previous commentators have alluded (forms 22–23 and 25) may be *Nadslúaig*, a member of the Dál nAraí (see county introduction) who is said to have met St Patrick (see *Trip. Life (Stokes)* 166–8 and *Trias Thaum.* 147). The stress in this male personal name would fall on the second syllable, however. In addition, this second syllable would be at variance with historical forms.

The following was recorded in 1838:

> In Carneatly, and holding of John Hill and company, there stood an ancient mound composed chiefly of earth, and on the summit of which were discovered about 2 feet beneath the surface a paved causeway 5 feet long and 3 feet broad, but destroyed in cut-

ting a road through the mound some years back. Here also was found an earthen urn containing bones and ashes (*OSM* xxiv 117).

Carnmoon *Carnán Muáin*
D 0943 "*Muán*'s cairn"

1. Carnammone	Hib. Reg. Cary	1657c
2. Cornanmmone	DS (Par. Map) 54	1657c
3. Carnemoan	Census 18	1659
4. Cornammonne	BSD 169	1661
5. (?)Carnamahin	Court of Claims §923	1662c
6. (?)Carnamhim	Court of Claims §923	1662c
7. Carnanmoan, the Quarter of	Decree of Innocence 431	1663
8. Carnemone 1 Qur.	Lapsed Money Book 156	1663
9. Carnanimone	ASE 116a §19	1668
10. (?)Carthmone parcell	ASE 116b §19	1668
11. Carmoone	HMR Ant. 7	1669
12. Carnemony	Hib. Del. Antrim	1672c
13. Carnemone	PRONI D2977/3A/2/1/7	1681
14. Cornemone	Ant. Forfeit.	1700
15. Carnemonie	Religious Survey	1734
16. Carneymoon	Stewart's Survey 14	1734
17. Carnymoon	C. McG. (OSNB) B 17	1734
18. Carnymoan	Lendrick Map	1780
19. Carnemoon	Bnd. Sur. (OSNB) B 17	1830
20. Carnemoon	OSNB B 17	1831
21. Carnmoan	Tithe Applot. 6	1833
22. Carneymoon	OSRNB sh.4, 1	1855c
23. Carnmoon "bogmount"; carn-heap, móna-bog	Rev. Connolly 518	1814
24. Carn Múghaine "Mugania's carn or sepulchral heap"	J O'D (OSNB) B 17	1831
25. Carn moin "The cairn of the bogs"	Ó Dubhthaigh 134	1905
26. "cairn of the moss"	Dallat's Ramoan 26	1973
27. karn'muːn	Local pronunciation	1993

Many forms indicate the former existence of a central syllable which has been omitted in the modern anglicized name. *Carnán*, a development from *carn* "cairn" but probably of similar meaning (cf. **Carnanmore** in Other Names, Ballintoy and **Carnanmore** in Other Names, Culfeightrin) seems the most likely first element. In 1838, the Ordnance Survey recorded the following:

In Carnmoon and on an eminence on the holding of Jean Lester, and contiguous to the sea-shore, there stood an ancient cairn of stones called Cairnmoon, and gave name to the townland. This cairn was locally considered a seat for fairies and in consequence regarded as a very gentle spot, but the cairn is at present destroyed (*OSM* xxiv 120).

The historical forms do not sufficiently reflect *muine* "thicket; brushwood, scrub; hill" (see *Ó Dónaill, GUH* 46 n.5) or gen. forms of *móin* "turf, peat; bogland, moor" (*Ó Dónaill*) for us to regard them as possible final elements. A raising of [o̯] vowels to [ʌ] in the local dialect was noticed by Holmer (see *Irish of the Glens* 17), but one would not expect this feature to have occurred as early as form 11 might otherwise suggest. The male personal name *Muán* (earlier *Muadhán*) which occurs also in the parish name **Ramoan** thus seems most likely to have formed the final element. It also appears to feature in the south-west Co. Antrim townland name **Carnmacmoin**/*Carn Mhic Mhuáin* "carn of the son of *Muán*" (*PNI* iv 173). The female personal name *Múin* (earlier *Mughain*; gen. *M(h)úna* (cf. Ó Maolfabhail 1990, 168 sv. *Dún Múna*)) may represent a further possible final element, but it is absent from east Ulster genealogies and hagiography, and seems to be associated more with Munster (see Ó Corráin & Maguire 1981, 140). The further name *Maon* is also unlikely (*PNI ibid.*). The final vowels in forms 12 and 15 may indicate scribal errors or a reinterpretation of the name.

Carnsampson	*Carn Samsain*	
D 0840	"Samson's cairn"	
1. Carnesampson	Hib. Reg. Cary	1657c
2. Cornesampsonne	DS (Par. Map) 57	1657c
3. Carnsamson	Census 18	1659
4. Cornesampson	BSD 169	1661
5. Carnsamson	Lapsed Money Book 156	1663
6. Cornesampeon	ASE 116a §19	1668
7. Carnsamson	HMR Ant. 8	1669
8. Carnasamson	Hib. Del. Antrim	1672c
9. CarneSamson	PRONI D2977/3A/2/1/7	1681
10. Carnsamson	Ant. Forfeit.	1700
11. Carnsamson	Religious Survey	1734
12. Carnsamson	Stewart's Survey 1	1734
13. Carnsamson	C. McG. (OSNB) B 17	1734
14. Carsamson	Merchant's Book 18	1752
15. Carnsampsons	Lendrick Map	1780
16. Carnsampson	Bnd. Sur. (OSNB) B 17	1830
17. Carnsampson	OSNB B 17	1831
18. Carnsampson "Sampson's mount"	Rev. Connolly 518	1814
19. "Sampson's carn"	J O'D (OSNB) B 17	1831
20. ˌkɑrnˈsamsən	Local pronunciation	1993

The male personal name *Samsan* (earlier *Samson*) is rare in Irish, although we may note that the death of a *Samson*, descendant of *Corcran*, was recorded in the *Annals of Ulster* in 735 (*AU* i 192). It possibly occurs in the Co. Wexford townland name Ballysamson (*Census 1851*). The use of *Samson* as a personal name in Celtic England (see below) and in Wales (see Bartrum 1966, 212) has been attested. Nicolaisen (1976, 56) has recorded the place-name *Bruthach an t-Samsain* which he translates "Samson's Brae" in North Uist where, "according to local tradition, a very strong man is supposed to have lived in the past". The second vowel of the personal name would have developed to *a* due to its unstressed position (cf. *Murlach*, the Mod. Ir. form of **Murlough Bay** in Other Names, Culfeightrin).

Forms 18–9 suggest that *carn* "cairn" is qualified here by the English surname Sampson. MacLysaght (1991, 264) says of this surname that it "appears fairly frequently in medieval Irish records from the early 14th century both in Leinster and Munster . . . but is now scattered". The English surname derives ultimately from the name of a Welsh saint which became "popular in Yorkshire and eastern counties and also in the Welsh border counties" (Reaney 1987, 305). It is absent from the local sources, however. The Scottish surname Simson, some variants of which developed an intrusive *p* (Black 1946, 727) is attested locally from the mid-1600s: there was a John Simson living in the neighbouring parish of Ballintoy in 1669 (*HMR Ant.* 2). However, Simson is not reflected in the forms. An original form such as *Corr na Seamsán* "round hill of the wood-sorrel" (see *Dinneen* sv. *seamsóg*) might be considered, but there are difficulties with this, including the central *e* in early forms, which is unlikely to represent a medial vowel as *carn* seems to have been rendered *carne* in most mid-17th-century English sources.

The following was recorded in 1838:

> In Carnsampson, and situated in the remains of bog in the holding of William Baily, there stood a small mound of earth and stones, and locally called Knocknahullar, but now reduced to a mere ruin (*OSM* xxiv 117).

This may have been the original cairn of the townland name. *Cnoc na hIolaire* "hill of the eagle" appears to be the origin of *Knocknahullar*. *Iolar* "eagle" is a fem. noun in Scottish Gaelic (*Dwelly* sv. *iolair*) and was also fem. in Rathlin (*Irish of Rathlin* 195 sv. *fiolar*).

Clare
D 1042

Clár Caisleáin
"level place of the castle(?)"

1. Clarecastle, land of	PRONI D2977/3A/2/1/1A	1605
2. Claircaslen	PRONI D2977/3A/2/1/2	1611
3. Clarecastlenun	Inq. Ult. (Antrim) §64 Car. I	1635
4. Clane	Hib. Reg. Cary	1657c
5. Clarr	Census 18	1659
6. Clane	BSD 170	1661
7. Clarecastle	Court of Claims §923	1662c
8. Clare Castle, the 40 acres of	Court of Claims §923	1662c
9. Clare Castle, the fforty acres of	Decree of Innocence 431	1663
10. Clare	Lapsed Money Book 156	1663
11. Clune and Carnconny	ASE 116a §19	1668
12. Claircastle	HMR Ant. 7	1669
13. Clane	Hib. Del. Antrim	1672c
14. Clare	Ballycastle Map	1720c
15. Clare	Religious Survey	1734
16. Clare	Stewart's Survey 1	1734
17. Clare	C. McG. (OSNB)B 17	1734
18. Clare	Taylor and Skinner 270	1777
19. Clare	Lendrick Map	1780
20. Clare	Bnd. Sur. (OSNB) B 17	1830
21. Clare, clar-level spot	Rev. Connolly 518	1814
22. Clár "a level plain"	J O'D (OSNB) B 17	1831

23. Clar "The plain"	Ó Dubhthaigh 134	1905
24. Clár "a board, a plain"	Rev. Magill 12	1923
25. 'klɑr	Local pronunciation	1993

In place-names, *clár* is usually "applied locally to a flat piece of land" (*Joyce* i 427). *Dinneen* translates it as "a level surface, a plain; a slab, a plate, a tablet; a flat country, a large district" (*Dinneen*). The townland name *Clár Aidhne* (anglicized Clarina) in Co. Limerick has been translated "the flat place of *Aidhne*" (Ó Maolfabhail 1990, 110). In O. Ir. *clár* was used "of a variety of flat objects normally made of wood" (*DIL* sv.), and in place-names the sense "bridge" is attested (Flanagan & Flanagan 1994, 54; see also **Clare Mountain** below). There is some doubt over what its exact meaning was in this case, however.

The following was recorded in 1838:

> In Clare and holding of John McCurdy, and about 4 furlongs south west of the old castle of Duinaneeny [*sic*], there stood an ancient castle of considerable extent said to have been founded and for a series of time inhabited by a Scotch clan of the McNeils, who held some tract of land in the neighbourhood. It was called Clare Castle. A large portion of the walls, together with the fruit garden, existed in the recollection of some of the local inhabitants now residing near the site of the castle . . . (*OSM* xxiv 123; cf. also *O'Laverty* iv 399).

It is to this building that forms 1–3, 7–9 and 15 presumably allude.

Clare Mountain	*An Clár*	
D 1336	"open expanse(?)"	
1. Clarie	Religious Survey	1734
2. Clare (Mountain)	C. McG. (OSNB) B 17	1734
3. Clare (Mountain)	Bnd. Sur. (OSNB) B 17	1830
4. Clár "a level plain"	J O'D (OSNB) B 17	1831
5. klɑr'mɔuʔən	Local pronunciation	1993

This townland lies in the south of the parish and is clearly not related to the previous townland. Topographically, it is situated on the eastern slopes of Knocklayd Mountain. The English suffix is surely a late addition to this name to distinguish it from Clare. It resembles somewhat the use of *sliabh* "mountain" in Scottish Gaelic to denote "extended heath, alpine plain, moorish ground; extensive tract of dry moorland; mountain grass, moor bent grass; face of a hill" (Nicolaisen 1969, 11).

The Irish form depends on the reliability of form 1. We might argue that forms 2–3 were affected in spelling by analogy with the previous townland name. *DIL* lists *clárach* as a collective noun meaning "boards, beams; wood", although it might normally be translated "level place" (*Joyce* i 428) in place-names. *Clárach* anglicized claragh is a reasonably common townland name and name element (*Census 1851*). It is listed by *DIL* as a masc. noun, but **Clare** in north-west Co. Down derives from *Cláraigh*, an oblique form of a fem. variant (*PNI* vi 285). The further masc. noun *cláradh* "boards, planking, woodwork; wooden palisading(?); wooden building(?)" (*DIL* sv. *cláradh*) does not appear to be attested in place-

names. Form 1 could contain an obsolete second element, but in the absence of more definite evidence, is probably best interpreted as containing a misleading scribal error.

It remains uncertain, however, to what *clár* originally referred. The usual meaning in
place-names, "a flat piece of land; a plain" (see *PNI* iv 36), seems unlikely here. *Dinneen* gives
clár several meanings including "a large district" (see **Clare** townland above); Clare
Mountain is a relatively small townland but we might consider a meaning such as "open
expanse of land". It is also possible that the original name referred to a bridge such as
Glenshesk Bridge (see Other Names), which connects this townland with Drumacullin in
Culfeightrin (see **Clare**). "The county of Clare was so called from the village of the same
name; and the tradition of the people is, that it was called Clare from a board formerly placed
across the river Fergus to serve as a bridge" (*Joyce loc. cit.*).

Cloghanmurry

D 0837

Cloch Dhún Muirígh
"(stone) castle of Murray's fort"

1.	Cloghdrummory	Hib. Reg. Cary	1657c
2.	Cloghdunmory	DS (Par. Map) 53	1657c
3.	Cloghdunmurre	Census 19	1659
4.	Ballinclogh of Dunmurrry	Court of Claims §923	1662c
5.	Balleclogh Dunmire	Court of Claims §923	1662c
6.	Balleclogh Dunmire	Decree of Innocence 431	1663
7.	Cloghdumnory 1 Qur	Lapsed Money Book 156	1663
8.	Cloughdunmory	ASE 116b §19	1668
9.	Cloghanmurry	HMR Ant. 3	1669
10.	Cloghhdunmurry	Hib. Del. Antrim	1672c
11.	Cloghdunmury	PRONI D2977/3A/2/1/3	1676
12.	Cloghdumnory	Ant. Forfeit.	1700
13.	Cloghermurry	Stewart's Survey 15	1734
14.	Cloghanmurry	Stewart's Survey 17	1734
15.	Cloughanmurry	C. McG. (OSNB)	1734
16.	Cloghdemurrie	Religious Survey	1734
17.	Cloughamurry	Lendrick Map	1780
18.	Cloghanmany otherwise Cloghdimurry	PRONI D2977/3A/2/1/40	1812
19.	Cloughanmurry	Bnd. Sur. (OSNB) B 17	1830
20.	Cloughenmurry	Tithe Applot. 4	1833
21.	Cloghdunmurry	OSRNB sh.8, 2	1855c
22.	Clogh in murray "virgin's stone"; clogh-stone, muirrha-virgin	Rev. Connolly 518	1814
23.	Clochán Muireadhaigh	J O'D (OSNB) B 17	1831
24.	Clochan mhuire "The carn of Mary"	OSRNB sh.8, 2	1855c
25.	Clochan Mhuiridhigh "Murray's stepping-stones"	Ó Dubhthaigh 135	1905
26.	Cloch dúin Muiridhigh	Ó Dubhthaigh 135	1905
27.	Cloghanmurry "the stone fort of Murry"	PSAMNI 11	1940
28.	ˌklɑxən'mo̜ri	Local pronunciation	1993

The first element *cloch* "is often applied to a large and conspicuous stone, or to a stone of some historical or cultural significance, [or to] a stone building, such as a castle" in place-names (*PNI* v 15; see also **Cloghcorr** in Ballintoy). Early forms indicate the existence of the medial element *dún* "fort". The (probably lenited) *d* has since been lost, but it was still remembered by some locals in the 1850s (form 21). Although there may have existed two separate names (and possibly divisions) prior to an amalgamation, forms 4–6 may merely indicate a prefixed *bally-* townland marker, a common feature of 17th-century documenta-tion (see *PNI* iv 103). The compound *clochdhún* "stony fort" might also be considered as a possible first element although it does not appear to be otherwise attested.

The personal name *Muiríoch* (formerly *Muiredach*) "was one of the more popular early names, and the name could be anglicized Murry or Murray" (Ó Corráin & Maguire 1991, 141). This occurs elsewhere in the south Antrim townland name *Dún Muirígh*, anglicized **Dunmurry** (*GÉ* 100).

The Ordnance Survey recorded in 1838 that:

> In Cloghanmurry and holding of Robert Thompson, and situated on the summit of a lofty round hill, west of and contiguous to the old road leading from Ballycastle to Ballymoney, there stand the ruins of an ancient castle locally called Cloghduinmurry Castle . . . Local tradition says that this castle was founded by the McQuillans and inhabited by them for a series of time, but that it was consumed by fire during the early rebellions of the country (*OSM* xxiv 105–6).

The site, however, was described in 1940 by the Archaeological Survey as consisting of noth-ing more than "a glacial hillock of hard clay" (*PSAMNI* 11).

Coolkenny	*Cúil Chaonaigh*	
D 0839	"corner of moss"	
1. Coulkeny	Inq. Ult. (Antrim) §73 Car. I	1635
2. Culkeyne	Hib. Reg. Cary	1657c
3. Culkeyne als Meerebane	DS (Par. Map) 57	1657c
4. Culkeney	Census 18	1659
5. Culkeny	Court of Claims §923	1662c
6. Coolekeny	Court of Claims §923	1662c
7. Coolekeny, the Towne Land of	Decree of Innocence 431	1663
8. Killkeyne als Myerbane	Lapsed Money Book 156	1663
9. Cullkeine	Lapsed Money Book 156	1663
10. Culkeyne	ASE 116b §19	1668
11. Coolekenny	HMR Ant. 5	1669
12. Coulkeyne	Hib. Del. Antrim	1672c
13. Culkeny	PRONI D2977/3A/2/1/3	1676
14. Cullkeine	Ant. Forfeit.	1700
15. Kilkeyne als Myerbane	Ant. Forfeit.	1700
16. Cullkeny	Reg. Deeds abstracts i §265	1722
17. Coolkeeny	Stewart's Survey 15	1734
18. Coolkeeny	C. McG. (OSNB) B 17	1734
19. Coulkenny	Lendrick Map	1780
20. Cullkenny	PRONI D2977/3A/2/1/40	1812
21. Coul Kinney	Ire. Ex. Eng. ii 230	1823

22.	Kulkenny	Bnd. Sur. (OSNB) B 17	1830
23.	Culkeeny	Tithe App. Book 8	1833
24.	Coolkinny "corner of McKinny"	Rev. Connolly 518	1814
25.	Cúil Cionaoith "Kenny's corner or angle"	J O'D (OSNB) B 17	1831
26.	ˌkulˈkɛni	Local pronunciation	1993
27.	ˌkulˈkini	Local pronunciation	1993

Regarding the first element in this name, see **Coolaveely** in Culfeightrin.

A number of the early forms suggest the second element was monosyllabic. However, these come mainly from related sources and can be dismissed as containing scribal errors. The personal name *Cionaodh* which is possibly originally of "Pictish" origin and is usually anglicized as Kenneth (Ó Corráin & Maguire 1981, 52) may have formed this second element. However, we would not expect its first vowel to have developed to [ʌ] or [i] (see *Irish of the Glens* 28 §28), as suggested by forms from 1734 on. The male personal name *Cainneach* has been anglicized Kenny elsewhere in Ireland (*ibid.*, 43), but again, many anglicized forms do not reflect this name. Except before specific consonants, Irish *ai* was usually anglicized as *a* locally. The final element, therefore, seems most likely to be the gen. form of *caonach* "moss".

Forms 3, 8 and 15 may be based on *maigh* "plain" (see **Moyarget Lower**) plus the meaningless suffix *-(e)ar* (see Ó Máille 1987, 32, 35) plus the adjective *bán* "white": *Maighear Bán*.

Corvally   *An Corrbhaile*

D 0943   "the prominent townland"

1.	Corvalle	Hib. Reg. Cary	1657c
2.	Carvally	DS (Par. Map) 54	1657c
3.	Corvally	Census 18	1659
4.	Corvally	BSD 168	1661
5.	Corvaile	Court of Claims §923	1662c
6.	Corvally, the twenty acres of	Decree of Innocence 431	1663
7.	Corvally	Lapsed Money Book 156	1663
8.	Corvally	ASE 116a §19	1668
9.	Corwelly	HMR Ant. 6	1669
10.	Corvally	Hib. Del. Antrim	1672c
11.	Corvally	PRONI D2977/3A/2/1/6	1681
12.	Corvally	Ant. Forfeit.	1700
13.	Corvally	Religious Survey	1734
14.	Corbally	Stewart's Survey 3	1734
15.	Corbally	C. McG. (OSNB) B 17	1734
16.	Cornally alias Corvally, the quarter land of	PRONI D2977/3A/2/1/33A	1737
17.	Corvally	Lendrick Map	1780
18.	Corvally	PRONI D2977/3A/2/1/40	1812
19.	Corvelly	Bnd. Sur. (OSNB) B 17	1830
20.	Corbally	Tithe Applot. 7	1833

21. Carvally "place of weeds"; Carran-weed, Bhalla-town	Rev. Connolly 519	1814
22. Corrbile "round hill of the old tree"	J O'D (OSNB) B 17	1831
23. Cor-Bhaile "round hill of the town"	Rev. Magill 12	1923
24. "the townland of the little round hill"	Dallat's Ramoan 26	1973
25. ˈkɔrvəli	Local pronunciation	1993

The prefix *corr* may variously mean "odd; tapering, pointed; angular, projecting; rounded, curved" (*Ó Dónaill*). The borders of this townland, which is located on the south-eastern slopes of Knocklayd, taper from the summit of this mountain. The lower borders are irregular, variously curved and angular. *Corrbhaile*, anglicized Corbally in Co. Waterford (*L. Log. P. Láirge* 27) and **Curley** in Co. Down (*PNI* i 18), for example, is found throughout Ireland. It has been variously translated "prominent townland" (*ibid.*) and "the noticeable townland" (*Ó Maolfabhail* 1990, 141). Mac Giolla Easpaig (1986, 75) suggests that the prefix in the Co. Donegal townland name *An Corrmhín* could represent "uneven".

Cregganboy
D 0943

An Creagán Buí
"the yellow rocky place"

1. Cornebane als Creganboy, quarter land of	DS (Par. Map) 53	1657c
2. Cregenboy	Census 18	1659
3. Creginboy	HMR Ant. 7	1661
4. Creganboy	PRONI D2977/3A/2/1/19	1709
5. Craignaboy	Religious Survey	1734
6. Creganbuey	Stewart's Survey 14	1734
7. Creggaboy	C. McG. (OSNB) B 17	1734
8. Creganboy, quarter land of	PRONI D2977/3A/2/1/34	1737
9. Creganbuy	Lendrick Map	1780
10. Craiganbuey	Bnd. Sur. (OSNB) B 17	1830
11. Creganbuy	OSNB B 17	1831
12. Creganbuoy	Tithe Applot. 7	1833
13. Creganbuy "Yellow rock"; cregan-rock, buy-yellow	Rev. Connolly 518	1814
14. Creagán Buidhe "yellow rock"	J O'D (OSNB) B 17	1831
15. "the little white rocks"	Dallat's Ramoan 26	1973
16. ˌkrɛgənˈbɔi	Local pronunciation	1993

The word *creagán* is variously translated "a little rock; a rocky or stony place; a blank spot in a growing crop" (*Dinneen*) and "rocky eminence; (patch of) stony, barren ground" (*Ó Dónaill*). In place-names it is common in every part of Ireland except the south-east (*PNI* iv 102); examples include the Co. Armagh and Co. Louth parish names of *An Creagán* (*L. Log. Lú* 2). See also **Craigban** in Culfeightrin.

Doonfin *Dún Finn(?)*
D 1334 *"Fionn's fort"*

1. Dúin Fionn i nGleann Seisg, ós coinne	Ultach 5:3, 6	1928
2. Doonefen	Hib. Reg. Cary	1657c
3. Downfinne als Tullos	ASE 116b §19	1668
4. Doonfinn	Stewart's Survey 2	1734
5. Dunfin	Sur. A.E. 80	1782
6. Doonfinn	Bnd. Sur. (OSNB) B 17	1830
7. Dún Finn "Finn's dún or fort"	J O'D (OSNB) B 17	1831
8. Dun Finn "The fort of Finn (MacCool)"	Ó Dubhthaigh 137	1905
9. Dún Fionn "white fort"	Rev. Magill 13	1923
10. "Finn's fort"	Dallat's Ramoan 26	1973
11. dun'fï·n	Local pronunciation	1993

The first element in this place-name may be qualified by the adjective *fionn* "white, pale, fair (of hue)" (*Dinneen*). Examples of its use elsewhere in place-names include *Cloch Fhionn* (**Cloghfin** x2) in Co. Derry (*PNI* v 15, 118), *Teampall Fionn* (**Whitechurch**) in Co. Down (*PNI* ii 72–3), *An Mhainistir Fhionn* (**Whiteabbey**) "white monastery" in Co. Antrim, and *Droim Fionn* (Drumfin) "white ridge" in Co. Sligo (*GÉ* 135, 93). *Fionn* (gen. *F(h)inn*) being also the personal name of the legendary *Fionn Mac Cumhail* (see, for example, Ó hÓgáin 1990, 213–24), there was no doubt locally that it was to him that the place-name referred when the Ordnance Survey interviewed local inhabitants in the 1830s. The historical variants do not exhibit lenition of the *f* as has happened in late forms of the Co. Limerick townland name *Cnoc Fhinn* (anglicized Knockeen) "the hill of Fionn" (Ó Maolfabhail 1990, 128), but this can be interpreted as a survival of an earlier grammatical feature (note form 7), while a lenited *f* is often delenited in the process of anglicization in any event (cf. **Craigfad** in Culfeightrin).

The fort in question was described as follows in 1838:

> In Doonfin, and the holding of Pat McCormack, there stands a fort locally called Duinfinn. It is composed chiefly of earth and approaches to oval shape, 15 by 10 yards on the top, and stand[s] 3 to 8 feet above the level of a natural and lofty hill on which it is situate . . . This fort gave name to the townland . . . dedicated by name to that celebrated chief of the Irish Phoenicians called Finn Macuill (*OSM* ix 114–5).

The Ordnance Survey also record some of the local lore surrounding it, including how *Fionn* tragically killed his own hound on this site:

> However, before his departure from the above fort he composed some beautiful poems which he dedicated to his favourite greyhound Brann, so early and so long his companion in Phoenician hunting and sundry other exploits. The poetry here alluded to is still recorded in the Irish poems and much esteemed. The glens and mountains in this district of the country are said to have been the Irish Phoenician's latter seat of amusement and hunting (*ibid.*).

The Ordnance Survey recorded the similar subtownland name of Dunfinn in Carnsampson in c. 1855 (*OSRNB* sh.8, 2).

Drumavoley   *Droim Ghabhla(?)*
D 1340   "ridge of the fork"

1. Drumgolly	Hib. Reg. Cary	1657c
2. Drunigholy	DS (Par. Map) 57	1657c
3. Drumgnoly	Census 18	1659
4. Drumgholly	BSD 168	1661
5. Drumholly	Lapsed Money Book 156	1663
6. Drumgowly	HMR Ant. 6	1669
7. Drumgolly	Hib. Del. Antrim	1672c
8. Drumegally	PRONI D2977/3A/2/8	1683
9. Drumnagoly	PRONI D2977/3A/2/19/1	1709
10. Drumagoly	Hill's Stewarts 11	1720
11. Drimayouly	Stewart's Survey 2	1734
12. Drumnagola	Hill's Stewarts 220	1741c
13. Drimawoley	Lendrick Map (OSNB) B 17	1780
14. Drumnagola	PRONI D2977/3A/2/1/40	1812
15. Drimavoley	Bnd. Sur. (OSNB) B 17	1830
17. Drumawoley	Tithe Applot. 9	1833

18. Drummawolley "behind the ascent"; Drum-back, ghoolla-shoulder	Rev. Connolly 518	1814
19. Druim a' mhullaigh "ridge of the summit"	J O'D (OSNB) B 17	1831
20. Druim an bhuaile "The ridge of the booley"	Ó Dubhthaigh 137	1905
21. "the hill ridge of the booleying"	Dallat's Ramoan 26	1973
22. ˌdrɔməˈvoli	Local pronunciation	1993

The phonetic change which affected the final element appears to have begun in the 1700s (form 11). The Co. Westmeath townland name of Rathwire derives from *Ráth Ghuaire* (Walsh 1957, 45–6), and exhibits a somewhat similar change. We may also note the further example of **Craigavole** in Co. Derry which derives from *Creig an Ghuail* (*Éire Thuaidh*). The final element may have been latterly reinterpreted as *Droim an Bhólaigh* "ridge of the cattle/person of the surname Bole". There was a Daniell Bole living here in 1669 (*HMR Ant.* 6; regarding this surname, see MacLysaght 1985, 20–1 and Black 1946, 87).

While several possible origins could be postulated for the first element, it seems most likely to have been *droim* "ridge", and that the inital consonant of the following element was lenited (possibly due to the use of the name in the dat. case), resulting in a development from [g] to [ɣ] and eventually to [w]/[v]. Forms 9, 12 and 14 may indicate a late introduction of a medial feminine definite article, and suggest that the *n* latterly assimilated to the *m* of *droim*. These forms appear to be related however, and may contain copies of misspellings.

The most likely final element in this name is *gabhla*, a gen. sing. form of *gabhal* (*DIL* sv. *gobul*). The *-(e)y* endings thus represent the final [ə] vowel. *Gabhal* normally denotes "a fork, anything forked" (*Dinneen*), but as with the south-west Co. Antrim name *Gort Gabhail*

(**Gortgole**) "field of the fork" (*PNI* iv 248–9) it is difficult to identify the exact topographical feature. *DIL* (sv. *ibid.*) lists several meanings for *gabhal*, including "a forked branch of a tree; a bifurcation or angle in a glen, pass, etc.; the spit of land between two rivers (?); a branch of a river, an arm or inlet of the sea forming a creek or river estuary". We could consider other possible final elements however, including the gen. sing. (*gabhlai*) of *gabhlach* "forked implement" (*Ó Dónaill*) or "stall or pen, as for cattle" (*Dinneen*), and perhaps a syncopated gen. form of *gabhal* plus the collective suffix *-ach*, with the meaning "forked place" or "place of forks". Some small streams which run through or border this townland feed the Glenshesk River, which forms its eastern boundary.

Drumawillin
D 1140

Droim an Mhuilinn
"ridge of the mill"

1. Drumwilliam	Hib. Reg. Cary	1657c
2. Drumwillin	DS (Par. Map) 53	1657c
3. Drumniwillin	Census 18	1659
4. Drumwilliam	BSD 169	1661
5. Drum William	Lapsed Money Book 156	1663
6. Drumwilliam	ASE 116a §19	1668
7. Drumoselin	HMR Ant. 8	1669
8. Drum William	Ant. Forfeit.	1700
9. Drumawillen	Grand Jury Pres. (Ant.) 44	1713
10. Drimvillen	Hill's Stewarts 11	1720
11. Drumawillen	PRONI D2977/3A/2/1/27	1720
12. Drimawillin	Stewart's Survey 1	1734
13. Drumawillin	PRONI D2977/3A/2/1/32	1735
14. Drumawillin	PRONI D2977/3A/2/1/34	1737
15. Drumawillen	Hill's Stewarts 15	1740
16. Drumawillen	Hill's Stewarts 16	1742
17. Drumawillen	Hill's Stewarts 16	1728
18. Drumawillin	Merchant's Book 1	1751
19. Drumawolien	Lendrick Map	1780
20. Drumawillin	Bnd. Sur. (OSNB) B 17	1830
21. Drumnawillian "behind the mill"; mullhan-mill	Rev. Connolly 518	1814
22. Druim an Mhuillinn "ridge of the mill"	J O'D (OSNB) B 17	1831
23. Druim a' mhuilinn "The ridge of the mill"	Ó Dubhthaigh 137	1905
24. Druim a mhuilinn "ridge of the mill"	Rev. Magill 14	1923
25. "hill of the mill"	Dallat's Ramoan 26	1973
26. ˌdrɔməˈwïlən	Local pronunciation	1993

Muileann is translated "a mill, a factory, a quern or handmill" by *Dinneen*. The element *william* in forms 1, 4–6 and 8, which come from related sources, indicates the substitution for the Irish element of the closest sounding English word by surveyors, or the copying of a scribal error.

This townland was the site of one of four flax mills which were operating in the parish at the time of the Ordnance Survey in the 1830s (*OSM* xxiv 97). It was on the Tow River (see Other Names), which flows through the centre of the territory. The historical forms predate the age of flax, of course, although it may have occupied the site of a former mill. The *Down Survey* parish map of c. 1657 shows a mill on the river just north of this territory in what is now Town Parks townland (*DS (Par. Map)* 53). Land divisions around a mill in the town are mentioned in some 17th-19th-century sources (for example, *Mill Holm* and *Mill Freehold* in *Stewart's Survey* 1; see also **Mill Five Acres** in Armoy).

Drumeeny	*Droim Fhinnigh*	
D 1339	"*Finneach*'s ridge"	

1. Druim Findich, Enán in	Tírechán 349	700c
2. inDruim [Fh]indich, Enán	Trip. Life (Stokes) 162	900c
3. Druim-Indich, Ecclesiam de	Trias Thaum. 146b	1647
4. Druim indich	Trias Thaum. 182b	1647
5. Druimindeich	Mon. Hib. 10	1779
6. Dromenagh	Inq. Ult. (Antrim) §100 Car. I	1635
7. Druminine	Hib. Reg. Cary	1657c
8. Drumnenyne	DS (Par. Map) 54	1657c
9. Drumniy	Census 18	1659
10. Drumnenyne	BSD 168	1661
11. Drumnenine	Lapsed Money Book 156	1663
12. Drumnemyne	ASE 116a §19	1668
13. Dromeny	HMR Ant. 6	1669
14. Drumine	Hib. Del. Antrim	1672c
15. Drumnenine	Ant. Forfeit.	1700
16. Drummeeny	PRONI D2977/3A/2/1/27	1720
17. Drummie	Religious Survey	1734
18. Drimeeny	Stewart's Survey 1	1734
19. Drimeeny	C. McG. (OSNB) B 17	1734
20. Drimanunny	Lendrick Map	1780
21. Druminneney	PRONI D2977/3A/2/1/40	1812
22. Drimeeny	Bnd. Sur. (OSNB) B 17	1830
23. Drumeeny	OSNB B 17	1831
24. Driminney "behind the height"; Drim-back, inney-height	Rev. Connolly 518	1814
25. Druimínidhe "little ridges"	J O'D (OSNB) B 17	1831
26. Druim aonaigh "The ridge of the asssembly"	Ó Dubhthaigh 137	1905
27. "St. Enan's hill"	Dallat's Ramoan 25	1973
28. ˌdrɔmˈinjə	Local pronunciation	1993

The early Irish forms (1–2) relate to the founding of a church here by St Patrick to which he appointed *Éanán* (O.Ir. *Énán*). Colgan suggested that this Éanán was the son of *Muán* who is commemorated in the parish name Ramoan (see the parish introduction). The personal name *Finneach* (O.Ir. *Findech*) which features in the townland name, is a "male and female [name] . . . derived either from *finn* 'fair' or from *finnech* 'having a lot of hair'" (Ó Corráin & Maguire 1981, 102 sv. *Finnech*). Forms 7–8, 10–12 and 15 appear to be based on *Droim Éanáin* "Éanán's ridge", but they come from related sources and may contain scribal errors.

The Ordnance Survey recorded the following in 1838:

> In Drumeeny and holding of Hugh Laverty and co., and about 1 mile south west of Bonamarge [*sic*] ancient church, there stands the remains of an ancient grave-yard and supposed ancient church, locally called Kille Enan. This graveyard was situated on a gentle elavation contiguous to the River Shesk, and contained about two roods of ground. It was enclosed by a thick stone and clay fence . . . About the centre of the grave-yard stood the ruins of some ancient building supposed to have been a church. It stood 30 by 21 feet on the outside (*OSM* ix 109).

It was also recorded that:

> In Drumeeny and holding of John Thompson, and situated on a handsome eminence about 150 yards north west of the ancient church and graveyard, there stands the ruins of another ancient church which measures 28 feet 8 inches by 15 feet 2 inches inside, walls run together by grouted mortar of a superior quality . . . This building is locally called Cloughneingobban, and thought to [have] been erected by Gobban Seir's daughter . . . However, the old residents call and believe it to be an ancient church, one of the first two of stone and lime work founded in this part of the country, and also to have been for some time the seat of nuns. It is probable that [Kille Enan] . . . was disused and superseded by this more modern erection of stone and lime work (*ibid.* 110–1; see also O'Laverty iv 422–4).

The anglicized form *Kille Enan*, which Reeves wrote as *Killeenan* in 1847 (*EA* 285, 386), may derive from *Cill Éanáin* "Éanán's church". *Cloughneingobban* is probably based on *Cloch Níon Ghobáin* "(stone) castle of the daughter of *Gobán Saor*"; *Gobán Saor* is the master artificer to whom various buildings throughout the country are ascribed (see Ó hÓgáin 1991, 241–43).

Drummans
D 1037

Na Dromanna
"the ridges"

1. Dromanas, the quarter land called	PRONI D2977/3A/2/1/2	1611
2. Dromana	Inq. Ult. (Antrim) §64 Car. I	1635
3. Dromonts	Census 18	1659
4. Dromana	Court of Claims §923	1662c
5. Dramana, the quarter of	Court of Claims §923	1662c
6. Drumana, the qtr. of	Decree of Innocence 431	1663
7. Dromine als Broome	ASE 116a §19	1668
8. Drumence	HMR Ant. 7	1669
9. Drumans	Religious Survey	1734
10. Drumans	Stewart's Survey 15	1734
11. Drummans	Lendricks Map	1780
12. Drummans	Bnd. Sur. (OSNB) B 17	1830

13. Drumonds	Tithe Applot. 11	1833
14. Drummans "hidden spot"	Rev. Connolly 518	1814
15. Dromáin "small ridge"	J O'D (OSNB) B 17	1831
16. Dromáin "small ridge"	J O'D (OSNB) B 17	1831
17. "the little hills"	Dallat's Ramoan 26	1973
18. 'dromǝns	Local pronunciation	1993

While Dallat has interpreted the form *Drummans* as implying a pl. diminutive of *droim* "ridge" (form 17), early forms indicate the simple pl. *dromanna* "ridges". This form was used first in the later Mid. Irish period (*DIL* sv. *druim(m)*). The English plural suffix appeared unusually early (form 1). The eminences in question are probably those found in the west of the townland at the foot of the western slopes of Knocklayd.

Glebe	An English form	
D 1040		
1. Church	Census 18	1659
2. Glibland	HMR Ant. 7	1669
3. Gleab	Religious Survey	1734
4. Churchfarm, Glebe	Stewart's Survey 1	1734
5. Glebe	Bnd. Sur. (OSNB) B 17	1830
6. 'glib	Local pronunciation	1993

In 1657, there was a "20 acre glebe adjoining the church worth £2 yearly" (*Inq. Par. Ant.* 2). The Ordnance Survey recorded the following in 1835:

> The Rector is supported by his tithes which are only charged on hay and grain of every description. He has got an excellent glebe house and a glebe of 44 acres, 2 roods and 14 perches of excellent arable land (*OSM* xxiv 99).

The glebe house was originally built in 1809 (*Lewis' Top. Dict.* 443).

Gortamaddy or White Hall	*Gort an Mhadaidh*	
D 1041	"field of the dog"	
1. Gorteemaddee	DS (Par. Map) 53	1657c
2. Gortamady	DS (Par. Map) 54	1657c
3. Gorteemadree	DS (Par. Map) 57	1657c
4. Gortamady	Census 18	1659
5. Gortreemddree	BSD 170	1661
6. Gortmadre, ¾ of Novilly called	Lapsed Money Book 156	1663
7. Gorteon Maddry	ASE 116b §19	1668
8. Gortamady	HMR Ant. 7	1669
9. Gartmady	PRONI D2977/3A/2/1/3	1676
10. Gartemaddy	Ballycastle Map	1720c
11. Gortmadie	Religious Survey	1734

12. Gartemaddy	Stewart's Survey 1	1734
13. Gartamady	Stewart's Survey 14	1734
14. Gartamady	C. McG. (OSNB) B 17	1734
15. Gortomaddy	Lendrick Map	1780
16. Gartamady	PRONI D2977/3A/2/1/40	1812
17. Gartamaddy or Whitehall	Bnd. Sur. (OSNB) B 17	1830
18. Gortemaddy	Tithe Applot. 11	1833
19. Gort na Madadh "field of the dogs"	J O'D (OSNB) B 17	1831
20. Gort-a'-mhadaigh "field of the dog"	Joyce iii 373	1913
21. Gortnamaddy "the field of the dog"	Dallat's Ramoan 26	1973
22. 'hwəit hɔːl	Local pronunciation	1993
23. ˌgɔrtə'madi	Local pronunciation	1993

Regarding *gort* "a field" (*Dinneen*), see also **Gortmillish** in Armoy.

Forms 3, 5 and 7 which appear to reflect *madra* "dog" (sometimes "wolf" in place-names; see Price 1949, 169–70; and *ibid.* 1953, 224) come from related sources and are more likely to indicate the copying of a scribal error. *Madadh* is the more usual form in Ulster (O'Rahilly 1932, 240). Joyce has noted that in place-names which feature animals, sometimes "a single animal is put forward to stand for many or all" (*Joyce* iii 11). The consistent lack of lenition of the first consonant of the final element is indicative of the process of anglicization. The Co. Down townland name *Lag an Mhadaidh* (*GÉ* 120) has been anglicized **Legamaddy**, for example. The central *-ee-* in forms 1, 3 and 5 might suggest that the final element in this place-name was the gen. form of the rare surname *Ó Madaidh*, but again, these forms are related and the spellings must be regarded as entirely unreliable.

The English alternative to this Irish place-name only appears in the sources in 1830 but seems to have almost replaced the older form. The name may derive from "a neat gentleman's seat with a small demesne attached and present residence of Mrs Kirkpatrick" of the same name (*OSRNB* sh.8, 2), while Dallat has suggested that the name incorporates the surname White (*Pers. comm.* 04.10.1995).

Gortconny
D 0842

Gort Connaidh
"field of the fire-wood"

1. Gortconnyn	Inq. Ult. (Antrim) §50 Car. I	1635
2. Carneconny	Hib. Reg. Cary	1657c
3. Carnetonny	DS (Par. Map) 57	1657c
4. Kircony	Census 18	1659
5. Carneconny	BSD 170	1661
6. Carnconny	Lapsed Money Book 156	1663
7. Cartconen	Decree of Innocence 440	1663
8. Carnconny, Clune and	ASE 116b §19	1668
9. Kirconny	HMR Ant. 7	1669
10. Gortconey	PRONI D2977/3A/2/1/9A	1693
11. Gartconny	Reg. Deeds Abstracts i §265	1722

12. Gortconie	Religious Survey	1734
13. Gartcony	Stewart's Survey 14	1734
14. Gartaconny	C. McG. (OSNB) B 17	1734
15. Garconny	Lendrick Map	1780
16. Gartconny	Bnd. Sur. (OSNB) B 17	1830
17. Gartconney "rabbit field"; gort-garden, connain-rabbit	Rev. Connolly 518	1814
18. Gort chonaidh "field of the fire-wood"	J O'D (OSNB) B 17	1831
19. Gort a chonnaidh "field of the firewood"	Rev. Magill 17	1923
20. "the field of the firewood"	Dallat's Ramoan 26	1973
21. ˌgo̞rtˈkon̠ːɪ	LASID i xiv	1958
22. ˌgo̞rtˈkɔni	Local pronunciation	1993

The absence of a central definite article militates somewhat against accepting *coinín/coiní* "rabbit" as the final element (both forms were recorded in the late local dialect; see *Antrim Notebooks* i 106 and *Irish of the Glens* 106).

Gort Connaidh "field of the fire-wood" is the most likely origin. Joyce notes other instances of *connadh* "wood; fuel, fire-wood" (*Dinneen*) in place-names, including Cloonconny "meaning fire-wood meadow" in Co. Roscomman (*Joyce* ii 351–2). We may bear in mind however that the final element was the gen. form (*conaigh*) of *conach* "murrain; hydrophobia" (see *DIL* sv.; note also *conach* "elephant hawk moth" (*Dinneen*)). We could also consider that the second element was a personal name. Form 1, which comes from a normally reliable source, suggests the male personal name *Conaing*. This name is a borrowing from Anglo-Saxon *cynyng* "a king" (Ó Corráin & Maguire 1981, 56). We would not expect vocalization of the final [ŋ'] (cf. **Tenaghs**), in an unstressed position, and certainly not as early as c. 1657 (forms 2–3). However, we might account for a loss of the final *n* as being due to its unstressed position. The south Co. Derry townland name *Cúil Sáráin* "Sáran's recess" is standardized as **Coolsaragh** in English. The palatalized *n* was lost in this case sometime between 1663 and 1767 (*PNI* v 118–9). Toner notes the loss of a final *n* in the further names of Islandeady in Co. Mayo and **Ednego** in Co. Down, and suggests the Derry example could be explained as "the result of an omission in writing of the contraction frequently used to represent *n* in early documents" (*ibid.*). The reinterpretation here of the final element as the gen. of *connadh* "firewood", or *coiní* "rabbit" (by analogy with the neighbouring **Gortamaddy**, perhaps), could also be contributing factors. In the absence of more early forms ending in -*n*, however, it is best to regard form 1 as anomalous and base our judgement on later forms.

The *carn*- and *kir*- elements in some early forms indicate some copying of scribal errors. Perhaps place-name elements in the neighbouring townlands of Carnmoon and Carnduff were confused by surveyors. Hogan (*Onom. Goed.* 448) equated references to a *Gort Conaigh* in early Irish sources with this name, but these appear to have referred instead to a monastery in Cremorne barony in Co. Monaghan (*AFM* i 337 n.c).

Kilcreg
D 1240

Cill Chreige
"burial-ground of the rocky hill"

1. Kilkreage	Hib. Reg. Cary	1657c

2. Killkreg	BSD 169	1661
3. Kilireg	Court of Claims §923	1662c
4. Killgeige, the quarter of	Court of Claims §923	1662c
3. Killgregg	Lapsed Money Book 156	1663
4. Killgreege	ASE 116b §19	1668
5. Kilkreagh	Hib. Del. Antrim	1672c
6. Killgregg	Ant. Forfeit.	1700
7. Killcreg, quarter land of	PRONI D2977/3A/2/1/18	1708
8. Killcregg	Ballycastle Map	1720c
9. Killycreg	Religious Survey	1734
10. Killcregg	Stewart's Survey 1	1734
11. Killcreagh	C. McG. (OSNB) B 17	1734
12. Kilcregs	Lendrick Map (OSNB) B 17	1780
13. Kilcreg	Bnd. Sur. (OSNB) B 17	1830
14. Killcraig	Tithe Applot. 13	1833
15. Killecreig	OSM xxiv 113	1838
16. Kilcreg "cell of the rock"; ceall-cell, creg-rock	Rev. Connolly 519	1814
17. Coill creige "wood of the rock"	J O'D (OSNB) B 17	1831
18. Cill craige "church of the rock"	Rev. Magill 17	1923
19. "the church of the rock"	Dallat's Ramoan 26	1973
20. kïlˈkrɛːg	Local pronunciation	1993

The Ordnance Survey recorded the following in 1838:

> On a rocky eminence in Kilcreg, and on the holding of Daniel McBride, there stands an ancient graveyard locally called Killecreig which gives its name to the townland. It contained about a quarter of a rood of ground and was enclosed by a stone and clay fence, and well occupied by graves and rude headstones at a former period, but all now defaced and grown over with whins (*OSM* xxiv 113).

This suggests that *cill* "a burial-ground" formed the first element in this name. The gen. sing. of *creag* "rock/rocky eminence" (see **Craig** in Ballintoy) seems a more likely second element than the gen. pl. (*creag*). We may account for the absence from historical forms of the final syllable as being due to its unstressed position.

Kilrobert
D 1337

Cill Roibeaird
"Robert's burial-ground"

1. Killrobert	Inq. Ult. (Antrim) §100 Car. I	1635
2. Kilrobert	Hib. Reg. Cary	1657c
3. Killirobert	Census 18	1659
4. Kilrobert	BSD 168	1661
5. Kilbrobbert	Lapsed Money Book 156	1663
5. Killrobert	ASE 116a §19	1668
6. Kilrobert	HMR Ant. 6	1669
8. Kilrobert	Hib. Del. Ant.	1672c

7. Killrobt.	PRONI D2977/3A/2/1/6	1681
8. Killrobert	Ant. Forfeit.	1700
9. Killrobert	Stewart's Survey 2	1734
10. Killrobert	C. McG. (OSNB) B 17	1734
11. Killrobert	PRONI D2977/3A/2/1/33A	1737
12. Killrobert	Lendrick Map	1780
13. Kilrobert	Sur. A.E. 54	1782
14. Killrobert	Bnd. Sur. (OSNB) B 17	1830
15. Kilrobert "Robert's burying place"	Rev. Connolly 519	1814
16. Coill Roibeird "Robert's wood"	J O'D (OSNB) B 17	1831
17. ˌkïl'rɑbərt	Local pronunciation	1993

The Ordnance Survey recorded in 1838 that "tradition says that there was an ancient graveyard in Kilrobert, but no traces at present are to be seen" (*OSM* xxiv 116). Reeves noted in 1847 that "it is stated that a small burying ground for infants existed in Killrobert but their places are not now distinguishable, being under cultivation" (*EA* 284). It may thus be tentatively suggested that the first element of this name was originally *cill* "burial-ground", notwithstanding that form 3 could be interpreted as containing a variant form of *coill* (*coillidh*) "wood". The form *cillidh* appears to have been used for the nom. in late local Irish (see Killaleenan in Other Names, Culfeightrin), but it is doubtful whether this would have occurred as early as 1659. However, the *Census* is notorious for scribal errors. See also **Tornarobert** in Armoy.

Magheramore

D 0736

An Machaire Mór

"the large plain"

1. Magherimore	Hib. Reg. Cary	1657c
2. Magremor	Census 19	1659
3. Magherimore	BSD 169	1661
4. Magherimore	Lapsed Money Book 156	1663
5. Magheremore	ASE 116a §19	1668
6. Maghermore	HMR Ant. 6	1669
7. Moherimore	Hib. Del. Antrim	1672c
8. Magheramore	PRONI D2977/3A/2/1/3	1676
9. Magheriemore	Ant. Forfeit.	1700
10. Magheramor, one quarter of	PRONI D2977/3A/2/1/25	1714c
11. Machremore	Religious Survey	1734
12. Macheremore	Stewart's Survey 17	1734
13. Magheramore	Lendrick Map	1780
14. Maghremore	Bnd. Sur. (OSNB) B 17	1830
15. Maghermore	Tithe Applot. 14	1833
16. Magheramore "large field"; maghera-field, mohr-large	Rev. Connolly 519	1814
17. Machaire mór "great plain"	J O'D (OSNB) B 17	1831

18. "the great field"	Dallat's Ramoan 26	1973
19. ˌmɑxərəˈmoːr	Local pronunciation	1993

Machaire has several meanings incuding "plain, flat or lowlying country, field" (*Dinneen*); see also **Magherboy** in Ballintoy. The western part of this townland forms part of an extensive, undulating plain to the west of Knocklayd.

Moyarget Lower,   *Maigh Airgid*
Moyarget Upper   "plain of the silver"
D 0637, 0639

1. Myerget	Hib. Reg. Cary	1657c
2. Moyergitt, Upper Moyergitt	Census 18	1659
3. Myerget	BSD 168	1661
4. Moyargit	Court of Claims §923	1662c
5. Moyargit, the ½ town of	Court of Claims §923	1662c
6. Moyargitt, the halfe towne of	Decree of Innocence 431	1663
7. Moyergitt	Lapsed Money Book 156	1663
8. Myergett	ASE 116a §19	1668
9. Lower Moyargett, Upper Moyargett Down	HMR Ant. 5	1669
10. Myerget	Hib. Del. Antrim	1672c
11. Moyergitt	PRONI D2977/3A/2/1/3	1676
12. Moyergitt	Ant. Forfeit.	1700
13. Murragatt	Religious Survey	1734
14. Moyergitt	Stewart's Survey 17	1734
15. Moyarget	C. McG. (OSNB)B 17	1734
16. Moyergitt	Merchant's Book 5	1751
17. Moyargets	Lendrick Map	1780
18. two Moyargitts	PRONI D2977/3A/2/1/40	1812
19. Moyargit, Lower; Moyargit,	Upper Bnd. Sur. (OSNB) B 17	1830
20. Moyarget (Upper), Moyarget (Lower), Moyarget (Hopkins)	Tithe Applot. 15–6	1833
21. Moyarget "silver field"; Moy-field, argidh-silver	Rev. Connolly 519	1814
22. Magh airgid "silver plain"	J O'D (OSNB) B 17	1831
23. Magh airgid "silver plain"	Rev. Magill 21	1923
24. Magh airgid "plain of the bright river"	Rev. Magill (JDCHS) v 84	1939
25. Maigh Airgid	AGMP 99	1969
26. "the silver plain"	Dallat's Ramoan 26	1973
27. ˌmɔiˈɑrgət	Local pronunciation	1993
28. ˈmïrgət	Local pronunciation	1996

The initial element of these townland names is *maigh*, an oblique form of *magh* "a plain, campus, or field, a level district" (*Dinneen*) which was adopted as the nominative. The second element was probably the gen. sing. of *airgead* "silver", a word which also came to mean "money". *Airgead* has been noted in other place-names including the Donegal townland name *Cruaich an Airgid* (anglicized Croaghanarget; O'Kane 1970, 76) and lake name *Loch an Airgid* (Lough Anarget) "lake of the money/silver" (Hughes 1987, 127), and the Rathlin Island subtownland names of *Sloc an Airgid* "hollow or gully of the money" (in Kinramer South; *Place-Names of Rathlin* 26) and *Cnoc an Airgid* or *Creig an Airgid* "the hill or rock of the silver or money" (in Knockans; *ibid.* 55). The use of *airgead* to denote "(the colour) silver" is attested (in compounds) in O.Ir. literature (*DIL* sv. *argat*) and might also be considered here (forms 22–4, 26).

The townlands of Moyarget Lower and Upper lie to the immediate north of Magheramore. Moyarget has been divided since at least 1659 (form 2).

| **Mullarts** | *Maolaird(?)* | |
| D 1339 | "bare hillock" | |

1. Toward	Hib. Reg. Cary	1657c
2. Towrard	DS (Par. Map) 57	1657c
3. Towrard	BSD 168	1661
4. Towzare	Lapsed Money Book 156	1663
5. Tourard	ASE 116a §19	1668
6. Mullarts	Lendrick Map	1780
7. Mullart	PRONI D2977/3A/2/1/40	1812
8. Mullarts	Bnd. Sur. (OSNB) B 17	1830
9. Mullart	Tithe Applot. 16	1833
10. Mullart "summit"; mulla-summit	Rev. Connolly 529	1814
11. Mullach Airt "Art's summit"	J O'D (OSNB) B 17	1831
12. Mularta "The dwarf elders"	Ó Dubhthaigh 184	1905
13. Mullaigh arda "high summits"	Rev. Magill 21	1923
14. "the place of the elders"	Dallat's Ramoan 26	1973
15. 'molərts	Local pronunciation	1993

Until the late 1600s, this townland was known as *Tuar Ard* "high cattle-field" (see **Tornabodagh** in Culfeightrin regarding the first element). Subsequently it disappeared in the sources, being considered part of Drumavoley or Drumeeny until 1780 (see Carleton 1991, 70–1).

As a palatal *d* has given rise to a *t* in other place-names (cf. **Duncarbit** in Culfeightrin), we may consider *Maolaird* as a possible original form. *Aird* is a feminine form of *ard* "height, hillock; top, high part" (*Ó Dónaill*) but is also a word meaning "promontory" (de hÓir 1965, 86). An elevated spur of land extends noticeably towards the Glenshesk River which forms the eastern boundary of this townland. On the basis of precedent the element *maol* would be more likely to represent the adjective/prefix "bald or bare" than the noun *maol* "rounded summit; hillock, knoll" (*Ó Dónaill* sv.) used in a noun plus noun compound (see Mac Giolla Easpaig 1981). *Maolghort* "bare field" might also be considered as an original form, although this represents a somewhat unusual mix of elements.

O'Reilly lists *mulurt* as a variant of *mulabhúr* "dwarf elder; *sambucus humilis*" (note forms 12 and 14). While this element would appear to represent an unusual origin of a townland name, we may note that the nom. sing. form *draighean* "blackthorn" occurs in two Co.

Antrim townland names which have been anglicized as **Dreen**. McKay suggests that *draighean* was used in a collective sense in these names, meaning "place of blackthorns" (*PNI* iv 200). The Irish forms of the dwarf elder cited in *O'Reilly* do not appear to be listed in any other dictionary, however, and its use in place-names may be otherwise unattested. Modern stress does not support the origins suggested in forms 11 and 13. *Mullach* "summit, height" (form 10) is unlikely to have formed the original place-name unless one accepts severe, and early, degeneration.

The English plural suffix may denote some internal division of the townland. Examples of palatal *d/t* in this position giving rise to an *s* ending in place-names appear to be rare. There is also a townland called **Mullarts** in the nearby parish of Layd (*Census 1851*), which may have a similar origin.

| **Novally** | *An Nuabhaile(?)* | |
| D 0941 | "the new townland" | |

1. Novilly	Hib. Reg. Cary	1657c
2. Movally	Census 18	1659
3. Novilly	BSD 170	1661
4. Moghvalle, the town and lands of	Court of Claims §923	1662c
5. Noaghvalle, the Towne and Land of	Decree of Innocence 431	1663
6. 3/4 of Novilly called Gortmadre	Lapsed Money Book 156	1663
7. Novally	ASE 116b §19	1668
8. Nobilly	HMR Ant. 7	1669
9. Novilly	Hib. Del. Antrim	1672c
10. Novally	PRONI D2977/3A/2/1/7	1676
11. Noullie	Religious Survey	1734
12. Novally	Stewart's Survey 14	1734
13. Novaly	Stewart's Survey 15	1734
14. Novally	C. McG. (OSNB) B 17	1734
15. Novally	Lendrick Map	1780
16. Novally	PRONI D2977/3A/2/1/40	1812
17. Novally	Bnd. Sur. (OSNB) B 17	1830
18. Novally "new town", nho-new	Rev. Connolly 519	1814
19. Nuabhaile "new town"	J O'D (OSNB) B 17	1831
20. "the new townland"	Dallat's Ramoan 26	1973
21. 'noːvəli	Local pronunciation	1993

An Eobhile "the yew tree" reflects the historical forms reasonably well. *Bile* "(scared) tree" (cf. **Toberbilly**) is masculine, but we could assume that the name survived in a calcified dative form. *DIL* (sv. *eó*) translates the somewhat similar compound *éochrann* as "a huge or ancient tree, a yew-tree". However, there are two problems with this form. Mac Giolla Easpaig (1981, 152) has noted that place-names of this noun plus noun compound type, which are probably pre-Christian in age, are generally not used with the definite article, although we might consider that this was adopted at a late stage. More importantly, he does not note any examples in which *bile* was used as an element. *Nuabhile* "new (sacred) tree", while grammatically plausible, is unlikely insofar as *bile* is used of old trees (cf. **Toberbilly**).

As most adjective plus noun compounds are believed to have been coined prior to the 12th century (Mac Giolla Easpaig 1984, 49), we might dismiss forms 18–20, because the use of *baile* "townland" in place-names post-dates this (see **Balleny** in Armoy). However, certain adjectives continued to be used in this position in place-names after the 12th century (cf. **Corvally**). It is possible that this is the only townland name in which *baile* is prefixed by *nua* "new". The *-gh-* in forms 4–5 may indicate the older forms of *nua*, *nuadh/nódh* (cf. **Ballynoe** in Rathlin, and **Tornaroan** in Culfeightrin).

Tavnaghboy	*Tamhnach Bhuí*	
D 1337	"yellow field"	
1. Tamhnach B(h)uidhe	Irish of the Glens 130	1940
2. Tawnaghboy	PRONI D2977/3A/2/1/6	1681
3. Tacoghboy	Religious Survey	1734
4. Taunaghbuey	Stewart's Survey 2	1734
5. Tavnaghbuy	C. McG. (OSNB) B 17	1734
6. Tannaghyboy alias Tannaughtboy	PRONI D2977/3A/2/1/33A	1737
7. Tamnaghbuy	Lendrick Map	1780
8. Tavnaghbuy	Sur. A.E. 54	1782
9. Taunaghbuey	Bnd. Sur. (OSNB) B 17	1830
10. Tamnaghbuoy	Tithe Applot. 18	1833
11. Tamhnach buidhe "yellow field"	J O'D (OSNB) B 17	1831
12. "the yellow grazing field"	Dallat's Ramoan 25	1973
13. tɑvnɑx vʎiə	Irish of the Glens 130	1940
14. ˌtɑvnəˈbɔi	Local pronunciation	1993

Toner notes that in Mod. Ir. *tamhnach* signifies "a grassy upland" or "an arable place in a mountain" (*PNI* v 197–8 sv. **Tamnymartin**), although it probably originally denoted "a clearing". Tavnaghboy is situated on the eastern slopes of Knocklayd. In the last century, it was noted in south Co. Derry that it meant "a cultivated spot in the middle of a wilderness" (and was equated with the Scottish croft) and it appears to have been used there also of places on relatively low, flat land (*ibid.*). It is translated "a cultivated or arable spot in a waste, a green field" by *Dinneen*.

Toberbilly	*Tobar Bile*	
D 0937	"well of the (scared) tree"	
1. Tubberbilly	Hib. Reg. Cary	1657c
2. Toberbilly	Census 19	1659
3. Tubberkilly	BSD 169	1661
4. Tubberbally	Lapsed Money Book 156	1663
5. Tobberbilly	ASE 116a §19	1668
6. Tubberkilly	HMR Ant. 6	1669
7. Tubberbilly	Hib. Del. Antrim	1672c
8. Toberbilly	PRONI D2977/3A/2/1/3	1676
9. Tobberbally	Ant. Forfeit.	1700

10. Toberbilley	Religious Survey	1734
11. Toberbilly	Stewart's Survey 15	1734
12. Toberbilly	C. McG. (OSNB) B 17	1734
13. Toberbilly	Lendrick Map	1780
14. Toberbilly,	Bnd. Sur. (OSNB) B 17	1830
15. Toberbilly "well near the border"; tober-well, billhe-elm	Rev. Connolly 519	1814
16. Tobar bile "well of the old tree"	J O'D (OSNB) B 17	1831
17. Tobar bile "The old tree well"	Ó Dubhthaigh 186	1905
18. Tober bile "well of the old tree"	Rev. Magill 24	1923
19. "the well of the ancient pagan tree"	Dallat's Ramoan 25	1973
20. ˌtobərˈbïli	Local pronunciation	1993

The existence or former existence of a *tobar* "a well, spring" was not alluded to in the *Ordnance Survey Memoirs*. A headstream of the Tow River rises in this townland.

The second element suggested in forms 15–9, the masc. noun *bile* "(large) tree; tree trunk" (*DIL*), has elsewhere been translated as "a sacred or historic tree; a tree, especially in a fort or beside a holy well" (*Dinneen*). *Bile* has been described by Lucas (1963, 16–7) as a tree "which was treated with a certain reverence which, normally, protected [it] from wilful damage". He further added that "individual trees can be grouped into a number of categories, including those associated with inauguration places, with ecclesiastical sites, with individual saints, with funerals and with holy wells" (1963, 16–7). Lucas (*ibid.*, 41) was of the opinion that this townland name indeed referred to some revered tree. It is perhaps noteworthy, in the absence of any recorded tradition associated with this name, that Connolly translated the second element as "elm" (form 15), notwithstanding that his interpretations are often inaccurate. There is another townland called **Toberbilly** in Kilraughts parish, barony of Dunluce Upper (*Census 1851*).

The fem. noun *bile* (earlier *bil*) "rim, border, edge" (*DIL* sv. *bil*) is used most often of vessels and clothes (see *Dinneen* sv.) and it is doubtful whether it was employed in place-names.

Town Parks An English form
D 1141

1. (?)The Castle parke of Ballicastle	DS (Par. Map) 54	1657c
2. (?)The Castle Parke	BSD 170	1661
3. (?)The Castle Parke	Lapsed Money Book 156	1663
4. (?)the castle and park	ASE 116a §19	1668
5. (?)Demesnes of Balycastle	PRONI D2977/3A/2/1/32	1735
6. Townparks	Bnd. Sur. (OSNB) B 17	1830
7. (?)Ballycastle Fields	Tithe Applot. 19	1833
8. təunˈparks	Local pronunciation	1993

In this townland lies the town of Ballycastle, itself a former townland which may originally have been coterminous with Town Parks (see **Ballycastle** in Other Names). The name appears in the sources for the first time in 1830 (form 6), although the divisions referred to in forms 1–4 and 7 appear to have corresponded to some of the modern territory. The modern townland comprises several obsolete divisions including Drumnacross, Drumargy, Gortrumine, Holm, Portbrittas and Stroanshesk, the names of which will be discussed in an article in a forthcoming edition of *Ainm*. **Leland** (see Other Names) possibly represents an anglicized form of an Irish name for another of these former divisions. See also **Dun a Mallaght** in Other Names.

There are some 60 townlands of this name throughout Ireland, including two in Co. Louth which have been gaelicized as *Páirceanna an Bhaile* (*L. Log. Lú* 18).

Turraloskin	*Tuar an Luscáin(?)*	
D 0838	"cattle-field of the small cave"	
1. Torilaskan	Hib. Reg. Cary	1657c
2. Torylaskan	DS (Par. Map) 53	1657c
3. Toriloskan	BSD 169	1661
4. Torrilosscan	Lapsed Money Book 156	1663
5. Torryleskan	ASE 116a §19	1668
6. Terryloskin	HMR Ant. 5	1669
7. Torelaskan	Hib. Del. Antrim	1672c
8. Torryloskan	PRONI D2977/3A/2/1/3	1676
9. Torriloscan	Ant. Forfeit.	1700
10. Torleskan	Religious Survey	1734
11. Turyluskan	Stewart's Survey 15	1734
12. Turryluskan	C. McG. (OSNB) B 17	1734
13. Touralooskin	Lendrick Map	1780
14. Torryloskan	PRONI D2977/3A/2/1/40	1812
15. Turraloskin	Bnd. Sur. (OSNB) B 17	1830
16. Tirrloskan "burnt land", tierra-land, losk-burnt	Rev. Connolly 519	1814
17. Tuar a' loscáin "green field of the burning"	J O'D (OSNB) B 17	1831
18. Tor-a'-loscáin "little hill of the burning"	Joyce iii 595	1913
19. "the hill of the burning"	Dallat's Ramoan 25	1973
20. ˌturəˈlɑskən	Local pronunciation	1993

Tuar "cattle-field; sheep-run; pasture, lea; bleaching-green" (*Ó Dónaill* sv.) is the most likely origin of the first element (see also **Tornabodagh** in Culfeightrin).

The final element may have been a variant form of *lusca* "underground dwelling" (*DIL*), "underground chamber, crypt, vault" (*Ó Dónaill*), or "cave" (*Joyce* iii 493). *Ó Dónaill* lists this as a masculine noun. *DIL* gives the gen. sing. form as *luscan* (*ibid.*), from which a similar nom. form might have developed by back formation. An otherwise unattested diminutive form *luscán* may have been locally current. McCahan (1900(e) 2) noted a cave on the Ramoan coast called *Loskin*; I have noted this name, which is used of Portnakillew, as [ˌðəˈlɔskən] (*Pers. comm.* 12.10.96). The preponderance of anglicized *-an* endings in the forms may indicate Irish *-án* (compare **Doonans** in Armoy and **Glenmakeerin** in Culfeightrin). A cave in the south-east of the townland was thus described in c. 1855:

A subterraneous passage running in a northerly direction for a considerable distance. It opens on the road from Ballycastle to Armoy. The entrance is about 2 feet broad and 3 feet high. A portion of this cave has been explored, and a number of chambers discovered therein. Some bone[s] supposed to be human and pieces of old metal were also found in it. Nothing is known locally relating to its use (*OSRNB* sh.8, 3).

O'Donovan's form *Tuar an Loisceáin* (16) may also be considered. *Loisceán* is a variant of *loiscreán* "fire for singeing corn; singed corn" (*Ó Dónaill*) but the meaning "burnt place/land" seems possible. A palatal *s* before *c* is often anglicized as *s* (see **Glenshesk** in Other Names). Genitive forms of *loscann* "frog" seem unlikely.

White Hall	An English form
or Gortamaddy	
D 1041	

See **Gortamaddy**.

OTHER NAMES

Altananam　　　　　　　　　*Allt an Anama*
D 1140　　　　　　　　　　　　"steep glen of the soul"

1. Altinamine	Hib. Reg. Cary	1657c
2. Alltinamine	BSD 169	1661
3. Altmamine	Lapsed Money Book 156	1663
4. Altinanie	ASE 116b §19	1668
5. Altunanum	HMR Ant 8	1669
6. Allnanum	PRONI D2977/3A/2/1/22	1709
7. Altenam	Stewart's Survey 1	1734
8. Altenanan	Stewart's Survey 2	1734
9. Altnanum	PRONI D2977/3A/2/1/32	1735
10. Altnanum	Merchant's Book 32	1752
11. Altinamin	Lendrick Map	1780
12. Altananine	PRONI D2977/3A/2/1/40	1812
13. Altenanum	Tithe Applot. 12	1833
14. Altananam	OSRNB sh.8, 3	1855c
15. "valley of the soul"	OSRNB sh.8, 3	1855c
16. "the height of the ghosts"	Dallat's Ramoan 25	1973

"The name of a subdivision of the townland of Ballywillin [*sic*], the principal part of which is in the occupation of Mr. John McCaughen. The name signifies the valley of the soul, but nothing is locally known as to how it originated" (*OSRNB* sh.8, 3). This former land division corresponded with "the northern part" of Drumawillin (Carleton 1991, 71 n.14).

Joyce was puzzled by the occurrence of *anam* "soul" in place-names: "Some believe that places with such names were bequeathed to some church or monastery for the soul's health of the donor [*sic*] or of some relative; while others again assert that the names originated in ghosts" (*Joyce* ii 466). He gives several examples of its occurrence in townland names, including **Killananima** in Leitrim and **Annaghananam** in Tyrone (*ibid.* 466–7).

Ballinanima (Massy) townland in Co. Limerick has the standard Irish form *Baile an Anama (Massy)* which has been translated "the town of the soul?" (Ó Maolfabhail 1990, 10–11).
    Regarding *allt* see **Altagore** in Culfeightrin.

Ballycastle
D 1241

Baile Chaisleáin
"townland of the castle"

1. the town of Somhairle, which is named Baile Caishlein	MacDonnells Antrim 134	1565
2. the town of Somhairle, Baile Caislein	MacDonnells Antrim 135	1565
3. mbun abhann Chnuic lán-álainn Leathaid, i	SMMD II, 43	1638c
4. Bhaile an Chaisleáin, de	Ultach 60:10, 7	1904
5. Baile an Chaisleáin	Claidheamh Soluis 29 Lún., L.5	1908
6. mBaile an Chaisleáin, i	Claidheamh Soluis 5 Fea., L.6	1910
7. Baile an Chaisleáin, ag	Claidheamh Soluis 9 Iúl, L.3	1910
8. Boile Chaislein	Antrim Notebooks i 108	1925c
9. Baile an Chaisil	Ultach 12:5, 2	1935
10. Baile'n Chaisleáin	Ultach 12:5, 13	1935
11. Baile Chaislein	Irish of the Glens 100	1940
12. Baile Chaisteal, in	Irish of Rathlin 135	1942
13. Baile an Chaisteil	Irish of Rathlin 162	1942
14. Baile Chaislein	Ultach 32:4, 2	1955
15. Marketown	MacDonnells Antrim 48	1551
16. (?)Nyw Castell in the Root, Sanhirly Boy his towne (sic)	MacDonnells Antrim 137	1565c
17. Market Town in the Glynns	CSP Ire. 355	1567
18. Market Town	CSP Ire. 378	1568
19. Market town, the Abbey called the	CSP Ire. 363	1568
20. Markettowne	Nowel's Ire. (1)	1570c
21. Markettown	Mercator's Ire.	1595
22. the Market Town or village called Dunynie and Ballycaslen	PRONI D2977/3A/2/1/2	1611
23. Baleecastle	CSP Ire. 1647–60 Addenda 163	1630
24. Ballycastle	Inq. Ult. (Antrim) §42 Car. I	1635
25. Ballycastill	Inq. Ult. (Antrim) §50 Car. I	1635
26. Duneneny and Ballycastle, markettownes of	Inq. Ult. (Antrim) §64 Car. I	1635
27. Ballicastle, Manor and Lordship of MacDonnells	Antrim 437	1637
28. Bally Castle, lordship of	Hill's Stewarts 150	1637
29. Bally Castell	Hill's Stewarts 86	1643
30. Ballycastle	Hickson's Ire. i 280	1652
31. Ballycastle	Hill's Stewarts 89	1652
32. Ballycastell	Hill's Stewarts 88–9	1652
33. Ballycastle	Civ. Surv. x §60	1655
34. Ballycastle village	Inq. Par. Ant. 2	1657

35. Ballicastle, The Castle parke of	DS (Par. Map) 54	1657c
36. Ballycastle	Census 18	1659
37. Ballycastle	BSD 170	1661
38. Ballicastle	Court of Claims §923	1662c
39. (?)Margie, the towne called	Decree of Innocence 431	1663
40. Ballicastle, Manor and Lordship of	Decree of Innocence 437	1663
41. Ballycastle, Tenements of	Lapsed Money Book 156	1663
42. Ballycastle, the lordship of	CSP Ire. 59, 67	1666
43. Ballycastle, ye lordship of	ASE 116a §19	1668
44. Ballycastle	HMR Ant. 5	1669
45. Ballycastle, Lordship of	PRONI D2977/3A/2/10/1	1678
46. Ballycastle	PRONI D2977/3A/2/1/4	1681
47. Bally Castle	Dobbs' Desc. Antrim 384, 386	1683
48. Ballycastle and Carntillagh, Mills of	PRONI D2977/3A/2/1/9A	1693
49. Ballycastle, The Manor of	PRONI D2977/3A/2/14/1	1696
50. Ballycastle	Irish Jacobites 55 §38v	1699
51. Ballycastle "Castletown"	Rev. Connolly 518	1814
52. Baile an chaislein "town of the castle"	J O'D (OSNB) B 17	1830
53. Ballycashlain "Castletown"	Lewis' Top. Dict. 461	1837
54. Baile Caiseil "Castle-town"	Ó Dubhthaigh 131	1905
55. Baile an Chaisleáin	Post-Sheanchas 28	1905
56. Baile caislein "town of the castle"	Rev. Magill 6	1923
57. "the town of the castle"	Dallat's Ramoan 25	1973
58. Baile an Chaistil	Ultach 50:8, 7	1973
59. Baile an Chaistil	GÉ 9	1989
60. bɔl'ə xwis'l'ən, xλ^js'l'ən	Irish of the Glens 19	1940
61. bɔl'ə xɛs'l'ən, xɪs'l'ən	Irish of the Glens 100	1940
62. əm bal'ə'xaʃt'ɛl	Irish of Rathlin 135	1942
63. ˌbali'kasəl	Local pronunciation	1993

Baile Caistéil "townland of the castle" reflects the majority of anglicized historical variants reasonably well and resembles the forms used in Rathlin earlier this century (forms 12–3). Holmer's form however (form 11), which featured an aspirated *c* due to the repeated use of the name in oblique cases, resembles the earliest historical variants (forms 1 and 2). Thus it appears that English surveyors substituted *caisleán* with *castle*. Ó Maolfabhail has pointed out that forms 1 and 2, taken from a letter written by Shane O'Neill or by his secretary Gearóid Flemynge, in Latin, may or may not reflect a local or personal dialect, or literary or even personal standardization; he therefore regards them as very dubious forms (*Ó Maolfabhail T re G* 370). However, historical forms of other local place-names indicate that *caisleán* was current in the early 1600s; see **Clare**, for example. There are other townlands called Ballycastle in counties Derry, Down, Mayo and Cork; the Mayo name derives from *Baile an Chaisil* (*GÉ* 11). There are, in addition, several places called Castletown scattered throughout the country, whose Irish form is normally *Baile an Chaisleáin* (*ibid.* 11–2).

Although forms 15 and 17–21 seem to be early English variants reflecting an important function of the town, Moran states that this name "was a corruption of the earlier name Mairge-town" (*Mon. Hib.* 4 n.9); the Margy River enters the sea to the immediate east of Ballycastle (see **Bonamargy** in Culfeightrin, and Ballycastle Bay in Other Names, Culfeightrin). It may indicate a translation of **Dunineny**, however.

The *Ordnance Survey Memoirs* recorded in 1831 that the castle in the modern name is:

> an ancient castle of the Mac Donnells, the ruins of which are to be seen near the church. It was erected in 1609 by Randall, Earl of Antrim, who was directed by James I to raise 'faire castels' at reasonable distances on his vast estates in this country . . . [that] the surrounding country might be the more speedily civilized and reduced to obedience. When Lord Antrim made Ballymagarry Castle his principal residence, Ballycastle was suffered to fall into decay. Very little of the castle now remains, the gable with a machicolated turret at the corner, close to the churchyard wall, being the only part now standing (*OSM* xxiv 90).

The remains of this castle were removed in 1853 (*OSRNB* sh.8, 3) or c. 1854 (Bigger 1901, 9; see also Jope 1951, 45). However, forms 1 and 2 (note also form 16), which date to 1565, suggest that some other castle inspired the name, and we may also note that Flanagan and Flanagan (1994, 41) suggest the element *caisleán* is used specifically of medieval and post-medieval castles. Dunineny is an obvious possibility (note especially form 22; see also **Dunineny Castle**, Other Names). Hill, however, suggests that Randal MacDonnell's castle occupied the site of an earlier castle built by the MacDonnells, called *Nyw Castell* (16) "which was thus distinguished from the very *old* structure on Dunanynie" (*MacDonnells Antrim* 137 n.53). It is not clear whether this earlier castle was built by Somhairle Buí MacDonnell (1505c-1589), who is referred to in forms 1, 2 and 16 (*ibid.* 121, 182; see also McCahan 1900(h)). Somhairle's residence, and place of death, was Dunineny Castle (*MacDonnells Antrim ibid.*).

Ballycastle lies almost entirely within the modern townland of Town Parks. The townland to which the name Ballycastle originally referred may have been coterminous with the modern townland of Town Parks, and comprised several obsolete divisions (see **Town Parks**), the names of which will be discussed in an article in a forthcoming edition of *Ainm*. In 1734, Ballycastle referred to a small division lying along the western banks of the Margy River (*Stewart's Survey* 1).

Bellennan　　　　　　　　　*Baile Uí Éanáin(?)*
D 0939　　　　　　　　　　　　"Heenan's townland"

1. Ballienan	DS (Par. Map) 54	1657c
2. Ballyennan	BSD 167	1661
3. Ballyonan	Lapsed Money Book 156	1663
4. Ballyennam	ASE 116a §19	1668
5. Ballinan	Hib. Del. Antrim	1672c
6. Bellennan	OSRNB sh.8, 2	1855c
7. ˌbɑlˈɛnən	Local pronunciation	1993

"A small farm village [in Carneatly] of two dwellings and out offices and in the occupation of John McNeile and Frances Todd" (*OSRNB* sh.8, 2).

Ó hEanáin/Ó hEidhneáin is a "scattered surname" (Woulfe 1923, 562, 565) but has been noted in Co. Down (MacLysaght 1985, 152). The shortening of stressed long vowels has been noted elsewhere (see **Balleny** in Armoy). *Éanán*, the male personal name on which the surname is based, is also a possible element. The surname *Ó hAnnáin* imay also be a possible second element in this name. This surname is usually anglicized as Hannan and in east Ulster is probably of Scottish origin (see MacLysaght 1985, 145 and Black 1945, 341–2). The raising of the [a] to [ɛ] in modern pronunciation might be explained as due to its proximity to *uí*, but might also indicate that a variant form of the name, *Ó hEannáin*, was used. We might also consider *Annán/Eannán*, the personal name from which the surname is derived. (In northern counties, surnames more commonly qualify *baile* than personal names).

Black Knowe	A Scots form	
D 0839		
1. Black Knowe	OSRNB sh.8, 2	1855c

"A small farm village of 3 dwellings [in Coolkenny], two of them being in the occupation of John Hayes and Archb. McAlister. It is so called from its being built upon what was formerly a series of black hillocks, called in the Scottish dialects *knowe*. Most of the hillocks are now reclaimed, but the village still retains the name which their original waste state suggested" (*OSRNB* sh.8, 2). *Knowe* is a "Scottish form of English *knoll*, a hillock, mound; in folklore often associated with fairies" (*Scot. Nat. Dict.*).

Capplecarry	*An Capall Carrach*	
D 1043	"the rock encrusted mare"	
1. Capplecarry	OSRNB sh.4, 1	1855c
2. Capall Carrach "the mangy horse"	OSRNB sh.4, 1	1855c
3. ˌkapəl'kari	Local pronunciation	1993

An Capall Carrach "the rock encrusted mare" seems to be the original form of this name. Perhaps the final [i] sound in modern forms developed by analogy with the barony name (see also **Castle Carra** in Culfeightrin). It refers to "a precipitous cliff with rugged shelving and projecting rocks [in Carnmoon]. The name is applied at times to the small bay underneath, as well as to the cliff, but it appears to be more particularly applied to the cliff. The name is supposed to have originated in the fanciful comparison of some of the projecting rocks to a mangy horse" (*OSRNB* sh.4, 1). Cappulcorragh, a townland name in Co. Mayo, may be of similar origin (*Census 1851*). See also **Legahapple Bridge** in Other Names, Armoy.

Carn an Truagh	Of uncertain origin	
D 1136		
1. (?)Lethead, Dun mBaedan a	Descendants Ir 322 §4	1200c
2. Carn-an-Tenagh	OSM xxiv 8	1838
3. Carn-na-Truagh	PSAMNI 11	1940
4. Cairn an Truagh "hillock of the three"	Hamilton's Letters 243	1822

5. Cairn-an-truagh "the hillock of the three"	OSM xxiv 86	1831
6. Carn an Thruir "the cairn of the three"	OSM xxiv 118	1838
7. ˌkɑrnəˈtruəx	Local pronunciation	1993
8. ðəˈkern	Local pronunciation	1996

The name of this cairn may be obsolete. The death of the three people alluded to in the discussion of **Knocklayd** (see Other Names, Armoy) was the inspiration for the original form suggested in forms 4 and 6: *Carn an Triúir* "cairn of the three" was reputedly built by each person who reached this spot "taking a stone and adding to it" (*OSM* xxiv 118; see also McCahan 1900(f), and *PSAMNI* 11). The few historical variants available do not reflect such an origin, however. The angl. forms may imply *Carn na Trua* "cairn of the pity", earlier *Carn na Truaighe/Truagha*, but the English *-gh* endings seem more likely to indicate Irish *-ch*, [x]. One might consider *Carn an Troch* "cairn of the condemned man" (see *Dinneen* sv. *trú*), but again, this does not correspond satisfactorily to the historical forms available.

Possible original forms include *Carn an Triúcha* "cairn of the cantred". The final element in this form is the gen. sing. of *triúcha* "Of a teritorial division, political unit, freq. transl. *cantred, barony*" (*DIL* sv. *tricha cét*) although we could also consider that the gen. pl. form *triúch* was used (see also Hogan 1929 regarding this element). In an early 17th-century text (*C. Conghail Cláir.* 100) the hero's lover is offered a *triocha céd* or cantred in north Antrim which the editor suggests would stretch "along the Antrim coast from Knocklayd to Dunseverick", but whether there is a link between this reference and the name of the cairn is not clear. *Carn na dTnúthach* "carn of the envious people" may be a further possible original form. However, the lack of satisfactory historical evidence prohibits conclusive interpretation.

Regarding form 1, see **Knocklayd** in Other Names, Armoy. The borders of 10 townlands radiate from this point.

Carnsaggart   *Carn Sagairt*
D 0842   "cairn of the priest"

1. Carnsegart	OSM xxiv 104	1838
2. Cairn Saggardh "priests heap"	Rev. Connolly 500	1814
3. Carn Sagairt "the priest's carn or heap"	J O'D (OSNB) B 17	1831
4. Carnsaggart "the Priest's Cairn"	O'Laverty iv 402	1887
5. Carn sagairt "The cairn of the priest"	Ó Dubhthaigh 134	1905
6. "the carn of the priest"	Dallat's Ramoan 25	1973
7. ˌkɑrnˈsɑgərt	Local pronunciation	1993

The Ordnance Survey recorded the following in 1838:

In Gortconny and on the holding of James Kirkpatrick and contiguous to the road from Ballintoy to Ballycastle, there stands a rocky eminence locally called Carnsegart or 'the priest's cairn'. This hill is said to have been formerly a seat of Roman Catholic worship, and subsequently the scene of a severe battle in which one or more priests were killed (*OSM* xxiv 103–4).

A cairn of stones to commemorate the murder was destroyed in c. 1798 "to build fences . . . [where upon] an altar, composed of a long flat stone supported by small columns underneath [was discovered] . . . About 1 furlong west of it stood an ancient spring locally called the Priest's Well, but it is at present closed up with stones" (*ibid.*). Regarding the removal of the altar see *ibid.*

Carn Sagart "cairn of the priests" might also be considered. The absence of a definite article in this name seems unusual, although we might postulate that it was recently lost through elision. We might also consider that the name represents a reinterpretation of an original name which featured, for example, a personal name. This is difficult to do in the absence of historical forms, however.

Carrickmannon	*Carraig Mhanann*	
D 0944	"*Manann's* rock"	
1. Carraic (Creig) Mhanannain	Irish of the Glens 121	1940
2. (?)Baptistes rock	Boazio's Map (BM)	1599
3. Carrickmannon Rock	Lendrick Map	1780
4. (?)Carrick ronan B.	Dubourdieu Map	1812
5. Craig Mananan, a large rock called	OSM xxiv 34	1838
6. Carrickmannanon	OSRNB sh.4, 1	1855c
7. Carrickmannanan "the rock of Mannanan"	O'Laverty iv 340	1887
8. kurik′ (kreg′) əvɑnɑn	Irish of the Glens 121	1940
9. ˌkarəgˈmɑnən	Local pronunciation	1993
10. ˌðə carək ˈrok (sic)	Local pronunciation	1996

The second element of this name appears to derive from *Manannán* "name of the Irish sea-god" (*DIL*) and "otherworld lord and mythical mariner" (Ó hÓgáin 1990, 286), rather than *meannán* "kid goat; pointed rock" (*Ó Dónaill sv.*). It is possible forms 3–4, 8 and 9 indicate the loss by haplology of a final syllable and that *Carraig Mhanannáin* constituted the earlier Irish form. It is also possible, however, that forms 1, 5 and 6 have been somewhat standardized. *Dinneen* (sv. *oileán*) gives *Oileán Mhanann(áin)* as the Irish name for the Isle of Man. It was recorded in 1838 that:

[this rock] is frequently hidden by the rise of the tide and so dangerous to all vessels coming in contact with it that all mariners coming along the north east coast of Antrim exert all their skill to evade it; for it is not only considered dangerous as other rocks but even subject to some enchantments which all who know or hear of it dread. The aforesaid Mananan, to whose name it is dedicated, is said to have drownded himself here, and he being one of the most extaordinary magicians ever to have frequented the north east coast. Even after his death, he was believed by the old Irish here to prosecute his magic tricks about the rocks here alluded to . . . (*OSM* xxiv 34).

It lies approximately .75 km off the coast from Kinbane or White Head.

Doon
D 1043

Dún Mhic Grioghair
"MacGreer's fort"

1. Dunmaccrue Fort	Hib. Reg. Cary	1657c
2. Drumnacrewre, a fforte called	DS (Par. Map) 54	1657c
3. Dunmacure Fort	Hib. Del. Antrim	1672c
4. Duinnagregor Castle	OSM xxiv 119	1838
5. Doon	OSRNB sh.4, 1	1855c
6. Doney Gregor Head	OSRNB sh.4, 1	1855c
7. Dun, a rock	OSRNB sh.4, 1	1855c
8. dun	Local pronunciation	1993

"Duinnagregor is a promontory or headland situated in Carnduff, and holding of Archy Boyd, and projecting several yards into the sea . . . It was also the seat of an ancient castle or fortress . . . which was dedicated to the founder's name . . . there is not a vestige at present to be seen, though it is said to have been of considerable size" (*OSM* xxiv 119).

Forms 1–3 come from related sources and probably contain some copying of scribal errors. However, they may suggest that *dún* "fort; promontory fort" (Ó Dónaill) was qualified by a form of the surname MacGregor. Bell (1988, 84 sv. Greer) has noted that MacGregor is a rare name in Ulster. The MacGregor clan was outlawed in Scotland in 1603, and many of the clan adopted new surnames, of which Greer has been numerous in North Ulster since the Plantation (MacLysaght 1985, 136). There was a George McGreyar living in Rathlin in 1669 (*HMR Ant.* 11). Some late forms (4 and 6) resemble *Dún Mhic Griogair*. The place-name has since been shortened to *Doon*.

Dun a Mallaght
D 1241

Dún na Mallacht
"fort of the curses"

1. (?)Dromnemallaght	Inq. Ult. (Antrim) §101 Car.I	1635
2. Dunamollaght	Ballycastle Map [1720c]	1720c
3. Dunamollaght	Stewart's Survey 1	1734
4. Dunmallacht	Merchant's Book 17	1752
5. Dunmalet	Lendrick Map	1780
6. Drumamollaght	PRONI D2977/3A/2/1/3A	1752
7. (?)Drumnamaight	Tithe Applot. 9	1833
8. Dunnamallachd, "the fort of the curse"	O'Laverty iv 417	1887
9. Dún Mallacht, "fort of the curses"	Ó Dubhthaigh 137	1905
10. (?)Drom-na-mallaght, "the ridge of the curse"	Antrim Place Names 84	1913
11. Dún a Mallacht, "fort of the curse"	Rev. Magill 15	1923
12. "the fort of the curse"	Dallat's Ramoan 25	1973

13. ˌdọnəˈmaləxt	Local pronunciation	1996
14. ˌdọnəˈmalət	Local pronunciation	1996

This fort in Town Parks was supposedly named "in consequence of some executions said to have taken place there during the Irish rebellions of the country" (*OSM* xxiv 122). O'Laverty describes this site as "an earthen mound which seems originally to have been circular, about 11 yards in diameter on the top and rising from 10 to 30 feet above the surface of the ground on which it stands. The fine old mound was much injured by Hugh Boyd, Esq., M.P., who erected on its summit a 'Tea House' which has long since disappeared" (*O'Laverty* iv 417–8). *Dún na Mallachta* "fort of the curse", with the loss of the final unstressed vowel, may also be a possibility. Joyce noted several place-names containing *mallacht* (*Joyce* ii 479–80). **Drumnamallaght** townland, for example, is in Ballymoney parish.

Dunineny Castle
D 1142

A hybrid form

1. Dún an Aonuigh	LCABuidhe 247 §113	1645c
2. (?)Druim an Aonaigh	Ultach 5:3, 7	1928
3. Donanany, the fort of	MacDonnells Antrim 170	1584
4. fort Donanynie	O'Laverty iv 400–1	1584
5. Donanany, the ward of	O'Laverty iv 401	1584
6. Dunanerry Ca.	Ulster Map [1590c]	1590c
7. Dunannaney	Jobson's Ulster (TCD)	1590c
8. Don Onene	Jobson's Ulster (TCD)	1590c
9. Donaneroni Ca	Boazio's Map (BM)	1599
10. Donanewny	Treatise on Ire. (NLI) 11	1599c
11. Dunanene	Bartlett Maps (Esch. Co. Maps) 1	1603
12. Dunynie, the fort called	PRONI D2977/3A/2/1/1A	1605
13. Dunanenye	Norden's Map	1610
14. Dunanerony	Speed's Antrim & Down	1610
15. Dunanerony	Speed's Ireland	1610
16. Dononerony	Speed's Ulster	1610
17. the Market Town or village called Dunynie and Ballycaslen	PRONI D2977/3A/2/1/2	1611
18. Donaneny, Downenenye	Ulst. Roll Gaol Deliv. 265	1613
19. Duneneny and Ballycastle, markettownes of	Inq. Ult. (Antrim) §64 Car.I	1635
20. Dunynyny, Neale de	Inq. Ult. (Antrim) §117 Car.I	1637
21. Dunininy, the fourth of	Court of Claims §923	1662c
21. Dunaniny	Stewart's Survey	1734
22. (?)Dunaine	PRONI D2977/3A/2/1/40	1812
23. Duninneeny	Hamilton's Letters 243	1822
24. Duninneeny "The castle on the height"	Rev. Connolly 506	1814
25. Dun-an-aenaighe "the fort of the assembly or fair"	O'Laverty iv 399	1887

270

26. Dún an Aonaigh "fort of the fair"	Rev. Magill 13	1923
27. ˌdɔnəniniˈkasəl	Local pronunciation	1993
28. ˌduniniˈkasəl	Local pronunciation	1996

Dún an Aonaigh "fort of the fair" (form 1) is the original form. The ruins of a castle on this site were traditionally believed to have been the residence of Alexander MacDonnell (*MacDonnells Antrim* 38), who died in 1513 (*ibid.* 36). It has been suggested that the castle was abandoned shortly after the death of Somhairle Buí MacDonnell in the late 1500s (*PSAMNI* 7). Regarding the castle, see also *OSM* xxiv 119 and 122–3 and *O'Laverty* iv 399–401. See also under **Ballycastle**.

Glenshesk,	*Gleann Seisc*	
Glenshesk Bridge,	"barren valley"	
Glenshesk River		
D 1437, 1436, 1340		

1. ghlenna seisg, Maidhm	ALC ii 388	1565
2. Gleann-Seisg	Ultach 4:2, 3	1927
3. nGleann Seisg, i	Ultach 4:4, 3	1927
4. Glinne Seisg, 'Ac Giolla Bhrighide	Ultach 4:6, 7	1927
5. nGleann Seisg, i	Ultach 5:3, 6	1928
6. (?)Bunglenseske	Inq. Ult. (Antrim) §98 Car. I	1635
7. Glanshesk River	Hib. Reg. Cary	1657c
8. The River Glensheske	Hib. Reg. Cary	1657c
9. River of Glensheisk	DS (Par. Map) 55	1657c
10. Balleglinteske	Court of Claims §923	1662c
11. Balleglintesske	Court of Claims §923	1662c
12. Balleghlintesk, the towneland called	Decree of Innocence 431	1663
13. Glensheske	HMR Ant. 10	1669
14. Glenshesk flu	Hib. Del. Antrim	1672c
15. Glensheck R	Ire. Map	1711
16. Glenshesk, the river of	Grand Jury Pres. (Ant.) 44	1713
17. Glenshesk River	Taylor and Skinner 273	1777
18. Glenshesk river	Lendrick Map	1780
19. Glenshy River	Dubourdieu Map	1812
20. Glenshesk	PRONI D2977/3A/2/1/40	1812
21. Glenshesk river	OSRNB sh.9, 2	1855c
22. Glenshesk Bridge	OSRNB sh.9, 2	1855c
23. Gleann Seisce "valley of the sedge"	J O'D (OSNB) B 24 B 37	1831
24. Gleann Seisg "the sedgy glen"	Ó Dubhthaigh 180	1905
25. Gleann Seisg	Alasdair Mac Colla 74	1914
26. glɛnˈʃɛsk	Local pronunciation	1993

While most of the historical forms of the valley name reflect O'Donovan's interpretation (form 23), form 1 indicates that the adj. *seasc* "barren, unfruitful" qualified the masc. form of *gleann*. Form 4 suggests that *gleann* latterly took a fem. form locally, although the reliability of Irish forms from early editions of *An tUltach* is in doubt (see also below). Irish *ea* was pronounced [ɛ] before *s* locally (cf. **Craigban** in Culfeigthrin), but we might also consider that the adj. was in the variant form *seisc* (see Ó Dónaill sv.), as Irish [ʃ] before [k] is often anglicized as *s* rather than *sh* (see **Prolusk** in Ballintoy). The somewhat similar Co. Down townland name of **Drumsesk** appears to derive from *Droim Seasc* "barren ridge" (*PNI* ii 144).

Form 6 features the first element *bun* "bottom of river or valley (etc.)", suggesting the place-name *Bun Ghleann Seisc/Bun Gleanna Seisc* "bottom of the barren valley" was formerly current (see also **Ballyberidagh North** in Culfeightrin). Several possible original Irish forms could be postulated for the former townland alluded to in forms 10–2, including *Baile Ghleann tSeisc* "townland of the barren valley"; there may have been a variant form of Glenshesk current in which *gleann* (gen. *glinne*) was feminine. Notwithstanding that a tall *s* is often mistranscribed as a *t*, it is also possible that this form represents a mistranscription of *Balleghlintesh*, and that it referred instead to **Glentaisie** (see below). The territory alluded to in form 13 covered the seven townlands of Broughmore, Coolaveely, Craigban, Drumacullin, Duncarbit, Greenan and Tenaghs (Carleton 1991, 66).

The river marks the greater part of the boundary between the parishes of Culfeightrin and Ramoan, and was described in *OSRNB* (sh.9, 2) as follows: "A mountain river with rapid current and running through several townlands . . . It is named from the glen through which it runs. It enters the sea at Ballycastle Quays but is only called Glenshesk River as far north as Drumahaman Bridge, hence it is called Margy River". In c. 1855, the bridge was described as "a new stone bridge with one arch over the Glenshesk River, and on the new road from Ballycastle to Breen" (*OSRNB ibid.*). It connects the townlands of Clare Mountain in Ramoan and Drumacullin in Culfeightrin. See also **Clare Mountain**, which may have been named from the bridge.

The event referred to in form 1 is the same as that in form 1 of **Glentaisie**.

Glentaisie	*Gleann Taise*		
D 1039	*"Taise*'s valley(?)"		
1. glinne taisi, san maidhm sin	AFM v 1606	1565	
2. (?) Balleghlintesk, the towneland called	Decree of Innocence 431	1663	
3. Gleann Taise "The glen of 'Taise'"	Ó Dubhthaigh 180	1905	
4. ˌglɛnˈteːsi	Local pronunciation	1993	

Dallat (1973, 25) has recorded that Taisie was the name of a princess who lived in a palace in Broom More (see also *O'Laverty* iv 384). This figure is called *Taisi Thaoibhgheal* in a text written c. 1600 in which she was reputed to have lived somewhere near here in a residence called *Dún Taisi* (*C. Congháil Cláir.* 100). Regarding this story which is located locally, see *ibid.*; for a brief and rough translation into English, see *MacDonnells Antrim* 393–404. MacSweeny describes the name Taisi Thaoibhgheal as "a common one in Irish story" (*C. Congháil Cláir.* 201). *Taisi* would be standardized as *Taise* in Mod. Ir.

The lack of historical forms hampers interpretation. It seems possible however that the second element was *taise* "wraith, apparition, ghost; remains, relics; ruins" (*Ó Dónaill* sv.), its gen. pl. (*taisí*), or *taise* "dampness, moistness" (*ibid.*), and that the name was reinterpreted as a female personal name. We might also consider that the second element records the gen. form of a name for the river now called the **Tow River**, and for which we could postulate the nom. form *An Tais*, although this is highly speculative.

Glentaisie may be something of a resurrected place-name. It does not appear in any 19th-century Ordnance Survey literature, and we would not have expected Irish *ai* to be raised and lengthened to [eː]. Modern pronunciation appears to be based on the English spelling. This valley has also been called *Glentow* (see, for example, McCahan 1900(f)), but this may represent a recently constructed name (see **Tow River**). The event alluded to in form 1 is the defeat by Shane O'Neill's army of MacDonnell forces.

Grey Stone, The	An English form	
D 0740		

This is in Moyarget Upper. The Ordnance Survey noted a standing stone of this name in Carnlelis in Ballintoy (*OSM* xxiv 27).

Island, The	An English form(?)	
D 0836		

1. The Island	OSRNB sh.8, 2	1855c
2. The Isle	OSRNB sh.8, 2	1855c
3. The Isle of Magheramore	OSRNB sh.8, 2	1855c
4. ðəˈailənd	Local pronunciation	1993

"A small compact village [in Magheramore] of farm houses on either side of the old road from Ballycastle to Armoy. It was so called from its being nearly detatched by bog from the remainder of the townland . . . This village is often called 'The Isle', and 'The Isle of Magheramore'" (*OSRNB* sh.8, 2). Regarding the element *island* in place-names, which is often translated from Irish *oileán*, see **Island Macallan** in Ballintoy. See also **Annagh** in *PNI* v 72.

Kanestown	An English form	
D 0638		

1. ˈkenstọn	Local pronunciation	1996

Kane is but one anglicized variant of *Ó Catháin*, "a leading sept in Ulster up to the time of the Plantation" associated especially with north Co. Derry and north-west Co. Antrim (MacLysaght 1985, 170; see also, for example, Mullin & Mullan 1966 *passim*). There were people of this surname in Ballintoy, Ballyberidagh, Glenshesk and Rathlin in 1669 (*HMR Ant.* 4, 10–1). Roger O'Cahan was one of 15 "owners of lands" in Culfeightrin parish in 1660 (*MacDonnells Antrim* 466). See also *PRONI D2977/3A/2/11/1, ibid. /3/2A,* 1 and *ibid. /23/1*.

There are still Kanes living in this hamlet (*Pers. comm.* 26.2.94), which is in Moyarget Upper.

Kilcrue Cross   A hybrid form
D 0938

1. Killnacrue	EA 386	1847
2. Kilcrue	OSRNB sh.8, 2	1855c
3. Kille Acrue, or "the horseshoe graveyard"	OSM xxiv 104	1838
4. ˌkïlkruːˈkrɔs	Local pronunciation	1993

The Ordnance Survey recorded the following in 1838:

> In Turraloskin and holding of Samuel Hill, and situated in a valley about 1 furlong west of the old road leading from Ballycastle to Ballymoney, there stands the site of an ancient graveyard locally called Kille Acrue or the 'horseshoe graveyard'. It contained about 1 rood of ground and was enclosed by a thick stone wall . . . nearly in its centre stands a stone column . . . locally called the Priest's Headstone . . . On the flat or south west side of this stone is cut a large and handsome figure of the cross . . . About 7 yards north of the cross stood the supposed ruins of an ancient church, which stood nearly square, 16 by 16 feet inside . . . No others than still-born children have been buried [in the graveyard] in the memory of the present generation (*OSM* xxiv 104–5).

Regarding a prophecy pertaining to interference with The Priest's Headstone, see *ibid.* In c. 1855, it was recorded:

> [Kilcrue is] an ancient burying ground, said to have been named from its being situated near a stream in which there was a bend or curve resembling a horse shoe. It has long ceased to be a place of interment. The site of the ancient graves was however undisturbed about 36 years ago when the present occupant, Samuel Hill, destroyed and tilled the ground . . . (*OSRNB* sh.8, 2).

We can assume the first element of this name to be *cill* "a church, a graveyard, a burial place" (*Dinneen*; see also **Killaleenan** in Other Names, Culfeightrin, regarding the use of the derived form *cillidh*).

Forms 1–3 show much variation. Form 3 suggests the presence of a masc. definite article, form 1 suggests the fem. definite article and form 2 might suggest there was no article. We might also consider that the final element was a gen. pl. and that nazalization of the *c* was omitted from anglicized forms.

On the basis of the information recorded in the *Ordnance Survey Memoirs, Cill na Crú/Cill Chrú* "burial ground of the (horse-)shoe" might be postulated as original forms. *Crú* "a horse's shoe; an iron heel-tip" (*Dinneen*) is usually a masc. noun, but Ó Dónaill lists a fem. variant. *Crú* was earlier *crudh*, and had several gen. pl. forms including *crudha*, which could be modernized to *crú* (the modern standard form is *cruite* (Ó Dónaill)). *Cill na gCrú* "burial ground of the horse-shoes" can thus also be considered as a possible original form.

Cill na gCnumh "burial ground of the maggots" is another possibility (compare the townland name of **Culnagrew** in Co. Derry which appears to derive from *Cúil na gCnumh* "recess of the maggots" (*PNI* v 144–5)), although velar *mh* seems to have been consistently pronounced [v] locally (*Irish of the Glens* 125 sv. *reamhar, samhradh*). *Cill na gCraobh* "burial ground of the trees" might also be considered but again final velar *bh* appears to have been consistently pronounced [v] (*ibid.* 128, 130 sv. *sliabh, taobh*).

The subtownland name of **Cruephort** in Kebble in Rathlin Island may derive from *Crúphort* "horse-shoe (like) port" (*Place-Names of Rathlin* 17).

Kinbane or White Head, Kinbane Castle D 0944	*An Cionn Bán* "the white headland"	
1. Keanbaan, the castill of	MacDonnells Antrim 51	1551
2. white heade, The	Nowel's Ire. (2)	1570
3. Whitehead	MacDonnells Antrim 418	1575
4. Ca. Whithead	Ulster Map	1590c
5. Whitehead	Dartmouth Map 5	1590c
6. White head	Dartmouth Map 6	1590c
7. Whithead	Dartmouth Map 25	1590c
8. Whithead Ca.	Boazio's Map (BM)	1599
9. White head	Bartlett Maps (Esch. Co. Maps) 1	1603
10. Whithed Ca	Norden's Map	1610
11. White head	Speed's Ulster	1610
12. Kinbane Castle or White head	Hib. Reg. Cary	1657c
13. Coanbane	Court of Claims §923	1662c
14. Ceanbane, the quarters of land of	Court of Claims §923	1662c
15. Ceanbane, Land of	Decree of Innocence 431	1663
16. Rinbane C:	Hib. Del. Antrim	1672c
17. Kinbane salmon fishing	PRONI D2977/3A/2/1/19	1709
18. Kinbane	Ire. Map	1711
19. Kinbane, Salmon fishing of	PRONI D2977/3A/2/1/34	1737
20. Kinbaan Head	Lendrick Map	1780
21. Kinbaan	Shaw Mason's Par. Sur. 161	1814
22. Kenbaan head, or Whitehead	Hamilton's Letters 245	1822
23. Kinbane or White Hd.	OSRNB sh.4, 1	1855c
24. Kinbane Castle	OSRNB sh.4, 1	1855c
25. Kinbane "White Head"	Rev. Connolly 506	1814
26. Ceann bán "white head"	J O'D (OSNB) B 17	1831
27. Ceann bán "The White head"	Ó Dubhthaigh 182	1905
28. Ceann bán "White head or end"	Rev. Magill 18	1923
29. ˌkïnbaːnˈheːd	Local pronunciation	1993
30. ˌkïnbeːnˈheːd	Local pronunciation	1996

An Cionn Bán "the white headland" is the most north-westerly point in Ramoan. In c. 1855 it was described as "a bold headland being the north point of a peninsula or promontory that runs into the sea. It is connected with the mainland by a narrow strip of rocks, over which the sea washes when the tide is in. It is so called from the white limestone rocks in the face of the cliffs forming the headland" (*OSRNB* sh.4, 1). *Kinbane Head* appears to be used much more widely than *White Head*.

Regarding the use of *cionn/ceann* in place-names, see **Kinmeen** in Other Names, Ballintoy, and **Kinkeel** in Rathlin. Regarding the castle on this headland (forms 1, 3, 8–9, 11, 13, 21), see *OSM* 119–22 and *PSAMNI* 5–6. It was apparently built by Colla MacDonnell (d. 1558; *MacDonnells Antrim* 52) in 1547 (*PSAMNI* 6) or c. 1551 (*MacDonnells Antrim* 51).

Leland An English form(?)
D 1141

1. Lealand	Hib. Reg. Cary	1657c
2. Lealand, quarter of Drumgee called	DS (Par. Map) 53	1657c
3. Lealand	BSD 169	1661
4. Lealand	Lapsed Money Book 157	1663
5. Lealand	ASE 116b §19	1668
6. Leland, quarterland of	PRONI D2977/3A/2/1/18	1708
7. Lealan	Ballycastle Map	1720c
8. Lellan	Religious Survey	1734
9. Lealan	Stewart's Survey 1	1734
10. Lelan alias Leland, the quarter of	PRONI D2977/3A/2/1/32	1735
11. Lelan	Lendrick Map	1780
12. Leland	PRONI D2977/3A/2/1/40	1812
13. Lealand	Tithe Applot. 14	1833
14. Leland	OSRNB sh.8, 3	1855c
15. ˈlɛlənd	Local pronunciation	1996

"This was the ancient name of Town Parks . . . The name is now applied only to the west portion of it – to a couple of farms – one of which is in the occupation of Mr. William McLees . . ." (*OSRNB* sh.8, 3). The name has been recently adopted for a housing development on the southern outskirts of Ballycastle.

A compound of English *lea* "grassland; pasture" (*Longman Dict.*) plus *land* is perhaps the most obvious possible origin. Original Irish forms such as *Liathlann* "grey land" can also be considered. *Lann* is attested as meaning "land or ground" in a number of pre-Christian compound names. With the introduction of Christianity it acquired the new meaning "church" (Flanagan & Flanagan 1994, 104). This territory probably lay next to the modern townland of Glebe in which lies the site of the Patrician church of Ramoan. We might also consider that the first element was *leath* "lopsided; one-sided; half-; one of a pair" (*Ó Dónaill* sv.).

Little Black Sythe A Scots/English form
D 1141

Sythe is a variant spelling of *sithe*, an obsolete form of both of the English words *scythe* and *side* (*OED*). It is also a variant spelling of *saithe* "fry of the codfish, the coal-fish" (*ibid.*). The latter word derives from Old Norse *seithr* "coalfish" (*Longman Dict.*; note also Irish *saián* (earlier *saoidheán*) "young coal-fish" (*Ó Dónaill*)). *Sythe* is also a Scottish dialectal form (from *sieve*) meaning "a (milk) strainer" (*Scot. Nat. Dict.*). The place-name refers to a small coastal outcrop of rock in Clare. There is an outcrop of rock called Great Black Sythe to the south-east of here (*OS 1:10,000*).

Lough Park　　　　　　　　　　A Scots/English form(?)
D 0841

This place-name denotes a district in the north of Novally. As the name does not appear in Ordnance Survey literature from the 19th century, it is difficult to discern whether the name contains Irish elements (*loch* "lake" and *páirc* "field"), surnames (Lough (see MacLysaght 1985, 198) or Park (see Bell 1988, 212)), or is a local dialectal form of recent construction. There is no apparent lake in the area.

Nelly's Cave　　　　　　　　　An English form
D 1043

A coastal place-name in Carnduff. Nelly was originally a pet-form of the female personal name Helen.

Port Calliagh　　　　　　　　*Port Cailleach*
D 1142　　　　　　　　　　　　"port of the hags/nuns"

1. Port caillighe "Port of the old woman"	Rev. Magill 22	1923
2. ˌportˈkaljəx	Local pronunciation	1993

Port Cailleach "port of old women or hags/nuns" is the likely original form of this place-name which is found on the rocky coastline north-west of Ballycastle. There was no convent nearby (although see **Drumeeny**), but a figure known as "the black nun of Bonamargy" who lived at some period in Bonamargy friary featured in local lore in the 1830s (*OSM* xxiv 63). The memoirs also call her "Sheelagh Dubh Nivilone" (*Síle Dhubh Ní Mhaoileoin*) or "Black Julia Malone" and say she was "a native of the province of Connaught and [that] she sometimes had her own sister as companion at Bonamargy" (*ibid.*; see also *McSkimin (DPJ)* and *Hill's Bun na Mairge*). *Cailleach* is a generic in the Irish names of several plants and animals but is apparently always qualified in these contexts (see, for example, *Dinneen* sv.). See also **Coskemnacally, Lisnacalliagh**, and **Portadoon** in Other Names, Culfeightrin.

Portcarn　　　　　　　　　　*Port Cairn*
D 1043　　　　　　　　　　　　"port of the cairn"

1. Portcarn	OSRNB sh.4, 1	1855c
2. port cairn "port of the carns or heaps"	OSRNB sh.4, 1	1855c
3. ˌportˈkarn	Local pronunciation	1993

This coastal place-name is found in the townland of Carnduff, but it is uncertain to what *carn* "heap, mound, cairn" the name originally referred. The Ordnance Survey noted in c. 1855 that it was "a small port where boats can only land in calm weather. There is an easy descent to it from the land side; and broken sea weeds which come in with the tide [are collected here]" (*OSRNB* sh.4, 1).

| **Portnakillew** | *Port na Coilleadh* | |
| D 0943 | "port of the wood" | |

1. Poernakillew	OSRNB sh.4, 1	1855c
2. Port na killy	OSRNB sh.4, 1	1855c
3. port na coille "port of the wood"	OSRNB sh.4, 1	1855c
4. ˌpɔrtnəˈkïlju	Local pronunciation	1993
5. ˌðəˈlɔskən	Local pronunciation	1996

"A port in which boats land in calm weather to collect and cut seaweed. It is called from a wood on the contiguous shore" (*OSRNB* sh.4, 1).

Port na Coilleadh "port of the wood" is the most likely origin. McCahan (1900(e) 2) describes a place somewhere near here, which he calls *Port-na-Cilian*, as being "richly wooded . . . planted by a family named Tennant, who formerly owned the property". He may in fact have been referring to Portnakillew. *Coilleadh* is a variant gen. sing. of *coill* "a wood, a grove" (*Dinneen*). Regarding form 5, see **Turraloskin**.

| **Sproule's Town** | An English form | |
| D 0737 | | |

1. Sproules Town	OSRNB sh.8, 2	1855c
2. ˈsprulstọn	Local pronunciation	1996

"A small farm village [in Moyarget Lower] situate on hilly ground, and so called from its having been for a length of time in the sole occupation of families named Sproule – there are none of the name now in it . . ." (*OSRNB* sh.8, 2).

The surname Sproule has "been in Cos. Donegal and Derry since the early seventeenth century" (MacLysaght 1985, 277). Black (1946, 743) lists Sproule as a variant of Spreull, "an old Dunbartonshire family on record since the late 1200s, which later spread throughout southern Scotland".

| **Trench**, The | An English form |
| D 0939 | |

In 1838, the Ordnance Survey recorded that "In Carnsampson, and holding of Robert Hill, there stood a strong fort or fortress locally called the Trench. Beneath this fort stood a cave and at one side of it a small lake, but the entire is now disfigured and superseded by houses, gardens and modern planting" (*OSM* xxiv 116).

| **Tow River** | *An Tó(?)* | |
| D 1140 | "the silent river" | |

1. Gleann tsamhadh, glen of sorrel	Ó Dubhthaigh 187	1905

It is possible that the name of this river has a similar origin to that of the river Tay in Scotland which derives from a word spelt *tóe* "silent" in O. Ir. (*DIL*). Watson (1926, 51) comments on the latter river name: "it was doubtless primarily the name of a goddess, 'The Silent One'" (*An Treasaigh* "the fierce one" angl. **Trassey River,** in the Mournes, is of different construction; see *PNI* iii 173). The Mod. Ir. form of our river name could be either *An Tó* or *An Tua* (both of which could be anglicized *tow*).

There was a flax mill on this river in the 1800s (see **Drumawillin**) and local historian Cahal Dallat has suggested that the river could have taken its name from the discarding of waste tow or flax into the water (*Pers. comm.* 26.2.94). Hill has suggested that this name is a corruption of the second element in **Glentaisie** (see above), the name of the valley through which this river flows (*MacDonnells Antrim* 133). The name Glentow appears only very recently in the sources (see Glentaisie). It may derive from *Gleann Tó* "valley of the river *Tó*" although it could alternatively represent a recently constructed name. Form 1 would have been anglicized *Glentavey* locally (see **Corratavey** in Other Names, Culfeightrin).

White Head   An English form
D 0944

See **Kinbane**.

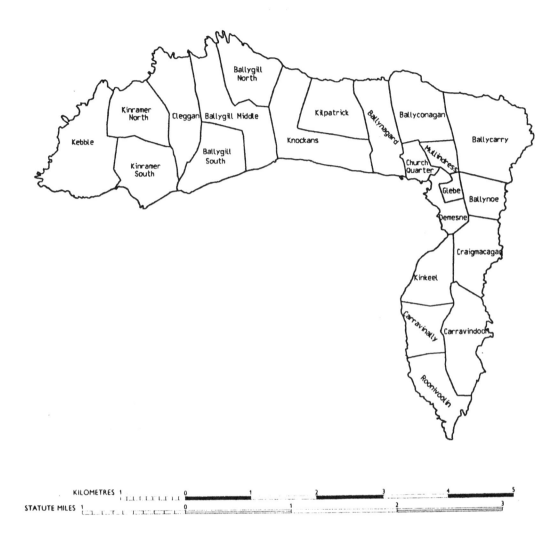

Parish of Rathlin Island

Townlands

Ballycarry
Ballyconagan
Ballygill Middle
Ballygill North
Ballygill South
Ballynagard
Ballynoe
Carravinally
Carravindoon
Church Quarter
Cleggan

Craigmacagan
Demesne
Glebe
Kebble
Kilpatrick
Kinkeel
Kinramer North
Kinramer South
Knockans
Mullindress
Roonivoolin

Based upon Ordnance Survey 1:50,000 mapping, with permission of the Director of the Ordnance Survey of Northern Ireland, Crown copyright preserved.

PARISH OF RATHLIN ISLAND

The main harbour of Rathlin Island lies over six miles north of Ballycastle, but the island is only about three miles distant from the mainland (Benmore or Fair Head) at its southern-most point (*Lewis' Top. Dict.* 460). It contains 22 townlands and c. 3,398 acres (*OSM* xxiv 127).

A biography of the six-century St *Comgall* of Bangor claims he attempted to land on the island but was forcibly prevented by the inhabitants (*VSSH (Plummer)* ii 18 §l; *EA* 249; forms 24, 37–39 below). O'Laverty suggests that he later succeeded in founding a church here, and that "the rectorial tithes of the island belonged to his successors, the abbots of Bangor, until the suppression of that abbey" (*O'Laverty* iv 353). This he bases on the "tradition of the islanders", and says that this church "formerly stood on the site at present occupied by the Protestant Church" (see below, and **Church Quarter** townland). Colgan supposed St *Colm Cille* to have founded a religious establishment here (*Trias Thaum.* 361a). Archdall follows Colgan: "he founded a church here, and placed over it Colman, the deacon, who was the son of Roi" (*Mon. Hib.* 20). However, O'Donovan (*AFM* i 251 n.e) points out that Colm Cille appears to have founded the church on the homonymously named *Reachrainn*, which lies off the coast of Co. Dublin and which has latterly been known in English as Lambay Island (cf. for example, *Anecdota Oxon.* 29 §959, *BCC* 96 §99 and *EA* 249), although Colm Cille may have visited Rathlin (*Adamnán's Columba* 436 §93b, Sharpe 1995, 264).

The earliest reference to Rathlin in Irish sources seems to be in 630 when *Segéne*, Abbot of Iona founded the church of *Reachrainn* (*AFM* i 250; form 1). While this is likely to have been the island off Antrim, subsequent references to abbots of *Reachrainn* in the annals could refer to either Rathlin or Lambay. Reeves assumed the following references to refer most certainly to the Antrim Rathlin: forms 1–3, 5–10, 12–19, 21–23 (*EA* 249–50; he excludes forms 25–27; for a list of the abbots mentioned in the annals see *ibid.*). Form 16, which refers to the burning of *Reachrainn* by "plunderers" (probably Vikings; *AFM* i 396–7), was assumed by O'Donovan to be more likely to refer to Lambay Island (*ibid.* i 397n). Similarly, for form 21, which associates Reachrainn with Durrow in Ballycowan barony in Co. Offaly, O'Donovan understood Lambay, although Reeves opted for Rathlin. In this par-ticular case (and hence also in form 22), as Colm Cille also founded a monastery in Durrow, it seems more likely to be referring to Lambay (*EA* 250). Conversely, O'Donovan claimed a reference to *Reachru* in 1038 (form 25), which records further plundering by foreigners, is more likely to have been Rathlin as Lambay was already in Viking hands at this time (*AFM* ii 834 n.s). This problem of identification extends to the martyrologies (forms 20, 30–1, 51–52). For example, the death of *Murghal mac Ninneadha* Abbot of *Reachrainn* is noted in 764 (*AFM* i 366) and is mentioned in forms 31 and 52, but again, the location of this *Reachrainn* is uncertain.

Earliest references to Rathlin in non-Irish sources may include form 121, written by an unknown Italian geographer in the 7th century. This form is possibly based on earlier works, such as those by Pliny and Ptolemy (forms 120 and 122 respectively). Earliest manuscript copies of Pliny's *Naturalis Historiae* date to c. 500 (Newsome 1964, xvi); the earliest extant copies of the work of the latter scholar date only to the 13th century (Mac an Bhaird 1991–93, 1). As Mac an Bhaird (1991–3, 16–9) points out however, these references may refer to Lambay or perhaps even indicate that there was an island in the Western Isles of Scotland called *Reachrainn*. In 1213 (form 123), the island was granted along with other Irish lands to one Alan de Galweia by King John of England (see barony introduction), and the name appears in confirmatory deeds in 1215 and 1220 (forms 125–6). An inquisition in 1278 (form 127; see barony introduction) fixed the rent of the island at two thirds of 1d.

(*CDI* §1500), while an inquisition of 1279 determined that the island was in the hands of John Biset "son and heir of John, held of Richard de Burgo" (*Cal. Inq. Post Mortem* I 63b §28 and *EA* 288). In c. 1319 the island was amongst land forfeited by Hugh Biset "for joining the rebellious Scots" and was granted to John de Athy (*Cal. Rot. Pat.* 84b; cf. also *EA* 288):

> Grant in Fee to John de Athy, of the land and tenements, late of Hugh Biset, in the island of Raghery in Ireland, and which are in the king's hands as an escheat, the said Hugh being an adherent of the Scots (*CPR* 12 Ed. II 271; cf. also *Inq. Earl. Ulster* 130).

The island was presumably soon reclaimed by the Bisets, or by the MacDonnells who acquired much of north-east Co. Antrim in 1399 (see barony introduction). Later English forms include those relating to Séamus and Colla MacDonnell's repulse in 1551 of an English attack on the island (*CSP Ire.* 116; cf. also *AFM* v 1520), and massacres of the inhabitants by English armies in c. 1557 (*O'Laverty* iv 360), in 1575 (*ibid.* 363) and in 1598 (*CSP Ire.* 109). O'Rahilly (1932, 164n) believed the modern dialect of the island to have been introduced from Scotland after the 1575 massacre (see also *Irish of Rathlin* 132–3). Indeed, there does not appear to be any place-name on the island of particularly old construction (although see **Cross Skreen** in Other Names, Culfeightrin; see also **Roonivoolin**). By the late 1500s the island was considered "half of a barony" or half of a "tuogh", being combined with Armoy to form a cinament (see introduction to Armoy, and the barony introduction).

Along with Ballintoy, Rathlin was formerly annexed to Billy parish in medieval times, which accounts for the absence of a reference to Rathlin in the *Ecclesiastical Taxation* of 1302–6 (*Eccles. Tax.* 78 n.p). The island appears to have come under the administration of the Catholic parish of Armoy sometime subsequent to the Dissolution in the mid-16th century, until c. 1782 (see *O'Laverty* iv 387–91; see also JDCHS (anon.) 1930, 53). Regarding its position as a Church of Ireland parish, after the Dissolution "the rectorial tithes of the island of Raghlin, which had been appropriate to the abbey of Bangor, were granted to Rice Aphugh; subsequently to John Thomas Hibbots; and in 1605 to Sir James Hamilton. In the King's Books the vicarage of Raughlins is taxed at 16s. 8d." (*EA* 288; Reeves neglected to source this information, but see *CPR Jas I* 38b, 73a). A report from 1622 recorded, however: "Graunge de Rawlines; the 2d part of all tithes impropriate to the Abbey of Bangor, & are possest by the Earl of Antrym. Noe vicar nor curate, it not being able to mayteyne one . . ." (*Ulster Visit. (Reeves)* 288; cf. also *EA* 289, and *Inq. Par. Ant.* 2). Sometime subsequent to 1633, when "Raughlins, Insula maris, Vicaria vacante" was entered in a further diocesan report (*Regal Visit. (Reeves)* 125; form 258), the island became "an appendage to the [Church of Ireland] parish of Ballintoy, which was itself united to Billy until 1745 . . . The Act of Council, severing Raghery from Ballintoy, and constituting the new church, which was built upon the site of the old one in Ballynoe [*sic*], parochial, is dated April 20, 1722" (*EA* 289).

The most complete work to date on the subtownland names of Rathlin (*Place-names of Rathlin*) has been published by Dónall Mac Giolla Easpaig in *Ainm* and is cited extensively below.

PARISH NAME

Rathlin Island   *Reachlainn*
D 1550   meaning uncertain

1. Rechrainne, ecclaise	AFM i 250	630

2.	(?)Rechrann, eclesiam	A. Tigern i 183	634
3.	Rechru	Thes. Pal. ii 273 §24	713c
4.	Rechrea, in	Thes. Pal. ii 279 §19	713c
5.	(?)Reachraine, epscop	AFM i 336	734
6.	(?)Rechrainne, episcopis	AU i 198	738
7.	(?)Rechrainne, abb	AFM i 338	738
8.	(?)Rechrainne, espoc	A. Tigern i 243	738
9.	(?)Rechrainne, abbatis	AU i 202	742
10.	(?)Reachrainne, abb	AFM i 346	743
11.	(?)Reclaindi, abbas	A. Tigern. i 250	747
12.	(?)Reachrainne, abb	AFM i 366	764
13.	(?)Reachrainne, abbatis	AU i 234	768
14.	(?)Reachrainne, abb	AFM i 372	768
15.	(?)Reachrainne, princeps	AU i 240	772
16.	(?)Reachrainde, Losccaadh	AFM i 396	790
17.	(?)Rechrainne, Loscadh	AU i 274	794
18.	(?)Reachrainne, abb	AFM i 402	794
19.	(?)Rechrainne, abbas	AU i 280	798
20.	(?)Rechraind, Colman mac Roe o	Mart. Tal. June 16, p.50	830c
21.	(?)Reachrainne & Dearmaighe	AFM i 478	848
22.	(?)Rechrand & Dermaighe, abbas	AU i 356	849
23.	(?)Reachrainne, abb	AFM ii 700	973
24.	Reachraynd	VSSH (Plummer) ii, 18 §1	1000c
25.	Reachru	AFM ii 834	1038
26.	Reachrainne, hi	AFM ii 848	1045
27.	(?)rRechrain, i	AIF 208 §5	1045
28.	Rachraind, a	Cath MT 26 §13	1050c
29.	(?)Rechrainne, Ronan	CSH 153 §707.915	1125c
30.	(?)Rechraind, Colman mac Rói i	Mart. Gorm., June 16 p.116	1170c
31.	(?)Murgal mac Uinnedha (sic), ab Reachrainne	Mart. Gorm., Sept. 29 p.186	1170c
32.	Rechrannd	VSSH (Plummer) ii, 18 §1	1450c
33.	Rechru	Scottish Saints (Pinkerton) i 87	1450c
34.	Rachlainn nó Rachrinn	Acallam (Stokes) 13 §416	1450c
35.	Rachlaind nó Rachrain	Acallam (Stokes) 103 §3644	1450c
36.	Rac[h]ruind atuaid, a	Acallam (Stokes) 140 §5122	1450c
37.	Reachraynd	C. Kilken. fol. 93b c.1 I.44 (EA)	1450c
38.	Reachrain, insula nomine	Fleming Collect. 311b (EA)	1450c
39.	Rechrannd	VSSH (Plummer) ii, 18 §l n.9	1450c
40.	(?)Rachlainn	SG i 103	1485c
41.	rachlainn, rachrainn	SG i 175	1485c
42.	Rechraind, hi	L. Gabála iv 22 §291	1525c
43.	Reachrainn na ríoghraidhe, i	Poems of Giolla Brighde 46 §23	1541
44.	reachrainn, co	AFM v 1520	1551
45.	ó Rachluinn a ccrích Alban	Poems on the Butlers 75 l.1779	1599
46.	Rachruinn, Inis na m-Barc risa raiter	C. Conghail Cláir. 72	1600c
47.	Rachroinn, go	C. Conghail Cláir. 84	1600c
48.	Rachlann, clár	LCABuidhe 159 §168	1617c

49. Reachroinn, leattuath dona seacht ttuathoibh se	MacDonnells (Ó Cuív) 144	1618
50. (?)Rachluinn	LCABuidhe 52 §10	1618c
51. (?)Colman, mac Roi, ó Reachrainn	Mart. Don. June 16, p.170	1630c
52. (?)Murghal, mac Ninnedha, abb Rechrainne	Mart. Don. Sept. 29, p.262	1630c
53. Reachrainn	Céitinn i 198	1633c
54. Raclinâ insula, in	Brit. Eccles. Ant. 958, 1149	1639
55. Reachraind	Brit. Eccels. Ant. 958	1639
56. Rechreyn	Brit. Eccles. Ant. 958	1639
57. Ro-chrinne	Brit. Eccles. Ant. 958	1639
58. Reachrann, ecclesiam	An. Roscrea 148 §55	1640c
59. Rechrea, in	Trias Thaum. 361a	1647
60. Rachrea, In	Trias Thaum. 384a	1647
61. Rechrainn, alijs Rechlandia, Insula Dalriediæ in Ultoniâ	Trias Thaum. 494a	1647
62. Rechrannensem Ecclesium	Trias Thaum. 498a	1647
63. Recrannensi, De Ecclesia	Trias Thaum. 509b	1647
64. Recrannensis, Abbas	Trias Thaum. 509b, 510a	1647
65. Rechrannia	Trias Thaum. 510a	1647
66. Rechranensis, Abbas	Trias Thaum. 510a	1647
67. Abbas Rechranniensis	Trias Thaum. 510a	1647
68. (?)Rachrainn, i	L. Gen. DF 45, 66	1650
69. Rachlonn Dál Ríatta	Acallam (Ní Shéaghdha) i 36 §8	1650c
70. Rachrainn	Acallam (Ní Shéaghdha) i 160 §7	1650c
71. (?)Recrann et Dermaighe, Ab	Chron. Scot. 150	1650c
72. Rachluinn, ó	Duanaire Dh. Bh. ii 68	1674c
73. Rachrainn	LS C vi 2 (RIA) (de hÓir)	1750c
74. Rachlainn	LS 23 N 6 (RIA) (de hÓir)	1750c
75. (?)Rachlainn, i	SG i 282	1847
76. Oilean Rachlan	Mac Bionaid LS 118 §74	1857c
77. Reacra	Mulcahy's Rathlin 60	1889
78. hOileán Racharaigh, go	Ultach 60:10, 7	1904
79. Oileán Reachrann	Seanfhocail 3	1907
80. Reachrann, beannacht Rí	Seanfhocail 65 §702	1907
81. Reachra, in	Claidheamh Soluis 18 Bea., L.6	1907
82. Reachra, Gaedhilg	Claidheamh Soluis 8 Mei., L.5	1907
83. Reachra, ó	Claidheamh Soluis 8 Mei., L.5	1907
84. Reachraigh, I nOileán	Claidheamh Soluis 21 Nol., L.7	1907
85. 'Oilean Reachra'	Claidheamh Soluis 22 Lún., L.11	1908
86. Reachaire	Claidheamh Soluis 22 Lún., L.11	1908
87. Reachrainn, go	Claidheamh Soluis 29 Lún., L.5	1908
88. Reachrann, Oileán	Claidheamh Soluis 16 Aib., L.3	1910
89. Rachrainn, go	Claidheamh Soluis 16 Aib., L.3	1910
90. 'Rachra'	Claidheamh Soluis 16 Aib., L.5	1910
91. 'Reachra'	Claidheamh Soluis 9 Iúl, L.3	1910
92. Reachrann, do Choisde	Claidheamh Soluis 9 Iúl, L.3	1910
93. Reachrainn, ar	Claidheamh Soluis 9 Iúl, L.3	1910
94. Rachreann, Sgéaltan X	Athchló Uladh iii	1910

95. Rachra'	Athchló Uladh iii	1910
96. Rachreann, sean-fhocal	Claidheamh Soluis 1 Ean., L.5	1911
97. Rachlann, de chuid	Claidheamh Soluis 17 Mei., L.1	1911
98. Rachlainn, i	Claidheamh Soluis 17 Mei., L.1	1911
99. Reachrann, Gaedhilg	Claidheamh Soluis 1 Iúl, L.4	1911
100. Reachrainn, i	Claidheamh Soluis 1 Iúl, L.4	1911
101. Reachrainn, as	Claidheamh Soluis 10 Fea., L.1	1912
102. Reachrann, canamhain	Claidheamh Soluis 10 Fea., L.1	1912
103. Rachlainn	Claidheamh Soluis 24 Fea., L.4	1912
104. Tugtar ar an oileán 'Rachlainn' nó 'Reachlainn' agus go minic 'Rachbhainn' acht bíonn 'Reachrannach' ar an duine a rugadh ann . . . ní abairthear 'Reachrainn'	Claidheamh Soluis 24 Fea., L.4	1912
105. Rachlainn	Claidheamh Soluis 27 Aib., L.6	1912
106. Rachlann, cainnt	Claidheamh Soluis 27 Aib., L.6	1912
107. Rachrainn, ann	Claidheamh Soluis 27 Iúl, L.5	1912
108. Rachlainn, i	Claidheamh Soluis 27 Iúl, L.5	1912
109. Rachrann, Oileán	Claidheamh Soluis 22 Fea., L.6	1913
110. Rachrainn, ceoil ó	Claidheamh Soluis 19 Iúl, L.3	1913
111. Reachlainn, ó	Ultach 4:5, 2	1927
112. Reachlainn	Filí agus Felons 70	1934
113. Reachlainn, toigh ann an	Irish of Rathlin 135	1942
114. Reachlainn, go	Irish of Rathlin 135	1942
115. Reachlainn, o	Irish of Rathlin 139	1942
116. Reachlainn	Irish of Rathlin 149, 225	1942
117. Reachraidh	Irish of Rathlin 225	1942
118. Oileán Reachrann	Ultach 31:4, 4	1954
119. oileán Reachrann	Ultach 32:4, 2	1955
120. (?)Ricina	Naturalis Historiae Lib. iv Cap xvi	500c
121. (?)Regaina	Ravenna Cosmog. 44b	690c
122. (?)Rikenna	Geographia II.2.10	1200c
123. Rathliñ Insuł de	Rott. Litt. Pat. 98a §6	1213
124. Rathrim, Inter alia Insulam de	Cal. Carew MSS v 352	1213
125. Rachrun, the Island of	CDI §564	1215
126. Rachrun, the Island of	CDI §942	1220
127. Island of Racry	CDI §1500	1278
128. Rachry, the island of	Cal. Car. MSS vi 352	1278c
129. Racry	Cal. Inq. Post Mortem i 63b §28	1279
130. Insula de Raghery in Hibnia	Cal. Rot. Pat. 84b	1319c
131. the island of Raghery in Ireland	CPR 12 Ed. II 271	1319c
132. Insula in Rughrie in Hibernica	Cal. Carew MSS v 353	1319c
133. Ragrin	Dalorto's Map (Taylor)	1325
134. ragri	Italian Maps 425	1339
135. ragri	Italian Maps 425	1367
136. Rauchryne	Bruce 77–9, 81, 94	1375c
137. abrini	Italian Maps 425	1384

138. ragrany	Italian Maps 425	1426
139. rathgyrn (or) rachgyrn	Bruce 94	1487
140. ragrini	Italian Maps 425	1497
141. ragrini	Italian Maps 425	1513
142. Raghlin	EA 288	1550c
143. Raghlin Island	CSP Ire. 116	1551
144. Raghlin, the Island of	MacDonnells Antrim 47	1551c
145. Rathlyns, the	Cal. Carew MSS 243	1553
146. Rathlens, the	Cal. Carew MSS 243	1553
147. Raghlyns, the Island of	O'Laverty iv 360	1557c
148. Raghlin Island	CSP Ire. 265	1565
149. Raghlin island	CSP Ire. 266	1565
150. Raghline	MacDonnells Antrim 139	1565c
151. Raghlin	Goghe's Map	1567
152. Raghlin Island, the	CSP Ire. 361	1568
153. Raghlins, The	CSP Ire. 362, 375, 383	1568
154. Raghlin	CSP Ire. 364	1568
155. Raghlins, the	O'Laverty iv 361	1568
156. Raghlins, the	MacDonnells Antrim 153	1569
157. Raghlins	CSP Ire. 372	1586
158. Raghlin	CSP Ire. 393	1568
159. Raghlins, the	CSP Ire. 420	1569
160. Raughlyn, the ile of	SSP 108 §2	1569
161. Rawghlyn, the	SSP 127 §75.8	1569
162. Rawghlyne	SSP 127 §75.8	1569
163. Raughlines, the Glynes with the	Fiants Eliz. §1530	1570
164. raughlayes	Antrim Coast Sketch	1570c
165. Great Ranggline	North Ulster Coast Map	1570c
166. great Ranghline	Ulster Map	1570c
167. Raghlins, ye	Nowel's Ire. (1)	1570c
168. Raghelions, the Glynnes and the	Fiants Eliz. §2326	1573
169. Raghlin Island, the	CSP Ire. 518	1573
170. Clandeboy, the Route, the Glynns, Raghlin, &c.	CSP Ire. 507	1573
171. Rowghe Glinnes or the Rofflins, the islands called	Cal. Carew MSS 439	1573
172. Raughlins	Cal. Carew MSS 441	1573
173. Raughlins, the isle of	Cal. Carew MSS 442	1573
174. Ricnea, Raclin	Ortelius Map	1573
175. Racklyn	Ortelius Map	1573
176. Raghlyns, the	Cal. Carew MSS 471	1574
177. Raghlins, the	CSP Ire. 47, 77	1575
178. Raghlins, the castle of the	CSP Ire. 87	1575
179. Rawghlins, island of the	Cal. Carew MSS 16	1575
180. Raughlins, island of the	Cal. Carew MSS 21	1575
181. Rawghlins, island of the	Cal. Carew MSS 19	1575
182. Raughlins, island of the	Cal. Carew MSS 23	1575
183. Raghlins, the	O'Laverty iv 363	1575
184. Raghrs	Nowel's Ire. (2)	1576

286

185. Rawlins Island, the	Walsing. Letter-Book 188	1579
186. Raughlins, the	Walsing. Letter-Book 197	1579
187. Raghlins, the	Cal. Carew MSS 201	1580
188. Raghlins, the island of	Cal. Carew MSS 351	1583
189. Raghlyns, the Island of	Cal. Carew MSS 359, 501	1583
190. Rawlins, the	Cal. Carew MSS 38, 383	1584
191. Raughlin, The	Cal. Carew MSS 380	1584
192. Raghlins, the	CSP Ire. 556	1585
193. Raghlins, The island of the	CSP Ire. 562	1585
194. the Ile of Raghlins is counted half a barony	Bagenal's Descr. Ulst. 155	1586
195. Racklyn	Italian Maps of Ire. 425	1589
196. Raghlins	Italian Maps of Ire. 425	1590
197. Raughlins	Sea Chart	1590c
198. Ratlinges, the	Ulster Map	1590c
199. Raghlins, The	Dartmouth Map 5	1590c
200. Raughlins	Dartmouth Map 6	1590c
201. Ricnea per Ptolomeum, the Raghlins	Dartmouth Map 25	1590c
202. Ragrins	Jobson's Ulster (TCD)	1590c
203. Raffelines	Jobson's Ulster (TCD)	1590c
204. Raghlins	Hondius Map	1591
205. Raghlyn	Mercator's Ire.	1595
206. Raghlins, the	CSP Ire. 109	1598
207. The Sound of Roughlen consisting of two islands	CSP Ire. (1601–03) 67	1598
208. Raghlins	Boazio's Map (BM)	1599
209. Raughlines, the ile of	Treatice of Ire. (Butler) 22	1599c
210. Raughlines, the	Treatice of Ire. (Butler) 23	1599c
211. Raghlins, The	Treatise on Ire. (NLI) 11	1599c
212. Raughlins, The	Treatise on Ire. (NLI) 110	1599c
213. Raghlins, the	CSP Ire. 274	1601
214. Raughlins, the island called	CPR Jas I 38b	1603
215. Armoy and Raghlines, the cynamond of	CPR Jas I 58a	1603
216. Raghlins, the island of	CPR Jas I 65b	1603
217. Raghlins, Ricnea	Bartlett Maps (Esch. Co. Maps) 1	1603
218. Raghlin, the Island of	CSP Ire. 137	1604
219. Raughlin, the Island of	CSP Ire. 137	1604
220. Raughlins, the	Lodge RR Jas. I i 63	1604
221. Rathlyns, the island of	CSP Ire. 158	1604
222. Raughlins, island called the	CPR Jas I 73a	1605
223. Racklyn	Mercator's/Hole's Ire.	1610
224. Raghlins, The	Speed's Antrim & Down	1610
225. Raghlins, The	Speed's Ulster	1610
226. Raghlyn	Speed's Ireland	1610
227. Armoy and Raghlynns, the tough called the Cinemond	LP 8 Jas. I (PRONI)	1610
228. Raghlinns, the entire island of	LP 8 Jas. I (PRONI)	1610
229. Raghlins	Norden's Map	1610c

230. Raughlins, the	CSP Ire. 57, 58, 59	1615
231. Raghlines	CSP Ire. 43	1615
232. Rathlin, the island of	CSP Ire. 215	1615
233. Ranchoyn	Bruce 78	1616
234. Raughring	Bruce 94	1616
235. Raghlyns, the isle of	Cal. Carew MSS 340	1617
236. Raughlyns, island of	Cal. Carew MSS 340	1617
237. Rathlyn, the island of	Cal. Carew MSS 351	1617
238. Rathlin, Insula de	Cal. Carew MSS 352	1617
239. Rathrim, the island of	Cal. Carew MSS 352	1617
240. Rathrim, Inter alia Insulam de	Cal. Carew MSS 352	1617
241. Rughrie in Hibernica, Insula in	Cal. Carew MSS 353	1617
242. Raghlin, the island of	Cal. Carew MSS 353	1617
243. the island of Raghlin, Rathrim or Raghery	Cal. Carew MSS 355	1617
244. Rathlin, island of	Cal. Carew MSS 355	1617
245. Raghlins, the Island of the	Cal. Carew MSS 356	1617
246. the island of the Rauchlins, one of the Hebrides	Cal. Carew MSS 356	1617
247. Raughlin	Cal. Carew MSS 358, 359	1617
248. Raghlin	Cal. Carew MSS 358	1617
249. Rathlin, the Isle of	Cal. Carew MSS 360, 362	1617
250. Rathlins, the	Cal. Carew MSS 362	1617
251. Rathlyn, the isalnd of	Cal. Carew MSS 366	1618
252. Rathroin, the island of	Cal. Carew MSS 374	1618
253. Rachroin	Cal. Carew MSS 375	1618
254. Raughlin, the island of	CSP Ire. 324	1621
255. Rawlines, Graunge de	Ulster Visit. (Reeves) 288	1622
256. Raghlins, the Island of the	Cal. Carew MSS 438	1623
257. Raghlins, the	Cal. Carew MSS 438	1623
258. Raughlins	Regal Visit. (Reeves) 125	1633
259. Rachlyns, the Iyland of	MacDonnells Antrim 437	1637
260. Rachlins, the island of	Hill's Stewarts 150	1637
261. Rachraye, isle of	Lib. Muner. iv 145a	1641
262. Raughlin, the	Rebellion Letters 8	1642
263. Ragheries, the	Hickson's Ire. i 289	1652
264. Roghlyn, the island of	Civ. Surv. x §60	1655
265. Rahglins	Inq. Par. Ant. 2	1657
266. Raghlin Island	Inq. Par. Ant. 4	1657
267. Rathline, Parish of	Hib. Reg. Cary	1657c
268. Raghlin, Parish and Island of	DS (Par. Map) 60	1657c
269. Rathline Castle	DS (Par. Map) 60	1657c
270. Rathry, the Iland of	Census 19	1659
271. Racklyn, the island of	CSP Ire. 70	1660
272. Raghlin Island	BSD 176	1661
273. Raghlins, Island of	Hill's Stewarts 147	1662
274. Raghline	Court of Claims §923	1662c
275. Raghlins, the island of	Court of Claims §923	1662c

276. Raghlins, the Finamont of Armoy and the Raghlins	Court of Claims §923	1662c
277. Rackins, the Island of	CSP Ire. 697	1662c
278. Rathlins, the Island of	Decree of Innocence 437	1663
279. Raghlins, the sinamount of Armoy and the	Decree of Innocence 431	1663
280. Rathlone, the island of	CSP Ire. 59	1666
281. Rathloane	CSP Ire. 67	1666
282. Racheryes, Island of	HMR (1666) 100	1666
283. Rathcline, ye island of	ASE 116a §19	1668
284. Rathline-Island	ASE 117a §19	1668
285. Raghery Island	HMR Ant. 11	1669
286. Rachrin	Bruce 78	1670
287. Rathlin	Hib. Del. Antrim	1672c
288. Racklyns, Iland of	PRONI D2977/3A/2/10/1	1678
289. Rathlyn	A. Clonmac. 177	1684
290. Rathlin	Lamb Maps Co. Antrim	1690c
291. Regaina	Ravenna Cosmog. 44b	1690c
292. Raclinda	RSH 24	1697
293. the Isle of Rachline, or	Rauchrin HSN 77	1697
294. Raghlins	Irish Jacobites 55 §38v	1699
295. Rachri Island	Lhuyd's Tour 222	1699
296. Rathlin	Ire. Map	1711
297. Rathlin, Island of	Hill's Stewarts 11	1720
298. Raghlin	Rathlin Catechism 175	1721
299. Raghlin, the Island of	EA 289	1722
300. the Island or Territory of Raghlin otherwise Raghery	PRONI D2977/3A/2/26/1A	1746
301. Raghlin or Rahery, Mill of	PRONI D2977/3A/2/26/1A	1746
302. Rachry	Merchant's Book 1	1751
303. Rachlin	Merchant's Book 32	1752
304. Raghlin	O'Laverty iv 389	1766
305. Raghery	Hamilton's Letters 3	1784
306. Rachra I.	Ire. Map	1790c
307. Rathlin or Raughlin	Clark's Rathlin 129	1808
308. Raghery, Island of	Statist. Sur. Ant. 450	1812
309. Raghery	OSNB B 32	1827
310. Raghery	Murphy's Rathlin 11	1953c
311. Rathery	Murphy's Rathlin 11	1953c
312. Rackery	Murphy's Rathlin 14	1953c
313. Rathlin	Murphy's Rathlin 83	1953c
314. Rathlin, or Rachery	Murphy's Rathlin vi	1987
315. Ro-chrinne "from the multitude of trees with which it abounded in ancient times"	Brit. Eccles. Ant. 958/Mon. Hib19 n.c	1639
316. Ragh-Erin, or "fort of Erin"	Hamilton's Letters 3	1784
317. Riada + lean "tribe or habitation in the water"	Hamilton's Letters 245	1822

318. Raghery "the best spar in a ship"	OSM xxiv 131	1835
319. Reachlaind "rocky island"	J O'D (OSNB) B 32	1827
320. Reachra (Rachra, Rachla)	Post-Sheanchas 108	1905
321. Reachra	Alasdair Mac Colla 75	1914
322. Reithere "Place of rams"	Rev. Magill 23	1923
323. "Notched Island", cf. Welsh rhygnu		
'to scrape'	Ravenna Cosmog. 44b	1949
324. Reachrainn, Reachraidh	Áitainm. Uladh 10	1963
325. Reachlainn	Reachlainn (de hÓir) 22	1966
326. "Rugged Island"	Dallat's Rathlin 26	1973
327. Reachlainn	GÉ 150	1989
328. rɑxəri	Irish of Rathlin 225	1942
329. rɑheri	Irish of Rathlin 225	1942
330. rɑxərin′	Irish of Rathlin 225	1942
331. rɑxlin′	Irish of Rathlin 225	1942
332. rɑhŋin	Irish of Rathlin 225	1942
333. rɑːxlɑn	LASID i xivc	1958
334. ′rɑxəriː	Reachlainn (de hÓir) 24	1966
335. ′rɑxlin′	Reachlain (de hÓir) 24	1966
336. ′rɑx(ə)riː	Local pronunciation	1993
337. ′rɑθlïn	Local pronunciation	1993

As noted in the introduction, Lambay Island is called *Reachrainn* in Irish. Hughes and Hannon (*PNI* ii 97–8, 220–1) have noted other places of similar name: Rathlin O'Byrne Island off the south-west coast of Co. Donegal (Mod. Ir. *Reachlainn Uí Bhirn*; *GÉ* 150); a "long finger shaped" promontory (surrounded by water in winter) in Lough Neagh in Co. Armagh, called **Rathlin Island**; a "partly submerged reef or promontory" in Strangford Lough, called **The Ragheries** (for which Hughes gives the Irish form of *An Dá Reachraidh*); and "a number of large stones . . . just off the shore", also in Strangford Lough, called *Raghorie* in 17th-century sources and thought by Hannon to derive from Irish *Reachraidh*, who also noted that "in this area, [this element] appears to mean 'rocky reef'" (see *ibid.* 220–1). We may further note that the townland of Raghra in Co. Offaly has the Mod. Ir. form *Reachra* (*L. Log. Uíbh Fhailí* 33). It appears from the incidence of these names that O'Donovan may have been broadly correct in his interpretation (form 319).

O'Rahilly (1946, 14 n.4) believed *Rechrann* to be the oldest form of the name, and that it later developed to *Rechru* (form 3). He suggested the name might "go back to *Rikorinā* or the like" in proto-Celtic. Anderson and Anderson (*Adomnán's Columba* 148) noted that "Rechru is the Irish nominative of an *ION*-stem; its suffixless dative Rechre is implied in the Latin ablative Reachrea" (form 4). Hughes suggests that *rechra* or *rechru* constituted the original Irish name (*PNI* ii 97). Whatever about the oldest form, de hÓir (*Reachlainn (de hÓir)* 24–5) noted that in the case of the Antrim Rathlin, both anglicized forms *Raghlin* and *Raghery* have been used for centuries. He took the first of these to represent a development from *Reachra* (earlier *Rechra*) to *Reachrainn*, with gen. form *Reachrann* or *Reachrainne*. The later change of the second *r* to *l* could presumably be ascribed to dissimilation. De hÓir also suggested that while the *Raghery* variant could have developed naturally from *Reachra* in Irish, it would be unusual for two separate Irish forms to have survived side by side for so long, and that it could represent *reachra* plus Norse *ey* "island". The latter element appears in other Irish island names such as Lambay and Dalkey (*Reachlainn (de hÓir)* 25). Viking place-names in Ireland, or Viking forms of Irish place-names, were often adopted by the English in preference to the Irish forms (*ibid.*), and according to de hÓir's argument the two name types *Raghlin* and *Raghery* belonged to different languages. *Raghery* must have been latterly adopted into Irish, however (forms 328–9); Holmer (*Irish of Rathlin* 225) spelt the Irish form of this as *Reachraidh* (form 117). Hughes (*PNI* ii 97–8), on the other hand, believed *Reachraidh* to represent a later Irish reflex of an original *Rechru/Rechra*. It seems possible, however, that the various Raghery/Rathlin names in Ireland could have derived from any of these origins.

The standard anglicized form is based on the Irish form *Reachlainn*; -th- may have arisen originally from a misrendering of -ch- (note form 123 dated to 1213). The use of the English plural suffix dates at least to 1553 (forms 145–6). Murphy (*Murphy's Rathlin* 1) recorded here in c. 1953 that "old people said that at one time there were two islands in Rathlin. Instances of shingles in the land where the division was supposed to have existed are quoted . . . [another informant] said it was a Scottish tradition. He said: 'They call it the 'Two Rackeries'. The reason is if you're off the island you can see right over to the channel and it looks as if the sea did run through it. That's how it gets 'The Two Rackeries'".

TOWNLAND NAMES

Ballycarry   *Baile Caraidh*
D 1551   "townland of the rocky ford(?)"

1. Baile Caraidh	Irish of Rathlin 171	1942	
2. Ballikerry	Hib. Reg. Cary	1657c	
3. Ballyceery	DS (Par. Map) 60	1657c	
4. Ballycary	Census 19	1659	
5. Ballykerry	BSD 176	1661	
6. Balleierry	Court of Claims §923	1662c	
7. Ballecerry, the fi town of	Court of Claims §923	1662c	
8. Balecarry, the halfe towne of	Decree of Innocence 431	1663	
9. Ballykerry ½ townland	Lapsed Money Book 158	1663	
10. Ballykerry	ASE 117a §19	1668	
11. Ballycarry	HMR Ant. 11	1669	
12. Ballikery	Hib. Del. Antrim	1672c	
13. Ballycarey	Hill's Stewarts 11	1720	
14. Ballykery	Maritime Map	1776	
15. B: carry	Lendrick Map	1780	
16. B:Carry	Rathlin Vestry Book 28	1780	
17. Old T. Ballycarry	Rathlin Vestry Book 56	1792	
18. Ballycarry	Rathlin Vestry Book 60	1794	
19. Ballykarry	PRONI D2977/3A/2/1/40	1812	
20. East B.Carry; S. B.Carry; N B.Carry	New Rent (Law)	1820	
21. Ballycanry	Bnd. Sur. (OSNB) 32	1827c	
22. Baile Uí Chainigh "Canny's town"	J O'D (OSNB) B 32	1827	
23. Baile carrac "the crooked bally"	Duncan 133	1906	
24. Baile caradh "Town of the weir"	Rev. Magill 6	1923	

25. Crooked "rugged town"	O'Boyle 44	1939
26. "the crooked townland"	Dallat's Rathin 26	1973
27. Baile Carraigh "the town of the rough ground"	Place-Names of Rathlin 64	1989
28. bal'ə 'kari	Irish of Rathlin 171	1942
29. ˌbali'kari	Local pronunciation	1996

Forms 21 and 22 are unusual in that they deviate from all the remaining Irish and anglicized historical variants. One suspects that form 22 is an interpretation based on one or two mistranscribed forms. Holmer's *caraidh* (form 1) is a variant of *cora* "weir; rocky crossing place in river; rocky ridge extending into sea or lake" (*Ó Dónaill*). This element could have applied originally to some spot on an eastward falling stream which runs through this townland. Examples of Irish *o* being lowered to [a] have been noted by O'Rahilly (1932, 192–3). We may note here the similar examples of **Ballycarry** in south Co. Antrim, which has the Mod. Ir. form *Baile Cora* (*GÉ* 17), and the barony name Cary, *Cothraí* in Irish. *Cora* is the standard nom. of this word, although *Ó Dónaill* gives *cara* as a variant. *Caraidh*, which Holmer translated as "weir (?)" (*Irish of Rathlin* 171) would have originally been a dat. form; Holmer noted it as a nom. form, and as meaning "weir; dam" on the mainland (*Irish of the Glens* 104). Its use in the gen. sing. in this place-name is unusual, and form 28 may indicate a late degenerate form (we would not be suprised at the normal gen. sing. forms *cora/coradh* being anglicized as *-carry*). Other examples of dative forms being used for the gen. in Rathlin Irish were recorded by Holmer (cf. *Irish of Rathlin* 176 sv. *coille* and 240 sv. *teanga*). There is a parallel in the place-name recorded by Holmer on the mainland and which he spelt *Cnuc na Caraidh* ([krʌk nə kari]; presumably **Knocknacarry** in Layd parish; *Irish of the Glens* 42). It seems unlikely that the final element here was the gen. pl. form *coraí*. Mac Giolla Easpaig's form (27) suggests the name contains a substantive form of the adj. *carrach* "rock-incrusted, rocky" (*Ó Dónaill*) meaning "rough ground", but this noun may be otherwise unattested. We could also consider *cairre*, which *Dinneen* gives as a gen. of *carr* "an uneven surface" (*Ó Dónaill* gives only *carra* as a gen. of this word).

Early forms which suggest that the first syllable in the second element was [ɛ] or even [i] come from related sources and probably reflect the copying of scribal errors.

Ballyconagan *Baile Coinneagáin*
D 1451 "*Coinneagán*'s townland"

1. Baile Coineagan	Irish of Rathlin 177	1942
2. Ballivergan	Hib. Reg. Cary	1657c
3. Ballynafirgan	Census 19	1659
4. Ballyvergan	BSD 176	1661
5. Ballevargan	Court of Claims §923	1662c
6. Ballevaragna	Court of Claims §923	1662c
7. Ballevaragna, the towne land called	Decree of Innocence 431	1663
8. Ballyvergan 1 Towne Land	Lapsed Money Book 158	1663
9. Ballyvergan	ASE 117a §19	1668
10. Ballynalarger	HMR Ant. 11	1669
11. Ballivergan	Hib. Del. Antrim	1672c
12. Ballynavargan	Hill's Stewarts 11	1720

13. B: conagan	Lendrick Map	1780
14. N. Qr Ballyconnagan	Rathlin Vestry Book 36	1782
15. Ballyconnagan	Rathlin Vestry Book 38	1783
16. Ballyconnagan	Rathlin Vestry Book 49	1789
17. Ballyconagan	New Rent (Law)	1820
18. Ballyconagen	Bnd. Sur. (OSNB) B 32	1827c
19. Ballyconigan	Tithe Applot. 7	1833
20. Baile Uí Choineagáin "O'Conigan's town"	J O'D (OSNB) B 32	1827
21. Baile cuineochan "personal name"	Duncan 133	1906
22. Baile na bhfargain "Town of the oak shrubbery"	Rev. Magill 7	1923
23. "Townland of the rabbits"	O'Boyle 44	1939
24. "the townland of Conaghan"	Dallat's Rathlin 26	1973
25. Baile Coinneagáin "town of Coinneagán"	Place-Names of Rathlin 59	1989
26. bal′ə kɔn′agən	Irish of Rathlin 177	1942
27. bal′ə na vargən	Irish of Rathlin 192	1942
28. bal na varəgən	Irish of Rathlin 192	1942
29. bal′ə faragən	Irish of Rathlin 192	1942
30. balə ′kʌn′əkən′	Place-Names of Rathlin 59	1989
31. ˌbali′konəgən	Local pronunciation	1996

Forms 21 and 24–5 suggest that the second element in this townland name was a personal name. The male personal name *Coindecc[á]n* which appears in the *Annals of the Four Masters* in 1081 was given the modern form of *Coinneag[á]n* by O'Donovan (*AFM* ii 916–7; another instance of this name is *Coinnecan* in *AU* i 428, 914 AD). *Cuinneagán* and *Connagán*, which gave rise to the surnames MacCunnegan and O'Cunnegan (MacLysaght 1985, 70), are variant forms of the same name. Woulfe (1923, 347) regards both as diminutives of the male personal name *Conn* (Ó Corráin & Maguire 1981, 58). The further surnames Conegan and Kinegan are derived from Irish forms of the Scottish settler surname Cunningham (MacLysaght *ibid.*), and so we may consider that this place-name contains a gaelicized form of this latter surname. We might not normally expect a Scottish settler surname to qualify a *baile*- name, but massacres of the islanders and resettling may have occured three times in the late 1500s alone (see parish introduction), while it may be significant that the name appears only in 1780 (form 13).

Form 20 suggests that the second element represents the gen. pl. *coineogan* "(of the) rabbits" (*Irish of Rathlin* 177 sv. *coineog*). The absence of a medial definite article might not necessarily militate against such a form (cf. **Ballygill North**), but it is clear that Holmer himself did not suspect such an origin, and Mac Giolla Easpaig's phonetic form (30) indicates a final palatalized *n*.

The forms predating 1780 are based on *Baile na bhFargán* "townland of the ledges/steep slopes with ledges" (cf. Ó Dónaill sv. *fargán*). Holmer recorded that *Ballynavargan* was "the old name of Mullindress" (*Irish of Rathlin* 192) but it appears more likely that this name formerly covered both Ballyconagen and Mullindress townlands. He recorded several forms of the name (forms 27–9), and spelt the final element in the nom. case as *faireacan* (with the translation) "ledge or terrace in rocks" (*ibid.*). Dinneen has this word as *farragán* "a shelving rock place, a ledge or terrace; na Farragain, a townland in Lettermacward [Donegal]".

Ballygill Middle,
Ballygill North,
Ballygill South
D 1253, 1252, 1151

Baile Ghaill
"townland of the foreigner"

1. (?)Baile an Ghaedhea[i]l	Irish of Rathlin 198	1942
2. Baile Ghoill	Irish of Rathlin 199	1942
3. Ceathramh an Fhancaigh	Irish of Rathlin 82	1942
4. Ceathramh an Fhainc (?)	Irish of Rathlin 193	1942
5. Balligile	Hib. Reg. Cary	1657c
6. Balligill	DS (Par. Map) 59	1657c
7. Ballygill	DS (Par. Map) 60	1657c
8. Ballywilly	Census 19	1659
9. Balligill	BSD 176	1661
10. Ballegill	Court of Claims §923	1662c
11. Ballegill, the towne land	Decree of Innocence 431	1663
12. Ballygill	Lapsed Money Book 158	1663
13. Ballygill	ASE 117a §19	1668
14. Ballaghall	HMR Ant. 11	1669
15. Balligile	Hib. Del. Antrim	1672c
16. Ballygial	Hill's Stewarts 11	1720
17. North Ba[lly]gill	Rathlin Vestry Book 1	1769
18. Ballygill	Rathlin Vestry Book 8	1773
19. Ballygill	Rathlin Vestry Book 12	1774
20. Ballygill	Maritime Map	1776
21. B: gile	Lendrick Map	1780
22. S. Ballygill	Rathlin Vestry Book 28	1780
23. Middle Ballygill	Rathlin Vestry Book 33	1781
24. N. Ballygill	Rathlin Vestry Book 36	1782
25. M. Ballygill	Rathlin Vestry Book 38	1783
26. S. Ballygill	Rathlin Vestry Book 63	1795
27. M. B.Gill; So. B.Gill; No. B.Gill	New Rent (Law)	1820
28. Ballygill North, Ballygill Middle, Ballygill South	Bnd. Sur. (OSNB) B 32	1827c
29. Ballygeel North, Ballygeel East, Ballygeel Middle, Ballygeel South	Tithe Applot. 3	1833
30. Ballygill "Gill's town"	J O'D (OSNB) B 32	1827
31. Baile geal "The bright town"	Ó Dubhthaigh 132	1905
32. Baile gaidhl "the townland frequented by certain sea-gulls"	Duncan 133	1906
33. " . . . of the hostages"	O'Boyle 44	1939
34. "the townland of brightness" (limestone)	Dallat's Rathlin 26	1973
35. Baile Ghaill (Láir) "the town of the foreigner"	Place-Names of Rathlin 38	1989
36. Baile Ghaill Thuaidh	Place-Names of Rathlin 44	1989
37. Baile Ghaill Theas	Place-Names of Rathlin 48	1989

38. Ceathramh an Fhanca "the quarter of the sheep-fold"	Place-Names of Rathlin 47	1989
39. (?)bɑlʹə ɣEːjəl	Irish of Rathlin 198	1942
40. bɑlʹə ˈɣEilʹ	Irish of Rathlin 199	1942
41. kʹɑrəv ə naŋki	Irish of Rathlin 82	1942
42. kʹɑrəv ə nɛŋkʹə	Irish of Rathlin 193	1942
43. ˌbɑliˈgil	Local pronunciation	1996

Holmer noted *gall* locally as meaning "lowlander, native of the 'low country' [i.e. the Scottish Lowlands]", and recorded a nom. pl. form (*gaill*), also used as the gen. sing., as [gEilʹ] (*Irish of Rathlin* 199). Hamilton (1974, 283) recorded the nom. pl. in the Irish of Tory Island as [nə gïLʹ] which also reflects somewhat the historical forms here. *Dinneen* translates *gall* as "a foreigner; applied in succession to Gauls, Franks, Danes, Normans and English; a Protestant". The aspiration of the *g* could be attributed to the use of the name in the dat. case. The somewhat less common *gall* "monolith, pillar-stone" (*Dinneen*) or "castle" (cf. *PNI* iv 178–9) might be also be considered as a possible final element (*Dinneen* has this as a fem. noun with gen. sing. *gaille*, although Ó Dónaill has it as a masc. noun, gen. sing. *gaill*. *Dwelly* also has it as masc. noun). Holmer also recorded that *gall* was used in Rathlin to denote "a small kind of sea-gull, called kittiwake" (*Irish of Rathlin* 199) and that this was the popular understanding of the final element in this name. The obsolete meanings "cock; swan" have been attested for *gall* in Scottish Gaelic (*Dwelly*). Somewhat similarly, *Albanach* "Scotsman; Protestant, Presbyterian" (*Ó Dónaill*) was also used in Rathlin to denote "a kind of puffin, called 'wild parrot'" (*Irish of Rathlin* 158). Holmer believed *gall* "kittiwake" occurred in the subtownland name **Carrickagile** (see Other Names), but not here.

O'Donovan suggested that the male personal name *Goll* (gen. *Ghoill*) formed the second element. There is no apparent tradition regarding such a figure (cf. *Suí Ghoill* in *PNI* v 163–4). The absence of a medial definite article in the place-name might indeed appear to favour a *baile* plus personal name structure, but several *baile-* names on the mainland are followed by sing. and pl. nouns without the definite article (cf. **Ballyberidagh** in Culfeightrin and **Ballycastle** in Ramoan, for example). Holmer regarded forms 1 and 39, which could be interpreted as *Baile Ghae(i)l* "townland of the Irishman(-men)/Highlander(s)" as particularly dubious forms. Forms 5, 16 and 29 might otherwise suggest *Baile Ghiall* "townland of (the) hostages" (cf. *Ráth Giall* "fort of (the) hostages", anglicized **Rathgill**, in *PNI* ii 166–7; *Irish of Rathlin* 52 §81), but must be regarded as anomalous.

We could account for form 8 by noting that intervocalic [ɣ]/[g] has changed to [w] elsewhere locally (cf. **Drumavoley** and **Ballydurnian** in Ramoan), but as the *Census* is in any event a very unreliable source, it is probably best explained as containing scribal errors. Forms 3–4, 38 and 40–41 refer to a name by which Ballygill North was commonly known (*Place-Names of Rathlin* 47), and which we may standardize as *Ceathrú an Fhanca* "quarterland of the sheep-pen". *Dinneen* suggests that *fanca* "a sheep pen" is an Antrim variant of *ban(n)c* "a bank of a stream; a bench, a seat; a bank, as of turf . . ." or *panc* "the cow-market at a fair" (note Scottish Gaelic *fang* (*Dwelly*) and Scots English *fank* (*Scot. Nat. Dict.*), both of similar meaning to *fanca*).

Ballynagard
D 1539

Baile na gCeard
"townland of the artificers"

1. Baile nan gCeard	Irish of Rathlin 173	1942

2. Ballnagard	Rathlin Vestry Book 44	1787
3. Ballynagard	New Rent (Law)	1820
4. Ballinagard	Bnd. Sur. (OSNB) B 32	1827c
5. Baile na g-Ceárd "town of the artificers"	J O'D (OSNB) B32	1827
6. Baile-na-g-ceard "from certain tinsmiths"	Duncan 133	1906
7. "Townland of the smith"	O'Boyle 44	1939
8. "townland of the tinsmiths"	Dallat's Rathlin 26	1973
9. Baile na gCeard "the town of the tradesmen"	Place-Names of Rathlin 58	1989
10. bɑl′ə naŋ g′ɛrd	Irish of Rathlin 173	1942
11. ˌbɑlnəˈgjɑrd	Local pronunciation	1995

Holmer recorded the word *ceard* (nom. pl. *ceardan*) as meaning "tinker, also a garrulous woman" (*Irish of Rathlin* 173). *Dinneen* translates this word as "a worker, a mechanic, a tinker, a smith; a poet, an artist". *Dwelly* (sv. *cèard*) has it as "tinker; smith, brazier, any tradesman working at smith-work of any kind [usually in composition, as *fear-cèaird*, a tradesman]; mechanic; blackguard". See also **Ballynagard** in Culfeightrin.

Ballynoe	*Baile Nua*	
D 1550	"new townland"	
1. Baile Nó	Irish of Rathlin 220	1942
2. Ballinar	Hib. Reg. Cary	1657c
3. Ballynoa	DS (Par. Map) 60	1657c
4. Ballymore	Census 19	1659
5. Ballinoa	BSD 176	1661
6. Ballenod	Court of Claims §923	1662c
7. Ballenoe	Court of Claims §923	1662c
8. Ballanoe, the towneland called	Decree of Innocence 431	1663
9. (?)Ballyneagh, 1 Towne Land	Lapsed Money Book 158	1663
10. Ballynea	ASE 117a §19	1668
11. Ballynoe	Hill's Stewarts 11	1720
12. Ballano	Rathlin Vestry Book 8	1773
13. Ballanoo	Rathlin Vestry Book 12	1774
14. Balinoe	Maritime Map	1776
15. Ballanoo	Rathlin Vestry Book 22	1778
16. Ballynoe	PRONI D2977/3A/2/1/40	1812
17. Ballynoe	New Rent (Law)	1820
18. Ballynoe	Bnd. Sur. (OSNB) B 32	1827c
19. Baile Nua "New town"	J O'D (OSNB) B 32	1827
20. Baile nuadh	Duncan 133	1906
21. Baile nuadh "New town"	Rev. Magill 7	1923
22. An Baile Nua "the new town"	Place-Names of Rathlin 69	1989

23. bɛl′ə ′nɔ·ə	Irish of Rathlin 42	1942
24. bɑl′ə ′nɔ·ə	Irish of Rathlin 220	1942
25. bɑlə′noː	Place-Names of Rathlin 69	1989
26. ˌbɑlə′noː	Local pronunciation	1996

Holmer noted that *nua* "new" was hardly used in the local dialect, although he did record it in a phrase meaning "brand new" which he spelt as *úr nó* ([ʌːr nɔ·ə]; *Irish of Rathlin* 220). Form 9 may represent an obsolete place-name; it referred to a territory of 179 acres, while the modern townland occupies just over 80 acres. Of course, townland territories change over time, and it could alternatively reflect the older forms of *nua, nuadh/nódh* (*Irish of Rathlin* 52 §81).

Carravinally
D 1549

Ceathrú na hEaladh
"quarterland of the pillar-stone(?)"

1. an Ealaidh	Irish of Rathlin 190	1942
2. an Ealaidh, air	Irish of Rathlin 190	1942
3. Ally	Rathlin Vestry Book 6	1772
4. Ally	Rathlin Vestry Book 8	1773
5. Carivenhala	Maritime Map	1776
6. Alley	New Rent (Law)	1820
7. Ally	Hamilton's Letters 246	1822
8. Carrivanally	Bnd. Sur. (OSNB) B 32	1827c
9. Corvanally	Tithe Applot. 15	1833
10. Ceathramhadha na hAille "Cliff quarter"	J O'D (OSNB) B 32	1827
11. Cearmhadh-na-n-ealaidhe "the quarterland of the swans"	Duncan 133	1906
12. "Quarterland of the lake"	O'Boyle 44	1939
13. "the quarterland of the swans"	Dallat's Rathlin 26	1973
14. An Ealaidh or Ceathramh na hEaladh, meaning uncertain	Place-Names of Rathlin 83	1989
15. ə ′n′ɑlɪ	Irish of Rathlin 190	1942
16. er ə ′n′ɑlɪ	Irish of Rathlin 190	1942
17. er ə ′n′ɑɲi	Irish of Rathlin 190	1942
18. ˌkarïvən′ali	Local pronunciation	1995
19. ′ali	Local pronunciation	1995

The use of the final element on its own appears to rule out more obvious possibilities regarding its origin. However, forms 15–7 suggest that the final element in the townland name began indeed with *ea*, while form 5 suggests that we are dealing with a feminine noun (we might otherwise have interpreted form 1 as indicating a petrified masc. dat. form). We may consider that this element represents a development of the fem. noun *eala* "mute swan; pillar[ed] stone; sanctuary" (*Dwelly* sv.). *Dwelly* gives *ealaidh* as the gen. sing. form, but we might postulate that there developed here a similar dat. form which was adopted as the nom. (compare *cill<cillidh* in **Killaleenan** in Other Names, Culfeightrin; see also **Ballycarry**

above). *Ealaidh* in this case would more probably represent "pillar-stone" or perhaps by extension "place of the pillar-stone". The meaning "sanctuary" (which, along with the meaning "pillar-stone" may be attested previously only in the Scottish Gaelic of the Western Isles) seems less likely. It would have the gen. form *ealadh* (note form 14), which is reflected in Irish forms of **Ally Lough** (see Other Names). These latter Irish forms discount the unattested collective noun *ealach* (dat. *ealaigh*) "place of swans/pillar-stones" as a possible origin of this element. *Dwelly*'s *eala* "pillar-stone" appears to represent a development of the fem. noun *ail* "stone, rock" (*Ó Dónaill*).

Mac Giolla Easpaig has noted that the official English form of this name is seldom used (*Place-Names of Rathlin* 83), and this also appears to have been the case in Holmer's time (forms 15–7). This official form suggests that *An Ealaidh* remained undeclined following *ceathrú* (earlier *ceathramha*) "quarterland", latterly at least (cf. **Sroanderrig** in Other Names).

Carravindoon	*Ceathrú an Dúin*	
D 1549	"quarterland of the fort"	
1. Karvandoan	Rathlin Vestry Book 15	1775
2. Carvandoan	Rathlin Vestry Book 26	1779
3. Carvandoan	Rathlin Vestry Book 44	1787
4. Carrivandoon	Bnd. Sur. (OSNB) B 32	1827c
5. Carvendoon	Tithe Applot. 15	1833
6. Ceathramha an Dúin	J O'D (OSNB) B 32	1827
7. Cearmhadh-an-dúin "the quarterland of the fort"	Duncan 133	1906
8. "Quarterland of the fort"	O'Boyle 44	1939
9. "the quarterland of the fort"	Dallat's Rathlin 26	1973
10. Ceathramh an Dúin "the quarter of the fort"	Place-Names of Rathlin 81	1989
11. ˌkarvən'duːn	Local pronunciation	1995

Mac Giolla Easpaig noted that "no trace of the fort remains", but suggests that two minor names in this townland, **Doon Bay** (see Other Names) and Doon Point, referred to the same *dún*. It seems possible that the *dún* in this case referred figuratively to columnar basaltic rock formations at Doon Point (see, for example, **Portandoon**, a subtownland name in Kebble, in Other Names). This territory was formerly a quarterland (*ceathrú*, earlier *ceathramha*), probably of Ballynoe, which explains its absence from 17th-century sources (Carleton 1991, 72).

Church Quarter	An English form	
D 1451		
1. Church Quarter	Rathlin Vestry Book 41	1784
2. Church Qr	Rathlin Vestry Book 51	1790
3. Church Qr	Rathlin Vestry Book 54	1791
4. Church Qr.	New Rent (Law)	1820

5. Church Quarter	Bnd. Sur. (OSNB) B 32	1827c
6. tʃɔrtʃ 'kwɔrtər	Local pronunciation	1996

The use of this townland name may be in decline. Church Quarter was formerly a constituent part of Ballyconagan (Carleton 1991, 72). In 1830 it was recorded that in this townland "there stands an Established church and about [200 yards] north of [this] there is a Roman Catholic chapel" (*OSM* xxiv 128) while in 1838 the Ordnance Survey noted:

> The Church is a neat modern building 58 feet long and 28 wide. It would accomodate about 150 persons. At its western extremity there is a small square tower . . . The Roman Catholic chapel is situated in the same townland . . . it is a plain substantial building 42 feet long and 20 feet wide, and capable of accomodating 400 persons. There is a gallery in it (*ibid.* 131).

O'Laverty later noted that the Protestant church occupied the site of the pre-Reformation Catholic church and recorded the tradition that:

> the ancient church was known by the names of *Seipeal Cooil* . . . and *Teampoll Cooil* . . . That, therefore, was the site where St. Cooal, or Comgall, the founder of [the monastery of] Bangor, erected about the year 580 the 'cell' or little church (*O'Laverty* iv 374).

Séipéal Chomhaill "St Comhall's chapel/church" and *Teampall Chomhaill* (of similar meaning) would be modern forms of the names collected by O'Laverty, if we accepted that the final elements were indeed the saint's name (earlier nom. *Comgall*). The church does appear to have had some medieval connection with the monastery of Bangor (see parish introduction).

Mac Giolla Easpaig has also noted the further minor names of *Leac na Cille* "flag[-stone] of the church or cemetery" and *Toigh an Aifrinn* "the church (lit. the mass house)" in this townland (*Place-Names of Rathlin* 62–3). The former of these refers to a rock which extends into the sea at the Protestant church. See also **Church Bay** in Other Names.

Cleggan
D 1151

Cloigeann
"skull-shaped hill(?)"

1. Claigeann	Irish of Rathlin 175	1942
2. Claigeann, go	Irish of Rathlin 175	1942
3. Cleggan	Rathlin Vestry Book 6	1772
4. Claggan	Rathlin Vestry Book 8	1773
5. Claggan	Maritime Map	1776
6. Claggan	Rathlin Vestry Book 24	1779
7. Cleggan	Rathlin Vestry Book 62	1794
8. Clagan	New Rent (Law)	1820
9. Cleggan (Recent)	Bnd. Sur. (OSNB) B 32	1827c
10. Claggin	Tithe Applot. 1	1833
11. Claigeann "hard rock hill"	J O'D (OSNB) B 32	1827

12. "Round hill"	O'Boyle 44	1939
13. An Chloigeann "the skull"	Place-Names of Rathlin 28	1989
14. klɛd'ən	Irish of Rathlin 175	1942
15. klɑg'ən	Irish of Rathlin 175	1942
16. kŋɑg'ən	Irish of Rathlin 175	1942
17. klag'ən	LASID i xiv	1958
18. 'klagən	Local pronunciation	1996

The use of *cloigeann* in place-names is discussed under **Cleggan** in Armoy. *Cloigeann* appears to have been generally masculine although it was feminine in Rathlin Irish. Holmer recorded a minor place-name, of uncertain location, which he spelt *Druim na Claiginne* (*Irish of Rathlin* 175). However, this townland name does not appear to have been used with the definite article (form 2).

Craigmacagan *Creag Mhic Ágáin*
D 1549 "*Mac Ágáin*'s rock"

1. Creag Macagan	Irish of Rathlin 180	1942
2. Cregmacaggan	Rathlin Vestry Book 16	1776
3. Cregmacagan	Rathlin Vestry Book 63	1795
4. Craigmacagan	New Rent (Law)	1820
5. Craigmacagan	Bnd. Sur. (OSNB) B 32	1827c
6. Creag mic Agáin "MacAgan's rock"	J O'D (OSNB) B 32	1827
7. Carraig-mic-Cagáin	Duncan 133	1906
8. Creag Mhic Agáin "the rock of Mac Agáin"	Place-Names of Rathlin 75	1989
9. kreg mɑ'kagən	Irish of Rathlin 180	1942
10. kreg mɑ'kag'ən	Irish of Rathlin 213	1942
11. krəmə'k'agən	Place-Names of Rathlin 75	1989
12. 'kreːgmə'kagən	Local pronunciation	1995

Mac Ágáin may be an otherwise unattested surname (MacLysaght 1985, Woulfe 1923, Black 1946). The somewhat similar *Ó hÁgáin*, anglicized O'Hagan, is an Ulster variant of *Ó hÓgáin*, anglicized O'Hogan (Woulfe 1923, 547). All these surnames derive from the male personal name *Ógán* "youth, lad" (*ibid.* and Ó Corráin & Maguire 1981, 148). The palatalization of the medial [k] in form 11 may represent a late development. Form 10 was recorded from an English speaker.

Regarding the first element in this name, see **Craig** in Ballintoy.

Demesne A English form
D 1551

1. (?)the Park	Rathlin Vestry Book 46	1788
2. (?)Park	New Rent (Law)	1820
3. Demesne	Bnd. Sur. (OSNB) B 32	1827c

4. Demesne	Tithe App. Book 17	1833
5. dəm'eːən	Local pronunciation	1995

This townland of over 62 acres was previously part of Ballynoe and Ballyconagan townlands (Carleton 1991, 72). In 1838, one Reverend Valentine Griffith lived here "in a neat little 1–storey cottage comfortably fitted up" (*OSM* xxiv 131), but the townland may have been carved out originally for the Gage family who became landlords of the island when they purchased it from Alexander MacDonnell, fifth Earl of Antrim, in 1740 (*O'Laverty* iv 371). The Gage residence is in the neighbouring townland of Church Quarter (*OSM* xxiv 128). Forms 1 and 2 may derive from Irish *An Pháirc* "the field". See **White Park** in Ballintoy.

Glebe
D 1551

An English form

1. Glebe	Bnd. Sur. (OSNB) B 32	1827c
2. Glebe	Tithe App. Book 17	1833
3. 'glib	Local pronunciation	1995

In 1838, the Ordnance Survey noted that "the rector is supported by his tithes and glebe, and 30 pounds per annum from Primate Boulter's fund" (OSM xxiv 132). The glebe contains 24 acres, 1 rood and 22 perches.

Kebble
D 0951

An Caibeal
"the chapel"

1. Caibeal, an	Irish of Rathlin 45	1942
2. Chaibeal, anns a'	Irish of Rathlin 170	1942
3. Chaibeal, tá mé dol a	Irish of Rathlin 170	1942
4. Cabbal	Rathlin Vestry Book 15	1775
5. Cabball	Rathlin Vestry Book 26	1779
6. Cabbel	Rathlin Vestry Book 49	1789
7. Cabal	New Rent (Law)	1820
8. Kibble	Bnd. Sur. (OSNB) B 32	1827c
9. Kebble	Tithe Applot. 1	1833
10. Caibiol "a burying-ground"	Duncan 133	1906
11. "a burying ground"	Dallat's Rathlin 27	1973
12. An Caibeal "the chapel"	Place-Names of Rathlin 7	1989
13. əŋ kɑbjəl	Irish of Rathlin 45	1942
14. sə xɑbjəl	Irish of Rathlin 170	1942
15. tɑː mi dol ə xɑbjəl	Irish of Rathlin 170	1942
16. k'jɑbəl	Place-Names of Rathlin 7	1989
17. 'kɑbəl	Local pronunciation	1996

Caibeal is translated "chapel; family burial ground" by *Dwelly*. There is otherwise no apparent ecclesiastical tradition of any kind associated with the townland. Mac Giolla Easpaig (*Place-Names of Rathlin* 70) noted a further instance of this element in the subtownland place-name of *Baile an Chabail* in Ballynoe.

In c. 1953 Murphy (*Murphy's Rathlin* 8) recorded the following etymology which features an interpretation of the name based on the English word *cabal* "a clandestine or unofficial group of people forming a faction, esp. in political intrigue" (*Longman Dict.*) :

'Doesn't that townland mean 'Council'? There's another at the other end. The story here was that when the Norsemen were coming that the people at the two ends of the island held a council there as to what to do' (cf. also *ibid.* 174).

This townland was previously considered a constituent part of Kinramer in mid-17th-century sources (Carleton 1991, 72).

Kilpatrick D 1351	*Cill Phádraig* "St Patrick's church"	
1. gCille Pháraic, in	Irish of Rathlin 66	1942
2. Kilpatrick	Hib. Reg. Cary	1657c
3. Repatrick	Census 19	1659
4. Killpatrick	BSD 176	1661
5. Killpatricke	Court of Claims §923	1662c
6. Kilpatricke	Court of Claims §923	1662c
7. Killpatrick, the towne land called	Decree of Innocence 431	1663
8. Killpatrick	Lapsed Money Book 158	1663
9. Killpatricke	ASE 117a §19	1668
10. Kilpatricke	HMR Ant. 11	1669
11. Killpatrick	Hib. Del. Antrim	1672c
12. Killpatrick	Hill's Stewarts 11	1720
13. Kilpatrick	Maritime Map	1776
14. Kilpatrick	Rathlin Vestry Book 43	1786
15. Killpatrick	PRONI D2977/3A/2/1/40	1812
16. Kilpatrick	New Rent (Law)	1820
17. Kilpatrick	Bnd. Sur. (OSNB) B 32	1827c
18. Cill Phádraig "Patrick's Church"	J O'D (OSNB) B 32	1827
19. Cill Phadraig "The church of Patrick"	Ó Dubhthaigh 181	1905
20. Cill Pádraig "Church of Patrick"	Rev. Magill 18	1923
21. Cill Phádraig "the church of (Saint) Patrick"	Place-Names of Rathlin 57	1989
22. ən gʹilʹə ˈfaːrikʹ	Irish of Rathlin 66, 174	1942
23. ˌkïlˈpatrïk	Local pronunciation	1996

Cill "a church, a churchyard, a burial place; cell, house" (*Dinneen*) was translated by Holmer as "church with cemetery" (*Irish of Rathlin* 174). O'Laverty noted regarding this townland:

302

No indications of a church or graveyard have been dicovered in Kilpatrick, but it has been used for many years as a stock-farm for Mr. Gage, and consequently there was no disturbance of its soil to bring to light such indications. In this townland there is a little field sloping to the south in which there is a hill called Altbeg, and on it a large stone on which Mass was celebrated during times of persecution (*O'Laverty* iv 379).

This stone was once the site of "the principal Mass Station" on the island (*ibid.* 385), and was called *Cloch an Aifrinn* "stone of the mass (mass-stone)" (*Place-names of Rathlin* 58). Holmer (*Irish of Rathlin* 221) and Mac Giolla Easpaig recorded in this townland the minor place-name of *Cnoc Phádraig* "the hill of (Saint) Patrick", where the saint is said to have preached (*Place-Names of Rathlin* 57).

Kinkeel	*An Ceann Caol*	
D 1449	"the narrow end"	
1. Ceann Caol, an	Irish of Rathlin 172	1942
2. Killcuile	Hib. Reg. Cary	1657c
3. Killcuille	DS (Par. Map) 57	1657c
4. Killcuile	BSD 176	1661
5. (?)Ceane	Court of Claims §923	1662c
6. Coankill, the townlands of	Court of Claims §923	1662c
7. Ceankill, the townelands of	Decree of Innocence 431	1663
8. Killcuille	ASE 117a §19	1668
9. Kilcuil	Hib. Del. Antrim	1672c
10. Kankiel	Hill's Stewarts 11	1720
11. Kinkeel	Rathlin Vestry Book 1	1769
12. Kenkele	Maritime Map	1776
13. Kinkeil	Rathlin Vestry Book 42	1785
14. Kinkeill	Rathlin Vestry Book 60	1794
15. Kinkoule	PRONI D2977/3A/2/1/40	1812
16. Kinkeel	New Rent (Law)	1820
17. Kinkeel	Bnd. Sur. (OSNB) B 32	1827c
18. Ceann Caol "narrow head"	J O'D (OSNB) B 32	1827
19. Ceann Caol "The slender head"	Ó Dubhthaigh 181	1905
20. Ceann Caol "slender head"	Rev. Magill 18	1923
21. "Narrow end of the island"	O'Boyle 44	1939
22. An Ceann Caol "the narrow end"	Place-Names of Rathlin 78	1989
23. əŋ k'aːn keːl	Irish of Rathlin 172	1942
24. k'ınˈkıːl	Place-Names of Rathlin 78	1989
25. kïnˈkeːl	Local pronunciation	1996

The earliest forms of this place-name might suggest that the first element was originally *cill* "church, burying ground" or *coill* "wood". Variants from similar sources of the townland name **Kinramer** also take a *kil-* form, while one source features both *kil-* and *kin-* forms on different pages (see forms 6–7, Kinramer). The *kil-* forms are probably best explained as scribal errors; they occur only in related sources. Notably, Mac Giolla Easpaig recently noted the two variants [k'ɪl'ˈkiːl] and [k'ɪn'kiːl] when recording the subtownland name of Kinkeel Lough (*Place-Names of Rathlin* 81), but the first of these may feature an assimilation of consonants. There is no apparent recorded ecclesiastical tradition associated with the townland, although the place-name seems to have once referred to the entire southern extremity of the island. It is now a much smaller territory on the eastern shore of Church Bay.

Ó Maolfabhail (1987, 7–8) suggests that *ceann*, which is now often used as "head(-land)", had also among other connotations, a meaning similar to that of *beann* "cliff, peak" (cf. **Benmore or Fair Head**, in Other Names, Culfeightrin). Considering the original area to which the place-name referred, the meaning "end, extremity" also seems applicable. The southern arm of the island, now called in English *The Lower End*, was referred to in Irish both as *An Ceann Caol* and *An Ceann úd Thios* while the north-western part of the island, now called *The Upper End*, was referred to both as *An Ceann R(e)amhar* and *An Ceann úd Thuas* (see *Irish of Rathlin* 172; see also *Iarsmaí ó Reachrainn* 252).

Forms 18–22 suggest that the adj. *caol* "narrow, slender, thin" formed the final element and this indeed seems most likely. It is supported by Holmer's recording (form 23; see *Irish of Rathlin* 43 §59 regarding local pronunciation of *ao*). Regarding less likely elements see *Cill Chaoil*/**Kinkeel** in *PNI* iii 13–7 and **Altachuile** in Other Names. Ó Maolfabhail notes that *ceann* is normally qualified by a noun, but that adjectives occur in *ceann*- names in some instances in northern counties and more commonly in Scotland (Ó Maolfabhail 1987, 76; cf. also **Kinramer**, and **Kinbane or White Head** in Other Names, Ramoan).

Kinramer North,
Kinramer South
D 1152, 1151

An Ceann Ramhar
"the thick end"

1.	gCinn Reamhair, i	Claidheamh Soluis 8 Mei., L.5	1907
2.	gCeann Reamhar, i	Athchló Uladh iii	1910
3.	Ceann Reamhar, in	Irish of Rathlin 66	1942
4.	Ceann Reamhar, an	Irish of Rathlin 225	1942
5.	Chinn Rámhar, 'uin a'	Iarsmaí ó Reachrainn 251	1948
6.	Kilrainire	Hib. Reg. Cary	1657c
7.	Kilraver	DS (Par. Map) 57	1657c
8.	Keanereavor	DS (Par. Map) 60	1657c
9.	Rovever	Census 19	1659
10.	Keanereavor	BSD 176	1661
11.	Ceanriver	Court of Claims §923	1662c
12.	Kearaver	Court of Claims §923	1662c
13.	Kearamer, the towne called	Decree of Innocence 431	1663
14.	Keawramer	Lapsed Money Book 158	1663
15.	(?)Kandaver	ASE 117a §19	1668
16.	Kilramer	HMR Ant. 11	1669
17.	Killrainure	Hib. Del. Antrim	1672c
18.	Kenramer	Hill's Stewarts 11	1720
19.	Kenrammer	Maritime Map	1776
20.	South Kinramer	Rathlin Vestry Book 16	1776
21.	N. Kinrammer	Rathlin Vestry Book 22	1778

22. Kinramer	Lendrick Map	1780
23. South Kinramer	Rathlin Vestry Book 51	1790
24. South Kinramer	Rathlin Vestry Book 54	1791
25. N. Kinrammer	Rathlin Vestry Book 56	1792
26. N. Kinrammer	Rathlin Vestry Book 57	1793
27. The Kenramer or western end	Hamilton's Letters 19	1784
28. So. Kinramer, No. Kinramer	New Rent (Law)	1820
29. Kinramher North, Kinramher	South Bnd. Sur. (OSNB) B 32	1827c
30. Kinrammer So, Kinrammer	North Tithe Applot. 1	1833
31. Kinravagh	Murphy's Rathlin 39	1953c
32. Cean-ramber "the large head or promontory"	Hamilton's Letters 19	1784
33. Ken-ramer "the great end"	Hamiltons' Letters 246	1822
34. Ceann Ramhar	J O'D (OSNB) B 32	1827
35. Ceann ramhar "The thick (fat) head"	Ó Dubhthaigh 181	1905
36. Cionn ramhor "thick head"	Duncan 133	1906
37. Ceann ramhar "thick end"	Rev. Magill 18	1923
38. "thick or broad head"	Dallat's Rathlin 27	1973
39. Ceann Ramhar Thuaidh "the thick end"	Place-Names of Rathlin 21	1989
40. Ceann Ramhar Theas	Place-Names of Rathlin 24	1989
41. əŋ k'an ra̯ṽ∂r, rɑuər	Irish of Rathlin 225	1942
42. ˌkïn'ramər	Local pronunciation	1996
43. ˌkïn'ravər	Local pronunciation	1996

Early forms of this name which contain a first element of the type *kil-* may be misleading. Early forms of **Kinkeel** are similar and while some linguistic explanation for the change could be found, it is probably best to account for them as being repeated scribal errors. The element *ceann*, which features in all the later forms and pronunciations, is dicussed under Kinkeel.

The English forms suggest that the second element *ramhar* "fat, thick" suffered early delenition of the medial *mh* (form 13). While some of the forms containing *-ramer* may be scribal errors or copies of scribal errors, the use of *m* rather than *v* probably reflects the voiced labio-dental nasal vowel ([ṽ]), whose nasal quality rendered an acoustic effect that Holmer described as "almost mv" (*Irish of Rathlin* 31). Other examples of the anglicization of *ramhar* as *ramer* probably include the townland name **Cullenramer** in Donaghmore parish, Co. Tyrone (Ó Máille 1960, 58) and **Muckleramer** in south Antrim (*PNI* iv 56–8). Joyce cites further examples of this phenomenon, which he regards as delenition, and suggests that it is confined to the northern half of Ireland (*Joyce* ii 419–20).

Kinramer appears to have once referred to the greater part of the north-western extremity of the island although today Kebble is the most north-westerly territory. Evidence for the division of Kinramer appears in the sources only in 1776 (form 19).

Knockan
D 1351

An Cnocán
"the hillock"

1. Cnocán	Antiquities of Rathlin 42	1911

2. An Cnocan	Irish of Rathlin 176	1942
3. Knockans	Rathlin Vestry Book 4	1770
4. Nockans	Rathlin Vestry Book 13	1774
5. Knockan	Lendrick Map	1780
6. Nockans	Rathlin Vestry Book 41	1784
7. Knockans	New Rent (Law)	1820
8. Knockan	Hamilton's Letters 246	1822
9. Knockans	Bnd. Sur. (OSNB) B 32	1827c
10. Cnocáin "hillocks"	J O'D (OSNB) B 32	1827
11. Cnocain "The little hills"	Ó Dubhthaigh 182	1905
12. Cnocain "Hillock"	Rev. Magill 19	1923
13. "Little Hills"	O'Boyle 44	1939
14. An Cnocán "the hillock"	Place-Names of Rathlin 52	1989
15. əŋ 'krɔkən	Irish of Rathlin 176	1942
16. 'nɔkəns	Local pronunciation	1995

The pronunciation of this name collected by Holmer (form 15) shows that *cnocán* "hillock, heap" (*Ó Dónaill*) was used in the nom. sing. case and not the nom. pl. as had been previously suggested (forms 10–3). The addition of the English plural suffix, probably due to some internal division of the territory or the development of more than one hamlet in the townland, had already occurred by 1770 (form 3). See also **Knockans** in Armoy.

Mullindress
D 1551

Maoil na nDreas
"hillock of the brambles"

1. Mullindress	Maritime Map	1776
2. Mullindress	Bnd. Sur. (OSNB) B 32	1827c
3. Mallandress	Tithe App. Book 9	1833
4. Mullan Dreasa "Bramble Hill"	J O'D (OSNB) B 32	1827
5. Maol-an-druis (brier)	Duncan 133	1906
6. "Height of the briars"	O'Boyle 44	1939
7. "Place of briars"	Dallat's Rathlin 27	1973
8. Maoil na nDreas "the hill of the brambles"	Place-Names of Rathlin 62	1989
9. mʌlən'drɛs	Place-Names of Rathlin 62	1989
10. ˌmolən'drɛs	Local pronunciation	1995

Mac Giolla Easpaig suggests that the first element in this place-name was *maoil* "rounded summit; hillock, knoll". We could also consider a variant of this word, *maol* (*Ó Dónaill*). Dwelly translates *maol* as "brow of a rock; cape, promontory, mull". The Ordnance Survey recorded in c. 1855 that Mullindress village was situated at "the south base of a low rocky hill" (*OSRNB* sh.1, 2). *Maolán* "low rounded hill, knoll", *maoileann* "rounded summit; hillock, knoll" and *mullán* "elevated ground, hillock" might also be considered as first elements. On the mainland, Holmer noted a [ʌ] vowel (form 9) where something like [ǫ] might otherwise be expected (e.g. *muc* [mʌk]; *Irish of the Glens* 17–8): probably a late linguistic development (post 1700). This feature also occured in Rathlin (*Irish of Rathlin* 28, 182–3). Unfortunately, Holmer does not appear to have recorded this particular place-name, so *maoil* has been followed here. Ó Maolfabhail (1986, 11) has shown how a word *maoil* "current or (sea-)stream" could have given rise to some nearby place-names, including the administrative name of Moyle in Antrim, and Mull of Kintyre in Scotland. The modern townland of Mullindress is separated from Church Bay only by the relatively new territories of Glebe and Church Quarter. However, *maoil* "current" is not likely here.

Mac Giolla Easpaig's suggested form (8) implies that the first *n* had been lost due to its position following the *l* of *maoil*, as it is already missing in the earliest variant (form 1, 1776). Since Rathlin Irish generally followed Scottish Gaelic in the construction of the gen. pl. case (see *Irish of Rathlin* 65), we would not expect the nazalization of the *d* in the final element. For example, Holmer recorded the somewhat similar subtownland place-name *Inean nan Dreas* as [inɛn nɑn dres] (*ibid.* 187; regarding the first element *inean* recté *ingeán* see **Inannanooan** in Other Names). The final element was probably the gen. pl. *dreas* "brambles, briars". *Dreas* is also a variant form of *dris* "prickly, cantankerous person" and *dras* "dross", while *Dwelly* also lists the additional meaning (from Mid-Perthshire Gaelic) for *dreas* of "place, stead". For various reasons, none of these latter meanings appears very likely in this case.

Roonivoolin
D 1548

Rubha na bhFaoileann
"headland of the seagulls"

1. Rudha na bhFaoileann	Irish of Rathlin 193	1942
2. Runavoolen	Rathlin Vestry Book 4	1770
3. Roonavolin	Rathlin Vestry Book 46	1788
4. Ronovolin	New Rent (Law)	1820
5. Roonivoolin	Bnd. Sur. (OSNB) B 32	1827c
6. Runavoolin	Tithe Applot. 17	1833
7. Roin a mhullain "division of the hill"	J O'D (OSNB) B 32	1827
8. Rú-na-bhFaoileann	Duncan 134	1906
9. "Point of the island"	O'Boyle 44	1939
10. "The point of the boolies"	Dallat's Rathlin 27	1973
11. Rubha na bhFaoileann "the point of the seagulls"	Place-Names of Rathlin 86	1989
12. rʌə nɑ vʌːlʹən	Irish of Rathlin 193	1942
13. ˌrunəˈvulʹn	Local pronunciation	1995

The first element of this name is *rubha* "a salient, a point (of a spear, a fort, land, etc.), peninsula" (*Dinneen*). *Dwelly* has this word as *rudha* (note form 1) which he translates as "point of land, promontory". Discussing the uncertain origin of this word, however, Hughes has noted the possible further meanings "land of the (herb) rue; brake or thicket; clearing", and translated the Ards townland name of *Rubha Riabhach* (anglicized **Rowreagh**) as "variegated clearing" (*PNI* ii 94–5). Mac Giolla Easpaig has noted that the *rubha* of Roonivoolin is further recorded in the subtownland name of **Rue Point** (see Other Names), a headland which marks the southernmost extremity of both the townland and the island (*Place-Names of Rathlin* 88). The Culfeightrin subtownland name of **Ruebane** also refers to a coastal salient.

Faoileann "seagull" (*Dinneen*) or "common white gull; mew" (*Dwelly*) has the standard modern form *faoileán* (*Ó Dónaill*). There was no distinction in Rathlin Irish between *n* and *nn* (*Irish of Rathlin* 55 §89), but there was a distinction between unstressed *ea* and unstressed *(e)á* (*ibid. passim*). Holmer suggested that the use of the gen. pl. article *na* rather than *nan* (the form *nam* was not recorded locally by Holmer; cf. also **Mullindress**) may be explained by the name being of a late origin, although he later conversely suggests that the absence of *nan* in some local place-names of similar construction such as the subtownland name of *Sloc na gCailleach* (anglicized **Sloaknacalliagh**; in Roonivoolin) may indicate an "earlier stage in the history of eclipsis" (*ibid.* 65). Normally townland names are of a much older vintage than subtownland names, but in Rathlin it is to be seen that few of the townland names have historical forms predating 1750. Holmer's *Sloc na gCailleach* was believed to refer to "the scene of terrible crimes during the Campbell massacres of 1642" when a Scottish chieftain "invaded the island and precipitated all the old women in the south part of the island into this gulf. Hence the name – Sloaknacallagh or the gulf or chasm of the old women" (*OSRNB* sh.1,3). Without historical forms of the subtownland name, however, we can say nothing of its linguistic origin or development.

OTHER NAMES

Ally Lough
D 1448

A hybrid form

1. Loch na h-Ealadh	Irish of Rathlin 54, 68, 190	1942
2. Lochan na h-Ealadh	Irish of Rathlin 190	1942
3. Loch Aille "lake of the cliff"	J O'D (OSRNB) sh.1, 3	1852
4. Loch-na-n-ealaidhe "the lake of the swans"	Duncan 132	1906
5. Loch na hEaladh "the lake of Ealaidh"	Place-Names of Rathlin 85	1989
6. lox na çaləg	Irish of Rathlin 54, 68, 190	1942
7. loxan na çaləg	Irish of Rathlin 190	1942
8. ale'lox	Place-Names of Rathlin 85	1989

"A small fresh water lough north of Ushet Lough from which it receives an inlet. It is named from the townland of Carivanally but is contracted and only called Ally Lough. Locally and in ordinary conversation the townland is only named Ally also" (*OSRNB* sh.1, 3).

Final *-adh* often yielded [əg] in late Rathlin Irish, but on some occasions was "quiescent" (*Irish of Rathlin* 52–3). See **Carravinally** townland. Form 6 represents the Irish form of the name.

Altachuile Bay   A hybrid form
D 1352

1. Allt a Chuidhil (?)	Irish of Rathlin 182	1942
2. Altachuile Bay	OSRNB sh.1, 2	1852
3. Alt a choill "cliff of hazel"	J O'D (OSRNB) sh.1, 2	1852
4. Allt an Chaoil "the cliff of the narrow inlet"	Place-Names of Rathlin 58	1989
5. ɑlt ə xɪːl	Irish of Rathlin 182	1942
6. altə'xʎːl'	Place-Names of Rathlin 58	1989
7. ˌaltə'hwil	Local pronunciation	1996

Forms 1 and 3–7 refer to a coastal cliff in Ballynagard, from which the inlet was named. Considering the pronunciations in forms 5–6, form 4 seems most likely to represent the original form of the Irish elements. *Caol* (gen. sing. *caoil*) is translated "strait; inlet of the sea; marshy plain" by *DIL*; the second of these meanings is most likely. Considering form 1 of **Altacorry Bay** below, it is possible that there formerly existed the Irish form *Bé Allt an Chaoil*. Holmer tentatively suggested that this name contained *cuidhil* "spinning wheel" (*Irish of Rathlin* 182).

Altacorry Bay   A hybrid form
D 1552

1. Bay Allt an Choire	Irish of Rathlin 177	1942
2. Altacuirry Bay	OSRNB sh.1, 2	1852
3. Altahuirry Bay	OSRNB sh.1, 2	1852
4. Bé Allt an Choire "the bay of (the cliff of the cauldron or whirlpool)"	Place-Names of Rathlin 66–7	1989
5. beː alt ə xor'ə	Irish of Rathlin 177	1942
6. beː aŋt ə xor'ə	Irish of Rathlin 177	1942
7. ˌaltnə'hori	Local pronunciation	1996

This derives from the cliff name Altacorry in Ballycarry (to which form 7 more correctly refers). Mac Giolla Easpaig's standard Irish form (4) uses *bé* "bay" as a masc. Rathlin variant of *bá* "bay" (see also **Cooraghy Bay**). Altacorry apparently derives its name from the sea current *Coire Bhreacáin* (*Place-Names of Rathlin* 64), some historical forms of which follow:

1. carubdis Brecani,	Adamnán's Columba 222 §16b	710c
2. Coire Breccáin	Met. Dinds. iv 80	1100c
3. coire Breccan, i	Liber Hymn. i 107 §4–5	1110c

4. caribdis Brecani	Adamnán's Columba 222 §16a	1195c
5. vortice Brecain, in	Adamnán's Columba 222 §16a	1195c
6. Coire Breacan	Uí Mhaine (Hogan) 163a 2	1390c
7. [Co]ire Breccain	BB 398a 33	1390c
8. Coiri breacain	L. Lec. 253a 1	1397c
9. Coire Brecain	San. Corm. 13	1510c
10. Coire Brecain	Betha CC. 378 §352	1532
11. Charybdis Breccani	Scottish Saints (Pinkerton) 87	1550c
12. Corebreacayn	Trias Thaum. 458a	1648
13. coire bhreacáin	Mulcahy's Rathlin 44	1889
14. Coire Bhreacain	Antiquities of Rathlin 46	1911
15. Coire Bhreacain	Irish of the Glens 106	1942
16. Koora-vracken	Murphy's Rathlin 60	1953c
17. Coire bhreacain "Brecan's cauldron"	Ó Dubhthaigh 136	1905
18. Coire bhreacain "Brecan's cauldron"	Rev. Magill 12	1923
19. kɔrʹə vrɑkɑn	Irish of the Glens 106	1942

Sanas Cormaic (see form 9) describes *Breacán* as a grandson of *Niall Naoi-Ghiallach*, the King of Tara who died in c. 454 AD (Ó hÓgáin 1991, 322). Breacán was believed to have drowned here with a fleet of fifty currachs, inspiring the name (*San. Corm.* 13–4; see also *EA* 289–92 and Watson 1926, 63, 95). Reeves (*EA* 386–7) believed the Norse place-name *Jǫlduhlaup*, which appears in the Icelandic saga *Landnámabok* and was said to be three days sail south of southern Iceland, to refer to this current. He translated the name as "the running" or "breaking of waves". The Norse means "mare's leap", however (*Pers. comm.* 15.01.96). Ó Tuathail (1950, 155–6) suggests it was translated from an existing Irish name, and postulates Slyne Head in Co. Galway.

Altandivan Bay
D 1153

A hybrid form

1. Allt an Duibhean	Irish of Rathlin 188, 192	1942
2. Altandivan Bay	OSRNB sh.1, 1	1852
3. Ba Alt an Dubhain "the bay of the dark glen"	J O'D (OSRNB) sh.1, 1	1852
4. Bé Allt an Duibhéin "the bay of (the cliff of the cormorant)"	Place-Names of Rathlin 28–9	1989
5. ɑlt ən dɪvɛn	Irish of Rathlin 188, 192	1942
6. aɲt ən dɪvɛn	Irish of Rathlin 188	1942
7. ɑltəˈdʌvən	Place-Names of Rathlin 28	1989
8. ˌaltənˈdivən	Local pronunciation	1996

"A small bay which boatmen visit in the summer season to cut seaweeds and burn kelp ... It is bounded on the north by a towering cliff, which intercepts the sun's rays, thus throwing a dark shadow on it. From this circumstance the name is supposed to have been derived" (*OSRNB* sh.1, 1).

A standard Irish form is given in form 4. Forms 1 and 5–8 refer to the cliff in Cleggan which gave the bay its name. See also **Mallandeevan** in Other Names, Culfeightrin. A development of *dubh* "black" plus the substantive suffix *-án* to *duibheán* "black place" might be considered (note form 3).

Arkill Bay   A hybrid form
D 1649

1. Archill Bay	Lendrick Map	1780
2. Earcail "a pillar"	J O'D (OSRNB) sh.1, 2	1852
3. Arcill "anchor"	O'Boyle 46	1939
4. Bé an Aircill "the bay of Aircill"	Place-Names of Rathlin 76	1989–9
5. ˌɑrkəlˈbeː	Place-Names of Rathlin 76	1989
6. ˌarkïl	Local pronunciation	1996

Arkill Bay lies beside "a small rocky headland jutting into the sea" called Arkill Point (*OSRNB* sh.1, 2), in Craigmacagan.

Holmer recorded the further subtownland place-name of *Lag an Aircill* as [lɑg ə nɑrˈkʹilʹ] (*Irish of Rathlin* 157). Mac Giolla Easpaig (*Place-Names of Rathlin* 76) suggests that *Arkill* may be derived from the fem. noun *faircill* "a cover, a lid" (gen. sing. forms *faircille* and *faircle* (*Dinneen*)) or the masc. noun *fairceallach* "a stump, a lump" (gen. sing. *fairceallaigh(e)*; *ibid.*). It seems more likely to derive from a variant of the (probably related) masc. noun *earcail* (gen. sing. *earcail*) "a prop, stay, post or pillar; a boat- or punt-pole" (*Dinneen*). A fem. form of this word was used in the Scottish Gaelic of Mid-Perthshire: *earchaill* "prop, post, pillar" (*Dwelly*). *An tAirceal(l)* seems to be the original name here.

Bracken's Cave   A hybrid form
D 1650

1. Uamh Breacain	Irish of Rathlin 167	1942
2. Brecan's oova	Mulcahy's Rathlin 44	1889
3. Uaimh ui bhreacain	Duncan 133	1906
4. Uamha Breacáin "the cave of Breacán"	Place-Names of Rathlin 64	1989
5. ʌəv brʹakən (-ɑn)	Irish of Rathlin 167	1942
6. ˌbrakənzˈkeːv	Place-Names of Rathlin 64	1989
7. brakənzˈkeːv	Local pronunciation	1996

See **Altacorry Bay** regarding the figure *Breacán*. Mac Giolla Easpaig recorded locally that this place-name, which is in Ballycarry, should be marked north of Portawillin on

311

Ordnance Survey maps (*Place-Names of Rathlin* 53, 64). The standard English form is a translation of the original Irish name.

Ó Dónaill lists *uamha* as a variant gen. sing. and nom. pl. of *uaimh* "cave; souterrain, underground escape passage; underground chamber", but *Dinneen* gives it as a nom. sing. (gen. *uamhadh/uamhan*) and it may have been this form that was used in the place-name (see also **Owey Doo**). Holmer noted several nom. sing. forms of this word: *uamh, uamha, uamhach, uamhaidh* (*Irish of Rathlin* 246). Mac Giolla Easpaig's suggested form (4) leaves the *b* unlenited as indicated by Holmer's recorded pronunciation. Holmer also recorded the further place-name *Leac Breac[á]in* "*Breacán*'s flag-stone" ([lʹɑkə brʹɑkən]; *Irish of Rathlin* 167).

Bruce's Castle	An English form	
D 1651		

1. (?)Raghlins, the castle of the	CSP Ire. 87	1575
2. Rathline Castle	DS (Par. Map) 73	1657c
3. Bruce C.	Maritime Map	1776
4. Bruce Castle	Lendrick Map	1780
5. Bruce Castle	Dubourdieu Map	1822
6. The Castle	Murphy's Rathlin 46	1953c

This castle gave rise to the Irish forms *Ceathrú an Chaistéil* (called *ye Castle Quarter* in the *Rathlin Vestry Book* 33 in 1781), *Port an Chaistéil* "the port of the castle" and *Leac an Chaistéil* "the flagstone of the castle" (see *Place-Names of Rathlin* 65, 69). It is located in the townland of Ballycarry, and is named after Robert Bruce who fled to Rathlin from Scotland in the early 1300s (*OSM* xxiv 129). The strict antiquity of the castle is not known, however (*PSAMNI* 1). **Bruce's Hill** in south-west Co. Antrim is named after Edward, brother of Robert (*PNI* iv 155–6).

Bruce's Cave	An English form	
D 1650		

1. Bruce's Cave	OSRNB sh.1, 2	1852
2. br(ʌ)səs kʹeːv	Irish of Rathlin 34	1942
3. brʌsəsˈkeːv	Place-Names of Rathlin 65	1989
4. bruzəzˈkeːv	Local pronunciation	1996

This cave is said to have been frequented by Robert Bruce during his sojourn in Rathlin (*OSRNB* sh.1, 2). It is in Ballycarry.

Bull Point	*Gob an Tairbh*	
D 0850	"point of the bull"	

1. Gob an Tairbh	Irish of Rathlin 202	1942
2. Bull	Maritime Map	1776
3. Bull Pt.	Lendrick Map	1780
4. Bull Point	Dubourdieu Map	1812

5. Builg "bellows"	Ó Dubhthaigh 133	1905
6. Gob an Tairbh "the point of the bull"	Place-Names of Rathlin 17	1989
7. gob ə tɛrʹv	Irish of Rathlin 202	1942
8. ðə 'bol̩	Local pronunciation	1996

This is named from a rock in Kebble called *The Bull*, a "large insulated rock rising from the sea, and so named from it being fantastically likened to a bull . . ." (*OSRNB* sh.1, 1). It appears that this rock was known as *An Tarbh* "the bull" in Irish. Another rock north-east of here is called *The Cow* (*ibid.*), which also appears to be a translation from Irish *An Bhó* "the cow" (*Place-Names of Rathlin* 16; cf. also **Portnaboe**).

Cantruan	*Ceann tSrutháin*	
D 1553	"headland of the current"	
1. Ceann (an) t-Shruthan	Irish of Rathlin 237	1942
2. Ken Truan	Hamilton's Letters 246	1822
3. Cantruan	OSRNB sh.1, 2	1852c
4. Ceann tSruthain "head of the current"	OSRNB (OD) sh.1, 2	1852c
5. Ceann an tSrutháin "the headland of the current or stream"	Place-Names of Rathlin 61	1989
6. kʹan trʌ̃an	Irish of Rathlin 237	1942
7. kʹən'trʌ̃ːɛn	Place-Names of Rathlin 61	1989
8. kïn'truən	Local pronunciation	1996

"A bold prominent and precipitous headland overhanging the sea. The name appears to signify the 'headland of the current' and is supposed to be derived, or so named, from a powerful current which is continually running at its base" (*OSRNB* sh.1, 2). It lies in Ballyconagan.

A medial definite article in this name may have been lost by haplology. It is also possible that the *t* was used, as a result of analogy, in the dat. or gen. case. *Carn tSiail* (anglicized **Carnteel**) in Co. Tyrone and *Cionn tSáile* (anglicized Kinsale) in Co. Cork are somewhat similar (*GÉ* 45, 62). See also **Stroan** in Armoy.

Carrickagile	*Carraig an Ghaill*	
D 1650	"rock of the foreigner(?)"	
1. Carraic an Ghoill	Irish of Rathlin 37	1942
2. Carraic na Goill	Irish of Rathlin 171	1942
3. Carraic nan Goill	Irish of Rathlin 199	1942
4. Carraig-a-gadhl (a certain type of sea-gull)	Duncan 133	1906

5. Carraig an Ghaill "the rock of the foreigner"	Place-Names of Rathlin 70	1989
6. karik′ ə ail	Irish of Rathlin 37	1942
7. karik na gɛil	Irish of Rathlin 171	1942
8. karik′ na gɛil	Irish of Rathlin 199	1942
9. karik′ə'ɣail	Place-Names of Rathlin 70	1989

This is in Ballynoe. The phonetic forms suggest several possibilites. Holmer believed the last element in this name to be a gen. form of *gall* "kittiwake" (*Irish of Rathlin* 199). See also **Ballygill Middle**.

Church Bay
D 1450

Bé na hEaglaise/An Loch
"bay of the church/the lake"

1. Bé na h-Eaglaise	Irish of Rathlin 12	1942
2. An Locha, usually called	Irish of Rathlin 12	1942
3. Bay na h-Eaglaise	Irish of Rathlin 189	1942
4. Loch(a), An	Irish of Rathlin 211	1942
5. Locha, air an	Irish of Rathlin 211	1942
6. Chapall bay	Dartmouth Map 25	1590c
7. church bay	Maritime Map	1776
8. church Bay	Lendrick Map	1780
9. Bé na hEaglaise "the bay of the church"	Place-Names of Rathlin 75	1989
10. An Locha "the lough"	Place-Names of Rathlin 75	1989
11. beːi na heglɪʃ	Irish of Rathlin 189	1942
12. ən lox(ə)	Irish of Rathlin 211	1942
13. er ə ŋoxə	Irish of Rathlin 211	1942
14. beːnəheglɪʃ	LASID iv 18	1969
15. ˌtʃɔrtʃ 'beː	Local pronunciation	1996

See **Church Quarter** townland.

Cloghadoo
D 1449

Na Clocha Dubha
"the black stones"

1. na Clocha Dubh	Irish of Rathlin 80, 175	1942
2. Cloghadoo	OSRNB sh.1, 3	1852
3. the Cloghadoos	Irish of Rathlin 80, 175	1942
4. Clocha Dubha "black stones"	J O'D (OSRNB) sh.1, 3	1852
5. Clocha Dubha; Black stones at shore-a good landmark	O'Boyle 47	1939

6. Na Clocha Dubha "the black stones"	Place-Names of Rathlin 83	1989
7. na klɔxə dʎ	Irish of Rathlin 80, 175	1942
8. klɑxə'dʎ	Place-Names of Rathlin 83	1989
9. ˌðə 'clɔxə'duz	Local pronunciation	1996

"A cluster of prominent rocks [in Carravinally] at the low-water line. They serve as landmarks for boatmen and are so called from their aspect which is black" (*OSRNB* sh.1, 3).

Cooraghy Bay
D 1050   A hybrid form

1. Curachaig	Irish of Rathlin 183	1942
2. Bé Cuarachaidh "the bay of (the crooked field)"	Place-Names of Rathlin 19	1989
3. kʎrɑhe(ː)g	Irish of Rathlin 183	1942
4. kʎrɑhəg	Irish of Rathin 183	1942
5. kʎrɑəg	Irish of Rathlin 183	1942
6. 'kʎːrəhi	Place-Names of Rathlin 19	1989
7. 'kʎːrəgi	Place-Names of Rathlin 19	1989

Forms 1 and 3–7 refer to the place-name *Cuarachadh* (anglicized **Cooraghy**) "crooked field", in Kebble, from which the bay took its name. Holmer also recorded the subtownland name which he spelt as *Bealach Churachaig* (standard Mod. Ir. *Bealach Chuarachaidh* "the road of the crooked field" (*Place-Names of Rathlin* 19)) as [bjɑlɑx xʎrɑhɛg] (*Irish of Rathlin* 163), in which *Cuarachadh* remains apparently undeclined (cf. *ibid.* 52–3 §81).
A standard Irish form of the name is given in form 2.

Derginan Point
D 0952   A hybrid form

1. Deargan Point	OSRNB sh.1, 1	1852
2. Dearginan Point	OSRNB sh.1, 1	1852
3. Dearganán "point of the red nook or chasm"	J O'D (OSRNB) sh.1, 1	1852
4. 'dʒɑrgən pɑint	Place-Names of Rathlin 11	1989

This headland, which is in Kebble, takes its name from nearby **Derginan**. Mac Giolla Easpaig gives Derginan the Irish form *An Deargán* "the reddish place" (*Place-Names of Rathlin* 11), that is, *dearg* "red" plus the substantive suffix *-án*. However, he notes that it could represent a contraction of *Deargingeán* "red *ingeán*". Form 2 suggests indeed that *Deargingeán* was the original form and that it has suffered the loss of a final unstressed syllable. Regarding *ingeán*, which Mac Giolla Easpaig spelt as *ineán*, and which derives ultimately from an oblique form of *eang* "track, trace; strip of land" plus the diminutive suffix *-án*, see **Inannanooan**. See also **Sroanderrig**.

Doon Bay D 1548	A hybrid form	
1. the bay	Hib. Reg. Cary	1657c
2. Bé an Dúin "the bay of the fort"	Place-Names of Rathlin 81–2	1989
3. dʌːnˈbeː	Place-Names of Rathlin 81	1989

See also **Carravindoon**, in which this bay is located. The bay is named from the headland (called **Doon Point**) which forms its northern extremity (*OSRNB* sh.1, 3):

1. Dundchuny Rock	Hib. Reg. Cary	1657c
2. Dundedhuny, A rock called	DS (Par. Map) 60	1657c
3. Dundedhuny Rock	Hib. Del. Ant.	1672c
4. Doon Point	Dubourdieu Map	1822
5. Pointe an Dúin "the point of the. fort"	Place-Names of Rathlin 82	1989
6. dʌːn paint	Place-Names of Rathlin 82	1989
7. duːn	Local pronunciation	1996

The original Irish form of variants 1–3 is uncertain.

Doonmore D 1152	*Dún Mór* "big fort"	
1. An Dún Mór "the big fort"	Place-Names of Rathlin 47	1989
2. ðə ˈfort	Place-Names of Rathlin 47	1989

This name refers to a "detached hill with steep sides and a flat summit. It is circular in outline and closely resembles an old fort . . . The foundations of a wall 10 feet broad are traceable all around the edge of the hill. It has evidently been a fort of considerable importance in former ages" (*OSRNB* sh.1, 1; cf. also *PSAMNI* 1). It lies in Ballygill North.

East Lighthouse D 1652	An English form	
1. (?)tigh soluis	Mulcahy's Rathlin 44	1889
2. ty soluish	Mulcahy's Rathlin 44	1889
3. the east	Murphy's Rathlin 70	1953c
4. the East Light	Murphy's Rathlin 70	1953c
5. ðə ˈist	Local pronunciation	1996

This is in Ballycarry, at Altacorry Head (see **Altacorry Bay**). Forms 1–2, which indicate that the Irish form *(An) Toigh Solais* "(the) lighthouse" was formerly current, could alternatively have applied to the **West Lighthouse** or the **South Lighthouse**. As with mainland Irish (cf. **White House** in Culfeightrin), *toigh* had replaced *teach* "house" as the local nom. form (*Irish of Rathlin* 242).

Farganlack or Lack Point	*Fargán na Leac*	
D 1053	"ledge of the flat rocks"	
1. Lack	Lendrick Map	1780
2. Farragannaleck	OSRNB sh.1, 48	1852
3. Puinte Farragannaleca "rugged rocky point of the flags"	J O'D (OSRNB) sh.1, 1	1852
4. Fargán na Leac "the ledge of the flags"	Place-Names of Rathlin 29	1989
5. fargənə'lek	Place-Names of Rathlin 29	1989
6. 'leːk	Local pronunciation	1996

"A bold rocky headland [in Cleggan] projecting into the sea. It has been so named from the rugged character of the rocks along its face and from ledges of rocks which the country people call 'lacks' running into the sea, from its north and west base" (*OSRNB* sh.1, 1). Regarding the first element in this name see **Ballyconagan**; a form of the final element recurs in the Culfeightrin townland name of **Cushleake Mountain Middle**.

Illancarragh Bay	A hybrid form	
D 1648		
1. Illancarragh Bay	OSRNB sh.1, 3	1852
2. "the crooked rock (island)"	Dallat's Rathlin 27	1973
3. Bé an Oileáin Charraigh "the bay of Oileán Carrach"	Place-Names of Rathlin 82	1989
4. eljɛn'karəx'beː	Place-Names of Rathlin 82	1989

This bay is named from "a rocky point running into the sea . . . connected with [Rathlin] by a low ledge of rocks over which the sea washes . . . [and which it surrounds] at high tides" (*OSRNB* sh.1, 3), called Illancarragh. The bay is "situate between Doon point and Illandcarragh [*sic*] . . . Boats enter it to cut seaweeds but there is no place of landing along it" (*ibid.*). Mac Giolla Easpaig gives the Irish form of Illancarragh as *An tOileán Carrach* "the rugged island" (*Place-Names of Rathlin* 82; cf. also *Irish of Rathlin* 171 and *O'Boyle* 46). A standard form of the name of the bay is given in form 3.

Inannanooan	*Ingeán na nUan*	
D 1651	"cove of the lambs"	
1. Inannanooan	OSRNB sh.1, 2	1852

2. -na n-uan "of the lambs"	J O'D (OSRNB) sh.1, 2	1852
3. "nook or glen of the lambs"	OSRNB sh.1, 2	1852
4. Íneán na nUan "ínean of the lambs"	Place-Names of Rathlin 66	1989

"An inward curve in the cliff at the coastline [in Ballycarry]. It signifies the nook or glen of the lambs" (*OSRNB* sh.1, 2).

Mac Giolla Easpaig (*Place-Names of Rathlin* 5) noted that the term which he spelt as *ineán* referred to "a steep grassy path or access leading to the shore between two cliffs. This feature was very important in earlier times as many of the cliff shores were inaccessible from the sea except in the calmest of weather. The element is also found on the island of Arran". Toner (1994–5 *passim*) has more recently argued that the masc. noun *ineán* represents in fact two distinct underlying words in Rathlin, both of which should be properly spelt *ingeán*. In those instances where it denotes "a green way down to the sea between rocks", it is derived from *eang* "track, trace". In some instances it is seen to denote "cove, harbour", however, and in these cases is derived from *eang* "a strip of land" (> "strip of land by the sea" > "cove, harbour"). Both words consist of a dat. form *ing* plus the diminutive suffix *án*. Toner also noted that *innean*, a masc. variant of *inneoin* "anvil; bluff; small landing creek" (*Irish of Rathlin* 206 sv.; note also Dinneen sv. *inneoin* "pool"), which would be indistinguishable from *ingeán* in unstressed position, could lie behind some names of the *inan-* type, and may also be considered here. See also **Derginan** Point.

Killeany
D 1251

Cill Éanna
"*Éanna*'s burial ground"

1. Cill Eannaigh	Irish of Rathlin 82	1942
2. Cill Éanna (?)	Irish of Rathlin 174	1942
3. Cill Éannaigh (?)	Irish of Rathlin 190	1942
4. Cille na Léanaidh (?)	Irish of Rathlin 209	1942
5. Killeany	OSRNB sh.1, 2	1852
6. Cill Éinne "St. Eany's church"	J O'D (OSRNB) sh.1, 2	1852
7. "Eanna's church?"	Irish of Rathlin 82	1942
8. Cill Éinne "church or burial place of (Saint) Éinne"	Place-Names of Rathlin 44	1989
9. ki'l'ɛːni	Irish of Rathlin 82, 174, 190	1942
10. k'i'l'ə na l'ɛni	Irish of Rathlin 190, 209	1942
11. ˌkïl'ɛni	Local pronunciation	1996

"A small port where boats land in calm weather to cut seaweeds and burn kelp. There is also a small dry beach at it where they can be drawn up in case of their being overtaken by storms" (*OSRNB* sh.1, 2).

O'Boyle noted in 1947 that there was "an old graveyard" here (*O'Boyle* 51), although there is no other record of an ecclesiastical association with this place. Form 4 suggests that the final element was based on the masc. noun *léana* "a meadow, swampy ground, a lawn, a field" (*Dinneen*). Dinneen notes a fem. variant of this word; a gen. *-idh* ending might have developed by analogy. However, as Holmer's forms are somewhat late, and as *cill* is often qualified by a personal name, we must regard form 4 as representing a late development, possibly based on reinterpretation. *Cill Eanaigh* "burial-ground of the bog" might be considered although the first vowel of the final element appears to have been accented. *Éanna*, a male personal name which may mean something like "bird-like" (Ó Corráin & Maguire 1981, 86), seems the most likely origin. There was no distinction in late Rathlin Irish between *n* and *nn* (*Irish of Rathlin* 55 §89), and *éa* was commonly pronounced [ɛː] (*ibid.* 45). Considering the apparent local uncertainty regarding this place-name (forms 4, 10), the [i] ending may indicate a development in the gen. case by analogy, rather than indicating that *Éanna* took a local form such as *Éannach/Éannaidh* in the nom. (form 3). Neither *Éinne* (forms 6 and 8), a variant of *Éanna*, nor the female saint's name *Eithne* is reflected in the phonetic forms (9–10; see also **Balleny** in Armoy). The north-west Co. Down name **Killaney** derives from *Cill Eidhnigh* "ivy-covered church" but again, the final element in the Down name, an oblique form of *eidhneach*, is not reflected in the phonetic forms here.

Lack Point	A hybrid form	
D 1053		

See **Farganlack**.

Loughnanskan	*Lochán na nEascann*	
D 1152	"small lake of the eels"	
1. Lochan na n-Easconn	Irish of Rathlin 190	1942
2. Loughaneaskan	OSRNB sh.1, 1	1852
3. Loughnaneaskan	OSRNB sh.1, 1	1852
4. Cleggan Loch	Irish of Rathlin 190	1942
5. Loch na n-eascainn "lake of the eels"	J O'D (OSRNB) sh.1, 1	1852
6. Loch na nEascann "the lake of the eels"	Place-Names of Rathlin 31	1989
7. lohɑn nɑ neskɑn	Irish of Rathlin 190	1942
8. lọxnənöskən	LASID iv 18	1969
9. lɔxnəˈneːsgɑn	Place-Names of Rathlin 31	1989
10. ˌklagənˈlɔx	Local pronunciation	1996

"A fresh water lough in a mountain district [in Cleggan] having one small outlet which flows north and enters the sea at Altadivan Bay. It abounds in eels and hence the name Loughnaneaskan or lake of the eels" (*OSRNB* sh.1, 1).

Maddygalla	*An Madadh Alla*	
D 1548	"the wolf"	
1. Madadh Alla	Irish of Rathlin 81	1942
2. Madadh Alla, an	Irish of Rathlin 213	1942
3. Madagalla	OSRNB sh.1, 3	1852

4. Maadda-gaala-ban	Murphy's Rathlin 64	1953c
5. Maadda-gaala	Murphy's Rathlin 64	1953c
6. Madaidhe Geala "white dogs"	J O'D (OSRNB) sh.1, 3	1852
7. Maide geala "the white sticks or wattles"	Ó Dubhthaigh 184	1905
8. Madaidh geala	Duncan 133	1906
9. Maide geala "white sticks"	Rev. Magill 21	1923
10. "white dogs (rock)"	Dallat's Rathlin 27	1973
11. An Madadh Alla "the wolf"	Place-Names of Rathlin 81	1989
12. madə'grɑlə	Irish of Rathlin 37	1942
13. madə'ɣɑlə	Irish of Rathlin 213	1942
14. ə madə'ɣɑlɪ	Irish of Rathlin 213	1942
15. madə'ɣɑlə	Place-Names of Rathlin 81	1989
16. ˌmadə'galə	Local pronunciation	1996

This is a "low ledge of rocks running into the sea, and covered at high water" (*OSRNB* sh.1, 3), in Carravindoon.

The Irish form given above follows Mac Giolla Easpaig (form 11), who notes that *Dwelly* gives *madadh-allaidh/all* "wolf". O'Laverty recorded the name *Maca Tire* "wolves" for some boulders in Craigmacagan (*O'Laverty* iv 377; regarding these latter rocks see *Murphy's Rathlin* 181 and *Place-Names of Rathlin* 76). In Rathlin Irish, *dh* and *gh* in final position and following a broad vowel were usually pronounced [g] (*Irish of Rathlin* 52 §81). Occasionally, they were pronounced [ɣ], a sound which caused difficulty to local speakers and which could thus lead them to be rendered as [gr] (form 12) or suppressed altogether (*ibid.* 37 §51).

Mill Bay
D 1540

Bé an Mhuilinn
"bay of the mill"

1. Bay a' Mhuilinn	Irish of Rathlin 163	1942
2. Mill Bay	Lendrick Map	1780
3. Mill Bay	Dubourdieu Map	1812
4. Mill Bay	OSRNB sh.1, 3	1852
5. Bé an Mhuilinn "the bay of the mill"	Place-Names of Rathlin 75	1989
6. beː ə vʌl'in	Irish of Rathlin 163	1942
7. ˌmïl 'beː	Local pronunciation	1996

"A small bay [in Demesne] where boats land and are drawn up from storms. It is named from a small corn mill at its S.E. end" (*OSRNB* sh.1, 3).

The earliest reference to this mill appears to be in 1746 (*PRONI D2977/3A/2/26/1A: Mill of Raghlin or Raghery*). In 1838, this was the only mill on the island, propelled by a breast water-wheel 12' in diameter and 1' 10" broad (*OSM* xxiv 131).

| **Owey Doo** | *Uamha Dhubhthaigh(?)* | |
| D 1448 | "*Dubhthach*'s cave" | |

1. Uamha (an) Dubhthaigh (?)	Irish of Rathlin 188	1942
2. Oweydooey	OSRNB sh.1, 1	1852
3. (?)Ivagooey	Murphy's Rathlin 121	1953c
4. Uamhaidh Dubh "black cove"	J O'D (OSRNB) sh.1, 1	1852
5. Uaimh dubh "black cave"	Duncan 133	1906
6. "black cave"	Dallat's Rathlin 27	1973
7. Uamha Dubhthaigh "the cave of Dubhthach"	Place-Names of Rathlin 84	1989
8. ʎavə dʎˑi	Irish of Rathlin 188	1942
9. ʎavə n dʎˑi	Irish of Rathlin 188	1942
10. ʎəviˈdʎː	Place-Names of Rathlin 84	1989

"A small port or cove [in Caravinally] at the west base of a steep precipitous cliff. It signifies the dark cove and is so called from the blackish aspect of the rocks along it" (*OSRNB* sh.1, 1).

Murphy recorded that five brothers called Black were buried at a place called *Ivagooey* (form 3) which may be Owey Doo (*Murphy's Rathlin* 121). The surname Ó *Dubhthaigh* is derived from the male personal name *Dubhthach*, and is common in all the provinces except Munster (MacLysaght 1985, 92 sv. O'Duffy). In Rathlin, it may represent a gaelicization of the Scottish name Black (also a common English name) "connected with three clans – Lamont, MacGregor and MacLean of Duart" (*ibid.* 18). We might not have expected -*bhth*- to yield [f] here (compare *lobhtha* [loˑə] in *Irish of Rathlin* 211). However, it is not certain whether an adjectival form of the surname such as *An Dubhthach* gave rise to the form *Uamha an Dubhthaigh* "Black's cave", as suggested in form 1. O'Boyle also noted the subtownland place-name *Lagadooey* (O'Boyle 45) in this townland, which might be interpreted as containing a similar form of the surname. Form 3 could be interpreted as *Uamha Uí Dhubhthaigh* "Black's cave". *Uamha Dhubhthaigh* "*Dubhthach*'s cave" (form 7) represents a third possibility, as we can account for the medial [n] in form 9 as resulting from the close proximity of a nasal consonant (compare *i n-áit* [NaːNʹtʹ] in south Co. Donegal (Wagner 1959, 49 §134), for example), or from reinterpretation. A fourth possibility is *Uamha Dhubhaigh* "cave of the dark place" (cf. **Doey Plantation** in Other Names, Culfeightrin).

| **Park Cove** | A hybrid form | |
| D 1447 | | |

1. Park Cove	OSRNB sh.1, 3	1852
2. cove of the park or field	OSRNB sh.1, 3	1852
3. Uamha na Páirce, the cave of the field	Place-Names of Rathlin 87	1989
4. parkˈkoːv	Place-Names of Rathlin 87	1989

321

"A small narrow precipitous cove [in Roonivoolin]. It signifies the cove of the park and is named from an adjacent field called the park – pairk in Irish" (*OSRNB* sh.1, 3).

Portandoon
D 0851

Port an Dúin
"port of the fort"

1. Portandoon	OSRNB sh.1, 1	1852
2. Port-an-dinya	Murphy's Rathlin 27	1953c
3. Port an Dúin "port or harbour of the doon or rock"	OSRNB sh.1, 1 (OD)	1852
4. Port an Dúin "the port of the fort"	Place-Names of Rathlin 14	1989
5. portNə'dʌːn	Place-Names of Rathlin 14	1989

"A small port [in Kebble] where boats land in calm weather to cut weeds for kelp. It is situated between the rocks called Doonmore and Carrickagarry and is called from the former rock which stands at the north side of the entrance to it" (*OSRNB* sh.1, 1). The former rock name was recorded in the *Down Survey* (*Hib. Reg.*) of c. 1657 as *Dunmore* ("a rock where falcons breed"), and called *Doonore* in a later source (*Ire. Map [1711]*). The rock was described in 1852 as follows: "A large insulated rock rising abruptly – perpendicularly apparently – from the sea and to a considerable height. It is flat on [the] summit but is apparently inaccessible . . . It is separated from the mainland by a narrow channel – It signifies 'the great rock'" (*OSRNB* sh.1, 1). It is uncertain whether form 2 indicates that *dún* latterly took a variant genitive form.

Portantonnish
D 1448

Port an tSonais
"port of the good luck"

1. Purt an t-Shonais	Irish of Rathlin 236	1942
2. Portantonnish	OSRNB sh.1, 3	1852
3. Port an tSonais "The port of fortune or good-luck"	J O'D (OSRNB) sh.1, 3	1852
4. Port-a-t-sonais "the lucky port"	Duncan 134	1906
5. Port an tSonais "The port of good luck"	O'Boyle 46	1939
6. "the lucky port"	Dallat's Rathlin 27	1973
7. Port an tSonais "the port of the luck"	Place-Names of Rathlin 84	1989
8. pʌrt ən tɔniʃ	Irish of Rathlin 236	1942
9. portən'tɔnəʃ	Place-Names of Rathlin 84	1989

"A small open port [in Carravinally] without any shelter, being bounded by low ledges of rock. Boats can only enter it in very calm weather. It signifies the fortunate port but nothing is known of the circumstance that led to its application" (*OSRNB* sh.1, 3).

| **Portawillin** | *Port an Mhuilinn* | |
| D 1651 | "port of the mill" | |

1. Purt an Mhuilinn	Irish of Rathlin 218	1942
2. Portawillin	OSRNB sh.1, 2	1852
3. Port a Mhuillin "port of the mill"	J O'D (OSRNB) sh.1, 2	1852
4. Port-a-mhuilinn	Duncan 134	1906
5. "Port of the mill"	Dallat's Rathlin 27	1973
6. Port an Mhuilinn "the port of the mill"	Place-Names of Rathlin 65	1989
7. pʌrt ə vʌlʹin	Irish of Rathlin 218	1942
8. portnəˈvʌljin	Place-Names of Rathlin 65	1989

"A small port [in Ballycarry] where boats land and are drawn up from storms . . . It has been named from a corn mill, now in ruins, which stood close to it on the beach on [its] W. side" (*OSRNB* sh.1, 2).

| **Portcastle** | *Port an Chaistéil* | |
| D 1651 | "port of the castle" | |

1. Purt an Chaisteail	Irish of Rathlin 170	1942
2. Portacastel	OSRNB sh.1, 2	1852
3. Port a Chaisleain "port of the castle"	J O'D (OSRNB) sh.1, 2	1852
4. Port an Chaistil "the port of the castle"	Place-Names of Rathlin 65	1989
5. pʌrt ə xaʃtʹɛl	Irish of Rathlin 170	1942

"A small port [in Ballycarry] on the south of Bruce's Castle and close to it. It is called from said Castle . . ." (*OSRNB* sh.1, 2). See also **Bruce's Castle**.

| **Portnaboe** | *Port na Bó* | |
| D 0851 | "port of the cow" | |

1. Purt na Bó	Irish of Rathlin 165	1942
2. Portnaboe	OSRNB sh.1, 1	1852
3. Port na Bó "port of the cow"	J O'D (OSRNB) sh.1, 1	1852
4. Port na Bó "the port of the cow"	Place-Names of Rathlin 16	1989
5. pʌrt na bɔː	Irish of Rathlin 165	1942
6. portnəˈbɔː	Place-Names of Rathlin 16	1989

"The entrance from sea to [this port] is between rocks called The Bull and The Cow, and it has been named from the later . . ." (*OSRNB* sh.1, 1). See also **Bull Point**.

Portnaminnan
D 1650

Port na Meannán
"port of the kids"

1. Purt na Meannan	Irish of Rathlin 55, 216	1942
2. Portnameanan	OSRNB sh.1, 2	1852
3. Port na Mionnán "port of the kids"	J O'D (OSRNB) sh.1, 2	1852
4. Port-na-mionán "the port of the kids"	Duncan 134	1906
5. Port na mionán "kid port"	O'Boyle 47	1939
6. "the port of the kids"	Dallat's Rathlin 27	1973
7. Port na Meannán "the port of the kids"	Place-Names of Rathlin 78	1989
8. pʌrt na mjanən	Irish of Rathlin 55, 216	1942
9. portnə'm'janən	Place-Names of Rathlin 78	1989

"A small port [in Demesne] formed by an inward curve in the coast line. Boats do not land in it except in calm weather when they come to cut seaweeds" (*OSRNB* sh.1, 2).

Rathlin Sound
D 1147

A hybrid form

1. an Caolas	Irish of Rathlin 171	1942
2. Sound of Roughlen consisting of two islands, the	CSP Ire. 676	1598
3. Sound, The	Treatise on Ire. (NLI) 11	1599c
4. Deucally donian Sea, The	DS (Par. Map) 58	1657c
5. Sound, The	Norden's Map	1610
6. Sound, The	Lendrick Map	1780
7. Caolas Reachlainne	Éire Thuaidh	1988
8. əŋ kEːləs	Irish of Rathlin 171	1942

Caolas is translated "strait; narrow water" by *Ó Dónaill*; Holmer translated the place-name (form 1) as "the Channel" (*Irish of Rathin* 171). On the mainland, Holmer noted the sea-current name *Sloc na Mara* was an "eddy between Rathlin and Fair Head" (*Irish of the Glens* 128). In 1942 he recorded it in Rathlin as *Sloc na Marann* "pit(?) of the seas", and noted that it referred to "a rough place in the sea, off the south point" (i.e. Rue Point; *Irish of Rathlin* 234), but that it was originally applied to "a place inland" (*ibid.*). The historical forms of this name follow:

1. sluc na mara	Mulcahy's Rathlin 44	1889
2. slóc na Maran, (or) mara	Mulcahy's Rathlin 60	1889
3. Sloc na Mara	Antiquaties of Rathlin 46	1911
4. Sloc na Marann (Morann)	Irish of the Glens 121 ,128	1940
5. Sloc na Moran (Mara)	Irish of Rathlin 234	1942
6. Sluc na mara	Iarsmaí o Reachrainn 255	1948–52
7. sloch na Moran in Rachri Island	Llyud's Tour 222	1699
8. Sloghnamorra	EA 289	1847
9. Sloak-na-marrin	Murphy's Rathlin 163	1953c
10. Sluck-na-marra	Murphy's Rathlin 163	1953c
11. Slug-na-mara "gulp of the sea"	EA 289	1847
12. Slug na marra (Sloughnamarra), "the swallow of the sea"	Ó Dubhthaigh 185	1905
13. Sloc na mara "swallow hole of the sea"	Rev. Magill 23	1923
14. Sloc na Mara "the channel between Rathlin Island and the mainland"	Dinneen	1927
15. "The Gulf of the Mariner"	Murphy's Rathlin 163	1953c
16. slɔk na marən (mɔrən)	Irish of the Glens 128	1940
17. slɔk na mɔrən (seldom marən)	Irish of Rathlin 41	1942
18. slɔk na mɔrən (seldom marə)	Irish of Rathlin 234	1942

Forms 16–8 appear to reflect a gen. pl. (*marann*) of *muir* "sea" (*DIL*). As the pl. suffix -*anna* only became common in the 17th and 18th centuries (McCone *et al* 1994, 451), we may have here an unusually early example of it in a place-name (note form 7). Holmer suggested that the place-name was analogous to the gen. pl. of nouns of the fifth declension which, if the nom. pl. ended in -*a*, was formed by dropping the final vowel (*Irish of the Glens* 46). We could also consider that forms 16–7 reflect a reduced form of the Scottish Gaelic gen. pl. *marannan* (*Dwelly* sv. *muir*). Holmer translated the first element *sloc* as "gully" (*Irish of Rathlin* 234). *Dinneen* translates *sloc* as "a hole, a pit, a hollow, a slough" while *Dwelly* gives the further meanings "grave; dungeon; pool, gutter, ditch". Murphy (*Murphy's Rathlin* 163) recorded: "'The French fleet was lost in Sloak-na-marrin: that's how it got its name'". For other sea-current names around Rathlin, see *Irish of Rathlin* svv. *slugan* "vortex" and *Geogan*, **Altacorry Bay**, *Murphy's Rathlin* 58–60, and *Mulcahy's Rathlin*.

Rue Point
D 1547

An Rubha
"the headland"

1. An Rubha	Irish of Rathlin 227	1942
2. Rue Point, The	Murphy's Rathlin 87	1953c
3. Rubha "The rue (herb) point"	Ó Dubhthaigh 185	1905
4. Rubha "headland"	Ó Dubhthaigh 189	1905

5. An Rubha "the point"	Place-Names of Rathlin 88	1989
6. ən rʌə	Irish of Rathlin 227	1942
7. rʌː pɑint	Place-Names of Rathlin 88	1989
8. ðə 'ruː	Local pronunciation	1996

This name is a shortened form of *Rubha na bhFaoileann* (*Place-Names of Rathlin* 88). See
Roonivoolin.

Ruecallan	*Rubha Chailean(?)*	
D 0952	"headland of the girls"	
1. Ruecallan	OSRNB sh.1, 1	1852
2. "the noisy or clamorous point"	OSRNB sh.1, 1	1852
3. Rubha Callainn "Callan's point"	J O'D (OSRNB) sh.1, 1	1852
4. Rubha Challáin "the point of the noise", or "the point of Callán"	Place-Names of Rathlin 8	1989
5. Rubha an Chailín "the point of the girl"	Place-Names of Rathlin 8	1989
6. rʌː'xɑlən	Place-Names of Rathlin 8	1989

This is in Kebble. Inland from this point are the two further place-names written *Rubha Challáin Ard* and *Rubha Challáin Íseal* by Mac Giolla Easpaig (*Place-Names of Rathlin* 8). Holmer recorded the latter of these as [(fiː) rʌə xɑl'ɛn iːʃəN] ((faoi) *Rudha Chailean Iseal*; *Irish of Rathlin* 207), and it is because of this pronunciation that Mac Giolla Easpaig suggests the further possible origin in form 5. Holmer recorded *cailín* "girl" as [kɑl'ɛn] locally (*Irish of Rathlin* 170) which we could probably represent orthographically as *caileán* (compare *goirtean* in *ibid.* 202). *Caile*, pl. *cailean* ([kɑl'ən]) was also used (ibid). On the mainland he recorded it as [kɛl'ən/kɑl'ən] and spelt it as *cailean* (*Irish of the Glens* 103). As both form 6 and Holmer's recording (see above) suggest that the final consonant was unpalatalized, we might suggest that the second element in Ruecallan is a variant gen. pl. *cailean/caileán* "of the girls". The lenited *c* (form 6) could be explained as being due to the use of the name in oblique cases.

O'Donovan gave the Irish form *Port an Challáin* "port of the noise or tumult" for the Ballintoy subtownland name **Portacallan** (*OSRNB* sh.3, 2). O'Boyle noted that *Callán* was the name of an "enchanted steed" which was killed at a place he calls *Loch Callán* (*sic*) in Knockans (*O'Boyle* 50), but no tradition of this appears to have been recorded in relation to Ruecallan (regarding this supernatural animal see *Murphy's Rathlin* 179–80). Forms 2–4 are at variance with Holmer's phonetic recordings, however. See **Roonivoolin** regarding the element *rubha*.

Ruenascarrive	*Rubha na Scarbh*	
D 1650	"headland of the cormorants"	
1. Ruenascarrive	OSRNB sh.1, 2	1852
2. Rubha na Scairbh "point of the cormorants"	J O'D (OSRNB) sh.1, 2	1852

3. Rú-na-scarbh "cormorant point"	Duncan 134	1906
4. (Caisdeal) Rún na Sgairbh	O'Boyle 47	1939
5. Rún na Sgairbhe "Port of the cormorants"	O'Boyle 48	1939
6. "cormorant point"	Dallat's Rathlin 27	1973
7. Rubha na Scarbh "the point of the cormorants"	Place-Names of Rathlin 77	1989
8. rʎənəˈsgɑrəv	Place-Names of Rathlin 77	1989

"A low rocky headland [in Craigmacagan] running into the sea and so called from the sea fowl called scarfs or cormorants, perching upon it" (*OSRNB* sh.1, 2).

Dinneen gives *scarbh* as "a cormorant, a shag (*Antrim*); *Old Norse* skafr [r. skarfr], green cormorant", while Holmer also noted the word locally (*Irish of Rathlin* 229; see also *Dwelly* sv. *sgarbh*). We may also note in this context a subtownland name in Town Parks in Ramoan recorded by the Ordnance Survey as **Craignascarf**, being a "long ledge of rock running into the sea" and ascribed the Irish form *Creag na Scarbh* "rock of the cormorants" by O'Donovan (*OSRNB* sh.5). The phonetically similar *scairbh/scarbh* (gen. sing. *scairbhe*) "shallow (in river, lake, sea) with shingly bottom; shingly beach; reef covered by shallow water" (*Ó Dónaill*) could also be considered as a possible final element, however. A variant form of this word pronounced [skörvi] and meaning "rough stony ground or place" was recorded by Holmer in the subtownland name he spelt as *Scairbhigh Dhomh'all ic Airteoir*, which we could standardize as *Scairbhigh Dhónaill Mhic Artúir* "Dónall MacArthur's rough ground" (*Irish of Rathlin* 229).

Skerriagh
D 1253

Sceir Riabhach
"brindled skerry"

1. Sceir Riabhach	Irish of Rathlin 225	1942
2. Skerriagh	OSRNB sh.1, 1	1852
3. Sceir Iagh "a sharp sea rock, an island"	OSRNB sh.1, 1	1852
4. Sceireach "rocky"	J O'D (OSRNB) sh.1, 1	1852
5. Sceir Riabhach "the brindled skerry"	Place-Names of Rathlin 45	1989
6. skʹer riɑx	Irish of Rathlin 225	1942
7. sgʹɛrˈriəx	Place-Names of Rathlin 45	1989

"A long narrow insulated rock [in Ballygill North] rising out of the sea. It stands from 6 to 8 chains from the shore, and at the north base of a towering precipitous cliff. It has been so named from its shelving scraggy appearance. It is never covered by the sea. In stormy weather the sea breaks over it" (*OSRNB* sh.1, 1). Holmer recorded the further minor names *An Sceir Dhubh* "the black skerry" and *An Sceir Bhán* "the white skerry" locally (*Irish of Rathlin* 229).

South Lighthouse D 1447	An English form	
1. (?)tigh soluis	Mulcahy's Rathlin 44	1889
2. (?)ty soluish	Mulcahy's Rathlin 44	1889
3. ðə ˈsəuθ	Local pronuciation	1996

This is in Roonivoolin at **Rue Point** (called *The Rue*). See **East Lighthouse** regarding forms 1–2.

Sroanderrig D 1050	Of uncertain origin	
1. Sróin an Deargain	Irish of Rathlin 64	1942
2. Sróin an Deargan	Irish of Rathlin 184	1942
3. Sróin Deargan	Irish of Rathlin 184	1942
4. Sroandeargig	OSRNB sh.1, 1	1852
5. Srón Deargaig "the reddish snout"	J O'D (OSRNB) sh.1, 1	1852
6. Sron-dearg "red point"	Duncan 134	1906
7. "red point"	Dallat's Rathlin 27	1973
8. Srón Dearg "the red nose"	Place-Names of Rathlin 24	1989
9. srɔːnʹ ən dʒɑrgən	Irish of Rathlin 64, 184	1942
10. srɔːnʹ dʒɑɾɣəɲ	Irish of Rathlin 184	1942
11. srɔːnˈdʒarəg	Place-Names of Rathlin 24	1989
12. ˌsɛnˈdʒɛrəg	Local pronunciation	1996

"A bold prominent precipitous headland so named from reddish clay or ochre appearing along its face" (*OSRNB* sh.1, 1). This is in Kinramer South.

Joyce has noted that *srón* "nose" may also be applied to "a hill-point, from shape" (*Joyce* iii 562). *Dwelly* lists several meanings for *srón*, including "promontory, headland running from a mountain to a 'strath'; ridge of a hill", while *Dinneen* also notes the meanings "a tail out of rock, etc.; a promontory". *Sróin* (form 1) was originally the dat. sing. form.

It is possible that there existed an original place-name *An Deargeang/Dearging* "the red cove(?)", in which *eang*, originally "track, trace; strip of land" (*DIL* sv. *eng*; cf. also **Innananooan**), was prefixed by *dearg* "red". *Srón (na) Deargeanga* "headland of the red cove" could thus be postulated as the Irish form for Sroanderrig. *Eang* could have developed to [ən] in unstressed position, but also appears to have given *eag* in dialects of Irish and Scottish Gaelic (*Ó Dónaill, Dwelly* sv.); *ng* between broad vowels was normally pronounced [g] in Rathlin Irish (*Irish of Rathlin* 56 §90). This might explain the variation between forms 4 and 9. It appears that the final element was not declined in forms 9–10 (compare *Cúl an Chreig Mhór* in *Place-Names of Rathlin* 35). The modern form has been shortened by syncope. See also **Derignan Point**, and **Knocknagarvan** townland in Ballintoy.

Among other possible original forms, we could consider *Srón an Deargáin* "headland of the red patch" and *Srón Deargán* "headland of the sea-bream" (see *Ó Dónaill* sv. *deargán* and

Derignan Point), and account for the assorted anomalies in Holmer's forms as being indicative of the weak state of the language. The understanding among Irish speakers in the 1940s appears to have been that this name referred to "an ancient hero" called *Brian Dearg* or *Brian Deargan* (*Irish of Rathlin* 184 sv. *deargan*): *Srón (an) Deargáin* "(the) *Deargán*'s headland" are thus further possible forms.

Sroannamaddy	*Srón an Mhadaidh*	
D 0950	"headland of the dog"	

One might also consider *Srón na Madadh* "nose of the dogs" as a possibility (cf. *Bruach na Madadh*, a subtownland name in south-east Co. Down, anglicized **Broughnamaddy**; *PNI* iii 127), but -*adh* was ususally pronounced [g] in late Rathlin Irish (*Irish of Rathlin* 52 §81). This headland is in Kebble.

Stackamore	*Staca Mór*	
D 1552	"big stack"	

1. Stac Mór	Irish of Rathlin 237	1942
2. Stackamore	OSRNB sh.1, 2	1852
3. "large stack or stook"	OSRNB sh.1, 2	1852
4. Stáca mór "big stack"	J O'D (OSRNB) sh.1, 2	1852
5. Stac Mór "Big rock"	O'Boyle 49	1946
6. An Staca Mór "the big stack"	Place-Names of Rathlin 60	1989
7. stakə moːr	Irish of Rathlin 237	1942
8. sdakə'moːr	Place-Names of Rathlin 60	1989

"A large rock [in Ballyconagan] rising abruptly at the low-water line. It is situated at the N. base of a towering cliff. The sea washes its north base. It is so called from its resemblence to a stack or stook" (*OSRNB* sh.1, 2).

Stroanlea	*An tSrón Liath*	
D 1150	"the grey headland"	

1. Sroanlea	OSRNB sh.1, 2	1852
2. Srón Liath "grey nose"	J O'D (OSRNB) sh.1, 2	1852
3. Srón Liath "grey rock – shaped like a nose"	O'Boyle 51	1946
4. An tSrón Liath "the grey nose"	Place-Names of Rathlin 49	1989
5. struən 'lia	Place-Names of Rathlin 49	1989

"A bold prominent headland [in Ballygill South] jutting into the sea and so named from its greyish aspect and from its being fantastically likened to a nose or snout" (*OSRNB* sh.1, 2). See also **Sroanderrig** above. The *t* in modern pronunciation is a late intrusion.

| **Ushet Lough** | Of uncertain origin | |
| D 1448 | | |

1. Loch na h-Usaide	Irish of Rathlin 247	1942
2. Logh	Hib. Reg. Cary	1657c
3. Ushet	Maritime Map	1776
4. Roonivoolin lake	OSM xxiv 127	1838
5. Ushet Lough	OSRNB sh.1, 2	1852
6. (from) usáid "use"	Duncan 134	1906
7. Loch na hUsaide "the lake of		
Usaid"	Place-Names of Rathlin 89	1989
8. lox na hʌsidʒə	Irish of Rathlin 247	1942
9. loha na hʌsədʒ	Irish of Rathlin 247	1942
10. 'oʃəd'lox	Place-Names of Rathlin 89	1989
11. 'oʃət	Local pronunciation	1996

"A large fresh water lough said to have been named from a landing-place called 'Ushet Port' a short distance south of it . . ." (*OSRNB* sh.1, 2). The lake was descibed in 1830 as being "extra-parochial" (*OSM* xxiv 127).

The place-name *An Usaid*, which gave this lake its name (and to which form 11 more correctly refers), was recorded as [ʌsɛdʒ] and [(sə n)ʌsadʒ] by Holmer (*Irish of Rathlin* 247), and was described as a subdivision of Roonivoolin by Mac Giolla Easpaig, who was uncertain of its etymology (*Place-Names of Rathlin* 88). The use of Ushet as a place-name in its own right militates against the etymology in form 6 of **Ushet Port** which suggests that it derived from *úsáid* "use, usage", although there may be a parallel in the Co. Meath town name **Nobber**, from *An Obair* (literally "the work") "the construction" (*IPN* 242). **Ushet Point** also features this element (see below). A reinterpretation of the name based on this etymology may have given rise to distorted pronunciations. A derivation from *òs* "mouth or outlet of a river; bar or sandbank in harbour" (*Dwelly*) plus the locative suffix *-aid* (see Watson 1926, 444) might be considered. Note also *Cloch na hUsaide*, which has been translated "the stone of the barrell", in Tory Island (Hamilton 1974, 229). Ushet is unlikely to represent a noun plus noun compound place-name, as it is unlikely that a name of this structure would have survived in Rathlin, where all the names with the exception of the island name appear to be of relatively recent vintage.

| **Ushet Point** | A hybrid form | |
| D 1547 | | |

1. Ushet Point	OSRNB sh.1, 3	1852
2. Pointe na hUsaide "the point of		
Usaid"	Place-Names of Rathlin 88	1989
3. ʌsəd paint	Place-Names of Rathlin 88	1989

"A low rocky point or headland [in Roonivoolin] pointing southward and bounding the entrance on E. side to Ushet Port, from which it is named" (*OSRNB* sh.1, 3). See **Ushet Lough**.

Ushet Port   A hybrid form
D 1547

1. Bay, The	Hib. Del. Antrim	1672c
2. Ushet Haven	Lendrick Map	1780
3. Ushet Haven	Map Antrim	1807
4. Ushet Haven	Dubourdieu Map	1812
5. Ushet Port	OSRNB sh.1, 3	1852
6. The port of use or accomodation	OSRNB sh.1, 3	1852
7. ˈʌsəd port	Place-Names of Rathlin 88	1989

"It is the principal landing-place in the south part of the island" (*OSRNB* sh.1, 3). This is in Roonivoolin. See **Ushet Lough**.

West Lighthouse   An English form
D 0952

1. (an) toigh soluis	Irish of Rathlin 33, 236	1942
2. (?)tigh soluis	Mulcahy's Rathlin 44	1889
3. The West Light	Murphy's Rathlin 21	1953c
4. ðə ˈwɛst	Local pronunciation	1996

This is in Kebble, at *Cnoc an Tairbh* "hill of the bull" (angl. **Crockantirrive**; see *Place-names of Rathlin* 20; see also **Bull Point** above). See also **East Lighthouse** regarding form 2.

APPENDIX A

ASPECTS OF IRISH GRAMMAR RELEVANT TO PLACE-NAMES

The following types of place-names can be identified:

1. Those which consist of a noun only:

> Sabhall "a barn" (Saul, Dn)
> Tuaim "a tumulus" (Toome, Ant.)

There is no indefinite article in Irish, that is, there is no word for *a*, e.g. *Sabhall* means "barn" or "a barn".

English nouns generally have only two forms, singular and plural, and the plural is normally formed by adding s, e.g. *wall, walls; road, roads.* Occasionally a different ending is added – *ox, oxen* – and occasionally the word is changed internally – *man, men;* sometimes there is both addition and internal change – *brother, brethren.* Irish nouns have not only distinctive forms for the plural but also for the genitive singular and sometimes for the dative and vocative as well. These distinctive forms are made by addition, by internal change and sometimes by both. Five principal types of noun change are identified in Irish and nouns are therefore divided into five major groups known as *declensions.* Examples of change will be seen later.

2. Singular article + masculine noun:

> An Clár "the plain" (Clare, Arm.)
> An Gleann "the valley" (Glen, Der.)

The only article in Irish is the definite article, that is, the word corresponding to *the* in English.

The singular article *an* "the" prefixes *t* to masculine nouns beginning with a vowel in certain cases. The nouns *éadan* "front, forehead" and *iúr* "yew tree", for example, appear in the place-names:

> An tÉadan "the face (of a hill)" (Eden, Ant.)
> An tIúr "the yew tree" (Newry, Dn)

3. Singular article + feminine noun:

> An Chloch "the stone" (Clough, Dn)
> An Bhreacach "the speckled place" (Brockagh, Der.)

The article *an* aspirates the first consonant of a following feminine noun.

Aspiration is indicated by putting *h* after the consonant *(cloch* "a stone"; *an chloch* "the stone") and the sound of that consonant is modified, just as in English the sound of *p*, as in the word *praise,* is changed when *h* is added, as in the word *phrase.* Only *b, c, d, f, g, m, p, s,* and *t* are aspirated. The other consonants, and vowels, are not aspirated.

The singular article *an* does not affect feminine nouns beginning with a vowel, e.g.

> An Eaglais "the church" (Eglish, Tyr.)

4. Masculine noun + adjective:

> Domhnach Mór "great church" (Donaghmore, Tyr.)
> Lios Liath "grey ring fort" (Lislea, Arm.)

In Irish the adjective normally follows the noun (but see §8).

5. Feminine noun + adjective:

> Bearn Mhín "smooth gap" (Barnmeen, Dn)
> Doire Fhada "long oak-wood" (Derryadd, Arm.)

The first consonant of the adjective is aspirated after a feminine noun.

6. Singular article + masculine noun + adjective:

> An Caisleán Riabhach "the brindled castle" (Castlereagh, Dn)
> An Baile Meánach "the middle town" (Ballymena, Ant.)

7. Singular article + feminine noun + adjective:

> An Charraig Mhór "the large rock" (Carrickmore, Tyr.)
> An Chloch Fhionn "the white stone" (Cloghfin, Tyr.)

Note that the first consonant of the feminine noun is aspirated after the definite article as in §3 above and that the adjective is aspirated after the feminine noun as in §5 above.

8. Adjective + noun:

> Fionnshliabh "white mountain" (Finlieve, Dn)
> Seanchill "old church" (Shankill, Ant.)

Sometimes an adjective precedes a noun. In such cases the two words are generally written as one and the second noun is usually aspirated. In compounds aspiration sometimes does not occur when *d, t* or *s* is preceded by *d, n, t, l* or *s*.

9. Article + adjective + noun:

> An Seanmhullach "the old summit" (Castledawson, Der.)
> An Ghlasdromainn "the green ridge" (Glasdrumman, Dn)

Dromainn is a feminine noun and the initial consonant of the compound is aspirated in accordance with §3 above.

10. Masculine noun + genitive singular of noun:

> Srath Gabhláin "(the) river valley of (the) fork" (Stragolan, Fer.)
> Port Rois "(the) harbour of (the) headland" (Portrush, Ant.)

These two examples contain the genitive singular forms of the nouns *gabhlán* and *ros*. Many nouns form the genitive singular by inserting *i* before the final consonant.

11. Feminine noun + genitive singular of noun:

> Maigh Bhile "(the) plain of (the) sacred tree" (Movilla, Dn)
> Cill Shléibhe "(the) church of (the) mountain" (Killevy, Arm.)

Note that in these examples the qualifying genitive is aspirated after the feminine noun. However the forms *maigh* and *cill* are also both old datives, and in the older language aspiration followed any dative singular noun.

Two other types of genitive are illustrated here: many nouns which end in a vowel, like *bile*, do not change at all, whereas others, like *sliabh*, form their genitive by adding *e* (and sometimes an internal change is necessary).

12. Noun + *an* + genitive singular:

> Léim an Mhadaidh "(the) leap of the dog" (Limavady, Der.)
> Baile an tSéipéil "(the) town of the chapel" (Chapeltown, Dn)

The noun *an madadh* "the dog" has a genitive *an mhadaidh* "of the dog". Note that, as well as the end of the noun changing as in §10 above, the genitive is aspirated after *an*.

Instead of aspirating *s* the article *an* prefixes *t* to it: *an sac* "the sack", *an tsaic* "of the sack"; *an séipéal* "the chapel", *an tséipéil* "of the chapel".

13. Noun + *na* + genitive singular:

> Muileann na Cloiche "(the) mill of the stone/the stone mill" (Clogh Mills, Ant.)
> Cúil na Baice "(the) corner/angle of the river bend" (Cullybackey, Ant.)

The genitive singular feminine article is *na*. It does not aspirate the following noun: *an chloch* "the stone", *na cloiche* "of the stone".

It prefixes *h*, however, to words beginning with a vowel e.g.

> Baile na hInse "(the) town of the water-meadow" (Ballynahinch, Dn)

The genitive in all these examples is formed by adding *e* to the nominative singular and making a slight internal adjustment.

14. Plural noun:

> Botha "huts" (Boho, Fer.)

The plural form of a substantial group of nouns in Irish is formed by adding *-a*. In the examples in §15 below an internal adjustment has also to be made.

15. *Na* + plural noun:

> Na Creaga "the rocks" (Craigs, Ant.)
> Na Cealla "the churches" (Kells, Ant.)

Na is also the plural article. *Creaga* and *cealla* are the plural forms of the nouns *creig* "rock" and *cill* "church".

16. Noun + genitive plural:

> Droim Bearach "(the) ridge of (the) heifers" (Dromara, Dn)
> Port Muc "(the) harbour of (the) pigs" (Portmuck, Ant.)

As in the case of *bearach* "a heifer" and *muc* "a pig" the genitive plural form is the same as the nominative singular.

17. Noun + *na* + genitive plural:

> Lios na gCearrbhach "(the) fort/enclosure of the gamblers" (Lisburn, Dn)
> Lios na nDaróg "(the) fort/enclosure of the little oaks" (Lisnarick, Fer.)

After *na* the first letter of the following genitive plural is eclipsed. Eclipsis involves adding to the beginning of a word a consonant which obliterates the sound of the original consonant, e.g.

bó "a cow", pronounced like English "bow" (and arrow)

(na) mbó "(of the) cows", pronounced like "mow"

The following are the changes which take place:

Written letter	Is eclipsed by
b	m
c	g
d	n
f	bh
g	ng
p	b
t	d
vowel	n

The other consonants are not eclipsed, e.g.

Áth na Long "(the) ford of the ships" (Annalong, Dn)

18. Noun + genitive of personal name:

Dún Muirígh "*Muiríoch's* fort" (Dunmurry, Ant.)
Boith Mhéabha "Maeve's hut" (Bovevagh, Der.)

In the older language the genitive of a personal name was not aspirated after a masculine noun but it was after a feminine noun. In the above examples *dún* is masculine and *boith* is feminine. In current Irish aspiration of the personal name is also usual after a masculine noun and this is reflected in many place-names in areas where Irish survived until quite recently, e.g.

Ard Mhacha, interpreted as "the height of *Macha*" (Armagh, Arm.)

19. Noun + genitive singular of *Ó* surname:

Baile Uí Dhonnaíle "Donnelly's townland" (Castlecaulfield, Tyr.)
Coill Uí Chiaragáin "Kerrigan's wood" (Killykergan, Der.)

Surnames in *Ó*, e.g. Ó Dochartaigh "(O') Doherty", Ó Flannagáin "Flanagan", etc. form their genitive by changing *Ó* to *Uí* and aspirating the second element – Uí Dhochartaigh, Uí Fhlannagáin .

20. Noun + genitive singular of *Mac* surname:

Lios Mhic Dhuibhleacháin "*Mac Duibhleacháin's* fort/enclosure"
(Lisnagelvin, Der.)
Baile Mhic Gabhann "*Mac Gabhann's* town (angl. McGowan, Smith, etc.)
(Ballygowan, Dn)

Surnames in *Mac*, e.g. Mac Dónaill "McDonnell", Mac Muiris "Morrison, Fitzmaurice", etc. form their genitive by changing *Mac* to *Mhic* and aspirating the second element (except those beginning with *C* or *G*).

21. Noun + genitive plural of Ó surname:

> Doire Ó gConaíle "the oak-wood of the Ó *Conaíle* family (angl. Connelly)" (Derrygonnelly, Fer.)

In the genitive plural of Ó surnames the second element is eclipsed.

22. Neuter noun + genitive or adjective:

> Sliabh gCuillinn "mountain of (the) steep slope" (Slieve Gullion, Arm.)
> Loch gCaol "(the) narrow lake" (Loughguile, Ant.)

The neuter gender no longer exists in Irish but traces of it are found in place-names. The initials of nouns and adjectives were eclipsed after neuter nouns.

APPENDIX B

LAND UNITS

TERRITORIAL DIVISIONS IN IRELAND

The old administrative system, used in the arrangement of these books, consisted of land units in descending order of size: province, county, barony, parish and townland. Theoretically at least the units fit inside each other, townlands into parishes, parishes into baronies, baronies into counties. This system began piecemeal, with the names of the provinces dating back to prehistoric times, while the institution of counties and baronies dates from the 13th to the 17th century, though the names used are often the names of earlier tribal groups or settlements. Parishes originate not as a secular land-unit, but as part of the territorial organization of the Christian Church. There they form the smallest unit in the system which, in descending order of size, goes from provinces to dioceses to deaneries to parishes. Some Irish parishes derive from churches founded by St Patrick and early saints, and appear as parish units in Anglo-Norman church records: parish units are thus older than counties and baronies. Townlands make their first appearance as small land units listed in Anglo-Norman records. However the evidence suggests that land units of this type (which had various local names) are of pre-Norman native origin.

The 17th-century historian Geoffrey Keating outlined a native land-holding system based on the *tríocha céad* or "thirty hundreds", each divided in Ulster into about 28 *baile biadhtaigh* "lands of a food-provider" or "ballybetaghs", and about 463 *seisrigh* "six-horse plough-teams" or "seisreachs" *(Céitinn* iv 112f.). The term *tríocha céad,* which seems to relate to the size of the army an area could muster, is not prominent in English accounts, though there is a barony called Trough *(Tríocha)* in Co. Monaghan. The ballybetagh (land of a farmer legally obliged to feed his lord and retinue while travelling through the area) is mentioned in Plantation documents for west Ulster, and there is some evidence, from townlands grouped in multiples of three and four, that it existed in Armagh, Antrim and Down (McErlean 1983, 318).

Boundaries of large areas, such as provinces and dioceses, are often denoted in early Irish sources by means of two or four extreme points (Hogan 1910, 279–280; *Céitinn* iii 302). There was also a detailed native tradition of boundary description, listing landmarks such as streams, hills, trees and bogs. This can be demonstrated as early as the 8th century in Tírechán's record of a land grant to St Patrick *(Trip. Life (Stokes)* ii 338–9),[1] and as late as the 17th century, when native experts guided those surveying and mapping Ireland for the English administration. The boundary marks on the ground were carefully maintained, as illustrated in the *Perambulation of Iveagh* in 1618 *(Inq. Ult.* xliii), according to which the guide broke the plough of a man found ploughing up a boundary. However very often Irish texts, for example the "Book of Rights" *(Lebor na Cert),* the "topographical" poems by Seaán Mór Ó Dubhagáin and Giolla-na-naomh Ó hUidhrín *(Topog. Poems),* and "The rights of O'Neill" *(Ceart Uí Néill),* refer to territories by the names of the peoples inhabiting them. This custom has been preserved to the present in some place-names, particularly those of provinces and baronies.

SECULAR ADMINISTRATIVE DIVISIONS

Townlands

Twelfth-century charters provide the earliest documentary evidence for the existence in Ireland of small land units, although we do not know what these units were called. Keating's smallest unit, the *seisreach,* a division of the ballybetagh, is given as 120 acres (the word *acra* is apparently borrowed from English). The size of the *seisreach* seems to have been approximately that of a modern townland, but the word does not occur much outside Keating's *schema.* Many other terms appear in the sources: *ceathrú* "quarter" (often a quarter of a ballybetagh), *baile bó* "land providing one cow as rent" (usually a twelfth of a ballybetagh), *seiseach* "sixth" and *trian* "third" (apparently divisions of a ballyboe). In most of Ulster the ballyboe and its subdivisions are the precursors of the modern townlands, and were referred to in Latin sources as *villa* or *carucata,* and in English as "town" or "ploughland" (the term used for similar units in 11th-century England in the Domesday Book). The Irish term *baile* (see below) seems to have been treated as equivalent to English "town", which had originally meant "settlement (and lands appertaining)"; and the compound term "townland" seems to have been adopted to make the intended meaning clear. It was used in 19th-century Ireland as a blanket term for various local words. In the area of Fermanagh and Monaghan the term for the local unit was "tate". In an English document of 1591 it is stated that the tate was 60 acres in size and that there were sixteen tates in the ballybetagh *(Fiants Eliz.* §5674). Tate appears in place-names in composition with Gaelic elements, but was regarded by Reeves (1861, 484) as a pre-1600 English borrowing into Irish.

There is no evidence for the use of the word *baile* in the formation of place-names before the middle of the 12th century. The earliest examples are found in a charter dating to c. 1150 in the Book of Kells which relates to lands belonging to the monastery of Kells. At this period *baile* seems to mean "a piece of land" and is not restricted to its present-day meaning "hamlet, group of houses", much less "town, village". After the coming of the Normans, *baile* appears more frequently in place-names, until it finally becomes the most prevalent type of townland name. By the 14th century, *baile* had acquired its present-day meaning of "town", probably in reference to small medieval towns, or settlements that had arisen in the vicinity of castles. Price suggests that the proliferation of the use of the word in place-names was a result of the arrival of settlers and their use of the word "town" *(tūn)* in giving names to their lands (Price 1963, 124). When the Irish revival took place in the 14th century many English-language names were translated into Irish and "town" was generally replaced by *baile.* The proportion of *baile* names is greatest in those parts of Ireland which had been overrun by the Anglo-Normans but subsequently gaelicized, and is lowest in the counties of mid-Ulster in which there was little or no English settlement *(ibid.* 125).

Despite attempts at schematization none of the units which predated the modern townlands was of uniform size, and it is clear from the native sources that evaluation was based on an area of good land together with a variable amount of uncultivated land. Thus townlands on bad land are usually larger than those on good land. The average size of a townland in Ireland as a whole is 325 acres, and 357 acres in the six counties of Northern Ireland, though these averages include huge townlands like Slievedoo (4551 acres, Co. Tyrone) and tiny townlands like Acre McCricket (4 acres, Co. Down). There is also considerable local variation: townlands in Co. Down average 457 acres (based on the ballyboe), compared to 184 acres (based on the tate) in Fermanagh (Reeves 1861, 490).

Parishes

Early accounts of the lives of saints such as Patrick and Columcille refer to many church foundations. It seems that land was often given for early churches beside routeways, or on the boundaries of tribal territories. Some of the same church names appear as the names of medieval parishes in the papal taxation of 1302–06 *(Eccles. Tax.).* Some parish names include ecclesiastical elements such as *ceall, domhnach, lann,* all meaning "church", *díseart* "hermitage" and *tearmann* "sanctuary", but others are secular in origin. Parish bounds are not given in the papal taxation, but parishes vary considerably in size, probably depending on the wealth or influence of the local church. The medieval ecclesiastical parishes seem to have come into existence after the reform of the native Irish church in the course of the 12th century; in Anglo-Norman areas such as Skreen in Co. Meath the parochial system had already been adopted by the early 13th century (Otway-Ruthven 1964, 111–22). After the Reformation the medieval parish boundaries were continued by the established Church of Ireland, and used by the government as the bounds of civil parishes, a secular land unit forming the major division of a barony. (The boundaries of modern Roman Catholic parishes have often been drawn afresh, to suit the population of worshippers).

As well as the area inhabited by local worshippers, lands belonging to a medieval church often became part of its parish. These were usually close by, but it is quite common, even in the early 19th century when some rationalization had occurred, for parishes to include detached lands at some distance from the main body (Power 1947, 222–3). Kilclief in the barony of Lecale, Co. Down, for example, has five separate detached townlands, while Ballytrustan in the Upper Ards and Trory in Co. Fermanagh are divided into several parts. While an average parish might contain 30 townlands, parishes vary in the number of townlands they contained; for example, Ballykinler in Co. Down contained only 3 townlands, while Aghalurcher contained 237 townlands (including several islands) in Co. Fermanagh plus 17 townlands in Co. Tyrone. Although most of its townlands are fairly small, Aghalurcher is still much larger than Ballykinler. There were usually several parishes within a barony (on average 5 or 6, but, for example, only 2 in the barony of Dufferin, Co. Down, and 18 in the barony of Loughinsholin, Co. Derry). Occasional parishes constituted an entire barony, as did Kilkeel, for example, which is coterminous with the barony of Mourne. However parish units also frequently extended across rivers, which were often used as obvious natural boundaries for counties and baronies: Newry across the Newry River, Clonfeacle over the Blackwater, Artrea over the Ballinderry River, Blaris over the Lagan. This means that civil parishes may be in more than one barony, and sometimes in more than one county.

Baronies

The process of bringing Irish tribal kingdoms into the feudal system as "baronies" under chieftains owing allegiance to the English crown began during the medieval period, although the system was not extended throughout Ulster until the early 17th century. Many of the baronies established in the later administrative system have population names: Oneilland, Irish *Uí Nialláin* "descendants of Niallán" (Arm.); Keenaght, Irish *Cianachta* "descendants of Cian" (Der.); Clankelly, Irish *Clann Cheallaigh* "Ceallach's children" (Fer.). Others have the names of historically important castles or towns: Dungannon (O'Neills, Tyr.), Dunluce (MacDonnells, Antr.), Castlereagh (Clandeboy O'Neills, Down). The barony of Loughinsholin (Der.) is named after an island fortification or crannog, *Loch Inse Uí Fhloinn* "the lake of O'Flynn's island", although by the 17th century the island was inhabited by the O'Hagans, and the O'Flynn area of influence had moved east of the Bann.

The barony system was revised and co-ordinated at the same time as the counties, so that later baronies always fit inside the county bounds. Both counties and baronies appear on maps from 1590 on. These later baronies may contain more than one older district, and other district or population names used in the 16th and 17th centuries, such as *Clancan* and *Clanbrassil* in Armagh, *Slutkellies* in Down, and *Munterbirn* and *Munterevlin* in Tyrone, gradually fell out of use. Baronies were not of uniform size, though in many cases large baronies have been subdivided to make the size more regular. The barony of Dungannon in Co. Tyrone has three sections (Lower, Middle and Upper) while Iveagh in Co. Down has been divided into four (Lower, Lower Half; Lower, Upper Half; Upper, Lower Half; Upper,

Upper Half). The number of baronies in a county in Ulster varies between five in Co. Monaghan and fifteen in Co. Antrim. Armagh, Fermanagh and Tyrone have eight.

Counties

Over the centuries following the Anglo-Norman invasion the English government created a new administrative system in Ireland, adapting the native divisions of provinces, tribal districts (as baronies), parishes and townlands, and dividing each province of Ireland into counties. The counties were equivalent to the shire in England, where a sheriff exercized jurisdiction on behalf of the King. To begin with the county system applied to only those areas where English rule was strong, but was eventually extended, through the reigns of Elizabeth and James I, to cover the whole of the country. Although a commission to shire Ulster was set up in 1585 *(Fiants Eliz. §4763)*, the situation in 1604 was expressed, rather hopefully, in a document in the state papers:

> "each province, except Ulster and other uncivil parts of the realm, is subdued into counties, and each county into baronies and hundreds, and every barony into parishes, consisting of manors, towns and villages after the manner of England."
> *(CSP Ire. 1603–6, 231).*

Most of the counties created in the north were given the names of important towns: Antrim, Armagh, Coleraine (later Londonderry), Down, Donegal, Monaghan and Cavan. Fermanagh and Tyrone, however, have population names. *Fir Manach* "the men of the *Manaig*" (probably the *Menapii* of Ptolemy's *Geography)* had been important in the area before the Maguires. *Tír Eoghain* "Eoghan's land" derives its name from the *Cenél nEógain* branch of the *Uí Néill*, who had expanded southwards from *Inis Eógain* (Inishowen) during the centuries and whose dominant position continued right up until the Plantation. Counties were generally formed out of an amalgam of smaller territorial units, some of which were preserved as baronies within each county.[2] The bounds of these older units were often of long standing, and usually followed obvious physical features, like the lower Bann, the Blackwater, and the Newry River.

Down and Antrim, as part of the feudal Earldom of Ulster (see below) had been treated as counties since the 13th or 14th century (Falkiner 1903, 189; *Inq. Earldom Ulster* ii 141, iii 60). However other districts within the earldom could also be called counties, and up to the mid-16th-century the whole area was sometimes called the "county of Ulster" *(Cal. Carew MSS* 1515–74, 223–4). The settling of Down and Antrim with their modern bounds began in 1570–1 *(Fiants Eliz. §1530, §1736)*. Coleraine had also been the centre of an Anglo-Norman county *(Inq. Earldom Ulster* iv 127). Jobson's map of 1590 shows *Antrym, Armagh, Colrane, Downe, Manahan, Farmanaugh, Terconnel,* and *Upper and Nether Terone* as the names of counties. However, Ulster west of the Bann was still referred to as "four seigniories" (Armagh? plus *Terreconnell, Tyren, Formannoche)* in 1603 *(Cal. Carew MSS* 1601–3, 446–454), although Tyrone had been divided into baronies from 1591 *(Colton Vis.* 125–130). Armagh was settled into baronies in 1605 *(CSP Ire.* 1603–6, 318). The "nine counties of Ulster" were first listed in 1608: *Dunegal or Tirconnel, Tirone, Colraine, Antrim, Downe, Ardmagh, Cavan, Monoghan,* and *Fermanagh (CSP Ire.* 1606–8, 401), and these counties are shown on Hole's adaptation of Mercator's map of Ireland for Camden's atlas *Britannia* (1610). The county of Coleraine was renamed as a result of the plantation grant to the London companies. Under the terms of the formal grant of the area in 1613, the barony of Loughinsholin, which had hitherto been part of Tyrone, was amalgamated with the old county of Coleraine, and Londonderry was made the new county name (Moody 1939, 122–3).

Provinces

Gaelic Ireland, in prehistory and in early historic times, was made up of many small native kingdoms (called *tuatha)*, but a sense of the underlying unity of the island is evident from the name of the earliest division in Ireland, that represented by the four modern provinces of Connaught, Leinster, Munster and Ulster. In Irish each is called *cúige* (older *cóiced)* "a fifth", followed by a district or population name. *Cúige Chonnacht* means "the fifth of the Connaughtmen" *Cúige Laighean* "the fifth of the Leinstermen", *Cúige Mumhan* "the fifth of Munster", *Cúige Uladh* "the fifth of the Ulstermen". The connection between population and place-names is evident at this very early stage. The ancient fifth "fifth" making up the whole was that of Meath, in Irish *Midhe* "middle". The division into these five provinces was taken over when Henry II of England invaded Ireland: Leinster, (North and South) Munster, Connaught, Ulster and Meath *quasi in medio regni positum* (as if placed in the middle of the kingdom), but the number was reduced by the 17th century to the modern four *(CSP Ire.* 1603–6 §402, 231), by incorporating Meath in Leinster.

The Province of Ulster

As mentioned above, the province of Ulster took its name from the tribal name *Ulaid* "Ulstermen" (Flanagan 1978(d)). The earliest record of the tribal name is the form quoted by the 2nd-century Greek geographer Ptolemy, as *Uoluntii* (O'Rahilly 1946, 7). The precise origin of the English form of the name is obscure, though it has been suggested that it derives from something like *Ulaðstir,* an unusual combination of the original Irish name plus the Norse possessive suffix *-s* and the Irish word *tír* "land" (Sommerfelt 1958, 223–227). Ptolemy mentions various other tribes in the north of Ireland, but it appears that the *Ulaid* were the dominant group.

The ancient province of the Ulstermen, according to the native boundary description, stretched south to a line running between the courses of the rivers *Drobaís* (Drowse, on the border between Donegal and Leitrim) and *Bóann* (Boyne, Co. Meath). The "fifth" of the legendary king of the Ulaid, Conchobar, *(Cóiced Conchobair)* thus included modern Co. Louth (Hogan 1910, 279b). It became contracted in historical times, as a result of the expansion of the *Uí Néill* "descendants of Niall", who drove the rulers of the Ulaid from the provincial capital at *Emain Macha* (Navan fort near Armagh) across the Bann into modern Antrim and Down.[3] From the 5th century the area stretching south from Derry and Tyrone to Monaghan and most of Louth belonged to a confederation of tribes called the *Airgialla,* who have been described "as a satellite state of the Uí Néill" (Byrne 1973, 73). Three groups of Uí Néill established themselves in the west, *Cenél Conaill* "Conall's kin" in south Donegal, *Cenél nEndae* in the area around Raphoe, and *Cenél nEógain* in Inishowen *(Inis Eógain* "Eógan's island"). On the north coast, east of the river Foyle, the *Cianachta* maintained a separate identity, despite continuing pressure from *Cenél nEógain.*

East of the Bann the *Dál Fiatach* (the historic Ulaid) shared the kingship of the reduced Ulster with *Dál nAraide* and *Uí Echach Coba,* both originally *Cruthin* tribes.[4] In the 12th century the Anglo-Norman conquest of Antrim and Down resulted in the creation of a feudal lordship of the area under the English crown called the Earldom of Ulster. During the same period the kings of Cenél nEógain had extended their influence eastward, and after the extinction of the Dál Fiatach kingship in the 13th century they assumed the title of *rí Ulad* "king of the Ulaid" to forward their claim to be kings of the whole of the North. It is this greater Ulster which was the basis for the modern province, although there was some doubt at the beginning of the 17th century as to whether or not this included Co. Louth. By the time of the Plantation in 1609 Ulster had been stabilized as nine counties and Louth had been incorporated into the neighbouring province of Leinster.

ECCLESIASTICAL ADMINISTRATIVE DIVISIONS

Dioceses

Under the Roman Empire Christianity developed an administrative structure of dioceses led by bishops based in the local towns. In early Christian Ireland a bishop was provided for each *tuath,* but since the main centres of population were the monasteries established by the church, the bishop often became part of the monastic community, with less power than the abbot. The invasion of the Anglo-Normans in the 12th century encouraged the re-organization and reform of the native church along continental lines, and by the beginning of the 14th century the territories and boundaries for Irish bishops and dioceses had been settled. Most dioceses are named after important church or monastic foundations: Armagh, Clogher, Connor, Derry, Down, Dromore, Kilmore and Raphoe in the North. The ancient secular province of Ulster was included in the ecclesiastical province of Armagh, which became the chief church in Ireland. The bounds of individual dioceses within the province reflect older tribal areas, for example Derry reflects the development of *Cenél nEógain,* Dromore *Uí Echach Coba.* In the 8th century *Dál Fiatach,* who had settled in east Down, pushed northward into the land of *Dál nAraide,* and the bounds of the diocese of Down reflect their expansion as far north as the river *Ollarba* (the Larne Water). The diocesan bounds differ from those of similarly-named later counties because by the time the county boundaries were settled in the 17th century the leaders of many of the larger native territories had been overthrown. County boundaries were generally not based on large native kingdoms but were put together from an amalgam of smaller districts.

Deaneries

The medieval church divided dioceses into rural deaneries, the names of which often derive from old population names. *Blaethwyc* (modern Newtownards) in the diocese of Down, for example, derives from *Uí Blathmaic* "the descendants of Blathmac", whereas *Turtrye,* in the diocese of Connor, derives from *Uí Thuirtre* "the descendants of (Fiachra) Tort". The deaneries of Tullyhogue (Irish *Tulach Óc*) in the diocese of Armagh and *Maulyne* (Irish *Mag Line)* in Connor are named after royal sites. *Mag Line* was the seat of the *Dal nAraide* and *Tulach Óc* was probably the original seat of the Uí Thuirtre, whose area of influence had by this time moved east across the Bann, as the deanery name reveals. The deanery of Inishowen reflects the earlier homeland of the Cenél nEógain. Deanery names are often a useful source of information on important tribal groups of medieval times. Some of these same population names were used later as the names of baronies, while in other cases the earlier population group had lost its influence and the area had become known by another name.

TRIBAL AND FAMILY NAMES

Many personal or population names of various forms have been used as place-names or parts of place-names in Ireland, from provinces, counties, deaneries and baronies to townlands. As with different types of land divisions, different types of family names have come into being at various times.

The names of early Irish tribal groupings were sometimes simple plurals, for example *Ulaid, Cruthin,* and sometimes the personal name of an ancestor or some other element in composition with various suffixes: *Connachta, Dartraige, Latharna.* Other types prefixed *uí* "grandsons", *cenél* "kin", *clann* "children", *dál* "share of", *moccu* "descendants", *síol* "seed", *sliocht* "line" to the name of the ancestor, for example *Dál nAraide* "share of (Fiacha)

Araide", and *Uí Néill* "grandsons of Niall", who are supposedly descended from the 5th-century *Niall Noígiallach* "Niall of the Nine Hostages".

In early Ireland individuals were often identified by patronymics formed by using *mac* "son of" or *ó* (earlier *ua)* "grandson" plus the name of the father or grandfather, rather than by giving the name of the larger group to which the individual belonged. Thus the most straightforward interpretation of *Eoghan mac Néill* is "Eoghan son of Niall", *Eoghan ó Néill* "Eoghan grandson of Niall". Sometimes the same formation can occur with female names. However, in the course of the 10th and 11th centuries patronymics began to be used as surnames. In Modern Irish orthography surnames are distinguished from simple patronymics by using capital *M* or *Ó*: *Eoghan Ó Néill* "Eoghan O'Neill", *Eoghan Mac Néill* "Eoghan MacNeill". However, in early documents, in either Irish or English, it is often difficult to distinguish between surnames and patronymics. This is particularly true of sources such as the *Fiants* where a name such as Donagh M'Donagh may represent the patronymic Donagh, son of Donagh, or the surname Donagh MacDonagh.

As families expanded it was common for different branches to develop their own particular surnames. Some of these have survived to the present, while others, which may have been important enough in their time to be incorporated in place-names, have either died out or been assimilated by similar, more vigorous surnames. In cases such as this the place-name itself may be the only evidence for the former existence of a particular surname in the locality.

Kay Muhr

(1) See also *Geinealach Chorca Laidhe* (O'Donovan 1849, 48–56); *Crichad an Caoilli* (Power 1932, 43–47).

(2) See *Fiants Eliz.* §1736 (1570) for Co. Down; *Colton Vis.* 125–30 (1591) for Cos Derry and Tyrone.

(3) North-east Derry and Louth were also held by the Ulaid, but their influence had been reduced to Down, Antrim and north Louth by the 7th century (Flanagan 1978(d), 41).

(4) The *Cruthin* were a population group widespread in the north of Ireland. The name is of the same origin as "Briton".

ABBREVIATIONS

acc.	Accusative	Mod. Eng.	Modern English
adj.	Adjective	Mod. Ir.	Modern Irish
al.	Alias	MS(S)	Manuscript(s)
angl.	Anglicized	n.	(Foot)note
Ant.	Co. Antrim	neut.	Neuter
Arm.	Co. Armagh	NLI	National Library of
art. cit.	In the article cited		Ireland, Dublin
BM	British Museum	no(s).	Number(s)
c.	About	nom.	Nominative
cf.	Compare	O. Eng.	Old English
Co(s).	County (-ies)	O. Ir.	Old Irish
col.	Column	op. cit.	In the work cited
coll.	Collective	OSI	Ordnance Survey, Dublin
d.	Died	OSNI	Ordnance Survey, Belfast
dat.	Dative	p(p).	Page(s)
Der.	Co. Derry	par.	Parish
Dn	Co. Down	pass.	Here and there
eag.	Eagarthóir/Curtha in	pers. comm.	personal comment
	eagar ag	pl.	Plural
ed.	Edited by	PRO	Public Record Office,
edn	Edition		London
Eng.	English	PROI	Public Record Office, Dublin
et pass.	And elsewhere	PRONI	Public Record Office,
et var.	And variations (thereon)		Belfast
f.	Following page	pt	Part
fem.	Feminine	r.	Correctly
Fer.	Co. Fermanagh	RIA	Royal Irish Academy,
ff.	Folios/Following pages		Dublin
fol.	Folio	s.	Shilling
gen.	Genitive	sa.	Under the year
HMSO	Her Majesty's Stationery	sect.	Section
	Office	ser.	Series
ibid.	In the same place	sic	As in source
IE	Indo-European	sing.	Singular
iml.	Imleabhar	SS	Saints
IPA	International Phonetic	St	Saint
	Alphabet	sv(v).	Under the word(s)
1(l).	Line(s)	TCD	Trinity College, Dublin
lit.	Literally	trans.	Translated by
loc.	Locative	Tyr.	Co. Tyrone
loc. cit.	In the place cited	uimh.	Uimhir
Lr.	Lower	Up.	Upper
masc.	Masculine	viz.	Namely
Mid. Eng.	Middle English	voc.	Vocative
Mid. Ir.	Middle Irish	vol(s).	Volume(s)

PRIMARY BIBLIOGRAPHY

Acallam (Ní Shéaghdha)   *Agallamh na Seanórach*, ed. Nessa Ní Shéaghdha, 3 vols (Baile Átha Cliath 1942–5).

Acallam (O'Grady)   *Acallamh na Senórach*, ed. S.H. O'Grady from the Book of Lismore, *SG* vol. i 94–233 (text), ii 101–265, 557–65 (translation and notes).

Acallam (Stokes)   *Acallamh na Senórach*, ed. Whitley Stokes, from the Book of Lismore and Laud 610 (*IT* 4 pt 1, Leipzig 1900), completing the text ed. by O'Grady.

Account Twescard (Orpen)   "The account of Henry de Mandeville, 'Custos of Twescard', 1259-61", in Orpen 1911–20, iii, 288–90.

Account Tweskard (Curtis)   "Sheriff's Accounts of the Honor of Dungarvan, of Tweskard in Ulster, and of County Waterford, 1261–3", ed. Edmund Curtis in *PRIA* xxxix (1929), sect. C, 1–17.

A. Clonmac.   *Annals of Clonmacnoise, being Annals of Ireland from the earliest period to AD 1408*, translated into English AD 1647 by Conell Mageoghan and ed. by Denis Murphy (1st edn. 1896; reprint Wales 1993).

A. Conn.   *Annála Connacht: the annals of Connacht (AD 1224–1522)*, ed. A. Martin Freeman (Dublin 1944).

Acta SS Colgan   *Acta sanctorum veteris et majoris Scotiae seu Hiberniae*, John Colgan (Lovanii 1645).

Adomnán's Columba   *Adomnán's Life of Columba*, ed. and translated by A.O. Anderson and M.O. Anderson, revised by M.O. Anderson (Oxford 1991; 1st edn. London 1961).

AFM   *Annála Ríoghachta Éireann: annals of the Kingdom of Ireland by the Four Masters from the earliest period to the year 1616*, ed. John O'Donovan, 7 vols (Dublin 1848–51; reprint 1990).

AGMP   *Ainmneacha Gaeilge na mBailte Poist*, Oifig an tSoláthair (BÁC 1969).

AIF   *The Annals of Inisfallen*, ed. Seán Mac Airt (Dublin 1951).

Ainm   *Ainm: bulletin of the Ulster Place-name Society* (Belfast 1986–).

Áitainm. Uladh	"Áitainmneacha Chúige Uladh", Bearnárd Ó Dubhthaigh, *Feasta*, Eanáir 1963, 14–8, Feabhra 1963, 9–12, 24.
Alasdair Mac Colla	*Alasdair Mac Colla*, Seosamh Laoide (Baile Átha Cliath 1914).
ALC	*The annals of Loch Cé: a chronicle of Irish affairs from AD 1014 to AD 1590*, ed. William Hennessy, 2 vols (London 1871; reprint, Dublin 1939).
ALI	*Acts of the Lord of the Isles 1336–1493*, ed. Jean Munro and R.W. Munro (Edinburgh 1986).
Anal. Hib.	*Analecta Hibernica* (Dublin 1930–69; Shannon 1970–).
An. Roscrea	"The Annals of Roscrea", ed. D. Gleeson and S. MacAirt, *PRIA* lix (1957–9), sect. C, 137–80.
Ant. Forfeit.	"List of townlands on estates of Randal Lord Marquis of Antrim and Sir Martin Nowell, apparently drawn up in connection with forfeitures, ca 1700", PRONI T473/1, 81–94.
Antiquities of Rathlin	"Some Antiquities of Rathlin", Henry Morris, *UJA* ser. 2, vol. 17 (1911), 39–46.
Antrim Coast Sketch	*Sketch of the coast of Antrim*, c. 1570, NLI (Mss.), Map 16.L.5(51).
Antrim Notebooks	"Séamus Ó Duilearga's Antrim Notebooks – 1: Texts", *ZCP* 40 (1984), 74–117, and "Séamus Ó Duilearga's Antrim Notebooks – 2: Language", *ZCP* 42 (1987), 138–218, ed. Seosamh Watson.
Antrim Place Names	"A Few Antrim Place Names", ed. 'Bheirt Fhear', *An Chraobh Rua*, Bealtaine 1913, 83–6.
Arch. Hib.	*Archivium Hibernicum; or, Irish historical records*, ser. 1, vols i–vii (Maynooth 1912–21); ser. 2, vol. viii– (1941–).
ASE	"Abstracts of grants of lands and other hereditaments under the acts of settlement and explanation, AD 1666–84" compiled by John Lodge and published in the appendix to the *15th Annual report from the commissioners... respecting the public records of Ireland* (1825).
Athchló Uladh	*Athchló Uladh*, eag. Gearóid Mac Giolla Domhnaigh agus Gearóid Stockman (Muineachán 1991).

A. Tigern.	*The annals of Tigernach*, ed. W. Stokes, 2 vols (Felinfach 1993), reprinted from from *Rev. Celt.* xvi (1895), 374–419; xvii (1896), 6–33, 116–263, 337–420; xviii (1897), 9–59, 150–303, 374–91.
AU	*Annála Uladh: annals of Ulster; otherwise Annála Senait, annals of Senait: a chronicle of Irish affairs, 431–1131, 1155–1541*, ed. William Hennessy and Bartholomew MacCarthy, 4 vols (Dublin 1887–1901).
Bagenal's Descr. Ulst.	"Marshall Bagenal's Description of Ulster, anno 1586", ed. Herbert F. Hore, *UJA* ser. 1, vol. 2 (1854), 137–60.
Ballycastle Map [1720c]	*Map of Ballycastle and district*, copied by G.A. Wilson, PRONI T1051/1. PRONI dates this to c. 1720, but it seems more likely to be a copy of *Stewart's Survey* (Map 1) of 1734.
Bartlett Maps (Esch. Co. Maps) 1	One of three maps by Richard Bartlett published with the *Esch. Co. Maps*: (i) *A Generalle Description of Ulster*; (PRO MPF 35–37; copies in PRONI T1652/1–3). These maps have been dated to 1603 by G.A. Hayes-McCoy, *Ulster and Other Irish Maps, c. 1600*, p. 2, n. 13 (Dublin 1964).
BB	*Book of Ballymote* (AD 1390c), ed. R. Atkinson (Dublin 1887).
BCC	*Betha Colaim Cille, Life of Columcille, compiled by Manus O'Donnell in 1532*, ed. and translated from the manuscript Rawlinson B.514 in the Bodleian Library, Oxford, by A. O'Kelleher and G. Schoepperle (Illinois 1918).
Béaloid.	*Béaloideas: the journal of the Folklore of Ireland Society* (Dublin 1927–).
Bigger's Bun na Mairge	*Bun na Mairge*, by F.J. Bigger, a special volume published with *UJA* ser. 2, vol. 4 (1898).
Bnd. Sur. (OSNB)	Boundary Survey sketch maps, c. 1825–30, cited in *OSNB, passim*.
Boazio's Map (BM)	*Gennerall discription or Chart of Irelande*, AD 1599, by Baptista Boazio. Three impressions are known, one in the British Museum (Cotton MS, Augustus I, vol. ii. no. 30), one in TCD (MS 1209.2), and a third in private hands.
Boazio's Map (NG)	Reprint of *Boazio's Map (BM)* published in Ortelius' *Theatrum Orbis Terranum* from 1606 on. Copy from Neptune Gallery, Dublin, reprinted with *AFM* 1990.

Book of Lismore (Hogan)   Forms from the *Book of Lismore*, c. 1400, quoted by Hogan in *Onom. Goed.*

Brit. Eccles. Ant.   *Britannicarum Ecclesiarum Antiquitates*, by Jacobo Usserio (James Ussher; Dublinii 1639).

Bruce   *The Bruce, or, The Book of the Most Excellent and Noble Prince, Robert De Broyss, King of Scots... compiled by Master John Barbour archdeacon of Aberdeen, AD 1375*, with a preface, Notes and Glossarial Index by Rev. Walter Skeat, 2 vols (Edinburgh 1894).

BSD   *Book of survey & distribution, AD 1661: Armagh, Down & Antrim* (Quit Rent Office copy), PRONI T370/A.

BUPNS   *Bulletin of the Ulster Place–Name Society*, ser. 1, vols 1–5 (Belfast 1952–7); ser. 2, vols 1–4 (1978–82).

Cal. Carew MSS   *Calendar of the Carew Manuscripts preserved in the Archiepiscopal Library at Lambeth*, ed. J.S. Brewer and W. Bullen, 6 vols (London 1867–73).

Cal. Inq. Post Mortem   *Calendarium Inquisitionum Post Mortem sive Escaetarum*, ed. John Caley and John Bayley, 4 vols (London 1806–28).

Cal. Ir. Council   "Calendar of the Irish Council Book, 1 March 1581 to 1 July 1586, made by John P. Prendergast between 1867 and 1869", ed. D.B. Quinn, *Anal. Hib.* 24 (1967), 93–180.

Cal. Rot. Pat.   *Calendarium Rotulorum Patentium in turi Londinensi*, ed. John Topham (London 1802).

Cath MT   *Cath Muige Tuired*, ed. Elizabeth A. Gray, *ITS* lii (Dublin 1983).

C. Conghail Cláir.   *Caithréim Conghail Cláiringhnigh: Martial career of Conghal Cláiringhneach*, ed. Patrick M. MacSweeney, *ITS* v (London 1904).

CDI   *Calendar of Documents relating to Ireland, 1171–1307*, ed. H.S. Sweetman and G.F. Handcock, 5 vols (London 1875–86).

Ceart Uí Néill   *Ceart Uí Néill*, ed. Myles Dillon, *Stud. Celt.* 1 (1966) 1–18. Trans. Éamonn Ó Doibhlin, "*Ceart Uí Néill*, a discussion and translation of the document", *S. Ard Mh.* vol. 5, no. 2 (1970) 324–58.

Céitinn	*Foras Feasa ar Eirinn: the history of Ireland by Seathrún Céitinn (Geoffrey Keating)*, ed. Rev. Patrick S. Dinneen, 4 vols, *ITS* (London 1902–14).
Celtica	*Celtica*, Dublin Institute for Advanced Studies (Dublin 1946–).
Census	*A census of Ireland, circa 1659, with supplementary material from the poll money ordinances (1660–1)*, ed. Séamus Pender, Dublin 1939).
Census 1851	*Census of Ireland, 1851. General alphabetical index to the townlands and towns, parishes and baronies of Ireland...* (Dublin 1904).
CGH	*Corpus genealogiarum Hiberniae*, vol. 1, ed. M.A. O'Brien (Dublin 1962).
Childe's Larry Bane	"A promontory fort on the Antrim Coast", V. Gordon Childe, *Antiquaries Journal* xvi, April 1936, 179–98.
Chronicle of Ire.	*The Chronicle of Ireland, 1584–1608, by Sir James Perrott*, ed. Herbert Wood (Dublin 1933).
Chron. Scot.	*Chronicum Scotorum, a Chronicle of Irish Affairs from Earliest Times to 1135; with a supplement, containing the events from 1141 to 1150*, ed. William Hennessy (London 1866).
Cín Lae Ó M.	*Cín lae Ó Mealláin*, ed. Tadhg Ó Donnchadha (alias Torna), *Anal. Hib.* 3 (1931), 1–61.
Civ. Surv.	*The Civil Survey, AD 1654–6*, ed. Robert C. Simmington, 10 vols, Irish Manuscripts Commission (Dublin 1931–61).
C. Kilken. 93b c.1 I.44 (EA)	Manuscript quoted by Reeves in *EA* 249, and dated to the 15th century in *VSSH (Plummer)* i, p.xii– xiv.
Claidheamh Soluis	*An Claidheamh Soluis* (Baile Átha Cliath 1899–1932).
Clark's Rathlin	*Rathlin – Disputed Island*, Wallace Clark (Waterford 1971).
C. McG. (OSNB)	A survey by one C. McGildowney Esq. in 1734, cited extensively in the *OSNB*. It is possible that this is a copy of *Stewart's Survey* of 1734.
Cogadh GG	*Cogadh Gaedhal re Gallaibh: the war of the Gaedhil with the Gaill*, ed. J.H. Todd (London 1867).

Colton Vis.

Acts of Archbishop Colton in his metropolitical visitation of the diocese of Derry, AD 1397, ed. William Reeves (Dublin 1850).

Court of Claims

"Claims of Innocence...", a manuscript kept in the Public Library of Armagh containing the proceedings of the Court of Claims of 1662–3 set up under an Act of Settlement (cf. *Catalogue of Manuscripts in the Public Library of Armagh*, ed. James Dean (1928), p. 11). A copy of this manuscript called *Court of Claims: Submissions and Evidence*, ed. Geraldine Tallon, will be published by the Irish Manuscripts Commission.

CPR Ed. I

Calendar of the Patent Rolls preserved in the Public Record Office, prepared under the supervision of the Deputy Keeper of the Records. Edward I 1272–1307, 4 vols (London 1893–1901).

CPR Ed. II

Calendar of the Patent Rolls preserved in the Public Record Office, prepared under the supervision of the Deputy Keeper of the Records. Edward II 1307–1327, 5 vols (London 1894–1904).

CPR Jas I

Irish patent rolls of James I: facsimile of the Irish record commissioner's calendar prepared prior to 1830, with a foreward by M.C. Griffith (Dublin 1966).

CRR

Cath Ruis na Ríg For Bóinn, with Preface, Translation and indices..., ed. Edmund Hogan, Todd Lecture Series vol. 4 (Dublin 1892).

CSH

Corpus genealogiarum sanctorum Hiberniae, ed. Pádraig Ó Riain (Dublin 1985).

CSP Ire.

Calendar of the state papers relating to Ireland, 1509–1670, ed. H.C. Hamilton, E.G. Atkinson, R.P. Mahaffy, C.P. Russell and J.P. Prendergast, 24 vols (London 1860–1912)

Culfeightrin Map [1789]

"Three maps of part of the estate belonging to heirs of the late Hugh McCollum, Co. Antrim; surveyed by John McCloy in 1789", PRONI D543/3.

Culfeightrin Map [1812]

"A map of the estate of John White, surveyed by William Martin in 1812"; PRONI D543/5.

Dallat's Armoy

"Placenames in County Antrim. Townlands in the Parish of Armoy", Cahal Dallat, *Glynns* vol. 14 (1986), 53–4.

Dallat's Culfeightrin

"Placenames in the Parish of Culfeightrin", Cahal Dallat, *Glynns* vol. 9 (1981), 33–36.

Dallat's Glens	*The Road to The Glens*, Cahal Dallat (Belfast 1989).
Dallat's Ramoan	See *Dallat's Rathlin*.
Dallat's Rathlin	"Placenames in Ramoan and Rathlin Island", Cahal Dallat, *Glynns* vol. 1 (1973), 25–28.
Dalorto's Map (Taylor)	Form from "a chart of Western European coasts by Angellino de Dalorto of Florence, drawn in 1325", quoted in "The Place–Name 'Rathlin'" by A.B. Taylor in *Clark's Rathlin* 174 (See also *Italian Maps of Ire.* 408 sv. Angelino Dulcert).
Dan. Force	*The Danish Force in Ireland 1690–1691*, ed. K. Danaher and J.G. Simms (Dublin 1962).
Dartmouth Map	A maritime chart/map of Ireland dating to 1590 preserved in the National Maritime Museum, Greenwich (England), Dartmouth Collection nos. 5–7.
Dartmouth Map 25	"Map of the Northern half of Ireland, c. 1590"; a copy in NLI (Mss.), Map 16.L.33(16). Preserved in the National Maritime Museum, Greenwich (England), Dartmouth Collection no. 25.
DCCU	*Dhá Chéad de Cheoltaibh Uladh*, eag. Énrí Ó Muirgheasa (Baile Átha Cliath, 1969, 2nd edn; 1st edn 1934).
Death Tales (Meyer)	"Death Tales of the Ulster Heroes", ed K. Meyer, Todd Lecture Series vol. xiv, December 1906.
de Courcy Charters	"Two unpublished Charters of John de Courcy, Princeps Ulidae", ed. E. Curtis, *PBNHPS* (1928–9), 2–9.
Decree of Innocence	*Decree of Innocence in favour of the Marquis of Antrim*, 1663, in *MacDonnells Antrim* 430–444.
De Hibernia & Antiq.	*De Hibernia & Antiquitatibus ejus, Disquisitones...* by Jacobi Waræi (James Ware; Londini 1654).
Descendants Ir	"The history of the descendants of Ir", 2 parts, ed. Magaret Dobbs, *ZCP* xiii (1921), 308–59; xiv (1923), 44–144.
Dieckhoff	*A Pronouncing Dictionary of Scottish Gaelic*, H.C. Dieckhoff (2nd edn Glasgow 1992; 1st edn London 1932).
DIL	*Dictionary of the Irish Language: compact edition* (Dublin 1983).

Dinneen

Foclóir Gaedhilge agus Béarla: an Irish–English dictionary, Rev. Patrick S. Dinneen (Dublin 1904; reprint with additions 1927 and 1934).

Dobbs' Desc. Antrim

A Briefe Description of the County of Antrim, begun the 3rd of May, 1683, by Richard Dobbs, appendix ii in *MacDonnells Antrim* 377–89.

Donatus Moneyus

"Brussels Ms. 3947: Donatus Moneyus, De Provincia Hiberniae S. Francisci", ed. Rev. B. Jennings, *Anal Hib.* 6 (1934), 12–138.

Dongl. Ann

Donegal Annual: journal of the County Donegal Historical Society (1947–).

Dower Charter

"Dower Charter of John de Courcy's wife", ed. Jocelyn Otway-Ruthven, *UJA* ser. 3, vol. 12 (1949), 77–81.

DS (Par. Map)

Copies of William Petty's original *Down Survey* parish maps of c. 1657, made by D. O'Brien in 1787, PRONI D597/2.

Duan. Dh. Bh.

"Duanaire Dháibhidh Uí Bhruadair", ed. John C. MacErlean, 3 vols, *ITS* xi, xiii, xviii (Dublin 1908–17).

Dubourdieu Map

A map of County Antrim, opposite p. 1 of *Statist. Sur. Ant.*

Duncan

"Gaelic Place Names in Antrim", James Duncan, *UJA* ser. 2, vol. 12 (1906), 131–34.

Dwelly

The illustrated Gaelic–English dictionary, Edward Dwelly, 3 vols (Glasgow 1901–11; reprint 1920).

EA

Ecclesiastical Antiquities of Down, Connor and Dromore, consisting of a taxation of those dioceses compiled in the year 1306, ed. William Reeves (Dublin 1848).

Eccles. Tax.

"Ecclesiastical Taxation of the Dioceses of Down, Connor, and Dromore", ed. William Reeves, *EA* 2–119.

Eccles. Tax. (CDI)

"Ecclesiastical taxation of Ireland", ed. H.S. Sweetman & G.F. Handcock, *Calendar of documents relating to Ireland...*, *1302–07* (London 1886), 202–323.

Éigse

Éigse: a journal of Irish studies (Dublin 1939–).

Éire Thuaidh

Éire Thuaidh/Ireland North: a cultural map and gazetteer of Irish place-names, Ordnance Survey of Northern Ireland (Belfast 1988).

Esch. Co. Map	*Barony maps of the escheated counties in Ireland, AD 1609*, 28 maps, PRO. Published as *The Irish Historical Atlas*, Sir Henry James, Ordnance Survey (Southampton 1861).
Ét. Celt.	Études Celtiques (Paris 1936–).
Exch. Accounts Ulst.	"Ancient exchequer accounts of Ulster", *UJA* ser. 1, vol. iii (1855), 155–62.
Féil. Torna	*Féilscríbhinn Torna .i. tráchtaisí léanta in onóir don Ollamh Tadhg Ua Donnchadha...*, eag. Séamus Pender (Corcaigh 1947).
Fél. Óeng.	*Félire Óengusso Céli Dé: the martyrology of Oengus the culdee*, ed. Whitley Stokes (London 1905; reprint 1984).
Fiants Eliz.	"Calendar and index to the fiants of the reign of Elizabeth I", appendix to the *11–13th, 15–18th and 21–22nd Reports of the Deputy Keeper of public records in Ireland* (Dublin 1879–81, 1883–86, 1889–90).
Filí agus Felons	*Filí agus Felons*, Seosamh Mac Grianna, eag. Nollaig Mac Congáil (Co. Mhaigh Eo 1987).
Fleming Collect. 311b (EA)	Manuscript cited by Reeves in *EA* 249, and dated to the 15th century in *VSSH (Plummer)* i, p. xii–xiv.
Forfeit. Estates	"Abstracts of the conveyances from the trustees of the forfeited estates and interests in Ireland in 1668", appendix to the *15th Annual report from the commissioners... respecting the public records of Ireland* (1825), 348–99.
GÉ	*Gasaitéar na hÉireann/Gazetteer of Ireland: ainmneacha ionad daonra agus gnéithe aiceanta*, Brainse Logainmneacha na Suirbhéireachta Ordanáis (Baile Átha Cliath 1989).
Geneal. Tracts	*Genealogical Tracts*, ed. Toirdhealbhach Ó Raithbheartaigh (Dublin 1932).
Geographia	*Claudi Ptolemaei, Geographia codicibus Recognovit, Prolegomenis, annotatione indicibus, tabulis instruxit...*, Carolus Müllerus, 2 vols (Parisiis 1883).
GJ	*Gaelic Journal: Irisleabhar na Gaedhilge*, 19 vols (Dublin 1882–1909).
Glynns	*The Glynns: Journal of the Glens of Antrim Historical Society* (1973–).

Goghe's Map

Hibernia: Insula non procul ab Anglia vulgare Hirlandia vocata, AD 1567, by John Goghe, PRO London MPF 68. Reproduced in *SP Hen. VIII* vol. ii, pt. 3.

GOI

A Grammar of Old Irish, Rudolf Thurneysen, trans. D.A. Binchy and O. Bergin (Dublin 1946).

Grand Jury Pres.

Grand Jury Presentment Books for Co. Antrim (1711–1800), PRONI ANT 4/1/1–6. The earliest book (1711–21) is paginated but a number of later volumes are not and the entries are differentiated by date or by session, e.g. Summer 1793.

Grants for the A.E.

"Grants for Lives Renewable", 1814, listing lands on the Antrim Estate, PRONI T473/1, 133.

GUH

Gleanings from Ulster History by Séamus Ó Ceallaigh (Cork 1951), enlarged edition published by Ballinascreen Historical Society (1994).

Hamilton's Letters

Letters concerning the northern coast of the county of Antrim... and an itinerary and guide to the Giants Causeway (from 1822), Rev. William Hamilton (Coleraine 1839; 1st edn c. 1788).

Harris Collectanea

"Harris: Collectanea de Rebus Hibernicus", ed. C. McNeill, *Anal. Hib.* 6 (1934), 248–450.

Hermathena

Hermathena: a Dublin University review (Dublin 1873–).

Hib. Del. Antrim

Hiberniae Delineatio: an atlas of Ireland by William Petty comprised of one map of Ireland, 4 maps of provinces and 32 county maps. It was engraved c. 1685 and first published in London c. 1685 (Goblet 1932, viii). A facsimile reprint was published in Newcastle–Upon–Tyne in 1968 and a further reprint, with critical introduction by J.H. Andrews, in Shannon, 1970.

Hib. Reg.

Hibernia Regnum: a set of 214 barony maps of Ireland dating to the period AD 1655–59. These maps were drawn at the same time as the official parish maps which illustrated the Down Survey of William Petty. The original parish maps have been lost but the *Hibernia Regnum* maps are preserved in the Bibliothèque Nationale, Paris (Goblet 1932, v–x). Photographic facsimiles of these maps were published by the Ordnance Survey, Southampton in 1908. A copy of the Cary map is kept in PRONI T2313/1/11.

Hickson's Ire.	"Ireland in the Seventeenth Century, or the Irish Massacres of 1641–2, their causes and results", Mary Hickson, 2 vols (London 1898).
Hill's Bun na Mairge	"The Ruins of Bun–Na–Mairge (in the county of Antrim): Gleanings of their history", George Hill, *UJA* ser. 1, vol. 8 (1860), 14–26.
Hill's Stewarts	"The Stewarts of Ballintoy, with notices of other families of the District", Rev. G. Hill, *UJA* ser. 2, vol. 6 (1900), 17–23, 78–89, 142–61, 218–23; vol. 7 (1901), 7–17.
HMR Ant.	Hearth–money Rolls for the county of Antrim, AD 1669, PRONI T307A.
HMR Ant. (1666)	Hearth–money Rolls for the county of Antrim, AD 1666, PRONI T3022/4/1.
Hondius Map	*Hyberniae Novissima Descriptio*, AD 1591, drawn up by Jodocus Hondius and engraved by Pieter van den Keere, reprinted by the Linen Hall Library, Belfast in 1983.
HSN	*Historiae Scoticae Nomenclatura, Latino–vernacula*, Christophorus Irvinus (Edinburgi 1697).
Iarsmaí ó Reachrainn	"Iarsmaí ó Oileán Reachrann", C. Ó Cuinn, *Éigse* vi (1948–52), 248–256.
Inq. Earl. Ulster	"The Earldom of Ulster", Goddard H. Orpen, *JRSAI* xliii (1913) 30–46, 133–43; xliv (1914) 51–66; xlv (1915) 123–42.
Inq. Par. Ant.	*Inquisition into the parishes of Co. Antrim*, 1657, an inquisition held during the Commonwealth by the Commission of the Great Seal of Ireland for dividing and uniting parishes. Representative Church Body Library, Dublin, MS. Libr. 26, also PRONI T808 14886.
Inq. Ult.	*Inquisitionum in officio rotulorum cancellariae Hiberniae asservatorum repertorium*, vol. ii (Ulster), ed. James Hardiman (Dublin 1829).
IPN	*Irish Place Names*, Deirdre Flanagan and Laurence Flanagan (Dublin 1994).
Ire. Ex. Eng.	*Ireland Exhibited to England, in a political and moral survey of her population*, A. Atkinson, 2 vols (London 1823).
Ire. Map [1711]	Map of Ireland, "printed in London by Senex and others, in 1711"; NLI (Mss.), Map 16.L.10(5).

Ire. Map [1790c] "Ortelius improved or a new map of Ireland wherein are inserted the principal families of Irish and English extract... by Charles O'Connor, Dublin, late 18th century"; NLI (Mss.), Map 16.L.10(5(b)).

Irish Geography *Irish Geography: bulletin of the Geographical Society of Ireland* (Dublin 1944–).

Irish Jacobites "Irish Jacobites: Lists from TCD Ms N.1.3", ed. J.G. Simms, *Anal. Hib.* 22 (1960), 13–125.

Irish of Rathlin *The Irish language in Rathlin Island, Co. Antrim*, Nils M. Holmer, Todd Lecture Series xviii (Dublin 1942).

Irish of the Glens *On Some Relics of The Irish Dialect Spoken in the Glens of Antrim*, Nils M. Holmer (Uppsala 1940).

Iris. MN *Irisleabhar Mhuighe Nuadhad* (Maynooth, 1907–).

IT *Irische Texte*, Leipzig (1880–1909).

Italian Maps "Early Italian Maps of Ireland from 1300 to 1600, with notes on foreign settlers and trade", by Thomas Johnston Westropp, *PRIA* xxx (1912–13), sect. C, 361–428.

ITS *Irish Texts Society*, London and Dublin (1899–).

Jas I to Connor Cath. (EA) Grant of James I to the cathedral of Connor, AD 1609, ed. William Reeves, *EA* 313–4.

JDCHS *Journal of the Down and Connor Historical Society*, 10 vols (Belfast 1928–39).

J Louth AS *Journal of the County Louth Archaeological Society* (Dundalk 1904–).

Jobson's Ulster (BM) A map of Ulster by Francis Jobson, c. 1590, preserved in the British Museum, Cotton MS. Augustus i, vol. ii, no. 19.

Jobson's Ulster (TCD) A set of three maps of Ulster by Francis Jobson, the first of which dates to AD 1590, TCD MS 1209, 15–17.

J O'D (OSNB) Irish and anglicized forms of names attributed to John O'Donovan in the *OSNB*.

J O'D (OSRNB) Irish and anglicized forms of names attributed to John O'Donovan in the *OSRNB*.

Joyce *The Origin and History of Irish names of Places*, P.W. Joyce, 3 vols (Dublin 1869–1913).

JRSAI	*Journal of the Royal Society of Antiquaries of Ireland* (Dublin 1849–).
Lamb Maps	*A Geographical Description of ye Kingdom of Ireland Collected from ye actual Survey made by Sir William Petty…Containing one General Mapp of ye whole Kingdom, with four Provincial Mapps, & 32 County mapps…Engraven & Published for ye benefit of ye Publique* by Francis Lamb (London c. 1690).
Lapsed Money Book	"Lapsed Money Book" regarding payment of debts to 'Sir Martin Noell et als', c. 1663, listing townland names in the baronies of Dunluce Lower and Cary, acreages, and sums levied per townland; published in *Hill's Stewarts*, 150–56.
LASID	*Linguistic atlas and survey of Irish dialects*, Heinrich Wagner and Colm Ó Baoill, 4 vols (Dublin 1958–69).
LCABuidhe	*Leabhar Cloinne Aodha Buidhe*, ed. Tadhg Ó Donnchadha alias Torna (Dublin 1931).
Leabhar na gCeart (JOD)	*Leabhar na gCeart, The Book of Rights*, ed. John O'Donovan (Dublin 1847).
Lebor Bretnach (van Hamel)	*Lebor Bretnach, the Irish version of the Historia Britonum ascribed to Nennius*, ed. A.G. van Hamel (Baile Átha Cliath [1932]).
Lebor na Cert	*Lebor na Cert: the Book of Rights*, ed. Myles Dillon, *ITS* xlvi (Dublin 1962).
Lendrick Map	Lendrick's map of Co. Antrim (1780), PRONI T1971/1.
Lendrick Map (OSNB)	Forms quoted in the *OSNB* but which are absent from the original map by J. Lendrick.
Letters Patent Jas I (Reeves)	Letters Patent of James I, 20th July, 1609, "by which the several chapters of Down, Connor and Dromore were erected", quoted by William Reeves in PRONI DIO/1/24/2, 238.
L. Gabála	*Lebor Gabála Érenn*, ed. R.A.S. Macalister, 5 vols, *ITS* xxiv, xxxv, xxxix, xli, xliv (Dublin 1938–56).
L. Gen. DF	*Leabhar Genealach an Dubhaltaigh Mhic Fhirbhisigh* ed. N. Ó Muraíle (forthcoming).

LGD Map	*Local government district series showing townlands and wards within the various districts and showing the layout of the OS 1:10,000 sheets*, Ordnance Survey of Northern Ireland (Belfast 1974).
Lhuyd's Tour	"The Tour of Edward Lhuyd in Ireland in 1699 and 1700", ed. J.L. Campbell, *Celtica* 5 (1960), 218–28.
Liber Dublin.	*Liber Dubliniensis: Chapter documents of the Irish Franciscans 1719–1875*, ed. Anselm Faulkner (Killiney 1978).
Liber Hymn.	*The Irish Liber Hymnorum*, ed. from the Mss. with translations, notes and glossary by J.H. Bernard and R. Atkinson, 2 vols; vol. 1, Henry Bradshaw Society vol. xiii; vol. 2, Henry Bradshaw Society vol. xiv (London 1898).
Liber Louvan.	*Liber Louvaniensis, A Collection of Franciscan Documents 1621–1717*, ed. Cathaldus Giblin (Dublin 1956).
Liber Munerum	*Liber Munerum Publicorum Hiberniae, Ab An 1152 usque ad 1827, or the Establishment of Ireland, ...*being the Report of Rawley Lascalles, of the Middle Temple, Barrister at Law, 5 vols (London 1852).
Lives of the Saints (Stokes)	*Anecdota Oxoniensia, Lives of the Saints from the Book of Lismore*, ed. W. Stokes (Oxford 1890).
LL	*The Book of Leinster, formerly Lebar na Núachongbála*, ed. R.I Best, O. Bergin, M.A. O'Brien and A. O'Sullivan, 6 vols (Dublin 1954– 83).
L. Lec.	*The Book of Lecan: Leabhar Mór Mhic Fhir Bhisigh Leacain*, (AD 1397c), facsimile edition ed. K. Mulchrone (Dublin 1937).
L. Log. C. Chainnigh	*Liostaí Logainmneacha: Contae Chill Chainnigh/County Kilkenny*, arna ullmhú ag Brainse Logainmneacha na Suirbhéireachta Ordanáis (Baile Átha Cliath 1993).
L. Log. Lú	*Liostaí Logainmneacha: Contae Lú/County Louth*, arna ullmhú ag Brainse Logainmneacha na Suirbhéireachta Ordanáis (Baile Átha Cliath 1991).
L. Log. Luimnigh	*Liostaí Logainmneacha: Contae Luimnigh/County Limerick*, arna ullmhú ag Brainse Logainmneacha na Suirbhéireachta Ordanáis (Baile Átha Cliath 1991).
L. Log. Mhuineacháin	*Liostaí Logainmneacha: Contae Mhuineacháin/County Monaghan*, arna ullmhú ag Brainse Logainmneacha na Suirbhéireachta Ordanáis (Baile Átha Cliath 1996).

L. Log. P. Láirge	*Liostaí Logainmneacha: Contae Phort Láirge/County Waterford*, arna ullmhú ag Brainse Logainmneacha na Suirbhéireachta Ordanáis (Baile Átha Cliath 1991).
L. Log. Uíbh Fhailí	*Liostaí Logainmneacha: Contae Uíbh Fhailí/County Offaly*, arna ullmhú ag Brainse Logainmneacha na Suirbhéireachta Ordanáis (Baile Átha Cliath 1994).
Lodge RR	John Lodge's *Record of the Rolls*: being "an exact list of the Patent Rolls remaining of record in the Office of the Rolls of His Majesty's High Court of Chancery in Ireland", transcribed in 1755, vols. ii–x (Jas I – George II), PRONI 1a 53 51 – 1a 53 59/MIS 42.
Longman Dict.	*Longman Dictionary of the English Language* (Harlow 1984, 2nd edn 1991).
LP 8 Jas I (PRONI)	A copy of "Letters Patent of James I to Randall McDonnell, Earl of Antrim of Dunluce, dated 11th of December 1610", regranting lands first granted in 1604 (*CPR Jas I* 58); PRONI D1835/55.
LS C vi 2 (RIA) (de hÓir)	18th–century manuscript cited by de hÓir in *Reachlainn (de hÓir)* 24.
LS 23 N 6 (RIA) (de hÓir)	18th–centiry manuscript cited in by de hÓir in *Reachlainn (de hÓir)* 24.
LU	*Lebor na hUidre, Book of the Dun Cow*, ed. R.I. Best and O. Bergin (Dublin 1929).
Mac Bionaid LS	*Lámhscríbhinn staire an Bhionadaigh, comhrac na nGael agus na nGall le chéile*, eag. Réamonn Ó Muirí (Baile Átha Cliath 1994).
MacDonnells Antrim	*Historical account of the MacDonnells of Antrim, including notices of some other septs, Irish and Scottish*, Rev. George Hill (Belfast 1873; reprint Ballycastle 1978).
MacDonnells (Ó Cuív)	"Some Irish items relating to the MacDonnells of Antrim", Brian Ó Cuív, *Celtica* xvi (1984), 139–56.
MacErlean	"The Synod of Ráith Breasail, boundaries of the dioceses of Ireland [AD 1110 or 1118]", J. MacErlean, *Arch. Hib.* ser. 1, vol. 3 (1914), 1–33.
MacQuillan of the Route	"The MacQuillan or Mandeville Lords of the Route", Edmund Curtis, *PRIA* xliv (1938), sect. C, 99–113.
Map Antrim	A map of Co. Antrim dating from 1807, PRONI T1129/234 (Edinburgh 1807).

Maritime Map	"Maritime Map", AD 1794, depicting Rathlin Island, by M. MacKenzie, published in part in *Clark's Rathlin* 124.
Mart. Don.	*The martyrology of Donegal: a calendar of the saints of Ireland*, trans. John O'Donovan, ed. James H. Todd and William Reeves (Dublin 1864).
Mart. Gorm.	*Félire Húi Gormáin: the martyrology of Gorman*, ed. Whitley Stokes (London 1895).
Mart. Tal.	*The Martyrology of Tallaght*, ed. R.I Best and H.J. Lawlor (London 1931).
McSkimin (DPJ)	"Abbey of Bona–Marga", Samuel McSkimin, *The Dublin Penny Journal* no. 41, vol. 1 (April 6, 1833), 321–2.
Mercator's/Hole's Ire.	A map of Ireland, AD 1610, drawn by Gerard Mercator and engraved by William Hole, and published in William Camden's atlas *Britannia, sive florentissimorum regnorum Angliae, Scotiae, Hiberniae, et insularum adiacentium...* Mercator's Ire. (1595) *Irlandiae Regnum*, by Gerard Mercator, first published in his atlas entitled *Atlas sive Cosmographicae Meditationes de Fabrica Mundi et Fabricati Figura*, AD 1595.
Merchant's Book	Account Book of a Ballycastle Merchant, 1751–1754, PRONI T1044.
Met. Dinds.	*The Metrical Dindshenchas*, ed. Edward J. Gwynn, 5 vols (Dublin 1903–35).
Miscell. Ann.	*Miscellaneous Irish Annals (AD 1114–1437)*, ed. Séamus Ó hInnse (Dublin 1903–35).
Mon. Hib.	*Monasticon Hibernicum: or a history of the abbeys, priories and other religious houses in Ireland*, Mervyn Archdall, 3 vols (Dublin 1786). New edn, ed. Patrick F. Moran (Dublin 1873–6).
Mulcahy's Rathlin	"A visit to Rathlin" (and) "Second voyage to Recra (Rathlin Island)", Rev. D. Mulcahy, in *GJ* iv (1889), 44, 60.
Murphy's Rathlin	*Rathlin: Island of Blood and Enchantment, The Folklore of Rathlin*, Michael J. Murphy (Dundalk 1987).
Naturalis Historiae	*Naturalis Historiae*, C. Pliny secundi, 4 vols (Hamburg 1851).
New Rent (Law)	"New Rent from 1820", ed. Rev. H.I. Law, in Law (1940–3), 93–4.

Nomina	*Nomina: a journal of name studies relating to Great Britain and Ireland*, Council for Name Studies in Great Britain and Ireland (Hull 1977–85; Cambridge 1986–).
Norden's Map	"The plott of Irelande with the confines", formerly included in *A discription of Ireland*, c. 1610, by John Norden. This map has been preserved in the State Paper Office but is now in PRO London MPF 67. It is reproduced in *SP Hen. VIII* vol. ii, pt. 3.
Norsk Tids.	*Norsk tidsskrift for sprovidenskap*, under medvirkning av Olaf Broch..., utgitt av Carl J.S. Marstrander (Oslo 1928).
North Ulster Coast Map	A map of the north coast of Ulster, c. 1570, NLI(Mss.), Map 16.L.5(56).
Nowel's Ire. (1)	A map of Ireland, c. 1570, attributed to Laurence Nowel, dean of Lichfield (d. 1576). British Museum Cotton MS, Domitian A18, f. 97. Reproduced by the Ordnance Survey, Southampton.
Nowel's Ire. (2)	A map of Ireland, c. 1570, attributed to Laurence Nowel, dean of Litchfield (d. 1576). British Museum Cotton MS, Domitian A18, f.97. Reproduced by the Ordnance Survey, Southampton.
O'Boyle	"Place Names of Rathlin", James O'Boyle, *JDCHS* vol. 10 (1939), 44–54.
Ó Dónaill	*Foclóir Gaeilge–Béarla*, eag. Niall Ó Dónaill (Baile Átha Cliath 1977).
O'Donovan (DPJ)	Irish forms of place–names suggested by John O'Donovan in *McSkimin (DPJ)*.
Ó Dubhthaigh	"Gaelic Place–Names in the Glens of Antrim", S. Ó Dubhthaigh, *UJA* ser. 2, vol. 11 (1905), 130–8, 180–9; also published as *Gaelic Place–names in the Glens of Antrim*, ed. F.J. Bigger (Belfast 1906).
OED	*Oxford English Dictionary*, ed. J.A. Simpson and E.S.C. Weiner, 19 vols (2nd edn. Oxford, 1959).
O'Flaherty's Ogygia	*Ogygia: seu, Rerum Hibernicarum Chronologia...*, Roderico O Flaherti (Londini 1685).
Ogygia Vindicated	*The Ogygia Vindicated: against the objections of Sir George Mac Kenzie, King's Advocate for Scotland in the reign of King James II*, C. O'Connor (Dublin 1775).

O'Laverty

An historical account of the diocese of Down and Connor ancient and modern, Rev. James O'Laverty, 5 vols (Dublin 1878–95).

Ó Maolfabhail (Grianán)

"Grianán i logainmneacha", Art Ó Maolfabhail, *Dinnsean.* iml. vi, uimh. 2 (1974), 60–75.

Ó Maolfabhail (T re G)

"An logainm *Tóin re Gaoith*", *S. Ard Mh.* vol. 10, no. 2, 366–79.

Onoma

Onoma: bibliographical and information bulletin, International Centre of Onomastics (Louvain 1950–).

Onom. Goed.

Onomasticon Goedelicum locorum et tribuum Hiberniae et Scotiae, Edmund Hogan (Dublin 1910).

O'Reilly

An Irish–English dictionary, Edward O'Reilly. Revised and corrected, with a supplement by John O'Donovan (Dublin 1864).

Ortelius Map

Eryn. Hiberniae, Britannicae Insulae, Nova Descripto. Irlandt by William Ortelius. Published in the second edition of his *Theatrum Orbis Terrarum* (Antwerp 1573).

OS 1:10,000

The Ordnance Survey 1:10,000 series maps, Ordnance Survey of Northern Ireland (Belfast 1968–).

OS 1:50,000

The Ordnance Survey 1:50,000 series maps, also known as *The Discoverer Series*, Ordnance Survey of Northern Ireland (Belfast 1978–88).

OSCNB

Contouring Name Books in the Ordnance Survey, Phoenix Park, Dublin.

OSM

Ordnance Survey Memoirs of Ireland, ed. Angélique Day and Patrick McWilliams (Belfast 1990–).

OSNB

Name–books compiled during the progress of the Ordnance Survey in 1827–35 and preserved in the Ordnance Survey, Phoenix Park, Dublin.

OSNB Inf.

Informants for the Irish forms of place–names in the *OSNB*.

OSRNB

Ordnance Survey revision name books, compiled c. 1855–8. They list under the OS 6–inch sheet number the minor place–names on that sheet and include descriptive remarks and in some cases information on the origin of the place–names. Originals in Ordnance Survey Headquarters, Phoenix Park, Dublin.

363

PBNHPS	*Proceedings and reports of the Belfast Natural History and Philosophical Society*, 74 vols (1873–1955).
Pers. comm.	Personal communications with Cahal Dallat 06.1.93, 26.2.94 and 4.10.95; Brendan Jennings 27.10.95; Peter Montgomery, 6.12.95; Rosemary Power 15.1.96; Nevin Taggart 12.2.96; Fionntán Mac Giolla Chiaráin 12.03.96; Maria Paterson 02.06.96; Gerard Burns and Peggy McLyster 07.10.96; Sammy Wilkinson 12.10.96.
Place–Names of Rathlin	"The Place–Names of Rathlin Island", Dónall Mac Giolla Easpaig, *Ainm* 3 (1988), 3–73.
PNI	*Place–names of Northern Ireland*, The Northern Ireland Place–Name Project, Queen's University, Belfast, vols 1– (Belfast 1992–).
Poems Giolla Brighde	*The Poems of Giolla Brighde Mac Con Midhe*, ed. N.J.A. Williams, Irish Texts Society vol. li (Dublin 1980).
Poems on the Butlers	*Poems on the Butlers, of Ormond, Cahir and Dunboyne (AD 1400–1650)*, ed. James Carney (Dublin 1945).
Post–Sheanchas	*Post–Sheanchas i n–a bhfuil cúigí, dúithchí, conntaethe, & bailte puist na hÉireann*, Seosamh Laoide (Baile Átha Cliath 1905).
PRIA	*Proceedings of the Royal Irish Academy* (Dublin 1836–). Published in three sections since 1902 (section C: archaeology, linguistics and literature).
PRONI D2977/3A/2	Collection of land indentures relating to the Antrim Estate (1611–1812).
PSAMNI	*A Preliminary Survey of the Ancient Monuments of Northern Ireland*, ed. D.A. Chart (1940).
Rathlin Catechism	"The Rathlin Catechism", ed. C. Ó Dochartaigh, *ZCP* 35 (1976), 175–233.
Rathlin Vestry Book	*Rathlin Vestry Book 1769–95*, PRONI T861.
Ravenna Cosmog.	"The British Section of the Ravenna Cosmography", I.A. Richmond, *Archaeologia* 93 (1949), 1–50.
Reachlainn (de hÓir)	"As Cartlann na Logainmneacha: Rathlin Island, Reachlainn", Eamonn de hÓir, *Dinnsean.* iml. 1, uimh. 1, Meith. 1966, 22–5.
Rebellion Letters	*Letters and Papers relating to the Irish Rebellion between 1642–46*, ed. James Hogan (Dublin 1936).

Regal Visit. (Reeves)

Regal visitation of Down, Connor & Dromore, AD 1633–34, transcribed by William Reeves, and collated and corrected from originals in the Prerogative Office [now the Record Office] Dublin, PRONI DIO/1/24/2

Reg. Cromer

"Archbishop Cromer's register", ed. L.P. Murray, *J Louth AS* vii (1929–32), 516–24; viii (1933–6), 38–49, 169–88, 257–74, 322–51; ix (1937–40), 36–41, 124–30; x (1941–44), 116–27, completed by Aubrey Gwynn, 165–79.

Reg. Deeds abstracts

Registry of Deeds, Dublin. Abstracts of wills, 1708–1832, ed. P. Beryl Eustace and Eilish Ellis, 3 vols (Dublin 1954–84).

Religious Census

"Religious Census, Antrim and Down, 1740–1810", NLI (Mss.), Ms. 44173.

Religious Survey

"Religious Survey of the Barroney of Cary", Séamus Ó Casaide Mss., NLI (Mss.), Ms. 5456. That part of the survey dealing with the parish of Culfeightrin has been published in "A Religious Census of the Barony of Cary, 1734", ed. H. Doyle, *Glynns* 21 (1993), 65–6; Armoy in *ibid.* vol. 22 (1994), 53–8; Ramoan in *ibid.* vol. 23 (1995), 55–62.

Rennes Dinds.

"The prose tales in the Rennes Dindsenchas", ed. Whitley Stokes, *Rev. Celt.* xv (1894), 272–336, 418–84; xvi (1895), 31–83, 135–67, 269–312.

Report of the A.E.

"Extract from a report on the estate of the Antrim family, mainly in Co. Antrim, 1812" PRONI T2325/6, 112–114.

Rev. Celt.

Révue Celtique, 51 vols (Paris 1870–1934).

Rev. Connolly

"Place–names of Ramoan", Rev. L. Connolly in *Shaw Mason's Par. Sur.* ii 518–9.

Rev. Magill

The Nine Glens of Antrim, Rachrai and the Route; Placenames and their Meanings, Rev. P. Magill (1923).

Rev. Magill (JDCHS)

"Irish Place Names in County Antrim", by Rev. P. Magill, in five parts; *JDCHS* vi (1934) 62–71, vii (1935) 75–84, viii (1936) 82–9, ix (1938) 73–6, vol. x (1939) 83–90.

Rot. Litt. Pat.

Rotuli literarum patentium in Turri Londinensi asservati. Accurante Thomas Duffy Hardy. Vol. I, Pars I. Ab anno MCCI ad annum MCCXVI... (London 1835).

RSH

Rerum Scoticarum Historia, Georgio Buchanano (1697).

San. Chorm.	*Sanas Chormaic, Cormac's Glossary*, trans. John O'Donovan, ed. W. Stokes (Calcutta 1868).
San. Corm. (YBL)	"Cormac's Glossary from Lebor Brecc", in *Three Irish Glossaries*, ed W. Stokes (London 1862).
S. Ard Mh.	*Seanchas Ard Mhacha*: journal of the Armagh Diocesan Historical Society (Armagh 1954–).
Scot. Nat. Dict.	*Scottish National Dictionary*, ed. W. Grant (1926–46) and D.D. Murison (1946–76), 10 vols (Edinburgh).
Scottish Saints (Pinkerton)	*John Pinkerton's Lives of the Scottish Saints* (Londini 1789), revised and enlarged by W.M. Metcalfe, 2 vols (Paisley 1884).
SCtSiadhail	*Seachrán Chairn tSiadhail: amhrán ilcheardaidheachta agus seanchas síor–chuartaidheachta...*, eag. Seosamh Laoide (Baile Átha Cliath 1904).
Sea Chart [1590c]	*A sea chart of the coast of Munster, Leynster and Ulster, Irelande.* "This chart appears to have been formed in the reign of Elizabeth"; NLI (Mss.), Map 16.L.10(6).
Seanfhocail	*Seanfhocail Uladh*, eag. Enrí Ó Muirgheasa (Baile Átha Cliath 1907).
Senchus Fer n–Alban	"Senchus Fer n–Alban, part 1", John Bannerman, *Celtica* 7 (1966), 142–62.
SG	*Silva Gadelica*, ed. S.H. O'Grady, 2 vols, vol. i texts, vol. ii translations, London 1892.
Shaw Mason's Par. Sur.	*A statistical account, or parochial survey of Ireland, drawn up from the communications of the clergy*, William Shaw Mason, vols. i and ii (Dublin 1814); including "the Sectarian Population of Ballintoy, taken 1803", 170–1, and a "List of Incumbents, extracted from the First Fruits' Records" (Ramoan), 516–7.
Sidney's Memoir	"Sir Henry Sidney's Memoir of his Government of Ireland, 1583; Memoir or narrative addressed to Sir Francis Walsingham, 1583", ed. anon., *UJA* ser. 1, vol. 3 (1855), 33–52, 85–109, 336–57.
SMMD II	"The Early Modern version of Scéla Mucce Meic Da Thó – Tempus, Locus, Persona et Causa scribendi", Caoimhín Breatnach, *Ériu* xli (1990), 37–60.

Speed's Antrim & Down

A map entitled *Antrym and Downe*, AD 1610, by John Speed. Reproduced in *UJA* ser. 1, vol. i (1853) between pp. 123 and 124.

Speed's Ireland

The Kingdome of Irland devided into severall Provinces and then againe devided into Counties. Newly described, AD 1610, by John Speed. Also published in his atlas *The Theatre of the Empire of Great Britain* (Sudbury & Humble 1612).

Speed's Ulster

The Province Ulster Described, AD 1610, by John Speed. Also published in his atlas *The Theatre of the Empire of Great Britain* (Sudbury & Humble 1612).

SP Hen. VIII

State papers published under the authority of His Majesty's Commission: King Henry VIII, 11 vols (London 1830–52).

SSP

Sydney State Papers 1565–1608 by Sir James Perrott, ed. Herbert Wood (Dublin 1962).

Statist. Sur. Ant.

Statistical Survey of the County of Antrim with observations on the means of improvement, Rev. John Dubourdieu (Dublin 1812).

Stewart's Survey

A Book of Maps of ye Barony of Cary in ye County of Antrim... surveyed in the Year 1734 by Archb Stewart, in PRONI T1703/1–2. See also "A Catalogue of the 18th and early 19th Century Estate Maps in the Antrim Estate Office, Glenarm, Co. Antrim" ed. J. Frey, *UJA* ser. 3, vol. 16 (1953), 95–100.

Stud. Celt.

Studia Celtica. Published on behalf of the Board of Celtic Studies of the University of Wales (Cardiff 1966–).

Sur. A.E.

Maps of part of the Earl of Antrim's Estate in the Barony of Carey, by John O'Hara. These maps have been dated to 1782 by Frey in "A Catalogue of the 18th and early 19th Century Estate Maps in the Antrim Estate Office, Glenarm, Co. Antrim", ed. J. Frey, *UJA* ser. 3, vol. 16 (1953), 100–102. The copy in PRONI T1703/2 resembles a continuation of *Stewart's Survey* of 1734.

Taylor and Skinner

Maps of the Roads of Ireland, surveyed 1777, by George Taylor and Andrew Skinner (Dublin 1778).

TBC (Rec. I)

Táin Bó Cúailnge Recension I, ed. Cecile O'Rahilly (Dublin 1976).

Terrier (Reeves)

Terrier or Ledger book of Down and Connor, c. 1615, trans. William Reeves, PRONI DIO/1/24/2/3.

367

Thes. Pal.	*Thesaurus Palaeohibernicus: a collection of Old–Irish glosses, scholia and prose and verse*, ed. by Whitley Stokes and John Strachan, 2 vols (reprint, Dublin 1975).
Thurloe Papers	"Reports on the Rawlinson Collection of Manuscripts preserved in the Bodliean Library, Oxford", ed. C. McNeill, *Anal. Hib.* 1 (1930), 12–117.
Tíreachán	Tíreachán's Collections c. 700, ed. W. Stokes in *Trip. Life (Stokes)* ii, 302–33.
Tithe Applot.	*Tithe Applotment Books* for Co. Antrim (1824–38), PRONI FIN5A/21 (Armoy); FIN5A/27 (Ballintoy); FIN5A/87 (Culfeightrin); FIN5A/235 (Ramoan); FIN/238 (Rathlin Island).
Topog. Poems	*Topographical poems: by Seaán Mór Ó Dubhagáin and Giolla–na–Naomh Ó hUidhrín*, ed. James Carney (Dublin 1943).
Topog. Poems (JOD)	*The topographical poems of John O'Dubhagain and Giolla na Naomh O'Huidhrin*, ed. John O'Donovan for the Irish Archaeological and Celtic Society (Dublin 1862).
Treatice of Ire. (Butler)	"A Treatice of Ireland; by John Dymmok, ca 1599", ed. Rev. Richard Butler, in Tracts Relating to Ireland, printed for the Irish Archaeological Society, vol. 2 (Dublin 1842).
Treatise on Ire. (NLI)	*Treatise on Ireland*, by John Dymok, c. 1599, NLI (Mss.), Ms. 669.
Trias. Thaum.	*Triadis Thaumaturgae seu divorum Patricii, Columbae et Brigidae... acta, tom* ii, John Colgan (Lovanii 1647).
Trien. Visit. (Boyle)	Boyle's *Triennial visitation of Down, Connor and Dromore*, AD 1679, transcribed by William Reeves, PRONI DIO/1/24/16/1, pp. 34–49.
Trien. Visit. (Bramhall)	Bramhall's *Triennial visitation of Down, Connor and Dromore*, AD 1661, transcribed by William Reeves, PRONI DIO/1/24/16/1, pp. 1–16.
Trien. Visit. (Margetson)	Margetson's *Triennial visitation of Down, Connor, and Dromore*, AD 1664, transcribed by William Reeves, PRONI DIO/1/24/16/1, pp. 19–33.
Trip. Life (Stokes)	*The Tripartite Life of Saint Patrick, with other documents relating to that saint*, ed. W. Stokes, 2 vols (London 1887).

UF	*Ulster Folklife*. Published by the Committee on Ulster Folklife and Traditions (Belfast 1955–).
Uí Mhaine (Hogan)	Forms from *Leabhar Uí Mhaine*, a 14th-century vellum quoted by Hogan in *Onom. Goed. passim*.
UJA	*Ulster Journal of Archaeology*, 1st ser., 9 vols (Belfast 1853–62); 2nd ser., 17 vols (1894–1911); 3rd ser. (1938–).
Ulster Map [1570c]	Map of Ulster, c. 1570, in PRONI T1483/6.
Ulster Map [1590c]	*A true description of the North part of Ireland*. "A Ms. Map of the Province of Ulster, in the reign of Queen Elizabeth...", NLI (Mss.), Map 16.L.10(14).
Ulster Visit. (Reeves)	*The state of the diocese of Down and Connor, 1622, as returned by Bishop Robert Echlin to the royal commissioners*, copied from TCD E.3.6. by William Reeves, PRONI DIO/1/24/1.
Ulst. Roll Gaol Deliv.	"Ulster roll of gaol delivery, 1613–1618", ed. James F. Ferguson, *UJA* ser. 1, vol. 1 (1853) 260–70; vol. 2 (1854) 25–8.
Ultach	*An tUltach: iris oifigiúil Chomhaltas Uladh* (1923–).
VSSH (Heist)	*Vitae Sanctorum Hiberniae ex codiceolim Salmanticensi nunc Bruxellensi*, ed. William W. Heist (Bruxelles 1965).
VSSH (Plummer)	*Vitae Sanctorum Hiberniae partim hactenus ineditae ad fidem codicum manuscriptorum...*, ed. Charles Plummer, 2 vols (Oxford 1910).
Walsing. Letter–Book	*The Walsingham Letter–Book, or, Register of Ireland, May 1578 to December 1579*, ed. James Hogan and N. McNeill O'Farrell (Dublin 1959).
Wright's Diary	"Extracts from a diary written during a scientific tour of County Antrim in 1806 (by) Samuel Wright", ed. Kevin J. O'Hagan, *Glynns* vol. 12 (1984), 29–32.
ZCP	*Zeitschrift für Celtische Philologie* (1897–).

SECONDARY BIBLIOGRAPHY

Abbott, T.K.	1900	*Catalogue of the Manuscripts in the Library of Trinity College*, ed. (Dublin and London).
Abbott, T.K. & Gwynn, E.J.	1921	*Catalogue of the Irish Manuscripts in the Library of the Trinity College, Dublin*, ed.s (Dublin and London).
Adams, G.B.	1974	"Irish in Ulster in 1891", *UF* 20, 65–70.
Andrews, J.H.	1974	"The maps of the escheated counties of Ulster, 1609–10", *PRIA* lxxiv, sect. C, 133–70.
	1975	*A paper landscape; the Ordnance Survey in nineteenth–century Ireland* (Oxford).
	1978	*Irish maps: the Irish heritage series, no. 18* (Dublin).
Arthurs, J.B.	1955–6	"The Ulster Place–name Society", *Onoma* vi 80–2.
B., G.	1857	"Surnames in the County Antrim", *UJA* ser. 1, vol. 5, 323–344.
Bannerman, John	1974	*Studies in the History of Dalriada* (Edinburgh).
Barber, Charles	1981	*Early Modern English* (London; 1st edn 1976).
Barber, H.	1903	*British Family Names* (London).
Bartrum, P.C.	1966	*Early Welsh Genealogical Tracts* (Cardiff).
Baumgarten, Rolf	1973	"Old Irish Personal Names: M.A. O'Brien's 'Rhyfls Lecture'–Notes, 1957", ed., *Celtica* x, 211–36.
Bradley, Joseph	1986	"A glossary of words from South Armagh and North Louth", *UF* 32, 91–4.
Bell, Robert	1988	*The book of Ulster surnames* (Belfast).
Bigger, F.J.	1902	"The Bally Castle, County Antrim", *UJA* ser. 2, vol. 8, 7–9.
	1908	"Séan O'Neill", *UJA* ser. 2 vol. 14, 97–99.
Bigger, F.J., & Fennell, W.J.	1898	"Culfeightrin Church, Diocese of Connor", *UJA* ser. 2, vol. 4, 1898, 178–180.
Black, G.F.	1946	*The Surnames of Scotland, their Origin, Meaning, and History* (New York).
Boyd, H.A.	1947	*Rathlin Island North of Antrim* (Ballycastle).
	1960	*A North Antrim Coastal Parish*.

	1968	*Old Ballycastle, and, Marconi and Ballycastle* (Belfast).
	1974	"DeanWilliam Henry'sTopographical Description of the Coast of County Antrim and N. Down c. 1740", ed., *Glynns* 2, 7–9.
	1978	"Irish Dalriada", *Glynns* 6, 27–33.

Byrne, F.J. 1973 *Irish Kings and High–Kings* (London 1973).

Campbell, Mary 1951 *Sea Wrack or Long–ago Tales of Rathlin Island* (Ballycastle).

Carleton, S.T. 1991 *Heads and Hearths: The hearth money rolls and poll tax returns for County Antrim 1660–69* (Belfast).

Childe, V.G. 1938 "Doonmore, a Castle Mound near Fair Head, Co. Antrim", *UJA* ser. 3, vol. 1, 122–135.

Corrigan, K. 1991 "The Glens and their speech", *Glynns* 19, 14–20.

Curtis, Edmund 1931 "The 'Bonnaght' of Ulster", *Hermathena* 46, 87–105.

de hÓir, Éamonn 1965 "Aird i Logainmneacha", *Dinnsean.* iml. i, uimh. 2, 79–86.

Evans, E.E. 1945 "Field Archaeology in the Ballycastle district", *UJA* ser. 3, vol. 8, 14–32.

Falkiner, C.L. 1903 "The counties of Ireland: an historical sketch of their origin, constitution, and gradual delimitation", *PRIA* xxiv, sect. C, 169–94.

Flanagan, Deirdre 1971 "The names of Downpatrick", *Dinnsean.* iml. 1, uimh. 1, 89–112.

1978(b) "Common elements in Irish place–names: *Baile*", *BUPNS* ser. 2, vol. 1, 8–13.

1978(d) "Transferred population or sept–names: *Ulaidh* (a quo Ulster)", *BUPNS* ser. 2, vol. 1, 40–3.

1979(a) "Common elements in Irish place–names: *Ceall, Cill*", *BUPNS* ser. 2, vol. 2, 1–8.

1979(f) "Review of *The meaning of Irish place names* by James O'Connell (Belfast 1978)", *BUPNS* ser. 2, vol. 2, 58–60.

1981–2(b) "Some guidelines to the use of Joyce's *Irish Names of Places*, vol. i" *BUPNS* ser. 2, vol. 4, 61–69.

1981–2(c) "A summary guide to the more commonly attested ecclesiastical elements in Place–Names", *BUPNS* ser. 2, vol. 4, 69–75.

Frey, J. 1953 "A catalogue of the Eighteenth and Early Nineteenth Century Estate Maps in the Antrim Estate Office, Glenarm, Co. Antrim", *UJA* ser. 3, vol. 16, 93–103.

| Greene, D. | 1983 | "Cró, crú and similar words", *Celtica* 15, 1–9. |

Gwynn, A. &
Hadcock, R.N.   1970   *Medieval Religious Houses: Ireland* (1st edn.; reprint 1988).

Gwynn, Lucias   1911   "The Life of St. Lasair", *Ériu* vol. 5, 73–109.

Hamilton, J.N.   1974   *The Irish of Tory Island* (Belfast).

Harvey, Anthony   1985   "The Significance of *Cothraige*", *Ériu* vol. 36, 1–9.

Hogan, Edmund   1910   *Onom. Goed.*

Hogan, J.   1929   "The trícha cét and related land measures", *PRIA* xxxviii, sect. C, 148–235.

Holmer, Nils M.   1957   *The Gaelic of Arran* (Dublin).
     1962   *The Gaelic of Kintyre* (reprint, Dublin 1981).

Hore, Herbert F.   1857–8   "The Bruces in Ireland", *UJA* ser. 1, vol. 5, 1–12, 128–36, vol. 6, 66–76.

Hughes, A.J.   1986   "Cloncayagh", *Ainm* i, 92–3.
     1987   "Loch an Airgid and Cruach an Airgid (Silver Hill)", *Ainm* ii, 127.
     1988   "Sheep, Ship in Place–Names, a Caveat", *Ainm* iii, 73–76.
     1989   "Old Irish mennán, bennán", *ZCP* vol. 43, 179–86.

JDCHS (anon.)   1930   "A note on the Parish of Rathlin", vol. iii, 52–3.

Jope, E.M.   1951   "Scottish influences in the North of Ireland: Castles with Scottish features, 1580–1640", *UJA* ser. 3, vol. 14, 31–47.

Law, Revd. H.I.   1940–3   *Rathlin, Island and Parish.*

Lawlor, H.C.   1938   "An Ancient Route: the Slighe Miodhluachra in Ulaidh", *UJA* ser. 3, vol. 1, 1–6.

Lucas, A.T.   1963   "The sacred trees of Ireland", *Journal of the Cork Historical and Archaeological Society*, vol. 68, 16–54.

McAleer, Patrick   1920   *Townland names of County Tyrone* (c.1920; reprint Portadown & Draperstown 1988).

Mac Aodha, B.S.   1989–90   "Some aspects of the toponymy of the Commeen district, Gweebara, Co. Donegal", *Ainm* iv, 172– 193.

Mac an Bhaird, Alan   1978   An unpublished article on the difference between Irish *alt* and *allt*, presently in the Place–Names Office, Ordnance Survey, Dublin.

McCahan, Robert	1900(a)	*Ballintoy, Carrick–A–Rede and Whitepark Bay* (Coleraine).
	1900(b)	*Bunnamairge Friary* (Coleraine).
	1900(c)	*Fair Head and the valley of Glendun* (Coleraine).
	1900(d)	*History of Rathlin Island* (Coleraine).
	1900(e)	*Kenbaan Castle and Dunananie Castle* (Coleraine).
	1900(f)	*Knocklayd Mountain and the Valley of Glentow* (Coleraine).
	1900(g)	*The Life of Shane O'Neill* (Coleraine).
	1900(h)	*The Valley of Glenshesk* (Coleraine).

Mac Cárthaigh, M. 1964 "Gamhar – a 'winter' stream", *Dinnsean.* iml. 1, uimh. 2, 43.

MacConaill, M.A. 1922–3 "The people of Rachrai", *JBNHPS*, 4–7.

McCone, Kim *et al.* 1994 *Stair na Gaeilge* (Maigh Nuad).

Mac Dhónaill, Tadhg 1995 *Cnuasach de Logainmneacha agus de Scéalta faoi charachtair Rann na Feirste*, tráchtas B.A. (Onór.; Ollscoil Uladh, Cúil Raithin).

McDonnell, H. 1987 "Glenarm Friary and the Bissetts", *Glynns* 15, 34–49.

McErlean, Thomas 1983 "The Irish townland system of landscape organisation" in *Landscape archaeology in Ireland*, ed. Terence Reeves–Smyth and Fred Hamond, 315–39 (Oxford).

McGill, D. 1988 "Early Salt–making in Ballycastle District", *Glynns* vol. 16, 17–21.

Mac Giolla Easpaig, D. 1981 "Noun + Noun Compounds in Irish Placenames", *Ét. Celt.* xviii, 151–163.

1984 "Logainmneacha na Rosann", *Dongl. Ann.* vol. 36, 48–60.

1986 "Logainmneacha Ghaoth Dobhair", *Scáthlán* vol. 3, 64–88.

McKavanagh, Patrick J. 1979 "The Franciscans in County Antrim", *Glynns* vol. 7, 5–8.

McKay, P. 1987 "Documentary Sources for County Antrim Place–Names", *Ainm* ii, 114–120.

1989–90 "Some field–names from the parishes of Drummaul and Duneane, Co. Antrim", *Ainm* iv, 211–216.

McKeown, Rev. L. 1930 "Franciscan Friaries of Down and Antrim", *JDCHS* iii, 1930, 36–52

MacKillop, Donald 1989 *Sea–names of Berneray. Ainmean–Mhara Bhearnaraigh* (Inverness; reprinted from *Transactions of the Gaelic Society of Inverness* vol. lvi).

McKinley, R. 1981 *The Surnames of Lancashire*, English Surnames Series 4 (London).

MacLysaght, Edward 1985   *The Surnames of Ireland* (fourth edn, Dublin 1985; 1st edn 1957).

Mac Néill, E.   1907   "Moco, Maccu", *Ériu* vol. 3, 42–49.
       1919   *Phases of Irish History* (Dublin).
       1932   "The Vita Tripartita of St. Patrick", *Ériu* vol. 11, 1–41.
       1933   "The Pretanic Background in Britain and Ireland", *JRSAI* lxiii part 1, (vol. iii, 7th ser.), 1–28.

MacNeill, J.   1911   "Early Irish population groups: their nomenclature, classification and chronology", *PRIA* xxix, sect. C, 59–114.

Mahr, A.   1937   "New aspects and problems in Irish Prehistory", *Proceedings of the Prehistoric Society* vol. 3, part 2, 261–436.

Marshall, J.J.   1905   "The Dialect of Ulster", *UJA* ser. 2, vol. 11, 64–70, 122–125, 175–179.

Mason, William Shaw 1814–9   *A statistical account or parochial survey of Ireland... in 3 vols* (Dublin, Edinburgh).

Moody, T.W.   1939   *The Londonderry plantation, 1609–41: the city of London and the plantation in Ulster* (Belfast).

Morton, Deirdre   1954(a)   "Documentary sources for Co. Antrim place–names", *BUPNS* ser.1, vol. 2, 23–29.
       1954(b)   "Some early maps of Co. Antrim", *BUPNS* ser. 1, vol. 2, 56–59.
       1956–7   "Tuath–Divisions in the Baronies of Belfast and Massereene" *BUPNS* ser. 1, vol. iv 38–44; v, 6–12.

Mullin, T.H. &
Mallin, J.E.   1984   *The Ulster Clans, O'Mullan, O'Kane and O'Mellan* (reprint, Limavady; 1st edn. Chippenham 1966).

Munn, A.M.   1925   *Notes on the place names of the parishes and townlands of the County of Londonderry* (1925; reprint Ballinascreen 1985).

Newsome, J.   1964   *Pliny's Natural History. A selection from Philemon Holland's translation* (Oxford 1964).

Ní Chogaráin,
Éadaoin   1994   "Cursaí staire agus logainmneacha i bparóiste Oirthear Maighe i gContae Aontroma", tráchtas B. Oid. (Coláiste Mhuire, Béal Feirste).

Nicolaisen, W.F.H.   1969   *The Distribution of Certain Gaelic Mountain–Names*, reprinted from the *Transactions of the Gaelic Society of Inverness* xlv (Stirling).
       1976   *Scottish Place–Names, their Study and Significance* (London).

Nolan, William   1982   *Tracing the Past* (Dublin).
    1986   *The Shaping of Ireland, The geographical perspective* (Cork).

Nolan, William,
Ronayne, Liam &
Dunlevy, Máiread   1995   *Donegal, History and Society*, ed.s (Dublin)

Ó Baoill, Colm   1978   *Contributions to a comparative study of Ulster Irish and Scottish Gaelic* (Belfast).

Ó Catháin, S. &
O'Flanagan, P.   1975   *The Living Landscape* (Dublin).

Ó Ceallaigh, S.   1950   "Notes on Place–Names in Derry and Tyrone", *Celtica* i, 118–140.

Ó Cearbhaill, P.   1989–90   "Áth na gCarbad", *Ainm* iv, 194–199.
    1991–93   "Sheep, Ship", *Ainm* v, 33–6.

Ó Corráin, D. &
Maguire, F.   1981   *Gaelic Personal Names* (Dublin).

Ó Cuív, Brian   1986   *Aspects of Irish personal names* (Dublin) [reprinted from *Celtica* xviii (1986) 151–84].

Ó Dochartaigh, C.   1987   *Dialects of Ulster Irish* (Belfast).

Ó Doibhlin,
An tAth. Éamon   1971   "O Neill's 'Own Country' and its Families", *S. Ard Mh.* vol. 6, no. 1, 23.

Ó Domhnaill, Niall   1952   *Na Glúnta Rosannacha* (Baile Átha Cliath).

O'Donovan, John   1849   *Miscellany of the Celtic Society...*(Dublin).
    1857   "Original letters in the Irish and Latin languages, by Shane O'Neill, Prince of Tyrone...", *UJA* ser. 1, vol. 5, 259–73.

O'Donovan, J.
& O'Daly, J.   1849–51   "Original Irish Poetry. Panegyric on Thomas Butler, the tenth Earl of Ormonde", *JRSAI* i, 470–85.

Ó Droighneáin,
Muiris   1982   *An Sloinnteoir Gaeilge agus an tAinmneoir* (3ú eag.; 1ú eag., 1966)

Ó Foghludha,
Risteard   1935   *Log–ainmneacha .i. dictionary of Irish place–names...* (Dublin).

O'Kane, J.   1970   "Placenames of Inniskeel and Kilteevoge (a placename study of two parishes in Central Donegal)", *ZCP* xxxi, 59–145.

Ó hÓgáin, D.	1987	"Magic Attributes of the Hero", in *The Heroic Process*, ed. Bo Almqvist, Séamas Ó Catháin and Pádraig Ó Héalaí (Co. Dublin), 207–42.
	1990	*Myth, Legend and Romance. An Encyclopaedia of the Irish Folk Tradition* (New York).
Ó hUrmoltaigh, Nollaig	1967	"Logainmneacha as Toraí, Tír Chonaill", *Dinnsean.* iml. ii, uimh. 4, 99–106,
Ó Máille, Tomás	1936	*An Béal Beo* (Baile Átha Cliath).
Ó Máille, T.S.	1953–4	"The name Béal Átha Seanaigh", *Dongl. Ann.* vol. 2, 499–501.
	1957	"Ára mar áitainm", *Galvia* iv, 54–65.
	1958	"Aichill in áitainmneacha", *JRSAI* lxxxvii, 93– 100.
	1960	"Cuilleann in áitainmneacha", *Béaloid.* xxviii, 50–64.
	1981–2	"Avish and Evish", *BUPNS* ser. 2, vol. 4, 1–5.
	1987	"Place–Name elements in –ar", *Ainm* ii, 27–36.
	1989–90	"Irish place–names in –as, –es, –is, –os, –us", *Ainm* iv, 126–164.
Ó Mainnín, M.B.	1989–90	"The element *island* in Ulster place–names", *Ainm* iv, 200–210.
Ó Maolfabhail, Art	1986	"Maoil i logainmneacha – focal a chiallaíonn sruth?", *Ainm* i, 3–13.
	1985	"Baill choirp mar logainmneacha: Droim", *Comhar* (Iúl), 22.
	1987	"Baill choirp mar logainmneacha", *Ainm* ii, 76– 82.
	1990	*Logainmneacha na hÉireann, Iml. 1: Contae Luimnigh*, (Baile Átha Cliath 1990).
Ó Murchadha, Diarmuid	1994–5	"*Sódh* i Logainmneacha", *Éigse* xxviii, 129–134.
O'Neill, Moira	1906	*Songs of the Glens of Antrim* (12th impression; London)
O'Rahilly, T.F.	1930	"Notes on Middle Irish Pronunciation", *Hermathena* xx, 152–195.
	1932	*Irish Dialects Past and Present* (Dublin; reprint 1976).
	1933	"Notes on Irish place–names", *Hermathena* xxiii, 196–220.
	1946	*Early Irish History and Mythology* (Dublin; reprint 1976).
Ó Searcaigh, S.	1925	*Foghraidheacht Ghaedhilge an Tuaiscirt* (Baile Átha Cliath agus Béal Feirste).
Ó Tuathail, Éamonn	1950(a)	"Varia", *Éigse* vi, 155–64.
	1950(b)	"The River Shannon poetically described by Michael Brennan", *Éigse* vi, 193–240, 275–313.

Orpen, G.H.	1894	"Ptolemy's Map of Ireland", *JRSAI* (fifth ser.) iv, 115–28.
	1911–20	*Ireland under the Normans, 1169–1333*, 4 vols (Oxford; reprint 1968).
Otway–Ruthven, A.J.	1964	"Parochial development in the rural deanery of Skreen", *JRSAI* xciv, 111–22.
Petty, William	1672	*The political anatomy of Ireland* (1672), reprinted in *Tracts and treatises illustrative of Ireland*, vol. ii, 72–3 (Dublin 1860–1).
Power, Patrick	1932	*Crìchad an chaoilli: being the topography of ancient Fermoy* (Cork).
	1947	"The bounds and extent of Irish parishes", *Féil. Torna* 218–23.
	1952	*Place–Names of the Decies* (2nd edn Cork; 1st edn London 1907).
Price, Liam	1945–67	*The place–names of County Wicklow*, 7 vols (Dublin).
	1963	"A note on the use of the word *baile* in place–names", *Celtica* vi, 119–126.
Rankin, J. Fred	1984	"Templastragh", *Glynns* vol. 12, 40–9.
Reaney, P.H.	1958	*A dictionary of British surnames* (London).
Reeves, William	1861	"On the townland distribution of Ireland" *PRIA* vii, 473–90.
Reid, Professor	1957	"A note on *cinament*", *BUPNS* ser. 1, vol. v, 12.
Roberts, A.	1988	"Bonamargy and the Scottish Mission", *Glynns* vol. 16, 33–40.
Sellar, W.D.H.	1973	"The Earliest Campbells – Norman, Briton or Gael?", *Scottish Studies* vol. 17, part 2, 109– 125.
Sharpe, Richard	1995	*Adomnán of Iona. Life of Columba*, trans. (London).
Simms, Anngret & Simms, Katherine	1990	*Kells* (Dublin).
Skene, William F.	1867	*Chronicles of the Picts, Chronicles of the Scots, and other early memorials of Scottish history*, ed. (Edinburgh 1867).
Smyth, J. & Whelan, Kevin	1988	*Common Ground, essays on the historical geography of Ireland, presented to T. Jones Hughes*, ed.s (Cork).

| Sommerfelt, Alf | 1929 | "South Armagh Irish", *Norsk Tids.* ii, 107–91. |
| | 1958 | "The English forms of the names of the main provinces of Ireland", *Lochlann* i 223–7. |

Spencer, F.C.   1945   "Place Names of the Barony of Coshma", *North Munster Antiquarian Journal* vol. 4, no. 4 (Autumn), 152–63.

Stockman, G.   1986   "Giorrú Gutaí Fada Aiceannta i nGaeilge Chúige Uladh", in *Féilscríbhinn Thomáis de Bhaldraithe*, ed. Seosamh Watson, 11–18 (Baile Átha Cliath 1986).
     1991   "Focail: Loisc", *Ultach* iml. 68, uimh. 3 (Márta), 26.

Stockman, Gerard &
Wagner, Heinrich   1968   "Contributions to a Study of Tyrone Irish", *Lochlann* iii, 43–236.

Taylor, Isaac   1896   *Names and their histories* (1896), reprinted in the Everyman edition of his *Words and places* (1911).

Taylor, Simon   1995   *Settlement–Names in Fife*, PhD (University of Edinburgh).

Toner, Gregory   1991–3   "*Money* in the place–names of east Ulster", *Ainm* v 52–8.
     1994–5   "An Eilimint **Íneán* i Logainmneacha Reachlainne", *Ainm* vi, 32–37.

Uí Fhlannagáin, D.   1982   "Béal Feirste agus ainmneacha laistigh", in *Topothesia, essays in honour of T.S. Ó Máille*, 45–64.

Wagner, Heinrich   1959   *Gaeilge Theilinn* (Baile Átha Cliath).

Walsh, Paul   1957   *The Placenames of Westmeath* (Dublin).

Walsh, T. &
Conynham, D.P.   1898   *Ecclesiastical History of Ireland* (New York).

Watson, W.J.   1926   *Celtic Placenames of Scotland* (Edinburgh).

Williams, B.B.   1985   "Excavations at Drumnakeel, Co. Antrim", *UJA* ser. 3, vol. 48, 51–61.

Williams, B.B. &
Robinson, P.S.   1983   "The excavation of bronze age cists and a medieval booley house at Glenmakeerin, County Antrim, and a discussion of Booleying in North Antrim", *UJA* ser. 3, vol. 46, 29–40.

Woulfe, Patrick   1923   *Sloinnte Gaedheal is Gall: Irish names and surnames; collected and edited with explanatory and historical notes* (Dublin).

GLOSSARY OF TECHNICAL TERMS

advowson   The right of presenting a clergyman to a vacant benefice.

affricate   A plosive pronounced in conjunction with a fricative; e.g. the sounds spelt with *(t)ch* or *-dge* in English.

alveolar   Pronounced with the tip of the tongue touching the ridge of hard flesh behind the upper teeth; e.g. *t* in the English word *tea*.

analogy   The replacement of a form by another in imitation of words of a similar class; e.g. in imitation of *bake – baked, fake – faked, rake – raked* a child or foreigner might create a form *shaked*.

anglicize   Make English in form; e.g. in place-names the Irish word *baile* "homestead, townland" is anglicized *bally*.

annal   A record of events in chronological order, according to the date of the year.

annates   Later known as First Fruits; a tax paid, initially to the Pope, by a clergyman on appointment to a benefice.

apocope   The loss of the end of a word.

aspiration   (i) The forcing of air through a narrow passage thereby creating a frictional sound; e.g. *gh* in the word *lough* as pronounced in Ireland and Scotland is an aspirated consonant, (ii) the modification of a consonant sound in this way, indicated in Irish writing by putting *h* after the consonant; e.g. *p* aspirated resembles the *ph* sound at the beginning of *phantom;* also called **lenition.**

assimilation   The replacing of a sound in one syllable by another to make it similar to a sound in another syllable; e.g. in some dialects of Irish the *r* in the first syllable of the Latin *sermon-* was changed to *n* in imitation of the *n* in the second syllable, giving a form *seanmóin.*

ballybetagh   Irish *baile biataigh* "land of a food-provider", native land unit, the holder of which had a duty to maintain his lord and retinue when travelling in the area (*Colton Vis.* 130).

ballyboe   Irish *baile bó* "land of a cow", a land unit equivalent to a modern townland, possibly so-named as supplying the yearly rent of one cow (*Colton Vis.* 130).

barony   In Ireland an administrative unit midway in size between a county and a civil parish, originally the landholding of a feudal baron (*EA* 62).

benefice   An ecclesiastical office to which income is attached.

bilabial   Articulated by bringing the two lips together; e.g. the *p* in the English word *pea*.

Brittonic   Relating to the branch of Celtic languages which includes Welsh, Cornish and Breton.

calendar   A précis of an historical document or documents with its contents arranged according to date.

carrow   Irish *ceathru* "a quarter". See **quarter.**

cartography   The science of map-making.

cartouche   An ornamental frame round the title etc. of a map.

carucate   Latin *carucata* "ploughland", a territorial unit, the equivalent of a townland.

Celtic   Relating to the (language of the) Irish, Scots, Manx, Welsh, Cornish, Bretons, and Gauls.

centralized   Pronounced with the centre of the tongue raised; e.g. the vowel sound at the beginning of *again* or at the end of *the.*

cess   Tax.

cinament   A territorial unit of lesser size than a **tuogh** (which see). Three derivations have been suggested: (i) from Irish *cine* "a family", (*cineamhain?*) (*EA* 388); (ii) from French *scindement* "cutting up, division" (Morton 1956–7, 39); (iii) from French *(a)ceignement* "enclosure(?)" (Reid 1957, 12).

civil parish   An administrative unit based on the medieval parish.

cluster   See **consonant cluster.**

coarb   Irish *comharba,* originally the heir of an ecclesiastical office, later a high-ranking hereditary tenant of church land under the bishop. The coarb may be in charge of other ecclesiastical tenants called **erenaghs,** which see.

compound   A word consisting of two or more verbal elements; e.g. *aircraft, housework.*

consonant   (i) An element of the alphabet which is not a vowel, e.g. *c, j, x,* etc., (ii) a speech sound in which the passage of air through the mouth or nose is impeded, e.g. at the lips (*b, p, or m*), at the teeth (*s, z*), etc.

consonant cluster   A group of two or more consonants; e.g. *bl* in *blood, ndl* in *handle, lfths* in *twelfths.*

contraction   (i) The shortening of a word or words normally by the omission of one or more sounds, (ii) a contracted word; e.g. *good-bye is* a contraction of *God be with you; can not* is contracted to *can't.*

county   Feudal land division, equivalent to an English shire, created by the English administration in Ireland as the major subdivision of an Irish province.

deanery   Properly called a rural deanery, an ecclesiastical division of people or land administered by a rural dean.

declension   A group of nouns whose case-endings vary according to a fixed pattern. (There are five declensions in modern Irish).

delenition   Sounding or writing a consonant as if it were not aspirated; see **aspiration.**

dental   A sound pronounced with the tip of the tongue touching the upper teeth; e.g. *th* in the English *thumb*.

devoicing   Removing the sound caused by the resonance of vocal cords; see **voiced.**

dialect   A variety of a language in a given area with distinctive vocabulary, pronunciation or grammatical forms.

digraph   A group of two letters expressing a single sound; e.g. *ea* in English *team* or *ph* in English *photograph*.

diocese   The area or population over which a bishop has ecclesiastical authority.

diphthong   A union of two vowel sounds pronounced in one syllable; e.g. *oi* in English *boil*. (Note that a diphthong cannot be sung on a single sustained note without changing the position of the mouth).

dissimilation   The replacing of a sound in one syllable by another to make it different from a sound in another syllable e.g. Loughbrickland comes from an original Irish form, *Loch Bricrenn*.

eclipsis   The replacement in Irish of one sound by another in initial position as the result of the influence of the previous word; e.g. the *c* of Irish *cór* "choir" (pronounced like English *core)* is eclipsed by *g* in the phrase *i gcór* "in a choir" due to the influence of the preposition *i*, and *gcór* is pronounced like English *gore*; also called **nasalization.**

elision   The omission of a sound in pronunciation; e.g. the *d* is elided in the word *handkerchief*.

emphasis   See **stress.**

epenthetic vowel   A vowel sound inserted within a word; e.g. in Ireland an extra vowel is generally inserted between the *l* and *m* of the word *film*.

eponymous   adjective referring to the real or legendary person from whom a tribe or family etc. has derived its name, for example Niall *Noígiallach*, "of the nine hostages", is the eponymous ancestor of the tribal name *Uí Néill*.

erenagh   Irish *airchinnech* "steward", hereditary officer in charge of church lands, later a tenant to the bishop *(Colton Vis.* 4–5).

escheat   Revert to the feudal overlord, in Ireland usually forfeit to the English crown.

etymology   The facts relating to the formation and meaning of a word.

fiant   A warrant for the making out of a grant under the royal seal, or (letters) patent.

381

fricative   A speech sound formed by narrowing the passage of air from the mouth so that audible friction is produced; e.g. *gh* in Irish and Scottish *lough.*

Gaelic   Relating to the branch of Celtic languages which includes Irish, Scottish Gaelic and Manx.

glebe   The house and land (and its revenue) provided for the clergyman of a parish.

glide   A sound produced when the organs of speech are moving from the position for one speech sound to the position for another; e.g. in pronouncing the word *deluge* there is a *y*-like glide between the *l* and the *u.*

gloss   A word or phrase inserted in a manuscript to explain a part of the text.

Goedelic = Gaelic   which see.

grange   Anglo-Norman term for farm land providing food or revenue for a feudal lord, frequently a monastery.

haplology   The omission of a syllable beside another with a similar sound; e.g. *lib(ra)ry, deteri(or)ated.*

hearth money   A tax on the number of hearths used by a household.

impropriator   The person to whom rectorial tithes of a monastery etc. were granted after the Dissolution.

inflect   To vary the form of a word to indicate a different grammatical relationship; e.g. *man* singular, *men* plural.

inquisition   A judicial inquiry, here usually into the possessions of an individual at death.

International Phonetic Alphabet   The system of phonetic transcription advocated by the International Phonetic Association.

labial = bilabial which see.

lenition   See **aspiration.**

lexicon   The complete word content of a language.

lowering   Changing a vowel sound by dropping the tongue slightly in the mouth; e.g. pronouncing *doctor* as *dactor.*

manor   Feudal estate (Anglo–Norman and Plantation), smaller than a barony, entitling the landowner to jurisdiction over his tenants at a manor court.

martyrology   Irish *féilire*, also translated "calendar", a list of names of saints giving the days on which their feasts are to be celebrated.

mearing   A boundary.

metathesis   The transposition of sounds in a word; e.g. saying *elascit* instead of *elastic*.

moiety   French *moitié,* "the half of", also a part or portion of any size.

morphology   The study of the grammatical structure of words.

nasalization   See **eclipsis.**

oblique   Having a grammatical form other than nominative singular.

onomasticon   A list of proper names, usually places.

orthography   Normal spelling.

palatal   A sound produced with the tongue raised towards the hard palate.

parish   A subdivision of a diocese served by a single main church or clergyman.

patent   (or letters patent), an official document conferring a right or privilege, frequently here a grant of land.

patronymic   A name derived from that of the father.

phonemic   Relating to the system of phonetic oppositions in the speech sounds of a language, which make, in English for example, *soap* a different word from *soup,* and *pin* a different word from *bin.*

phonetic   Relating to vocal sound.

phonology   The study of the sound features of a language.

plosive   A sound formed by closing the air passage and then releasing the air flow suddenly, causing an explosive sound; e.g. *p* in English *pipe.*

ploughland   Medieval English land unit of about 120 acres, equivalent to a townland.

prebend   An endowment, often in land, for the maintenance of a canon or prebendary, a senior churchman who assisted the bishop or had duties in the cathedral.

precinct   *Ad hoc* land division (usually a number of townlands) used in Plantation grants.

prefix   A verbal element placed at the beginning of a word which modifies the meaning of the word; e.g. *un-* in *unlikely.*

proportion   *Ad hoc* land division (usually a number of townlands) used in Plantation grants.

province   Irish *cúige* "a fifth": the largest administrative division in Ireland, of which there are now four (Ulster, Leinster, Connaught, Munster) but were once five.

quarter   Land unit often a quarter of the ballybetagh, and thus containing three or four townlands, but sometimes referring to a subdivision of a townland. See also **carrow.**

raising   Changing a vowel sound by lifting the tongue higher in the mouth; e.g. pronouncing *bag* as *beg.*

realize   Pronounce; e.g. *-adh* at the end of verbal nouns in Ulster Irish is realized as English *-oo.*

rectory   A parish under the care of a rector supported by its tithes; if the rector cannot reside in the parish he appoints and supports a resident vicar.

reduction   (i) Shortening of a vowel sound; e.g. the vowel sound in *board* is reduced in the word *cupboard*, (ii) = **contraction** which see.

register   A document providing a chronological record of the transactions of an individual or organization.

rounded   Pronounced with pouting lips; e.g. the vowel sounds in *oar* and *ooze.*

Scots   A dialect of Anglo-Saxon which developed independently in lowland Scotland from the 11th to the 16th centuries. By the time of the Union of Crowns in 1603 it was markedly different from southern English.

seize   To put in legal possession of property, especially land.

semantic   Relating to the meaning of words.

semivowel   A sound such as *y* or *w* at the beginning of words like *yet, wet,* etc.

sept   Subgroup of people, for instance of a tribe or ruling family.

sessiagh   Irish *seiseach* "a sixth", usually referring to a subdivision of a townland or similar unit. Apparently three sessiaghs were equivalent to a ballyboe (*Colton Vis.* 130).

shift of stress   The transfer of emphasis from one syllable to another; e.g. *Belfast* was originally stressed on the second syllable *fast* but because of shift of stress many people now pronounce it **Bel**/*fast*. See **stress.**

stem   (dental, o-, etc.) Classification of nouns based on the form of their endings before the Old Irish period.

stress   The degree of force with which a syllable is pronounced. For example, the name Antrim is stressed on the first syllable while Tyrone is stressed on the second.

subdenomination   A smaller land division, usually a division of a townland.

substantive   A noun.

suffix   A verbal element placed at the end of a word which modifies the meaning of the word; e.g. *-less* in *senseless.*

syllable   A unit of pronunciation containing one vowel sound which may be preceded or followed by a consonant or consonants; e.g. *I*, *my*, *hill*, have one syllable; *outside*, *table*, *ceiling* have two; *sympathy*, *understand*, *telephone* have three, etc.

syncopation   The omission of a short unstressed vowel or digraph when a syllable beginning with a vowel is added; e.g. *tiger+ess* becomes *tigress*.

tate   A small land unit once used in parts of Ulster, treated as equivalent to a townland, although only half the size.

termon   Irish *tearmann*, land belonging to the Church, with privilege of sanctuary (providing safety from arrest for repentant criminals), usually held for the bishop by a coarb as hereditary tenant.

terrier   A list of the names of lands held by the Church or other body.

tithes   Taxes paid to the Church. Under the native system they were shared between parish clergy and erenagh (as the tenant of the bishop), under the English administration they were payable to the local clergyman of the Established Church.

topography   The configuration of a land surface, including its relief and the position of its features.

toponymy   Place-names as a subject for study.

townland   The common term or English translation for a variety of small local land units; the smallest unit in the 19th-century Irish administrative system.

transcription   An indication by written symbols of the precise sound of an utterance.

tuogh   Irish *tuath* "tribe, tribal kingdom", a population or territorial unit.

unrounded   Articulated with the lips spread or in neutral position; see **rounded**.

velar   Articulated with the back of the tongue touching the soft palate; e.g. *c* in *cool*.

vicarage   A parish in the charge of a vicar, the deputy either for a rector who received some of the revenue but resided elsewhere, or for a monastery or cathedral or lay impropriator.

visitation   An inspection of (church) lands, usually carried out for a bishop (ecclesiastical or episcopal visitation) or for the Crown (regal visitation).

vocalization   The changing of a consonant sound into a vowel sound by widening the air passage; akin to the disappearance of *r* in Southern English pronunciation of words like *bird*, *worm*, *car*.

voiced   Sounded with resonance of the vocal cords. (A test for voicing can be made by closing the ears with the fingers and uttering a consonant sound. e.g. *ssss*, *zzzz*, *ffff*, *vvvv*. If a buzzing or humming sound is heard the consonant is voiced; if not it is voiceless).

voiceless   See **voiced.**

INDEX TO IRISH PLACE-NAMES
(with pronunciation guide)

The following guide to the pronunciation of Irish forms suggested in this book is only approximate. Words are to be sounded as though written in English. The following symbols have the values shown:

ă	as in *above, coma*
ā	as in *father, draught*
ċ	as in *lough, Bach*
ch	as in *chip, church*
ġ	does not occur in English. To approximate this sound try gargling without water, or consider the following: *lock* is to *lough* as *log* is to *loġ*. If you cannot manage this sound just pronounce it like *g* in **go**.
gh	as in *lough, Bach*; not as in *foghorn*
ī	as in *five, line*
ky	as in *cure, McKeown*
ly	at beginning of words as in *brilliant, million*
ō	as in *boar, sore*
ow	as in *now, plough*

Stress is indicated by writing the vowel in the stressed syllable in bold, e.g., Arm**a**gh, Ballym**e**na, L**u**rgan.

Place-Name	Rough Guide	Page
Allt na Darach	alt nă daragh	170
Allt na Muc	alt nă muck	36
Allt Shíle	alt heelă	169
Ardach	ardăgh	230
Ardach Mór	ardăgh mor	110
Ard Tí Mhic Cormaic	ard tee vick corrămick	51
Baile an Daim	ballăn dam	112
Baile an Leá	ballăn lay	52
Baile an Locháin	ballăn loughine	112
Baile an Loig	ballăn lig	231
Baile an Tuathaigh	ballăn Tooăhee	47
Baile Bhairéadach	ballăn waraydăgh	114
Baile Bheannacht	ballă vanăċt	120
Baile Bhuí	ballă wee	121
Baile Caraidh	ballă karee	291
Baile Chaisleáin	ballă ċashline	263
Baile Cloicheach	ballă klighyăgh	114
Baile Coinneagáin	ballă kinyagine	292
Baile Ghaill	ballă ġill	294
Baile na bhFargán	ballv nă varăgan	293
Baile na gCeard	ballă nă gyard	115
Baile na gCeard	ballă nă gyard	295
Baile na gCloch	ballă nă glogh	116
Baile na Sráide	ballă nă srādjă	53
Baile Nua	ballă nooa	296
Baile Pádraig	ballă pādrăg	117
Baile Riabhach, An	ăn ballă reewagh	118
Baile Tirim, An	ăn ballă chirăm	119
Baile Uí Éanáin	ballee ayănine	265
Baile Uí Éinigh	ballee aynee	18
Baile Uí Bhaothalaigh	ballee weehălee	232
Baile Uí Dhoirnín	ballee ġornyin	230
Barr Mín, An	ăn bar meen	123
Bealach na Creamhaí	ballăgh nă krawee	83
Bealach Chuarachaidh	ballăgh ċooăraghee	315
Bearnais	bārnăsh	123
Bé Allt an Choire	bay alt ăn ċoră	309
Bé Allt an Chaoil	bay alt ăn ċeel	309
Bé Allt an Duibhéin	bay alt ăn divayn	310
Bé an Aircill	bay ăn arkyil	311
Bé an Dúin	bay ăn doon	316
Bé an Mhuilinn	bay ăn willin	320
Bé an Oileáin Charraigh	bay ăn illine ċaree	317
Bé Cuarachaidh	bay kooraghee	315
Bé na hEaglaise	bay nă heglishă	314
Bhinn Bhán, An	ăn vin wān	174
Bhinn Mhór, An	ăn vin wore	172

Place-Name	Rough Guide	Page
Ceathrú an Dúin	kyahroo ăn doon	178
Ceathrú an Dúin	kyahroo an doon	298
Ceathrú an Fhanca	kyahroo ăn ankă	295
Ceathrú Chlocháin	kyahroo ċloghine	214
Cheathrú Chrua, An	ăn ċahroo ċrooă	56
Cheathrú Gharbh, An	ăn ċahroo ġaroo	151
Ceathrúin Leithlis	kyahroon lelish	55
Ceathrú na hEaladh	kyahroo nă haloo	297
Cheathrú Riabhach, An	ăn ċahroo reewăgh	215
Ceathrú Uí Laifeartaigh	kyahroo ee lafartee	22
Cill an Líonáin	kill ăn lyeeonine	192
Cill Chreige	kill ċregyă	253
Cill Chruaiche	kill ċrooăghyă	27
Cill na Crú	kill nă kroo	274
Cill Éanna	kill ayănnă	318
Cill Éanáin	kill ayănine	250
Cill Eoin	kill oine	137
Cill Liúca	kill lyooka	192
Cill Mochroma	kill moghromă	93
Cill Mochomóg	kill moghomog	69
Cill Phádraig	kill phādrig	302
Cill Roibeaird	kill robardge	254
Cionn Mín, An	ăn kyun meen	93
Cionn Bán, An	ăn kyun bāne	275
Chillidh Bheag, An	ăn ċillee veg	102
Chill Mhaol, An	ăn ċill weel	218
Chruach Bheag, An	ăn ċrooăgh veg	61
Chruach Mhór, An	ăn ċrooăgh wore	62
Claondoire	kleendiră	38
Clár, An	ăn klāre	241
Clár, An	ăn klāre	87
Clár Caisleáin	klāre kashline	240
Clocha Dubha, Na	nă kloghă doowă	314
Cloch an Aifrinn	klogh ăn afrin	303
Cloch Chorr	klogh ċorr	58
Cloch Dhún Muirígh	klogh ġoon muree	242
Cloch Ghilbeirt	klogh yilbirch	97
Cloch Níon Ghobáin	klogh neeon ġobine	250
Cloigeann	kligan	23
Cloigeann	kligan	299
Cloigneach	klignyagh	57
Cloigneach	klignyagh	215
Cnoc an Aoil	krock ăn eel	181
Cnoc an Choiléir	krock ăn ċulyer	88
Cnoc an Chártha	krock ăn ċārhă	38
Cnoc an Óir	krock ăn ōre	182
Cnoc an Tí Mhóir	krock ăn chee wore	182

Place-Name	Rough Guide	Page
Tarbh, An	ăn taroo	313
Teampall Chomhaill	champal ċōwill	299
Tamhnach Bhuí	townăgh wee	259
Teampall Lasrach	champal lasragh	79
Teangach	changagh	160
Tír Mhaoilĺn	cheer weelyeen	161
Tobar Bile	tubber billă	259
Tobar Caoch, An	ăn tubber keegh	81
Toigh an Aifrinn	tee ăn afrin	299
Toigh Bán, An	ăn tee bāne	166
Toigh Ghilbeirt	tee yilbirch	97
Toigh Solais, An	ăn tee sulish	331
Tor	torr	206
Tor Corr	torr corr	162
Tor Taidhg	torr tayg	207
Tor Uí Bhranáin	torr ee vranine	207
Tor Glas	torr glas	162
Tor na bhFiach	torr nă veeăgh	206
Tuar an Luscáin	tuăr ăn luskine	261
Tuar na gCró	tuăr nă gro	102
Tuar na mBodach	tuăr nă muddagh	163
Tuar na Móna	tuăr na mōnă	163
Tuar na Ruán	tuăr nă rooan	164
Tuar na Roibeard	tuăr nă robard	35
Tuar Riabhach	tuăr reewăgh	34
Tulach Pádraig	tulagh pādrig	20
Tulaigh Chorra	tulee ċorră	33
Uamha Breacáin	ooă brakine	311
Uamha Dhubhthaigh	ooă ġoofee	321
Uamha na Páirce	ooă nă pārkyă	321
Ucht Briste Croí	uċt brishchă kree	200
Usaid, An	ăn oosădge	330

PLACE-NAME INDEX

Sheet numbers are given below for the OS 1:50,000 map only when the name occurs on that map. Not all the townlands discussed in this volume appear on the published 1:50,000 map and no sheet number appears for those names. The sheet numbers for the 1:10,000 series and the earlier 6-inch series, which is still important for historical research, are supplied for townlands, although not for other names. For these, follow the townland in which they occur.

Place-Name	1:50,000	1:10,000	6 inch	Page
Clare Mountain	5	15, 16	8, 9	241
Clare Wood	5			87
Cleggan	5	3	1	299
Cleggan	5	15	8, 9, 13, 14	23
Clegnagh	5	1, 7, 8	4	215
Clegnagh	5	14	7, 8	57
Clinery Burn	5			38
Cloghadoo	5			314
Cloghanmurry		8, 15	8	242
Cloghcorr	5	8	4, 8	58
Colliery Bay	5			179
Coolanlough	5			180
Coolaveely	5	9, 16	9	132
Coolkenny	5	8	8	243
Coolmaghra	5	8	4	58
Coolnagoppoge	5	9	9, 10	133
Coolnagorr	4/5			87
Coolranny	5	10, 17	10	134
Cooraghy Bay	5			315
Corratavey Bridge	5			180
Corrymellagh		17	10, 15	134
Corvally	5	15, 16	8, 9, 14	244
Craig	5	1, 7	3	59
Craigalappan	5	7, 8	4, 8	60
Craiganee	5	2, 8	4 ,8	61
Craigban	5	16	9	135
Craigfad	5	9	5	135
Craigmacagan	5	3	1	300
Craignagolman	5			87
Cregganboy	5	8	4	245
Croaghbeg		7	3, 7	61
Croaghmore	5	7	3, 7, 8	61
Crockachara	5			38
Crockacollier	5			88
Crockan Point	5			182
Crockanaskista Burn	5			181
Crockanore	5			182
Crockateemore	5			182
Crockatinny	5			39
Crocknahorna	5			224
Cromaghs	5	15	13	23
Cross	5	9	5	136
Cross Bridge	5			88
Culfeightrin				106
Curragh	5	17	15	137
Curramoney	4/5	7, 8, 14, 15	8	63
Currysheskin	5	1, 7	3	64

Place-Name	1:50,000	1:10,000	6 inch	Page
Larry Bane Head	5			96
Leckpatrick	5			193
Legacapple Burn	5			194
Legahapple Bridge	5			43
Leland				276
Lemnagh Beg	5	7	3, 4	73
Lemnagh More	5	7	3, 4	74
Ligadaughtan	5	17	10	157
Limepark	5			43
Lisbellanagroagh Beg	4/5	7	3	74
Lisbellanagroagh More	4/5	7	3	76
Lismorrity	5	15	8, 13	220
Lisnacalliagh	5			194
Lisnagat		14	7, 8	220
Little Black Sythe	5			276
Long Causeway	5			96
Long Gilbert	5			97
Losset	5	9	9	158
Lough Bridge	5			195
Lough Doo	5			195
Lough Fadden	5			196
Lough Park	5			277
Lough na Crannagh	5			196
Lough-a-verrie	5			97
Loughan	5	10, 17	10	158
Loughareema (Vanishing Lake)	5			195
Loughnanskan	5			319
Low Carn	5			98
Low Town	5			43
Maddygalla	5			319
Magheraboy		1, 2, 7, 8	4	76
Magheraboy	5			197
Magheracashel	5	8	4, 8	76
Magheramore		15	8	255
Magherindonnell		9	9	159
Magherintemple	5			131
Maghernahar	5	8	4, 8	77
Maghralough	5			98
Mallanadeevan	5			197
Manister	5	14, 15	8, 13	221
Mazes	5	15	8, 13	222
Mill Bay	5			320
Mill Five Acres		15	13	29
Mill Town	5			198
Milltown Burn	5			198
Monanclogh	5	15	8	29

Place-Names of Northern Ireland,
edited by Professor Gerard Stockman.

Vol. I   Newry and South-West Down (1992) 217pp
Gregory Toner and Mícheál B. Ó Mainnín
ISBN 085389 449 3 (HB) ISBN 085389 432 9(PB)

Vol. II   The Ards Peninsula (1992) 301pp
A.J. Hughes and R.J. Hannan
ISBN 085389 4507 (HB) ISBN 085389 4337 (PB)

Vol. III   The Mournes (1993) 246pp
Mícheál B. Ó Mainnín
ISBN 085389 4515 (HB) ISBN 085389 4485 (PB)

Vol. IV   The Baronies of Toome (1995) 313pp
Patrick McKay
ISBN 085389 5686 (HB) ISBN 085389 5694 (PB)

Vol. V   The Moyola Valley (1996) 283pp
Gregory Toner
ISBN 085389 6127 (HB) ISBN 085389 6135 (PB)

Vol. VI   North-West Down/Iveagh (1996) 422pp
Kay Muhr
ISBN 085389 5708 (HB) ISBN 085389 5716 (PB)

Vol. VIII   Armagh City (forthcoming)
Mícheál B. Ó Mainnín